Islamic Legal Interpretation

CENTER FOR MIDDLE EASTERN STUDIES

HARVARD STUDIES IN ISLAMIC LAW

Islamic Legal Interpretation

MUFTIS AND THEIR FATWAS

Edited by

Muhammad Khalid Masud

Brinkley Messick

David S. Powers

Harvard University Press

Cambridge, Massachusetts

London, England

1996

Printed in the United States of America

Library of Congress Cataloging-in-Publication Data

Islamic legal interpretation : muftis and their fatwas /
edited by Muhammad Khalid Masud, Brinkley Messick, David S. Powers.
p. cm. — (Harvard studies in Islamic law)
Includes bibliographical references (p.) and index.
ISBN 0-674-46870-8 (alk. paper)
1. Fatwās—History. 2. Islamic law—History.
I. Masud, Muhammad Khalid, 1939– . II. Messick, Brinkley Morris.
III. Powers, David Stephan. IV. Series. LAW <ISLAM Isla 1996>
340.5'9'09—dc20 95-46771

Contents

Preface

Legal interpretation sheds light not only on the law and its methods but also on society and the human relations surrounding the cases construed. Weighing doctrine and fact, interpreters formulate opinions that leave marks on the discourses of their jurist colleagues, on their communities, and on the world at large. To examine a culturally specific form of legal interpretation, then, is to raise issues of an interdisciplinary and comparative nature concerning law, society, and history.

In 1985, the Joint Committee for the Comparative Study of Muslim Societies, established by the Social Science Research Council and the American Council of Learned Societies, began to discuss the Islamic institution of the fatwa, or legal opinion. In response to a suggestion by William R. Roff, the committee decided to direct its energy and resources toward an international conference on the institution of fatwa giving as it has manifested itself throughout history in different Muslim societies. "The Making of a Fatwa," organized by Muhammad Khalid Masud, was convened January 10–13, 1990, in Granada, Spain, where seventeen scholars presented papers.

Following the conference, we assumed the task of preparing a volume on the fatwa project. In an attempt to achieve a greater balance of period, region, school of law, language, and legal issue, the editors solicited contributions from additional scholars who had not participated in the conference. Each contributor was asked to translate a short fatwa and write a brief chapter based on the translation, a mandate that was intended to lend thematic consistency to the volume and to heighten its value as a sourcebook of Islamic legal cases. Contributors also were asked to pay attention to the institutional context in which the fatwa was issued, the sources cited by the mufti, the language and rhetorical strategies employed, the method of reasoning, and the intended audience. Within these constraints, contributors were free to write their chapters from the perspective of their respective disciplines, which include law, Islamic studies, history, and anthropology.

The first section of the volume contains two chapters of a general and theoretical nature. In the first, we survey the state of the field in the study of fatwas and muftis, sketching the history, structure, and modern transformation of this important Islamic institution. In a more specialized manner, the second chapter, by Wael B. Hallaq examines a segment of the history of the institution within one branch of the legal tradition, that of the Sunnis. The remaining twenty-six chapters, each focused on a particular fatwa, are grouped chronologically according to the lifetime of the issuing mufti, as follows: pre-modern, early modern (nineteenth and early twentieth centuries), and modern.

As the fatwa project comes to an end in the form of this first case-based volume on Islamic legal interpretation, we gratefully acknowledge the vision and support of the Social Science Research Council, of SSRC Staff Associate David Szanton, and of the members of the Committee on the Comparative Study of Muslim Societies. We also thank the two anonymous readers of the manuscript for their many helpful comments and suggestions. Finally, we express our gratitude to Aida Donald, Elizabeth Suttell, Julie Ericksen Hagen, and Kate Brick of Harvard University Press for their encouragement and expert editorial assistance.

Muhammad Khalid Masud
Brinkley Messick
David S. Powers

PART ONE

Theoretical Perspectives

CHAPTER ONE

Muftis, Fatwas, and Islamic Legal Interpretation

MUHAMMAD KHALID MASUD, BRINKLEY MESSICK, DAVID S. POWERS

> When they ask you for a pronouncement [*yastaftūnaka*] . . .
> Say: "God pronounces to you [*yuftīkum*] . . ."
>
> QURAN 4:126

> Question the people of remembrance, if you do not know.
>
> QURAN 16:43

An important division of juristic labor marks the relation of the *sharīʿa,* or Islamic law, to the concrete world of human affairs. Across time and space, two distinct categories of legal interpreters have stood at the meeting points of law and fact. The domain of legal procedure, including adversarial cases, rules of evidence, binding judgments, and state enforcement, belongs to the judge *(qāḍī);* the issuance of nonbinding advisory opinions (*fatāwā,* or *fatwās*) to an individual questioner *(mustaftī),* whether in connection with litigation or not, is the separate domain of the jurisconsult (*muftī*). In their different venues, both qadis and muftis have specialized in handling the everyday traffic in conflicts and questions falling within the purview of the shariʿa.

Compared to qadis, muftis have received little attention in Western scholarship, in part because of the litigation-oriented expectations of many observers for whom the role of the jurisconsult is unfamiliar,[1] and in part because, in many historical settings, the activity of the mufti was far less institutionalized than that of the qadi. Whereas qadis always were appointed, salaried officials who dispensed justice in public tribunals, many muftis operated privately and unobtrusively without any ties to the political authorities, while others were officially appointed. The significance of the work of the muftis—whether private or public—rests on the high degree of authority that could be carried by their opinions, which represent the closest Islamic equivalent to the familiar Anglo-American legal mechanism of case-law precedent.

Research focused on muftis and their fatwas is integral to current efforts to refine our understanding of the history of Islamic law. In pre-modern times, the umbrella of the shariʿa encompassed not only ritual law but also criminal law and a wide range of contracts. Derived from the Quran and the Sunna (the exemplary behavior of the Prophet Muhammad as recorded in narrative reports, or hadith),[2] the shariʿa developed by means of human juristic efforts into a comprehensive and detailed corpus of law that was continuously adjusted to changing circumstances. While the more theoretical aspect of the shariʿa is embodied in the literatures dealing with the "branches" of substantive law *(furūʿ al-fiqh)* and with the "roots" of legal methodology and jurisprudence *(uṣūl al-fiqh)*, its more practical aspect is embodied in fatwas issued by muftis in response to questions posed by individuals in connection with ongoing human affairs. As the corpus of substantive law and jurisprudence grew, acquiring both multiple levels of commentary and authoritative summaries, the accumulation of fatwas issued by muftis in diverse social and historical settings served to stimulate the development of the shariʿa from below, in response to the specific needs of particular Muslim communities.[3]

In its many historical manifestations, the muftiship exhibits both a number of consistent family resemblances and, especially on its public side, considerable institutional diversity. As interpreters, individual muftis displayed varying degrees of juristic proficiency and different discursive styles. They issued fatwas in response to a wide range of questions emanating from individual Muslims of every status, including qadis and political authorities such as the caliph or sultan. Reflecting the importance of fatwa giving *(iftāʾ)* in the Islamic legal system, both the activity of the mufti and the fatwa genre have been analyzed by Muslim intellectuals of various eras. In this chapter, we outline the history of iftaʾ and examine its structure, to help situate the specific worlds invoked by the contributors to this volume.

The Formative Period

The Quran announces itself as a divine revelation communicated to humanity through the medium of the Prophet Muhammad. According to Islamic tradition, the Quran was revealed *seriatim* over a period of approximately twenty-three years. Muhammad received the first revelation, Sura 96 ("The Blood Clot"), in the year 610, and the last revelation, verse 176 of Sura 4 ("Women") shortly before his death in 632. The content of these revelations changed dramatically over time, reflecting a new phase in Muhammad's mission as a prophet and statesman. During the Meccan phase of his career (610–622), Muhammad's primary task was to announce the doctrine of the Oneness of God *(tawḥīd)* and to summon humanity to His worship and service. The Meccan verses therefore deal largely with the issues of *tawḥīd,* reward and punishment, and the last judgment. The hegira to Medina in 622 marks a watershed in Islamic history. In Medina, Muhammad established a religio-political community *(umma)* that accepted God as the ultimate source of authority for all human belief and action, and the verses revealed during this second phase of his career (622–632) deal increasingly with political, social, economic, and ritual matters.

Guided by the revelations, Muhammad instituted a series of rules and practices in the areas of ritual behavior, purity, social relations, and the economy. Inevitably, perhaps, these innovations occasionally met with expressions of incomprehension or resistance from members of the nascent Muslim community, some of whom continued to act in accordance with the customary practices of pre-Islamic Arabia. These reactions may be reflected in a literary structure that occurs repeatedly in the Quran: "When they ask you *(yas'alūnaka)* concerning . . . Say . . ."[4] This formulation, which encapsulates the basic features of what would become the classical Islamic activity of fatwa giving, was understood by subsequent generations of Muslim scholars in the following terms: One or more members of the community approach Muhammad and ask him for clarification regarding the continuing validity of a certain practice. Muhammad then awaits the reaction of the Divinity, who issues His response in the form of a revelation that becomes a verse of the Quran.[5] As represented in the Quran, the activity of consultation involves a three-way relationship between God, Muhammad, and the Muslim community, with Muhammad serving as the medium through which community members know God's laws and ordinances (cp. Shaltut 1988:5–14).

The Quran also contains the linguistic forms that would characterize the activity of legal consultation *(futyā)* in its classical manifestation, for it uses verbal forms derived from the root *f-t-y* in contexts having to do with asking questions and responding to them. An alternative to the above-mentioned literary structure occurs in two verses of Sura 4 ("Women"). Here, significantly, the verb *yas'alūnaka* is replaced by *yastaftūnaka,* and the resulting Divine pronouncement is signified by *yuftī* (the latter two verbs are derived from the root *f-t-y*). Thus, in verse 176, Muhammad receives the following instruction: "When they ask you for a pronouncement *(wa-yastaftūnaka).* Say: 'God pronounces to you *(yuftīkum)* concerning *al-kalāla . . .*'"; the verse proceeds to define the inheritance rights of siblings (on the problematic term "*kalāla,*" see Powers 1986:22–49). Similarly, in verse 126, God instructs Muhammad on the manner in which he should respond to people who ask him about the treatment of orphaned females. From the quranic usage of the verbs *aftā* and *istaftā*, it was only a short step to the terminology associated with the classical activity of legal consultation: mufti, *mustaftī* (questioner), futya (legal consultation), ifta' (fatwa giving), and *istiftā'* (request for a fatwa).[6]

A slightly different pattern of question and response is reflected in the hadith literature, where, typically, we find a Companion approaching Muhammad and asking him a question about a certain practice. Here, without awaiting the reaction of the Divinity, Muhammad responds immediately to his interlocutor, speaking in his own voice. The authoritative nature of his responses came to be understood as being based on verse 63 of Sura 4 ("Women"): "O Believers, obey God, obey the Messenger and those in authority among you." It is reported, for example, that al-Aqraʿ b. Habis (d. ca. 636) asked the Prophet, "O Messenger of God, is the pilgrimage to be performed every year or only once?" He replied, "Only once, and whoever does it more than once, that is an act of supererogation" (al-Azimabadi 1968–1969, 5:144). Similarly, it is reported that the Prophet was once standing in the pulpit of the mosque in Medina when a man asked him, "What is your opinion regarding the night prayer?" He replied, "Two [*rakʿa*s, or inclinations] at a time; and when one of you knows that the dawn [is near], he should add one [inclination], thereby causing his prayer to have an odd number of inclinations" (al-Bukhari 1862–1898, 1:130). Thus, in the hadith literature, a two-way relationship between Muhammad and the Muslim community complements the three-way relationship that characterizes the activity of question and response in the Quran. Underlying this relationship, of course, is the assumption that Muhammad is divinely inspired, infallible, and speaks in the name of God.

Muhammad's death in 632 marked an important shift in the dynamics of the consultative process. In Sura 33 ("The Confederates"), verse 40, the Quran designates Muhammad as "the Seal of the Prophets," a phrase that was understood to signify that God no longer would communicate with humanity, either directly through revelation or indirectly through a prophet. The Muslim community found itself separated from the voice of God and the immediate example of His Prophet. But in the aftermath of the Islamic conquests, as the Muslim community increased in size, spread across a wide geographical area, and became increasingly heterogeneous in its ethnic composition, there arose many new issues for which the Quran provided little or no instruction. In the period immediately following Muhammad's death, Muslims turned for guidance to his Companions, that is, to the men and women who had interacted with the Prophet and thus were best suited to determine what constituted proper Islamic behavior. Traditional sources identify approximately one hundred thirty Companions who are said to have functioned as muftis during the first century A.H./seventh century A.D. (al-Qasimi 1986:35). During his tenure as governor of the Yemen, Muʿadh b. Jabal (d. 640) is said to have issued fatwas on a wide variety of subjects relating both to the sacred and the profane (al-Bukhari 1928, 8:270). The Prophet's secretary, Zayd b. Thabit (d. 666), reportedly served as the leader of futya (and several other offices) in Medina between 634 and 666 (Ibn Saʿd, 1957–1968, 2: pt. 2:115–117). Among all the Companions, the distinction of being the most prolific mufti belongs to Ibn ʿAbbas (d. 687), whose fatwas reportedly were collected in twenty volumes by the great-grandson of the ʿAbbasid Caliph al-Maʾmun (al-Qasimi 1986:35).[7]

During the first/seventh century, futya was a widespread but largely undifferentiated activity that made an important contribution to the elaboration of a distinctive Islamic identity and lifestyle. The corpus of hadith compiled during the third/ninth century suggests that the activity of futya as practiced by Companions had been linked to the preservation of the prophetic Sunna. For example, it is reported that Masruq (d. 682) once asked the Prophet's wife, ʿAʾisha (d. 678), about the manner in which the Prophet had performed the night prayer. To this question she replied, "[Sometimes] seven [inclinations, sometimes] nine, and [sometimes] eleven" (al-Bukhari 1862–1898, 1:287–288). Similarly, it is reported that ʿAbd al-ʿAziz b. Rufayʿ (d. ca. 747) once asked Anas b. Malik (d. ca. 709), "Tell me about something about which you possess knowledge regarding the Prophet. Where did he perform the midday and afternoon prayers on the day of Tarwiyah?" (the day of providing oneself with water on 8 Dhu al-Hijja, during the performance of the pilgrimage). Anas replied, "At Mina."[8]

As the generation of Muhammad's Companions died out, the Muslim community was cut off from the guidance of men and women who had been in direct contact with the Prophet. But an important mechanism had been established for the accurate transmission of both the Quran and the prophetic hadith from one generation of Muslims to the next. This mechanism, which Graham (1993) calls the "*isnād* paradigm," places a high value on the human element in the process of transmitting knowledge from one generation to the next, with the result that Muslims of subsequent generations could experience a sense of personal connection with both the Quran and the hadith. Beginning in the second/eighth century, those Muslims who dedicated themselves to the preservation and analysis of Islamic knowledge (*ʿilm)* were designated as *ʿulamāʾ*, or scholars. The acquisition of knowledge came to be associated exclusively with individuals who devoted themselves to the study of the Quran, the hadith, and, increasingly, the "roots" and "branches" of substantive law, or *fiqh* (those who specialized in fiqh are known as *fuqahāʾ*). In Mecca, Medina, Damascus, the Yemen, and other centers of Islamic scholarship, men such as al-Shaʿbi (d. ca. 721–722), al-Zuhri (d. 742), Makhul (d. 734), and Taʾus (d. 720) generated discrete legal materials that were used by subsequent generations of scholars to create the fully developed system of Islamic law. Identifying themselves with "those in authority among you" *(ūlū al-amr)* mentioned in Quran 4:63 and with "the people of Remembrance" mentioned in Quran 16:43, this special class of literate scholars acquired religious authority analogous to that exercised by the Prophet. "The mufti," writes al-Shatibi (d. 1388), "stands before the Muslim community in the same place as the Prophet stood" (1969–1970, 4:224–225). One interpretation of Quran 16:43 holds that Muslims are under an obligation to consult with and seek advice from individuals known to possess knowledge and moral probity *(ʿadāla)* (al-Tabari 1954–1968, 14:108–109).

The complex interplay between futya, fiqh, and hadith is illustrated by a narrative report that preserves a conversation that reportedly took place in Kufa during the governorship of Bishr b. Marwan (690–694). The hadith specialist ʿAtaʾ b. al-Saʾib (d. 753–754) approached the Kufan qadi Shurayh (d. between 697 and 718), and said to him, "O Abu Umayya, I need a fatwa from you." Taking care to inform ʿAtaʾ of his jurisdictional limitations, Shurayh replied, "O son of my brother, I am merely a qadi, not a mufti." But ʿAtaʾ persisted, explaining that he wanted not a judgment but an opinion regarding a dispute involving a third party who had designated his house as an endowment in an apparent effort to circumvent the quranic inheritance rules. Shurayh then entered the mosque and, as he was making his way toward the *maqṣūra* (a special enclosure or compartment), instructed one of his judicial assistants to inform ʿAtaʾ that "it is not permitted to create an endowment in circumvention of the shares of [inheritance awarded by] God—may He be glorified and exalted" (al-Tahawi 1968, 4:96, ll. 18–21; cf. al-Bayhaqi 1968, 6:162, ll. 27–31). This last statement, attributed here to Shurayh, subsequently was reformulated as a prophetic hadith (ibid., 6:162, ll. 23–25).

Institutional Manifestations

Futya began as a private activity that was independent of any state control. To a large extent, it was the scholars themselves who regulated their own activities and determined their own professional standards. To issue a fatwa, all that was required of a person was religious knowledge and piety *(taqwā)*. In the words of a North African mufti, "Anyone who is learned and whose religious sentiments are recognized may issue fatwas" (al-Wansharisi 1981–1983, 8:236). Acting in a private capacity, muftis provided authoritative advice for Muslims unfamiliar with the detailed provisions of Islamic law or uncertain that their behavior conformed to what was considered to be properly Islamic. Simultaneously, however, some muftis became members of the judicial administration, and the activity of futya acquired a public and official nature (Ibn Khaldun 1958, 1:452).

Already in Umayyad times (661–750) muftis served as legal consultants for qadis and issued fatwas at the request of provincial governors. The governor of Ailah, Ruzayq b. Hukaym, reportedly wrote to al-Zuhri in Wadi al-Qura, asking whether he should hold the Friday prayer service for the benefit of black slaves who worked certain lands that he managed. Al-Zuhri wrote back instructing Ruzayq that he should indeed hold the Friday service, citing as support for his opinion a Sunna of the Prophet (al-Bukhari 1862–1898, 1:227–228). By the late Umayyad period, fatwa giving also had become an important instrument of political criticism. It is reported, for example, that Saʿid b. al-Jubayr (d. 714) issued a fatwa in which he criticized the tyrannical behavior of al-Hajjaj, and that, despite being threatened with death, the mufti steadfastly refused to recant (al-Qarafi 1989). Nearly a century later, al-Muntasir (d. 862) felt it necessary to secure a fatwa from leading Iraqi jurists before setting in motion the plot that led to the assassination of his father, Caliph al-Mutawakkil (d. 861). In view of the increasing importance of futya as a mechanism of religious legitimization, it is perhaps not surprising that central governments sought to establish a measure of control over the activity. To this end, caliphs (and, later, sultans) began to designate jurists who were deemed qualified to serve the government in an official or semiofficial capacity.

Although a number of contributions to this volume record specific characteristics of futya as practiced in different times and places in the pre-modern era (see Part II), a comparative history of this activity between the tenth and the sixteenth centuries has yet to be written. The following remarks therefore have the limited objectives of indicating the sources for and tracing the broad regional outlines of this history.

The fundamental source of information on the activities of muftis is the collections of their fatwas, which began to appear in the second half of the tenth century and have been produced in a continuous and unending stream until the present (see al-Nadim 1970, 1:493ff.; Hajji Khalifa 1941–1955, 2:1218–1231, 2 [supplement]:155–158; Brockelmann 1943–1949, index, s.v. *fatāwā;* and Sezgin 1967–, 2: index, s.vv. *fatāwā, fatwā, nawāzil*). Each collection is identified with a particular school *(madhhab)* of legal thought. In Sunni Islam, the Hanafi, Maliki, Shafiʿi, and Hanbali schools emerged as authoritative, taking the names of the jurists Abu Hanifa (d. 767), Malik b. Anas (d. 795), Muhammad al-Shafiʿi (d. 820), and Ibn Hanbal (d. 855), respectively. Among the Shiʿis, fatwa collections likewise pertain to specific interpretive communities, such as the Jaʿfaris (or "Twelvers"), named for the Imam Jaʿfar b. Muhammad al-Sadiq, d. 765 (see Tabataba'i 1984). Each of the schools produced biographical dictionaries that constitute important historical sources on the lives of muftis and other jurists and specify the names of teachers, texts studied, students, writings, and positions held.[9]

One of the earliest fatwa collections, the *Kitāb al-Nawāzil* compiled by Abu Layth al-Samarqandi (d. 983), contains fatwas issued by a wide range of Hanafi jurists. Subsequently, it became more common for the students of a single jurist to collect fatwas issued by their master and arrange them according to legal categories. Thus, the fatwas of al-Natifi (d. 1054) appeared as the *Majmaʿ al-nawāzil wa'l-wāqiʿāt,* and those of Qadikhan (d. 1195) as *Fatāwā Qāḍīkhān,* to mention only two of the most famous Hanafi collections. As the titles of these two texts indicate, the terms "*fatāwā*" and "*nawāzil*" (cases) were used interchangeably to signify legal opinions issued by jurisprudents (*Encyclopaedia of Islam,* 2nd ed. 1992, s.v. Nāzila).

Some geographic regions have historical associations with particular schools of legal thought. In the Islamic West (Andalusia and North Africa), the Maliki school prevailed (see Chapters 3, 4, and 8 in this volume). Among the early Maliki collections are the fatwas of the Cordovan mufti Ibn Sahl (d. 1093), collected as the *Kitāb al-Nawāzil* (see Azemmouri 1973), and those of Ibn Rushd (d. 1126), known as *Fatāwā Ibn Rushd.* Arguably the single most important collection of Maliki fatwas is the *Kitāb al-Miʿyār* of Ahmad al-Wansharisi (d. 1508), which, like most classical collections, is arranged according to the standard categories of Islamic law. But whereas other collections contain the relatively limited output of individual muftis living in a particular time and place, the *Miʿyār* contains approximately six thousand fatwas issued by hundreds of muftis (including some thirty issued by the compiler himself) who lived between 1000 and 1496 in the major cities of Ifriqiya, the Maghrib, and al-Andalus. This masssive corpus has been used by historians as a source for social, economic, and religious history (Brunschvig 1940–1947; Idris 1962; Kably 1986; Lagardère 1990) and, to a lesser extent, for legal thought and practice (Powers 1990a, 1990b, 1992, 1993).

The emergence of the fatwa collection as a discrete literary genre points to the increasingly important role played by muftis in the judicial process. Islamic legal doctrine generally encourages qadis to consult with legal experts before issuing a judicial decision *(ḥukm),* especially in difficult, unusual, or sensitive cases (al-Khassaf 1978:105), such as those involving the possible imposition of the death penalty (Powers 1993:94–95). This practice manifests itself most clearly in the Islamic West, where judicial advisers *(mushāwarūn)* customarily were attached to each court. These advisers, who constituted the qadi's consilium *(shūra),* issued fatwas at the request of judges, and the institution of the shura became an essential feature of Maliki judicial administration in al-Andalus and the Maghrib. Although formally appointed by the caliph or emir, judicial advisers often were chosen directly by individual qadis (Tyan 1955:251–253; Marin 1985a; Powers 1990a:240, 253). The primary function of these mushawarun was to insure that Islamic legal standards were being applied in the courts, and they accordingly played a key role in the process of Islamic judicial review (Powers 1992). In addition, they issued fatwas on policy issues at the request of the political authorities.

Little has been written about the activities of muftis in the central Islamic lands in the period between the eighth and the twelfth centuries, although numerous sources exist to fill in this gap. We are somewhat better informed about the Mamluk period (1250–1516) in Egypt and Syria, although even here the activity of futya has yet to be studied systematically (see Tyan 1960:224). Under the Mamluks, futya was largely a private activity that was performed independently of state control (see Chapters 6 and 7 in this volume). The sole prerequisite was the possession of the necessary moral and intellectual qualifications, as confirmed by established jurists. Private muftis issued written fatwas in response to requests from the individual parties to a dispute and from qadis. It was not uncommon for muftis to attend shariʿa courts where qadis might consult with them before issuing their judgments, especially in difficult cases. But the Mamluks did not appoint muftis to the qadi courts, although they did appoint a relatively small number of muftis to serve in the *maẓālim* tribunals, special courts of justice established by the sultan and his governors (Tyan 1965:866; Nielsen 1990:933–935). The Mamluk sultans also seem to have employed a small number of muftis who advised them on matters of policy, a function that may have given rise to the office of shaykh ul-islam under the Ottomans, and they appointed muftis to reinforce their political authority in the principal cities (Gibb and Bowen 1957, 1:2:134–135).

The activity of futya during the Ottoman period (1516–1918) is well documented in several important studies (Kramers 1934; Gibb and Bowen 1957, 1:2:133–138; Walsh 1965; Heyd 1969; Krüger 1978; Repp 1986; Johansen 1993). Initially Ottoman muftis acted in a private capacity and were independent of the state. As the state expanded and developed into an empire, Hanafi legal doctrine was adopted and muftis gradually were incorporated into an increasingly centralized judicial administration. Beginning in the reign of Murad II (1421–1451), a single mufti, designated shaykh ul-islam, came to be recognized as the ultimate source of authority in matters relating to the shariʿa (Walsh 1965:867).[10] By the time of Selim I (1512–1520), the shaykh ul-islam exercised considerable moral influence in the capital city of Istanbul. These developments culminated in the reign of Sulayman (1520–1566), under whom the shaykh ul-islam became responsible for a complex hierarchy of jurists scattered throughout the empire. As the demand for *fetvas* (the Ottoman Turkish form of fatwa) increased, the office of shaykh ul-islam underwent a process of bureaucratization. The sultan established an official department for issuing fetvas, with a professional staff headed by the fetva supervisor *(fetvā emīnī)*. The efficiency of this department is reflected in the report that in the sixteenth century, the shaykh ul-islam issued an average of 350 responses to inquiries, twice weekly; Abu al-Suʿud, who served as shaykh ul-islam from 1545 to 1574, is reported to have claimed that on at least two occasions he wrote more than 1,400 fetvas in a single day (Heyd 1969:46). The fetvas issued by the shaykh ul-islam were systematically recorded in registers, and those issued by certain distinguished shaykhs, such as Abu al-Suʿud, were collected in book form.

Sensitive to the legitimizing function of a fetva, the Ottoman Sultans customarily would not proceed with any important decision relating to either foreign or domestic policy without first securing a legal opinion from the shaykh ul-islam. In 1516, Selim I requested a fetva from ʿAli al-Jamali authorizing an attack on the Mamluks of Egypt; in 1570 Selim II obtained a fetva from Abu al-Suʿud authorizing the Ottoman armies to attack the Venetians. Similarly, the consumption of coffee was made licit in a fetva issued by Abu al-Suʿud; the operation of a printing-press was authorized in a fetva issued by ʿAbd Allah Effendi in 1727; and the nineteenth-century legal and administrative reforms embodied in the *Niẓām-i Jadīd* were given legitimacy by a fetva issued by Esʿad Effendi (Kramers 1934, 4:277).

Within the empire, there was considerable variation in the activity of muftis located in Istanbul, in the Anatolian and European provinces, and in the Arab provinces. For example, the shaykh ul-islam generally did not cite any legal authorities in his fetvas, which tended to be brief and often consisted of merely "yes" or "no" (see Chapter 11). Provincial muftis, on the other hand, did support their views with citations from earlier legal authorities and texts (Heyd 1969:45). Two of the most important collections of Ottoman fatwas are provincial texts: Ibn ʿAbidin's abridged version of the fatwas of the Damascene mufti Hamid al-ʿImadi, entitled *al-ʿUqūd al-durriyya fī tanqīḥ al-fatāwā al-ḥāmidiyya* (1883), and the fatwas of the Syrian mufti Khayr al-Din al-Ramli, compiled by his son and entitled *al-Fatāwā al-khayriyya li-nafʿ al-bariyya* (1883); on the latter, see Chapter 10. Further, there appears to have been a sharp difference in the status and function of muftis in different parts of the empire. In the Anatolian and European provinces, muftis generally were not members of the ʿulamaʾ class but rather were local elders, holding no official position, who were called on to confer authority on judgments issued by qadis, who frequently were outsiders; in the Arab provinces, on the other hand, muftis tended to be scholars appointed by the shaykh ul-islam and recognized by the local authorities as the chief religious and judicial officers (Walsh 1965:867).

Further east, in Iran, Central Asia, and South Asia, the institutional history of futya is not well documented. In particular, we are poorly informed about the function of muftis in Shiʿi circles, including Twelver groups located in Iran (see Chapter 22) and southern Iraq, the Caucausus, and India (see Chapter 14). To the tension familiar in the Sunni world between the interpretive authority of the jurists and the temporal authority of the state (see, for example, Ibn Khaldun 1958, 3:314) is added, among Twelver Shiʿis, the issue of "deputed authority" during the occultation *(ghayba)* of the Imam (Calmard 1991a:549–550). And in addition to concepts of juristic preeminence *(riyāsa)* common to both Sunni and Shiʿi jurists, the latter elaborated a series of specialized notions of authority and hierarchy, culminating in the title of *marjaʿ-i taqlīd*. This term refers to a single, typically private jurist "who is to be considered during his lifetime, by virtue of his qualities and his wisdom, a model for reference" (Calmard 1991a:548).

Although the precise historical origins of the institution are unclear, in more recent times the *marjaʿ-i taqlīd* has been responsible for guiding his followers by issuing fatwas, which are complemented by other, fatwa-like genres, including both practical treatises *(risāla-yi ʿamaliyya)* and works intended to clarify problems of daily life *(tawḍīḥ al-masāʾil)*. Together, these genres constitute the distinctive discursive context of the high-level Shiʿi fatwa (Calmard 1991a:554; Tabatabaʾi 1984:60). Among the more than fifty fatwa collections of the Jaʿfari school listed by Tabatabaʾi (1984:95–100), two have acquired particular importance in contemporary times. As part of a characteristic orientation toward such authoritative works, leading twentieth-century jurists have written marginal glosses, to indicate slight differences of opinion, on the collected fatwas of al-Yazidi (d. 1919), *al-ʿUrwa al-wuthqā* (in Arabic), and of al-Burujirdi (d. 1961), *Tawḍīḥ al-masāʾil* (in Persian).

In Safavid Iran (1501–1722), Twelver Shiʿism became the state religion, and jurists occupied a range of positions, some of which may have included public fatwa-issuing functions. Although the office of shaykh ul-islam under the Safavids appears similar in many respects to its Ottoman counterpart, it is uncertain whether such officials issued fatwas. In Timurid Central Asia, however, an official bearing this title was in charge of all religious matters, including futya: "no legal document or fatwa could be issued without his signature" (Ando, 1995). Among other important Safavid religious officials, the *ṣadr* has been characterized as "similar to the mufti of the Turks" (Chardin, cited in Minorsky 1943:111), while in pre-modern India an incumbent *ṣadr* was described as "the mufti of the guarded territories [*muftī mamālik-i maḥrūsa*]" (Blochmann 1939:284).

Shiʿis generally use the terms "mujtahid" (practitioner of *ijtihād*) and "*faqīh*" (legal specialist) in a manner synonymous with "mufti" (see Sangilaji 1335/1916:18; Calmard 1991b:295–304). Among the Twelvers, the Akhbaris and the Usulis were contending subschools: the former reject ijtihad outright; the latter advocate ijtihad and have been predominant for the last 300 years (Tabataba'i 1984; Calmard 1991b). Other Shiʿi subschools include the Twelver Shaykhis (Chapter 13) and the non-Twelver Zaydis of Yemen (Chapter 28).

In the Indian subcontinent and Central Asia, the Hanafi school of Sunni Islam predominated (see Chapters 15, 16, 17, and 21). Although several contemporary scholars (e.g., Ahmad 1941; Qureshi 1958) treat muftis as an integral part of the pre-modern Indian judicial system, suggesting that they were attached to the qadi courts at all levels, this conclusion is not borne out by the primary sources (Masud 1984). Husaini (1952:203) and Ibn Hasan (1967:315) observe that although muftis are mentioned frequently in the sources, they were not regular officials, and judges could seek legal opinions from any well-known scholar.

In this region, the term "fatwa" often denoted an authoritative and accepted opinion of the Hanafi school, not necessarily an opinion issued in response to a question. Pre-modern Indian fatwa collections bear the names of rulers, indicating the status of these texts as authoritative opinions potentially enforceable in state courts. Of eleven major Indian fatwa collections cited by Bhatti (1973:30), the more important are the *Fatāwā Ghiyāthiyya* of Da'ud b. Yusuf, dedicated to Ghiyath al-Din Balban (1265–1287); the *Fatāwā Qarakhānī* of Sadr al-Din Yaʿqub Muzaffar Kirmani, compiled in question-and-answer form by Maqbul Qarakhan, on the order of Sultan Jalal al-Din Firuz Shah Khilji (1290–1295); the *Fatāwā Tātārkhāniyya* of ʿAlim b. ʿAla' (d. 1384), dedicated to Amir Tatarkhan, who solicited the compilation at the behest of Sultan Ghiyath al-Din Tughlaq (1320–1325); and the *Fatāwā Bābarī* or *Ẓāhiriyya* of Nur al-Din al-Khwafi, dedicated to Sultan Zahir al-Din Babur (1483–1530), who ordered its compilation. Such sources are utilized in a recent historical study of public endowments in Central Asia (McChesney 1991).

Also listed by Bhatti and of singular importance is *al-Fatāwā al-ʿĀlimgīriyya,* which ranks next in authority to the *Hidāya,* the leading doctrinal law book of the Hanafis (both texts were translated into Urdu and English and were used in colonial British courts). This famous collection, assembled by a committee of forty scholars headed by Shaykh Nizam of Burhanpur (d. 1679), was undertaken at the command of the Mughal emperor, Awrangzeb ʿAlamgir (1618–1707). It contains a systematic arrangement of authoritative Hanafi doctrine, which was previously scattered in a number of legal works (Ansari 1965). Technically, the collection mostly comprises legal doctrine (fiqh). Strictly speaking, it is not a fatwa collection, for it neither addresses specific questions nor takes the form of answers to questions.[11] However, in a usage specific to Central Asia and India, a work was characterized as a "fatwa" collection if it concentrated on issues that arose in practice. Such a work's specific association with the issuance of fatwas derived from the fact that it represented authoritative Hanafi doctrine *(al-muftā bihi)* on every subject for which a fatwa might be issued. As Schacht has observed (1971:477), the two distinctive features of Indian fatwa collections are state sponsorship and authoritative status (in his view, the Indian "fatwa" collections should be considered systematic works of Islamic law).

Adab al-Mufti

Turning from the historical diversity of institutional forms taken by the muftiship, we now examine the basic identity of the mufti, the formal requirements of the position, and the character of the interpretive relation between muftis and questioners. These matters have been the subject of systematic thought on the part of Muslim social and legal theorists.[12] The *uṣūl al-fiqh* literature provides standard discussions of the qualifications and status of the mufti, defined in connection with the key activity of legal interpretation.[13] In addition, a small number of works treat the specialized subject of *adab al-muftī,* which elaborates on the detailed features of the mufti's position and on the processes of the interpretive interchange.[14] Although the adab al-mufti treatises provide an extensive treatment of the structures and functions of the muftiship, they describe an institution that is fully mature, timeless, and highly ideal in character, paying little attention to historical developments or to the actual circumstances of muftis in specific local settings. An analogous and better known genre concerned with the judgeship, the *adab al-qāḍī* literature, sometimes touches on the role of the mufti, but mainly to distinguish it from that of the judge.[15] In a unique work that integrates aspects of these two specialized fields, Shihab al-Din al-Qarafi (d. 1285) provides a synthetic analysis that compares muftis and judges and elucidates the conceptual differences between fatwas and judgments (al-Qarafi 1967; see also Jackson 1991, 1992). Finally, as several of the chapters in this volume demonstrate, analytic statements and brief typologies of muftis and fatwa giving occasionally occur in the fatwas themselves.

As is true of the works on the judgeship, the adab al-mufti treatises typically open with a discussion of the countervailing significance and peril of the position (see, for example, al-Nawawi 1988:13–14; al-ʿAmili 1988–1989:136–137). These dual qualities consist, on the one hand, of a firm societal obligation *(farḍ kifāya)* to produce interpreters of the shariʿa, and on the other, an acknowledgment that engaging in this type of interpretation inevitably exposes the mufti to the possibility of (divinely punished) error. On the positive side, the mufti is identified as "the heir of the prophets" and "the signatory for God Almighty"[16] and as standing "between God Almighty and His creatures" (al-Qasimi 1986:44). Al-Shatibi (n.d., 4:244) regards the mufti as a legislator *(shāriʿ),* a title otherwise reserved for the Prophet Muhammad. In general, it is agreed that a mufti's "reward is great," as indicated by the well-known hadith "If an interpreter is right he receives two rewards; if he is mistaken he receives one reward."

On the other hand, the adab al-mufti treatises mention several types of caution *(taḥdhīr),* including quranic verses that warn generally against providing false information; prophetic hadith, such as "The most reckless of you in issuing fatwas is the most sure to go to Hell" (Ibn Khaldun 1958, 1:452); and cautionary statements attributed to important early practitioners, including the founders of major Sunni law schools. When it was observed that he did not respond to a questioner, al-Shafiʿi is said to have remarked that he would not do so "until I know whether silence or a response is better." Ahmad b. Hanbal was reported to answer "I don't know," even in matters in which he was aware of the various possible positions. Commenting on how few his responses were in comparison to the number of questions posed to him, Malik reportedly observed, "He who responds to a matter should, before answering, reflect upon Paradise, Hell, and his own salvation, and [only] then respond." Reticence on the part of the jurist became a mark of qualification and integrity (al-Nawawi 1988:16).

The adab al-mufti treatises generally distinguish several levels of competence in relation to ijtihad, or interpretation (see Chapter 2), the highest being the absolute *(muṭlaq)* or independent *(mustaqill)* mufti. The status of mujtahid, proudly claimed by some great Muslim jurists but cautiously declined by others, represents the fullest realization of shariʿa knowledge and its associated intellectual skills. It is the absolute, independent mufti-mujtahid who fulfills the societal obligation to produce interpreters of the shariʿa. This exemplar engages in unfettered ijtihad based on knowledge of the following sources: the Quran (especially the legal verses, including the abrogating and abrogated verses, and the specific and general); the Sunna, together with the biography of the Prophet; hadith reports, especially those relating to legal matters, and the biographies of transmitters; the fiqh literature, including both its applied branches *(furūʿ)* and its theoretical roots *(uṣūl),* and its areas of consensus *(ijmāʿ)* and disagreement; and the Arabic language, including grammar, syntax, and the related linguistic sciences.[17] The basic interpretive techniques of the independent mufti combine the capacity to identify relevant shariʿa source texts, such as quranic verses or prophetic hadiths, with various methods of reasoning or derivation from those texts, to ascertain the legal assessment or rule *(ḥukm)* applicable to the specific matter in question. At this level, it is strictly forbidden to assume the posture of *taqlīd,* that is, to follow the opinions of others or of an established school of law.

Although documented for earlier periods (Hallaq 1984), in later periods this ideal status was considered by some Sunnis to be unattainable.[18] The typical mufti, in any case, tended to have more modest qualifications, and the treatises accordingly discuss lower levels of "nonindependent" or "affiliated" *(muntasib)* muftis and their respective characteristics.[19] Below the top level of the independent mujtahid, a mufti was classified as *muqallid* (practitioner of *taqlīd*), an interpreter who responded within the framework of an existing school *(madhhab)* of shariʿa thought, using as his source texts the leading opinions of that school. With regard to this level, the adab al-mufti treatises emphasize the proper acquisition of the requisite knowledge through the basic instructional mechanism of memorization, with the principal texts being the authoritative manuals of the particular schools.[20] Whereas the independent mufti interpreted directly from the sacredly constituted original sources, the Quran and Sunna, the nonindependent mufti worked from the humanly authored texts of school founders and leading disciples. In reponding to questions posed about the shariʿa, the independent muftis could create opinions recognized as novel and original. By contrast, affiliated muftis either selected from among or simply transmitted already existing opinions.

Employing the fatwa medium itself, Ibn Rushd responded to a question that arose among twelfth-century Maliki jurists of Tangier concerning the qualifications for muftis. In his fatwa he offers a three-tiered typology, beginning, at the lowest level, with the simple memorizers of Maliki doctrine, followed by those who, in addition, were able to distinguish whether opinions were in conformity with the school, and finally, at the highest level, by those who could derive rules from the original sources (cited in Powers 1993:96–98). Beyond such elaborations of ideal levels, Muslim scholars occasionally comment on the actual capacities of historical muftis. "In our days," Qadi Khan (1893, 1:2) writes in the twelfth-century subcontinent, "when a mufti of our [Hanafi] school is asked about a problem or questioned about an event, he should follow the school and issue his fatwa according to the doctrines of our jurists." A thirteenth-century adab al-mufti theorist, al-Nawawi (1988:26), notes in passing that some assert that "after the era of al-Shafiʿi [d. 820] no independent muftis have been found." Another thirteenth-century mufti, al-Qarafi (1967:29), refers to the mufti muqallid as the type existing "in our times." A late seventeenth-century treatise from the subcontinent states that, technically, "what is called a fatwa in our days is not in fact so, it is rather quoting the statement of a mufti [mujtahid] for the benefit of the questioner" (quoted in Masud 1984:146;

cf. al-Nawawi 1988:41). As Heyd (1969:54) reminds us, distinct levels of fatwa giving were required in practice: "The fatwa in Islam not only served as a means to explain and apply the law in complicated cases; it was also used simply to state it for people who were not in a position to look up a lawbook themselves."

A separate section of the adab al-mufti treatises sets forth the formal "conditions" *(shurūṭ)* required of candidates for the position. The specifics of these conditions highlight an initial set of differences between a mufti and a judge. In one such text (al-Nawawi 1988:19) the conditions are that the candidate "be an adult, Muslim, trusted, reliable, free of the causes of sin and defects of character, a jurist in identity, sound of mind, firm in thought, correct in behavior and derivation, [and] alert." The passage continues: "Equally [suitable] are a free man, a slave, a woman, a blind man, and a mute—if he can write or if his gestures are understood." Beyond the generally more stringent moral requirements and higher intellectual standards of the position, the mufti was distinguished from the judge in that the incumbent could be, in theory, a woman or a slave.[21]

Other distinctive features of the muftiship emerge from technical contrasts with the judgeship. Although both muftis and judges interpret the shariʿa, their respective positions are defined by the specific status of their interpretive acts. Al-Qarafi (1967:30–31) provides a useful differentiation of the mufti's fatwa and the judge's judgment. Whereas the mufti's interpretive work follows *adilla,* that is, indications in textual sources (such as the Quran and hadith), that of the judge follows evidential *ḥijāj,* which include testimony, acknowledgment, and oath. As a consequence, fatwas and judgments represent different orientations to the relationship of law and fact. In a fatwa, the factual description, as provided by the questioner, is taken as given, as the point of departure for an interpretive solution that engages the sources of law (or the authoritative opinions of a particular school). In a judgment, competing factual versions put forward by the litigants are themselves the crux of the problem, and sorting them out is the judge's central task. Schematically put (somewhat in the manner of al-Qarafi), fatwas mainly provide determinations of law, assuming a set of facts, while judgments mainly provide determinations of fact, assuming a set of laws.

Fatwas and judgments are also distinguished in ways that derive, in part, from the nature of an appearance before a mufti as opposed to a qadi. The basic circumstances of format—individuals appearing singly to pose questions to the mufti versus pairs of adversaries coming before the judge—are associated with a fundamental difference in the status of the ensuing judicial act: a fatwa is not binding, while a judgment is. The binding *(ilzām)* quality of the judgment, which is to be expected of formal court rulings, is further defined by means of a linguistic analysis (see especially al-Qarafi 1967:46–

64). In this perspective, a judgment is a "creative" *(inshā'ī)* or performative act, a quality it shares with other categories of legal speech acts, such as testimony and binding contractual utterances. Very different as a discursive act is the "informational" *(khabarī)* or communicative nature of the fatwa.[22] In this respect, a mufti is comparable to a transmitter of hadith (al-Nawawi 1988:19; al-Qasimi 1986:53) or to a translator (al-Qarafi 1967:29, 84).

Whereas a judgment entails direct action, a fatwa provides access to shariʿa knowledge in the form of a considered opinion. Whereas a judgment carries the presumption of finality, a fatwa enters a world of competing opinions.[23] The authority of a judgment is narrowly specific *(khāṣṣ)*, applying only to a particular case and its participants, while that of a fatwa is general *(ʿāmm)*, potentially extending beyond the circumstances of the given questioner to govern all equivalent cases (Ibn al-Qayyim al-Jawziyya 1969, 1:38; see Ibn Taymiyya 1381/1961, 3:238–240). Accordingly, while copies of judgment texts issued in court cases were entered into local shariʿa court records, there was no concept of precedent entailed in such rulings, and thus no system of publishing or referencing. Broader in both address and applicability, important fatwas, by contrast, frequently were collected in book form and cited across space and time. Despite their nonbinding and informational qualities, then, fatwas often had a significant impact on the law, and it is in this light that the burden of the mufti as a human interpreter of God's law may be seen as even greater than that of the judge (see Ibn al-Qayyim al-Jawziyya 1969, 1:38).

While the terms of a judge's jurisdiction, specified as part of the delegation of authority *(wilāya)* in his appointment, typically included hearing particular cases arising in substantive areas of the shariʿa, such as transactions (*muʿāmalāt*), injuries *(jināyāt)*, and quranic crimes *(ḥudūd)*, what was the corresponding terrain of the mufti? Al-Nawawi (1988:24) considers the absolute mufti to be competent in "all the chapters of the shariʿa," but he also mentions the (contested) notion of a specialized mufti competent "in a particular chapter," such as inheritance. Al-Qarafi (1967:23–24) makes an interesting distinction: a judge gives binding rulings only with respect to conflicts that entail interests of "this world" *(al-dunyā)*, not those of "the hereafter" *(al-ākhira)*. In the different, informational medium of their fatwas, by contrast, muftis address questions pertaining to both categories, irrespective of their basis in a conflict. According to al-Qarafi (1925–1926, 4:48), all matters connected with ritual law *(ʿibādāt)*, including ablutions, prayer, tithes, fasting, and pilgrimage, fall exclusively within the domain of the mufti. In speculations on the possibility of judges issuing fatwas, it is agreed that this could only occur in connection with nonjusticiable matters, such as rituals (al-Nawawi 1988:22; Jad al-Haqq 1980, 1:22). In certain regional legal cultures, muftis have given responses in domains lying well beyond the conventional boundaries of the fiqh, including such fields as mysticism. Masud (1984:143,150) argues generally that the scope of fatwas is considerably broader than that of fiqh and is best compared to the breadth of subject matter encountered in the hadith. Some early theorists would limit the response range of muftis, however. Al-Nawawi (1988:65–69), for example, identifies *kalām* (theology) as a problematic field. He reports that some muftis responded to theological questions by saying, "This is not included in our knowledge," "We did not sit [to give fatwas] for this," or "A question other than this I will take." Al-Nawawi (1988:69–70) also cites two earlier adab al-mufti writers who maintained that the mufti should refer questions relating to quranic exegesis *(tafsīr)* to specialists in exegesis, unless they pertained directly to legal rules *(aḥkām)*. In addition to their regular shariʿa-oriented activities, Ottoman muftis also addressed a number of subjects, including sultans' firmans and matters relating to taxation, crime, agriculture, and procedure that were regulated by state law *(qānūn)*.[24]

Both judges and muftis are strictly forbidden to accept bribes *(rashwa);* judges may not accept gifts of any kind, since their rulings have binding force. While official muftis were salaried or received fees (Heyd 1969:52–53), the prevailing conception concerning private muftis was that they should give fatwas for free (Ibn al-Qayyim al-Jawziyya 1969, 2:262; *al-Fatāwā al-ʿĀlamgīriyya,* cited in Masud 1984:149, cf. 140; Zafir al-Din 1962, 1:93ff.), just as teachers ideally were to provide instruction without receiving payment. Of his work issuing fatwas, al-Shawkani (d. 1834) stated, "I acquired knowledge without a price and I wanted to give it thus" (cited in Messick 1993:145). One solution to providing appropriate income for muftis and teachers was to establish pious endowments for their support.[25] The adab al-mufti writers such as al-Nawawi (1988:39–41; see Masud 1984:149) discuss several issues relating to income, including support from the treasury *(bayt al-māl),* fees collected from questioners, collective support by the community, and gifts.

Questions and Answers

Behind the encounter of mustafti and mufti, the posing of a query and the giving of a fatwa, lies a complex social and interpretive relation. Entering into this important relationship is not always a simple matter. As noted earlier, from the perspective of the jurists, individuals qualified to be muftis are sometimes reluctant to serve or else doubt their own qualifications. Malik is reported to have said, "I did not issue fatwas until seventy individuals swore to me that I was qualified" (cited in al-Nawawi 1988:18). It was in theory the Great Imam, or caliph, the spiritual-temporal leader of the Muslim community, who appointed (public) muftis (al-Qarafi 1967:32; Ibn Khaldun 1958, 1:451). In his adab al-mufti treatise, al-Nawawi (1988:17–

18) briefly mentions how the Imam ought to go about making appointments and regulating existing muftis. "To ascertain if an individual is competent for *al-futyā,* the Imam was to make inquiries among the scholars of his [the candidate's] era." Muftis found to be incompetent are to be officially prohibited from issuing fatwas and punished if they persist (see Tyan 1965:866; Schacht 1964:126). On the private side, although muftis do not receive any specialized training, their activities can be regulated by teachers through the granting of licenses to teach and issue fatwas (al-Qalqashandi 1919, 14:322ff.).

The questioner confronts the problems of finding a mufti and of deciding which of several to approach. Like the caliph, but from a very different societal position, the questioner may have to make inquiries and even conduct "research." Travel might be necessary: "For a single question, many in the earlier generations used to journey days and nights," al-Nawawi (1988:71) remarks. The questioner's task is to assess a potential mufti's scholarly reputation, ideally basing his or her choice on secure public information as to the qualifications of the individual, not just for knowledge or teaching but specifically for fatwa giving. An uneducated questioner faces an obvious difficulty in evaluating information about scholarly credentials. The treatises urge caution in relying on the views of laymen about juristic qualifications and also raise the posssibility of misrepresentation *(talbīs).* The solutions offered to the questioner include relying on his or her own sense of the mufti's piety *(diyāna)* or on information provided by a just person (*ʿādil*). However, since muftis typically are well known, such concerns are mainly theoretical in nature.

Equally theoretical, but more directly relevant to understanding the social relation of knowledge and power, is the conceptual distinction between the mufti and the mustafti, involving diametrically opposed statuses with respect to the key activity of shariʿa interpretation. In a concise *uṣūl* work, al-Juwayni (1906:38) says that while the mufti must be a qualified interpreter and cannot be a doctrinal follower (muqallid), the questioner cannot be an interpreter and must be a follower. Al-Nawawi (1988:71) describes the questioner as follows: "Anyone not at the level of the mufti with respect to the shariʿa rules asked about is a questioner, a doctrinal follower of the one who gives him a fatwa." Further, in the event of an occurence necessitating knowledge of a shariʿa principle, such an individual is formally obligated to seek an opinion. Especially in pre-modern societies, this sharp differentiation of interpretive roles echoed wider hierarchical differences between the scholar and the uninformed *(jāhil)* or nonspecialist (*ʿāmmī*). In diverse historical settings of restricted literacy and restricted control of the essential cultural capital that shariʿa knowledge represents, the relation between mufti and questioner is a relation of power.

As an expression of the social honor vested in muftis, they are to be approached with correct comportment and the appropriate gestures of deference and respect (al-Nawawi 1988:83; see also Chapter 21 in this volume). Since muftis should be exemplary moral figures, a sinner *(fāsiq)* is disqualified from the post.[26] Al-Shatibi (n.d., 4:246, 261) understands the mufti to be a guide and a leader, and he therefore considers the mufti's personal actions to constitute fatwas. Specifically, a mufti's own practice must not be contrary to the fatwas he issues, nor should it contradict the doctrines of his school of law. At the fatwa-giving session *(majlis)*, the mufti must be attentive to his appearance and demeanor. Proper dress (al-Qarafi 1967:271) and a dignified and calm manner are required. Like judges, muftis should not engage in interpretive work when their physical states are disturbed by anger, hunger, or fatigue. Just as judges are to strive for equality of treatment of the adversaries who come before them, muftis are to answer questioners without preference and in the order in which they arrive. Implicitly acknowledging that fatwas frequently are issued in connection with adversarial disputes, al-Nawawi (1988:54) cautions muftis to avoid favoritism.

While interest in shariʿa interpretation inevitably gravitates toward the fatwa and the potential exercise therein of ijtihad, the interpretive process between mufti and questioner begins with the posing of the question. Questions are of great significance, because they are the means by which concrete concerns and quandaries are formally brought to the attention of qualified legal specialists. Due to the access they provide to the "actual" problems of specific societies, questions posed to muftis are important sources for research. Far from representing simple windows on reality, however, many questions are themselves carefully constructed, containing motivated and selective renderings of the facts and issues. The variations on this theme are many, including purely didactic questions, drafting by the scholarly or literate for the untutored, and, at the extreme, trick questions, or a series of slightly differing questions, designed to elicit a desired response (see Chapter 6). In the highly institutionalized Ottoman case, where the intention was to facilitate brief replies, often a simple "yes" or "no," the reformulation of the question by official scribes "became a decisive stage in the preparation of the fatwa" (Heyd 1969:49).

It is a characteristic feature of fatwa giving that the question not only initiates the mufti's interpretive activity but also constrains it. As muftis must answer according to what is asked, their field of response is largely determined by the formulation of the question. Since the mufti is not an investigator of the facts, these are taken as given. In addition, while the issues involved ought to be ones that have actually arisen and should not be purely hypothetical or imaginary (Heyd 1969:53–54; Masud 1984:137, 148),[27] questions are commonly posed in general terms, using the names of fictional individuals, such as Zayd and ʿAmr (Heyd 1969:41), or simply "a man" or "a woman." Such usage of generic descriptions and fictional names distances the query from the particular evidential circumstances of the questioner. Yet in many settings, the mufti is confronted personally by the questioner, whose name appears below the text of the question. In this distinctive juxtaposition of the abstract and the actual, questions delimit the fatwa as a genre of legal response.

Before getting into the process of formulating an answer, the mufti must comprehend the question. Crucial to this comprehension is knowledge of local customs and colloquial language (see al-Qarafi 1967:231–253). Changing linguistic conventions and differences between a questioner's manifest expression and actual intent are typical problems. Unlike the judge, the mufti is instructed not to proceed on the basis of his own "knowledge about the real situation," unless this is directly reflected in the formulation of the question (al-Nawawi 1988:46). If uncertainty regarding the question persists, the mufti may ask for elucidation or append a caveat to his response, such as "this [is the answer] if the matter is thus" (al-Nawawi 1988:45; see al-Wansharisi 1981–1983, cited in Powers 1993:91). Ottoman opinions were given by muftis "according to what [the questioners] made known [to them]" (Heyd 1969:51). Before delivering the fatwa to the questioner, the mufti should read his response to, and seek the advice of, qualified individuals present with him at the fatwa-giving session (al-Nawawi 1988:48).

In the event that a mufti has no answer, a model fatwa-giving license presented by al-Qalqashandi (1919, 14:325) exhorts the incumbent not to "refrain from saying, concerning what he does not know, 'I do not know.'" On the other hand, both public and private muftis regularly respond to routine informational questions. Heyd (1969:54) writes, "A large number of Ottoman fatwas deal with very simple legal questions the reply to which is obvious and free from any doubt." Part of the fatwa-issuing work of many noted scholars typically is devoted to the giving of ordinary opinions to private questioners. In ninteenth-century Yemen, al-Shawkani refers both to his major fatwas, which were collected and preserved as a book, and to his "shorter" fatwas, which he said "could never be counted" and which were not recorded (cited in Messick 1993:150). As grand mufti of Egypt at the turn of the twentieth century, Muhammad ʿAbduh "revived a moribund practice of granting opinions to private individuals on their problems of belief and practice, and in this regard he issued a number of controversial fatwas" (Kerr 1966:104).

Thus far, a written form for the question has been assumed; oral communication involves other considerations. Since this form of delivery leaves no documentary trace, the historical incidence of oral questions and answers is unknown. The single reported instance concerns the extremely bureaucratized Ottoman system, where in the late period questioners could request an oral fatwa from a specially designated functionary (Heyd 1969:47). The earlier adab al-mufti writers discuss some implications of oral exchanges between mufti and questioner, and verbal and written fatwas are presented as options (al-Nawawi 1988:44; see al-Qalqashandi 1919, 14:325). One theoretical justification of a mufti's income invokes the difference between obligatory oral fatwas, given for free, and supplemental written fatwas, given for a fee (al-Nawawi 1988:39; *al-Fatāwā al-ʿĀlamgīriyya,* cited in Masud 1984:149).

In general, where reduction to writing limits the scope of inquiry by restricting the mufti's view of the facts, oral communication can be open-ended. The treatises specifically recommend use of the spoken word to achieve at least a minimal level of comprehension when this is a problem (al-Nawawi 1988:46, 63). Recourse to the spoken medium is also helpful in a number of difficult situations. "If it becomes apparent to the mufti that the answer goes against the objective of the questioner, and if [the questioner] refuses to have [the answer] written on his paper, then [the mufti] should limit himself to an oral reply" (al-Nawawi 1988:54). In the delicate situation of a mufti's being shown an inaccurate (written) fatwa obtained from another mufti by a questioner who refuses to have it corrected, a recommended option is to respond orally (al-Nawawi 1988:61; see Chapter 6 in this volume). Advocating an oral response to laymen who inquire about extremely complicated or technical issues, al-Qarafi (1967:283) remarks, "The tongue communicates that which the pen cannot, because it is alive while the pen is dead."

As the chapters in this volume illustrate, actual fatwas assume a variety of local forms, differing in language and literary style, conventions of inclusion and exclusion, and usage of characteristic rubrics. The work of Uriel Heyd (1969) on the Ottoman period remains the most thorough examination of the textual aspects of a single fatwa-giving tradition. At the level of phrase selection, the adab al-mufti treatises provide samplers of appropriate invocations of the divinity (see Heyd 1969:38–39, on the Ottoman *daʿvet*), opening and closing honorifics, terms of address for figures such as the sultan, and formulas for emphasis. They also discuss the mufti's disclaimer, some version of which, such as *allāhu aʿlam,* "God knows best," is characteristic of virtually all fatwas.

The adab al-mufti treatises also address issues relating to form and content. Important variations among fatwas derive either from differences among muftis, discussed earlier, or from differences among questioners. In addressing nonspecialists, muftis are to be concise and informal, while in responding to scholars, especially judges, a fuller technical discussion typically is required (see Chapters 5, 15, and 16). Fatwas may consist of one-word answers, such as "true," "false," and "permitted"; otherwise, in answering laymen, the mufti should convey his opinion in a mode of expression *(ʿibāra)* that is both clear and correct (al-Nawawi 1988:48). Where some authors do not require the mufti to specify the opinion's basis *(ḥujja, dalīl)* if the questioner is a nonspecialist, al-Nawawi (1988:64) says, "It is not objectionable for the mufti to indicate the *ḥujja* in his fatwa if it is a text that is clear and short" (see also Rashid Rida 1970–1971, 4:1258–1259). Similarly, the mufti is not required to mention his methods of reasoning *("ṭarīq al-ijtihād wa-wajhat al-qiyās wa'l-istidlāl")* unless the intended recipient is a jurist (al-Nawawi 1988:64). Another view holds that such citations should be avoided so as to distinguish the fatwa genre from other types of composition (al-Nawawi 1988:65; see also al-Qaradawi 1982:25). As muftis commonly are affiliated with particular schools of law, in some historical settings they cite authors of authoritative works in their fatwas. Qadi Khan (1893, 1:3) states that a mufti muqallid should accept the opinion of "the best jurist" of his school and "attribute his answer to him." In later Ottoman times, muftis of the capital did not cite authorities, while provincial muftis characteristically did (Heyd 1969:44–45). Together with the recognition of distinct local traditions of Muslim legal writing, technical considerations, such as the status of the recipient, help clarify some of the variation observed within the fatwa genre. A fatwa that does not cite any source text or engage in formal reasoning thus may be seen as intended for a nonspecialist, rather than, as in the view of Weber (1978:797), the work of a judicial oracle. Complex fatwas delivered to scholars and judges, however, are frequently highly implicit in other ways, and challenge us to read for culturally specific styles of argumentation (see Chapter 8).

The material qualities of fatwas as writings also have drawn attention (e.g., al-Nawawi 1988:46–49, 54, 60; al-Qarafi 1967:254–256, 264–266). Beginning with the desideratum of a balanced, consistent, and clear script, ideally using the same pen throughout, the goal is to assure the authority of the written fatwa text. Recommendations as to the physical placement of writing on the paper and, specifically, the danger of leaving open spaces or mistakes and other defects in either the question or the answer address concerns about forgery and legal stratagems. To avoid a potential stratagem *(ḥīla)*, the mufti is cautioned not to use two pieces of paper, but to write on either the margin or the back side of the same piece. As handwriting and signature are the authoritative mark of the individual, when they are consistent an opinion can be conclusively identified. While questions often are written out by a scribe or by someone other than the questioner, the fatwa text and the signature must be in the mufti's own hand (Heyd 1969:42–43). The paper itself, which may contain previous fatwas, is the property of the questioner and should not be taken away or crossed out without the questioner's permission. In provincial Yemen, questioners present their question to the mufti on a small piece of paper. The mufti answers immediately, in the space left above the question, and then hands the paper back to the questioner, who departs with it (Messick 1993; Chapter 28 in this volume).

If constructing the question is the initial step in the interpretive process, deconstructing the answer is the last. When the questioner does not understand the fatwa, al-Nawawi (1988:63) counsels the mufti to detain him until he does. Frequently, questioners take their fatwas to individuals in the mufti's entourage, or to others, to have them read or explicated (see Chapter 16). Supplementary or follow-up questions, asking for further details or anticipating implications, are also documented in a number of settings (Heyd 1969:43; Chapter 15, this volume). To the extent that fatwas are contestable (see Chapters 3, 8, and 17), a dissatisfied questioner might approach another mufti for a second opinion, while opponents might seek out different muftis to vindicate their respective positions. Al-Nawawi (1988:36) discusses the legal implications of a fatwa's subsequent revision (see Chapter 16). If the mufti revises the fatwa because it is contrary to the Quran, the Sunna, or consensus, the questioner must be informed (see Jad al-Haqq 1980, 1:23–24). If the mufti revises the fatwa on other grounds, the old fatwa may still be valid, if based on ijtihad, and there is no obligation to inform the questioner. Once a questioner has been informed of a revision, however, he or she must follow the new fatwa.

Modern Muftis

How have muftis and the issuance of fatwas fared in modern times? Assessments range from a finding of general "obsolescence" (Tyan 1965:866) to arguments for revitalization and a new mission.[28] This volume, which contains a significant variety of "modern" fatwas, issued in ninteenth- and early twentieth-century contexts of colonial rule and reformist debate (see Part III) and in more contemporary times (Part IV), permits a complex, comparative view of continuities and changes. While the specific detail regarding local settings and circumstances is to be found in the individual chapters, some of the broader currents of the developments surrounding modern muftis and their fatwas may be summarized here.

Of the fundamental changes that have had a direct impact on muftis, perhaps none is more important than the transformation in the essential character of knowledge and its means of transmission. Curricular and organizational changes in educational institutions have meant that the shariʿa, or fiqh, formerly the centerpiece of advanced instruction and of Muslim knowledge itself, has been largely displaced by a spectrum of "secular" subjects, many derived from Western models. Typically, the study of fiqh has been removed to Islamic institutes or to specialized law schools, where it competes with offerings in Western-style law. Rather than muftis, lawyers and law professors are the legal professionals now produced by most mainstream educational systems. While muftis inhabited a social world characterized by patterns of sharply restricted literacy and unequal distribution of the essential shariʿa-based knowledge, contemporary societies are well on the way to generalized literacy (Eickelman 1992) and reliance on a variety of new and specialized forms of expertise. To the extent that the shariʿa remains relevant or authoritative, it is usually in the domain of family law, as recast in codes, an alteration far more consequential than the move to a new framework of numbered articles might seem to indicate. Beginning with the Ottoman civil code (the *Majalla*) of the late ninteenth century, and continuing in colonial and nation-state contexts, codification powerfully harnessed shariʿa materials, adapting them to the different epistemology and categories of international legal standards. In the process, a key dimension of interpretive authority passed from the hands of individual jurists, including muftis, to the collective bodies of national legislatures.

The situations of modern muftis, both public and private, vary according to the type of overarching legal and political system in which they operate, as well as according to their educational formation. While the extremely elaborate bureaucratic hierarchies associated with the office of the Ottoman shaykh ul-islam no longer exist (the office was abolished in 1924), patterns of formalization and rationalization are nevertheless characteristic of twentieth-century public muftiships found across the Muslim world. "Grand" muftis and muftis of the republic are currently found in a variety of nation-states, with the incumbents usually serving under government appointments and with their activity regulated by legislation.[29] While the establishment of the Egyptian grand mufti dates to the late ninteenth century, state muftis were not appointed until after the middle of this century in a number of other nations, including Saudi Arabia (1953), Lebanon (1955), Malaysia (1955), Yemen (1962), and Indonesia (1975). In some institutional contexts, fatwa giving is now closely associated with religious propagation and guidance activities (*daʿwa* and *irshād*).[30] Formal instructional programs and apprenticeships for the training of muftis have been established in institutions such as Azhar University in Egypt and Dar al-ʿUlum in Karachi, which has a specialized two-year program of courses in iftaʾ (Danish 1978:772–775; Chapter 16, this volume). On the other hand, the modern era has also seen fatwa giving by individuals, such as Maudoodi, who had no traditional training. Elsewhere, it has been asserted that authority in matters of shariʿa interpretation should no longer be restricted to the ʿulamaʾ. In some quarters, muftis in particular have borne the brunt of political criticism.[31]

A significant modern organizational development is the appearance of specialized committees charged with collective fatwa giving. Institutions with titles such as Dar al-ifta' have appeared in many countries (see Chapters 16, 17, 18, 20, 23, 26). In his discussion of the "fatwa organization [*hay'a*] in the contemporary age," Shaltut (1974:14) refers to two such Egyptian institutions, one based at Azhar University.[32] Other notable fatwa committees include that established by the World Muslim League in Mecca, the Fatwa Committee of the Organization of Islamic Countries, and the Council of Islamic Ideology in Pakistan.[33]

While the roles of mufti and judge, and their respective legal products, the fatwa and the judgment, have remained distinct, at times their interrelationship has proved quite complicated. This is illustrated for the twentieth century by the assumptions underpinning a procedural code (based on an Egyptian law of 1931) enacted in Lahj (South Yemen) in 1949. Article 100 of this code states, "No qadi [judge] might issue a fatwa in any claim due to be heard (or which had been heard) by any court of law, any fatwa issued contrary to this rule should be entirely disregarded, and no court should regard itself as in any way bound by a fatwa issued before litigation began" (Anderson 1970:33). As was true of a variety of pre-modern historical settings, notably the Andalusian *shūra,* modern muftis have been attached directly to courts and have delivered opinions in connection with trial proceedings.[34] Contemporary Indonesia (see Chapter 20) offers a variant in which fatwas are issued by the Islamic courts themselves.[35]

Another possible relationship between mufti and judge, and fatwa and judgment, was illustrated by the situation in Iraq before the drafting of the personal status code in the middle of this century. As in pre-modern contexts, such as in Morocco (see Chapter 8), previously issued fatwas were treated by jurists as a source of established legal rules to guide court outcomes. Collections of fatwas "given at different times, in reference to heterogeneous circumstances" (Anderson 1953:44) were considered authoritative and were applied in case rulings by Iraqi judges no longer qualified as mujtahids competent to carry out their own independent interpretations of the law. In contemporary states, the relationship between muftis and court activity depends on the status of shariʿa-based law in the national jurisdictions and also on the existence of a formal legislative mandate.

Fatwas have continued to figure at key historical junctures as appropriate vehicles for expressing shariʿa views of major political events. When issued at the behest of governments, fatwas have served as the ultimate statements of shariʿa principle, defining or supporting general policies. Thus fatwas were obtained at the outbreak of World War I in 1914 (Peters 1979:90–92) and before the Gulf War of 1990 (Chapter 27). As in earlier centuries, an entire branch of modern fatwa activity concerns religious and doctrinal disputes, set in contexts of colonial rule and Islamic reform movements (see

Chapters 12, 14, 17, 19). In very recent years, the fatwa has become a worldwide media phenomenon, especially in connection with the assassination of Anwar al-Sadat and the condemnation of Salman Rushdie (Appignanesi and Maitland 1990; Fischer and Abedi 1990; Asad 1990). In a broader and far less spectacular sense, the fatwas of modern muftis have directly and indirectly registered Muslim reactions to and initiatives in the modern world. New technologies such as the phonograph (Snouck Hurgronje 1915; Masud 1969), birth control policies (Schieffelin 1965; al-Qalqili 1969:"*hāʾ*"), smoking (al-Shawkani 1969:47–48; Al al-Shaykh 1979; Calmard 1991a:552), interest banking (Chapter 26), and immigration (Shaltut 1974; al-Qalqili 1969; see also Masud 1990:42) have all been addressed in fatwas. To back up his statement that his recent collection of 200 Saudi fatwas "should be found in every house," a compiler (al-Shuwadafi 1408/1987–1988:4) offers examples of relevant topics covered: selling blood, administering medical treatment with alcohol, eating imported chicken, wearing pants and jackets, working in banks, Muslim women going to Muslim and non-Muslim doctors, eating butter from Holland, drinking Coca-Cola, and dealing with nationalization.

Departing from the range of coverage found in older fatwa collections, some recently published volumes, bearing subtitles such as *Studies [dirāsāt] in the Problems of the Contemporary Muslim* (Shaltut 1974; see also Lemke 1980 and Zebiri 1983), include innovative sections devoted to "social issues" or "social relations." These cover such topics as moon exploration, communism and Islam, religion and development, music and singing, and suicide (Shaltut 1974); minimum wage rates, beer drinking, television watching, and representational art (al-Qaradawi 1982). In the meantime, the relative importance of the old-style fatwa categories appears to be shifting. More than half of the material in collections of fatwas issued by central Middle Eastern muftis such as Makhluf (1965), Shaltut (1974), al-Qaradawi (1982), and Ibn Baz (Ibn Baz et al. 1988) now falls into "religious" categories, that is, ritual law, creed *(ʿaqāʾid),* and quranic exegesis. Reflecting the smaller place occupied by the shariʿa in many civil law regimes, the formerly prominent transactions *(muʿāmalāt)* sections are reduced to less than 5 percent of the total in these volumes, while coverage of family law (marriage, divorce, inheritance, and endowments) still represents as much as 25 percent of the fatwas. In sum, while the scope of the modern fatwa appears broader in social address, it has at the same time become more specialized in "religious" issues and, with the exception of the interest maintained in family law, generally less concerned with strictly legal issues.[36]

Many modern muftis consciously have revised the discourse of their fatwas to accommodate their perceptions of new societal conditions. Echoing a move first seen in the Ottoman Majalla in the last century, in which some usages of the fiqh were replaced by a more widely understood idiom, muftis now tend to utilize more accessible and contemporary language in their fatwas, although they frequently hold to the distinction between laymen *(ʿawāmm)* and scholars. "We have endeavored to attain simple and clear expression," writes Makhluf (1965:9). A principle for al-Qaradawi (1982:15) is to "address people in the language of the age." While many contemporary muftis strive for simplicity and concision, they also are more apt to introduce supporting examples and even comparative material from other religions or philosophies. Reflecting the growth of specialized modern knowledge and disciplines, muftis occasionally must draw on lay experts (Chapter 26). Many muftis are concerned about the relevance of their fatwa work. As a consequence, some avoid answering questions lacking in social benefit or contemporary importance, such as questions about the measurements of Paradise (Shaltut 1974:14) or the relative merits of the Family versus the Companions of the Prophet or the createdness of the Quran (al-Qaradawi 1982:18–30). As a relatively "liberal" mufti, al-Qaradawi seeks common ground between contemporary extremes, represented by those "who want to change everything" and those "who want to forbid everything."

Some contemporary muftis describe their freedom from the constraints of interpretive school (madhhab) doctrine (see Makhluf 1965:9; Shaltut 1974:15; al-Qaradawi 1982:10). Such muftis refer directly to the source texts of the Quran and the Sunna of the Prophet, without citing the positions of the old schools. Al-Qaradawi (1982:11) refers to an equivalent conception of Ibn al-Qayyim al-Jawziyya in identifying his own interpretive work as involving "*al-ijtihād al-juzʾī*," an applied ijtihad connected with detailed matters. Addressing the question of the necessity of ijtihad, al-Qalqili (1969:"*tāʾ*") states that it is inevitable that muftis will be asked about matters not precisely covered by particular source texts, and that they must then interpretively extract principles from the available sources. For their part, and in a manner parallel to the new panels of judges that replaced the single qadi in some modern jurisdictions, fatwa-giving committees exercise a novel form of collective ijtihad (see Masud, 1995).

A more subtle but nevertheless fundamental shift in the way in which muftis operate concerns the media in which contemporary fatwas are delivered. Where the options were formerly handwritten and oral, they now include print and the broadcast media. While the authoritative fatwas of noted pre-modern muftis were collected and circulated in limited fashion as manuscripts, the fatwas of influential modern muftis (and also many famous predecessors) now appear in print and achieve extremely widespread distribution. The adoption of print technology occurred comparatively late in the central part of the Muslim world, and was marked (in the Ottoman Empire) by the issuance of an authorizing fatwa in 1727 (Kramers 1934, 4:277; Kut 1991:800). Print is important not only for the publication of fatwa collections in book form but also for the wider dissemination of fatwas in newpapers, magazines, and journals, as well as for the gazetting of many opinions in the public legal record. The fatwas of many modern muftis have been published individually in newspapers and later collected in book form. Associated generally with the rise of the nation-state and the growth of mass markets (B. Anderson 1983), print heralds a number of basic discursive changes, including a shift in authorial voice, new rhetorical forms, and a greatly expanded and differently constituted readership (Messick 1993:115–131; Robinson 1993).

Dissemination through the print medium may be transnational as well as national in character, reaching Muslims around the world with a new rapidity. Transnational fatwas tend to rephrase specific local or national problems to speak to the common experiences of widely differing communities. In the early years of the twentieth century, Muhammad Rashid Rida (d. 1935) issued a famous series of fatwas in his publication *al-Manār*.[37] Beginning in 1903, first under the title "Question and Fatwa," and later "Fatwas of *al-Manār*," Rida responded to a wide variety of queries sent in by readers from all corners of the Muslim world. His general method was to rely directly on Quran and hadith, and then on "reason" *(ʿaql)*, and his principal aim was to foster Islamic unity. Collected now in six volumes (Rida 1970), the 2,592 fatwas first published in the pages of *al-Manār* constitute a remarkable record of the preoccupations and interests of early twentieth-century Muslims.

Fatwas are regularly broadcast on radio and television services, and reproduced on audio and video cassettes (Eickelman 1989). These media take the changes brought by print an important step further. Unlike the print medium, literacy is not a requirement for listeners and viewers. For this reason, the broadcast media place a further demand on the authors of fatwas to use more accessible language and, depending on the range of reception, to address concerns in a manner relevant to a mass audience, either national or international in scope (Chapter 28). It is apparent, however, that the issuance of fatwas in the electronic media age retains some of the institution's former character as a societal barometer, as modern muftis respond to the specific concerns and the changing worldly circumstances of their questioners. Al-Qaradawi (1982:33–35; see also Shaltut 1974:15) has commented on his broadcasting work. Citing the earlier community-building work of the print mufti Muhammad Rashid Rida, he endeavors to find ways for his listeners and viewers to "come together where we agree, and forgive one another where we do not." Although he advocates exacting analysis and debate, he maintains that radio and television are not the appropriate media for these activities. Al-Qaradawi also notes an interesting new phenomenon associated with his broadcasts: he receives more requests for fatwas from women than from men.[38]

One further characteristic of the contemporary age is the striking reuse of terminology,[39] and the institutional language of the muftiship is no exception. Although perhaps not exclusively a modern phenomenon, the extension of the sense of the term "mufti" to designate not only a legal interpreter but also a political figure has occurred in the cases of the former mufti of Jerusalem (Mattar 1987; Hopwood 1980) and the mufti of the republic in midcentury Lebanon, who became, by legislative decree, the general "religious leader" of the Muslim community (Tyan 1965). A still wider departure from the general notion of ifta' is the term's usage in the late Ottoman Empire as a rubric for codification (Berkes 1964:169; Mahmassani 1961:41). In the present day, the old concept of istifta' (request for a fatwa) is reemployed to refer to a popular referendum or plebicite.

CHAPTER TWO

Ifta' and Ijtihad in Sunni Legal Theory: A Developmental Account

WAEL B. HALLAQ

Since its beginnings, Islamic legal theory has concerned itself with the establishment of principles and precepts that govern the procedure of ijtihad, or legal interpretation, from the initial stages of juridical reasoning and legal causation down to the promulgation of rulings and their implementation. The institution of ifta' and its practitioner, the mufti, were central to that part of legal theory that dealt with the modalities of transmitting the outcome of ijtihad from the domain of the legal profession down to the public. For it was chiefly in their capacity as muftis that the jurists of Islam could communicate the mundane results of their legal constructions to the *mukallafūn,* those on whom the observation of the law was incumbent, and without whom the law would have had no existential purpose.

The close link between ifta' and ijtihad explains why the early theoreticians stipulated that to qualify as a jurisconsult, one first had to be a mujtahid. It is with the chronological juristic discussions of this requirement that I am concerned in this chapter, though I shall also address the issue as a case study of the adaptation of theoretical discourse to juridical practices in the real world.

I begin with the celebrated al-Shafiʿi (d. 820), who does not explicitly state that a mufti must be capable of ijtihad, but nonetheless enumerates the branches of knowledge in which one must be proficient in order to qualify as a mufti. It turns out that these branches are precisely those at which the mujtahid must be adept, and they include skilled knowledge of the Quran, of the Prophet's Sunna, the Arabic language, the legal questions subject to consensus, and the art of legal reasoning *(qiyās)* (al-Shafiʿi 1325/1907–1908, 7:274).

More than two centuries later, the requirement remained unchanged. Abu al-Husayn al-Basri (d. 1044) explicitly maintains that for a jurist to qualify as a mufti, he must be a mujtahid; and to reach the rank of ijtihad, an encompassing knowledge of legal reasoning is a prerequisite. Al-Basri, however, subsumes virtually all branches of rational and textual knowledge under the general category of legal reasoning, since reasoning about the law, he argues, requires expert knowledge of the revealed texts, of the sciences that treat them—such as those of abrogation *(al-nāsikh wa'l-mansūkh)* and transmission of hadith—and of the methods of establishing and verifying the *ratio legis* (*'illa*) of a case of law (al-Basri 1964–1965, 2:929–931). Only when all these sciences and texts have been mastered may one be permitted to issue fatwas. The sole exception to this, al-Basri maintains, is a jurist who is adept at such sciences and texts only insofar as they pertain to the law of inheritance. In this case, he may be allowed to issue fatwas in this area alone, since inheritance cases and wills rarely bear on other branches of the law (ibid., 2:932). With this exception, a mufti must fulfill the requirement of ijtihad, the implication being that a mufti, when asked to issue a fatwa, must not follow the teachings of other jurists but should, rather, formulate his own opinion on the question addressed to him.[1] This is quite different from a situation in which a layman requests the mufti-mujtahid merely to state the opinion of other jurists concerning an issue, in which case he, the mufti, must comply with such a request and must name the authority who held the opinion (ibid., 2:932). In all other cases, ifta' clearly means for al-Basri the exercise of ijtihad, for if a mufti issues a fatwa through taqlid, namely, by following the authority and doctrines of others, then he is considered a muqallid. As al-Basri sees it, the logical conclusion of allowing a muqallid to practice ifta' is grave, since it means that laymen, who are commonly defined as muqallids, are permitted to issue fatwas, whether for themselves or for others, on the basis of the writings of earlier jurists—a conclusion that is utterly objectionable (ibid., 2:932).[2]

All other eleventh-century jurists who include a discussion of this matter in their works (and who have been surveyed), maintain, directly or indirectly, that ijtihad is a prerequisite for fatwa giving. While al-Shirazi (d. 1083), like al-Shafi'i, enumerates the sciences and texts the mufti must master (and they are again identical to those the mujtahid ought to know; al-Shirazi 1988, 2:1033), al-Baji (d. 1081) insists, after having given a similar list of sciences, that any jurist who falls short of mastering even a part of these fields of legal knowledge must not be permitted to practice ifta' (1986: 722). And al-Mawardi (d. 1058) predicated both ifta' and *qaḍā'* on the attainment of ijtihad (1971–1972, 1:637). In his commentary on al-Shafi'i's *Risāla,* Abu Muhammad al-Juwayni (d. 1046), the father of Imam al-Haramayn, is reported to have held that "he who commits to memory all of al-Shafiʿi's writings and those of other jurists, but who does not understand their true meanings, is permitted neither to practice ijtihad nor to draw inferences about the law. He will not be qualified as a mufti [*lā yakūn min ahl al-fatwā*], and it is not permissible for him to issue fatwas" (cited in al-Shawkani n.d.[a]:270–271).

Similarly, in his *Burhān,* Imam al-Haramayn al-Juwayni (d. 1085) not only uses the terms "mufti" and "mujtahid" interchangeably but also reports that jurists by and large have required muftis to possess masterly knowledge of both the texts containing the law and the methods of legal reasoning that are necessary for deriving *(istinbāṭ)* rules for novel legal cases.[3] In al-Juwayni's own view, a mufti must be able to derive the legal norms for new cases, and this requires that he be adept at exegesis *(tafsīr)* and language. Though a mufti need not memorize the hadith, he must be able to locate what is necessary for solving legal issues in the commonly accredited collections. Finally, he must be well versed in the science of *uṣūl al-fiqh,* which lays down the methodology and principles of the law (al-Juwayni 1979, 2:1332–1333). In his rather short work, *al-Waraqāt,* al-Juwayni summarizes his views by saying that the mufti must have an all-embracing knowledge of ijtihad *("kāmil al-āla fīʾl-ijtihād")* (n.d.: 14).

In his *al-Mustaṣfā,* al-Ghazzali (d. 1111) implies only that the mufti must be able to practice ijtihad, and he quotes with approval a statement from al-Baqillani (d. 1013), to the effect that a layman can choose any of two muftis' opinions, since both must be mujtahids (1904, 2:391). In *al-Mankhūl,* however, he treats the qualifications of the mujtahid as the first subchapter of *kitāb al-fatwā* (1980:462). Later on he declares that "the mufti is he who has complete mastery of the shariʿa rules embedded in the revealed texts as well as of those discovered by means of legal reasoning [*man istaqalla bi-aḥkām al-sharīʿa naṣṣan waʾistinbāṭan*]" (1980:463, 465). From this, as well as from two other instances in which al-Ghazzali assumes the mufti to be a mujtahid (1980:478, ll. 2, 9–10), one can safely state that he follows in the footsteps of his predecessors in affirming that to be a mufti is to be nothing short of a mujtahid.

About a century after al-Ghazzali, an interesting change occurs in the jurists' treatment of the issue. Although al-Amidi (d. 1234) approaches the problem in the same vein as did his precursors, and although he insists in the beginning of his discussion on the same requirement (1968, 3:245), he later allocates a separate space for the question *(masʾala)* of "whether a non-mujtahid is permitted to issue fatwas according to the school of a mujtahid." Immediately thereafter he adds the significant phrase "as it is the custom nowadays" (1968, 3:254). After having discussed the disagreements among jurists with regard to the matter, he argues that a mujtahid within a legal school *(mujtahid fī'l-madhhab)* who is knowledgeable of the methodology of the independent mujtahid *(mustaqill)* he follows, and who is capable of deriving rules in accordance with this methodology and defending his position in scholarly debates *(munāẓara)*, is entitled to practice ifta'. In support of this opinion, al-Amidi cites what he calls an indubitable consensus of all generations of Muslim scholars (1968, 3:255).

Al-Amidi's discussion indicates three significant changes that took place no later than the middle of the thirteenth century. First he speaks of a juristic disagreement that before the twelfth century must have been, if it existed at all, so marginal that no author we know cared to mention it. While Abu al-Husayn al-Basri and "other *uṣūlī*s" are mentioned as jurists who stood on the side demanding ijtihad, al-Amidi does not name those who took the other side. Second, according to al-Amidi, a less than independent mujtahid may occupy the office of ifta', whereas earlier jurists (with the partial exception of al-Basri) assumed that unqualified ijtihad was indispensable. Third, in al-Amidi and, as we shall see, in others—and this is quite significant—a new section is created and exclusively consecrated for discussing the permissibility (or impermissibility) of issuing fatwas by a jurisconsult who is not a mujtahid.[4]

While al-Amidi's discourse denotes a change with regard to the ijtihad qualification of the mufti, he continues to insist that a jurisconsult must at least be a *mujtahid fī'l-madhhab.* A younger contemporary of al-Amidi, however, goes further. In his *Muntahā al-wuṣūl,* Ibn al-Hajib (d. 1248) concedes that a jurist who is "knowledgeable of a madhhab and is able to reason properly, but who is not himself a mujtahid within the legal school of a mujtahid" (not a "*mujtahid fī'l-madhhab*") is entitled to issue fatwas (1908:165).

A contemporary of Ibn al-Hajib takes yet another step in articulating the change. Ibn al-Salah al-Shahrazuri (d. 1245) wrote an entire treatise dedicated to the institution and practice of futya, and at the outset he makes the significant remark that what he has to say in the work applies to his own times and age (1986, 1:6). Indeed in the course of his work he often points to the actual juridical practices and conditions prevailing in his era.

Ibn al-Salah divides muftis into two kinds, one independent, the other not. The former are equated with the mujtahid mustaqill who follows the teachings and methodology of no one else, and who has established his own legal school (madhhab). This sort of mufti, Ibn al-Salah tells us, has long become extinct (1986, 1:21–28, 29, l. 3). The latter kind, in Ibn al-Salah's classification, may in turn be divided into four types. First is the mufti who enjoys all the qualities of the mujtahid mustaqill but does not have his own legal school. The immediate followers *(aṣḥāb)* of the schools' eponyms are said to have belonged to this category (1986, 1:29ff.). Second is the mufti whose ijtihad is exclusively limited to the methodology laid down by the mujtahid mustaqill but who is capable of deriving, on the basis of this methodology, legal norms for cases hitherto unsolved. This mufti is commonly known as the *mujtahid fī'l-madhhab.* The ifta' of such muftis, Ibn al-Salah remarks, is and has been the normative practice.[5] Third is the jurisconsult who masters and can defend the teachings of the mujtahid he follows, but whose abilities in ijtihad are unequal to those belonging to the two preceding categories. Last is the mufti who is knowledgeable of the teachings of his school but is weak in methodology and legal reasoning. Should such a mufti encounter a yet unsolved case, he must attempt to reach a solution for it if the case presents no particular difficulty. But if the case proves to be too abstruse, he should not solve it but should instead pass it on to a mujtahid. However, this type of mufti, Ibn al-Salah observes, in reality rarely encounters such difficult cases (1986, 1:36–37).

Having completed the classification of the types of muftis, Ibn al-Salah goes on to say that no other types of jurisconsults should issue fatwas. But this is not all. Ibn al-Salah raises, in the name of a hypothetical interlocutor, a real question as to whether a jurist who is a muqallid can issue fatwas, should he be the only jurisconsult available in town. The interlocutor maintains that the muqallid should do so, since it is preferable for a layman to act on such a fatwa than to be left to his own devices. However, Ibn al-Salah neither agrees nor disagrees with the interlocutor. He argues that a layman should, if he can, seek a solution in another locality where a qualified mufti is to be found. But what if such muftis do not exist at all? Ibn al-Salah ostensibly avoids a direct answer to this question. By citing the opinion of some anonymous associates *(aṣḥāb),* he seems to agree with the interlocutor, though grudgingly and vaguely, in allowing a mere muqallid to issue fatwas (1986, 1:39–40).

By the middle of the thirteenth century, the concession allowing muqallids to occupy the office of ifta' seems to have become commonplace. Ibn ʿAbd al-Salam (d. 1261), issuing an actual fatwa himself as to who is entitled to be a mufti, takes in outline the same position adopted by his older contemporary Ibn al-Salah. If a mufti does not meet the condition of absolute ijtihad, Ibn ʿAbd al-Salam maintains, then he may be a *mujtahid fī'l-madhhab.* Failing this, he may still issue a fatwa on points of law where he feels, beyond any shade of doubt, that he is competent. Should the case under question fall in an area of the law where he is not so competent, but where he has rarely been mistaken and the likelihood of an error is quite slim, then he is permitted to serve as a mufti. In all other cases, Ibn ʿAbd al-Salam insists, he should be banned from doing so (cited in al-Wansharisi 1981–1983, 11:110).

Ibn Daqiq al-ʿId (d. 1302), however, is reported to have gone so far as to maintain that "predicating futya on the attainment of ijtihad leads to immense difficulties [*ḥaraj ʿaẓīm*] as well as to a situation in which people will indulge themselves in their own pleasures. Therefore, we hold that if the mufti is just [*ʿadl*] and is knowledgeable of the school of the mujtahid whom he cites in his fatwa, then this is sufficient . . . Indeed, in these times of ours, there is a consensus on this type of fatwa"[6] (cited in Ibn Amir al-Hajj 1899, 3:348; al-Shawkani n.d.[a]:270).

The great majority of theoreticians who flourished subsequent to those thus far discussed make the same concession to the mufti-muqallid. In the remaining part of this chapter, I shall deal with a number of them. I should hasten to add, however, that their works are either based on theories expounded by the eleventh- and twelfth-century jurists already discussed, or they are later commentaries *(shurūḥ)* on such works. By probing the changes and modifications that the later commentators have made in their commentaries and supercommentaries, we can learn something not only about the particular subject with which we are concerned but also about the significance of commentaries in the study of *uṣūl al-fiqh*.

Al-Juwayni explicitly equates the mufti with the mujtahid. Commenting on al-Juwayni's *al-Waraqāt,* al-Mahalli (d. 1459) follows in the footsteps of al-Juwayni. But in his supercommentary on al-Mahalli, al-ʿAbbadi observes that the two earlier authors meant by the phrase "the mufti, namely, the mujtahid" either that the mufti must be a mujtahid, or that a mufti may be a mujtahid whenever it is possible for him to be one. Al-ʿAbbadi, however, immediately goes on to say that the second interpretation is more likely.[7]

Later on in the discussion, al-ʿAbbadi comes back to the issue. He quotes the works of a number of predecessors in this regard, but, significantly, none of them is earlier than that of al-Amidi. Having discussed the concession the latter has made to the mufti who is a *mujtahid fīʾl-madhhab,* he moves on to cite Taj al-Din al-Subki (d. 1369), who has on this issue, he says, a number of followers. According to al-ʿAbbadi, al-Subki maintains that the bone of contention lies with the question of whether the "*mujtahid al-fatwā* who is adept at the school of an eponym and who can give preponderance to one legal opinion of that eponym over another" can sit for iftaʾ. The correct view, al-Subki maintains, is that he may do so out of necessity, when a mujtahid is not to be found. Al-ʿAbbadi also maintains that in another work, al-Subki allows a muqallid to issue fatwas even if he is not able to give preponderance to one view over another. Furthermore, such a mufti is under no obligation to cite the authorities from whom he borrows. (Incidentally, early jurists abhorred the practice of omitting the names of such authorities).[8] Al-ʿAbbadi quotes an anonymous commentator on al-Subki as saying that this sort of ifta' has been the prevailing practice in later times *("al-aʿṣār al-muta'akhkhira")*. In what seems to be an attempt to bolster al-Subki's views, al-ʿAbbadi quotes a certain commentator on *al-Muhadhdhab* who essentially makes the same argument (al-ʿAbbadi n.d.:244–245).[9]

In al-ʿAbbadi's supercommentary there are at least three issues worth noting. First, it is curious that in a supercommentary on al-Juwayni and al-Mahalli, other authors like al-Subki and al-Amidi should occupy such a paramount place. It is clear, however, that by incorporating them into his discussion, al-ʿAbbadi hoped to mitigate the strict demands laid down centuries before by al-Juwayni and his like. Second, the sequence of quoting later authors parallels an increasing adaptation to a reality in which muftis were by and large muqallids. While al-Amidi, the first to be cited, admitted the ifta' of a *mujtahid fī'l-madhhab,* the commentator on *al-Muhadhdhab,* being last, went as far as permitting a muqallid par excellence to practice ifta'. Third, in al-Subki, and as accepted by al-ʿAbbadi, the expression *"mujtahid al-fatwā"* is used to refer to a muqallid.

One should note in passing that in *Jamʿ al-jawāmiʿ*, al-Subki allows a muqallid to sit for ifta', provided he is knowledgeable of the means by which the doctrines of his school have been reached (al-Bannani 1970, 2:397). Needless to say, al-Subki deems legitimate the ifta' of what has been called by al-Amidi a *mujtahid fī'l-madhhab.* Al-Mahalli, who commented on al-Subki's work, adds that the practice of issuing the latter type of fatwa has been prevalent throughout the ages and has not been censured (ibid., 2:397). When speaking of the former type, he also notes that "it has been prevalent in recent times" (ibid., 2:398).

Commenting on both al-Mahalli and al-Subki, al-Bannani (d. 1784) observes, interestingly, that a jurisconsult who is knowledgeable in the law of his school but cannot derive rulings for new legal cases is commonly called by the jurists a *mujtahid al-fatwā.* Al-Bannani, to be sure, realizes that the compound expression is self-contradictory, but he does not seem to offer any explanation (ibid., 2:398). However, in his supercommentary on al-Bannani, al-Shirbini (d. 1908) explains that the expression is merely conventional and does not connote the ordinary meaning of the terms (ibid., 2:398).

The changes and modifications brought about by al-ʿAbbadi on al-Juwayni's doctrine are by no means singular. A similar modification may be observed in the commentary of al-Iji (d. 1355) on Ibn al-Hajib's *Muntahā.* Following Ibn al-Hajib, al-Iji discerns four views held by the jurists as to the legitimacy of ifta' by muqallids, and he agrees with the first view, which permits a muqallid to practice ifta', provided he has mastered the teachings of his school and is able to reason correctly. He upholds this view on the grounds that "at all times, and repeatedly, jurisconsults who are not mujtahids have issued fatwas. No one has abjured this [practice] and thus it has been subject to consensus [*ʿijmāʾ*]" (al-Iji 1974, 2:308). Al-Iji's claim that a consensus has been reached is serious, for invoking the sanction of this powerful authority is tantamount to asserting that the legitimacy of the practice is conclusive and lies beyond the realm of probability. But al-Iji's claim is difficult to substantiate, since he himself acknowledges that the jurists disagree on the matter. In fact, this is precisely the objection al-Taftazani (d. 1388) voices against al-Iji. In his supercommentary on al-Iji's *Sharḥ,* he insists that such a consensus has not been reached, since there are jurists who do abjure this practice (al-Iji 1974, 2:308, ll. 35–36).

Furthermore, al-Iji does not subscribe to the second view held by a certain group of jurists—namely, that a muqallid can serve as a jurisconsult if and only if a mujtahid is nowhere to be found.[10] Nor does he accept the third view, which allows a muqallid—whatever his professional qualifications may be—to issue fatwas. And he obviously rejects the fourth view, which denies muqallids any place in this capacity (al-Iji 1974, 2:308). In addition to the argument from consensus in support of his position, al-Iji adds (particularly against those who argue that a muqallid is merely a layman) that if the muqallid is adept at the teachings of his school, then he is not a layman ignorant of legal science but is, rather, adequately qualified to perform the task that iftaʾ involves (ibid., 1974, 2:309).

The four views reported by al-Amidi, Ibn al-Hajib, and al-Iji seem to have become an integral part of the jurists' discussions, at least since the beginning of the thirteenth century. In his commentary on al-Baydawi's (d. 1286) *Minhāj al-wuṣūl,* al-Isnawi (d. 1370) speaks of the same views, but adds a new element to the issue. He maintains that the controversy recorded by al-Amidi and Ibn al-Hajib has been with regard to the muqallid of a living mujtahid, and that the issue of a jurisconsult who is a muqallid of a dead mujtahid is altogether different (al-Isnawi 1899, 3:331). On this last point, another controversy has arisen, and it seems that there are two parties to it. The first party maintains that it is not lawful for a mufti-muqallid to follow the teachings of a dead mujtahid, since the latter has, in effect, no opinion *(lā qawla lahu)* to be accounted for by the succeeding jurists; the reason for this is that the opinion of a dead mujtahid does not count in the consensus of a later generation. However, a living mujtahid who holds, on a legal question, an opinion that differs from all other opinions will prevent a consensus from taking place. Therefore, since the opinions of a dead mujtahid do not count, the mufti should not resort to them in issuing fatwas.

The second party, on the other hand, argues for the validity of iftaʾ according to the teachings of a dead mujtahid. One of its spokesmen was al-Baydawi himself who held in justification of this position that "since mujtahids do not exist at the present age, consensus has been concluded on the practice of this kind of iftaʾ" (1899, 3:331, ll. 4–7). Al-Isnawi, however, maintains that al-Baydawi's line of argument is weak, because consensus may be reached only by mujtahids, and since these no longer exist, any alleged consensus is invalid. The correct justification of this position, he argues, is that the barring of such a practice is detrimental to the welfare of society. Whatever the reasoning behind their positions, both al-Baydawi and al-Isnawi adopted the view that a jurisconsult may be a muqallid, whether the mujtahid he follows is alive or dead (al-Isnawi and al-Baydawi 1899, 3:327–332).

Finally, I should note that this survey of the *uṣūl al-fiqh* literature shows that despite the overwhelming tendency of legal theoreticians to approve of the ifta' of muqallids, there were later jurists, like al-Amidi, who still insisted that a jurisconsult be a *mujtahid fī'l-madhhab*. As far as I know, al-Ansari (d. 1707) and the commentator on his work (1904, 3:303–304),[11] as well as al-Shawkani (n.d.[a]:269–271), constituted most of the exceptions. In the case of al-Shawkani, at least, we know that his insistence on the requirement of ijtihad stemmed from his systematic, "ideological" opposition to taqlid, which he deemed to be a vice with which the shariʿa had been inflicted.[12]

We have seen that in their discourse about the ijtihad qualifications of the mufti, Sunni legal theorists have articulated four positions that cannot be properly understood without reference to diachronic developments. The first position to dominate legal discourse lasted from the eighth to the eleventh century, when jurisconsults, in order to qualify for the office of futya, were required to be mujtahids. The second, advocated by al-Amidi, among others, reflected the concession made by a group of theoreticians to a reality in which, it was thought, mujtahids of the highest caliber no longer existed, and what was to be found were only mujtahids whose legal creativity was confined to the application of an already established methodology to new cases of law. The third accepted a muqallid in the role of a mufti, but only when a mujtahid was not available. The fourth approved of a mufti-muqallid, whether or not a mujtahid was to be found.

Chronologically, it is highly probable that the third position preceded the fourth. But that the first position emerged prior to the second, and the first two prior to the others, seems beyond doubt. The appearance in later legal literature of a chapter on the legality *(jawāz)* of the muqallid's ifta', and its complete absence from eleventh-century works is alone a cardinal piece of evidence to prove the point. To this evidence may be added the fact that the eleventh-century theorists were unanimous in their stipulation that a mufti had to be a mujtahid. Furthermore, they reported no opinion of any of their predecessors to the contrary.

If the chronology of the four positions is correct, as overwhelming evidence indicates, then it is possible to use their diachronic emergence as an indicator of the Muslim jurists' perception of their legal profession, if not of the changes that occurred within this profession. However, I must first point out that the majority of theoreticians I have studied did not fail to follow a certain pattern when discussing who qualified as a mufti. As a rule, they began with the requirement of ijtihad, be it limited or absolute, and then they moved, in a descending order, to the lowest rank of legal knowledge they deemed acceptable. For the early jurists, only the mujtahid properly so called qualified for ifta'; for al-Amidi and others, it was the *mujtahid fī'l-madhhab;* and for the majority of later theoreticians, it was ultimately taqlid that constituted the minimal requirement, though most of them first began by stipulating ijtihad.

The descending order of requirements perhaps best exemplifies the success of legal theory in striking a balance between the demands of religious idealism and the exigencies of reality. Whatever the requirements were in each period, they were in complete accord not only with the practice prevailing then, but also, and more important, with the theoreticians' perception of the professional and scholarly standards of their contemporary peers. For, as we have seen, the argument from *wuqūʿ* (the actual practice of the past)[13] was central in justifying the ifta' of the jurist who was less than a mujtahid. In fact, this argument was used, though unsuccessfully, to invoke a consensus in legitimizing the mufti-muqallid. It is partly the reality that gave rise to this argument and partly the general Muslim perception of continuous decline—which finds its "ideological" roots in a host of prophetic traditions—that were instrumental in the gradual transformation of discourse about the qualifications of the mufti.

But what does all this mean for us? Does it mean that all muftis throughout the first five centuries of Islam were mujtahids, or that legal theory in that period completely lost itself in a fanciful utopia? And does it mean that muftis after the eleventh century were muqallids? Of course, conclusive answers to these questions must await a thorough investigation into the legal contribution of individual muftis, and into the extent of their originality. Only then will we be able to ascertain the degree to which individual legal theories did or did not respond to legal practice. Nevertheless, the present study, coupled with our general knowledge of Islamic legal history, allow us to offer some brief, tentative answers.

There is no good reason to believe that legal theorists until the end of the eleventh century were less mindful of the prevailing juridical practices than were their successors. In other words, we have no choice but to assume that if the normative practices prior to the twelfth century were identical to those that existed earlier, the early theorists would have referred to them in their theories, and the argument from *wuqūʿ* would have played, as it did later, an important role in formulating theories about the qualifications of the mufti. This should not mean, however, that as a rule the muftis of the first five centuries were mujtahids, for this would not be a realistic historical assessment. Nor would it be accurate to argue that because later theory generally approved of the mufti-muqallid there could have been no muftis who practiced ijtihad. But it does mean that the early theorists' stipulation of ijtihad represented a desideratum that was neither impractical nor uncommon. The jurists of this period genuinely thought that attaining the rank of mujtahid was not only possible but indeed of frequent occurrence (Hallaq 1984:7–10). The issue, then, is not only one of objective reality but also one of self-perception. The absence from the early period of both the notion of the mujtahid's ranks and a deep-rooted and highly developed awareness of what later came to be known as *fasād al-zamān,* is evidence of this perception. The early jurists no more indulged themselves in a utopia than did their successors who, despite their being theorists, demonstrated a great deal of sensitivity toward the practices of their day. Thus, we are not entitled to maintain that early legal theories were purely academic, nor would we be correct in saying that the mufti was, in fact, always a mujtahid. Nor, still, would we be close to the truth if we argued that mujtahids were entirely absent in later times, for this not only runs counter to what we now know from the sources, but it also fails to make sense of the later theorists' nearly universal insistence on requiring the mufti first to be a mujtahid or, only when this was not possible, a muqallid.

Be that as it may, the changing discourse concerning the mufti's qualifications may not be as indicative of conditions in the real world as it is of the developments within *uṣūl al-fiqh* itself. This chapter demonstrates one of the instances in which Sunni legal theory succeeded in developing, at a later stage of its life, richly diverse views on a single issue, and also was able to adapt its discourse to a changing situation that grew ever more complex. This instructs us that an adequate understanding of the issues posed by *uṣūl al-fiqh* cannot be gained by means of studying any one particular author, for no single *uṣūlī* can, or should be, allowed to speak on behalf of the others. There is no substitute for a diachronic study that consults, at each stage, a variety of authors.[14]

PART TWO

The Pre-Modern Period

C H A P T E R   T H R E E

Learning at Mosques in al-Andalus

MANUELA MARÍN

The mosque is the central place in the life of any Muslim community. It is in the Friday mosque that the communal prayer is performed and the public sermon *(khuṭba)* is delivered to the assembly of worshippers. Historically, in addition to its religious role, the mosque became the site of the many communal activities relating to the exercise of political and judicial power and to the transmission of knowledge, perhaps because Islamic cities lacked the kind of public spaces found in the Greek and Roman metropolis, the agora and the forum (Pedersen 1986:640).

The Friday Mosque of Córdoba, one of the most important examples of Islamic architecture in the world, has been analyzed and studied by scholars, who have traced its history and evolution (Torres Balbás 1957). It is, indeed, a living monument; Umayyad emirs and caliphs added to its splendor and left their mark on the mosque, making it both a historical and an architectural monument. Founded by ʿAbd al-Rahman b. Muʿawiya, the first Umayyad emir of al-Andalus (r. 756–788), the mosque was enlarged by ʿAbd al-Rahman b. al-Hakam (r. 822–852); by ʿAbd al-Rahman b. Muhammad al-Nasir, the first Umayyad caliph (r. 912–961); by al-Hakam al-Mustansir (r. 961–976); and finally by al-Mansur b. Abi ʿAmir, actual ruler of the country during the caliphate of al-Mustansir's son, Hisham. To the original building, located on the site of a Christian church near the river and the city's Roman bridge, succesive emirs or caliphs added monumental gates, the minaret, the special place for the ruler's prayers, and other structures.

The Fatwa

In this chapter, I translate and analyze a fatwa that deals with the use of the mosque as a public place in which a nonreligious activity is undertaken.

The fatwa was originally recorded in the *Aḥkām* of Ahmad b. Muhammad b. Ziyad (d. 925), known both as Ibn Ziyad and as al-Habib, one of the most distinguished judges of Córdoba (Fierro 1992b); other members of his family served in the judicial administration. Although Ibn Ziyad's collection of judicial decisions is lost, some of those decisions are preserved in later sources, including the *al-Aḥkām al-kubrā* of the judge Abu al-Asbagh ʿIsa b. Sahl b. ʿAbd Allah al-Asadi (1022–1093), a collection of Andalusian fatwas and judicial decisions issued between the third/ninth century and the end of the fifth/eleventh century (Daga Portillo 1987).[1] Only partially edited,[2] the *Aḥkām* is an important source of information on Andalusian legal practice, social history, and religious life (Marín 1990).[3] The text of the fatwa, as transcribed by Ibn Sahl, reads as follows:

> From the *Aḥkām* [of Ibn Ziyad]:
>
> You [namely, Ibn Ziyad] have asked us [the undersigned advisers]—may God favor you and help you in what He has bestowed on you—about some people who sit in circles inside the Friday Mosque to give fatwas and hold discussions on subjects relating to religious knowledge. You have also mentioned that somebody complained to you, stating that those who sit in these circles are not entitled to these practices, because although staying [in mosques] is a duty, mosques are designed for prayer, and those assemblies may disturb people who are praying. This is what we think and say about this question—may God grant success:
>
> Although mosques are designed for prayer, discussions on religious knowledge and its branches in mosques are permitted according to what was done by the imams. It is recorded that Malik—may God have mercy upon him—used to sit in a circle on Fridays in the Mosque of the Prophet—God bless him and grant him peace—in Medina, until the imam appeared. At that moment, he would interrupt his futya and greet the imam. Religious knowledge indeed—may God honor you!—is the best thing, after the Book of God the Almighty, for people to gather and discuss.
>
> I have seen the mosques of the garrison towns [*amṣār*][4] in which the imams and other learned persons sat in circles. This was not considered to be a reprehensible action and did not raise any objection. So you can allow these persons to sit in circles in the mosque as they used to do, if God the Almighty wills.
>
> This is what has been said by [the advisers] ʿUbayd Allah b. Yahya, Ibn Lubaba, Muhammad b. Walid, and Saʿd b. Muʿadh.
>
> The judge [namely, Ibn Sahl] said:
>
> This answer allowing sitting in circles without restriction is not correct. This practice is to be permitted only if the participants include someone who is of solid understanding, knowledge, and religion, who can be trusted to speak about what is improper and to give legal counsel [fatwa] about what is not to be done. Whereas such a person speaks to his companions on the subjects he knows, the ignorant person realizes what he himself does not understand. In these conditions, it is allowed to him [the wise person] and those who listen to

him to sit down in learning circles, when it is not the time for prayers, to avoid disturbance to the worshippers.

Abu al-Bakhturi[5] mentioned that ʿAli b. Abi Talib—may God be pleased with him—entered a mosque and found there a man frightening [the people]. He asked, "What is that?" To which the answer was given, "A man who supplicates [God] for the people." "He is not," said ʿAli. "Rather, the man was saying, 'I am so-and-so, son of so-and-so, acknowledge who I am.'" ʿAli sent for him and asked, "Do you know the difference between the abrogating and the abrogated"?[6] "No," he replied. "Go out of our mosque then," ʿAli said, "and do not make any invocations in it." A similar story is transmitted by Ibn ʿAbbas.[7]

What they [the advisers] mentioned in their answer about Malik is wrong and mistaken; the same can be said of the entire answer, but we have abstained from additional explanations to avoid prolixity.

The Question

Unfortunately, the full text of the istiftaʾ, or question, is not included in the text transcribed by Ibn Sahl, probably because the *jawāb,* or answer, was sufficiently explicit with regard to the matter under discussion. The loss of the istiftaʾ means that we do not know either the identity of the person who posed the question or the reason the judge felt the need to seek advice. The answer suggests that an unidentified person presented a complaint to the judge, who decided to take the counsel of his advisers. We can only speculate that the anonymous plaintiff was an ascetic and pious man, perhaps one of those who spent his time in mosques, praying and reciting the Quran (Marín 1991 and 1992).

What was the complaint? Simply that people used to sit "in circles" *(mutaḥallaqūn)* in the mosque, discussing scholarly matters and issuing fatwas, thereby disturbing the worshippers. As mosques were designed for prayer, sitting in circles should be prohibited.[8]

The complaint is directed at the ʿulamaʾ, the "people of religious knowledge" *(ahl al-ʿilm)* who, from the earliest times, used to gather in mosques to disseminate their knowledge. As Makdisi has pointed out (1981:10), "the mosque, *masjid,* was the first institution of learning in Islam" in which assemblies *(majlis, ḥalqa)* of scholars took place. In al-Andalus, mosques frequently were used for the purpose of instruction (Ribera 1928). Although some scholars received their students in their own residences, the Friday mosque and smaller mosques scattered throughout a town were the preferred places of instruction.[9]

Teaching and discussing religious knowledge in mosques were common and well-established practices in al-Andalus. The anonymous plaintiff was denouncing a practice that had a long history in Córdoba, in al-Andalus, and in the East. The only ground for the complaint was that the plaintiff was a practicing ascetic who was disturbed by the assembly of scholars and who held the opinion that mosques were places dedicated exclusively to devotional practices. In fact, remaining in mosques to pray continuously was one of the most common practices of early ascetics in al-Andalus. Biographical sources mention the case of Yahya b. Qasim b. Hilal (d. 885 or 909), who prayed continuously in a particular mosque from morning to evening, leaving only to sleep briefly at his home (ʿIyad b. Musa 1981–1983?, 4:428). Many other ascetics are described as "attendants of mosques," persons who adopted the sacred space as their favorite residence, dedicating themselves to prayer and Quran recitation. In this context, the complaint may be regarded as a protest on the part of pious members of the Muslim community against an intrusion into "their" space.

The ʿulamaʾ had developed rules regulating their behavior while teaching or discussing religious knowledge in mosques. Malik b. Anas specified silence as one of the virtues of the student (Ibn Abi Zayd al-Qayrawani 1985:169), and Maliki scholars apparently endeavored not to raise their voice while teaching in schools. According to the well-known jurist and specialist in prophetic tradition (hadith), Ibn ʿAbd al-Barr (d. 1070), when Malik was asked about raising the voice while teaching, he manifested a strong dislike of the practice (which was common enough, apparently, to provoke a question to the master). It is true that Ibn ʿAbd al-Barr recorded the opinion of Abu Hanifa, who allowed a teacher to raise his voice in the mosque in order to facilitate a better understanding by the students (Ibn ʿAbd al-Barr 1968, 1:168). But since the Maliki school was dominant in al-Andalus, it would be unreasonable to explain the complaint in terms of a difference of opinion among scholars belonging to different law schools.

The Counsellors of the Judge

Having received the complaint, the judge turned to his advisers (mushawars), whose names are recorded at the end of their answer and who acted as muftis for the judge. The judge's council (shura) was composed of several eminent jurists who gave expert judicial advice on matters raised by the judge. These advisers played a key role in the administration of justice, a role for which there is no parallel in other pre-modern Muslim societies. From the time of ʿAbd al-Rahman b. al-Hakam (first half of the ninth century), advisers appear regularly in the biographical and historical sources, and some of them played a decisive role in Andalusian intellectual and political life (Marín 1985a). In the present case, Ibn Ziyad consulted with four jurists, ʿUbayd Allah b. Yahya, Ibn Lubaba, Muhammad b. Walid, and Saʿd b. Muʿadh, all of whom regularly served in this capacity.

ʿUbayd Allah b. Yahya (d. 909) was the son of Yahya b. Yahya (d. 848), himself a mushawar and one of the most influential jurists in the history of Umayyad al-Andalus (Marín 1985b). Like his father, ʿUbayd Allah was an outstanding intellectual figure. Although he did not write any book on law or other subjects, his transmission of Malik's *Muwaṭṭaʾ*, taken from his father, was regarded as the most accurate and reliable transmission of the text. In his capacity as a jurist, ʿUbayd Allah attracted a great number of disciples who disseminated his learning throughout al-Andalus. In addition to his knowledge of law, his high social position and wealth allowed ʿUbayd Allah to play an important role in political circles.

Curiously, neither Yahya nor his son ʿUbayd Allah ever held a judgeship or official position in any city of al-Andalus. Yahya b. Yahya was well aware of the possibilities open to a mushawar. On one occasion he advised the jurist Saʿid b. Hassan not to volunteer evidence against a judge but to wait until he was asked to give his opinion as a mushawar, so as to have a more decisive impact on the judgment (Marín 1985a:46). His son, ʿUbayd Allah, probably followed this "policy," refusing to serve as a judge but agreeing to give advice to judges. In this way, he played an influential role in the judicial process until the end of his long life.

Muhammad b. ʿUmar b. Lubaba (d. 926) (Marín 1988: no. 1283) was a man of wide-ranging interests. Besides law, he was an expert in Arabic grammar and poetry and had gathered many reports *(akhbār)* regarding the history of his country and the life of Andalusian scholars, much of which is recorded in later works, such as the *Tartīb al-madārik* of Qadi ʿIyad. Of client *(mawlā)* origins, Ibn Lubaba held the office of *ṣāḥib al-ṣalāt,* or master of prayer, in Córdoba and began his activity as a mushawar during the reign of the emir ʿAbd Allah, together with ʿUbayd Allah b. Yahya and other jurists. Following the death of ʿUbayd Allah at the beginning of the reign of al-Nasir, Ibn Lubaba became the only mushawar of Córdoba, and he generally was recognized as the most knowledgeable legal expert in the city. In the biographical sources, Ibn Lubaba is presented as a Maliki jurist with no interest in prophetic tradition. This was a common attitude among Andalusian jurists in this period, when the use of prophetic tradition as a source of legal authority was still a matter of debate (Fierro 1989a). But Ibn Lubaba's career reflects the changes that were taking place in al-Andalus; it is said that toward the end of his life he began to use prophetic traditions and to accept the Shafiʿi school.

The tension between law (fiqh) and prophetic tradition appears also in the biography of our third mushawar, Muhammad b. Walid b. Muhammad (d. 922), an expert on law and especially on contractual stipulations, but one who was also interested in literature (Marín 1988:no. 1353). The emir ʿAbd Allah held him in high esteem, and he was a respected mushawar. At the same time, he was accused by some of his biographers of forging prophetic traditions and of being a flatterer.

The fourth mushawar, Saʿd b. Muʿadh (d. 920) was a Córdoban jurist who was an expert on legal questions, or *masaʾil* (Marín 1988:no. 519). Significantly, the sources indicate that he used to sit in the Friday Mosque, where people attended his circle *(ḥalqa)* and listened to his teaching—that is, he participated in precisely the activity that was the subject of the complaint.

These four judicial advisers typify the social status and intellectual attitudes of the learned class. They occupied positions close to the source of political power, and they exercised their own power as custodians and transmitters of knowledge. Their knowledge, moreover, had an immediate effect on people's lives and behavior; their influence cannot be underestimated. In the present case, their answer was unanimous.

The Answer

In two short paragraphs, the judicial advisers stated clearly that teaching in mosques and gathering there to discuss religious knowledge must be permitted. The only authority quoted is Malik b. Anas, who himself used to sit in the Prophet's Mosque in Medina with his students. Malik nevertheless respected the times of prayer, ending his lesson when the imam entered the mosque to direct prayers. The mushawars did not quote other legal authorities, as was common in other cases. For them, the issue was clear. The pursuit of religious knowledge, they said, is the best of reasons for people to sit together and converse. At the end of the answer, one of the advisers added a personal comment, recalling how he had seen scholars sitting in mosques in the cities of the East and discussing religious knowledge without anyone raising an objection.[10] The mushawars therefore advised the judge to allow, without reservation, the sitting of scholars in the Friday mosque.

The advisers do not refer to the difference of opinion among Malikis and Hanafis. Malik b. Anas is invoked as a model of behavior, something to be expected from ʿUbayd Allah b. Yahya, whose father had transmitted the *Muwaṭṭaʾ* directly from Malik. As in other cases, Malik is the paramount authority and example for Andalusian jurists, whose intellectual prestige was based on their reliance on Maliki legal doctrine (Turki 1982). It was for this reason that these jurists objected to new trends of thought imported from the East, as when Baqi b. Makhlad (d. 889) tried to introduce the science of prophetic tradition. The same ʿUbayd Allah b. Yahya refused to serve as mushawar together with Baqi b. Makhlad, thereby demonstrating his distrust of someone who was not an adherent of the Maliki school.

Although we know of many cases in which judicial advisers held different and contrary opinions, in the present case no disagreement is mentioned, probably because the mushawars themselves operated in mosques, where their knowledge was recognized and disseminated among their disciples. Furthermore, mosques were public places; teaching in private residences did not provide the same kind of symbolic status. For the community of believers, the Friday mosque was the cult place par excellence, but it also played a pivotal role in the political life of the country. The attendance of the emir at prayers was accompanied by an elaborate ceremony that underlined his position in the community and was intended to impress itself on the minds of the worshippers. It was at the mosque that the sermon *(khuṭba)* was pronounced in the name of the ruler and public readings of war communiqués were made. The learned class used the mosque to disseminate religious knowledge; although their activities were not exclusively religious, they constituted a counterpart to the activities of the civil authority.

This was the answer given by the four mushawars who lived at the end of the ninth century. Two centuries later, when Ibn Sahl copied this document for inclusion in his own collection, he felt compelled to give his own opinion on the matter. Himself a judge and legal expert, Ibn Sahl disagreed with his predecessors, arguing that the general permission to assemble in the mosque should be restricted to very specific cases; such meetings should be allowed only when they are led by knowledgeable and trustworthy people. Ibn Sahl also claimed that the four mushawars misrepresented and distorted Malik's view on the subject.

Why should Ibn Sahl have opposed scholarly gatherings in mosques? In my opinion, the answer lies in the example given by Ibn Sahl to support his objection to such assemblies. He refers to a report that ʿAli b. Abi Talib had expelled from the mosque a man who was invoking God and frightening the people. This man no doubt was a storyteller *(qaṣṣāṣ)* and religious preacher, although the text does not specify this. The activities of such men are documented from early periods of Islamic history, when they were subjected to strong disapproval by many scholars. I assume that Ibn Sahl was opposed to this particular kind of gathering in which people sat around a person who was not an accepted scholar. A possible connection with asceticism recurs: one of the characteristics of Andalusian asceticism, beginning in the tenth century, was the increasing importance of assemblies in mosques to listen to public sermons and readings of pious books. In some cases, frightening people with statements about the Judgment Day and the punishment of sinners is mentioned as one of the leitmotifs of these sermons, following another well-established Islamic tradition. The disturbing elements contained in this kind of oratory may have caused scholars to distrust these assemblies, which were outside of their control. For Ibn Sahl, Muslims ought to meet in mosques only if they were properly directed by someone not likely to arouse dangerous emotions. In itself, Ibn Sahl's comment demonstrates the growing importance of these kinds of gatherings in mosques in al-Andalus. Two centuries earlier, scholars had not even considered this possibility, and they accepted and recommended assemblies of learned people in mosques.

C H A P T E R   F O U R

Caliphal Legitimacy and Expiation in al-Andalus

MARIBEL FIERRO

The usual place to look for authoritative legal opinions is in the special genre devoted to them, collections of fatwas. However, due to the wide range of topics treated by this genre and their bearing on every aspect of the private and social life of the individual, fatwas or material referring to them can be found elsewhere as well. The three cases studied here have been preserved in a legal-religious treatise not devoted specifically to fatwas; one of them also is recorded in a biographical dictionary. The fatwas dealt with are not recorded in their conventional form, as the narrative framework in which they are situated imposes its own standards of presentation. Therefore, what we have is the story of how fatwas were solicited; how the *faqīhs* (or muftis) answered, reacted to each other, and explained the motives for their legal opinions; and, in one case, how the inquirer reacted.

In his treatise against innovations, the Andalusian jurist al-Shatibi (d. 1388) records three instances in which Maliki jurists, including Malik b. Anas, were consulted on the subject of expiation *(kaffāra)* imposed on rulers (al-Shatibi 1914, 2:285–286). My translation of these three cases follows.

CASE 1

The first case is embedded in al-Shatibi's citation from another Andalusian author, Ibn Bashkuwal (d. 1183):[1]

> The Commander of the Faithful al-Hakam II[2] sent for the jurists [*al-fuqahā'*] and consulted them [*shāwarahum*] with regard to an affair that had happened to him. Al-Hakam II told them that he had approached one of his most beautiful women and had had sexual intercourse with her during the month

of Ramadan. The jurists advised that the caliph should feed the poor as expiation. Among the jurists, Ishaq b. Ibrahim kept silent. The Commander of the Faithful asked him: "What has the shaykh to say regarding the legal opinion of his companions?" Ishaq b. Ibrahim told him: "I do not agree with their opinion. I say that you should fast." The others replied to him: "Why, is it not the doctrine of Malik to give food to the poor?" Ishaq b. Ibrahim retorted: "You would remember better the doctrine of Malik if you were not busy trying to ingratiate yourselves with the Commander of the Faithful. Indeed, Malik ordered the expiation to be feeding the poor in the case of the person who has money. However, the Commander of the Faithful has no money of his own, because his money is the money of the Muslim treasury [*māl bayt al-muslimīn*]." The Commander of the Faithful accepted the expiation proposed by Ishaq b. Ibrahim and thanked him for it.

CASE 2

The first case, transmitted by Ibn Bashkuwal, is similar to another that involved al-Hakam II's predecessor, ʿAbd al-Rahman II.[3] Al-Shatibi gives an abridged version of this second case, which is preserved in a longer version by Qadi ʿIyad (d. 1149) in his biographical dictionary devoted to the scholars of the Maliki school of law (ʿIyad b. Musa 1981–1983?, 3:388):[4]

The emir of al-Andalus, ʿAbd al-Rahman II, had sexual intercourse with a young slave girl one day during the month of Ramadan. He repented afterward, summoning the jurist Yahya b. Yahya al-Laythi and the latter's companions, and asking them their opinion with regard to the requisite expiation for his transgression. Yahya b. Yahya was the first to answer, saying: "The emir—may God honor him—must fast for two consecutive months." Listening to him, the other jurists kept silent. But when they were on their own, they asked Yahya: "Why did you say that, excluding the other possible expiations among which he could have chosen, like feeding the poor and manumitting slaves?" Yahya answered: "Were we to open this door to him, he would find it easy to feed the poor and manumit slaves each day. But if we oblige him to do something that is more difficult to him, he will refrain from committing transgressions."

CASE 3

Al-Shatibi records another case involving a ruler and expiation, but not lust. This case is transmitted by the Egyptian Yahya b. Bukayr, a pupil of Malik b. Anas:[5]

The caliph al-Rashid[6] broke an oath that he had sworn. He assembled the scholars [*al-ʿulamāʾ*], who agreed that he should manumit a slave. Malik was also consulted and his answer was: "The expiation should be a fast of three days."

Sex, Fasting, and Expiation in Islam

In Islam, sexual intercourse is generally considered to be of two sorts, legal and illegal (Bousquet 1966; Bouhdiba 1975; Musallam 1983). If a man and a woman are legally married *(nikāḥ)*, the woman may have intercourse only with her husband, whereas the man may have intercourse with his other wives and his slave girls. Illegal intercourse includes homosexual relationships, and, as regards sexual relationships between males and females, *zinā*, a term often but not quite accurately translated as adultery (Bellamy 1979:30). A sexual relationship is permissible and legal only when there exists a recognized legal basis for it—that is, the marital tie between husband and wife or the right of ownership that a master has with his female slave concubine. Moreover, within the framework of licit intercourse, there are certain moments when sexual relationships are forbidden: while a woman is menstruating, during the pilgrimage, and during fasting (Bousquet 1966:163). When the sexual relationship takes place outside the legal framework defined by the religious law (shariʿa), that relationship is a criminal offense (Coulson 1979: 63).[7]

Fasting in Islam involves abstention from food as well as from sexual intercourse during the period of the fast—that is, roughly, during the day. To have sexual intercourse while performing the fast is considered to be a violation of the law and is therefore subject to expiation.

Expiation, *kaffāra*, is an act by which certain transgressions (a wrong action, a sin, or a crime) can be effaced: unintentional homicide; the *ẓihār* oath, which is pronounced for the repudiation of a wife (Santillana 1938, 1:269–271); violation of ritual duties; breaking a vow; breaking the fast.[8] The expiation may take the form of manumission of slaves, fasting, feeding the poor, or, in the case of transgression of the pilgrimage rites, sacrifice *(hady)*.[9] Al-Shatibi states that the aim of expiation is prevention *(al-zajr);* that is, to restrain people from transgressing the law again (al-Shatibi 1914, 2:285).

The Andalusian emir ʿAbd al-Rahman II, the protagonist of the second case, is described in the sources as a man who enjoyed and sought sex. The following anecdote is told about him: one night, during an expedition directed against the Christian frontier, ʿAbd al-Rahman II became sexually excited, and his desire was augmented by some verses recited by the poet ʿAbd al-Rahman b. al-Shamir. Feeling the urge to have sexual intercourse with one of his favorites, he left the command of the army to his son al-Hakam and returned to his palace at Córdoba, where he accomplished his desire (Ibn al-Qutiya 1926: 60–61/48–49).[10] ʿAbd al-Rahman II's breaking of the fast through unlawful sexual intercourse in case 2 fits well with his personality as reflected in this anecdote. I do not know of similar stories told about his descendant, al-Hakam II, the protagonist of the first case.[11]

The Legal Doctrine of the Fatwas

The jurists involved in all three cases are Malikis. The third case, which involves Malik b. Anas, is the starting point for the other two cases. Let us now examine, in reverse order, the legal reasoning and doctrine involved in the three cases.

CASE 3

The doctrine of Malik b. Anas (d. 795) in his legal treatise, *al-Muwaṭṭa'*, is as follows: If a man swears and repeats the oath and then breaks it, he must free a slave or clothe ten poor men; but if he swears the oath only once, he must feed ten poor men, giving each person one measure *(mudd)* of wheat, unless he does not have the means to do so, in which case he should fast for three days.[12] The latter is the expiation Malik himself chose for al-Rashid (the caliph who reportedly wanted to adopt Malik's *Muwaṭṭa'* as the canonical legal code).[13] The reason for Malik's choice is not stated explicitly. The fact that fasting is the expiation imposed on the person without the means for performing the other possible expiations may be taken as the reason behind Malik's decision, but nowhere is it attested that he considered the caliph to be a person without means. When recording this case, al-Shatibi comments that Malik's doctrine was the precedent followed by the jurist of Córdoba, Ishaq b. Ibrahim (see case 1), who stated explicitly that the Andalusian caliph had no money or possessions of his own. This may indicate that Malik (elsewhere) held the same view as expounded by Ishaq b. Ibrahim; alternatively, it is possible that the doctrine of the latter was projected backwards to the former. In any case, it is clear from what we have seen of Malik's doctrine that, in his opinion, the jurist had to take into account the economic means of the expiating person and choose the expiation appropriate to those means.

CASE 2

Yahya b. Yahya al-Masmudi al-Laythi (d. 848) was the most important of Malik's Andalusian pupils ('Iyad b. Musa 1981–1983?, 3:379–394; López Ortiz 1931:65–75). Of Berber origin, he is famous as the transmitter of Malik's *Muwaṭṭa'* in the version that came to be most widely known (Goldziher 1967–1971, 2:240–241; Sezgin 1967, 1:459–461). He obviously was familiar with Malik's doctrine on the expiation for breaking the fast of Ramadan as expounded in the *Muwaṭṭa'*: the manumission of a slave, feeding sixty poor men, or fasting for two consecutive months.[14] One of the cases recorded in the *Muwaṭṭa'* deals with breaking the fast by engaging in sexual intercourse: a bedouin came to the Prophet, beating his breast and pulling at his hair, saying that he had had intercourse with his wife during the month of Ramadan. The Prophet asked him whether he could manumit a slave. When he replied that he could not, the Prophet asked whether he could send a camel or a cow for sacrifice at the pilgrimage. When he again replied in the negative, the Prophet offered him a basket of dates to give away as charity. At this point the bedouin interjected that there was none more needy than he himself, so the Prophet gave the dates to him, telling him to fast for a day (Malik b. Anas 1981: 240–241, no. 30). In the version of the *Muwaṭṭa'* transmitted by the Hanafi jurist Muhammad b. al-Hasan al-Shaybani (d. 805), the expiation required for breaking the fast is specified as the manumission of a slave; if the person does not own a slave, then fasting for two consecutive months; if he cannot perform that fast, then he has to feed sixty poor people (Malik b. Anas 1979: 122–123, no. 349). Although this sequence does not refer specifically to the economic status of the expiator, it is clear that each of the three possibilities is regarded as an alternative to be applied as required by the expiator's economic situation and ability.

Thus, in Maliki law, fasting appears to be the appropriate expiation for transgressors who do not have the economic means to perform manumission or make a sacrifice. But economic solvency is not the reason given for Yahya b. Yahya's choice of one expiation from among the three mentioned in the *Muwaṭṭa'*. Rather, as explained in Qadi 'Iyad's version of the case, Yahya's choice was motivated by his independent legal reasoning: were the emir to be given the possibility of expiating his transgression by manumitting a slave or feeding the poor, that expiation would not dissuade him from transgressing the law again, for such expiations would involve no real exertion on the emir's part. Thus Yahya b. Yahya's legal reasoning seems to stem from common sense: expiation for the Andalusian jurist is a kind of punishment, implying some effort on the part of the transgressor that would restrain that person from transgressing the law in the future; because manumission or almsgiving require no exertion on a ruler's part, the only possibility left is fasting.[15] No mention is made of any precedent established by Yahya b. Yahya's teacher, Malik b. Anas. What we know about Yahya b. Yahya's personality suggests that the Andalusian jurist may have been making an independent judgment and choice, as he did on other occasions.[16]

CASE 1

Ishaq b. Ibrahim b. Masarra (d. 963 or 965) ('Iyad b. Musa 1981–1983?, 4:126–134; Fierro 1985: 89–95) was one of the jurists who was instrumental in imposing Maliki law as the "official" legal doctrine of the Umayyad caliphate in al-Andalus. He participated in the trial against the heretic Abu al-Khayr, who was accused of, among other things, being a follower of the Fatimids at a time when Umayyads and Fatimids were fighting for control of the Maghrib. Ishaq b. Ibrahim imposed the death penalty on Abu al-Khayr without granting him the possibility of challenging the witnesses who testified against him.[17] At first sight, in case 1 Ishaq b. Ibrahim appears to be acting with a similarly rigorous attitude, in this instance directed against the caliph. However, the underlying reason for his choice of expiation was not the same as that of Yahya b. Yahya.[18] Indeed, his choice stemmed from a countervailing consideration. Ishaq b. Ibrahim chose fasting as the only possible expiation on the ground that the caliph had no possessions of his own[19] and because Malik considered the other two forms of expiation as applicable exclusively to those who had money.[20] In other words, Ishaq b. Ibrahim was drawing an analogy between the Andalusian caliph and the destitute bedouin mentioned in the *Muwaṭṭa*ʾ to whom the Prophet showed benevolence by reducing his required expiation. Yahya b. Yahya, on the other hand, considered that it was too easy for a ruler to manumit a slave or to give food to the poor, suggesting that he took it for granted that a ruler was by definition wealthy, not poor. The most interesting point in Ishaq b. Ibrahim's legal opinion is that the Andalusian Umayyad caliph is presented as owning nothing and that no mention is made of the existence of private means that would allow him to undertake the expiations involving the payment of money or the manumission of slaves. This may be explained by the fact that Ishaq b. Ibrahim regarded al-Hakam II exclusively as caliph—that is, as a public figure with no private identity—and that he did not envisage the transgression committed by al-Hakam II as one related to his private capacity and thus to be expiated through use of private means. But this point also may be understood as reflecting something far more significant. Ishaq b. Ibrahim may have been suggesting with his fatwa that the first Umayyad, ʿAbd al-Rahman b. Muʿawiya,[21] had arrived in al-Andalus escaping from the ʿAbbasids and owning nothing, so that his descendants had no private resources: all their possessions belonged to the Public Treasury. Against this background, to state openly that the Andalusian Umayyads had private resources would be tantamount to admitting that they had appropriated for themselves resources that belonged to the Muslim community.

Caliphs and Scholars

I will now try to qualify my previous assertion that Yahya b. Yahya's legal reasoning stems from common sense. Yahya b. Yahya was attempting to impose proper legal and moral behavior on the ruler, and, consequently, the intention of his fatwa was to make that ruler expiate his transgression by expending the maximum possible effort. Had he wanted to ingratiate himself with the ruler, his attitude would have been different, the "common sense" in that case being to impose on the ruler the easiest expiation. In our story, Yahya b. Yahya appears as the ideal scholar *(ʿālim)* who communicates with the ruler exclusively with the aim of giving him advice that will keep him on the right path.[22] ʿAbd al-Rahman II, at the same time, appears as the ideal ruler who seeks the advice of scholars. Although our source does not indicate how ʿAbd al-Rahman II reacted to Yahya b. Yahya's fatwa, the context implies that he accepted the latter's opinion (whether or not he actually fasted for two consecutive months is another story). The fact that the case of ʿAbd al-Rahman II and Yahya b. Yahya reflects a state of affairs between ruler and scholars that can be described as ideal (the ruler seeks and accepts the role of scholars as advisers, counselors, and interpreters of the religious law) raises doubts about the historicity of the report. It is my opinion, however, that this report provides additional evidence bearing on our knowledge of ʿAbd al-Rahman II's policy toward scholars. Previously, ʿAbd al-Rahman II's father, the emir al-Hakam I,[23] had faced a revolt of the inhabitants of Córdoba that counted among its leaders a number of scholars. Although al-Hakam I had eventually suppressed the revolt, the experience had made him aware of the difficulties of ruling without the support of the scholars. His son learned the lesson well. ʿAbd al-Rahman II is reported to have fully accepted the scholars as the "heirs of the Prophet" and to have consulted them in all matters relating to religious law (Fierro 1992). In particular, ʿAbd al-Rahman II seems to have been the first Andalusian emir to establish a consultative body of scholars (shura) (Marín 1985a). One of the scholars who exerted a special influence on him was Yahya b. Yahya, whose opinion was decisive in the selection of the judges of Córdoba. Yahya b. Yahya had been involved in the rebellion against al-Hakam I. The severity of his fatwa against ʿAbd al-Rahman II and the reasons he gave for it may have been intended to demonstrate to the Andalusians that things had changed in the relationship between emir and scholars. It also may indicate Yahya's subconscious desire to make the son expiate the sin of the father.

The relationship between ruler and scholar is also reflected in Ishaq b. Ibrahim's legal opinion. The main difference between the first two cases lies in the differing characters of the respective rulers. Yahya b. Yahya dealt with an Umayyad who, like his predecessors, had not dared to adopt the caliphal title, albeit for different reasons, the most important being that ʿAbd al-Rahman II did not rule—and could not envisage ruling—in Mecca and Medina, two symbols of caliphal power by that time firmly in the hands of the ʿAbbasids (Fierro 1989b). Although the absence of the caliphal title was insignificant in practice, in theory it meant that the Umayyads' religio-political legitimacy was dubious and better left unmentioned. This situation is reflected in the lack of any legal discussion in al-Andalus as to how the Umayyad Andalusian emir fit within the framework of Islamic political theory. From a scholar's point of view, the existence of such an emir—indeed, of any emir—was better than his absence, because tyranny is better than anarchy. But the emir's legal *status* was not clear, and any discussion of his private resources and his administration of the Public Treasury would be risky.

By contrast, Ishaq b. Ibrahim dealt not with an emir whose status was better left unmentioned, but with a caliph, a ruler who was pivotal to the entire fabric of the ideal Islamic community. As such, the caliph was subject to the religious law; he had to expiate his transgressions. Indeed, he might be given the most difficult expiation to perform so as to deter him from falling again into temptation. But stating the underlying reason for the expiation (as Yahya b. Yahya had done) would not have been good for the Andalusian Umayyad caliphate, which had to establish its right to exist not only against the weak ʿAbbasid caliphate (which had proved incapable of protecting Mecca from the Qarmatians), but also against the growing power and charisma of the Fatimid caliph who, by definition, was an impeccable imam. For this reason, Ishaq b. Ibrahim was obliged to choose the most appropriate expiation for the Umayyad ruler *as a caliph*. Now, according to Sunni doctrine, a caliph owns nothing. Taking into account what has been said about the Andalusian Umayyads' lack of private resources, an analogy may be drawn between the caliph and the man who has no money and no possessions (that is, the destitute bedouin of Malik's *Muwaṭṭaʾ*). Whereas in practice the Umayyad state might be patrimonial, in theory the Public Treasury belonged to the Muslim community, and the caliph was merely charged with administering it. As noted, Ishaq b. Ibrahim played a decisive role in establishing Maliki doctrine as the official doctrine of the Umayyad caliphate in al-Andalus. He also was clearly interested in conferring legitimacy on that caliphate, and his fatwa served as a means to this end. At the same time, it appears that he used the fatwa to remind the caliph that the money he controlled and the possessions he enjoyed were merely a trust and that full ownership had not been granted to him. Viewed in this manner, Ishaq b. Ibrahim's fatwa becomes a document of the utmost importance insofar as it fills a gap in our knowledge regarding the manner in which the scholars conferred legitimacy on the Umayyad caliphate.

C H A P T E R   F I V E

Ibn Taymiyya on Leadership in the Ritual Prayer

BERNARD WEISS

Taqi al-Din ibn Taymiyya (1263–1328) was the most famous member of an eminent family of Hanbali scholars. His fame rests not only on the volume of his written works but also on the reformist spirit that informed many of those works. His outspoken criticisms of the established order were often irksome to the political authorities, resulting more than once in his imprisonment. The checkered character of his career militated against the writing of lengthy multivolume works, and though he did write a number of treatises of moderate length, the fatwa became for him a major vehicle for the expression of his ideas.

On reading the fatwas of Ibn Taymiyya, one finds the material to be in a middle zone between formal treatises and the truly practical fatwas that muftis produce in response to queries put to them concerning concrete situations. Fatwas of the latter type are not in the first instance literary productions, although they may become literature if collected into volumes. The collection of Ibn Taymiyya's fatwas entitled *al-Fatāwā al-Kubrā,* from which the fatwa to be examined here is taken, displays an Ibn Taymiyya who is very much a *writer* of fatwas, a writer who adopts the fatwa as a literary form. This is not to deny that he issued a great many fatwas to real people caught up in concrete legal and moral problems; this side of Ibn Taymiyya, however, does not shine forth from the pages of *al-Fatāwā al-Kubrā.*

The connection between literary fatwas and the major treatises of Islamic jurisprudence (both fiqh and *uṣūl al-fiqh*) is intimate. Both are subtypes within a larger literary genre that is best described as "jurisprudential dialectic." In both, one finds a format of *su'āl* (or *mas'ala*) and *jawāb*—question and answer—and a common method of argumentation in which the citation and interpretation of sacred texts plays a prominent role (both in arguments and in rebuttals or counterarguments). The connection between the two subgenres is reflected in the title of a major Indian work in Hanafi fiqh, *al-Fatāwā al-ʿAlamgīriyya,* which was composed under the orders of the Mughal emperor Awrangzeb during the seventeenth century. What distinguishes fatwa literature is its basic character as a collection of discrete units (the fatwas). Although the fatwas usually are grouped under topic headings and a particular fatwa may be quite long and complex in its argumentation, fatwa literature does not attain the degree of systemization that is found in the great treatises and, as a rule, does not admit of such highly extended argumentation as is found in *uṣūl al-fiqh* works.

The fatwa here to be examined shows that questions about worship could as appropriately occasion fatwas as questions about secular affairs *(umūr al-dunyā).*[1]

Question. Concerning the four schools of law: is the ritual prayer [performed] by certain ones of them [adherents of these schools] under the leadership of certain others valid or not? Did any of *al-salaf* [the pious ancestors] say that certain ones of them should not perform the prayer under the leadership of certain others? Is the one who says such a thing an innovator or not? If a prayer leader [*imām*] does something that he believes to be compatible with a valid performance of the prayer and the one being led in prayer [*ma'mūm*] believes it to be incompatible—if, for example, the imam has vomited, had a nosebleed, undergone cupping, touched his genitals, touched a woman out of desire, laughed during his prayer or eaten food touched by fire or camel meat and [in spite of this] performs the prayer without having washed, and the ma'mum believes that purification [by ablution] from all of this is obligatory—or if the imam does not recite the *bismillāh* ["In the name of the Merciful, the Compassionate"] or another *shahāda* ["There is no god but God, and Muhammad is the Prophet of God"] or does not say "Peace be unto You" at the end of the prayer, and the ma'mum believes all of that to be obligatory—is the prayer [performed] by the ma'mum valid in such a situation? If it has been stipulated that a mosque's imam must belong to a particular school of law but someone other than he [who happens to be present] has a better knowledge than he of the Quran and the Sunna and takes charge, is this permissible, and is a prayer [performed] under his leadership valid or not?

Answer. Praise be to God. Yes, indeed, the prayer of the one under the leadership of the other [in these cases] is valid, for the Companions [of the Prophet] and those who came after them in merit as well as the four Imams who came after these [established a precedent]. Some would perform the prayer under the leadership of the others even while they debated the aforementioned issues and other issues. None of the pious ancestors said that certain ones should not perform the prayer under the leadership of certain others. Whoever denies this is an errant innovator who opposes the Quran, the Sunna, and the consensus of the pious ancesters of the [Muslim] community and its Imams. Among the Companions and the Successors and those who came after them were some who recited the *bismillāh* and some who did not; some who recited it very loudly and some who did not; some who steadfastly performed the dawn prayer and some who did not; some who purified themselves [by washing] from cupping, nosebleed, and vomit and some who did not; some who purified themselves from touching their genitals, touching a woman out of desire, and some who did not; some who purified themselves from laughter during prayer and some who did not; some who purified themselves from eating camel's meat and some who did not. And yet they performed the prayer under each other's leadership. Similarly, Abu Hanifa and his followers and al-Shafiʿi and others would perform the prayer under the leadership of the Maliki imams of Medina even though these [imams] did not recite the *bismillāh* either to themselves or in a loud voice. Further, Abu Yusuf performed the prayer under the leadership of [Harun] al-Rashid immediately after the latter had undergone cupping and Malik had advised him [*aftāhu*] that he need not wash. Abu Yusuf performed the prayer under [Harun's] leadership and did not repeat [the prayer as a compensation]. Further, Ahmad ibn Hanbal used to observe purification from cupping and so was asked: "If blood was extracted from an imam and he did not wash, would you perform the prayer under his leadership?" To which he replied, "Why not? I perform the prayer under the leadership of Saʿid ibn al-Musayyib and Malik."

All these questions taken together entail two types of situations. The first is the situation in which the ma'mum does not know that something which his imam has done invalidates the prayer.[2] In such a situation, the ma'mum may, according to the agreement of the pious ancestors and the four Imams and others, [proceed to] perform the prayer. There is in regard to this no disagreement on the part of anyone of the earlier generations . . . For Muslims in the age of the Prophet and the caliphs continually performed the prayer under each others' leadership. Most of the imams did not draw a hard and fast line between the obligatory components of the prayer and the recommended components. Rather, they [simply went ahead and] performed the shariʿa-ordained prayer. If knowledge of this matter [that is, of what is required as opposed to what is merely recommended in prayer] were required, the prayers of most Muslims would be invalid. Such comprehension is not possible, for this subject is to a large extent moot, and the indicators [*adilla*] that pertain to it are obscure. Generally, to the extent that one who practices the religion [of Islam] is able to comprehend any of the dispute [over the details of prayer], he will not be certain which of two [opposing] opinions [is correct]. If certainty about one of two opinions were a requirement [an impossible situation would arise], since most people are incapable of such certainty. The one who holds the view [under consideration] is himself merely resting his case [taqlid] upon [the declarations of] one of the jurists. If he were asked for indicators from the shariʿa to show why his master's teaching is correct, as opposed to someone else's, he would be unable to respond. For this reason, the contrary opinion of such a person is not to be given serious consideration, for it is not the product of authentic scholarly endeavor [ijtihad].

The second situation is the situation in which the maʾmum is convinced that the imam has done something that for him [the ma'mum] is impermissible [in the context of valid prayer]—for example, he has touched his genitals or touched a woman out of desire, has been cupped, has had a nosebleed, or has vomited, and then performs the prayer without washing. This situation is the subject of a well-known debate. According to one view, the prayer of the maʾmum is not valid, the [alleged] reason being that the maʾmum believes the prayer of his imam to be invalid. This is the argument of those followers of Abu Hanifa, al-Shafiʿi, and Ahmad [ibn Hanbal], who hold this view. The second view is that the prayer of the ma'mum is valid. This is the view of most of the pious ancestors, and it is the doctrine of Malik. It is also an alternative view within the school of al-Shafiʿi and Ahmad—and, in fact, of Abu Hanifa. Most of the texts [that record opinions] of Ahmad favor this view.

This [latter view] is the correct one, for it is well established in the *Ṣaḥīḥ* and other works that the Prophet, may God's blessing and peace be upon him, said, "They [the imams] perform the prayer for your sake. If they perform it correctly, it is [credited] to you and to them; and if they perform it incorrectly, it is [credited] to you and [counted] against them." Thus he, may God's blessing and peace be upon him, made it clear that error on the part of the imam does not extend to the maʾmum. Furthermore, the maʾmum believes that what the imam does is permissible for him [the imam] and that he has not sinned in doing what he has done, for he [the imam] is either a mujtahid or the follower of a mujtahid. Moreover, he [the maʾmum] knows that error on the part of the imam has been forgiven by God, for the imam believes that his prayer is valid and that he has not sinned, since he does not repeat the prayer. Having judged this to be the case with the imam, the maʾmum may not rescind his judgment but rather will act upon it. If the imam has acted in accordance with his ijtihad—and God does not burden a soul except with what it is capable of—and the maʾmum has done what is required of him, the prayer of each of them is valid; and each of them has fulfilled a duty laid upon him. A following of [the lead of] the imam has occurred in the realm of external actions. The one who says that the maʾmum believes the prayer of the imam to be invalid is mistaken; for in fact the maʾmum believes that the imam has done what is required of him, that God has forgiven him that in regard to which he erred, and that the prayer is not invalid on that account . . .

[All of] this proves that what the imam does in error does not entail an invalidation of the prayer of the maʾmūm. And God knows best.

The fatwa deals with an issue that has practical importance for every devout Muslim concerned with correct performance of the ritual prayer. For a prayer to be valid, it must conform to certain requirements. An invalid prayer is tantamount to no prayer at all and thus constitutes, if no compensatory measures are taken, a sin of omission. The preferred prayer is always the prayer performed with others under the leadership of a prayer leader, or imam—in other words, the congregational prayer. One may perform the prayer in solitude under certain conditions, but whenever possible one should pray with others, not only at the Friday service but at other prayer times as well. Hence the ubiquity of places of prayer, whether finely constructed mosques or simple hallways in public buildings or even open spaces.

The issue considered in this fatwa is whether an invalid performance of the prayer on the part of the imam affects the validity of the prayer performed by the one being led, the maʾmum. "Invalid" here means invalid from the point of view of the maʾmum, not from the point of view of the imam. For this reason the issue has to do partly with prayer in a setting of sectarian diversity, a setting in which the imam and the maʾmum belong to different schools of law and thus perform the prayer in accordance with different understandings of the fundamental requirements. The opening phrase "concerning the four schools of law" excludes prayer settings in which the imam or the maʾmum or both belong to other schools, whether Sunni or Shiʿi. Ibn Taymiyya subscribed to a view of Islam that made normative the doctrine of the early generations of Muslim divines up through the "four Imams" (Abu Hanifa, Malik, al-Shafiʿi, Ibn Hanbal) and their immediate followers.

But minor differences of opinion could emerge within any particular school, and for this reason the issue should not be seen as limited to situations of sectarian diversity. Understood more broadly, it has to do with all situations in which any Muslim who adheres to normative Islam—in Ibn Taymiyya's reckoning, the Islam of the four schools—is performing the prayer under the leadership of an imam whose performance of the prayer diverges from what he, the ma'mum, understands to be correct prayer.

The issue is, on the other hand, limited to situations in which both imam and ma'mum are sincerely performing the prayer in what they believe to be the correct way. When a ma'mum is aware that the imam is a profligate who knowingly performs the prayer in an incorrect manner, an entirely different situation emerges that is beyond the scope of the present issue. Indeed, such a situation in all probability would not present an issue at all for Ibn Taymiyya, since he no doubt would see prayer under the leadership of a known profligate as incontestably invalid.

Ibn Taymiyya's discussion embraces two kinds of situations: the situation in which the maʾmum is not aware that the imam has done something that invalidates the prayer, and the situation in which the ma'mum is fully aware that the imam indeed has done something that invalidates the prayer. The former situation is, for Ibn Taymiyya, noncontroversial. For anything to be authentically and legitimately controversial, it must have been controversial during the time of the "ancients" *(mutaqaddimūn),* in which case an acceptable diversity of opinion may exist and any individual may hold any opinion within the spectrum of acceptable opinions. If something was noncontroversial among the "ancients" and people of a later generation seek to raise controversy, they are guilty of innovation *(bidʿa)*.

Ibn Taymiyya presents us with what amounts to a plea for reasonableness. The details of correct observance of the ritual prayer are so much debated among scholars that we cannot expect the ordinary Muslim unversed in scholarly niceties to be able to assume the posture of an infallible judge of the correctness of his imam's performance. In particular, scholars debate whether particular details are obligatory or merely recommended. How can we expect the ordinary Muslim to know into which of these categories a given detail falls? If, for example, the imam has had a nosebleed, and the ma'mum innocently supposes that the nosebleed does not invalidate the prayer, we should not, on the grounds that a body of scholarly opinion holds that it does invalidate it, deprive the ma'mum's prayer of its validity.

But what if the ma'mum happens to know that according to the doctrine of his school the nosebleed does invalidate the prayer, and is firmly convinced of the correctness of this doctrine? Here an entirely different situation arises, one that for Ibn Taymiyya occasions legitimate controversy, since it was debated not only in the generation of the four Imams, but also among the pious "ancestors" *(al-salaf)*.[3] Debate thus does not embroil one in innovation.

According to Ibn Taymiyya, some early Hanafis, Shafiʿis, and Hanbalis—and, by implication, a few "ancestors" before them—held that the prayer of the ma'mum in this sort of situation was not valid. What rendered it invalid, according to them, was the ma'mum's belief that the imam's prayer was invalid. One should not perform the prayer under the leadership of an imam if one truly believes the imam's prayer to be invalid. The perceived invalidity of an imam's prayer invalidated, on this view, the prayer performed under his leadership.

Ibn Taymiyya himself embraces the opposing view, which he regards as the view of the vast majority *(jumhūr)* of the pious ancestors. He sees the above-mentioned view as resting on a fallacious argument. It is not the case, he insists, that the ma'mum regards the imam's prayer in this kind of situation as invalid for the imam himself. If he truly regards the nosebleed as invalidating the prayer, this can apply only to his own prayer, not to that of another, for another Muslim—the imam or anyone else—may happen to subscribe to a different view of the effect of the nosebleed on the prayer. The ma'mum must therefore give the imam the benefit of the doubt. He must respect the integrity of the imam and assume that since the imam proceeded to perform the prayer without having undergone an ablution for the nosebleed, he considered the nosebleed as having no adverse effect on the validity of his prayer. Like the ma'mum himself, the imam is either a mujtahid (one who interprets the sources of the law for himself) or the follower of a mujtahid. Both ma'mum and imam are performing the prayer in accordance with their understanding of the requirements of correct prayer.

In sum, the ma'mum's prayer is valid in both of the two situations under consideration. Ibn Taymiyya's argument for the validity of the ma'mum's prayer in the situation in which he is unaware of anything that might invalidate the imam's prayer draws upon the principle of consensus. Although he does not use the standard term for consensus *(ijmāʿ)*, he does use a term often employed in its place, *ittifāq*, usually translated as agreement. The agreement to which he appeals is that of the pious ancestors—the Companions of the Prophet and the two succeeding generations—and that of the founders of the four schools of law and "others" *(ghayruhum)*. The "others" seem to be contemporaries of the four Imams. In stating that controversy first broke out among the "moderns," Ibn Taymiyya is saying in effect that among the "ancients"—the pious ancestors and the generation of the four Imams—there was complete agreement. In fact, he explicitly declares that there was no *khilāf mutaqaddim*, no disagreement among the ancients.

Any appeal to consensus among Muslim jurisprudents entails an implicit textual base. Ibn Taymiyya does not quote from any text of the sort normally used to support an appeal to consensus (such as a text containing a saying of an eminent Muslim for which an argument could be made that it expressed the opinion of all his contemporaries), but in asserting that the ancients were in agreement on the matter under consideration, he is making a claim that both he and his readers would understand to be sustainable with texts. It was common procedure among the learned of Islam not to accompany an appeal to consensus with citations from particular texts. But at the same time it was always assumed that citations could be made when called for. The texts functioned in two complementary ways. First of all, they provided positive evidence that the view or position under consideration was held by known scholars in the generation thought to have produced the consensus. Second, they were used as a clearinghouse to ascertain that none of the other scholars of that generation had objected to the position in question. The formula "I know of no one who disagreed with such-and-such" is widespread in the literature. It signifies: I do not know of any text in which disagreement with such-and-such is recorded. If one had textual evidence that a particular scholar or group of scholars in a given generation espoused a certain position, one could then use the *absence* of textual evidence of disagreement with this view to conclude that a consensus had occurred. Such a consensus was classified, in the jargon of the Muslim jurisprudents, as "tacit consensus" *(ijmāʿ sukūtī)*. It is to a tacit consensus that Ibn Taymiyya is here appealing.

In arguing for the validity of the maʾmum's prayer in a situation in which the maʾmum is convinced that the imam's prayer is invalid according to the doctrine of his own school (though not necessarily according to the imam's school), Ibn Taymiyya cannot appeal to consensus, since the ancients were not in agreement on this issue. He is thus constrained to find textual support either in the Quran or in the Sunna. It is to the Sunna that he turns, quoting the Prophet's saying, "They [the imams] perform the prayer for your sake. If they perform it correctly, it is [credited] to you and to them; and if they perform it incorrectly, it is [credited] to you and [counted] against them." Ibn Taymiyya does not take up his reader's time with a close interpretation of this saying but simply states in succinct language its import: error on the part of the imam does not extend to the maʾmum. From what follows we learn that the error in question is error from the point of view of the maʾmum's school, not from the point of view of the imam's. If the maʾmum were to pray without having performed an ablution for a nosebleed, the prayer would be invalid for him. This academic invalidity "does not extend" *(lā yataʿaddī)* to his actual prayer. It thus appears that Ibn Taymiyya interprets the phrase "and [counted] against them" as meaning not that the imam's prayer is invalid, but that the error committed is truly his error, not that of the maʾmum. As he subsequently points out, it is an error that is forgiven and thus does not invalidate the prayer.

In addition to citing a saying of the Prophet, Ibn Taymiyya appeals to a widely accepted principle of Islamic jurisprudence: when an individual Muslim truly believes that he is performing a duty in a correct way, God accepts his effort and considers the duty as fulfilled even if in fact it has been performed incorrectly. This principle represents Islamic jurisprudence's accommodation to the fallibility of human understanding of God's law, an understanding based on a vast and somewhat intractable textual corpus. It is this principle that provides the justification for the toleration of variation between the different schools of law. Where different understandings of the law arise among sincere and devout interpreters (mujtahids), *all* understandings are valid, even if exegetically incorrect. Whenever authentic scholarly exegesis yields multiple results, the correct interpretation is considered to be truly known—known with absolute certainty—only to God. An individual must, of course, perform his duties in accordance with his conviction as to what constitutes the correct interpretation, but he must do so in all humility, acknowledging that if indeed his interpretation happens to be the correct one he cannot know this with perfect assurance until the life to come. For this reason, he is not entitled in this life to castigate those who hold different views, for if the view of another happens to be incorrect but that person sincerely believes it to be correct, God will forgive the incorrectness and consider the duty fulfilled. No sin has occurred.

Ibn Taymiyya's fatwa affirms the open and tolerant spirit that existed within the confines of the four Sunni schools. Congregational prayer was vital to the integrity and well-being of the Muslim community. Scruples that militated against the expeditious performance of that prayer could not therefore be allowed to spread among the faithful. The fatwa was clearly prompted not by a purely individual "case," but by a communal problem in which all Muslims were involved. It is thus in the truest sense a popular fatwa, a fatwa for the people.

CHAPTER SIX

Use and Abuse of the Law: A Mufti's Response

NISSREEN HARAM

Ifta' under the Mamluks was an integral part of the judicial process and, as such, instrumental in the interpretation and application of legal doctrine. Fatwas made their way to court either directly at the request of a judge or via litigants. A valid fatwa by a qualified person constituted a strong legal argument in court and could be decisive to the outcome of disputes. Ifta' was not restricted to occupants of public office, but rather was open to all those who had the requisite educational and personal credentials (Tyan 1955: 248). Muftis, however, sought to exercise effective control over their practice. Like many other Muslim professional groups, muftis enjoyed the benefit of specialized *adab* (rule) manuals. The adab al-mufti works outlined the qualifications for ifta' and the rules and ethical norms governing its practice. Moreover, they furnished muftis with precautionary measures to prevent abuse of ifta' by unqualified individuals and unscrupulous petitioners.

The fatwa examined here will serve as a concrete illustration of the practical relevance and applicability of the adab al-mufti discourse at the time of its issuance (see Masud 1984). This fatwa was issued by Taqi al-Din al-Subki, father of the renowned Taj al-Din al-Subki, the author of *Ṭabaqāt al-Shāfiʿiyya.* Taqi al-Din was himself an outstanding Shafiʿi jurist and is credited with many novel contributions to his school's doctrine (al-Subki, Taj al-Din, n.d., 6:186ff.). Born in Egypt in 1284, al-Subki enjoyed an illustrious career there as a teacher-scholar and mufti[1] before being pressured by the Mamluk sultan to accept the judgeship of Damascus, a position he held for sixteen years, until shortly before his death in 1355. In Damascus, he also held two teaching posts and, for a short while, was the preacher at the Umayyad mosque. Throughout his career, al-Subki was a prolific jurist;

he issued fatwas regularly and composed some major works on law and jurisprudence, as well as numerous specialized treatises (al-Subki, Taj al-Din, n.d., 6:147ff.).

The source of this fatwa is *Fatāwā al-Subkī,* an anthology of al-Subki's writings that was put together shortly after his death. Besides fatwas, this collection includes summaries of judicial decisions, several legal treatises, and miscellaneous exegetical notes, which are apparently excerpts of an unfinished book. Published years ago,[2] *Fatāwā al-Subkī* has been virtually neglected by scholars, although it offers a remarkably rich and reliable testimony about the different aspects of the career of a prominent Muslim jurist and the legal system in which he operated (see Haram forthcoming). Like many other texts in the collection, the fatwa singled out for discussion here represents the transcript of a document issued to a specific petitioner regarding an actual dispute. As an unedited copy of an original fatwa,[3] this text faithfully preserves not only al-Subki's legal opinion about a particular point of law but also the mode in which he communicated his opinion. The latter feature proves to be of special significance in light of the circumstances that gave rise to the fatwa.[4]

> *Mas'ala:* What do the master scholars, may God assist them, say regarding the case of a carpetmaker to whom Zayd paid money to purchase whatever is needed for manufacturing carpets, and with whom Zayd determined the service fee. The artisan made the carpets, but delivered only some of them, claiming that the rest were stolen.[5] Is he obliged to incur the loss for what he claims to have perished?[6] Give us your fatwa, may you be rewarded [*aftūnā ma'jūrīn*] [P3].[7]
>
> He [al-Subki] answered, may God be content with him, by saying:[8]
>
> This *futyā* was presented to me last Friday in the Tayluni Mosque[9] after the prayers, although it was worded differently. In fact, it pertained to a different case [*ṣūra*], which is about a carpetmaker to whom Zayd paid money to manufacture some carpets. The carpetmaker delivered some of the carpets, but claimed that the rest had been destroyed. Is he obliged to incur the loss for what was destroyed [*hal yalzamuhu gharāmata ma talifa*]? This was the wording of the fatwa or something to this effect [*aw mā hādhā ma'nāhu*] [P1].
>
> So I wrote on the petition sheet:
>
>> This manufacturing contract [*al-istiṣnā'*] is invalid [*fāsid*][10] and the carpetmaker is unconditionally liable for the money until he refunds his client. Moreover, the damaged carpets are considered the property of the artisan. Therefore, he is the one liable for their loss [*min ḍamānihi*]. As for the carpets that are delivered, if the carpetmaker and the client are able to reach a mutual agreement regarding them, the carpetmaker may deduct their price from the money [already paid].

[This was my exact response] or something to this effect.

Then, on Saturday morning, as I was entering the class [*dars*] in al-Mansuriyya,[11] a *futyā* was presented to me [P2], bearing the same question about which I had written a fatwa earlier. Moreover, on the same sheet, there was also the writing [*khaṭṭ*] of someone stating that the carpetmaker is not liable [*lā yaḍman*] and that he is a fiduciary [*wa inna yadahu yad amāna*], or something to this effect. So, I returned the sheet to the courier, knowing that the fatwa was unworthy of my consideration. Later, when I entered the classroom, some people asked me to read the fatwa, but I declined to do so because I do not like to malign or bad-mouth anyone.

We nevertheless discussed the case without specifying the author of the fatwa. I mentioned to those people that this was a famous issue [*mas'ala*] that occurred frequently in cases of bookbinding and custom manufacturing of slippers, textiles, gowns, etc. According to al-Shafiʿi's doctrine, the aforementioned contract is invalid, while it is valid according to the doctrines of Malik and Abu Hanifa. Al-Shafiʿi states this explicitly in *al-Umm,* and our early colleagues [*al-aṣḥāb al-mutaqaddimūn*] mention it in their books. Malik and Abu Hanifa justify their position on the basis of customary practice and necessity. Al-Shafiʿi argues that this is an invalid contract of future sale [*salam*], and that it constitutes neither a sale of an object [*ʿayn*] nor employment for a service to be rendered upon an object. Thus the opinion that the money received [in payment for the carpets] is a deposit in trust [*amāna*], that the payer is liable for its loss [*min ḍamān al-dāfiʿ*], and that the recipient is not obliged to incur the loss is not upheld by anyone among the Muslims. Moreover, this opinion is not indicated by either the earlier or the later scholars, nor is it implied in their speech. Indeed, it is contrary to the consensus of scholars. Because, according to us, this contract is invalid, and since the valid form of this contract entails an unconditional liability [upon the recipient], then so does its invalid form. Thus, the received money falls under the recipient's unconditional liability according to the terms of unconditional liability applicable to invalid contracts [*fa-huwa maḍmūn ʿalā'l-qābiḍ ḍamān al-ʿuqūd al-fāsida*]. Moreover, according to the principles of Malik and Abu Hanifa, the money is received in a valid [synallagmatic] contract. Thus it is legally equivalent to the price received in a valid sale, or the fee received in a valid contract of employment, both of which are subject to the recipient's unconditional liability by the intrinsic terms of [synallagmatic] contracts [*maḍmūnān ḍamān al-ʿaqd*].

The opinion denying the applicability of the rules of unconditional liability to this case is not upheld by any group of jurists. It could have been maintained only by someone who does not possess even a smattering of knowledge. Indeed, such things are committed by someone combining two traits, one of which is laziness, a distracted mind, and ignorance about the shariʿa, its rules, the means of its attainment, and its sources. The second is a preoccupation with abridged books such as *al-Ḥāwī al-ṣaghīr* and its likes. Such a person tires and exhausts his mind in unraveling the words of these books, although he does not comprehend real fiqh. Yet he mistakenly believes himself to have attained fiqh and commits such blunders. The aforementioned book, *al-Ḥāwī,* and its like, are very good books that are useful for retrieving legal cases and indicating their rulings, although in a manner that yields cursory knowledge only. Such books are to serve as supplements for others. But it cannot be claimed that fiqh might be learned from them. The utmost that those who memorize such books may attain is some sort of virtue, but not fiqh. Virtue is of three kinds, one of which consists of knowing the detailed legal rules, learning them from the Book, the Sunna, and the sayings of recognized leaders, and knowing their basis. This is fiqh, and those who possess it are the ones called the ʿulamāʾ [*sic,* read *fuqahāʾ*]. The second kind of virtue consists of learning the religious sciences [*al-ʿulūm al-sharʿiyya*] in an absolute sense, without attaining detailed legal understanding, as is the case in exegesis, hadith, and theology [*uṣūl al-dīn*]. Those who possess this virtue are called ʿulamāʾ. The third kind is different from the former two kinds. It is a science that is close to craftsmanship. Although we may call those who possess it learned people [*fuḍalāʾ*], we may not call them either jurists or general scholars. Such people are often mistaken for jurists or general scholars, because others may fail to distinguish between the learned people, general scholars, and jurists. Those who occupy themselves with *al-Ḥāwī,* especially, belong to the third kind of scholars [*fuḍalāʾ*].

It was subsequently reported to me that the fatwa [denying the carpetmaker's liability] was reissued as a response to the case mentioned in this paper [i.e., in P3], and that other fatwas were solicited about it in the hope of finding someone who would endorse it. I do not know if anyone endorsed it. It was reported to me, and I am not sure whether it is true, that some people endorsed this fatwa, thinking that it involved the issue of the self-employed artisan [*masʾalat al-ajīr al-mushtarak*].[12] If this had indeed occurred, it would be indicative of a great deal of ignorance, and of remoteness from the essence of fiqh and from knowledge of peoples' conditions.

Then, this paper [*hādhihi ʾl-waraqa*] was presented to me together with another paper bearing the same question [P3],[13] as well as a fatwa in the handwriting of the same person who had issued the fatwa denying the carpetmaker's liability. The courier asked me: "Is this that one [P2] or a different one?" I said: "Indeed, it is a different one, for the question is different and the paper is different and does not even look like it [i.e., P2]." I was surprised that someone would act in this manner, since it is the habit of knowledgeable people to admit their mistakes, and not to immerse themselves in error or to act deceptively. Moreover, I was told that my usage of the word *istiṣnāʿ* [manufacturing contract] was criticized. Oh God, what ignorance! This expression is used by al-Shafiʿi in *al-Umm,* and by our early colleagues as well as other jurists, so how could this escape a jurist? It is more apt for someone like this to guard himself against falling into such things:

Not every man is qualified for battle
and registries require good scribes and accountants.[14]

Knowledge is difficult and not easily attained. Not all dispositions accept it. Indeed, some people spend their entire lives pursuing it without obtaining anything, while it is disclosed to others in a short time. It is a privilege that God bestows upon whomever He wills.

As for the question mentioned in this paper [P3], the aforementioned person had answered it by saying that the carpetmaker is not liable [*lā yalzamuhu al-ḍamān*] unless he was negligent in maintaining the carpets, because he is a fiduciary [*li-anna yadahu yad amāna*]. This answer would still be wrong in this case, presuming that the actual case is identical to the case depicted in the question. For if the actual case did not involve other than what is mentioned here, it would constitute an invalid agency [*wakāla*], since what is needed to produce carpets is unknown, and an agency regarding an unknown is invalid. Furthermore, if the agency is invalid, then everything the agent [*al-wakīl*] buys, be it wool or anything else, is his property and not that of the principal [*al-muwakkil*]. Thus, if the carpetmaker manufactures carpets with the wool, and if these carpets are destroyed, they would be the carpetmaker's loss. The carpetmaker is not in a fiduciary position vis-á-vis the carpets, since a fiduciary position would arise only if the carpets were someone else's property, whereas they belong to the carpetmaker. As for the money, it is in the hand of the agent, and the petitioner did not ask about it in any case. Therefore, the answer that the carpetmaker does not incur the loss for the carpets [*lā yaghram al-busūṭ*] and that he is a fiduciary is wrong. However, even if we presume that this agency is valid, and that the wool is the property of the payer, workmanship is subsumed under objects [*al-ṣanʿa mulḥaqa biʾl-aʿyān*]. The rule applicable to workmanship with respect to the issue of the fee is equivalent to the rule applicable to an object of sale with respect to the issue of the price; the artisan would be unconditionally responsible for it [the object of sale][15] and does not have a fiduciary capacity toward it [*yad al-ṣāniʿ ʿalayhi yad ḍamān lā yad amāna*]. Thus, to say that he has a fiduciary capacity is wrong. In order to determine the extent of the carpetmaker's liability, further specifications about the actual case are needed. The other mufti may have had a different case in mind. However he does not mention this [in his response]. Admittedly, the aforementioned answer may not be entirely wrong. Yet it is an unqualified statement where elaboration is due [*iṭlāq fī mawḍiʿ tafṣīl*]. We have been asked to provide an answer to what is mentioned in this paper [P3], and have given an elaboration and a clarification of the ruling, may God exalted be willing (Al-Subki, Taqi al-Din, n.d., 1:447–449).

Before I analyze this case, it will be useful to summarize the main events al-Subki relates in his response. Shortly before receiving the petition leading to the text translated above (i.e., P3; see note 7), al-Subki had received two other petitions (P1 and P2) pertaining to a slightly different version of the carpetmaker's case. In P1 and P2, it was indicated that the client paid the carpetmaker money to manufacture some carpets. But case P3 indicated that the client paid the carpetmaker money to purchase "whatever is needed" for making the carpets, and that he specified the carpetmaker's fee for this service. In responding to the first petition (P1), al-Subki issued a written fatwa maintaining that the carpetmaker should bear the entire loss for the damaged carpets. One day after he had issued this fatwa, al-Subki received another petition (P2) about the same case. This time, however, the petitioner wished to obtain al-Subki's *written* opinion regarding another fatwa on the petition sheet, which would absolve the artisan of any liability for the stolen carpets. Al-Subki evidently was well acquainted with the author of this fatwa and deemed him unqualified to issue legal advice. Moreover, he considered the fatwa entirely inadmissible. In the end, he denied the petitioner's request, declining to write any comments on the submitted sheet. Some time later, the other mufti reissued his first fatwa as a response to the second version of the case (P3). This fatwa was approved by some of those who were consulted about it. Finally, al-Subki himself was consulted about the modified case, and about the fatwa denying the carpetmaker's liability as applied to this new version. The text translated here represents al-Subki's response to this last petition.

Notwithstanding the apparent anonymity of the petitioner, al-Subki must have inferred, as the events unfolded, that the fatwas about the carpetmaker's liability were being solicited on the carpetmaker's behalf. Moreover, he probably considered the "re-presentation" of the case as an illegitimate attempt by the carpetmaker to use loopholes in the law to avoid having to compensate his client. Later on in this chapter I will examine how the carpetmaker's legal position in the second version of the case is improved. It will be shown how al-Subki's response to the last petition (P3), especially in its final part, reflects his concern to expose and defeat the petitioner's legal scheme. But first I wish to analyze al-Subki's responses to the first two petitions submitted to him about the case. Al-Subki's response to P1 highlights the problematic features of his response to P3. Moreover, his response to P2 is a concrete illustration of the practical significance of some important instructions in the mufti manuals pertaining to the regulation of ifta'.

Al-Subki must have perceived the first petition as an unsuspect and unproblematic request. The legal problem raised by the petitioner was familiar to him; it represented, as he explains, a type of problem that arose frequently between certain types of artisans and their clients in custom manufacturing contracts. Nothing in the formulation of the question warranted suspicion about the motives of the petitioner, whose identity was not disclosed. Thus al-Subki handled the case with no more than the conventional prudence required in issuing written fatwas.

From a legal point of view, the question was neither novel nor complex; it had a clear and uncontested solution in legal textbooks. Acting in conformity with the instructions in adab al-mufti works, al-Subki did not justify his opinion; the basis of his fatwa would have been quite apparent to the legal expert, and al-Subki was under no obligation to justify himself to the layperson (Ibn al-Salah al-Shahrazuri 1986, 1:82; al-Nawawi 1990: 64).

Al-Subki's fatwa was a rigorous and straightforward application of Shafiʿi doctrine. Its underlying reasoning may be explicated as follows. The contractual relationship between the carpetmaker and his client fits squarely under the definition of an *istiṣnāʿ*—a contract of custom manufacture—that is considered invalid in the Shafiʿi school. Being invalid, the contract between the artisan and his client does not result in the transfer of ownership. Thus the manufactured carpets are the artisan's property, and since these carpets were damaged in the artisan's possession, he alone incurs their loss. Moreover, an invalid sale contract does not create mutual obligations of exchange between the contracting parties. Therefore the client is not obligated to purchase the outstanding carpets.

As for the money received by the carpetmaker, it would have to be refunded because of the contract's invalidity (thus restoring things between contracting parties to their precontractual state). This is, however, only part of what al-Subki conveys in the terse statement about the money in his fatwa *("al-darāhim maḍmūna ʿalāʾl-akhdh")*. Al-Subki is also saying here that until the carpetmaker refunds the money, he will be unconditionally responsible for it. In other words, if this money were lost under any circumstances, the carpetmaker would incur the loss and would be obliged to compensate his client.

The carpetmaker's unconditional liability regarding the money is due to the fact that the money was received in a contract involving a bilateral exchange, a synallagmatic contract. Unconditional liability arises in this case, notwithstanding the invalidity of the contract, because according to a major Shafiʿi legal principle *(qāʿida fiqhiyya)*, the rules of liability applicable to assets that transfer hands in valid contracts are also applicable to the invalid counterparts of such contracts *("kull ʿaqd ṣaḥīḥuhu yaqtaḍī al-ḍamān fa-fāsiduhu kadhālika")* (al-Suyuti n.d.:308).[16]

Al-Subki's first fatwa is exhaustive insofar as it addresses all the implications of the case in question. He does not limit his answer strictly to the petitioner's specific question (should the carpetmaker incur the loss?). He also spells out the legal consequences of the invalid contract regarding the outstanding carpets and the money received. This is quite justifiable, since al-Subki must have considered, and rightly so, that providing this information was necessary to insure the proper resolution of the dispute at hand. However, al-Subki does not always volunteer legal information in this manner. Indeed, as shall be seen, in his fatwa about the second version of the carpetmaker's case (i.e., the last part of P3), he deliberately withholds from his petitioner significant legal information, which he feared the latter might misuse.

It will be recalled that al-Subki denied the petitioner's second request (P2), dismissing the courier without writing anything on the submitted sheet. Subsequently he explained to his students, by way of instruction, that the fatwa about which he was consulted in P2 was entirely inadmissible, as it ran against scholarly consensus. Yet this begs the question of why al-Subki declined to write his ready and effortless refutation on the petitioner's sheet.

Al-Subki states that he considered the fatwa on the petitioner's sheet unworthy of his consideration (*"laysat ahlan li-an araha"*). However, I would like to suggest here that al-Subki dismissed the petition about this fatwa not so much because the fatwa was wrong, but because of its author's poor credentials.[17] In other words, al-Subki would have issued a written response about this fatwa, *on the petitioner's sheet,* if this fatwa had been issued by a qualified jurist. Because it was not, he refused to write on the same sheet as the other mufti, and would have done so even if the latter's fatwa had been admissible. The instructions in the adab al-mufti works highlight these significations in al-Subki's response.

The adab manuals instruct muftis not to write anything on a petition sheet that bears a fatwa by an unqualified person (*"man laysa ahlan li'l-fatwā"*), regardless of the intrinsic merit of such a fatwa.[18] Cowriting on a sheet with an unqualified person, it is explained, implictly sanctions transgression on the domain of ifta'. Unqualified muftis are to be ignored and systematically ostracized.[19] At the same time, the manuals state that if a mufti discovers on a petition sheet a definite error in a fatwa by a qualified jurist, it is his duty to point this out, and to issue a valid fatwa on the same sheet, thereby forestalling a potential misapplication of the law. In fact, in such a case it is recommended that the mufti return the petition sheet to the author of the mistaken fatwa for revision. Muftis, however, are instructed not to comment on other fatwas by qualified jurists on the petition sheet, as these simply represent a different opinion and are otherwise admissible. (al-Nawawi 1990:60–62). Petition sheets are not intended to serve as a forum for juristic debate.

It is highly unlikely that the conformity between al-Subki's response to the second petition and the adab instructions is merely coincidental. *Fatāwā al-Subkī* includes two transcripts of petition sheets with fatwas by several jurists (al-Subki, Taqi al-Din, n.d., 1:467–472). These texts also indicate that al-Subki and his colleagues adhered in practice to the above described instructions. In both texts, divergent views are advanced by the muftis. Yet, with one justifiable exception, the muftis do not discuss other fatwas in their own response. Moreover, in one of those transcripts, Qutb al-Din al-Sunbati commits a definite error that, further down on the sheet, he retracts *(saḥḥaḥahā)* explicitly, adopting another view. In between al-Sunbati's fatwas, there are fatwas by al-Subki and Badr al-Din ibn Jamaʿa, one of whom must have been responsible for discovering the error and rerouting the petition back to al-Sunbati. Evidently, what accounts for the obvious disparity between the responses prompted by al-Sunbati's error and the one committed by the mufti in the carpetmaker's case is al-Sunbati's qualification: according to *Ṭabaqāt al-Shāfiʿiyya,* al-Sunbati was a well-known Shafiʿi jurist who had adequate credentials to issue fatwas.

Finally, in the carpetmaker's case, it seems that the petitioner understood al-Subki's response to P2 in this context; he realized that al-Subki would refuse in principle to write a fatwa on the same sheet with the other mufti. Therefore, in P3, this technical obstacle was removed by providing al-Subki with a separate sheet on which to write his response.

Under the Mamluks, iftaʾ was still largely an independent institution. Unlike judges, muftis did not have to be publicly appointed; fatwa giving was open to all those who were recognized by their fellow scholars as having the requisite intellectual and personal qualifications. The open character of this institution gave muftis their valued autonomy from the state, while allowing litigants and judges access to a larger pool of juristic resources. Notwithstanding its independence, iftaʾ was closely regulated by its own practitioners. Muftis adopted both moral and practical measures to curb unqualified incursions into their domain. The adab al-mufti manuals commence with a lengthy statement about the grave religious responsibility assumed in issuing fatwas and the dire eschatological consequences awaiting those who undertake the task without the requisite qualifications. Moreover, the manuals charge petitioners with the duty to consult only jurists with established credentials (Ibn al-Salah al-Shahrazuri 1986, 1:7ff., 85–86; al-Nawawi 1990:13ff., 71–72). Besides religious sanctions, though, muftis adopted practical measures such as the ones described here, which served to curb abuses of iftaʾ while preserving the pluralism characteristic of this institution.

I stated earlier that al-Subki perceived the changes made to the case as an illegitimate attempt by the petitioner to avoid his liability. These changes recharacterized the contractual relationship in the case at hand, and in light of the relevant legal doctrine, the new contractual relationship could have improved the carpetmaker's position.

The second version of the case [P3], it will be recalled, indicates that the client paid the carpetmaker money to purchase "whatever is needed" for the production of the carpets, and that the client designated the carpetmaker's fee for this service. These added specifications transform the legal nature of the relationship between the carpetmaker and the client from a contract of future sale to a contract of employment.

On closer examination of the additional specifications, one observes that the carpetmaker in the new version of the case is required to perform two services: purchase the primary material and apply his expertise to change this material into carpets. In performing the first service, the carpetmaker is considered an agent, since he does not derive any gain from buying the material for his client. As an agent, he acts on behalf of, and to the benefit of, his client. Therefore, whatever he buys in his capacity as an agent belongs to the client—assuming the agency is valid. In performing the second service, the carpetmaker is an employee; he sells a skill rather than a finished product. He profits exclusively from selling this skill, not from the difference between the price of the carpets and the cost of the material. Thus one may conclude that the final aim of the added specifications was to establish that the carpetmaker was an employee hired to manufacture carpets *from material provided by the client.* Presenting the case in this manner, as we shall see, would allow the carpetmaker to take advantage of some lenient liability rules associated with the self-employed artisan.

The question of a self-employed artisan's[20] liability toward objects he receives in conjunction with a contract of employment is a controversial one in Islamic law. Two main views were advocated regarding this issue: (1) the employee bears a strict liability toward his client's object, and thus he incurs the loss unconditionally for any damage to that object (that is, he is *ḍāmin*); (2) the employee bears a fiduciary liability vis-à-vis the object and therefore incurs the loss only for damages to the object due to negligence or transgression (that is, he is *amīn*) (al-Dimashqi 1960: 179; al-Baghdadi 1308/1892:27–28).[21]

How was this question treated in the Shafiʿi legal school? In the *Kitāb al-Umm,* al-Shafiʿi admits both of the above-mentioned views, since, as he explains, there is no decisive textual evidence to favor either one (al-Shafiʿi 1961, 3:261–262). Significantly, though, in later Shafiʿi works, it is said that al-Shafiʿi considered the employee a fiduciary but refrained from issuing fatwas to this effect because he feared that they might be abused. In light of this, Shafiʿi jurists mention both opinions about the employee's liability but assert that treating the employee as a fiduciary represents the stronger doctrine *("aẓhar al-qawlayn")* (al-Shirazi n.d., 2:408; al-Shirbini 1933, 2:351; al-Nawawi n.d., 5:228).

Shafiʿi jurists, moreover, addressed separately the issue of the employee's liability when an object is damaged after he has performed his service. In *al-Muhadhdhab,* al-Shirazi (d. 1003) maintains that the employee in such a case incurs either the loss for the material or the fee, but not both. He justifies this opinion in terms of earlier Shafiʿi doctrine, by linking the question of the fee to the employee's liability status (*amīn* versus *ḍāmin*). The employee loses his claim to the fee, al-Shirazi argues, if he is considered a fiduciary and merits it if he is held liable (al-Shirazi n.d., 2:409). Al-Shirazi's argument rests on the assumption that an employee fulfills his contractual obligation and merits his fee only by delivering the manufactured product *(maʿa al-taslīm),* and not merely by applying his expertise.

By contrast, Abu Zakariyya al-Nawawi (d. 1277) dissociates the question regarding the employee's eligibility for the fee from that of his liability for the damaged object. In *Rawḍat al-ṭālibīn,* he states that an artisan's workmanship may be conceived either as an effect *(athar)* or an object *(ʿayn).* If the workmanship is conceived as an effect, he maintains, the employee merits the fee, but otherwise he does not (al-Nawawi n.d., 5:231). The underlying rationale for al-Nawawi's rule is made clear in a fifteenth-century Shiʿi legal work. The *athar/ʿayn* distinction corresponds to two opinions about the nature of an artisan's obligation in a contract of employment; if workmanship is seen as an intangible effect, the employee fulfills his contractual obligation and merits the fee by applying his expertise. But if workmanship is treated as a tangible object, the employee fulfills his obligation only by delivering the product (al-Karaki 1410/1990, 7:274–276). By combining the latter two views about the nature of workmanship together with the two opinions about the employee's liability (that is, *ḍāmin* versus *amīn*), al-Nawawi advances four solutions to the question of liability for a *manufactured object.* The following two may be singled out as more authoritative, in view of al-Shafiʿi's preference to treat the employee as a fiduciary:

1. The employee is a fiduciary over the wool, but loses his claim to the fee (workmanship is *ʿayn*).
2. The employee is a fiduciary over *the carpets* and maintains his claim to the fee (workmanship is *athar*) (al-Nawawi n.d., 5:231).

The foregoing exposition clearly demonstrates that the carpetmaker's legal position in the second version of the case [P3] is significantly improved according to Shafiʿi legal doctrine. In fact, the fatwa denying the carpetmaker's liability in the second version seems justifiable, since it corresponds exactly to one of the stronger solutions advanced by al-Nawawi; it grants the employee a fiduciary status over the manufactured carpets, thereby absolving him of any liability for the material. Moreover, it does not deny him the fee.

In P3, it will be recalled, the petitioner solicited al-Subki's opinion about the new version of the case and about the fatwa denying the carpetmaker's liability as applied to this version. Al-Subki addresses the petitioner's specific request only after providing detailed background information about his earlier encounters with the case, clearly in an attempt to expose the petitioner's questionable motives. Finally, in the last part of his response to P3, he turns to the legal question raised by the petitioner.

Al-Subki insists that the fatwa denying the carpetmaker's liability in the new version of the case is wrong, notwithstanding the added specification. He argues, first, that the case as described in the question involves an invalid agency, which precludes the possibility of ascribing a fiduciary status to the carpetmaker. Then he maintains that the fatwa would still be wrong even if the agency were presumed to be valid.

The first half of al-Subki's argument is unobjectionable. Al-Subki's rejection of the agency conforms to the general doctrine that invalidates contracts of agency with an indeterminate object (al-Shirazi n.d., 1:350); al-Subki must have construed the clause "whatever is needed" to constitute an invalidating factor on the ground of indeterminacy. Thereafter, his reasoning constitutes a straightforward application of the rules regarding invalid contracts. An invalid agency, al-Subki says, does not transfer ownership. Thus it is not possible to say that the artisan has a fiduciary status with regard to the carpets, for the compelling reason that the damaged carpets were the artisan's property.

The second half of al-Subki's fatwa proves to be less compelling. To begin with, this part of his fatwa is quite obscure; it is extremely difficult to identify its line of reasoning. The expository difficulties in the argument, though, may have been partly resolved by my translation. Al-Subki's argument may be explicated as follows. Granting the carpetmaker a fiduciary position over the carpets in toto, as the other mufti did, makes him a fiduciary over his own workmanship. However, the legal status of the employee's workmanship in a contract of employment, with regard to the issue of compensation and liability, is analogous to that of a concrete object in a contract of sale. An artisan would be liable for his workmanship until he delivers it to the client, just as a vendor would be liable for the object of sale until he delivers it to the buyer. Thus it is wrong to say that the carpetmaker is a fiduciary in relation to his workmanship.

This part of al-Subki's response is not as readily justifiable in terms of Shafiʿi legal doctrine. Al-Subki is entitled to treat workmanship as an object and to issue a fatwa accordingly. However, he may not use such an inconclusive opinion to refute another fatwa based on a different but nonetheless admissible view of workmanship. Al-Subki must have been acquainted with the different opinions about workmanship expounded in al-Nawawi's *Rawḍat al-ṭālibīn*. He was, after all, an astute student of al-Nawawi and was already well acquainted with the latter's legal works at an early stage in his career (al-Subki, Taj al-Din, n.d., 6:156, 170). Why, then, does he overlook entirely this other view of workmanship in his fatwa?

It may be that the view of workmanship as an effect was considered admissible but weak by jurists after al-Nawawi. There is some evidence in the sources that points in this direction.[22] If this was indeed the case, al-Subki's objection to the other fatwa would be justifiable; according to adab al-mufti manuals, a jurist is not at liberty to choose any one of the opinions in the school regarding a particular point of law. Rather he should base his fatwa on the weightiest and most plausible opinion in his school *(al-arjaḥ, al-aṣaḥḥ)* (Ibn al-Salah al-Shahrazuri 1986, 1:60–61; al-Nawawi 1990:42).

Yet, even if we grant al-Subki the benefit of the doubt on this point, his fatwa about the second version of the case would still be problematic. This becomes apparent if one takes into account not only what al-Subki says in his fatwa but also how he says it—and what he conspicuously chooses not to say. Al-Subki, it may be noted, focuses strictly on the mistaken segment of the other fatwa and stresses only the liability of the artisan. However, he avoids conceding the improvement in the carpetmaker's position in the new case. Thus when he entertains the possibility that the agency involved in the transaction might be valid, he does not spell out the implications of this possibility regarding the wool. He moves directly to assert that ascribing a fiduciary status to the carpetmaker in this case would also be wrong, because it involves ascribing to him a fiduciary status over his workmanship. However, al-Subki does not state explicitly that if the agency were valid, the carpetmaker would not be liable for the wool—presuming no negligence on his part—since the wool in this case would be the property of his client. Al-Subki undoubtedly was aware of the implications of the new case regarding the wool. In fact, he indicates this at the end, when he concedes that the fatwa ascribing a fiduciary status to the carpetmaker may be valid in a qualified sense. However, he deliberately avoids explaining how this is so. Moreover, he defers providing a definite statement about the extent of the carpetmaker's liability on the unconvincing pretext of lacking specifications—presumably regarding the validity of the agency.[23] The negative and evasive character of al-Subki's fatwa about the second version of the case is unmistakable.[24]

Was al-Subki acting as a good mufti in issuing such a vague, incomplete, and biased fatwa about the second version of the case? From the narrow perspective of formal legal validity, the answer would not be in al-Subki's favor. However, if al-Subki's actions are interpreted in light of his concern to forestall an attempt to abuse the law, they would have solid justification in the norms of ifta' at his time.

Muslim jurists were well aware of the existence of loopholes in the corpus of legal doctrine. In recognition of this fact, the adab manuals instruct muftis against assisting petitioners to avoid liabilities that are dictated by the intended meaning of the law (Ibn al-Salah al-Shahrazuri 1986, 1:82, 47; al-Nawawi 1990:38, 54–55).[25] The mufti acting on the carpetmaker's behalf apparently furnished the latter with such objectionable legal advice, thereby violating a basic principle of ifta'. Al-Subki reacted to this misconduct in conformity with his adab culture. In the manuals, it is stated that a mufti may issue a fatwa that does not conform to the apparent meaning of the law *(al-ẓāhir)* if he suspects ill will on the petitioner's behalf. The example provided in the manuals to illustrate this principle is not clearly relevant to this case (al-Nawawi 1990:56). However, we need not limit ourselves to the adab works, since these are necessarily an incomplete record of the larger discourse about fatwa giving that existed at al-Subki's time. Indeed, an excellent illustration of the principle at hand is provided by the anecdote, cited above, about al-Shafiʿi's refusal to publicize his opinion about the employee's fiduciary status, for fear that it might be misused. The principle underlying this anecdote must have been an integral part of al-Subki's culture and education as a mufti, and was evidently the overriding consideration behind his actions in this case. Admittedly al-Subki did not go as far as misrepresenting the doctrine for the carpetmaker. However, he did not provide him with a full statement of the law, depriving him of written support for his attempt to evade his liability toward the client.

Moreover, al-Subki did not limit his response in P3 to the petitioner's question but also provided all the relevant background information about the carpetmaker's case. His decision to do so must have been informed by his professional training. Judging from the silence of the manuals on this issue, it seems that muftis were not expected to verify the facts of cases about which they were asked to issue fatwas. In general, they were only expected to provide a precise answer to the question posed by the petitioner; responsibility for verifying the applicability of a fatwa to the actual case fell to the judge. It was a different matter, however, if a mufti happened to know, or had reason to suspect, that the legal case as described by the petitioner *(ṣūrat-al-fatwā)* did not conform to the actual case *(ṣūrat al-ḥāl)*. In such an event, the manuals instruct the mufti not only to answer the petitioner's question but also to cite and provide the solution for what is suspected to be the actual case (Ibn al-Salah al-Shahrazuri 1986, 1:79). This is exactly the course al-Subki adopted.

The instructions in the manuals underscore the notion that a written fatwa was not to be treated merely as a medium for the mufti to communicate his opinion to the petitioner in a form that is preservable. A mufti had to keep in mind that a fatwa might be read by someone other than the petitioner. Thus muftis were advised to incorporate in their response all relevant information about the case. Moreover, they were to take all the precautionary measures to insure that their written fatwas would stand as autonomous and self-explanatory texts (Ibn al-Salah al-Shahrazuri 1986, 1:78; al-Nawawi 1990:45–46).[26] In this case, al-Subki clearly did not compose his answer only for the benefit of the petitioner or the other mufti assisting him, since most of the information he provided was already well known to those two readers. Rather, he also had in mind other potential readers who might be in a position to influence or decide the outcome of the case. The additional information al-Subki provided in his response would alert those readers to the petitioner's suspect motives. Moreover it placed his fatwa in its very particular context, thus justifying its problematic character.

CHAPTER SEVEN

Dhimmi Women and Mourning

SETH WARD

In 1337–1338, a trio of requests for fatwas was sent from Tripoli, in what is now Lebanon, to Taqi al-Din al-Subki (1284–1355) (al-Subki 1936, 2:594–632). Al-Subki was at the time a prominent Shafiʿi jurist and teacher living in his native Egypt; the following year he was appointed chief judge of Damascus and moved to Syria. The third fatwa in the set concerns whether non-Muslim women are subject to *iḥdād,* the prohibition of certain acts of personal grooming and of wearing bright dress or adornment during mourning.[1] The text reads as follows:

> The third question concerns a man who says, "The dhimmi woman is included in the general sense of Muhammad's statement, 'It is not permitted to a woman who believes in God and the Last Day to be in mourning more than three [days] except for her husband, whom she mourns for four months and ten [days].'" [This man] says, "The dhimmi woman is a believer in God and the Last Day" [and thus she is bound by Muhammad's statement]. Some of the jurists dispute him in this matter. He claims further that belief is of two types—absolute and with qualifications in meaning [*muqayyad*][2]—and that the Ahl al-dhimma are believers with qualifications.[3]
>
> He said, "This is the statement of the ʿulamaʾ," but when asked about who said it, he said, "I am not the one who must present his transmission, to ascribe it to a particular person."[4] He says, "If we hold that the derived Divine Laws [*furūʿ al-sharīʿa*] apply to unbelievers,[5] meaning that they are punished in the next world for not observing them, then what they observe of them in this world lightens their punishment in the next."
>
> When told that God has said, "Nor shall its chastisement be lightened for them" (Quran 35:36), he said, "The meaning [of the verse] is that it will not be lightened for them in a way they will feel."[6]

Is the man correct in his statements? Is he supported by a single statement of the scholars in this regard? If he is wrong, and persists in this belief, manifesting it openly and publicizing it, what must be done about him?

The answer:

God has said: "Fight those who believe not in God and the Last Day . . ." (Quran 9:29).[7] God has thus declared that the People of the Book believe neither in God nor in the Last Day. As the dhimmi woman is a member of the People of the Book, she does not believe. The ʿulama' have said that even if the People of the Book believe in the last day, they do not do so in the correct manner,[8] and therefore it is said that they do not believe. So too their faith in God is in the incorrect manner.[9] So one who says that the dhimmi woman believes in God and the Last Day is incorrect.

His saying that they are "believers with qualifications" indicates that he might be using the term "believer" metaphorically. For qualification is necessary only in a metaphor; a term used literally does not require qualification. For example, if I mean to use the word "wing" literally, it is left unqualified; but if I wish it to be understood metaphorically, it is qualified, as in "the wing of shame." Thus the man who made this claim is using an unqualified metaphor.

Regarding his statement that the dhimmi woman is included in the general reference of the hadith, "It is not permitted to a woman who believes in God and the Last Day" [i.e., when he says that the term "woman" does not exclude the dhimmi woman]: we should indeed say that she is included in the application of the ruling of the hadith. If we say that unbelievers are addressed by the derived laws, she is included in this ruling, but not, however, directly from its wording. For the subject of the ruling is qualified by the hadith as "the woman who believes in God and the Last Day"; no other woman may be included in the application of the wording. But the dhimmi woman is included in its rule, according to proofs showing that the infidel woman is bound [in this case] by what is incumbent upon the believing woman.

As for his ascription to the ʿulama', it is not out of the question that a statement to this effect might occur in the teaching of one of the scholars, in which case its meaning is the nonqualified metaphor, as mentioned by Ibn Qutayba and others. This is because all Creation is tied to God, as the Quran says, "If you ask them, 'Who created you?' they will say, 'God'" (43:87).

As for his statement that he is not the one who is required to present his source, we should not even discuss it, for two discussants should bear with each other, as they are brothers cooperating in the clarification of the Truth. A brother should not with contempt his brother resent. If one treats another roughly, the latter should nevertheless bear with him, and should not resent him but should treat him with gravity and honor, and should act civilly with him and call to him, and know that he is the cause of the increase of his knowledge, and a means for him to get closer to God.

Those who say that unbelievers are addressed by the derived laws declare that if [the unbelievers] refrain from them, their punishment in the next world will be doubled: they will be punished for refraining from Belief, and for refraining from required acts and doing forbidden acts. Those who say that persons in the state of unbelief are addressed only regarding belief itself say that they are punished only for their unbelief. Nevertheless there are various levels: some have a harsher punishment than others. Those who are at the lowest rung are punished more harshly than those above, for the levels of unbelief are dissimilar. But whatever we say about whether the unbelievers are addressed by the derived laws of Islam, it is not said that the punishment of those who are above them is lightened.

Even if we say that unbelievers are addressed by the derived laws, in the state of unbelief they cannot effect the obligatory acts for which intention [*niyya*] is a precondition, which cannot proceed from them [on account of their unbelief].[10] According to this they are punished absolutely for these acts. The man's statement that if they performed the [obligatory acts, their punishment] is lightened cannot apply to this type of act; if this is what he meant, then what he said is not so. But this can occur for obligatory acts for which religious intention is not a precondition, such as repaying debts, deposits, loans, seizures, and redemptions; and for avoiding prohibited acts. If they fulfilled these obligatory acts, they are not punished in the afterworld for refraining from them, as they did not. If they refrained from prohibited acts, they are not punished for performing them, for they did not perform them. But it is not said that this lightens the punishment they deserve for their unbelief; nothing is lightened of this punishment. This is the meaning of the quranic verse, "Nor shall its chastisement be lightened for them."

The man's statement that there will not be a lightening of the chastisement is inappropriate, as the meaning [of the quranic verse he quotes] is as we have indicated. No part of the punishment of Hell is light— may God save us from it! Some parts of it are harsher than others, but it is all harsh. We ask God for well-being!

As for the question of what must be done about the man if he is wrong or persists: nothing [specific] need be done, but rather, what is obligatory is cooperation in Truth and Right-Guidance, and mutual assistance, and that the servants of God be brothers.

I propose the following three-part program for assessing this fatwa. I shall first examine the general approach of the mufti as well as the nature of his futya. How does this fatwa fit into the work of the mufti? Because many fatwas are preserved in collections, much may be learned from the context of the fatwa in the collection and the principles of editing that appear to be at work there. I shall then explore the availability, plausibility, and context of details—both internal and external, legal and social—for the question, the answer, and the circumstances of its issuance. How does the fatwa (and fatwa giving) fit into its legal, historical, and social context? Finally, I shall critically examine the text itself, including the relation of the question to the answer.

The Collection

The Tripoli material was included in the fatwas collected, prepared, edited, and copied shortly after al-Subki's death (al-Subki 1936, 1:11 and 1:colophon). Al-Subki's collected fatwas contain a copyist's introduction, headings, editorial comments by this copyist and by al-Subki's son, and occasional remarks by al-Subki himself relevant to why or how he came to write a given fatwa. These items are of great value in evaluating the editorial process, al-Subki's approach, and other similar concerns.

A detailed discussion of these matters is beyond the scope of this chapter, but it is worth noting that both the copyist and al-Subki claimed to have taken great care in copying questions exactly from the handwriting of the questioner. Although al-Subki could be technical and legalistic in his fatwas, he also was aware of the popularity of the fatwa genre. Many of the opinions included in the fatwa collections are general, avoiding excessive technicality and aiming for an approach that can be applied to situations beyond the limited one depicted in the question. Furthermore, the copyist noted that he excercised what may be called an option of choice, including the item with the most general application when there were several fatwas dealing with similar topics (al-Subki 1936, 1:11).

The work of al-Subki and the editorial principles apparent in his collected fatwas indicate no reason to doubt this fatwa is a response to an actual, written question, one of a group on the subject of the application of Islamic law to various types of non-Muslims, an area of interest to the author. It is reasonable to assume that the author may have seen his response as directed to a general audience rather than to advanced students of shariʿa.

Legal, Historical, and Social Context

The question of the mourning practices allowed to, or encumbent upon, dhimmis is at most of tangential concern to Muslim jurists[11] and plays only a small role in the general Islamic understanding of death and its consequences.[12] *Iḥdād* in Islam pertains to women only. Al-Nawawi summarized the traditional Shafiʿi teaching on this subject as follows:[13]

> A widow's mourning consists first in her abstaining from personal adornment in bright-colored clothing even of a coarse material; although some jurists permit her to wear material of which the threads are dyed first and woven afterwards, whatever the color may be. A woman in mourning may legally wear all kinds of cloth, black or white, cotton, wool, linen or silk. Bright-colored stuff is not forbidden if not worn for adornment. Second, a woman in mourning must wear no ornaments of gold or silver or pearl.[14] She must abstain from perfumes on the body, on the clothes, in food, or in eyewash, she must

> not paint her eyes with antimony, except in cases of necessity, e.g. if she is bleary-eyed; nor may she use white lead, unguents, henna, etc. (al-Nawawi 1882–1884, 3:52–54; 1914: 371–372)

The obligatory period of mourning for a deceased husband is coterminous with that of the *ʿidda,* or period of separation after the term of a marriage; that is, four months and ten days; the widow does not observe *iḥdād* after this period, regardless of when she learned of her husband's death. And: "[A woman] may observe *iḥdād* for someone other than her husband for up to three days" (al-Nawawi 1882, 3:54; 1914:372). Minor differences on these points among the schools are beyond the scope of this chapter.

The law of mourning is based primarily on the hadith quoted in our question: "It is not permitted to a woman who believes in God and the Last Day to be in mourning more than three [days] except for her husband, whom she mourns for four months and ten [days]." This hadith, reported with minor variations, is cited in all the major collections (Wensinck et al. 1992, 1:430).

The Quran prohibits a widow from remarrying for the same length of time: "And those of you who die, leaving wives, they shall wait by themselves for four months and ten nights" (2:234).[15] By analogical extension *(qiyās),* the observance of *iḥdād* is linked to the observance of the *ʿidda,*[16] or, in the words of al-Shafiʿi (d. 820), "The general principle is: where there is *ʿidda* there is *iḥdād*" (1325/1907–1908, 5:232). Islam allows the marriage of a Muslim man and a free Jewish or Christian woman, so long as there is no additional problem that might prevent their marriage were she a Muslim. Jurists note that the Quran does not limit the application of the widows' *ʿidda* to believers. Again al-Shafiʿi: "Free women, Muslim or dhimmi, old or young, are all of identical status regarding *iḥdād,* as are Muslim slaves." Summarizing the rulings of almost all the schools, a modern jurist has observed that the dhimmi wife of a Muslim is expected to observe *ʿidda* and "anything obligatory upon the Muslim [widow] during the *ʿidda* is obligatory on the dhimmi woman, learned not from the hadith but from the generality of the Quranic verses" (Zaydan 1382/1963:435–436).

Against the standard view, other Muslim jurists have expressed opinions closer to that of the questioner in the fatwa. For example, the commentator al-Qastallani (d. 1517) understood the "woman who believes in God and the Last Day" in the hadith to include the dhimmi woman and further suggested that the same status applied to other non-Muslim women present in Islamic lands, the *muʿāhada* and *mustaʾmina* (1327/1909, 2:397).[17] While the Tripolitan disputant may be referring to an earlier scholar who espoused such views, this approach was very much a minority one, especially in al-Subki's Shafiʿi school.

As for the historical context, we can only speculate as to why the question under study was sent to al-Subki. I know of no historical information about a specific incident in Tripoli in 1337 (or at any other place or time) that is relevant to this issue.[18] Nor is al-Subki acting in an official capacity: although he was soon to become chief Shafiʿi qadi in Damascus, he was still living in Egypt at the time the fatwa was written, and was not a chief qadi there. (Note too that under the Mamluk administration, Tripoli was not within the jurisdiction of Damascus.)

Nevertheless, al-Subki was a noted teacher and judge with a continuing interest in questions concerning the application of Islamic teachings to issues involving non-Muslims. Al-Subki wrote on such issues as the status of children of unbelievers who die young, payments made by non-Muslims, synagogues and churches, and the shariʿa regarding the inheritance of nonbelievers.[19] He was interested in the question of whether non-Muslims are "addressed" by the detailed prescriptions of Islamic law, or only by the requirement to become believers. The other two questions sent to al-Subki with this text relate to the same issue. The first concerns the general application of Islamic law to non-Muslims and nonhumans(!). The second, a question about the wages of an employee who recently converted to Islam, has been discussed elsewhere (Ward 1986). Al-Subki's interest in dhimmi affairs may relate to a particularly vivid dream in the days of his youth (Ward 1984:11–12). He was already well known in greater Syria at the time of the fatwa; Ibn Kathir describes an extremely warm, popular welcome that he received on his arrival in Damascus the following year, one which would seem hardly likely for someone who was totally unknown (1966, 14:184). The best we can say is that al-Subki was perceived as an appropriate Shafiʿi to whom to address questions, including those dealing with the application of shariʿa categories to nonbelievers.

We have no real way of knowing who sent the question. The three Tripoli questions may or may not originate from the same mustafti, or questioner. Possibly they came from the Shafiʿi qadis who served in Tripoli at that time,[20] or from one Fakhr al-Din al-Maʾmun, who wrote to al-Subki from Tripoli the following year (al-Subki 1936, 2:545).[21]

The tone of the response may provide a clue to the type of audience the mufti felt he should address in this piece. This does not appear to be a particularly elevated legal discourse: essentially, the only source that is brought to bear on the issues is the Quran, and there is no detailed discussion of the ramifications of the subject of *iḥdād,* which ostensibly gave rise to the question. Nor is there any reference to legal sources on the nature or status of dhimmi beliefs. It seems unlikely that al-Subki would write in this manner to a learned colleague. If we recall al-Subki's awareness of the tendency of a fatwa to be circulated among the masses, this particular fatwa seems to belong to the class of "fatwas for the people." (The first and second Tripoli questions have a different tone: they refer to an array of sources and maintain a more complex level of intellectual or legal discussion. Perhaps this question came from a different questioner, or at any rate, al-Subki may have assumed that it did.)

In the fourteenth century, Muslims frequently treated dhimmis in a manner openly contradicting their legal status in a Muslim society. The sources mention several accounts of riots or anti-dhimmi actions occasioned by finely dressed non-Muslims, non-Muslims appearing too haughty in public, or non-Muslims dressing like Muslims. It is possible to conceive of Muslim reactions against various non-Muslim behaviors involving aspects of *iḥdād*—for example, dhimmi women improperly "wearing *iḥdād*" in public or wailing at the graveside after the third day, or, conversely, a dhimmi wife of a Muslim notable appearing in public too soon after her husband's death wearing fine clothing and jewelry. In short, there may have been a practical import to the man's claims, in the form of "commending good and prohibiting evil," encouraging or requiring dhimmi women to adopt the same mourning practices as Muslim women, or limiting their dress. Perhaps the reference in the question to preventing the man from publicizing his claims relates to some event that either led to a riot or might have led to one.

It should be stressed, however, that we cannot determine from the question alone that there was a practical side to this issue; there is no outside evidence, and al-Subki seems to treat the claimant's arguments from an academic perspective. Even if there was no practical ramification, it is hard to dissociate the question from the background of increasing pressure against non-Muslims, including polemics, pressure to convert, and riots (see, e.g., Tritton 1970; Baron 1980, esp. 174–193).

The Text

The views of the unnamed Tripolitan may be summarized as follows:

1. The dhimmi woman is bound by the hadith on *iḥdād*.
2. The dhimmi woman is a believer in God and the Last Day.
3. She believes in a qualified way.
4. This is the statement of the jurists.
5. He does not have to state the name of his source.

6. If Islamic law is directed at dhimmis, then dhimmis who perform acts required by the shariʿa are rewarded in the afterworld by the lightening of their punishment.

The starting point of the argument may be interpreted in several ways. The questioner merely asks "concerning a man who says the dhimmi woman is included within the general meaning" of the hadith about *iḥdād*. Knowing that the Shafiʿis and others teach that the dhimmi widow is obliged to observe *iḥdād* but not how they arrive at this ruling, the man may have concluded that the hadith teaches that the dhimmi woman is a believer in God and the Last Day. In other words, her belief in God and the Last Day is inferred from the fact that the hadith is said to apply to dhimmis. This is a kind of converse inference, although as such it is curiously similar to al-Subki's use of Quran 9:29 to show that those who pay the poll tax *(jizya)* do not believe in God and the Last Day.

The claimant's starting point may have been more straightforward: simply, the dhimmi woman believes in God and the Last Day. Since the hadith mentions these two beliefs but does not mention belief in Muhammad's mission, it applies to her even though she is not a Muslim. This reconstruction of the claimant's reasoning is more likely if the istiftaʾ is read as questioning the ruling itself, rather than its derivation.

Another possibility is that the Tripolitan knows the ruling and is explicitly rejecting the usual argument described above, by which the hadith is deemed not to be the direct source of the ruling.

Whatever the reason for the claim, the remainder of the fatwa turns on dhimmi belief; most points may be seen as applicable to the question of mourning, but there is no further explicit discussion of *iḥdād*. This is in line with al-Subki's interest in the status of nonbelievers and the relative unimportance of the legal issue.

The man next claimed that dhimmis can be called believers in the qualified sense, as reportedly confirmed by the scholars. This claim may relate to his views concerning belief, to the supposition that the hadith applies directly to the dhimmi woman, or to the notion that *iḥdād* in fact applies to the dhimmi woman. This last case, as we have seen, is precisely the view of scholars, although the man's reasoning differs from that usually adopted. Al-Subki discusses only the question of belief.

The term "qualified belief" *(īmān muqayyad)* sometimes occurs in discussions of the nature of belief. In such cases, it is used not for the belief of the non-Muslim, but for that of the Muslim, who, according to some authorities, must say, "I am a believer, if God wills."[22]

If the claimant's dispute with the jurists centered on his ideas about the belief status of non-Muslims, his statement about the limited belief of the dhimmi would be a response to the first counterclaim: that dhimmis can in no way be called believers. To the objection that he did not provide his source, he responded that he did not ascribe the view to a particular scholar and that, therefore, his claim should stand until disproved. In other words, he apparently felt that the burden of proof lay on anyone who asserted, contrary to his own assumption, that no dhimmi could ever believe in God and the Last Day, even in a qualified sense.

Al-Subki formulates this argument as if he were analyzing legal evidence. According to al-Subki, if a woman says "I was married" or "I was a man's wife" without specifying who her husband was, she is believed, but if she says "I was married to Zayd," she must prove that Zayd was her husband (1936, 2:385; see Ward 1984:203). Although this kind of argumentation may be the norm for verifying evidence, al-Subki rejects it here in connection with determining an actual point of law.[23]

The next issue raises the question of why dhimmis should bother to observe this hadith even if they are obligated to do so. Despite the discussions of whether dhimmi women should or should not observe the rules of *iḥdād* found in each of the schools, there does not seem to have been any practical implementation, such as adding this regulation to the stipulations regarding burials in the "Pact of ʿUmar." Presumably this is because mourning, like drinking wine and eating pork, are bodily acts that Islam does not deny to the dhimmis, even though such acts are forbidden to Muslims. Perhaps the man claimed that dhimmi observance of the rules of Islamic law applicable to them, including *iḥdād,* might benefit them by lightening their punishment in the next world. Alternatively, the question of punishment in the afterworld turns only on whether they were believers.

As I have mentioned, it is not possible to determine whether the problem raised in the question was academic or practical; we have no evidence of the latter, but no clearcut evidence against it, either. Al-Subki, at any rate, appears to assume that the important consideration is the furtherance of brotherhood among Muslims discussing points of law and theology.

In his answer, al-Subki changes the order of the clauses, addressing the claim that dhimmis are believers before addressing the interpretation of the hadith dealing with *iḥdād.* This may have been logically necessary, as his response to the claim hinges on his definition of the dhimmi as a nonbeliever. Be that as it may, the approach undercuts any significance that might have been attached to the correctness of the practical ruling espoused by the claimant: namely, that dhimmi women are bound by the hadith.

Use of the Quranic verse 9:29 to counter the assumption that dhimmis are believers is a strong but "popular" argument. Discussions of belief *(īmān)* do not usually cite this verse, using other methods to arrive at the conclusion that Islam is a precondition for belief, or, as it is sometimes put,

"Every believer *(mu'min)* is a Muslim, but not every Muslim is a believer *(mu'min)*" (cited, e.g., in al-Nawawi 1930 1:148). Muslim scholars allow that Jews and Christians profess belief *(yaʿtaqidūna)* in God and the afterworld, but their faith is incorrect, so it is not considered that they believe *(yu'minūna)*.

A polemical treatise that was probably written in the seventeenth century (in the form of a fatwa) was directed precisely against persons holding the point of view undertaken by the man from Tripoli (Perlmann 1982). The author, ʿAli al-Munayyar, had learned that certain Muslims consider Christianity and Judaism to be "divine" and (in Perlmann's words) "consequently feel it is wrong to call Jews and Christians infidels" (Perlmann 1982:182). Al-Munayyar adduced the example of people who believe a Christian who says, "There is no God but Allah," a statement which, he goes on to explain, is pure unbelief (1982:188). Al-Munayyar, like al-Subki in the fatwa under discussion, avoids legal argumentation, explaining that he wants to reach the simple folk; for this reason, instead of adducing proofs from jurists, logic, and the elaboration of Islamic beliefs, he presents *al-adilla al-sharʿiyya min kitāb Allāh al-ʿazīz* ("legal proofs from the noble book of God," 1982:189). Interestingly, the verse adduced by al-Subki is not cited in the substantial abstract of the text published by Perlmann. Al-Munayyar, who seems fairly aware of the beliefs claimed by Jews and Christians, repeatedly points out the contradictions between those proclaimed beliefs and what they *really* believe, as explained by God in the Quran.[24] Thus, understanding and analyzing their beliefs is of no avail: the Word of God establishes for all time that Jews and Christians can never be called believers, regardless of what they claim to believe.

Conclusion

In the absence of external information, I cannot determine whether the dispute recorded in the question was any more than an academic exercise. Al-Subki, a popular jurist, was known for his interest in the application of principles of Islamic law to the status of non-Muslims; perhaps this is why the istifta' was addressed to him.

The questioner may have sought al-Subki's help in order to convince an individual to desist from airing his views on a potentially controversial topic. The priorities of the mufti may not have been the same. Through deft rhetorical maneuvers (including reversing the order of the issues and downplaying the correctness of the original premise of the claimant's thesis) and by quoting a Quran text to define dhimmis unequivocably as unbelievers, he shows that he is primarily interested in the nature of the belief of the dhimmis and the application of Islamic law to them. Rather than discussing the technicalities of a particular practice, al-Subki presents a brief but telling excursus on belief, uncompromisingly rejecting an attempt to give at least limited validity to non-Muslims who proclaim belief in one God.[25]

For al-Subki, it was essential to remind his audience that a non-Muslim is at best a believer only in a qualified or metaphoric sense, regardless of views legitimately held under Islam about whether non-Muslims must obey a particular aspect of Islamic law, the merit of their doing so, or even whether non-Muslims can in some way believe in God.

This message is not surprising, for the status of belief has broad applications. There is no definite indication that the specific debate in Tripoli about the applicability of Islamic mourning (which engendered the fatwa request) was more than an academic exercise, but that is precisely the point. This fatwa exemplifies the manner in which a mufti can go beyond a moot question to address what he believes to be an important issue. This issue, moreover, bears closely on one of the important reasons that questions are addressed to a mufti—and that, in my opinion, the chapters in this volume clearly illustrate. For the mufti's expertise is especially valuable for defining the borders of Islam—what is inside and what is outside authentic Islamic concern and belief, and how to relate to them.

C H A P T E R E I G H T

The Art of the Legal Opinion: al-Wansharisi on *Tawlīj*

DAVID S. POWERS

Comparable in certain respects to an opinion issued by jurists in other societies, including our own, a fatwa is a discrete literary performance through which we may analyze the culture of the mufti, the rhetorical strategies that he employs, and his mode of reasoning (see White 1985, 1990). To illustrate the potential of a textual approach to fatwas that seeks to identify the juristic styles adopted by different muftis and the underlying cultural characteristics of fatwa giving in Muslim societies, I will translate an autograph fatwa of Ahmad al-Wansharisi (d. 1508) issued during the last quarter of the fifteenth century, characterize its juristic style, and attempt to break through the surface of the text to the interstices of the mufti's argument. I have chosen this fatwa, which is preserved in the *Kitāb al-Miʿyār,*[1] because it is of moderate length, includes a transcription of a legal document that facilitates the reconstruction of the dispute addressed by the mufti, and addresses a doctrinal issue that is of general interest—namely, the intergenerational transmission of property in premodern Muslim societies.

Islamic Inheritance Law

Islamic inheritance law, the *ʿilm al-faraʾiḍ,* or "science of the shares," places substantial constraints on the freedom of a person to determine the devolution of his (or her) property: bequests may not exceed one-third of an estate and may not be made in favor of any person who qualifies as a legal heir. The law's underlying ethos is reflected in a conversation that reportedly took place on the occasion of Muhammad's limiting bequests to one-third. When Saʿd b. Abi Waqqas asked the Prophet if he might bequeath his estate to persons other than his heirs, he responded, "It is better for you to leave your heirs rich than to leave them destitute, begging from others. Any expense that you incur, seeking thereby the face of God, will be rewarded—even the morsel of food that you put into your wife's mouth" (Muslim 1930, 11:76). Compulsory rules for the division of property have their basis in quranic verses that traditionally have been understood as recognizing two classes of heirs: "sharers," that is, those persons for whom the Quran specifies a fractional share of the estate (one or more daughters, a father, mother, or spouse—and, in the absence of children, one or more siblings), and agnates, who are arranged in a series of hierarchical classes. The division of an estate proceeds as follows: the qualifying sharers take their quranic entitlements, and the closest surviving male agnate inherits whatever remains. For example, if a man dies, leaving a wife, son, daughter, and brother, the wife and daughter inherit one-eighth and seven-twenty-fourths of the estate, respectively, as "sharers," and the son inherits the remaining seven-twelfths of the estate as the closest surviving agnate, totally excluding the brother from the inheritance. In theory, the person contemplating death is powerless to affect the relative entitlement of the heirs; he or she may not, for example, stipulate that the bulk of the estate will devolve on his or her son.

During the first centuries of Islamic history, Muslims throughout the Near East found themselves subject to these rules of partible inheritance, which, to the extent that they were applied in practice, resulted in the progressive fragmentation of wealth and capital. It is perhaps not surprising that Muslim proprietors found numerous ways to circumvent the inheritance rules and that they received important assistance in this regard from Muslim jurists. Working with and around the prophetic Sunna cited above, the jurists taught that the inheritance rules take effect only on property owned by the deceased at the moment they enter their deathbed illness, and that proprietors are free to dispose of their property in any way they wish prior to that moment. There are no restrictions on the amount of property that persons may alienate during their lifetime, whether in favor of their eventual heirs or anyone else, and Muslim proprietors may therefore shift assets to their desired heirs by means of a sale, gift, or acknowledgment of a debt—on the condition that these transactions conform to the requisite legal formalities. Frequently, however, a proprietor would pay lip service to these formalities while designing a transaction that created a merely nominal transfer of ownership. A transaction of this type was designated by the Maliki jurists as *tawlīj* (alternatively, *ta'līj*), a relatively obscure term that was understood as referring specifically to transactions between parents and children; thus, a medieval lexicographer glosses the expression *wallaja mālahu tawlījan* as "he gave (or transferred) his wealth to one of his children during his lifetime" (Ibn Manzur 1979, 2:400). By extension, the term "*tawlīj*" came to signify generally a "donation déguisée *illégale*" (Fagnan 1923:190 [emphasis mine]). In fact, the Maliki jurists adopted an equivocal attitude toward *tawlīj*. Although the practice technically was illegal, they would invalidate a transaction of this nature only if the plaintiff were able to establish its illegality on the basis of direct evidence (for example, if the witnesses to a transaction subsequently acknowledged its fraudulent nature) or if circumstantial evidence pointed unequivocally to its fraudulent nature. In the absence of such evidence, the transaction was presumed to be valid, and the recipient of the property needed only to swear an oath attesting to its legitimacy. By placing no restrictions on inter vivos transactions and by adopting a benign attitude toward *tawlīj*, the jurists accorded Muslim proprietors the freedom to dispose of their property as they saw fit.

Reconstruction of the Dispute

The Document

Islamic legal doctrine encourages a qadi who is confronted with a difficult case to consult with a mufti before issuing a judicial decision *(ḥukm)*. A qadi who requested a fatwa from a mufti customarily would attach to his question (istifta') copies of any documents relating to the case at hand; frequently, these transcriptions mentioned names of the people involved and were dated. One of the virtues of al-Wansharisi is that he occasionally recorded not only a particular question and answer but also any transcriptions of legal instruments that may have been attached to the istifta', making it possible to follow the process whereby documented events were transformed into the abstract and impersonal language of the law. (I assume that most fatwas in the *Mi'yār* that are formulated in abstract terms but not accompanied by such documents also have their source in real events and are not merely hypothetical cases constructed for scholastic purposes.) The fatwa to be examined here involves al-Wansharisi himself, who writes that he received a letter from the jurist Abu Zayd 'Abd al-Rahman b. Muhammad al-Ghasawi of Banu Burtal (whom I am unable to identify). The letter, al-Wansharisi adds, was written at the bottom of a legal document, which he reproduces as follows:

> Praise be to God. [This is] a copy of a document that reads, after "Praise be to God":
>
> 'Uthman b. al-Hasan, who is known as [the] Mahdi al-Kaniksi, summoned [witnesses to hear him attest] with regard to himself, several years subsequent to [the sale's] date, being in a state of sound [mind and body,] voluntarily, and legally capable [of conducting his affairs,] that he had sold all his properties [*amlākahu kullahā*], that is, lands and gardens together with their contents,

> namely, fruit-bearing and non-fruit-bearing date palm trees and all of their material appurtenances and abstract rights, wherever they be, in the town of Banu Kanikas and in the town of Banu Budarmayn, and that which is in Jabal Aʿrus and its jurisdictions, to the most pious scholar [*ṭālib*], Abu al-ʿAbbas Ahmad b. ʿAli b. Muhammad al-Nasiri. The testimony included [the seller's acknowledgment] that he had been paid [*takhallaṣa min*²] the entirety of the sale price for which he had sold [the properties] and that he had given the buyer a quittance with regard to the price for which it was sold, after receiving it [*baʿda qabḍihi*]. However, his witnesses did not know the amount of the price, because the acknowledger did not specify it at that time. The attestation [was given], after its import was made known, while he was in the described state. They recorded their testimony therein, [as] requested of them, in the month of God, al-Muharram, at the beginning of the year eight hundred and eighty [June 1475]. (al-Wansharisi 1981–1983, 6:83)

This document refers to a sale transacted between ʿUthman b. al-Hasan and Abu al-ʿAbbas Ahmad b. ʿAli b. Muhammad al-Nasiri. Of the former, we know only that he probably was a religious figure in the town of Banu Kanikas, where he was known as the "Mahdi al-Kaniksi," and that he was a man of wealth and means; of the latter, we know only that he was a jurist. The document provides no indication of the nature of the relationship between the two men (nor does it indicate the number, gender, and age of any children that ʿUthman b. al-Hasan may have had at the time of the sale). From the document, we learn that at an unspecified date prior to 1475, ʿUthman b. al-Hasan sold to al-Nasiri "all his properties"—fields and date palm orchards in the towns of Banu Kanikas, Banu Budarmayn, and Jabal Aʿrus and its environs (I am unable to identify these toponyms). For the sale to be valid, the buyer and seller needed only to have spoken certain prescribed formulas in the presence of two witnesses; no written documentation was required. Subsequently, in June 1475—while he was still sound of mind and body, and perhaps anticipating a challenge to the validity of the sale, ʿUthman had the terms of the sale certified by notary witnesses, in all likelihood in the presence of a qadi. The document that resulted from this procedure is known as an *ishhād,* or judicial certification (cf. Little 1984:224ff.).

The contents of the judicial certification point to the suspicious nature of the sale. The notary who drafted the *ishhād* specifies that the witnesses summoned by ʿUthman (who clearly were not the same individuals who had witnessed the sale itself) "did not know the amount of the price, because the acknowledger [ʿUthman] did not specify it at that time." Further, the *ishhād* makes no reference to the conveyance *(ḥiyāza)* of the property from the seller to the buyer, generally an essential feature of a valid sale. It is therefore conceivable that ʿUthman b. al-Hasan designed the transaction to make it appear that he had sold his properties to al-Nasiri and that the properties no longer belonged to him, while in fact he continued to use the properties and any revenues that they generated, as he had done prior to the "sale." (This, of course, is speculation, for the real facts of the case cannot be known to us and may not have been known to al-Wansharisi).

The Fatwa

Although the source contains no direct information regarding subsequent events, these may be partially reconstructed from the fatwa itself. ʿUthman b. al-Hasan died some time after 1475 but before 1496 (the latter being the year in which al-Wansharisi completed the *Miʿyār*), leaving as his heirs an unspecified number of sons and daughters. If ʿUthman did not convey the properties to al-Nasiri and did continue to use them until his death, then his children, who may have been minors at the time of the "sale," may have viewed the properties in question as part of their father's patrimony, to be inherited by them—as his heirs—upon his death. Be that as it may, the properties in question apparently were not treated as part of ʿUthman's estate (which would have comprised only those assets acquired subsequent to the date of the sale in question). For this reason, at his death, his children protested, alleging that the sale had been undertaken with the intention of disinheriting them in favor of al-Nasiri, who was not related to their father by ties of blood. In an attempt to recover what they considered to be rightfully theirs, they approached the jurist, al-Ghasawi, presumably the qadi of the locale in which they lived. In accordance with the rules of judicial procedure, al-Ghasawi would have summoned al-Nasiri. When both parties to the dispute were present, they would have told their stories to the qadi in the language of everyday discourse, of which no record survives, and in terms of the relations that existed between and among them, about which we can speculate: ʿUthman b. al-Hasan's honorific title (al-Mahdi al-Kaniksi) and al-Nasiri's status as a jurist suggest that the two men were situated in a network of religio-legal authority (a network that included al-Ghasawi and al-Wansharisi). As for the relations between ʿUthman and his children, the source does not indicate whether the children were minors dependent on their father when the sale was made or adults who were economically secure and self-sufficient, whether ʿUthman had made any provisions for his children in the form of premortem transactions, or whether he was known to have displayed any bias in favor of or against his children.

After listening to the respective claims and counterclaims, reviewing the documentary evidence, and, perhaps, asking some questions of his own, al-Ghasawi determined that the case raised a difficult point of law, and he decided to consult with a legal expert before issuing his judgment. He therefore sent the above-mentioned judicial certification to al-Wansharisi. Written at the bottom of the *ishhād* was his undated request for a legal opinion. In the *Miʿyār,* al-Wansharisi reproduces the istifta' as follows:

> The text of the question:
>
> Praise be to God. My Lord—may God be pleased with you [pl.]—your [pl.] response [is requested] with regard to the above document: Is it legally effective, [and] may it serve as the basis of a judicial decision, despite the fact that the witnesses were unaware of the amount of the price for which it was sold [and despite their not having] seen [the actual sale price]? Is the acknowledger's acknowledgment sufficient [to render] the sale valid, or not? How [should one treat], my Lord, the claim of the seller's heirs, who are the male and female children of his loins, that [the sale properties] were part of their inheritance, but [were sold] to the buyer by way of *al-ta'līj* [*ʿalā wajh al-ta'līj li'l-mubtāʿ*]? Should one accept their claim, and should the buyer—or his heirs after him—be required to establish the price that was paid on the basis of eyewitness testimony? Or should no consideration be given to their claim, and should the sale be assessed to be valid on the basis of his acknowledgment of their inheritance?[3] Your [pl.] response [is requested], my Lord—may you [pl.] be rewarded. Farewell—and may the mercy and blessings of the exalted God [be upon you]. (al-Wansharisi 1981–1983, 6:83–84)

The istifta' is carefully formulated, short, and to the point. Conscious of the conventions relating to a request for an advisory legal opinion, al-Ghasawi begins and ends his letter with conventional pious invocations, thereby situating the activity of consultation in a proper Islamic framework. Noteworthy is the manner in which he signals his subordination to al-Wansharisi, whom he addresses as "My Lord" and to whom he refers in the second person, plural. Also noteworthy is the manner in which the mustafti transforms the names of the litigants and whatever stories they may have told him into the abstract and impersonal language of legal discourse, as required by the conventions of futya: ʿUthman b. al-Hasan, (the) Mahdi al-Kaniksi, becomes "the seller"; the scholar, al-Nasiri, becomes "the buyer"; and ʿUthman's children become his "heirs" and "the children of his loins." The translation of the "facts" of the case into legal categories has the effect of masking status, gender, and age differences, thereby facilitating al-Ghasawi's adoption of an impartial attitude toward the litigants, as reflected in his alternately taking into account both sides of the dispute. Indeed, striving for impartiality appears to be a distinctive feature of the activity of Islamic justice.

Al-Ghasawi asks two questions. The first relates to the *ishhād* of 1475: Is the judicial certification a legally effective document on which a judicial decision may be based, its alleged defect notwithstanding? Al-Ghasawi subdivides this question into two parts: (a) Does the witnesses' ignorance of the sale price and their failure to observe its receipt invalidate their testimony—and, by implication, the sale?; (b) Is the seller's acknowledgment regarding the sale price sufficient to render the sale legally valid? The second question, which relates to the notion of *tawlīj,* is formulated carefully. Properly speaking, the sale transaction does not fall into the category of *tawlīj* because it does not involve a parent's shifting of assets from one child to another. But the plaintiffs sought to have the Muslim judicial authorities extend the meaning of the term *tawlīj* to include this type of transaction, for it was all the same to them whether their father had disinherited them in favor of another relative or of a total stranger. In this regard, al-Ghasawi asks whether one should accept the children's claim that their father had "sold" the property to al-Nasiri in an attempt to disinherit them *("ʿalā wajh al-taʾlīj liʾl-mubtāʿ").*[4] If so—and in the event that the buyer is unable to establish the sale price on the basis of eyewitness testimony—should one pass judgment in favor of the children? If not, is the seller's acknowledgment regarding the sale price sufficient to maintain the sale as valid?

In the *Miʿyār,* al-Wansharisi informs us that he offered the following response (for convenience, I shall present his response in several sections):

> I responded as follows:
>
> Praise be to God—may His majesty be exalted. I have studied the copy of the purchase document [*sic*][5] that is recorded above and the question that follows it, and I have examined their contents. The response—God, praised be He, is responsible for success, in His benevolence:
>
> Al-Matiti and the author of *al-Kāfī* stipulated that it is not necessary to mention the eyewitnessing of receipt, in a valid sale. They said, "There is no reason for that [viz., eyewitnessing] unless the purchaser is an arrogant person who is known [to engage in] coercion, compulsion, and violation [of the law] and [unless] the person who alleges that about him produces something by means of which his accusation may be confirmed, in which case, [the buyer] must then swear an oath that he paid the amount of the sale price confirmed by the testimony [*bayyina*], in the event that the attestation did not mention the eyewitnessing of the seller's receipt of the price."
>
> However, some of the writers of legal documents maintain that the eyewitnessing of receipt is incumbent upon every person who takes possession on behalf of someone other than himself, like the father, the executor, the proxy, and the custodian. [Eyewitnessing] also [is incumbent] with regard to the interdicted person's receipt of his maintenance, or [his receipt] of wealth for the purpose of testing him in commercial activity; for the postpubescent virgin's receipt of the prompt portion of her dower; and for the dumb and the blind. [The requirement also applies to] a person on his deathbed [who] sells [something] to his child. (ibid., p. 84)

The response, which opens with the customary pious invocations, was addressed specifically to al-Ghasawi and would have been fully intelligible only to a jurist familiar with legal discourse, the sources of legal authority, and the art of legal reasoning. Significantly, al-Wansharisi allowed al-Ghasawi to establish the terms of the argument, organizing his response in the order of the questions posed by the mustafti. Confident of his reader's ability to follow the thread of his reasoning, al-Wansharisi shifts abruptly from one topic to the next without signaling the direction of his argument (that is, without using verbal cues, such as, "in response to your first question," common in other fatwas).

The starting point of al-Wansharisi's substantive response to al-Ghasawi's query may be significant. Without making any reference to either the Quran or the hadith, the mufti finds textual authority for his response to al-Ghasawi's initial subquestion (Is the validity of a sale conditional on the witnesses' having observed the receipt of the sale price?) by citing a statement attributed to two jurists who lived in the middle of the eleventh and twelfth centuries, respectively: Ibn ʿAbd al-Barr (d. 1070), the author of *al-Kāfī,* a systematic treatise on Islamic law, and al-Matiti (d. 1174), the author of a treatise on legal documents. These two authorities held that eyewitnessing is required only in the abnormal circumstance of a buyer's being reputed to engage in "coercion, compulsion, and violation [of the law]." This observation implicitly touches on a potentially relevent issue, namely, the character of al-Nasiri, who had been accused of colluding with ʿUthman b. al-Hasan to deprive the latter's children of their lawful inheritance—behavior which, if substantiated, no doubt would qualify as a "violation of the law." Curiously, al-Wansharisi completely disregards this issue, passing immediately to the observation (in this case, irrelevant) that some notaries require eyewitnessing of a sale in which one of the parties to the transaction is acting on behalf of a third party—as, for example, a father acting on behalf of his child, an executor, a proxy, or a custodian (clearly not the case in the sale in question).

Turning next to al-Ghasawi's second question, relating to *tawlīj,* al-Wansharisi writes, in the continuation of his response:

> If this has been established, we say, next: If the purchaser immediately received all the properties to which reference was made that are specified in the document, the seller being in the described state, namely, full competence, then the seller's heirs who allege *ta'līj* have no argument, and the claim is absolutely without foundation. However, if he did not immediately receive that which was mentioned, but, rather, the "seller" continued to use, cultivate, and freely dispose of [the properties] until his death, [then there is merit to the claim]. This [view] is similar to what was stated by Ibn ʿAt in his *Ṭurar,* on the authority of Saʿid b. Malik: [1] Someone sold land to his son and summoned [witnesses to hear him attest] that he received the sale price [viz., on behalf of his minor son], but he did not bring forward the price [*māl*] and he did not show it to the witnesses; following his death, his heirs arose, claiming *ta'līj.* [The sale] is

effective if [the witnesses] acknowledged receipt [of the sale price]—even if the son was of the age of legal majority and the land remained in [the father's] possession until he died. [2] Some of the judges [discuss] the case of a person who purchased [something] from himself, on behalf of his minor son who was not known to possess any assets; when the father died, the heirs arose and claimed, "[The sale was intended] as *ta'līj*." Their claim has no basis, and that [sale] to the son is effective. [3] Then [Ibn ʿAt] said, on the authority of the legal adviser [*mushāwar;* viz., Saʿid b. Malik]: If a man buys properties and records them in the name of his son, who is not known to possess any assets, Malik requires that [the father] acknowledge [the sale] and attribute [the properties] to the son, even if the father cultivates them or resides in them until his death. This is the correct [opinion], which is in conformity with the judicial practice [*wa-bihi al-ʿamal*], because it is possible that the son possesses assets in a manner that is not known. Asbagh, [however,] treats it as *ta'līj*—[but his opinion] is of no consequence. End [of quote].

If the sale is binding in these three cases, and the acknowledgment of the receipt of the sale price is effective—even if no testimony confirms the presumption of receipt [*aṣālat al-qabḍ*], together with the fact that the person on behalf of whom the acknowledgment was made in all [three cases] is a child, which, generally, constitutes cause for suspicion of *ta'līj* and deception—then the binding nature of [the sale] in your [pl.] case, in which the buyer is a stranger with respect to the seller, is more appropriate and stronger. This is because no one would be suspected of diverting his wealth from a child of his loins to a stranger, because this is the opposite of human nature, namely, sympathy and affection [for the child]. Be that as it may, if the persons who allege *ta'līj* produce the testimony [of two witnesses] whose moral probity is satisfactory and whose testimony is acceptable, who testify on their behalf that they mediated the contract between the buyer and the seller, and they both concur that the apparent sale that they negotiated was merely a thing heard [*sumʿa*], without any basis in reality—or they say, "He acknowledged that [viz., the fictitious nature of the sale], in the presence of the buyer, subsequent to the sale"—or they say, "So-and-so and So-and-so summoned us [as witnesses to hear] their testimony in one of the two [above-mentioned] respects"—then they have grounds for a claim, as stated by Ibn Harir on the authority of Ibn Harith. [The transmission] was cited by Ibn ʿAt and others. (ibid., pp. 84–85)

To determine whether the sale should be classified as *tawlīj,* it is necessary to establish whether or not the seller immediately conveyed the fields and the date palm orchards to the buyer. As already noted, this detail is not specified in the *ishhād,* for which reason al-Wansharisi considers two alternative scenarios. If the seller did convey the property immediately, then there is no force to the claim of *tawlīj*. But if he did not—that is, if the seller continued to use the property in any way whatsoever—then there may be force to the claim. Al-Wansharisi finds textual authority for this formulation in three cases mentioned in the *Ṭurar* of Ibn ʿAt al-Shatibi (d. 1212), itself a commentary on *al-Wathāʾiq al-majmūʿa* of Ibn Fattuh (d. 1069). All three cases deal with a father who purchased property from himself on behalf of his minor child. In the first case, the witnesses did not observe the sale price, and the father retained possession of the property until his death; in the second and third cases, it is further specified that the minor on behalf of whom the purchase was made did not have any assets at the time of the transaction. In all three instances, when the father died, one of his heirs challenged the transaction on the ground that it constituted *tawlīj*. The legal authorities, however, upheld the validity of each transaction. (In the third case, a minority opinion is attributed to Asbagh [d. 839], who classified the sale as *tawlīj*. Ibn ʿAt, however, states that "his opinion is of absolutely no consequence." Significantly, al-Wansharisi does not pursue Asbagh's line of reasoning, which represents an alternative view).[6]

Commenting on the statement attributed to Ibn ʿAt, al-Wansharisi reasons that if an argument can be made for the validity of the sales mentioned in these three cases, an even stronger argument can be made for the validity of the sale in the case at hand (an example of an argument *ad minorum ad majorum*). At this point in the argument al-Wansharisi makes a subtle but important shift from the formal language of legal discourse to the simpler expression of everyday speech, observing that in the three cases mentioned by Ibn ʿAt, a father attempts to transfer assets from one child to another, whereas in the present case the buyer and seller are "strangers" who are not related to one another by blood. Al-Wansharisi makes a key *cultural* assumption, based on his understanding of human nature. Invoking the natural sympathy and affection that parents have for their children, he asserts that the absence of a blood relationship between the buyer and the seller creates a presumption of validity, for under normal circumstances, there is no reason to suspect that a father would disinherit his children in favor of a stranger. That is, al-Wansharisi assumes that because he knows who the seller is in relation to both the buyer and the plaintiffs, he can know with certainty how the seller will behave and what the seller would or would not do. On these cultural grounds, anyone who would argue that the sale in question should be classified as *tawlīj* goes against the normal presumption and bears the burden of proof. Such a claim must be substantiated by the explicit testimony of upright witnesses who attest that the buyer and seller colluded with one another and that the sale was intended as a legal fiction.

In the present case, al-Wansharisi continues, the claim of *tawlīj* is not supported by such evidence:

> As for the mere allegation of *taʾlīj* by the claimant—as appears from the weight [*quwwa*] of the question, it should not be taken into consideration and it should not be relied upon, unless circumstantial evidence [*qarāʾin*] manifests something

> that renders doubt, in which case the buyer should be offered the decisory oath regarding the true nature [*bāṭin*] of the case. If the testimony supports [the claim] of *ta'līj* in a general manner, without mentioning anything that was specified above, Ibn Harith said, "Most of the distinguished legal authorities [maintain: it] is not accepted unless given by scholars in the form of testimony." But Ibn Zarb held for the acceptability [of testimony given by nonscholars], giving as a reason for his position the fact that the moral probity of testimony should be presumed [*yuḥmal*] [here] to the extent that it is presumed with respect to someone whose lying is not evident. (ibid., pp. 85–86)

Here, al-Wansharisi appears to have arrived at the determination that the claim of *tawlīj* in the present case should be rejected because it is not supported by testimonial evidence. Seeking to make his answer as comprehensive as possible, however, he immediately presents a countervailing consideration: an unsubstantiated claim of *tawlīj* may be accepted if circumstantial evidence signals cause for suspicion. Unfortunately, al-Wansharisi does not specify what this circumstantial evidence might be, although we assume that he had in mind either the witnesses's failure to specify the sale price, or the seller's continuous use of the property until his death. In the event that circumstantial evidence does point toward *tawlīj*, the case would be resolved by having the buyer swear a decisory oath confirming the legitimacy of the sale; only if the buyer refused to swear would the presumption shift in favor of the plaintiffs. This procedural strategy would appear to favor al-Nasiri, who, merely by swearing the oath, could render the sale legally valid even if circumstantial evidence suggested that it was fictitious.

An additional level of al-Wansharisi's reasoning incorporates a fatwa issued by the Andalusian jurist Ibn al-Makwi (d. 1010) that introduces a distinction between deathbed and inter vivos transactions:

> In some of the *Nawāzil* books [there is a case relating to *tawlīj*]: Ibn al-Makwi was asked about someone who summoned [witnesses to hear him attest] with regard to himself, during his deathbed illness, that he had sold all his properties to his daughter's husband, and that he had received the sale price from him—it was such-and-such—and that he had no [heirs] other than that daughter and his wife, her mother. Then he died. He responded: If the seller feared [that he would die] from his sickness, then his [mere] acknowledgment of having received the sale price is not legally effective, unless eyewitnesses attest to its having been paid. End of quote.
>
> I said: The meaning is: had [the transaction taken place] while he was healthy or during the course of an illness that was not life-threatening, then the acknowledgment would have been effective [viz., without eyewitnessing]. This understanding is widespread and it is supported by the preceding transmission of Ibn ʿAt. In a manner similar to this response by Ibn al-Makwi, a fatwa was issued by Ibn al-Hajj and Abu Muhammad b. ʿAttab in the case of a man who sold a female servant to his wife during the course of the illness from which

> he died; the sale was certified, but receipt [of the sale price] was not seen [by the witnesses]. Ibn al-Hajj and Ibn ʿAttab issued a fatwa, when [the case] occurred in Córdoba, after the qadi, Ibn Hamdin, had consulted with them [*istashārahum*], holding for nullification of the sale and [recommending] that the female servant revert [to the estate as part of] the inheritance. But the two of them were opposed by Ibn Rushd and Asbagh b. Muhammad, who issued fatwas holding for the effectiveness of the sale and [the sale object's] belonging exclusively to the wife. As a result [of the disagreement], the qadi recommended a compromise solution: one-half of the servant was awarded to the wife and the other half was awarded to the estate. Some say: This was a good choice. (ibid., p. 86)

The case referred to Ibn al-Makwi deals with a father who, during his deathbed illness, summoned witnesses to hear him attest that he had sold all his properties to his daughter's husband, that he had received a specific sale price from the buyer, and that he had no heirs other than his daughter and his wife. When the sale was contested (presumably by his wife), Ibn al-Makwi reasoned that because the statement was uttered by the father on his deathbed, his acknowledgment *(iqrār)* of receipt of the sale price was legally effective only if the exchange had been observed by the witnesses. The relevance of this case to the case at hand (in which the acknowledgment was not made on the seller's deathbed) is immediately clarified by al-Wansharisi. Ibn al-Makwi required eyewitnessing of the sale price only because the sale was acknowledged on the seller's deathbed. Otherwise, al-Wansharisi observes, the father's acknowledgment of his receipt of the sale price would have been legally effective *without* eyewitnessing of the exchange (as in the first of the three cases cited above). As further support for this conclusion, al-Wansharisi refers to another Andalusian fatwa, issued about a century after that of Ibn al-Makwi. During his final deathbed illness, a husband sold his slave girl to his wife. Although the sale was certified, witnesses did not observe receipt of the sale price. Subsequently the sale was contested, and the case was brought before the Córdoban qadi Ibn Hamdin, who, before issuing his decision, consulted with the muftis Ibn al-Hajj and Ibn ʿAttab (both men died in 1126). The muftis advised the qadi that the sale was null and void and that the slave girl should revert to her master's estate. This case also suggests that if the transaction had not been conducted on the man's deathbed, the sale would have been valid, even though the witnesses did not observe the receipt of the sale price.

Having nearly finished his analysis, al-Wansharisi tests it by constructing the following hypothetical objection to his line of reasoning.

> *Objection:* Why did you not treat—in the case in question—the properties' remaining in the possession of the seller until his death [as a factor that] weakens the sale contract and nullifies it—if it is established that [the proper-

> ties] did remain in his possession until his death; and [why did you not] construe the seller's acknowledgment of the sale and receipt of the price in the sense that he intended not to give the buyer the aforementioned properties and [in the sense] that his summoning [of witnesses] for that purpose was a legal fiction, designed to circumvent the law governing property conveyance [*ḥiyāza*], which is the established legal custom [*sunna*], in the absence of which neither a gift nor any other type of unilateral monetary transaction becomes complete? This is the sense conveyed in the fatwas issued by all of the most eminent authorities and the leading muftis, [including] Abu Muhammad b. ʿAttab, Asbagh b. Muhammad, Abu ʿAbdallah b. al-Hajj, Abu al-Walid b. Rushd, when [a case] occurred in Córdoba, during the days of the qadi Abu al-Qasim b. Manzur, regarding a man who sold to a wife or to his female slave who had borne him a child [*umm walad*] half of his house, while he was in a state of health. He summoned [witnesses to hear him attest] to the sale for one hundred and fifty *ʿibādiyya mithqāl*s, and to the receipt of the entirety [of the sale price], but he continued to reside there until he died. [This is] also [the sense conveyed by] the transmission of Husayn b. ʿAsim on the authority of Ibn al-Qasim, which is the source text [*mustanad*] on which these noble legal authorities rely in their fatwa. The text of [the transmission] reads: Husayn said: I asked Ibn al-Qasim about someone who, while he was in a state of health, summoned [witnesses to hear him attest]: "I have sold this residence of mine to my wife, to my son, or to my heir, for a large sum of money"—but not one of the witnesses saw the sale price, and the residence remained in the possession of the seller until he died. [Ibn al-Qasim] replied: That is not permissible and that is not a [valid] sale. Rather, it constitutes *tawlīj,* an [act of] deception, and a bequest to an heir. End [of quote]. (ibid., pp. 86–87)

Here, al-Wansharisi asks his reader to imagine that the following facts have been established: the seller in the case at hand retained possession of the sale object until his death and admitted, in his acknowledgment of 1475, both that it was his intention *not* to give the properties to the buyer and that his summoning of witnesses was a legal fiction designed to circumvent the legal requirement relating to the conveyance of property. Under these circumstances, one might argue, the sale should be declared null and void. Indeed, this argument finds support in two cases. The first case occurred in twelfth-century Andalusia. While in a state of health, a man sold half of his house to either his wife or his *umm walad.* He summoned witnesses to hear him attest that the sale price was 150 *ʿibādī mithqāl*s and that the sale price had been received. The seller, however, continued to reside in the house until he died. The sale was invalidated by Ibn ʿAttab, Asbagh b. Muhammad, Ibn al-Hajj, and Ibn Rushd, presumably on the ground that the man's failure to convey the house to the buyer served as an indication of *tawlīj*. The second case, related by a certain Husayn b. ʿAsim on the authority of Ibn al-Qasim (d. 806), is the source text on which the four Andalusian jurists based their decision. While in a state of health, a man summoned witnesses to hear him attest that he had sold a residence belonging to him to his wife, to his son, or to his heir, for a large sum of money. But the witnesses did not see the sale price, and the residence remained in the seller's possession until his death. The sale was contested, and Ibn al-Qāsim declared it invalid on the grounds that it constituted *tawlīj,* a deception, and a bequest to an heir.

Al-Wansharisi's hypothetical objection was constructed so that it would collapse on inspection, as follows:

> *Reply:* In the case [discussed by] the distinguished legal authorities, the heir is a brother, and a document containing secondary testimony confirmed that the deceased brother had [manifested] continuous enmity for [the surviving brother] and that [the former] used to say, while he was alive, that he would not allow [his brother] to inherit any property from him. The buyer is either a wife or an *umm walad,* and in both cases this constitutes grounds for suspicion of bias and *ta'līj.* In the case in question, on the other hand, it is posited that the buyer is a stranger and that the heir is a child. As [in the case discussed by the distinguished legal authorities], in the case of Husayn b. ʿAsim, the buyer is a wife, or a child, or a parent. Therefore, it is necessary to nullify the sale in these two [cases] on account of the suspicion of *ta'līj,* because of the [three] aforementioned qualities [viz., *ta'līj,* deception, and a bequest to an heir]. Its nullification in the case in question is a consequence of [only] one of those qualities, namely, the seller's misappropriation of the sale object and its continuing in his possession until his death—if he [in fact] did so, because the consideration of something that relates to a third party does not necessitate its being taken into consideration with regard to himself—despite the fact that the transmission of Ibn ʿAsim contains exceptions in the school.[7] The distinguished legal authorities followed [his transmission] in their case only because of the magnitude of the intent to [engage in the practice of] *ta'līj* in their time and its diffusion in their place, and out of deference for the opinion of the Medinese—Ibn Kinana, al-Makhzumi, Ibn Abi Hazim, and Ibn Maslama—in the case of a man who, while he was in a state of health, acknowledged that he owed a debt to his child, to his wife, or to one of his heirs. Then, years later, he died, whereupon the heir demanded the [debt] that he had acknowledged in his favor. The Medinese said, "[The claim] is of no consequence, even if he made the acknowledgment on his behalf while he was in a state of health." Ibn Rushd said, "That which is known and widespread is that he possessed assets with regard to which he made an acknowledgment on his behalf, while he was in a state of health. God—praised be He—knows best. In Him resides success."
>
> Signed by the one who submits to You [pl.] frequently, the servant who asks for forgiveness, the one who is in need of God—praised be He: Ahmad b. Yahya b. ʿAbd al-Wahid b. ʿAli al-Wansharisi—may God grant him [*sic*] success. (ibid., pp. 87–88)

Bringing to bear his expert knowledge of Maliki fatwas, al-Wansharisi turns the tables on his imagined "opponent" by saying that he has failed to convey all of the facts relating to the first supporting case. The plaintiff was the seller's brother, and witnesses attested, after the fact, that the two men were known to have hated each other and that during his lifetime the seller used to say that he would not allow his brother to inherit any property from him (these details can be found in ibid., p. 79, where the fatwa is cited in full). The latter statement, viewed in conjunction with the fact that the "buyer" was the seller's wife or *umm walad,* strengthens the presumption that the seller was attempting to disinherit his brother. In other words, this case (as well as the source text related on the authority of Ibn al-Qasim) constitutes a textbook example of *tawlīj,* which explains why the jurists nullified the sale. Indeed, al-Wansharisi adds, the practice of *tawlīj* was widespread in twelfth-century Andalusia, where Maliki jurists sought to eradicate it out of deference to the Medinese jurists whom they regarded as their authorities. In the present case, on the other hand, the facts are different. Because the seller and the buyer are strangers who are not related to one another and the heirs are the seller's children, the sale in question cannot, properly speaking, be classified as *tawlīj* or even, as the plaintiffs had argued, quasi-*tawlīj.* It might still be invalidated—but only if the plaintiffs can demonstrate that the seller misappropriated the sale object by retaining possession of it and freely disposing of it until his death (and if, as al-Wansharisi fails to remind us, the defendant refuses to swear an oath attesting to the legitimacy of the transaction).

Al-Wansharisi's distinctive and characteristic signature, which emphasizes his subordinate and supplicatory status with respect to the Divinity, signals the end of his response—and of the documentation. Presumably al-Wansharisi sent the fatwa to al-Ghasawi, who, after studying it and seeking to determine which of the legal issues raised by the mufti were relevant to the case, issued his judgment, or *ḥukm.*[8]

Conclusion

In issuing a fatwa, the jurisprudent is summoned to draw on his expert knowledge of the multiple layers of the Islamic legal tradition in an effort to identify the legal rules and categories that govern a particular case. Like jurists in other cultures, the mufti locates legal authority in established sources that are external to himself. Inasmuch as Islamic law commonly is characterized and perceived as a sacred law in which legal doctrine invariably is grounded in the authority of the Quran and the prophetic Sunna, it is noteworthy that al-Wansharisi makes no reference whatsoever to either of these two sources, but rather situates the authority of his response in an impressive range of Maliki sources that includes doctrinal lawbooks, treatises dealing with legal formularies, earlier fatwas, and court practice,[9] especially as manifested in eighth-century Medina and twelfth-century al-

Andalus. Drawing on his extensive knowledge of these sources—knowledge that was sharpened as he compiled the *Miʿyār*—al-Wansharisi articulates the contemporary Maliki legal tradition by selecting from the thousands of available cases those he considered relevant to the case at hand, carefully arranging them in a unique narrative context.[10] The rhetorical art by which he proceeds in this particular literary performance involves the frequently abrupt and unannounced juxtaposition of parallel and contrasting cases, a characteristic form of Islamic legal argumentation (cf. Schacht 1964:205). Treating these cases as the relevant sources from which legal rules may be construed, al-Wansharisi applies the resulting rules to the case at hand. The mufti's contribution is to bring earlier cases to bear on the present case through an interpretive act embedded in a new literary composition, the fatwa, which, because it is formulated in general terms, has a timeless quality that facilitates the citation of other cases—formulated in similar terms—from, in this instance, eighth-century Medina, twelfth-century al-Andalus, and fifteenth-century Fez. By its very nature, such a literary work displays a dense intertextuality that is mediated and controlled by the mufti, through whom there emerges a layered voice representing the consensus of Muslim jurists as formed over a period of nearly eight centuries. Herein lies the authoritative nature of the mufti's discourse.

The juristic style adopted by al-Wansharisi in this particular fatwa appears to be characterized by openness, evenhandedness, and a willingness to suspend judgment.[11] Rather than commit himself to one or another version of "the truth," al-Wansharisi outlines the legal parameters of the case, tacking back and forth between the perspective of the plaintiffs and that of the defendant and between factual configurations found in earlier cases, so as to provide as full and comprehensive a statement as possible of the legal issues that must be taken into consideration before *any* judgment is issued; he also takes care to mention his doubts and uncertainties. (Further research may establish whether this juristic style is particular to al-Wansharisi, or characteristic of muftis in general.) Running below the linguistic surface of the text, however, are crosscurrents that one discerns when taking account of the information in the document attached to the istifta' and, fortuitously, transcribed by al-Wansharisi when he compiled the *Miʿyār.* The present case juxtaposes two legal norms: a father's obligation (imposed by the Quran and the Sunna) to provide for his children after his death; and an individual's right (sanctioned by the jurists) to dispose of his property during his lifetime in whatever manner he wishes. In his analysis al-Wansharisi expresses no overt interest in these norms or in the manner in which they relate to one another; I have noted his conspicuous silence with regard to both the quranic verses that establish the inheritance rights of children and the prophetic Sunna that establishes the underlying ethos of Islamic inheritance law.

Charged to ascertain the law (and not to judge the facts), al-Wansharisi devotes no overt attention to the human details of the case, specifically the plaintiffs' allegation that their father, 'Uthman b. al-Hasan, had colluded with al-Nasiri to deprive them of their lawful inheritance. Rather than consider the character of the buyer and seller, al-Wansharisi focuses his attention on formal, observable, and seemingly objective legal facts and legal relations: Did the transaction take place while the seller was sound of mind and body or while he was on his deathbed? Was the seller legally competent to undertake the transaction? Was he acting on his own behalf or on behalf of a third party? Was the sale price transferred to the seller, and did the seller immediately convey the property to the buyer? Is the plaintiffs' claim supported by the testimony of upright witnesses or, alternatively, by circumstantial evidence?

Al-Wansharisi's disregard for the specific human details of the case and for its normative, ethical, and Islamic dimensions may have conditioned his seemingly open and evenhanded juristic style, which focuses almost exclusively on one-dimensional legal considerations. As noted earlier, the principle figures in the case, with the exception of the plaintiffs, were members of a network of religio-legal authority that extended from the capital city of Fez to its surrounding countryside and beyond. Is it possible that al-Wansharisi's readiness to suspend judgment in this particular case was driven by his unwillingness to rebuke a fellow jurist, al-Nasiri, and a person who was known as the Mahdi al-Kaniksi? In support of this admittedly speculative hypothesis, I would like to draw attention to a subtle linguistic detail that bears on an important cultural assumption. Although al-Wansharisi speaks for the most part in the formal language of the law, a revealing shift occurs at a key juncture in the argument, where he confronts the contention of two Andalusian jurists who maintained that eyewitnessing of a sale is required in the case of individuals who are reputed to have engaged in a "violation." Perhaps in an effort to avoid the implications of this argument, al-Wansharisi shifts from the level of formal legal language to that of everyday discourse, asserting it to be unimaginable, on the basis of his understanding of human nature, that a father would disinherit his child in favor of a stranger. In other words, the absence of a blood relationship between the buyer and the seller constitutes prima facie evidence that the sale was valid, irrespective of the children's claim that their father had engaged in fraudulent behavior in order to disinherit them. This linguistic shift may be an indicator of juristic bias.[12]

The fatwas preserved in the *Miʿyār* represent a meeting point of legal theory and social practice, a moment in the ongoing process whereby legal theory is actualized. The case that I have analyzed points to the manner in which Muslim proprietors attempted to resist the perceived constraints of

Islamic inheritance law and the manner in which the jurists assisted them in this endeavor. From the fatwa, we learn that different forms of *tawlīj* were practiced in eighth-century Medina, were "widespread" in twelfth-century al-Andalus, and were employed in fifteenth-century Morocco. It is my sense that practices similar to those embodied in the Maliki doctrine of *tawlīj* have been common in Muslim societies at most times and in most places. Future research may qualify and refine this preliminary speculation.

C H A P T E R   N I N E

When Women Went to Mosques: al-Aydini on the Duration of Assessments

A. KEVIN REINHART

A fatwa is a lens through which any particular circumstance may be viewed, Islamically. Like a lens, a fatwa can focus the entire spectrum of Islamic knowledge on an issue, illuminating it and guiding Muslims to proper action in a changing world.

According to a stereotype common to Muslims and non-Muslims alike, "Islamic law" is immutable, unchanging, and timeless. But the fatwa by Muhammad al-Aydini examined here refutes this stereotype, because it is precisely about the moment in which a ruling that had formed part of Islamic law must change, because circumstances have changed. Al-Aydini's treatise is important because even though he belongs to the school that is the most conservative on the matter of reassessing old circumstances, he nonetheless recognizes that, far from being immutable, the assessments that constitute the human side of Islamic law can and must change if the prior assessment causes harm.

The entire apparatus of Islamic law is designed to produce assessments *(aḥkām)* of acts (on this, see further Reinhart 1983). The assessment, in turn, has its origin in indicants (*dalāʾil* or *adilla*)—individual stipulations or evidences in the Quran and Sunna, as well as in the Consensus (explicit or inferred)—of previous generations of scholars. The constellation of relevant indicants is called the "address" *(khiṭāb)* of God to the faithful. It might be thought that, once God had "addressed" a problem, the resulting assessment would be definitive. Muslim scholars realized, however, that this address was partially a human construct, for it was the mufti who chose the relevant indicants from the Quran and the ocean of Sunna and previous legal thought, and it was the mufti who assembled these indicants into the address and "opined" what the assessment must be. Consequently, all Sunni scholars recognized that the currency of law was "probability" *(ẓann)*, not certainty (see Reinhart 1983).

This admirably self-conscious epistemology made scholars both anxious and humble, but one practical consequence was that no prior assessment bound either a contemporary or a subsequent mufti or judge; rather, each *qualified* legist theoretically was obliged to reassess each question as it presented itself to him, without commitment to earlier rulings. The process of finding a problem's assessment is called ijtihad (literally, "exerting oneself" to find an assessment). In jurisprudential theory, each judicial and jurisprudential ruling ought to be an act of unfettered ijtihad. There is no doctrine of stare decisis in Islamic jurisprudence.

In reality, scholars recognized the value of other scholars' labors. With varying justifications and to various degrees, all allowed themselves to be informed by the works of previous scholarship. The Hanbali school was theoretically the most insistent on assessment de novo, the Hanafi school—to which al-Aydini belonged—was the most attentive to prior scholarship and jurisprudence, and the Shafiʿis and Malikis ranged somewhere in between. The Hanafis consequently seem to have been the most likely to compile and value fatwa collections.[1]

The title, "*Fatāwā* of so-and-so," may identify at least three quite different types of works:

1. Cryptic rulings on novel events, for example, a petition of inquiry followed by the scholar's "valid" or "void," "obligatory" or "proscribed," scrawled at the end; or prolix essays issued in response to a problem.

2. A regular handbook of Islamic law organized in the standard order (purity regulations followed by ritual prayer rules and so on); such texts usually contain a combination of précis and divertissements on fine points of law not previously discussed, or a presentation of the several possibilities found in the literature with an argument for the correctness of one of them.

3. A collection of minor treatises on topics in Islamic law and jurisprudence. These treatises are theoretical in form, though their inclusion in a book of fatwas suggests that they were composed in response to a specific situation or to a question posed, and were not merely musings on some topic of the author's fancy.

It is to this third category that al-Aydini's treatise belongs.

Al-Aydini's Collection of Fatwas

The title page of the collection reads, *"Fatāwā ʿĀlim Muḥammad al-Aydini,"*[2] and its topics include: "Dhimmis who glance at Muslim women [impertinently]"; "that the major ablution includes the minor one"; "the obligation of the poor to sacrifice on the feast of sacrifice"; "on the difference between the lands of the Sunnis and the lands of the Dissenters [*Rawāfiḍ*, that is, Shiʿa]"; "that the common Turkish phrase *'ṣabāḥın*[3] *khayr olsun'* [may your morning be good] is more than is prescribed by the Sunna"; and so forth. In the present instance, a fair rendition of the title page inscription might be "Miscellania of the Scholar Muhammad al-Aydini."

Miscellania are not necessarily trivia. The more quaint-seeming of these titles are best understood as demonstrations of the ongoing relevance of fiqh, the discipline of which al-Aydini, whoever he was, was a master. No social circumstance, not even vernacular greetings, was below the regard of the shariʿa. And matters of considerable social import—such as how to regard the nearly unprecedented fact of a domain within Islamdom identifying itself solely with Imami Shiʿism—are discussed here too.

Al-Aydini's theoretical discussions were considered important by subsequent generations of scholars. The text was known to Baghdadlı Pasha, as indicated by its inclusion in the *Zeyil-i Kashf-i Ẓunūn,* and it was found in the library of the Süleymaniye madrasa, the most prestigious in the hierarchy of Ottoman madrasas (Repp 1986:44, 62). Thus, it must have been read and studied by many generations of the Ottoman learned elite. This particular fatwa on "the duration of the assessment" is not unique in its class, but it is typical of the sort of fatwa in which the glacial progress in the theory and content of the shariʿa was achieved.

"On the Duration of the Assessment"

In the treatise entitled, "On the Duration of the Assessment" *(fī dawām al-ḥukm),* al-Aydini attempts to describe the "life span" of an assessment. Such a text can be understood completely only when we understand its immediate context—that is, what provoked it, for whom it was written, and so forth. These details we may never know. The larger context for this essay, however, is plain. It is the anxiety or humility occasioned by epistemological uncertainty.

Ordinarily, the phrase "duration of an assessment" refers to a ruling issued in response to an inquiry about the licitness of some practice; once the ruling is issued, the presumptive status of the practice remains thereafter the same. For instance, if a mufti rules that a commercial practice is valid, a merchant need not seek a second ruling when he wishes to repeat the same practice. Likewise, if a food is deemed illicit, a petitioner may not return later with the same food, or with a different specimen of the same food, hoping for a different assessment. The previous assessment, presumptively, stands. If, however, the prohibition of the food, or the commercial practice, subsequently becomes detrimental, al-Aydini, as we shall see, argues that the earlier assessment is revoked.

Al-Aydini realizes that this argument pulls in two directions. On the one hand, the principle is a conservative one that approximates stare decisis; that is, once a ruling has been issued, it remains generally effective. On the other hand, the flexibility inherent in the concept of the unconstrained mufti allows that the perception of a potential "deleterious consequence" *(fasād)* may lead to a radical reinvention of the law.

Indeed, as a demonstraton of just such a radical reinvention of the law, al-Aydini cites a hadith found in the "Sound" collections of prophetic Sunna assembled by Muslim and al-Bukhari [2] (note: numbers in square brackets refer to the relevant section of the accompanying translation). In a paragraph that may have important contemporary implications, he cheerfully admits that the Prophet categorically condemned interference with women's attendance at the mosque. He further adduces a hadith allowing menstruating women and *"dhawāt al-khudūr"*—that is, young, vulnerable, or unmarried women who ordinarily are kept from public view—to attend liturgical events at the two festivals of the Islamic year, though menstruous women were excluded from the actual site of worship. Suggested perhaps by the restrictions on women's attendance during their periods of ritual disorder, the founding fathers of Islamic jurisprudence ("our Imams") began to extend the restriction to women who might be occasions of public disorder. A later generation of scholars banned all women of whatever age from mosques on the grounds of possible "deleterious consequences."[4]

Likewise, the Prophet is understood unequivocally to have forbidden one to pick up property abandoned by mistake during the pilgrimage. But Ibn Wahb subsequently determined that one ought to pick up the abandoned property, presumably with the intention of returning it to its owner (see [8] and the sources cited there). Even more remarkable, an unequivocal quranic injunction to use the *zakāt* (alms tax) to support certain non-Muslim groups is frankly admitted to have been overturned by ʿUmar, with the agreement of Abu Bakr.

How does al-Aydini justify these changes—indeed, any changes—in the stipulations of Islamic law? How does he reconcile these particular changes, which might justifiably be regarded as socially conservative, with another principle of social conservatism—namely, the presumption that an assessment once made remains in force?

In [1] al-Aydini states his general principle for determining the continuance of an assessment: "The assessment perdures while its effective cause [ʿ*illa*] remains, so long as, in its continuance, no deleterious consequence [*fasād*] follows that would favor removing [the assessment] over its [continued] existence. [In that case, the assessment] is withdrawn."

This principle is represented in the following decision tree:

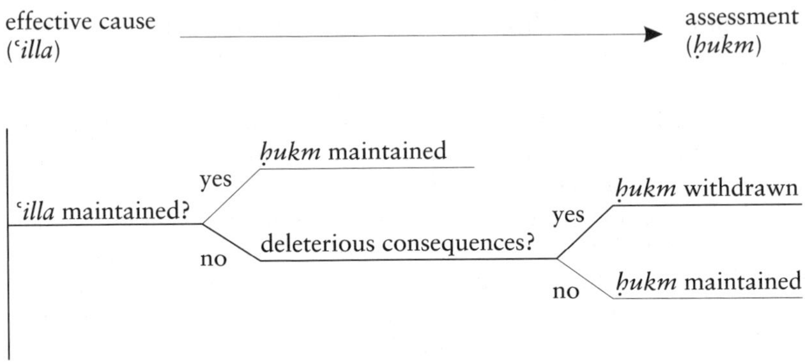

The existence of the ʿ*illa,* the effective cause or rationale, is clearly at the core of the argument. Al-Aydini assumes that his audience is familiar with the doctrine of the ʿ*illa,* which is among the slipperiest in all of Islamic jurisprudence (Weiss 1992:555ff.). Although space prevents a full discussion here, it is important to know that the ʿ*illa* is the underlying rationale for the rule; it is not the teleology of the rule but its formal ground. The most frequently cited example is wine *(khamr),* which is prohibited in the Quran without any specification of the characteristic that determines its impermissibility. Later jurists determined that it was that wine intoxicates (as opposed to its being red, liquid, or tart) that determines its prohibition. "Being intoxicating" is the ʿ*illa* for the ban on wine.

The ʿ*illa* stands at the center of shariʿa epistemology because the careful application of the rationale to novel situations ensures that the scope of the shariʿa remains coextensive with experience. When a novel situation occurs, one seeks the ʿ*illa* of a known ruling that is relevant to the new case. The first ruling is then brought to bear on the new situation. For example, most jurists prohibit the consumption of *nabīdh,* another fermented drink, on the ground that the ʿ*illa* for the prohibition of *khamr*—that it intoxicates—applies to *nabīdh* as well.[5]

While standing at the core of *sharʿī* epistemology, the ʿ*illa* is the most problematic link in the epistemological chain because there is no objective procedure for its determination. Why should the rationale for prohibiting *khamr* be that it is intoxicating and not, rather, that it is a product of the grape? More important, how can a jurist be certain that it is the ʿ*illa* of *khamr* that best applies to *nabīdh,* and not the permissibility of water, or the implicit permissibility of things unmentioned in Revelation? This uncertainty haunts Sunni Islamic legal epistemology and is one source of the anxiety I have mentioned.

In al-Aydini's view, once a satisfactory *ʿilla* has been located, the resulting assessment remains valid until and unless circumstances change in such a way that the rule becomes counterproductive. In that case, the deleterious consequence becomes the rationale for changing the rule. The deleterious consequence, as it were, becomes an indicant, similar to quranic indicants, that the assessment of the act ought to be changed. In the case of women entering a mosque, the menstruating woman and the secluded woman are deemed to be restricted because of the likelihood of a "deleterious consequence." Because, according to the Hanafis, a likelihood of a deleterious consequence exists if any woman attends the mosque, by extension of the original ruling they prohibit all women from entering a mosque. Implicit in this argument (as in the example of lost property) is the converse: if the deleterious consequence is removed and the nonattendence of women at public worship is estimated to be a greater harm than their attendance, then they may/must attend [3]. Once the initial assessment is made, however, it remains effective not merely until the deleterious consequence is removed, but, more conservatively, until the balance of harm shifts clearly in the other direction.

This radically conservative position may be what some critics have in mind when they refer to the rigidity of Islamic law. Although this mechanism maintains predictability, it does so at the cost of littering the legal environment with rulings whose rationale has ceased to exist, but whose efficacy is nevertheless maintained in the absence of a motive to the contrary.

Al-Aydini's essay can be read as an attempt to demonstrate how to avoid the shackles of tradition, or, conversely, as a justification for novel rules and unprecedented rulings. While the notions of precedent and duration of the assessment move in one direction, the doctrine of a reprehensible effect frees one from the heritage of Islamic law and puts any issue on the table for reconsideration, in light of the perceived deleterious consequence; in this manner, it contributes to slow but steady progress in the theory and content of the shariʿa. At the same time, there is no doubt that al-Aydini himself was a social conservative who viewed history within the framework of "the corruption of times" *(fasād al-zamān).* He invokes the notion of the duration of the assessment as a means to evade the liberality of the Islamic scriptural sources, not as a means to evade the oppressiveness of tradition: the examples he adduces all justify abandonment of a more equalitarian ethic in favor of one that particularizes the roles of women and non-Muslims.

In al-Aydini's treatise the flexibility of Islamic law is clearly demonstrated, but as his argument shows, the mutability of the shariʿa can be used by both conservatives and reformers. Nonetheless, the method of Islamic law permits both sorts of change, and in the end, sociology rather than divinity determines how Islamic law is applied to the particular world of men and women (Arabic text on facing pages).

Treatise Concerning the Duration of the Assessment of Muhammad al-Aydini[6]

In the name of God the Merciful the Compassionate, Glory be to Him the Most High. Praise God. Peace upon his chosen bondsmen.

[1] The assessment perdures while its effective cause [*ʿilla*] remains, so long as, in its continuance, no deleterious consequence [*fasād*] follows that would favor removing [the assessment] over its [continued] existence. [In that case, the assessment] is withdrawn, as is the case with the [Prophet's] preference [*istiḥbāb*] for the presence of women in the congregation at all [occasions of] worship.

[2] The Messenger of God—may God's blessing and peace be upon him—said, "Do not prevent the bondmaidens of God [from entering] the mosques of God." Muslim transmitted it from ʿAbdallah b. ʿUmar—may God be pleased with both of them.[7]

Umm ʿAtiyya—may God be pleased with her—said, "We were ordered to bring out menstruating women and 'shielded women'[8] on the day of the two festivals. Thus they would attend the assembly of Muslims and their invocations. [However,] the menstruating women kept away from [the women's] place of prayer." The two shaykhs [that is, al-Bukhari and Muslim] include it.[9]

Later, our Imams forbade young women [from attending] and later [scholars] extended [the prohibition] to them and [also] to older women at all worship because of the overwhelming increase [*ghalaba*] of a deleterious consequence at all times [in a woman's life]; [all this] according to what is in *Fatḥ al-qadīr* and elsewhere.[10]

[3] As [for the case in which the assessment's] effective cause ceases [to exist]: If the continuation of [the assessment] leads to deleterious consequences, or an indicator indicates [that the assessment's] withdrawal [ought to follow] because [the effective cause] has ceased [to exist], then [the assessment] is withdrawn. Otherwise, it is not [withdrawn].

[The method al-Aydini outlines is a conservative one: an initial assessment remains in force unless continuation of the assessment is more harmful than not. Even prophetic practice may be overtaken by changed circumstances.]

[4] The Shaykh and Imam, Kamaladdin Ibn al-Humam, pointed this out in sundry places in the commentary on the *Hidāya*. Let us adduce them [here]: He said in the chapter on the alms tax [*zakāt*] for fields and fruits:

> The *sharʿī* assessment does not require the existence [*qiyām*] of its *sharʿī* effective cause in order to remain in effect; it needs [the effective cause]

رسالة في دوام الحكم لمحمد الآيديني

Süleymaniye 1038/17 ff 23a-23b

بسم الله الرحمن الرحيم وبه سبحانه وتعلى

الحمد للّه وسلام على عباده الذين اصطفي.

[١] انه يدوم الحكم ما بقيت علـّته إلا ان يستتبع دوامه مفسدة يترجّح تركها على وجوده. فيرتفع حينئذ كاستحباب حضور النساء الجماعةَ في الصلوات كلها.

[٢] ققد قال رسول الله صلّى الله عليه وسلم «لا تمنعوا إماء الله مساجد الله.» أخرجه مسلم عن عبد الله ابن عمر رضي الله عنهما.

وقالت أُم عطيّة رضي الله عنها «أمرنا ان نخرّج الحُيَّض يوم العيدين وذوات الخدور. فيشهدن جماعة المسلمين ودعوتهم وتعتزل الحُيَّض عن مُصلاهن» اخرجه الشيخان [يعني البخاري و مسلم]

ثم أن ائمتنا منعوا الشوابّ والمتأخرين عمّموا لهن وللعجائز في جميع الصلوات[1] لغلبة الفساد في الاوقات كلها على ما في «فتح القدير» وغيره.

[٣] فإنْ زالت علته فإنْ تضمّن مفسدةً او دلّ دليل على ارتفاعه بزوالها يرتفع: وإلا فلا.

[٤] نبّه على ذلك الشيخ الإمام كمال الدين ابن الهمام في مواضع شتّي من شرح الهدايه.

[1] في الاصل: جميع الصلوت

> only at its initiation, as slavery is an effect of infidelity. Thereupon [the condition of slavery] remains, subsequent to [conversion to] Islam. [The same holds for] trotting[11] [in circumambulation of the Kaʿbah] and wrapping one's pilgrimage garment around the shoulder and armpit in circumambulation.[12]

[A state once initiated remains effective thereafter.]

> [5] [Ibn al-Humam] said in the chapter on the expenditure [of the alms tax] regarding the words of the *Hidāya:*
>
> > The efficacy of the quranic dictum, "Those whose hearts are to be reconciled" [Quran 9:60], has lost effect [among the list of authorized expenditures of the alms tax] because God Most High has so strengthened al-Islam that it has no need of them.
> >
> > On this basis a Consensus was reached—that is, by the Companions, during the caliphate of Abu Bakr al-Siddiq—may God be pleased with him: Had they not been in accord on this agreement [to abolish the expenditure], they would have forthrightly denounced it [Abu Bakr's change of policy].

[How is it that the dicta of the Quran itself are abrogated by changed circumstances? Here is the demonstration. Quran 9:60 lists among the licit uses of the *zakāt* "the inclination of hearts," meaning, attracting non-Muslims who might be well-inclined toward Muslims as a result of this kindness. It was, as one commentator says, "a struggle of the poor at that time," and as a result, giving money to infidels was appropriate. But during Abu Bakr's caliphate, ʿUmar refused a non-Muslim claim on the *zakāt* and Abu Bakr confirmed his refusal, thereby revoking a quranic stipulation on the ground of a change in the effective cause for the rule.[13]]

> Indeed, one must say that there could have been no Consensus [to this effect] unless it were grounded in their knowledge of an indicant suggesting that [the Quran rule] had been abrogated before the death of [Muhammad]—may God's blessing and peace be upon him, or suggesting that the assessment was restricted to [the period of] his lifetime—peace and blessings be upon him, or negating it with the cessation of its effective cause. They [must have] agreed upon its cessation after his death—may God's blessings and peace be upon him, or from the last gift that he gave them during his life—peace and blessings be upon him.

[Having adduced his example, al-Aydini must now explain how a Consensus may seemingly abrogate a quranic dictum. He also must explain, within his theory of the necessity of some positive sign to change an assessment, whence that sign came. It must have been there, he suggests, and it must have been part of the (lost) legacy of prophetic instruction to the Companions that makes the Consensus of the Companions so uniquely valuable.

فَلنُوردها: قال في باب زكوة الزروع والثمار.[٢] «الحكم الشرعي يستغني عن قيام علته الشرعية في بقائه وانما يفتقر اليها في ابتدائه كالرِقّ أثرُ الكفر، ثم يبقى بعد الاسلام. والرَمَل والاضطباع في الطوّاف.»[٣]

[٥] وقال في باب المصارف في قول الهداية: «وقد سقط منها {المؤلَّفة قلوبهم} لانّ الله تعالي اعزّ الاسلام واغنى عنهم». وعلى ذلك انعقد الاجماع أي اجماع الصحابة في خلافة // [٢٣ب] ابي بكر الصديق رضي الله عنه: فلو لا اتّفاق عقائدهم، لبادروا الى انكاره. نعم يجب على القول بانه لا اجماع إلا عن مستند علمهم بدليل أفاد نسخ ذلك [الحكم] قبل وفاته صلى الله عليه وسلم او أفاد تقييد الحكم بحياته صلعم او كونه منفياً بانتهاء علّته. وقد اتفقوا[٤] انتهاءها بعد وفاته صلعم او من آخر عطاء اعطاهموه حال حيواته صلعم.

[٦] أما تعليله بكونه[٥] معلّلاً بعلّة انتهت، فلا يصلح دليلاً يعتمد عليه في نفي الحكم المعلل لما تقدّمناه من ان الحكمَ لا يحتاج في بقائه الا بقاء علته لما عُرِف من الرقّ والاضطباع والرمل.

[٧] فلا بدّ في خصوص محلّ يقع فيهاالانتفاء عند الانتهاء[٦] من دليل يدلّ على ان هذا الحكم مما شُرِع مقيّداً بثبوته بثبوتها غير انه لا يلزمنا تعيينُه في محل الاجماع، بل إن ظهر وإلا وجب الحَكمُ بانه ثابت.

[٨] وقال في كتاب اللُقطة وقد ثبت في صحيح مسلم انه صلعم نهى عن لُقطَة الحاجّ.

---

[٢] في «الهداية» ١:١٠٩

[٣] شرح فتح القدير ٢:٢٥٢

[٤] في الاصل «القو»: Scribal error

[٥] او لكونه

[٦] في الاصل: الانتهاء عند الانتفاء

Surely Muhammad instructed them that this quranic stipulation would cease to be effective upon his death, or that this rule was to be discarded when it was no longer necessary.]

> [6] As for [supposing that one's withdrawing the assessment] is caused by an effective cause that has ceased [to exist,] it is evidentially improper to ground the cessation of the assessment in [the cessation of] its effective cause, because of what we have already [explained,] namely, that in order for an assessment to continue in effect, there is no need that the effective cause continue to exist, because of what is known of slavery, hitching up the pilgrimage garb, and trotting [in circumambulation].

[It cannot be simply that the effective cause—for example, the circumstances of the Muslims as poor strugglers—changed, since al-Aydini has argued that the assessment ought to continue in that case. No, there must have been a positive sign indicating the cessation of the rule derived from Quran 9:60.]

> [7] In special circumstances in which the assessment is to be withdrawn because of the disappearance [of the effective cause], there must be an indicant that *this* assessment is one of those of which it is stipulated that [the assessment's] being in force [depends on the effective cause's] being in force. However, this rule does not require us to define this [process] as being [unique to] the domain of Consensus. On the contrary, only if [an indicant of change] appears [does the assessment change]; otherwise one is compelled [to hold] that the assessment remains in force.[14]
>
> [8] [Ibn al-Humam also] said in *Kitāb al-Luqṭa:*[15]
>
> > It is established in the *Ṣaḥīḥ* of Muslim that [Muhammad]—may God's blessings and peace be upon him—forbade one to keep lost property found on the pilgrimage. Ibn Wahb[16] said: "That means, leave it until its owner [returns to] get it. But we do not do this at the present time because of the spread of [actual] thefts in Mecca, [even] in the precincts of the Kaʿbah. How much more likely is [the taking] of abandoned objects!
>
> [9] [As for] assessments whose imposition as law [*sharʿiyyatuhā*] is known by the appearance of a necessary condition [*sharṭ*]—when one knows subsequently of the establishment [*thubūt*] of its opposite, including a deleterious effect as an implication of its imposition as law, one knows of its cessation. This differs from [assessments] whose imposition as law is known by an occasion [*sabab*]: If you know of [this sort of assessment's] negation, [you are not thereby informed of a] deleterious consequence of [the assessment] remaining [in effect], since it does not entail [harm], as [we see from the case] of trotting and hitching [the pilgrimage garb] in circumambulation because of the presumption [*iẓhār*] of permanence.

[Here al-Aydini proposes a crucial distinction between changes that might result from a change in a necessary condition *(sharṭ)* and those that might

قال ابن وهب يعني تركَها حتى يجيء صاحبُها ولا عمل على هذا في هذا الزمان لفشو[٧] السرقة بمكّة في حوالي الكعبة فضلاً عن المتروك.

[٩] والاحكام اذا عُلِم شرعيتُها باعتبارِ شرط، ثمّ عُلِم ثبوت ضدّه متضمّناً مفسدةً بتقدير شرعيتها معه عُلم انقطاعها بخلاَف العلم بشرعيتها بسبب اذا علم انتفاؤه ولا مفسدةَ في البقاء فانه لاَ يلزم ذلك كالرمل والاضطباع في الطواف لاظهار الجلادة.

[١٠] تجزت الرسالة بعون الله سبحانه وتعالي وحسن توفيقه يوم الجمعة عاشر رمضان سنة اربع ومائة والف. [١١٠٤] ضمنت بالخير والظفر والشرف بجاه النبي الامين المختار عليه صلوات وسلام رب العالمين والحمد الله رب العالمين وصلي الله على سيدنا وسندنا محمد وعلي آله والصحابة اجمعين امين.

[٧] او لغشو

result from a changed occasion of performance *(sabab)*. A *sharṭ* is that without which an act is invalid, such as the ablution before ritual prayer. A *sabab* informs one that now is the appropriate time to perform an act, as, for example, when the sun crosses slightly from its zenith (or the shadow from a stick reappears after the sun's zenith); at that point one should pray the noon prayer. If the necessary condition ceases, then the act is by definition invalid. If the occasion of performance ceases to exist, then the obligation—in this case, to pray—remains in effect.]

> [10] I completed this treatise with the assistance of God—glory be to Him—the Most High and His good fortune, on Friday, 10 Ramadan 1104 [May 15, 1693].[17]
>
> Herein find blessing, success, and honor by the nobility of the Prophet, the trustworthy, the chosen one—may the blessings and peace of the Lord of the worlds be upon him.
>
> Praise to God, Lord of the worlds, and the blessing of God on our master and support, Muhammad and altogether on his family and Companions. Amen.

C H A P T E R   T E N

Child Marriage in Seventeenth-Century Palestine

HARALD MOTZKI

Child marriage was a common, licit, and variably practiced institution in many ancient cultures. It is known to have existed in ancient China, Japan, India, Babylonia, Rome, Athens, among the Jews, and in Christian Europe during the Middle Ages.[1] It is, therefore, not surprising to find this institution in premodern Muslim societies. In Islamic law, eligibility for marriage is defined, first, by physical criteria: the beginning of sexual maturity—for girls the first menstruation and for boys the first (nocturnal) seminal emission.[2] This is the lower limit of the phase that we call today "puberty."[3] In the Near East, this stage of physical maturity was reached by girls at the age of approximately twelve or thirteen and by boys at the age of thirteen or fourteen (see Motzki 1985:490–493). The first signs of sexual maturity, however, might appear at an earlier age. If the young person or his guardian made an acknowledgment regarding the occurence of menstruation or of a nocturnal seminal emission, this acknowledgment was accepted by the jurists on the condition that the person in question had reached the minimum age of sexual maturity: nine years for girls and twelve years for boys (see Motzki 1985:493–496). Marital cohabitation could legally take place at these minimum ages, but not before. If, on the other hand, the young person or his guardian did not make a claim regarding the arrival of sexual maturity, the jurists defined the maximum age at which a person is to be regarded as sexually mature: usually fifteen years for both sexes (in rare cases, seventeen years for girls and eighteen for boys).[4]

Consequently, in premodern Muslim societies an individual was considered to be marriageable at an age when, according to modern Western standards, he or she is only a child.[5] The difference between these two views lies in the definition of childhood; for the *fuqahā'*, the first signs of sexual maturity not only constitute proof that one has reached the marriageable age but also indicate the termination of childhood.[6] A person who has reached sexual maturity is normally regarded as an adult or major *(bāligh)*.[7] In Islamic law, the end of childhood is sealed by the beginning of puberty, whereas in modern Western legal thinking one becomes an adult only at the end of puberty. Thus, according to the modern Western understanding, the majority of Muslim first marriages concluded before the twentieth century would be classified as "child marriages." In the classical Islamic legal view, however, this label applies not to marriages in which one of the partners is of very young age, but to those in which he or she is a minor according to the Islamic definitions, that is, not yet sexually mature. The latter are the cases dealt with in this chapter.

In premodern Islamic law, marriage with a minor or between minors is allowed regardless of the age of the child in question, even with a baby.[8] The jurists differentiate, however, between the marriage contract *(ʿaqd al-nikāḥ)*, which the guardian of a child can conclude on the child's behalf, and consummation *(dukhūl)*, which must not take place until the partner in question is physically ready for it. Although this appears to suggest that the girl or boy should have either attained sexual maturity or reached the marriageable age prior to the wedding, we shall see below that the marriage might be consummated even earlier.[9]

The theoretical framework of Muslim child marriage, as just summarized, reflects the social practice in the Islamic heartland during the first three Islamic centuries—that is, at the time when the main body of Islamic law became established. Once established, these legal norms contributed to the subsequent consolidation and perpetuation of such social practices.

The Source

What impact did the Islamic rules regarding child marriage have on real life? How common were such marriages? For what reasons were they concluded? What problems resulted? These questions cannot be answered using the doctrinal law books, which contain only theoretical discussions of legal cases or normative rules concerning them. In the twentieth century, anthropological research has thrown some light on the realities of marriage in different Islamic countries. But for previous centuries, few sources provide any insight into the family life of Muslim peoples. Biographical dictionaries, chronicles, and traveler's accounts sometimes hint at the age of marriage and at the peculiarities of married life, but this information is mostly fragmentary. More valuable sources are the collections of judicial *responsa* (fatwas) that are preserved from many centuries and places. To demonstrate the usefulness of this genre of legal literature, I have chosen to focus here on the fatwas of the Hanafi scholar and mufti Khayr al-Din b. Ahmad al-Faruqi al-Ramli, who lived in seventeenth-century Palestine.[10]

Khayr al-Din was born in 1585 in Ramla, where he received his elementary education from a Shafiʿi scholar who was strongly attached to Sufism. Following in the footsteps of one of his elder brothers, he continued his education in Cairo at the venerable al-Azhar,[11] where he studied law (fiqh), hadith, Quran recitation, and grammar for six years. While he followed the lectures of scholars of different legal schools, he specialized—after some hesitation—in Hanafi law, the official school of law in the Ottoman Empire, and thus the most advantageous for a governmental career. Although he completed his study with great success, he returned to his native town of Ramla to serve as a private teacher and mufti. There he supported himself with the revenues of fruit and olive plantations that he planned and successfully managed with his family. In time he became one of the great landowners of the city, investing his money in local markets and real estate. As his renown as a scholar and mufti spread, he and the huge library he had built up attracted students not only from different parts of Syria but also from neighboring countries.

Al-Ramli's legal advice was in great demand and carried considerable weight in the qadi courts. He gave his fatwas free of charge to anyone who asked him. Both the questions and the answers were written down and preserved. During the course of Khayr al-Din's long life, this legal material must have grown quite large. Toward the end of his life, his son Muhyi al-Din began to sift through his father's fatwas and to arrange them according to the subject order of the authoritative Hanafi legal handbook, the *Hidāya* of al-Marghinani (d. 1196).[12] But Muhyi al-Din predeceased his father in 1661, having completed only the first chapters of the collection. Ibrahim b. Sulayman al-Jinini, one of Khayr al-Din's students, asked his master for permission to continue his son's work. It took al-Jinini about ten years to finish this work; it was completed a few months before the death of Khayr al-Din himself at the end of Ramadan in 1671.[13] The resulting collection, entitled *Kitāb al-fatāwā al-khayriyya li-nafʿ al-bariyya* (Comforting Legal Answers for the Benefit of Creation) was printed in Egypt as early as 1858; a second edition followed in 1882, indicating the esteem in which Khayr al-Din's fatwas were held.

A Fatwa

The Question. [The shaykh] was asked about a minor girl [*ṣaghīra*] who is just over three years old and [already] has a husband. She has a mother who is married to a stranger [*ajnabī*] [in relation to the girl's clan]. Otherwise, she has no agnates [*ʿaṣabāt*] or other relatives. Her husband fears concerning her that the mother and her husband shall leave [the place] with her and that his legal claim [*ḥaqquhu*] [on her] shall be lost, because both [the mother and her husband] are strangers [*gharībān*] [with regard to the place]. He also fears that the two of them will futilely [*bi'l-bāṭil*] consume her bridewealth [*mahruhā*].

Is the qadi justified or not in having [the girl] taken [away from her mother to a place] of his choice in order to bring her and her bridewealth to safety; in ordering the [girl's] husband to pay maintenance for her [*infāq ʿalayhā*] from her bridewealth until she is able to consummate the marriage [*ḥattā tuṭīqa'l-rijāl*]; and, then, in ordering a respected person who fulfills the function of an official witness at court [*ʿadl*] to take delivery of the remainder of her bridewealth from the husband and to hand it to her when she has become [sexually] mature [*balaghat*] and he [viz., the *ʿadl*] has determined that she is capable of managing her personal possessions [*rushduhā*]?

The Answer. [The shaykh] answered: Yes, the qadi has the right to do that. [The jurists] have explained in the chapter on the care [*ḥaḍāna*] [of children]: If a minor girl has no agnatic relatives [*ʿaṣaba*] and if no [relative] has the right to care [for the child], then the qadi is justified in having her taken wherever he wishes. Women whose [right to the] care [of a child] is set aside [*sāqiṭāt al-ḥaḍāna*] are like unrelated women [*ajnabiyyāt*]. This is transmitted in the *Majmaʿ al-fatāwā* from *al-Muḥīṭ*. How can this be otherwise in view of the [husband's] fear mentioned [in the question]? There is no disagreement on this [point]. God, however, knows best![14]

An Academic Case or a Real One?

The name of the questioner (mustafti) and of the persons and places involved in the case are not mentioned, and no dates are given. Does this mean that we are dealing with a theoretical construction of a legal case invented by a student or by the teacher himself in the course of academic lessons? Although some fatwas are in fact theoretical constructions, most are based on real cases, even if they have been stripped of details that would be of interest to historians. The reason for this absence of historical details is that fatwas are copied in order to preserve the solution to a specific legal problem, a solution that is, in principle, a timeless expression of legal science and a precedent for future generations of jurists and judges who may be confronted with the same or a similar problem. Besides, this absence of specific details lends the fatwa an aura of objectivity. In spite of this tendency, however, many questions preserve individual details indicating that these fatwas had arisen from real cases. The occurence of such details seems to be the only means to decide the question most crucial for the historian—namely, whether a fatwa or a fatwa collection is dealing with real-life or hypothetical cases. In addition, such details sometimes permit conclusions regarding the date, place, and persons involved.

In this case, the mention of the approximate age of the girl and the fact that not only the second husband but also the mother are described as "strangers" speaks in favor of a real case. Further, several factors suggest that the question was posed by a judge: the mustafti asks whether a qadi may intervene to the advantage of a minor girl, certain specific features of judicial procedure are mentioned in the question, and Khayr al-Din cites juridical sources in the fatwa in a manner that presumes that the mustafti possessed some legal knowledge. The action was probably brought to court by the girl's husband, since his "fears" are expressly stated.

The Social Context

The peculiarities of the case reveal much about the social reality of Muslim marriages in general, and of child marriages in particular. The question contains several hints that allow us to partially reconstruct the social context of the dispute. The text mentions a girl who is already married at the age of three, a phenomenon that was not exceptional in seventeenth-century Palestine, according to the evidence in our fatwa collection (see below). The girl's mother and father belonged to different clans and came from different villages. The girl's father had died either during his wife's pregnancy or some time after the birth of the child. Her marriage had been arranged either by her father or by her grandfather (also dead at the time the dispute arose). At an unspecified point in time following the birth of her child and the death of her husband, the girl's mother had married a man from a clan or village other than that of her former husband, the father of the child. (It was common in Muslim society for a widow or divorcée to remarry soon after her husband died or divorced her; see Motzki 1985:514–516). In such a case, however, a fundamental question arises: Who has the right to care for the child? The mother who married into a family unrelated to the child, or the relatives of its father? Two Islamic legal norms are here in conflict: the mother's right to care for the child, called *ḥaḍāna* (a term mentioned in the shaykh's answer), and the *wilāya,* the legal authority of the father and of the agnatic relatives over the child.

Let us assume that the first husband died during his wife's pregnancy or shortly after the birth of the girl, and that his widow remarried immediately. In this circumstance, the child could not be taken away from her mother, because she had the legal right to breast-feed her child, if she wished, until the child reached the age of two, the legal minimum for breast-feeding. This can be seen as part of the mother's right to *ḥaḍāna.* And even after a child has been weaned, the Sunni legal schools allow a child to be brought up by its mother for a certain time. The Hanafis permit it until the child is seven (boys) or nine (girls).[15] The right of the mother to bring up her child is, however, not unconditional, as we shall see.

The mother's right to care for her child conflicts with that of the father and the agnates to serve as the child's guardian. In Islamic law, a child must have a guardian *(walī)* who is responsible for his or her well-being and maintenance. The right of guardianship *(wilāya)* lies with the agnatic relatives of the child: in the first line, the father and the grandfathers. Even when the child lives with the mother, the guardian must be permitted to check the child's well-being. He may contest the mother's right to *ḥaḍāna* if he suspects that the child is not being cared for properly (see Motzki 1986:418–420). Consequently, the mother's right to bring up her child frequently is challenged if she proposes to move away from the guardian's place of residence or if she remarries with a man who is not related to the child.[16]

In this fatwa there are no agnatic relatives who may function as guardian. In such a circumstance, the right to guardianship may be assumed by the mother if she is able to do so. At this point, however, the girl's husband intervenes, fearing that the mother and her new husband will remove the girl from the place where he lives and that he will loose sight of his bride. The bridegroom expresses a sense of moral responsibility for his future wife, especially because there is no male guardian to supervise her upbringing. Of course, he also has financial interests to defend, because he obviously has already paid part of the bridewealth to the girl's family, a practice that is mentioned in several other fatwas relating to child marriage (see below). According to the Muslim jurists, however, the bridewealth belongs to the bride, not to her parents or to her guardian; the latter have the right only to hold the bridewealth in trust for her and to use it in case of need. Since there is no proper guardian, the bridegroom suspects that the property of his future bride might be misused.

The Solution

The mufti confirms and expands on the solution advanced by the mustafti (himself probably a judge) in question. Three points are instrumental. First, the girl has no guardian who is responsible for her maintenance, because there are no male agnatic relatives. Second, the girl's mother has lost her right to *ḥaḍāna,* because her second husband is not related to the girl. (The reason the mother forfeited her right to raise the child is not expressly stated in the shaykh's answer, but such reasons are mentioned in other fatwas and in the Hanafi legal handbooks.) Third, other women on whom the right to *ḥaḍāna* might devolve after the mother are either nonexistent, or unable or unwilling to assume the task.[17] The girl is, therefore, without any person legally responsible for her. In these circumstances, the mufti specifies, it is the right of the qadi, as the representative of the Muslim community, to choose persons qualified and willing to assume the tasks of raising the child *(ḥaḍāna)* and supervising her personal and financial well-being *(wilāya).*

The consequences of the qadi's intervention are sketched in his question. First, the girl will be taken away from her mother and given to another woman for care. From the perspective of the Muslim jurists, the rules of *ḥaḍāna* and *wilāya* have been established to protect the interests of the child. Thus, the prescription that a mother who remarries with a nonrelative loses her right to raise her child must be explained by the jurists' reasoning that it is better for a child to grow up with persons who really love her—these are, in Muslim society, the agnatic or cognatic relatives—than in a household of strangers, that is, nonrelatives. The necessary maternal care can, in the view of the jurists, be provided by any female relative of the child as well as by the mother. The fact that in this case a "strange" women is preferred to the mother is the logical consequence of Hanafi legal reasoning about the devolution of the right of *ḥaḍāna*.

Second, the husband of the child bride recovers the bridewealth that he had delivered to the bride's family at the time that the marriage contract was concluded. Although this is not expressly stated in the fatwa, it is implied by the fact that the girl's husband may be ordered to use the bridewealth to pay maintenance for her until the wedding takes place. This provision seems to be based on the legal rule that a child may, if necessary, be maintained from the child's own property (see Linant de Bellefonds 1973:115–116). The bridewealth is, indeed, the girl's property (see Motzki 1985:528–530). In this manner, the future husband acquires the function of a guardian *(walī)* for the girl.

Third, when the wedding takes place, the husband conveys the remaining part of the bridewealth to the qadi's deputy, the *ʿadl,* who is charged with preserving it for the girl until she reaches the age of majority. The reason for this is that once the marriage has been consummated, the husband must provide maintenance *(nafaqa)* for his wife out of his *own* property. The conveyance of the bridewealth to the *ʿadl* would be, surely, accompanied by an account of the expenditures.

The fatwa contains three expressions relating to maturity that require some comment. The first expression, *"ḥattā tuṭīqa'l-rijāl,"* means that the wedding may not take place until the girl is physically fit to engage in sexual intercourse. The second expression, *"balaghat,"* concerns the reaching of sexual maturity by the beginning of the menses. The age related to these two concepts can, but need not necessarily, coincide. According to the views of the jurists, physical fitness for the consummation of the marriage *(ḥattā tuṭīqa'l-rijāl)* may be reached earlier than real sexual maturity *(bulūgh),* which becomes manifest by the menses.[18] The third noteworthy expression in the fatwa is *rushd.* As I have already mentioned, sexual maturity is the first condition of majority. A second condition is *rushd,* the intellectual maturity to handle one's own property.[19] Only when both conditions, *bulūgh* and *rushd,* are fulfilled is one regarded by the jurists as really major and free to dispose of one's own property at will. Consequently, this fatwa specifies that only when the married girl has reached this capacity will she receive her bridewealth.

Formal Aspects

The language of the question is technical. This is not surprising, as a qadi appears to have been the questioner. The mufti responds, in turn, in legal terminology, citing legal sources as the basis of his opinion. Generally speaking, Khayr al-Din does not cite legal sources unless the questioner is trained to understand them. The sources mentioned in this fatwa are the chapter on *ḥaḍāna* in the legal handbooks of the Hanafi madhhab and the *Majmaʿ al-fatāwā,* probably a compilation of fatwas issued by one of Khayr al-Din's teachers, the Egyptian jurist Muhammad b. ʿUmar Shams al-Din b. Siraj al-Din al-Hanuti (d. 1601).[20] The fatwa indicates that the reference is based, in turn, on an earlier text, *al-Muḥīṭ.*[21] Finally, the mufti concludes his fatwa with a reference to consensus: "There is no disagreement on this [point]," referring, of course, to the consensus of Hanafi jurists.

Child Marriage in Palestine

Most of the questions submitted to Khayr al-Din and contained in the collection of his fatwas are likely to have emanated from his hometown, Ramla, and its surrounding jurisdictions. The questions, therefore, reflect the social reality of this region in the first three quarters of the seventeenth century. The fatwa under discussion here constitutes only a fragment of the evidence bearing on the subject of child marriage in seventeenth-century Palestine. The information that can be gleaned from this fatwa is limited: We learn that a marriage between an adult man and a female child was legally valid. The bridewealth was paid in advance, fully or in part, to the bride's parents, who might use it for her maintenance. The consummation of the marriage was suspended, and the child continued to live with her parents or guardians until she was physically capable of engaging in sexual intercourse. In the meantime, legal problems might arise if there occurred any change in the circumstances existing at the time of the marriage contract, as, for example, if the girl's father or guardian died.

A systematic study of Khayr al-Din's collection of fatwas yields considerable information on child marriage in seventeenth-century Palestine, only the highlights of which can be given here.[22] In *al-Fatāwā al-khayriyya,* a relatively large number of fatwas treat the subject of marriage in general. For this survey, I have taken into consideration only those whose question alludes to the topics of matchmaking, marriage, consummation of the marriage, weddings, and the like, altogether 145 (the numbers in parenthesis are absolute ones). Of these 145 texts, 39 percent (56) deal expressly with child marriage; in 21 percent (31), the maturity of one of the partners is stated or implied but nothing is said about the other; and in 40 percent (58), the question of maturity remains open. It would be hasty to conclude from these data that in the first two-thirds of the seventeenth century 40 percent of all marriages in Palestine, especially in the region of Ramla, involved at least one minor partner. The very nature of the legal subject suggests that such marriages are overrepresented in the corpus. We may nevertheless conclude from our sample that marriages in which one or both of the partners were minors were not uncommon in seventeenth-century Palestine.

In the majority of cases, these marriages were concluded by a father on behalf of his child.[23] This is not surprising, because in the eyes of the law a father is the person who is most qualified to perform this task. Other relatives, however, are also mentioned: the paternal grandfather, the older brother, the paternal half brother, the paternal or maternal uncle, the son of the paternal cousin, the husband of the maternal aunt, the *shaykh al-bilād* (*sic;* village chief), and the mother.[24] This list suggests that child marriages were also arranged when the father had died or been absent for a long time. Sometimes, however, he seems to have been bypassed on purpose (al-Ramli 1974, 1:24, second fatwa).

As seen in the fatwa discussed above, the bridewealth exchanged by virtue of the marriage contract played an important role in child marriages. Significant differences between the amount of the bridewealth of immature and mature girls, however, cannot be found. The value of the bridewealth for a minor bride fluctuates between less than 10 dirhams—the minimum required by Hanafi law—and 200 qurush.[25]

This fatwa concerned the marriage between an adult man and a female child. In theory, the minor partner could also be a boy. In practice, however, as the sample reveals, the minor partner in a child marriage was a usually a female—only about 18 percent (10) were boys.[26] In only 12 percent (7) of the marriages were both partners minors.[27]

Age at the time of the marriage contract varies between birth and the day of sexual maturity. For girls, the first day of life, three years, six years, and seven years are mentioned.[28] For boys, no age details are given. The interval between the date of the marriage contract and that of the wedding night could therefore vary widely. In this text, we have seen that it was not necessary to demonstrate the sexual maturity of the child, as reflected in her menstruation, in order for the marriage to be consummated. The corpus mentions twelve cases in which a wife was handed over to the husband and the marriage was consummated prior to the occurrence of her first menstrual period.[29] One text specifies that the wife was about nine years old at the moment when her marriage was consummated (al-Ramli 1974, 1:30, fourth fatwa). Boys also could be handed over for the consummation of marriage before attaining sexual maturity, but this is mentioned only once in the source (1:55, first fatwa).

The determination of when a child is able to "bear sexual intercourse" *(tuṭīqu'l-jimāʿ)* was made by the father or the guardian or—if the couple was already living together—by the adult partner (thus usually by a man). Disputes over this subject might emerge between the father of the bride and the bridegroom, if the father was of the opinion that the girl was not yet fit for sexual intercourse and declined to hand her over (al-Ramli 1974, 1:32, second fatwa).[30] In one case a father agreed to hand the girl over to her husband but it seems she was not ready for intercourse—at least not mentally—because she fled from her husband's house to that of her mother, who granted her shelter (1:32, third fatwa).[31]

A father's or guardian's willingness to marry his child or ward at such an early age may be explained by factors that vary according to class and environment. In many of the questions, financial factors play an important role. Often, the girl's father or the guardian demands and receives the bridewealth, in full or in part, at the time of the marriage contract.[32] According to Islamic law, he is then obliged to hold it in trust for the girl until she attains the age of majority and is competent to manage her property herself (see Linant de Bellefonds 1973:219–238). The fatwas show, however, that fathers and guardians often used the money for other purposes, for example, for their own consumption, to pay off a debt, to enable a son to marry, or for the girl's maintenance, education, and wedding.[33] Only the last use was justified according to the view of most Hanafis, including Khayr al-Din (see his answers in al-Ramli 1974, 1:69, eighth fatwa, and 70, third fatwa).

Whether motivated by poverty or greed, fathers or guardians arranged child marriages in an attempt to eliminate the cost of their daughter's or ward's maintenance, clothing, and education and to profit from the bridewealth, even if this was illegal. Sometimes they demanded additional maintenance from the bridegroom although the marriage had not yet been consummated (al-Ramli 1974, 1:34, second fatwa; 74, second fatwa). For these reasons, guardianship of a minor female ward was coveted, especially if she was attractive, as is indicated by legal disputes in which two men claimed the right of guardianship over a single ward.[34]

Other motives are more difficult to identify: sickness and the awareness of approaching death were sometimes decisive;[35] in other cases, disappointment over the birth of a daughter instead of a son or the wish to tighten the bond to a certain man or family was the decisive factor (al-Ramli 1974, 1:20, sixth and eighth fatwas). The two cases in this sample in which child marriages were arranged between a young man and his parallel female cousin—that is, his father's brother's daughter *(bint ʿamm)*—were perhaps motivated by this last reason. In both cases, both partners were minors (1:23, fourth fatwa; 24, sixth fatwa).[36]

Child marriage often gave rise to legal disputes. As already mentioned, some disputes had as their object the bridewealth and maintenance of the bride—especially the dates of payment, the use of the money, and the restitution of the rest of the bridewealth to the adult woman; other disputes involved the right to give a minor in marriage *in absentia patris;* still others related to the time when the girl was to be handed over to the husband or when the consummation of the marriage was to take place. The peculiarities of this type of marriage led, in addition, to several other characteristic problems. We have seen in the fatwa translated here that the interval between the conclusion of the marriage contract and the beginning of true married life might be very long, sometimes ten years or more. The danger was therefore great that the marriage would not reach its final goal, consummation. This might happen for several reasons: the death of one of the partners, leading to a dispute over the estate or inheritance;[37] a change of disposition by the adult partner or the guardian of the minor;[38] divorce *(ṭalāq);* divorce in return for the wife's renunciation of some of her rights *(khulʿ);* and denial of the validity of, or ignoring, the marriage contract. To these reasons must be added the right of a minor—commonly invoked—to have the marriage annuled when he or she became a major, if the contract had been concluded by persons other than the father or the grandfather.[39] The invocation of this right could lead to disputes between the parties involved, especially about financial claims. Of all the child marriages in the sample, 25 percent (14) failed before or shortly after the wedding. This high percentage probably does not reflect the true incidence of failed marriages. They seem to be overrepresented in the sample because successful marriages gave fewer causes for disputes. A certain tendency, however, is surely manifested in this high proportion of failure.

This sketch of Muslim marriage practice in Palestine during the seventeenth century gives an impression of how important the fatwa literature is for the social historian. The fatwas provide information about different aspects of child marriages among the lower and middle classes about which few data are available from the chronicles and biographical dictionaries: the frequency of the institution, the procedures involved, the proportions of girls and boys involved, the ages of the marriage partners, the motives for such marriages, and the problems that could arise from them. The questions, in particular, reflect the social circumstances and the daily happenings that confronted judges and muftis.

Although not all fatwa collections will be as productive as that of Khayr al-Din al-Ramli, systematic research on the extensive available fatwa literature will provide many insights into Muslim daily and family life during different periods of Islamic history, in many regions, and among different classes.

C H A P T E R   E L E V E N

Eleven Fetvas of the Ottoman Sheikh ul-Islam ʿAbdurrahim

COLIN IMBER

In the Ottoman Empire, collections of the *fetvas* issued by the *sheikh ul-islams*[1] from the second half of the sixteenth century until the end of the nineteenth came to form a distinctive branch of legal literature. Although some were anthologies, most contained the fetvas of a single sheikh ul-islam, together usually with the fetvas of his predecessors that he too had signed. The usually anonymous compilers of these collections grouped the fetvas under chapter headings, such as "Marriage," "Sale," or "Evidence," which correspond to the chapters in standard works of fiqh, beginning always with the "Chapter on Ritual Purification." Within each chapter, the compilers grouped fetvas together under headings and subheadings according to the subject matter. These usually reflect a division of material familiar from manuals of fiqh, although sometimes they relate to topics such as military fiefs or tax farming, which are specific to Ottoman law. In some collections, the compilers have added proof texts to some or all of the fetvas. So too have some of the owners of the volumes.

The careful and systematic arrangement of the collections is a testimony to the legal skills of their compilers.[2] The same skill is evident in the drafting of the fetvas themselves. This—and probably also the compilation of most of the collections—was the work of the permanent officials at the Fetva Office who, under the superintendence of the *fetvā emīni,* received the original questions from members of the public, the legal profession, or the government, and recast them in the form in which they came before the sheikh ul-islam.

The establishment of the Fetva Office, which survived as long as the empire itself, was largely, it seems, the work of the great sixteenth-century sheikh ul-islam Ebussuʿud (in office 1545–1574), and it is clear that from his time the issue of fetvas became a routine procedure. In Ebussuʿud's own fetvas, the text of the question is often fairly circumstantial and the text of the answer often detailed, as though he were trying to educate the questioner. However, the tendency after Ebussuʿud's time was for the *fetvā emīni*s to draft the question so as to omit any detail that was not strictly relevant to the legal point at issue, and usually in a format that required the sheikh ul-islam to add no more than a yes or no answer. Furthermore, given a knowledge of the law, the form of the question usually presupposed the answer. It is clear, too, that, in most cases, the *fetvā emīni* saved the sheikh ul-islam time by indicating to him in advance what answer was required (Heyd 1969). A result of this standardization of procedure is that after the time of Ebussuʿud, and especially from the early seventeenth century, Ottoman fetvas were the work not so much of the sheikh ul-islams who signed them as of the legal bureaucracy at the Fetva Office. It is the procedures of this bureaucracy that the collections reflect, and that the following fetvas exemplify.

The popularity of the collections was perhaps due in part to a respect for the office of the sheikh ul-islam—the supreme legal authority in the Ottoman Empire—and to the dignity attaching to the fetvas that its holders had signed. They must also have served the very practical purpose of providing a source of reference for the solution of legal problems. The arrangement of material according to familiar legal categories makes them easy to use, and since the fetvas by and large present solutions to practical problems that had arisen in an Ottoman context, they may, at least to practicing members of the Ottoman legal profession, have seemed more relevant, if less revered, than the classic works of fiqh. Above all, almost all the fetvas are in Turkish,[3] the language in which most legal proceedings in the Ottoman Empire were conducted, and for Turkish speakers they were easier to use than the standard manuals of fiqh, which are invariably in Arabic. It is possible, too, to imagine students of the law familiarizing themselves with legal problems through the medium of Turkish fetvas before graduating to the authoritative Arabic texts.

The fetvas discussed in this chapter are from an anonymously compiled collection of the fetvas of ʿAbdurrahim (1827, 2:214–215), who held office as sheikh ul-islam from 1715 to 1716. They appear in a single block and illustrate how a compiler would group together a series of fetvas relating to a specific legal problem. The question here is the legal status of mother and child when a man produces offspring by a female slave belonging to his wife.

The status of a female slave who has given birth to a child by her own master is an important feature of Islamic family law. If the master acknowledges the child as his, the child is free and the mother becomes his *umm walad*. He may not transfer ownership of her to another person, and on his death she too becomes free. The case of a man who has a child by a slave belonging to his wife might seem more problematic, but the law is equally clear. An earlier Hanafi mufti, the Transoxanian jurist Qadi Khan (d. 1196), gives an excellent summary of the rules, which apply equally if the slave belongs to the man's wife, parent, or grandparent (Qadi Khan 1973, 1:569):

> [A man] has intercourse with a female slave belonging to his wife, or with a female slave belonging to a parent or grandparent. If [the man] acknowledges the child as his, [the child] is not affiliated to him, but he avoids the fixed penalty [for unlawful intercourse] because of a *shubha*.[4]
>
> If he says: "The owner of the female slave made her licit to me," there is no affiliation unless the owner confirms that s/he made [the slave] licit to him, and that the child is by him. If s/he confirms him in both these things, [the child] is affiliated [to him]; but otherwise, it is not.
>
> But if the slave's owner contradicts him [in his claims], and he then acquires possession of the slave for a single day, then the child is affiliated to him.

Qadi Khan's first concern here is to establish whether a man's sexual relations with the slave attract the fixed penalty for illegal intercourse. They do not, since he has "quasi-ownership" *(shubhat al-milk)*[5] of a slave belonging to his wife, parent, or grandparent. If the slave belonged to a stranger, he would, in theory, be liable for punishment. Qadi Khan's second and, in practice, most important concern is to establish the rules for the affiliation of the child. First, the man must declare that the owner permitted him to have intercourse with the slave, and the owner must confirm him in this. Second, he must acknowledge that the child is his, and again the owner must confirm his acknowledgment. The child is affiliated to him only when these procedures are complete. The other route to affiliation is for the man subsequently to acquire ownership of the slave.

In his exposition of the case, Qadi Khan omits an important question that occurs in the Ottoman fetvas. This is whether, on affiliation, the child becomes free or remains a slave. The answer is that, since the mother does not become the man's *umm walad* and a child inherits its mother's status, the child is a slave. In an earlier section, however, Qadi Khan rules (1973, 1:569) on the case of a man who has a child by a female slave in quasi-ownership, when the child is affiliated to him and he subsequently takes possession of the slave. In this case, the slave becomes his *umm walad* and the child is freed.

In brief, if a man has a child by his wife's slave, the child is affiliated to him, provided he claims that his wife gave him permission to have intercourse with the slave and that the child is his, and provided that his wife confirms him in both these claims. The slave, however, continues in the possession of his wife, and the child too becomes his wife's slave. However, if the child is affiliated to him and he acquires ownership of the slave, she becomes his *umm walad* and the child is freed.

ʿAbdurrahim has eleven fetvas on this problem. The compiler has included them as a sequence in the "Chapter on Affiliation and the Status of the *umm walad* [*bāb fīʾl-nasab waʾl-istīlād*]."[6] The eight cases in which the husband claims that his wife gave him permission to have intercourse with the slave he has placed under the heading "Concerning a wife's permitting her husband to have intercourse with her female slave." The three cases where the husband has not made this claim he includes as the first items under the heading "Concerning intercourse with the female slave of a wife, father, son, etc., with and without permission." All the questions except for one are problems of affiliation, succession, and the legal status of the mother and child as slaves or free persons. The answers conform exactly to the Hanafi rules as Qadi Khan presented them.

The first two questions concern affiliation:

> (1) Hind grants her husband Zeyd permission to have intercourse with her female slave, Zeyneb. Zeyd has intercourse with Zeyneb and impregnates her, and she gives birth to a child. Zeyd claims: "The child is by me." Hind confirms that she granted permission and that the child is by Zeyd. Is the child affiliated to Zeyd?
>
> Answer: Yes. [3]

Here the man and his wife have met all the conditions for affiliation, which is not the case in the next example:

> (2) Zeyd takes possession of [*tutub*] his wife Hind's wholly owned female slave, Zeyneb. When Zeyneb produces a child, Zeyd claims: "I had intercourse with Zeyneb and made her my concubine with Hind's permission. The child is by me." However, Hind does not confirm that she granted Zeyd permission or confirm Zeyd in his claim [that the child is by him]. Is the child affiliated to Zeyd?
>
> Answer: No. [7]

There can be no affiliation because the wife has contradicted both of the relevant claims of her husband.

The next problem on affiliation is anomalous in that it refers to a man's child not by his wife's, but by a stranger's slave. The compiler no doubt included it here because there was nowhere else to put it, but in fact it is not out of place, since the two problems are identical. A wife's slave, like a stranger's, is separate from her husband's property, and the same rules for affiliation apply:

(3) Zeyd has intercourse with ʿAmr's wholly owned female slave, Hind, and says: "ʿAmr permitted me to have intercourse with her." When Hind produces a child, Zeyd claims: "The child is by me." However, if ʿAmr did not grant Zeyd permission and does not confirm him in his claim, is the child affiliated to Zeyd?
Answer: No. [8]

If the slave's owner had confirmed the man in his claims, then the child would have been affiliated. The only difference between this case and the case in which a man has a child by his wife's slave, is that a man does not have quasi-ownership of a stranger's slave and is therefore technically liable for the fixed penalty for unlawful intercourse. However, since the fixed penalty can never in reality be inflicted (Imber 1982), it is for practical purposes irrelevant, and the only legal distinction between intercourse with a wife's and a stranger's female slave disappears.

After affiliation, the next problem to worry questioners was the legal status of mother and child. Even when her child was not affiliated to the husband, some seem to have suspected that the slave mother might nonetheless become the husband's *umm walad* and that the child might therefore be free. This view presumably arose from an exaggerated respect for male authority and a belief that a man had rights over his wife's property, but it was plainly wrong:

(4) Without Hind's consent, Zeyd has intercourse with and impregnates his wife Hind's wholly owned female slave, Zeyneb. When Zeyneb produces a child, Zeyd dies. Did Zeyneb become Zeyd's *umm walad?*
Answer: No. [10]

(5) Zeyd has intercourse with and impregnates his wife, Hind's wholly owned female slave, Zeyneb, without Hind's permission. If Zeyneb produces a child, is the said child Hind's slave?
Answer: Yes. [9]

In these two cases, the child is not affiliated to the husband, but even if it were, it would make no difference, as the following fetva implies:

(6) Hind permits her husband, Zeyd, to have intercourse with her female slave, Zeyneb. Zeyd has intercourse with Zeyneb and impregnates her, and she produces a child by Zeyd. Is Hind still able to employ Zeyneb and her child as slaves?
Answer: Yes. [5]

Here the text of the question does not make it absolutely clear that the child is affiliated to the husband, but this is the obvious implication of the statement that the wife permitted her husband to have intercourse with the slave. In any case, the question is irrelevant. Whether the child is affiliated or not, both it and its mother are slaves.

In the next two fetvas in the series, the questioner, after enquiring whether the child is affiliated to the husband, does not ask whether the child is a slave, but whether it is an heir. The two questions are, however, related. If the child is affiliated but still a slave, it is not an heir, because a slave cannot own or inherit property. If the child is affiliated and free, it is automatically an heir:

> (7) Hind permits her husband Zeyd to have intercourse with her wholly owned female slave, Zeyneb. Zeyd has intercourse with Zeyneb and impregnates her, and she gives birth to a child. If Zeyd now dies, is the child affiliated to Zeyd, and does it inherit from Zeyd?
>
> Answer: If Zeyd claims [that the child is by him] and Hind then confirms [both] that she gave permission [for intercourse] and [also] that Zeyd claimed [paternity], then the child is affiliated to Zeyd. But if the child is not freed, then it is not an heir. [2]

However, only the owner—in this case the man's wife—can free the child, either by manumission or by transferring ownership of the slave to her husband. Furthermore, as the next fetva makes clear, manumission must take place before the husband's death:

> (8) With his wife Hind's permission, Zeyd takes her female slave, Zeyneb as a concubine. When Zeyneb produces a child, Zeyd claims [that it is by him]. Hind then confirms that she granted Zeyd permission and that the child is by Zeyd. However, Zeyd dies before Hind has freed the child. Is the said child affiliated to Zeyd and does it inherit from Zeyd?
>
> Answer: It is affiliated, but does not inherit. [1]

The child is not an heir, because it was still a slave at the time of its father's death. Subsequent manumission does not retroactively entitle it to a share in the estate.

The fetvas so far given seem to indicate that the normal procedure to establish affiliation was claim and confirmation. The less common method was to transfer ownership of the slave from the wife to the husband:

> (9) Zeyd has intercourse with his wife Hind's female slave, Zeyneb, and impregnates her. Later, when Zeyneb is pregnant, Hind sells her to Zeyd. Then, when she gives birth, Zeyd claims: "[The child] is by me." Is the said child affiliated to Zeyd?
>
> Answer: Yes. [6]

In this case, the slave gave birth when she was in the husband's ownership, and the husband acknowledged the child as his. She therefore, by the normal rules, becomes his *umm walad,* and the child is both affiliated and free. If, however, the husband acquires ownership of the slave after the birth of the child, ʿAbdurrahim offers a different solution:

> (10) Zeyd has intercourse with his wife Hind's female slave Zeyneb, without Hind's consent. When she later produces a child, Zeyd claims: "It is by me." If Zeyd then buys the child and Zeyneb from Hind, is the child affiliated to Zeyd and, when Zeyd dies, does it inherit from Zeyd?
> Answer: No, but when he buys the child, it becomes free. [11]

In this case, had the child been affiliated, the slave would have become the husband's *umm walad* at the time of purchase. The child would have become free and therefore entitled to inherit. However, since the wife did not consent to her husband's having intercourse with her slave, there is no affiliation. In the absence of her consent, intercourse with the slave was unlawful, and this explains ʿAbdurrahim's answer to the question. He is simply invoking the rule to be applied in a case in which a man fornicates with a female slave, which Qadi Khan (1973, 1:570) presents as follows: "A man fornicates with a female slave and she gives birth. He then buys her. By juristic preference [*istiḥsān*], she does not become his *umm walad.* [But] if he buys the child, it becomes free."

One fetva does not, strictly speaking, belong with the others in the group, since although the case arises when a man fathers a child by his wife's slave, the problem has nothing to do with affiliation, manumission, or inheritance:

> (11) Zeyd says to his wife Hind: "Permit me to have intercourse with your female slave, Zeyneb. Let me have intercourse with Zeyneb. If Zeyneb produces a child, I'll pay you so-and-so many akçes." Zeyd has intercourse with Zeyneb and she produces a child. If Zeyd dies before paying the [specified] sum of akçes, is Hind, on the basis of the aforementioned promise, able to take the [specified] sum of akçes from Zeyd's estate?
> Answer: No. [4]

The crux of the question here is whether the husband's promise is binding. If it is, then he becomes his wife's debtor and, on his death, she is entitled to receive the debt from his estate. The circumstances in which he made the promise are irrelevant to the solution of the problem, which is why the fetva is out of place in this series. Instead, the key to the question lies in whether the precise words the husband used in making the promise constitute a binding oath *(yamīn)*. The query is a reasonable one, since in one form of an oath the swearer imposes on himself a penalty to be activated on the fulfillment of a specified condition. In Qadi Khan's formulation (1973, 2:2), "An oath . . . is the stipulation of a valid condition and a valid penalty on which the oath is sworn." The husband's promise—"If Zeyneb produces a child, I'll pay you so-and-so many akçes"—takes the form of a penalty dependent on the fulfillment of a condition, and so there are grounds for considering it an oath. However, juristic discussion of oaths usually restricts the sense of a "valid penalty" to divorce (Imber 1993), manumission, and religious impositions (al-Marghinani 1965, 2:74, 87–89): for example, "If I do X, my wife is divorced / my slave is free / I am an infidel / I shall go on the hajj." In this instance, ʿAbdurrahim has clearly taken the restricted view and does not regard the payment of money as a valid penalty. The husband's promise is therefore non-binding, and the debt cannot be deducted from his estate.

A salient feature of Ottoman fetvas, as these examples demonstrate, is their anonymity. The identities of the original questioner, the officials who drafted the question in its existing format, and the protagonists in the case are all usually unknown. Another feature is their brevity. Both the question and the answer normally omit everything but the essentials of the case. A consequence of their brevity is that the fetvas illustrate points of law with great clarity, while a consequence of their anonymity is that they emphasize that the rulings of the sheikh ul-islams have a general validity, rather than a validity in a particular case.

For a modern reader with an interest in legal history, anonymity and concision have their drawbacks, since they obscure the processes whereby the fetvas came into existence. It is therefore impossible to comment with any real certainty on the social or legal background of the fetvas given here. The circumstance that they describe, of a man's producing a child by his wife's slave, cannot have been rare in Ottoman society, where slave ownership was commonplace. It was, however, as these fetvas show, a situation that caused problems of legal status and succession, and one may presume that these problems would come from time to time before the qadis' courts. If the qadi was uncertain of the solution to such a case, he could apply to the sheikh ul-islam's office for a fetva and pass judgment on the basis of the answer he received. This certainly appears to be what has happened in (1) and (2), for example, where the texts of the questions appear either to reproduce or to summarize statements that the husband and wife had made in court. In these two cases, the qadi presumably had passed the problem, together with the statements of husband and wife, to the Fetva Office, and later passed judgment in accordance with the sheikh ul-islam's reply. One may assume, too, that the important question of the child's status as an heir in (7), (8), and (10) had come before the qadi when the father died and his estate was divided. The form of the question in (8), for example, seems to suggest that a qadi had been asked to rule on whether a child was an heir of its father. He had before him evidence of the child's affiliation, but no evidence of manumission. Unable to decide on the case, he applied for an authoritative ruling from the sheikh ul-islam, who then issued a fetva.

If these assumptions are correct, these fetvas illustrate how, in Ottoman law, court cases could, in a sense, come to form legal precedents. Faced with a difficult case, a qadi might apply to the sheikh ul-islam for a definitive ruling. The sheikh ul-islam would issue a fetva. The proceedings would then conclude with a judgment given on the basis of this fetva, in which the question, although presented in concise and stylized language and cloaked in anonymity, would in fact reflect very precisely the particular legal problem that had arisen. The qadi's judgment, pronounced in court, had no validity beyond the case at hand, but the fetva, based on the same case, had a general validity and would provide qadis with authoritative guidance in similar cases in the future.

PART THREE

The Early Modern Period

C H A P T E R   T W E L V E

The Fatwas of Condemnation

JOHN RALPH WILLIS

The "fatwas of condemnation" constitute an extraordinarily provocative genre of *responsa* in the annals of Islam. They provoked action; they aroused rebuke; and they served to banish from the fold of Islam the most troublesome elements, who threatened to unravel the fabric that bound one Muslim to another. Indeed, there is a long and rancorous tradition of condemnation that threads down to our own times. The list of those condemned reads like a Who's Who of Muslim militants—al-Hallaj; al-Ghazzali; Ibn al-ʿArabi; Muhammad Ahmad; Mirza Ghulam Ahmad[1]—and, through the power of the poison (i.e., the fatwa), the wound to reputations was (in the case of many) judged almost incurable. Indeed, al-Hallaj (who endeavored to bring dogma into harmony with Greek philosophy on the strength of mystic experience) was denounced by the Muʿtazila, excommunicated by the Imamiyya, and roundly condemned by a fatwa issued by authorities from the Zahiriyya. Later, he was arrested and imprisoned by the ʿAbbasids of Baghdad. Following swiftly on another fatwa proclaimed by the Maliki qadi Abu ʿUmar, he was exposed on a gibbet (in a kind of Muslim crucifixion), decapitated, and burned in 309/922 (Massignon 1961:127). Ibn al-ʿArabi (d. 628/1240), whose manner and vision were also aligned with the mystics, was assailed as a dangerous innovator, and fatwas rushed from the pen of Ibn Taymiyya, Taqi al-Din al-Subki, and Badr al-Din b. Jamaʿa, among others (Ates 1971:710).

What these "militants" shared with countless others who cannot be mentioned here was a high individualism and an aversion to taqlid (following the opinion of another within a madhhab, or school of law)—an independence of approach that was to cast them in bad odor with the ʿulamaʾ of their day. Muhammad b. ʿAli al-Sanusi (1202/1787–1859),[2] the subject of this analysis (the so-called Grand Sanusi), achieved high rank on this infamous "honor roll" of *ghulāt,*[3] as he challenged some of the most deeply embedded practices in orthodox Islam. Like Ibn Taymiyya (d. 1328) and al-Ghazzali (d. 1111), to whom he displayed a natural and binding affinity, Muhammad al-Sanusi seems to have broken with taqlid from his earliest youth. One also senses in him an early disdain for the company of "kings" and an eager embrace of the leaders of the *ṭuruq,* or religious brotherhoods. Though learned in law and skilled in the reigning modes of scholarly expression, al-Sanusi's breadth of Sufistic sympathy extended to a constant quest for *baraka* (spiritual grace or charisma) and knowledge acquired from religious scholars, as exemplified by the number of associations he affected with leaders of religious brotherhoods.[4] But, as he allowed his reputation to engulf that of his rivals and engrossed to himself an alarming number of partisans, these actions served only to further alienate him and anger his enemies.

In the late 1830s, we find al-Sanusi traveling in the Hijaz, the favored disciple of Ahmad b. Idris al-Fasi (d. 1837), the celebrated founder of a popular brotherhood then thriving in the Muslim holy places. At the time of his death, the mantle of Ahmad b. Idris did no more than flutter over a host of aspirants before it descended in hot controversy on the figure of al-Sanusi. The followers of the deceased split in acrimony, Muhammad al-Sanusi gathering to himself the bulk of adherents (Ziadeh 1958:45; Martin 1976:102–104). Even before this period, however, the teachings of al-Sanusi had stirred rumblings of concern among the leading ʿulamāʾ. Of his abrupt departure from al-Azhar, Ziadeh (1958:39) has observed:

> He had intended to stay for some time in Egypt, where he would pursue his learning at al-Azhar. But al-Sanusi decided to leave the place in much shorter time than he had intended. He seems to have been disappointed there. For one thing he did not find al-Azhar as congenial as he had expected, as the Ulama were courtiers of Muhammad Ali or else attached to the great Ottoman officials in Cairo. For another, al-Sanusi did not meet with the consideration he thought he should receive, for after all, when he arrived at Cairo he had already been recognized as an "alim" in his own right in North Africa. His views were not favourably received by the Ulama, and he was publicly denounced by Shaykh al-Hanish as an innovator. Maybe the main disappointment he had there was the lack of spiritual activity and Sufi teachings at al-Azhar.

If Muhammad al-Sanusi failed in his attempts to obtain some recognition among the official clerisy of Egypt, he succeeded in securing their venomous opposition to his teachings. In 1843 (three years subsequent to his return to the Maghrib), a fatwa was issued at the instigation of Shaykh al-Hanish ("the snake") accelerating the revulsion against the doctrinal positions assumed by the Sanusiyya.[5] As we shall recognize, this message, replete with anathema and recrimination, signaled the early success of the Sanusiyya in Egypt and the Hijaz. And its tone of urgency suggests that the ʿulamāʾ of these lands felt strongly that immediate action should be mounted against al-Sanusi and his partisans.

The Question. What do the people of learning (who separate from the pure shariʿa every element of deviation and falsehood) say regarding a man [i.e., Muhammad al-Sanusi] who has appeared in the land of the Hijaz [en route] to the Maghrib [who has with him] a party of people who alight on the fringe of the land and incite the people to exalt the greatness of their shaykh and enter his brotherhood? These servants make every effort to act upon his wishes in the same way that servants attend to kings, so much so that they do not enter upon religious service under him except after repeated requests to him during a special period. They are not permitted to visit him except during specific hours. They assert that their way is the path [*ṭarīqa*] of the people. Those sent to him do not bear witness with him in the Friday prayer [i.e., he prays separately]. Whenever he resides in a country for an extended period, the prayer service lasts a long time. He does not attend the community prayer, nor does he [attend] other prayers in the mosque. He commands the people to follow the precepts of the Quran and the Sunna ["by word," but not by action]. Whenever devoted servants come to him, he says to that group that they should direct themselves toward someone who will present to them the *wird*[6] and write for them a special *dhikr*,[7] and he delivers it to them saying, cleave to the one who ranks over you, even if he is a tax collector. Those appointed over [these initiates] do not deter them from any disapproved action. And they call themselves "Shadhiliyya,"[8] and they read loudly the *bismillāh* [which is obligatory to all Muslims]. The imam breaks off speech after the greater part of the sacred pronouncement, and after the *fātiḥa* [first Sura of the Quran] there is a long interim. They make obligatory the reading on those who stand behind the imam which the substitute for the imam leads in a plain voice. They prolong the time of prostration beyond the legal prescriptions, so as to allow strangers to join them in prayer. They display a god-fearing quality as they stand a long time in prayer lifting their voices strongly and raising their hands. They contend that breaking the fast of Ramadan during the journey is better than fasting during it. They gather for the prayer and they shorten the length of it in accordance with the duration of their stay in a land, even if they remain a long time there. They assert that they are Malikis, yet the common people have had aroused in them a suspicion of the Maliki ʿulamaʾ owing to their [i.e., the Sanusis'] lack of familiarity with the requirements of the madhhab.[9]

They assert that this *wird* [of theirs] is sunna, and that he who disagrees with it is an innovator. Some of them, upon entering the prayer [*ṣalāt*], utter a shrill cry, and they do not rise up [and recover their senses] until the imam completes his prayer. Praying after a single *tayammum*[10] is made obligatory among them. They contend that the action of *tayammum* is not broken until the *wuḍū'*[11] is broken, and they maintain that all the actions of the *wuḍū'* are obligatory. For the most part, his most eager followers are drawn from the ranks of the emirs and other important people and their servants. [The Sanusis] do not render hospitality to guests unless they are from the class of Arab shaykhs, and from those who obtain their wealth illegally, or by deception. They eat and supply themselves provisions from what [the aforementioned] possess. To him who refrains from that unlawful [situation], they say, "you will not reach what the shaykh has reached" [or, "subsist on what the shaykh and his followers subsist on"].

O 'ulama' of Islam, Allah the Almighty has already made obligatory upon you that you should explain the truth and make clear the shari'a, and respond to every falsehood emanating from the quarter of the deceived. Make clear to us what the Imam Malik [b. Anas (d. 795)] and the people of the brotherhood have obliged us to do. Do not guide us except by what is well known. By your [guidance] do not misdirect the leaders and the common people. Be concise in your reply, and perhaps Allah will be pleased with you and lead to the straight path he who returns to the Prophet (may Allah be pleased with him) in a state of penitence.

The Reply. Our learned shaykh (may Allah the Almighty have mercy on him and encompass with mercy his words), Mustafa al-Bulaqi [see Brockelmann 1943–1949, 356; 1937–1942, 705] replied [to the above queries]: "Praise be to Allah. This closing off of the above-mentioned from the face of the aforementioned is an oppression of darkness. To assert that the path of the Sufis is like that is a lie upon them, since the perfect path of the people is clinging to the Messenger of Allah (may Allah bless him and grant him peace) and questing the moral temper of the noble descendants of the Messenger of Allah. The master of the humble people (may Allah bless him and grant him peace) indeed received in a friendly manner everyone who asked for a reception—even women and slaves—without reproach. He sat down with the poor and the homeless and others like them. Thus, to deny this tradition of common deliberation is to swerve from one's duty. The way of the people is not to depart from the following of the Prophet. If they depart from this emulation, the following of such people cannot be sanctioned. What is Islam, if not the book of Allah and the Sunna of His messenger? Everyone who contradicts the Quran and the Sunna is an apostate [and their acts are to no avail]. Gathering for the public prayer is confirmed Sunna, and its obligatory nature affirmed by the Imam Ahmad b. Hanbal [d. 855]. This man's absence from the witness of the Friday prayer and the public prayer is a grievous affair and an indication that he does not in fact follow the way of the Sufis. His absence from the community gathering for prayer and other [obligatory] gatherings of the people is disobedience [of the commandments of Allah]. What is to be gained from these wrongdoings [even] if he is present at these obligatory gatherings and held in contempt by Allah? For his people consider themselves in accordance with the law, whereas they are the purveyors of falsehood. He commands the commoners among the people to follow the Quran and the Sunna with words of truth (yet what he intends by this is falsehood and the abandoning of the obligatory legal rites [madhhabs], and the use of the laws from the Quran and the Sunna without intermediaries). This constitutes a deviation from the straight path. His advice to others on the strength of these views is an indication of his own ignorance, when it is known to everyone that [certain] texts [from Quran and Sunna] have been abrogated and other [texts] refuted owing to the opposition to those who related them, and still others abandoned due to strong opposition to them or to their replacement by stronger texts, or their confirmation by the four founding Imams [that is, the "founders" of the four madhhabs] in the face of opposition. What is held best is what is rendered accurate from the madhhabs of the founding Imams, because these legal rites contain people of high rank and long service—the people of truth and those concerned with the careful examination of it.

To abandon the accumulated opinion [taqlid] of these four canonical rites is to stray from the right path and to command by it the example of ignorance and rebellion. It is obligatory to follow the opinion of the learned from one of the four rites. These Sanusis deflect everyone from the true course of Sufism—the well-traced road verified by the religious texts. Initiates should possess in the first instance a clear knowledge of the religious tenets of Islam, then let those who wish to affiliate with a brotherhood (and who are entitled to that relationship)—let [them] do that, otherwise if [they] are unworthy of that relationship, it should be refused to [them].

It is obvious that the man [al-Sanusi] is ignorant of the obvious aspects of the shariʿa, and that he strays from the [true] path of the Sufis. From the vantage point of these circumstances, it is forbidden to enter into any agreement with him [along the lines discussed above], as it cannot be fulfilled legally, and it would be analogous to a sick man seeking a remedy from someone other than a physician. Alas! Perhaps man busies himself about that which would surely result in the loss of his carnal soul [*nafs*],[12] and he enters into this folly without forewarning.

As to the words of the bestower of the *wird*, "stay in your condition, even if it is one of disobedience [to the laws of Islam]," and these words are uttered in the absence of any encouragement to repent and to become reconciled to the duties of Islam—these actions are *ḥarām*—forbidden by every religious community [*milla*]. Those who became nonbelievers from the Banu Israʾil [viz., the Jews] were cursed by the language of David and ʿIsa b. Maryam [viz., Jesus, son of Mary] for the very reason that they rebelled against their community, displayed hostility toward it, and led others away from its prescriptions. And its leaders—how detestable are the actions of the Sanusis—their making loud the *bismillāh* during the *ṣalāt* of the canonical prayers—their remaining silent before *fātiḥa* prayer and after it [are also to be condemned, for] the recitation of the *fātiḥa* is obligatory and in accordance [with the teachings] of the Imams. Again, their remaining long in the prostrations or their performance of the prostrations in a heedless manner, as well as their loud pronouncement of the

Qanut[13] (and the raising of the hands during the course of it)—all of that is contrary to what is in the Maliki books, which are under our obedience. He who behaves thusly, and pretends to trace his beliefs back to our obedience, is [on the contrary] from the impostors. Breaking the fast [of Ramadan] during a journey—there is no need to emphasize that this is contrary to the text of the Holy Quran. It would seem that their doubt concerning this emanates from the hadith, "No good will come to those who fast during travel." The Imams have treated with forbearance those whom the fast truly damaged [during travel]. These people, owing to their ignorance, are unable to unite the signs evident in the texts on these matters. They contravene the law that is upon the people in these matters. [As for] their shortening the *ṣalāt* while remaining four days in a single place—whether through custom or belief in the canonical propriety of the practice—their prayers during this period are of no value, and their actions are contrary to the texts of the Malikis. Their contention that they are Malikis, despite this [abominable] practice, is an action contrary to the texts of the madhhab of Malik, and gives the lie to the clear evidence against them, while not in any way depriving the explanation that guides the Maliki texts of its clarity. The ʿulamaʾ of the madhhab do not conceal anything from the texts and indeed are not ignorant of them (or unlearned in regard to them). He who forms this [contrary] opinion with [the Sanusis] has upon him the obligation of repenting of this view because such a conjecture is blameworthy and offensive to the ʿulamaʾ of the Muslims. The further assertion of the [Sanusis] that their actions are Sunna, since [they are] in fact contrary to it, is itself an innovation [*bidʿa*]—and denial of the shariʿa is falsehood. The Imam Malik (may Allah be pleased with him), instructed the people in the Sunna and the following of it to perfection. The people of his madhhab strove to strengthen the people in the following of the Sunna. [In contrast] the actions of the [Sanusis] are contrary to what is obligatory upon the Malikiyya—and the books of the Malikiyya (praise be to Allah) are manifold, and their texts pure and unmingled concerning the replies which are appropriate to the actions of the Sanusis. He who wishes to demonstrate affection towards the Malikis, let him return to canonical texts [as interpreted by them]. The manner in which some of the Sanusis call out loudly at the commencement of prayer is a manifestation of mischief from Satan. [As for] their contention that performing prayers with a single ablution is legal, no Maliki has ever professed this—nor has any Maliki professed the belief that the Sanusis profess with regard to the constituent parts of the ablutions. For the most part, those who follow this man [al-Sanusi] are people of importance—worldly people, an indication that he is a dog from the dogs of this world (and a strike against his claims to be a Sufi [*taṣawwuf*] because the majority of the people who follow the prophets and the good people were from the poor and the weak among the populace). Devouring impure wealth is a transgression of the law. The arguments adduced by those who seek the favors of this shaykh and by those who are attached to them [in] opposition [to the real teachings of the prophets and the good people?] are an indication of their ignorance. [In any case,] adducing what is in the texts of the shariʿa does not turn on the action of this or that person nor on the sum [of the actions of many people] because the texts stand apart from the interpretation of them. These people, owing to their pursuance of the aims of this world and their performance of contradictory acts as a result of their setting themselves and their knowledge apart in it—these people have abandoned the straight path. [Hence,] may the [good] people abandon them and busy themselves with their madhhab, and not be misled by their falsehood against the [obligatory] madhhabs, nor led from the straight path and made to deviate from it. There is the obligation upon everyone from the land of Peace (in his religion and in the matter of his salvation from the anger of Allah, the Almighty)—to move far away from these people (and may the running away be intense). It is well known to everyone that the rank of independent reasoning [ijtihad] has been cut short for some time, and that there is not in this time anyone who has reached the degree of ijtihad. He who fancies that [he has attained this rank] has already brought ridicule upon himself, and Satan has made sport with him. Moreover, according to the divine laws of existence, can any intelligent person believe that he is greater than his predecessors to the point that he is prepared to follow his own opinions and abandon what is obligatory from the principles [of Islam]. The obligation on the custodians of Islamic customs (and on all those on whom Allah has extended His hands) is that they should keep away from these people and hinder them from harming the general populace and leading them astray and damaging the canonical madhhabs. If they do not leave, let us force them to leave the land, and send them far away from the pious people so that they might find relief from their evildoing and restore peace to their condition, if Allah wishes. And Allah is All-Knowing."

As we review the charges brought against Muhammad al-Sanusi and his followers, it will be noted that they fall into two principal categories: several of his teachings are denounced as dangerous innovations, and some of the ritual practices of the brotherhood are denounced further as having departed from the rigors of the Maliki convention and the pure path of the Islamic shariʿa. Still further, it will be noted that the tone of denunciation is unusually heated and personal—perhaps an indication of the haste with which this proclamation was conceived—surely a confirmation of the fact that the Grand Sanusi was not prepared to modify his voice to chime with that of the Maliki ʿulamaʾ. Moreover, this fatwa must be understood within the genre of fatwas of condemnation and, indeed, of "fatwas that never were."[14] This edict and others of the same classification seem to find their ancestry in the climate of uncertainty surrounding the weakness of Ottoman authority and the rapid rise of European activity in Africa, India, and the Middle East. Europeans were quick to grasp in the fatwa an effective means of suppressing dissent, in emulation of Muslim authorities who employed these acrimonious censures as a lash against deviation and tendencies toward ijtihad. But here, as with the other fatwas of condemnation mentioned above, one is plagued by a suspicion that there is more in this malediction than meets the eye. The Sanusiyya had begun to stress the view first put forth by Yahya b. Sharif al-Shafiʿi (d. 1277/1860) that no Muslim should live under a non-Muslim power and that *hijra*[15] from such lands was obligatory should they become part of the Abode of War *(dār al-ḥarb)*. Though further research is necessary on this question, it is not far-fetched to suggest that Muhammad al-Sanusi's association with ʿAbd al-Qadir[16] and the latter's advocation of *hijra* as a response to French activities in Algeria may well have had a role in the issuance of this censure of rebuke.

Clearly, what awakened the alarm of the ʿulamaʾ of Egypt and the Hijaz was Muhammad al-Sanusi's thinly veiled claims to ijtihad—claims which, if upheld, would have elevated him far above the reach of his compeers in the madhhab and disturbed the settled climax of subordination. The Grand Sanusi was not the first to lay claim to this distinction, nor was the Sanusiyya the first *ṭarīqa* to rival the authority of the traditional madhhabs. What compels our attention is that the Sanusiyya had begun to function as a madhhab and to claim for itself the distinction of a madhhab. Again, Muhammad al-Sanusi's attempt to make ijtihad the common property of all Muslims of high learning caught the contempt of conservatives such as Shaykh al-Hanish and Mustafa al-Bulaqi, who had fenced off ijtihad as a preserve of the Islamic past and cast down the Sanusiyya as a repository of shame and degradation. It had been argued that with the closing of the so-called "*bāb* of ijtihad" (the gate of free inquiry) no Muslim retained the right to interpret freely the original sources (Quran and hadith). Still again, Muhammad al-Sanusi's rejection of the consensus of learned scholars *(ijmāʿ)* was seen as an arrogant effort to turn his sight from the accumulated wisdom of the ancients—the legal precedents that had become the touchstones of taqlid.

Of course, this is only one side of the controversy. It was the "Grand" Sanusi's belief that the official ʿulamaʾ had forfeited their claims as inheritors of the Prophet and guarantors of his shariʿa. Over the minefield of their public scorn he treads deftly, isolating the truth as he perceived it, releasing its power against his detractors, depriving the objections of their force. The vanished prosperity—the low estate of the Muslim community *(umma)* across the map of nineteenth-century Islam—seemed a confirmation of this view. The Sanusiyya, he argued, was no more than a response to the despondency of the times.

Some of the ritual practices of the brotherhood are denounced further as having departed from the rigors of the Maliki code and the pure path of the Islamic shariʿa. The Sanusiyya stand accused of encouraging its followers to shorten certain prayers in the *ṣalāt* and dispensing with others altogether.

The fatwa also makes allusion to the raucous atmosphere that is said to have prevailed in their meetings and suggests that participants often passed into a feeling of stark detachment and took leave of their sensibilities. There is some evidence that serves to undermine this view. Several authors (though rather late in the chronology of this fatwa) have claimed that the Sanusiyya actually discouraged noisy *dhikr*s and indeed banned music, dancing, and extravagant movements of the extremities.[17] If this view is to be sanctioned, however, it must be done so with the caution that practices condemned in this fatwa might well have been abandoned in a later period as the Sanusiyya sought to tone down activities that left it open to continued rebuke.

Through his use of ijtihad, Muhammad al-Sanusi had hoped to establish an entente between sufism and fiqh, but in this effort he was to meet with the same failure that beset his predecessors, as his talents went unvalued among the official ʿulamaʾ. Again, though there may have been some effort to soften the more treasonable expressions, no real gesture of atonement was forthcoming from al-Sanusi, who seems to have done little to check the animosity of these feuds. Yet the Sanusiyya did not collapse under these objections, and the ambition of the Grand Sanusi found a footing in the numerous religious settlements (*zāwiya*s) that began to rise up on the periphery of settled authority.[18] It was in this sphere that the Sanusiyya were to effect some dramatic changes on the religious landscape until the revolution of Muʿammar al-Qadhdhafi put a period to their influence in modern Libya.

C H A P T E R   T H I R T E E N

Fatvas as Asymmetrical Dialogues: Muhammad Karim Khan Kirmani and His Questioners

SETRAG MANOUKIAN

Since the institutionalization of Twelver Shiʿism as the religion of the Iranian state in the Safavid period (1501–1722), the ʿulamaʾ have been a heterogeneous sector of society representing different theological and political positions. ʿUlamaʾ frequently criticize and contend with one another; in debating theological issues they also participate in political struggles to attain positions of authority. The authority of the ʿulamaʾ is based on the possibility of making independent judgments (ijtihad) on matters of jurisprudence. Only ʿulamaʾ who have attained the highest degree of religious and juridical knowledge (the mujtahids) can exercise this authority. Their directions and orders must be followed by the community of believers and by lower-ranking jurists. But these judgments are personal and remain valid only so long as the person who issued them is alive.[1]

The contemporary practice of ijtihad, embodying a form of analogical reasoning, is the outcome of struggles and debates within the Shiʿi religious centers that began in the sixteenth century. Broadly speaking, two different positions, each influenced by historical and political factors, developed in the eighteenth century: the Usuli and the Akhbari. The Usulis believed in the function of the mujtahid as a guide for the community and in the possibilities of applying personal interpretation to the texts. The Akhbaris, who dominated the shrines of Arab Iraq until the Qajar period (1785–1925) and were then reduced to a minority position, refused this power to the ʿulamaʾ, holding that the only authoritative sources were the Quran and the Sunna. Attributing more authority to the mujtahids, the Usuli position was more flexible politically, as it allowed religious leaders to express opinions and thus to influence worldly matters. The recognition of such authority opened the way to hierarchical structures. The concept of ijtihad thus was a strong tool the Usulis used to strengthen their power among the people and with respect to the state. During Qajar times, when the Usulis prevailed, the ʿulamaʾ secured their power base and acted as a counterpart and counterpower to Qajar rule (Scarcia 1958a; Cole 1985).

The founding figure of the Shaykhi school,[2] Shaykh Ahmad Ahsaʾi (1753–1826), was an Arab native of Bahrain who spent the last part of his life moving between the religious center of Karbala and different cities in Iran. Typically hosted by city notables, he sometimes had to flee because opposition arose against his presence in the town.[3] He had close relations with different members of the Qajar family and was on intimate terms with Muhammad ʿAli Mirza, governor of Kermanshah, where he spent several years. In the winter of 1808 he was invited to Tehran by the monarch, Fath ʿAli Shah. He left after spending the winter there.[4] Upon the death of Shaykh Ahmad, his intellectual approach was defended and developed by Sayyid Kazim Rashti (1798–1843), who based himself in Karbala, where he developed a following.[5] Sayyid Kazim's disciples included Hajj Muhammad Karim Khan Kirmani and the founder of the Bab movement, Sayyid Mirza ʿAli Muhammad. After the death of Sayyid Kazim, Hajj Muhammad became the guide of the school, transferring it to Kerman, where it exists to the present day.[6]

Several scholars have observed that the somewhat "fluid" thought of the founder was developed and modified by his immediate disciples and their descendents. The Shaykhis generally stress the importance of the spiritual dimension of faith and believe that the authority of God is always active and present among human beings. After the Prophet Muhammad and the Imams, a chain of intermediaries continued, one of whom is always present in the community of believers. Shaykh Ahmad was alleged to have had spiritual contacts with God and the Imams through the medium of dreams, which conferred on him a degree of "holiness." Subsequently, the school tended to limit this mediation to the presence on earth of a spiritual guide whose identity could not be detected.[7] Eventually the school was condemned as heretical by the Usulis, who emphasized the essentially Akhbari position of the Shaykhis regarding the problem of ijtihad. In accordance with their spiritualism, the Shaykhis rejected any formalistic approach that attributed more power to men than to the Quran and the Sunna, the only acknowledged sources of authority.[8]

As Scarcia points out (1958b:201–202), the political stance of the Shaykhis is a conservative one that rejects the authority of the mujtahids, thus limiting their autonomy. The "theologically modern and juridically conservative" stance of the school may explain why it attracted the sympathies of the Qajars as well as those of the "religious rebels" who were anticlerical and looked to the spiritual integrity of Shaykh Ahmad as opposed to the temporal avidity of the mujtahids. The relation between the dynasty and the school became closer when the school moved to Kerman with the third shaykh, Muhammad Karim Khan Kirmani, himself a member of the Qajar family.

Here I will examine several *fatvas* of Hajj Muhammad Karim Khan Kirmani (1809–1870) in an attempt to describe their historical and social context and to evaluate information about the mufti, Muhammad Karim, and the mustaftis, that is, the people who requested the fatvas. Whereas the mustaftis are totally unknown and "exist" only inside the texts, Muhammad Karim "exists" mostly outside the texts, as his answers give very little information about him. To re-create his role and his perspective, I turn to his autobiography and to information on the Shaykhis of Kerman.

Muhammad Karim Khan

The city of Kerman was the battlefield on which the final clashes were fought between the emerging Qajars and the Zands, the Shiraz-based regents who had authority over a large portion of Iranian territory in the second half of the eighteenth century. The definitive occupation of the town by the Qajars in 1794 resulted in a massacre of the population. To regain the trust of the population and to secure Qajar authority over the town, Fath ʿAli Shah Qajar appointed as governor of the town his first cousin Ibrahim Khan, known as Zahir al-Dawla, probably under the influence of his chief wife, Sunbul Baji, who belonged to a Turkish tribe of the Kerman area (Lambton 1986:164).

The local elite in Kerman, as elsewhere in Iran, was composed of prominent families whose power base was complex: members of the same family (or even single individuals) were at the same time landowners, tribal leaders, merchants, government officials, and religious leaders. This was true of Ibrahim Khan's family, which became very influential during the nineteenth century and remained influential until the revolution of 1979.[9] When Zahir al-Dawla settled down as governor, he acquired estates that had belonged to an influential local family, a common practice in Qajar times, when government officials used their position to acquire wealth and land and to become part of the local elite, often strengthening their positions through marriage. (Moreover, government offices tended to be hereditary.) Zahir al-Dawla is remembered for his good administration and for establishing a period of relative security in the province after decades of devastations and massacres (Bastani Parizi 1358/1979: 10-14). Among other initiatives, he instituted a madrasa in 1816 and summoned several scholars to teach there.[10]

Muhammad Karim Khan Kirmani, the son of Ibrahim Khan, was born on 18 Muharram 1225 (February 24, 1810). He wrote an incomplete autobiography in Arabic that contains an interesting narrative relating to his childhood and education.[11]

> During my childhood I was, as worldly people are, happy and satisfied. I belonged to the rank of nobles [*maqām-i karīmī*], and we were submerged in abundance. My father—blessed be he—desired the education of his children and especially my education because he was aware that I had great passion for learning the arts and sciences. He supplied me with everything necessary for the acquisition of science, including teachers and books. He also arranged discussions and even founded a great madrasa in Kerman—may God protect it from misfortunes—that today is known as the Madrasa Ibrahimiyya. He established many *vaqf*s[12] for [the *madrasa*] and for students there, appointed me administrator after him, and endowed many books, numbering more than 500 volumes. In addition, he stipulated that every year many books should be purchased from the budget of the *vaqf*. He settled me in that madrasa so that I would acquire an education. He prepared for me a separate house and appointed a servant for me, things that he did not supply to his other children. With all this richness and abundance, I was free of all preoccupations except for the study of science and literature. I used to sit with the ʿulamaʾ and the learned men and gain from what they had, and all of them made efforts to educate me. As a result, I possessed wealth and authority and I had none of the preoccupations that others have because everything was provided for me. For this reason, I was not involved with the things that the people of the transient world are [involved with], such as tricks and expedients, avidity, jealousy, and violence. I remained of good character and straight to the extent that at the beginning of learning I was the most clever and intelligent of my peers. (Ibrahimi 1957, 1:61–62)

Muhammad Karim's method of studying was to write a treatise on every book that he read. First he studied grammar, rhetoric, and logic, then mathematics and the natural sciences and, finally, several unspecified disciplines. In all of these he acquired knowledge equal to that of his teachers, and sometimes more. This broad education is reflected in the variety and quantity of Muhammad Karim's writings. In addition to works on theology and religion, he wrote on medicine, alchemy, the natural sciences, mathematics, and even wrote an essay on colors.

Muhammad Karim represents his father as having been decisive for his future: it was his father who secured his economic position and motivated him to study. Although it is uncertain whether his father ever met the founder of the school, Shaykh Ahmad Ahsaʾi, we know that he had indirect contact with him and was sympathetic to the shaykh's thought. Apologetic sources emphasize the relationship between the two men to create parallels between the spiritual and the physical fathers of Muhammad Karim.[13] The autobiography also draws an implicit analogy between the two fathers.

When Muhammad Karim has mastered the sciences, thereby completing his "external" education, his physical father dies and his spiritual father appears to complete his inner education: "So I was at the beginning of my adult age and at the maximum of abundance [when] God predestined that one of the disciples of Shaykh Ahmad should enter my country and sojourn here for a period of one year" (Ibrahimi 1957, 1:63). Muhammad Karim subsequently left Kerman for Karbala, where he studied with Sayyid Kazim, the successor to Shaykh Ahmad.

To establish his leadership in the Shaykhi school, Muhammad Karim had to compete with other disciples of Sayyid Kazim. This struggle engendered several submovements, as different disciples claimed to be the true followers of the mentor. The legitimacy of Muhammad Karim's leadership was the subject of several disputes. As late as 1957, one of his successors published a facsimile of the license *(ijāza)* to exercise ijtihad that Sayyid Kazim issued to Muhammad Karim to "put an end to the quarreling and disputes" (Ibrahimi 1957, 1:60).

After Muhammad Karim brought the Shaykhi school to Kerman, it acquired a definite family orientation, as all his successors came from his family.[14] The school increasingly acquired the character of what Scarcia has described as a "feudal" community, combining economic relations with loyalty to the head of the community/family as spiritual guide. The identification between the family and the school became more pronounced after the death of Muhammad Karim. Scarcia describes the school as an economic power toward which the lower classes of the town grew resentful, with the anger eventually taking the shape of religious intolerance. Theological differences between the Shaykhis and the mainstream Usulis became a means for the poor to express their anger against the rich, and the school became the target of several riots, the most serious one in 1905 (Scarcia 1963). Shaykhi communities founded by disciples of Muhammad Karim still exist in Iran and are composed mostly of middle-class people. In some cases, whole villages are Shaykhi (Scarcia 1958b:237–238).[15]

Fatvas

The collection of the fatvas issued by Muhammad Karim was assembled and edited by Zayn al-ʿAbidin Khan (1859–1942), son of Muhammad Karim and guide of the school after the death of his brother, Muhammad Khan (1846–1906).[16] It was the latter who ordered Zayn al-ʿAbidin to make the collection. In the introduction, Zayn al-ʿAbidin praises Muhammad Karim in hyperbolic fashion and then carefully describes the method that he followed in gathering the fatvas. Most of the fatvas were in Muhammad Karim's own handwriting; when this was not the case, the compiler included fatvas only if they had been written by a trustworthy person. The care taken in preparing an accurate text and the concern for authenticity may be related to the venerated status of Muhammad Karim and to the importance that the corpus of his writings has for the school.[17] Fatvas collected in this manner are especially useful if the reader is able to reconstruct the mufti's line of reasoning. To this end, details on many of the matters in question are included so that the steps leading to the final opinion may be retraced.

These fatvas do not deal with theological issues about which the opinion of Muhammad Karim might differ from that of other mujtahids. That is, these fatvas do not have a "Shaykhi" character. Rather, they deal with administrative proceedings of the Shaykhi community, for the most part pragmatic decisions relating to contentious matters. Muhammad Karim serves here as head of a community, a wise and holy man from whom people solicit advice. The mustafti may perceive the answer not only as an opinion on religious law, but also as a "solution" for one's problems and uncertainties, issued by a man of superior knowledge who is thought to be in direct contact with God and the Imams. The questions were often complex, and, for the purpose of clarification, an exchange may have taken place between the mustafti and Muhammad Karim, or possibly an intermediary. On a linguistic level, however, the questions and answers interact only partially. The questions are in colloquial Persian, the answers largely in the Arabic language of the legal-religious tradition that was spoken, written, and understood by only a limited number of scholars.[18] These linguistic differences vary from fatva to fatva and depend on the complexity of the issues discussed and the length of the question.

Most of the questions are presented in generic terms and contain detailed but concise information on the case. The average length of a question is seven lines. There is no single formula for requesting a fatva. The term *fatva* itself is seldom used; most of the mustaftis ask for a *ḥukm-i sharʿī,* a decree based on the shariʿa. The answers are usually shorter than the question, and typically begin with the invocation, "In the name of God the Merciful, the Compassionate." The fatvas deal with a variety of subjects and problems relating to legal procedure. For example:

> *Question:* If a dispute occurs between two persons, and the plaintiff wants to take the defendant to another district, regardless of whether or not a religious judge [*ḥākim-i sharʿ*] is present in that village, according to the shariʿa [*ḥukm-i sharʿī*] do the defendent's expenses [for the travel] have to be paid by him or by [the plaintiff]?
>
> *Answer:* In the name of God: If a judge is present there [viz., in the original district], he [viz., that judge] is the one who must judge [the case]. If there is no [judge], the plaintiff must pay the expenses. (p. 87)[19]

Other questions deal with problems of land or inheritance, often combined:

> *Question:* A woman who had inherited some land gave it to her husband. The husband died. They had children. Does this land currently belong exclusively to the wife, or to the children as well?
>
> *Answer:* In the name of God the Merciful the Compassionate: If [the land] belonged to the woman, it is hers, unless the contrary can be established. (p. 90)
>
> *Question:* A person purchased some land and, several years later, designated it as a *vaqf*. But [the purchaser] did not take the land from the seller, but rented it to him without any contract. Now the purchaser of the land is dead, and his sons claim that they do not know anything [about the *vaqf*]. Does the land belong to them, or is it a *vaqf?*
>
> *Answer:* In the name of God: That land is a *vaqf,* and peace be upon you. (p. 89)

Some questions are about marriage and divorce:

> *Question:* A woman lived for several years in a man's house, and then he died. Now another man claims that she is his wife, saying that the man [with whom she lived for several years] had taken her by force. Is this man now permitted to take her back [that is, without an intermediate marriage]?
>
> *Answer:* Yes, if he can produce evidence that he was married to her. (p. 89)

Some of the questions are longer and are formulated in the first person, with the mustafti describing his own problem; others are recounted by someone else involved in the case. The length of the questions is related to the complexity of the matter described.[20] The presence of rich details may be attributed to the perceived necessity to report all the information on which an answer is based. A professional jurist reading the fatva cannot understand it exclusively from the answer but must use the material provided in the question to reconstruct the mufti's mode of reasoning; only after he has done this may the reader or jurist adopt the fatva as his own.

It is in the longer questions that the shift from the colloquial Persian of the question to the mainly Arabic language of the answer is most conspicuous. Such linguistic shifts are particularly pronounced in a fatva on divorce (pp. 108–109) in which the question, which is mostly in colloquial Persian, contains several long phrases, shifts of grammatical subject, repetitions, and sudden transitions from indirect to direct speech. The narrative of the question unfolds according to the chronological order of the dispute. As circumstances change, the wife (whose words are cited in the first person) changes her defense strategy several times. In the answer, on the other hand, the vocabulary is almost entirely Arabic, as is some of the syntax, and the phrases are short and concise; the issue is analyzed theoretically and in formal, legal (not chronological) terms.

In those of his fatvas dealing with simple, legal issues, Muhammad Karim's answers are generally plain and direct and do not manifest any explicit analogical reasoning, as in the short fatvas quoted above and in the following fatva dealing with land tenure, the only fatva among those I read in which the mufti addresses himself directly to the questioner in the second-person plural.

A Fatva Dealing with Land

Some questions have a narrative rhythm and can be read as stories, although the end product is a highly mediated and constructed text that is remote from whatever dialogue may have occurred between Muhammad Karim and his interlocutor. While conveying only a fragmented and distorted image of the questioners, such texts nevertheless suggest what their concerns might have been.

> *Question:* There is a dry hamlet [*mazraʿa*][21] in Rafsanjan that has not been watered for almost twenty years. It is owned by many different people, none of whom thought—or thinks—to revive it [*iḥyāʾ*]. The well-maintained and watered lands in that hamlet, which is [called] ʿAli Abad, [are the property of] our qibla [viz., a person whom we honor and respect], the distinguished Hajj Muhammad Husayn. The distinguished Hajj gradually bought from several owners approximately half of the dry hamlet; some of the remaining owners gave him permission to appropriate it while some remained who could not be reached and who did not sell [the land] or give permission to appropriate it. The humble one [viz., the mustafti], the administrator of farming in ʿAli Abad, thought that the [remaining] dry [portion of the] hamlet legally might be appropriated according to the shariʿa, on the ground that a dry hamlet which the owners have abandoned, left, and have no intention of reviving may legally be appropriated. For two or three years I have been cultivating these lands as part of the ʿAli Abad [hamlet]. The dry hamlet also had a ruined garden whose trees the people had cut down and taken away and which had dried up due to the absence of water. After the humble individual repaired the walls and watered the plants, the trees became green and they now produce fruits. I keep the fruits for myself, and I consider it, too, to be the revival of wasteland [*iḥyāʾ-i mavāt*]. To sum up, I do not know whether or not these appropriations were licit. If they were not licit, may I rightfully act as guarantor of the property and fix the price of the produce that represents the shares [*sahm*] of those people who cannot be reached, if I pay the tax [*ṭasq*] on those lands? If [the appropriations were] not licit, what is the option legally to acquire those lands and the garden that now belong to the distinguished Hajj or for which he has permission from the owners? I request your honor to explain how to make the

appropriations licit so that no debt will be incumbent on the humble individual. May the grace and benediction of God be upon you.

Answer: In the name of God the Merciful the Compassionate: every bitterness ultimately results from negligence at the outset. The appropriation of people's property without the permission of the owners is not licit. What you heard about the appropriation of dried lands after three years refers to sterile and wasteland (*mavāt*). A land that is suited for cultivation is not wasteland. A garden whose plants have dried up or some of whose walls have been destroyed is not wasteland. Thus, everything you bought is yours and is common property [*mushāʿ*] between you [viz., the owners]. The rest has to be divided or permission must be given, or something similar, so that the appropriation becomes licit. (p. 185–186)

The questioner, a farmer who cultivated land for someone named Muhammad Husayn, revived nearby abandoned land and restored its garden on his own initiative. He maintains that since he has been cultivating the land for three years and nobody has claimed it, it now belongs to him. He is prepared to pay taxes on it but wants to be sure that everything is done legally. He refers to the practice of *iḥyāʾ* (literally "revivification"), a technical legal term signifying the revivification of wasteland and its resulting legal acquisition. Such land must be cultivated for three years, after which, if nobody claims it, it becomes the property of the revivifier.[22] But such was not the case here, and Muhammad Karim opines that because the land and the garden in question are not wasteland, the mustafti's claim to them is specious.

The fatva contains no information regarding the relation between the farmer and Muhammad Karim. The fact that the farmer comes from far away may mean that he had a special relation with the shaykh.[23] If he was a follower of the Shaykhi school, there is no evidence of this in the fatva. The farmer expresses great deference toward his landlord, Hajj Muhammad Husayn, whom he describes with the epithet "our qibla." At the same time, he acts in pursuit of his own interests and requests a decree sanctioning the status of the property that he wants to acquire for himself. Perhaps he sought the opinion of an undisputable authority in order to prevent retaliation from his landlord.

The scribe or notary who drafted the question was familiar with the law and with legal terminology. He uses technical legal terms such as *iḥyāʾ*, *mavāt, ṭasq* (a land tax), *sahm* (share), and *mushāʿ* (jointly owned property); he justifies the cultivating of the dried land by referring to the legal practice of *iḥyāʾ* (see the phrase beginning "on the ground that"); and he formulates the specific requests by dividing the issue into analytically consequential segments (if it is licit, if it is not, then). The notary also displays an interest in persuasive style and expression. For example, when referring to the "many different owners" who had no intention of reviving the dried land, he emphatically repeats the same verb, first in the past tense and then in the present, juxtaposing the owners' disinterest to the farmer's manifest concern. And he describes the revivification of the garden, the rebuilding of walls, and the watering of the trees until they became green again in terms that have poetic resonance.[24]

In his response, Muhammad Karim does not use sophisticated analogical reasoning to deny the farmer's request. The opening phrase ("every bitterness ultimately results from negligence at the outset") elegantly anticipates his legal assessment. From the outset, the land in question was not wasteland, and the term *"iḥyāʾ"* properly should not be applied to it. The incipit subtly conveys an ethical admonishment: you knew from the beginning that these lands were not wasteland. Although Muhammad Karim's decision is based on the shariʿa, it contains no theoretical argument, the matter being a simple and practical one. The tone of his answer is more advisory than legal.

The fatva takes the form of a dialogue, perhaps the outcome of conversations or interactions between several people. From the reader's perspective, the dialogue is asymmetrical. Although all fatvas are no doubt the products of several mediations and consequent interpretations, there are manifest differences between the question and the answer: the mustafti and the mufti literally speak a different language and have different concerns, perspectives, and interpretations of reality.[25] Most mustaftis probably could not understand the technical and mostly Arabic language of the answers. For example, in the longer divorce fatva mentioned above, it is unlikely that the woman understood the ground upon which Muhammad Karim allowed the man from whom she wanted a divorce to keep her. In the fatva delivered to the Rafsanjani farmer, on the other hand, Muhammad Karim Khan responds in a lower register that is more direct and less theoretically oriented.

If fatvas are in fact the products of dialogues, their fragmentary nature and factual omissions limit the possibility of reconstructing with any precision the contexts in which the dialogues were undertaken, leaving room only for hypotheses. For most mustaftis, the events described in the questions constituted an essential part of their lives. In asking for legal advice, they were seeking practical answers to issues that had the potential to transform their existence. Sometimes, however, it seems that they sought more than just a legal opinion—that they were seeking broader advice, counsel, and solutions to their problems. If such advice was proferred, it does not appear in the answers, which discuss problems in legal terms, as fatvas should, thereby reinforcing the gap between the questions and the answers. Muhammad Karim evaluates facts and situations according to their form. For him, facts and events are variables that he puts into perspective with sets of rules and then evaluates accordingly. Through analogical reasoning, he relocates the coordinates of a specific situation within an abstract system of rules. In a movement from practice to theory, each case adds new particulars and variants to the set of rules, thus providing material for further elaboration and expansion of the system. Unlike his questioners, Muhammad Karim never had to worry about "worldly matters" (as he writes in his autobiography). Taken together, the asymmetries of such fatvas provide an image of a complex, articulated, and variegated society, documenting, at a local level, different languages, statuses, attitudes, patterns of thought, and, finally, lives.

CHAPTER FOURTEEN

Sacred Space and Holy War in India

JUAN R. I. COLE

The motif of the usurped place of worship is an important element of South Asian popular culture and communal conflict. In the late twentieth century, Hindu communalist groups charged that the Baburi Mosque at Ayodhya, near Faizabad in the northern province of Uttar Pradesh, stood on the site of the birthplace of the holy figure Ram, and that medieval Muslim rulers had demolished the temple that used to commemorate that sacred spot. The ultimately successful campaign by Hindu fundamentalists to see the mosque razed has proved an explosive element in Indian politics, and has signaled a new assertiveness by the Hindu majority in the postcolonial era.[1]

In the 1850s a similar controversy agitated North India, but at that time the shoe was on the other foot. Ayodhya, then a town of about 7,000, was ruled by the Shiʿi king of Awadh (Oudh), a principality that had broken off from the defunct Mughal Empire and gradually had been surrounded by British-conquered territory, and the small town was the site of a Hindu temple to Hanuman, the monkey god of the Ramayana who aided Ram. Sunni Muslim activists of the time became convinced that the Hanumangarhi had been built atop the site of an old mosque, and they determined to tear it down and restore the mosque. This Sunni-Hindu conflict of more than a century ago posed a profound difficulty for the chief mujtahid, or Shiʿi jurisprudent of Awadh, Sayyid Muhammad Nasirabadi (1785–1867), since both Sunni and Shiʿi groups beseeched him for a fatwa on whether Muslims had a right to act independently of the state to redress the insult to Islam that they felt the Hanumangarhi represented.[2]

Sayyid Muhammad eventually delivered more than one juridical opinion (fatwa) on the issue, one of which survives in the original Persian. Many such fatwas were issued by Shiʿi clerics in nineteenth-century Awadh, and some were even collected and published in manuscript or lithograph form.[3] The form and social meaning of these opinions appears not to have differed in Shiʿism and Sunnism. They were pieces of extended, formal, legal reasoning applied to a concrete case and typically elicited by the question of a believer or litigant. They differed from the rulings of court judges (qadis) in having primarily moral rather than legal force, though they could become the basis for court judgments if adopted by a qadi. Muftis, the jurisprudents who issued the fatwas, derived their status from their reputation for great learning, though some were appointed by the state to issue official opinions (which then had greater legal force). In India, most often the state had been in Sunni hands, so that official muftis tended to be Sunnis; Shiʿi fatwas were more informal and tended to focus on internal community issues. In Shiʿi-ruled Awadh, however, the state appointed muftis from both branches of Islam, and the prestige of Lucknow's Shiʿi mujtahids or jurisprudents was very great.

Throughout the nineteenth century, North Indian fatwas were written in Persian, a language that was still widely cultivated by educated Indians, not excluding Hindus. They had to be translated into Urdu for the nonelite Muslims, but that would have been an easy task, given the grammatical similarities of Persian and Hindustani (the Hindi-Urdu of the time) and the large shared vocabulary between the two languages. Some of the official fatwas appear to have survived only in the British Government of India Archives, in the form of translations made for the British Resident (envoy) to Lucknow and for imperial officials in Calcutta. My translation of the text of Sayyid Muhammad's Persian fatwa is as follows:

> *Question:* What is your guidance concerning those who go to Faizabad to fight the Hindus? For they desire to take revenge on them for their uncivilized behavior with the mosque and the Quran. According to the Law, is it permissible for them to go there and fight, and will this be rewarded? Or is it forbidden?
>
> *Answer:* Without the participation and aid of the customary-law ruler or the Islamic-law ruler, such actions are in no wise permissible. God knows best. (Mashhadi 1896:109)

The ruling appears to be a simple Weberian statement of the monopoly on the use of force enjoyed by the state. In the context of nineteenth-century Islam, and more particularly the Usuli school of Shiʿi Islam, the fatwa serves to define the relationship of the Shiʿi jurisprudents to lay Muslims and to the Shiʿi-ruled state. The fatwa came at the end of a long process whereby the Shiʿi clergy in Awadh had managed to take control of the judiciary and to establish the dominance of the Usuli school, with its clericalist, elitist theory of jurisprudence.

Power and demography were at odds in Awadh, a country of some ten million inhabitants in 1855 that had its capital in the metropolis of Lucknow, one of the four largest Indian cities of the day. The vast Hindu majority of 88 percent consisted largely of rural peasants, and only their rajas and a few great merchants and government officials had much political influence. Most of the 12 percent who were Muslims belonged to the Sunni branch of the faith; they dominated the small towns (*qasabah*s) and accounted for a disproportionate number of the urban residents. They were prominent in skilled and unskilled trades, as butchers and tailors, and also represented many of the petty clerks and middle managers for the bureaucracy, as well as troops and officers in the army (see Bayly 1983). Yet Sunnis labored under some disadvantages under the Shiʿi government of Awadh. Only 3 to 10 percent of the Muslims were Shiʿi, but as coreligionists of the shah, they dominated high government offices and had control of the judiciary. As for the Hanumangarhi, a Western observer in the 1830s described it as a large, well-maintained building about a mile from the river, supported by an annual revenue of 50,000 rupees from an endowment in land created by the Awadh ruler Nawab Shujaʿuʾd-Dawlah (1754–1775). "No Musulman is permitted to enter its walls, and the revenues are absorbed by about 500 resident and itinerant bairagis [*vairagi*], and Hindu mendicants of all descriptions" (Butter 1839:163).

The trouble over the Hanumangarhi became serious enough in February of 1855 to be noticed by Major-General Outram, Calcutta's Resident in Lucknow. He wrote to the reigning king, Vajid ʿAli Shah (r. 1847–1856) that an activist in Faizabad named Shah Ghulam Husayn was bent on destroying the Hindu temple in nearby Ayodhya. He added that this man was being supported by a perhaps even more formidable ("diabolical" was the word he used) lieutenant known as "Mawlavi Sahib," the cleric. Shah Ghulam Husayn led a group from Faizabad that February to begin the work of building a mosque at the site of the shrine to the monkey god, but he was checked by the local government of Agha ʿAli Khan. The British believed that Ghulam Husayn and Mawlavi Sahib should be arrested for their agitations, to prevent a conflict in which blood surely would be spilled.[4] As despicable as advocating preventive detention may have been, the Resident's note demonstrated a sibylline foresight. The heat of summer came, and with it trouble. On July 28, 1855, 500 Muslims clashed at Ayodhya with some 8,000 Hindus (many of them holy men, or *vairagis*) and at least 80 persons were killed on each side, according to Captain Alexander Orr, the representative in Faizabad of the British Frontier Police.

Shah Ghulam Husayn had announced his intention to lead an attack on the vairagis at the Hanumangarhi after the noon prayers. Orr and the local Faizabad government attempted to convince him to take his followers instead to Lucknow, where they could present their complaints to the Muslim king. When Shah Ghulam Husayn refused, Orr requested that they wait five days so that he could get them a response from the nearby capital, hoping that he could bring in more police reinforcements in the meantime. At the time, the Frontier Police only had 150 men of all ranks in place. The fiery preacher refused to wait, and at around one o'clock, the crowd of Muslims met the Hindu holy men. Orr later reported that it was difficult to know who began the violence, though his investigations indicated that a Muslim fired the first shot. Once the shooting began, the outnumbered Muslims were quickly routed. Having led his followers into the confrontation, Shah Ghulam Husayn escaped, abandoning his people. Some of the Muslims ran to a mosque in the neighborhood, taking refuge in it. The enraged Hindus, however, refused to recognize this sanctuary. The vairagis surrounded the place of worship, broke in, and cut the Muslims to pieces. Thereafter Hindus rioted and ransacked the town until around six in the evening, when the violence subsided. Orr thought the Muslims involved to have been men of low caste "and bad character," from both Ayodhya and Faizabad. Their Hindu opponents included not only the holy men and supplicants at the temple, but also peasants from the estates of Hindu magnates such as Raja Man Singh and Rajkumar. Two days later, on July 30, a local government official, Mirza Aʿla ʿAli, and his men attempted to arrest the ringleaders of the Muslim rioters in Faizabad, suggesting that Shiʿi authorities and their clients had grown alarmed that the largely Sunni movement against the Hindus was endangering the stability of the Shiʿi-ruled state. The confrontation turned ugly, and Orr and the local police chief intervened to disperse the crowd.[5]

Vajid ʿAli Shah's response to the crisis was to vacillate and avoid strong action, in the hope that it would subside. He did dispatch the governor of Sultanpur and Faizabad, Agha ʿAli Khan, back to the provinces from the court. Although he claimed to have sought the arrest of Shah Ghulam Husayn, he declined to offer a reward for his apprehension, lest it be perceived publicly that the activist had been convicted without a trial. This indecisiveness pointed not to a flaw in the king's character, but to a political dilemma. He depended desperately on the Sunni-dominated army and the Sunni great landholders in the countryside, and could not afford to be seen taking the side of the subordinate and despised Hindus against them. As a Muslim ruler, he himself had a certain amount of sympathy for the Sunni activists' grievance. Early in his reign he had provoked a major demonstration by Hindu merchants and their followers when he ordered the demolition of several temples on the grounds that members of the Mahajan jewelers' caste had practiced child sacrifice there. The shah seemed unaware that these groups were extreme pacifists, perhaps even Jains, and that the rumors of human sacrifice were quite incredible in the circumstances. Six years later, he had not developed a sympathy for or understanding of the Hindus, and indeed he blamed the vairagis for the Ayodhya violence. Yet he needed the support of Hindus, as well, because they formed the majority of his subjects and because their rajas, merchants, and holy men were not without power. Moreover, the British worried a great deal about a Hindu uprising against a minority Muslim king, and they put pressure on Agha ʿAli Khan to mollify the followers of Ram and Hanuman.[6] In the end, he appointed a commission to investigate whether a mosque had indeed once stood on the site of the Hanumangarhi.

Many Muslims interpreted the clash of July 28 as a horrific massacre of Muslims in a mosque, a profanation by unlawful bloodshed of both a place of prayer and the holy Quran, which had been reposited there. According to Islamic law as interpreted in India at that time, the Hindus were at best a protected minority (provided they submitted to the political authority of the Muslims), and at worst idolaters who deserved only a choice between death and conversion. For them to have killed Muslims in a mosque in the midst of a Muslim-ruled realm proved too much to bear for many adherents of Islam, whatever the provocation. Vajid ʿAli's refusal to act decisively convinced many Sunni townspeople that they would have to take matters into their own hands. Muslim volunteers began departing the capital, Lucknow, for Faizabad in small groups. Two small-town preachers, Mawlavi Amir ʿAli of Amethi and Mawlavi Ramazan ʿAli, began grassroots organizing, collecting men from Bijnor and Malihabad, places with significant Sunni populations to Awadh's northwest, and gathering them in the small town of Amethi in preparation for a march on Faizabad. In Faizabad itself, Muslim clerics preached a jihad against the Hindus, and hundreds gathered about seven miles from the town, under the standard of Islam. Thousands more were ready to march from Faizabad, but the local governor had the bridge leading to Ayodhya from Faizabad blocked off.[7]

Less than a month later, on August 24, while passions over the Ayodhya events were still running high, the Festival of Sacrifice (ʿId al-Adha) was celebrated. At the holy-day prayers held that morning at the Shiʿi mosque in the complex of the Great Imambarah near old Lucknow, the chief mujtahid delivered a sermon to the hundreds of assembled worshippers, who included the great nobles and courtiers, in which he openly cursed Agha ʿAli Khan, the governor of Faizabad and Sultanpur, for having taken bribes from wealthy Hindus to decide the dispute in their favor.[8]

The chief mujtahid, having taken a strong stance in opposition to the equivocation of the shah and his chief minister, briefly became the cynosure of the Muslim activists, who beseeched him for fatwas. Two such exchanges are preserved in the British archives, and I reproduce them here with all the idiosyncrasies of their original orthography and punctuation:[9]

> The Soonees asked the High Priest [chief mujtahid] for his opinions on the following matter: Are those who were slain fighting against the infidels martyrs? Ought not Mussulmans to avenge their deaths? If any one attempts to prevent Mussulmans from so acting—what is your judgment on such conduct?
>
> Reply. - Princes of the Faith, who are believers and Mussulmans are bound to put an end to the wickedness of accursed kaffirs (infidels). God he knows. - Signed the High Priest.

Shiʿis sympathetic to the Sunni activists also sought a ruling:

> Question put to the High Priest by the Shiahs - Suppose a number of Mussulmans had taken up their abode in a Musjid [mosque]—and suppose they were unprepared—say sleeping, or praying—and suddenly a band of infidels were to attack, and slaughter them; so that the Musjid should be inundated with blood—and suppose the infidels were to make water in the Musjid, to tear a Koran to pieces—and to trample it underfoot—and were to subject the Koran to other indignities—and suppose an immense number of them (infidels) had assembled to slay any Mahomedans [who] from fear of their lives were to run away—then, in that case would it not be obligatory on all Mahomedans of these and other parts to fight with the aforesaid infidels?
>
> Reply. - God be our protector from the wickedness of Infidels! Upon the Rulers of the Moslems it is obligatory to repress the enormities of accursed kafirs. Signed by the High Priest.

In late August, the investigative commission came back with the explosive conclusion that no mosque had existed on the site of the Hanumangarhi for at least a generation, and that most likely none had ever been there. The chief minister, ʿAli Naqi Khan, wished to break up the alliance developing between the chief mujtahid and the activists by treating the commission's findings as mere preliminaries and giving it a new charge, designating Sayyid Muhammad Nasirabadi as its chairman. Outram, the Resident, insisted that the commission continue to report directly to the shah, but accepted the idea of adding the prominent Shiʿi cleric to it. When Outram pointedly questioned the chief minister about Nasirabadi's sermon and fatwas, ʿAli Naqi Khan replied that he had been sitting too far away to hear the sermon of August 24, and that the formulation of the questions left no room for any other answer. Whereas the British saw these rulings as inflammatory, insofar as they demanded government action against the Hindus, the Awadh government probably already perceived a crucial difference between the chief mujtahid's stance and that of the small-town Sunni preachers—the Shiʿi fatwas authorized state action rather than enjoining individuals to act on their own.[10]

Vajid ʿAli Shah attempted to reach a compromise with Amir ʿAli of Amethi, proposing to build a mosque resting on one wall of the Hindu temple, with a door on the opposite side. In this manner the interior of the Hanumangarhi would retain its sanctity. Amir ʿAli, at Amethi with his followers, gave the government a one-month deadline by which such building would have to be initiated or he would take action. When they heard of this plan in mid-September, the vairagis in Ayodhya rejected it forcefully, convincing the British that any attempt to implement it would result in more bloodshed.[11]

In late September the sacred month of Muharram arrived, with its potential for further communal violence. Shiʿis particularly honor this month, during which they commemorate with weeping and flagellation the martyrdom of the Prophet's grandson, Imam Husayn, sometimes cursing early Muslim figures revered by Sunnis. In Awadh, on the tenth of Muharram (ʿAshura'), both Shiʿis and Sunnis (and often Hindus) carried colorful bamboo and paper replicas of the Imam's tomb in the holy city of Karbala, and at the end of day-long processions, buried them in sacred burial grounds. As a sign of protest against the Hanumangarhi, Amir ʿAli called on Muslims not to bury their tomb replicas, called *taʿziya*s. In Kheri, in the Khayrabad province, Muslims deliberately neglected to bury fifteen *taʿziya*s on September 25, the tenth of Muharram, whereas in Zaydpur, where a local elite of Shiʿi descendants of the Prophet held great power, the Shiʿis insisted on burying their tomb replicas, refusing to play politics with this sacred ritual, and therefore clashing with Sunni adherents of Amir ʿAli. Communal rioting spread. On September 26, 2,000 Muslims rioted in Kheri, attacking a vairagi and his disciple, and slashing a cow with swords to show their contempt for an animal held holy by their opponents; in the subsequent week, 50 men were killed on both sides, Hindu temples were defiled, and cow's blood was spilled. Followers of Amir ʿAli in the *qasabah* town of Suhali also fought Hindus, attacking temples and destroying idols.[12]

The alarmed sovereign submitted a request to his chief mujtahid for a ruling on the Hanumangarhi dispute, formulated so as to stress the interests of the state:

> Suppose that some of the Faithful imagined that in former times, a mosque had been built in certain lands, possessed by Infidels and that they therefore laid claim to the said lands; that the claim had lain dormant for centuries in fact had never been advanced; either in the memory of man, or in the traditions of the Country; that the Infidels expressed their willingness and desire, to refer the claim to the arbitration and decision of the sovereign of the Country, himself

> a Mahomedan; that the Faithful rejecting these terms, sought by force of arms, to dispossess the Infidels and with that object assaulted them; but were beaten back, followed up, and in the heat of pursuit, slain wherever found. Are you of the opinion, under these circumstances, that any one of the subjects of the aforesaid Mohamedan is empowered by Law; to call the Faithful to arms, and to conduct a Holy war; When the Sovereign himself has not thought fit to proclaim the Jehad or to lead the religious movement, or to countenance it by any public act?
>
> Reply. - Under these circumstances the order for the waging of the Jehad does not apply; but the sovereign has the right to build the Musjid; and the Hindu Ryots ought not to disobey.
>
> —Sealed Syud Mahomed, High Priest[13]

Sunni supporters of Amir ʿAli alleged that the shah had summoned Sayyid Muhammad Nasirabadi with his brother, Sayyid Husayn, and pointed out to them that the efflorescence of Shiʿism in Awadh depended heavily on the Nishapuri dynasty, and that the high station enjoyed by the Shiʿi clergy was a result of the favors of the nawabs and shahs. These supporters further alleged that Vajid ʿAli Shah argued that the Hindus were a protected minority, dhimmis, and that it was not lawful for Muslims to attack them, and that in any case Shiʿi law maintained that holy war no longer was permissible during the Occultation of the Imam (Jan 1855:40–41). Even if this report of the shah's views is accurate (which is not certain), it seems unlikely that the chief mujtahid agreed in viewing the Hindus as dhimmis.

In the subsequent meeting between Outram and Vajid ʿAli Shah, the Resident conceded that Sayyid Muhammad Nasirabadi's disallowance of holy war was helpful, but objected that the last phrase authorizing government action against the Hindus was inflammatory. In reply, Vajid ʿAli blamed the trouble on the audacity of the Hindus. He said they were claiming more land for the Hanumangarhi than their official land grant warranted, that in fact they claimed all land trod by their monkey god, and that they had provoked a riot in the north of the realm (apparently referring to events in Kheri). The Resident did not let the remark pass, insisting that the shah reread the Shankar Dyal report, after which the sovereign admitted that Muslims did seem at fault.[14]

By the beginning of October, Vajid ʿAli, under strong British pressure, was denying he had ever pledged to build a mosque adjacent to the Hindu temple, though Amir ʿAli and the Sunni activists insisted that he had. On October 2, the Officiating Resident handed the shah a note warning him that he would be held personally responsible if he should attempt to build the mosque or if Muslims attacked Hindus. The shaken monarch agreed to do his duty. British officials suspected that Vajid ʿAli had counted on being able to employ British troops to quell the Hindus in the last instance, and his government had already broached the possibility of using them to put down Amir ʿAli's forces.[15] The British had now put him in the position of having to take the Hindu side against the Sunni activists, and of having to find a way to put them down militarily without provoking his largely Sunni army to split or rebel. On October 13, the shah issued a decree *(hukm-namah)* offering amnesty to the activists, but sentencing to death anyone who did not desist from the so-called holy war (Jan 1855:52–53).

In mid-October, Amir ʿAli and his followers began a procession through the small towns of Awadh toward Faizabad, having despaired of government intervention against the Hindus. The 1,800 men, 200 of them Sufi *murids* (disciples) of Amir ʿAli, camped at Daryabad. This area was garrisoned by 5,000 Shiʿi troops loyal to Vajid ʿAli Shah. The government dispatched a contingent of Sunni muftis to debate the activists publicly there. By late October, these muftis, high-powered clerics from the capital and from such respected Hanafi institutions as the Farangi Mahall seminary (on this institution, see Robinson 1984:152–183), managed to convince substantial numbers of Mawlavi Amir ʿAli's supporters to desert him. Those men who had sold their shops or given up their employment in order to join the movement remained the most hard-line. They were urged on by supporters outside Awadh such as the Begam of Bhopal (central India), who sent an elephant and funds for 300 men to Amir ʿAli at Daryabad. On November 7, Amir ʿAli and his forces attempted to advance toward Faizabad, but were met and defeated by Shiʿi army troops along with soldiers supplied by Shiʿi great landlords such as Mahmudabad. Some 400 activists died, among them Amir ʿAli, against 12 dead and 70 wounded among the government troops.[16]

Although many Sunnis came to revere Amir ʿAli as a martyr and a holy man, the Shiʿi clergy did not accept such claims. Someone asked Sayyid Husayn Nasirabadi, brother of the chief mujtahid, whether Amir ʿAli and his followers were saved and martyrs. He replied, "Only Twelver Shiʿis are saved, and no others can be, whether they are killed or die naturally" (Jan 1855:65).

The conflict over the Hanumangarhi in Ayodhya provides a fascinating set of insights into the workings of communalism in mid-nineteenth-century India. Militant leaders of the three religious communities attempted to mobilize their adherents by wielding religious symbols, often in a crude manner, focusing on what divided Indians rather than what united them. Urinating in a mosque, carving up a cow with a sword, refusing to bury *taʿziyas*—all these acts were intended to distinguish friends and enemies and to push the wavering off their fence. It is important to note that these events occurred against the background of a joint civic culture characterized by a high degree of eclecticism (for example, Sunnis, Shiʿis, and Hindus often joined together in Awadh to commemorate the martyrdom of Imam Husayn). In this crisis, however, members of the three communities turned such cooperation on its head. Instead of jointly burying *taʿziyas*, some Muslims refused to bury theirs at all. Yet agreement on such shifts was elusive, so that Sunnis and Shiʿis clashed over the propriety of leaving *taʿziyas* unburied, and a gesture meant by Sunnis to unite Muslims against Hindus served instead to divide the two branches of Islam, showing the ad hoc and tentative nature of the symbol reversals.

Perhaps the most striking aspect of the conflict is the vague allegation—lacking any convincing material or documentary proof—that the sacred space of one community had been usurped from that of another. Why should such an assertion be found credible? Surely at least one reason for its believability lay in a (perhaps unarticulated) conviction that the dominant, ruling community ought to control the disposition of sacred space. The large, well kept, and wealthy Hanumangarhi stood as an affront to some Muslims, those beset by status anxiety in particular. Especially prone to such anxieties were the lower-middle-class Sunnis, squeezed between the Shiʿi nobility and the Hindu merchants and rajas who supported the Ayodhya vairagis. It is common in North India for groups that see themselves as rightfully dominant but somehow denied their full privileges to express their resentment through competition over sacred space. If this interpretation is correct, then it is no accident that Sunni Muslim shopkeepers and artisans living under a Shiʿi Muslim government took the offensive in attempting to reassert their rights over a Hindu holy place in 1855, whereas in the Hindu-majority, Congress-dominated India of the late twentieth century, it was a predominantly lower-middle-class Hindu movement that tore down the Baburi Mosque on December 6, 1992, seeking to replace it with a temple to Ram.

What of the import of the fatwa for our understanding of Shiʿism? Sayyid Muhammad Nasirabadi was put in an extremely delicate position by the Ayodhya temple conflict. He clearly believed that the grievance of the Sunni activists was legitimate, and that a righteous Muslim government would in fact build a mosque on the site of the Hanumangarhi and would punish the Hindus who clashed with the Muslims on July 28. The moral dilemma arose when the British intervened to prevent the Muslim government from acting as it otherwise would have, for surely if left to their own devices Vajid ʿAli Shah and his minister, ʿAli Naqi Khan, would have built the mosque and penalized the vairagis. The question then became, what do you do if the duly constituted Muslim authorities neglect to carry out their duties?

Amir ʿAli and other Sunni activists believed the answer to that question was to take the law into their own hands. Sunni jurisprudence often does allow individual activism on moral issues, and there has frequently been an activist interpretation of the commandment to "enjoin the good and prohibit evil," as can be seen among the "volunteers" *(muṭawwaʿūn)* who enforce the command to pray and who police morals in Wahhabi Saudi Arabia. In Awadh, as in Iran, during the course of the nineteenth century, the clericalist Usuli school of jurisprudence won out among Shiʿis. Usulis believe that outside major ritual and legal obligations (such as the five pillars of witness to faith, prayer, fasting, alms giving, pilgrimage), law becomes too complex and subtle for lay believers to determine by themselves. They have an obligation, on these murkier issues, to ask the opinion of an upright, trained, and knowledgeable Shiʿi clergyman. The Usuli tradition therefore militates against independent lay activism, though a major clergyman can by his ruling authorize laypersons to take action.

The kind of lay and Sufi grassroots activism represented by the holy warriors in the *qasabah* towns was anathema to the chief mujtahid. Moreover, it certainly is true that most nineteenth-century Shiʿis believed that holy war could no longer be fought in the absence of an Imam (a divinely inspired descendant of the Prophet), and Twelvers believed the last Imam to have gone into occultation in the ninth century. Only in an instance in which the lands of Islam were attacked would most Shiʿi clerics authorize a "defensive jihad." From an Usuli Shiʿi point of view, then, only the duly constituted Shiʿi authorities could act in the Ayodhya dispute, which was not suitable grounds for holy war. Sayyid Muhammad Nasirabadi, who did his part by authorizing government action against the vairagis, could go no further except by endangering the stability of the minority, Shiʿi kingdom. Interestingly enough, he recognized that although the Shiʿi state in Awadh was a "common law" *(ʿurfi)* government, not having the divine sanction that would underpin the government of an Imam, it nevertheless had the authority to punish the vairagis and build the mosque. When it did not do so, the chief mujtahid was left with no choice, doctrinally or politically, except to acquiesce in this inaction, however wrong he might have thought it. The Shiʿi minority chose to stand with their shah, and to disallow the claims by Amir ʿAli's followers that he was a holy warrior and, later, a martyr. The fatwas of the chief mujtahid serve to underscore the falsity of the idea that the Shiʿi clergy have, throughout history, been opposed to the secular state.

C H A P T E R F I F T E E N

Two Fatwas on Hajj in British India

BARBARA D. METCALF

The following two fatwas are translated from Urdu.

Query. What of a person who goes to Noble Mecca on hajj and does not go to Medina the Radiant, thinking, "To go to Noble Medina is not a required duty [*farz-i wājib*] but rather a worthy act [*kār-i khayr*]. Moreover, why should I needlessly take such a dangerous route where there are marauding tribes from place to place and risk to property and life. A great deal of money would be spent as well—so what is the point?" Is such a person sinful or not?

Answer. Not to go to Medina because of such apprehension is a mark of lack of love for the Pride of the World, on whom be peace. No one abandons a worldly task out of such apprehension, so why abandon this pilgrimage? The road is not plundered every day; [safety] is a matter of chance—so that is no argument. Certainly, to go is not obligatory. Some people, at any rate, think this pilgrimage is a greater source of reward and blessing than lifting the hands in prayer and saying "āmīn" out loud. Do not give up going out of fear of controversy or concern for your reputation. Should you abandon this pilgrimage from such apprehension and supposition, or put it off, consider, then, which portion is that of full faith. It is a joy to spend money on good acts. To go from Mecca to Medina, traveling first class, costs only fifty rupees. Whoever takes account of fifty rupees and does not take account of the blessed sepulchre of the lord is a person of undoubtedly defective faith and love. Even if not a sinner, this person lacks faith in his basic nature. The end. Almighty Allah knows better. Rashid Ahmad, may he be forgiven.

Query. A person is such that he brings many religious benefits, for example, he teaches the Word of Allah, hadith, commentary, etc. Thanks to him, any mosque he is in is full. Is it better for him to undertake *hijrat* [migration] to the Noble Holy Places, or is his current occupation better? (Marginal note: from ʿAzizuddin Sahib, Moradabadi, 1311/1893)

Answer. If there is no harm to the religion of this learned person, and the populace receives religious benefit from him, it is better for him to stay than to undertake *hijrat* to Arabia. But Almighty Allah knows better. Rashid Ahmad, may he be forgiven (Rashid Ahmad Gangohi 1362/1943, 1:43–44).

These two fatwas were issued in the late nineteenth century in reply to questions posed in 1893.[1] ʿAzizuddin, the questioner, is from nearby Moradabad; Maulana Rashid Ahmad, the mufti, is based in Gangoh. Both are country towns in the Upper Doab area, one hundred miles or so from Delhi. ʿAzizuddin is the person most frequently noted as the source of questions to Rashid Ahmad in the published collection of his fatwas. Maulana Rashid Ahmad Gangohi (1829–1905) was one of the founders of the reformist madrasa at Deoband (1867). Known primarily as a scholar of hadith and Hanafi fiqh, he also served as a spiritual guide in the Chishti Sabiri lineage, which combined initiation and practices of other lineages, particularly the Naqshbandi Mujaddidi. He held no official position (Metcalf 1982: 76, 78–80).

Subject

The two fatwas comprise the entirety of the "Book of Hajj" in the first of three volumes of the 1943 edition of the fatwas.[2] A marginal notation to the second fatwa in the Deoband edition indicates that this is "A rule on *hijrat*" (Deoband ed., n.d.: 375).[3]

The choice of these two fatwas from the collection is arbitrary: virtually any fatwa could have been used to illustrate the same points. A rough count of the approximately three hundred fatwas in the first volume of the Delhi edition shows that they deal primarily with *ʿaqāʾid* (beliefs) and *ʿibādāt* (acts of worship), in itself a telling comment on the domains central to religious guidance at the height of colonial rule. These two fatwas therefore are typical.[4]

A major concern of the fatwas in this volume (and, in fact, in the other volumes as well) was to evaluate customs and beliefs related to Sufism, examining them to identify reprehensible innovation. Approximately one-third of the fatwas deal with issues related to Sufism: its importance, the primacy of the shariʿa, the role of the shaykh, the legitimacy of such practices as saying *ẓikr* aloud (repeating certain words and formulas in praise of God), conceiving of the image of the shaykh, pilgrimages to saints' graves, the celebration of the death anniversaries of the saints, and the customary recitation of the Fatiha. Roughly one-fifth are devoted to the correct performance of the canonical prayer, reviewing such issues as the correct time, the manner of ablution, procedures, the location of the funeral prayer, ceremonies of fixed days after death, and the character of the imam.

Others deal with fasting, reading the Quran, and—the two discussed here—the pilgrimage to Mecca. The fatwa thus served as a central tool for holding up everyday religious practices to the scrutiny of normative principles.

Several fatwas deal explicitly with relations to other Muslim groups, including the Ahl-i Hadith, the Shiʿa, and those who adhere to customary practices, later known as Barelvi; to a far lesser degree, they are concerned with Hindus and with the British (*pace* widespread scholarly assumption to the contrary). In fact, as is the case with the two fatwas under consideration, concerns with these Islamic groups, defined by religious orientation, underlay perhaps the majority of the questions answered.

In this regard, the fatwas implicitly resonate with two important themes. Just as fatwas on hajj are typical—in that the fatwas as a whole deal with issues of belief and obligations to Allah—typical, too, is the first fatwa's particular concern with the definition of correct practice and a correct spiritual disposition in contrast to the stance of other Muslims. The late nineteenth century was a time of intense proliferation of institutions and schools of thought among the ʿulamaʾ, who used new forms of organization, financial support, and communication to build Muslim communities in the context of colonial rule.

Thus the subject of the first fatwa is, implicitly, the teachings of the Ahl-i Hadith, whose reformist teachings also took shape among a group of ʿulamaʾ in late-nineteenth-century North India. The Ahl-i Hadith, influenced by certain strands of Arab reform, went against the predominant practice of Muslims in the subcontinent, who for the most part were Hanafi, to insist that the learned should consult Quran and hadith directly and not follow the rulings and commentaries of the various schools of law. Their opponents called them *ghayr muqallid,* those who do not follow taqlid, or guidance that has been historically given. They were most notorious for their particular practices in prayer, the lifting of hands and saying *āmīn,* which were not Hanafi practices. Observers often marveled at the fact that Muslims came to blows over seemingly trivial matters, not realizing that issues of textual and personal authority were in fact at stake in the forms of prayer that were followed.

The members of Ahl-i Hadith were on the whole more extreme than the Deobandis in their zeal to set a single standard of piety and behavior and in their relentless quest to eliminate all those customary practices that could be construed as reprehensible innovation. Placing the personality and teachings of the Prophet at the center of what they did, in the fashion of all the movements of this period, they stressed their proximity to him because of their devotion to hadith, from which they derived their name. Despite this devotion, they opposed pilgrimage *(ziyārat)* to the Prophet's tomb in Medina, as they opposed pilgrimage to all tombs. Thus Nawwab Siddiq Hasan

Khan (1832–1890), perhaps the best known leader of the Ahl-i Hadith in the late nineteenth century, insisted that no one should make a specific journey to visit the Prophet's tomb, perhaps leaving open the possibility of a visit should one have other reasons to be in Medina (Saeedullah 1973:139). In discouraging pilgrimage, the Ahl-i Hadith shared the orientation of contemporaneous reformers in the Hijaz influenced by Muhammad ibn ʿAbduʾl-Wahhab (1703–1787) and others who earlier had gone so far as to destroy the tomb of the Prophet. Like the Wahhabis, they valued the work of Ibn Taimiyya (1263–1328) and eschewed virtually all practices associated with Sufism (Metcalf 1982:264–296). But the members of Ahl-i Hadith tried to distance themselves from the Wahhabis, disclaiming their violence and their jurisprudential stance (as Hanbali). That Maulana Rashid Ahmad was particularly concerned to challenge and distance himself from the Ahl-i Hadith is also suggested by the introduction to the Deoband edition of the fatwas, where the editor notes that the *ṣāḥib-i fatāwā* shows respect for all four schools of law *(maẓāhib)* (p. 3).

The second fatwa carries a second implicit theme—namely, that in the context of British India one could be of great service to religion, sustain one's own religion unharmed while staying there, and, under these circumstances, feel no obligation to undertake migration to a Muslim-ruled land. The fatwa thus reflects the stance of the majority of Deobandis toward the colonial power (at least through the First World War): avoidance of any direct confrontation. Other fatwas suggest a moral superiority over British culture, permitting one to lie, since the basis of government was contrary to shariʿa; justifying an escape by someone unfairly imprisoned; denouncing missionaries for using bribery; and so forth (Metcalf 1982:153). Well into the twentieth century, however, Deobandis did not measure British practices or technologies as illegitimate in themselves but condemned them only if some aspect specifically countered shariʿa (Masud 1969). In a brief, one-sentence reply in another fatwa in this volume, Maulana Rashid Ahmad himself, noting that the majority of ʿulamaʾ considered "Hindustan" to be *dāruʾl-islām*, chose not to take a position on this point at all (p. 7). Overall, it was less with the British than with other Muslims that the ʿulamaʾ were concerned, as the first fatwa indicates.

Rhetoric and Sources

The tone of these two fatwas is typical of Deobandi rhetoric as a whole, with its goal to utilize a straightforward, simple language, ideally accessible to anyone. The fact that the ʿulamaʾ at this period wrote in Urdu is significant and should not be taken for granted. In fact, some of the fatwas in this volume are received, answered, and reproduced in Persian, which had long been the language of the governing and cosmopolitan classes. At Deoband, however, Persian was no longer taught as part of the education of the learned. The move to Urdu as the vernacular—and increasingly, by the end of the century, a specifically Muslim vernacular—was a result of the colonial framework of both formal decisions and implicit practice interacting with indigenous strategies of cultural reproduction (cf. Fabian 1991; Hardy 1972; Metcalf 1982:198, 206–210). It was precisely the deployment of Urdu in texts like this that was crucial in creating community and in identifying Urdu as a cultural symbol.

The accessible style of the fatwas is particularly evident in those that are in fact actual exchanges of letters. There is no effort to put all the questions and answers into a single format. Thus a letter will be reproduced with a marginal note that it was sent, "*mursala,*" by so-and-so, and the conventional greetings and conclusions are reproduced. Maulana Rashid Ahmad may be addressed as *makhdūm-i zamān, ḥaẓrat, maulānā*—lord of the age (a term often used in a Sufi context), the presence, the master—and he, in turn, signs himself *banda*—servant or slave.

In addition to their simplicity, the writings of the ʿulamaʾ not infrequently take on a mocking or ironic tone. Thus, here, Maulana Rashid Ahmad gently mocks those who would compare the merit of (inappropriate and divisive) practices in prayer with the merit of visiting "the blessed sepulchre of the lord." The terms of this comparison are what give us the conclusive clue that the fatwa is fundamentally "about" the Ahl-i Hadith, whose followers were identified precisely by this public behavior at prayer. Having asserted the relative value of the pilgrimage, Maulana Rashid Ahmad goes on to dismiss the whole rationale for not going. In so doing, he uses yet another typical strategy: imputing to those who do not go mere expediency instead of principle. Much of the debate of this period operated precisely in this style of (consciously) ignoring the premises of one's opponents (Metcalf 1982: 215–234). Imagine how infuriating it would be to be accused of caring about fifty rupees when you believed yourself driven by passion for prophetic example itself in not going to Medina—to say nothing of the same motivation for raising of hands and saying *āmīn* in prayer.

The tone of the answer, moreover, was also light-handed in judging those who differed. Here, Rashid Ahmad did not judge a person sinful who did not go to Medina; the Deobandis did not rush to call anyone deviant, let alone kafir, or infidel. Given the competition among the varying schools of thought in this period, each of which insisted that it came closer to the pattern of the Prophet and loved him most, the suggestion that the wrongdoer "only" showed "defective faith" and lack of "love for the Pride of the World" was damning enough: the very understatement makes the accusation more wounding. Maulana Rashid Ahmad's triumphant parry is framed, of course, by conventional modesty: God knows better; may the sins of the mufti be forgiven. Thus, behind the apparent simplicity lay a nuanced and pointed mode of argument valued in a culture that delighted in polished and clever language.

No sources are quoted to bolster the argument, suggesting (as does the simplicity of the language) an effort to gain a wide audience and, perhaps, an awareness of the extent to which people had fallen from a laudable standard of religious learning: in another fatwa in this volume, Maulana Rashid Ahmad explains that he does not cite arguments of hadith and fiqh because the knowledge of both the ordinary and the learned, *ʿawāmm* and *khawāṣṣ*, is defective (pp. 88–89). Although some fatwas in the collection mention a quranic verse or hadith, most do not.

A further reason that only a simple answer was given was the emphasis of the Deobandis on the position known as *taqlīd-i shakhṣī,* that each Muslim should follow a single scholar as a definitive guide to correct belief and practice. Parallel to this was the notion that each person should follow a single spiritual guide (*murshid,* or shaykh). These injunctions were intended to bolster the authority of individual ʿulamaʾ.

At times, however, Maulana Rashid Ahmad did turn to other scholars to bolster his opinion with testimonials, frequently with seals showing the date. On several occasions in these volumes, opinions are supported by the signatures of a dozen or more additional scholars, who often added a rhyming phrase in Arabic (e.g., *"al-jawāb ṣaḥīḥ wa-munkiruhu faẓīh,"* the answer is correct and the denier disgraceful) or a sentence in support. This was the case, for example, with a fatwa forbidding the customary celebration of the Prophet's birthday, a contended practice that was spreading, in part because it was espoused by a rival group of ʿulamaʾ. The editor, similarly, footnotes on occasion such significant elders of the Deobandis as Shaykh ʿAbdulʿaziz Dihlawi (d. 1824) or Hajji Imdaduʾllah (1817–1899) to render support.

The Deobandis took for granted that their arguments were based on Hanafi fiqh. Occasionally Maulana Rashid Ahmad would make a reference to another law school, for example on a minor matter like saying the *bismillāh* before reading each chapter of the Quran, when he was prepared to accept the practice of another school. He also stretched a point to make acceptable the Shafiʿi opinion allowing teachers to accept recompense for teaching Quran and hadith, an issue of importance to the ʿulamaʾ at a time when they did not enjoy official patronage: he called the Shafiʿi position fatwa, in the sense of what was decreed; the Hanafi, more difficult to practice, he termed piety, or *taqwā.* In general, however, the Deobandis condemned interscholastic eclecticism, for fear that it would encourage one to choose the easiest path and prevent the establishment of a single standard.

Such discussion, or discussion of such points as the Hanafi emphasis on ascertaining the *ḥaqīqa* (truth, essence) of a problem to identify its correct analogue, rarely entered into the fatwas themselves. Generally speaking, the early Deobandis did not feel any need to lay bare the framework of their analysis (Metcalf 1982: 141–143).

Institutional Context and Dissemination

The ʿulamaʾ of the late nineteenth century, in the wake of the decisive establishment of British rule following the Mutiny of 1857, turned away from any governing or political role and established themselves as guides to personal behavior and morality, defined by Islamic authority. Their teachings disseminated a self-conscious identification with Islamic symbols and built new communities, both among subgroups of Muslims (often defined by the various schools of thought, like the Deobandi, Barelvi, and Ahl-i Hadith, that were taking shape in the late nineteenth century) and among Muslims generally. Published fatwas, moreover, were central in defining appropriate codes of behavior at a hitherto unknown level of detail. The fatwas thus had no support from political powers, nor did those providing them have the authority of any official office. Muftis had only the authority of their learning and moral qualities, coupled with their identification with one or another school of thought.

Popularly supported schools to train ʿulamaʾ, who themselves would become learned in hadith and fiqh and in turn be able to offer fatwas, were the institutional foundation and base of Deobandi ʿulamaʾ like Maulana Rashid Ahmad. The madrasa at Deoband, founded in 1867, spawned some two dozen schools of similar orientation across India by the end of the century and, in its first hundred years, gave rise to several hundred more schools identified as Deobandi. Individuals not only consulted respected ʿulamaʾ associated with the school to secure fatwas but also began to solicit fatwas with the imprimatur of "Deoband" as well. In 1892 a formal *dāruʾl-iftāʾ* was established at the school, and an *ʿālim* was appointed as the school's mufti (Muhammad Tayyib 1965:99). This did not mean that others at the school did not offer fatwas, but only that the burden was now particularly focused on one person who had iftaʾ as his primary responsibility. Beginning in 1911, a register was established into which each question, along with its answer, was recorded. At the time of its centennial, the school counted a total of 269,215 fatwas that had been issued, proudly claiming to have provided answers to most of the questions on the very day they were received (Metcalf 1982: 146).

The dissemination of fatwas by means of lithographed books, along with religious publications generally, was critical to the creation of communities linked by religious style. The importance of publications in creating "imagined communities"—imagined in the sense that they are communities whose members are imagined rather than known on a face-to-face basis—has been argued by Benedict Anderson (1983) in relation to the emergence of nation-states. Printed works have been critical as well, however, in creating ethnically and religiously defined communities. As David Gilmartin (1990) has suggested, there emerged in British India what might be called a "particular" space, neither private nor public (in the sense of being open to all inhabitants of the geographic area), that defined group commonalities and group interests through what were at the time new modalities of communication and new institutional forms. Some of these "particular" communities, or variations of them, ultimately competed in a shared public space (Hardy 1971). "Indian Muslim" represents one significant community that occupied that space in the twentieth century. There was no direct link between the communities defined by the ʿulamaʾ and those that took on explicit political significance later, but to the extent that the ʿulamaʾ, and their publications, disseminated Islamic teachings and entered, as they did, into debates with non-Muslims, they surely made some contribution to what became politicized religious identities.

While a great deal is not known about the publishing histories of fatwa collections, Maulana Rashid Ahmad's fatwas were published at least by 1906, the year following his death, and were frequently reprinted thereafter. The Delhi edition published in the 1940s carried an announcement on the last page explaining that despite frequent reprintings, the volumes had been continuously snatched up and were therefore unavailable; the rights had been purchased by the Maktaba Rahimiyya, which intended to keep the volumes in print—and asked that no one pirate the text. A later edition by the Deoband branch of the company reorganized the three-volume format into one volume in order to make all fatwas relevant to a single subject available in one place.

The fatwas of the late nineteenth century, along with those of Shah ʿAbdul-ʿaziz from earlier in the century (Metcalf 1982: 46–52), appear to have taken on the character of "classics" and continue to be available in reprints in shops that deal in Urdu books. Important collections include those of Maulana ʿAbdu'l-Hayy Farangi Mahalli (d. 1304/1886–1887; *Fatāwā ʿAbduʾl Ḥayy Lakhnawī*), whose decisions were, broadly speaking, identified as Deobandi; Maulana Ashraf ʿAli Thanawi (1864–1943; *Fatāwā Imdādiyya*), a disciple of Maulana Rashid Ahmad; Nawwab Siddiq Hasan Khan (*Majmūʿa Fatāwā*), the Ahl-i Hadith leader; and Maulana Ahmad Riza Khan Barelvi (1856–1921; inter alia, *Fatāwā Rizwiyya*). The last named, an opponent of the Deobandis and a proponent of a more custom-laden religious style, was known for using fatwas against his opponents and for his great efforts to solicit support from scholars in the Hijaz to bolster his opinions. He did not, moreover, follow the pattern of offering a simple opinion, but made what were in fact his primary claims to authority with massive citations of Quran and hadith: his published fatwas fill a dozen volumes, each running to a thousand pages, with a single answer on occasion taking a hundred pages (Metcalf 1982: 308). The fatwas issued by the successive muftis at Deoband also have been published, running now into many volumes. A bibliography of religious works in Urdu lists some ninety-three collections of printed fatwas that were available in Urdu bookshops thirty years ago (Anjuman-i Taraqqi-yi Urdu 1961: 382–390).

The durability of these fatwas is not unrelated to their domain. As Masud has suggested (1969: 1), the fatwas of this period represent both a narrowing, away from issues related to rulership and the state, and a broadening, toward issues not only of religious obligation but also of moral opinion regarding a wide range of customary practices, relevant to the attempt of the ʿulamaʾ to define a purified and authoritative personal standard of faith and practice as the foundation of individual and communal life. To the extent that attention to correct individual practice remains at the heart of Muslim religious style, these fatwas continue to have relevance for the Urdu-speaking Muslims of the subcontinent.

CHAPTER SIXTEEN

Apostasy and Judicial Separation in British India

MUHAMMAD KHALID MASUD

In 1913, a Muslim husband applied to a British court in India for the restitution of conjugal rights when his in-laws refused to let his wife join him. His in-laws claimed that the woman had apostatized and thus, according to Islamic law, was no longer the claimant's wife. The judge asked the claimant to obtain a fatwa clarifying the position of Islamic law on the status of his marriage. The claimant therefore approached Mawlana Ashraf ʿAli Thanawi for a fatwa. Mawlana Thanawi (1863–1943) ruled that due to apostasy the marriage was annulled. A translation of the question and answer, as recorded in the *Imdād al-Fatāwā* (Thanawi 1965, 2:229–230), is given below.

> *Question:* What do the scholars of religion and the jurisconsults of the vigorous law say in the matter of Zayd [a fictitious name] who married a woman and brought her to his home? A few months after the consummation of the marriage, his wife's guardians came to take her back. Zayd sent her with them. Several days later, when Zayd asked her to return, her guardians declined, offering various excuses. After a few days, they flatly refused and demanded *khulʿ* [that is, divorce on payment of consideration by the wife]. Zayd had no alternative but to apply to the government [court] for his wife's return. When the guardians learned [about Zayd's application to the court] they immediately taught the woman words of unbelief. The woman uttered those words of unbelief. Now, the guardians have submitted to the court that the woman, as a sane and adult person, had uttered those words of unbelief, and hence her marriage contract with Zayd was no longer valid. Thus the plaintiff's request [for his wife's return to him] was not justified. Since the marriage was annulled, they could not return her. After this declaration, the judge asked Zayd to seek a fatwa. The judgment is withheld pending receipt of the fatwa. Now, the

question is, [with regard to] this woman who uttered the words of unbelief, whether as instructed by her guardians or on her own [initiative], with the intention to annul her marriage, is her marriage contract annulled according to God['s law] or not?

Response: Annulled. Uttering words of unbelief, intentionally and knowingly, whether one actually believes in those words or not, whether it is one's own view or someone else's instructions, necessarily constitutes unbelief in all cases. Since unbelief causes annulment of the marriage contract, the marriage [in question] is dissolved. At the same time the marriage contracts of those who instructed her words of unbelief are also annulled. The marriage contracts of all those who consented to such instruction are also annulled. The only difference [between the status of the marriage contract of Zayd's wife and that of the wives of those who taught her words of unbelief] is that according to the Shariʿa, Zayd's wife should be forced to embrace Islam and to marry the same first husband. She is not allowed to marry any other person. The wives of those who taught words of unbelief and of those who supported them, however, are allowed to marry whomever they wish after completing the *ʿiddat* [Arabic: *ʿidda,* the specified waiting period after the annulment of marriage].

Al-Durr al-Mukhtār reads as follows: A woman who is informed about the apostasy of her husband has the right to marry another man after the *ʿidda* . . . [al-Haskafi 1979, 3:332]. It continues: An apostate wife does not have the right to marry any person other than her husband. This is the most authoritative view [ibid., 335]. *Radd al-Muḥtār* adds: The jurists ruled that she will be forced to renew the marriage contract with the husband and that she will be punished by seventy-five lashes. This opinion was upheld by Qadi Khan in his *Fatāwā,* vol. 3, pp. 469, 470. Since the marriage contracts of all of them were annulled, the subsequent rules will apply to them as well. 4 Dhuʾl Qaʿda, 1331 H. [October 5, 1913].

Although it is not clear why the woman refused to return to her husband, it is obvious that she had used apostasy as a legal device to rid herself of him. Since the question emanated from the husband, we have no way of knowing the wife's side of the story. The question alludes to the use of apostasy as a legal device to annul a marriage, but it does not challenge the act of apostasy itself; rather, it focuses on the issue of whether or not apostasy annuls the marriage contract. The response clearly indicates that a wife's apostasy does annul the marriage. Without addressing the issue of motive or the wife's specific circumstances, it focuses on apostasy, its penalties, and its effects on marriage, adding details relating to the status of the marriages of the persons who assisted the apostatizing wife.

The 1913 fatwa was revised by the mufti in 1931. For convenience, I shall refer to the 1913 fatwa as "the first fatwa" and to the 1931 fatwa as "the revised fatwa." I have selected these two fatwas to illustrate some significant developments in ifta' in British India. An analysis of the circumstances leading to the revision of the fatwa provides an opportunity to observe the process of legal change in Islamic law, the impact of developments in the judicial institution, and the role of mufti in the development of legal doctrine. Ifta' in British India seems to have emerged as a parallel institution to the courts, but one also notes its complementary role of filling the gap that the British legal system had created in the administration of Muslim personal law. The question of judicial separation led the muftis to question the jurisdiction and validity of British judges and to redefine the role of the mufti in this judicial vacuum. These fatwas also indicate that the British courts accorded a specific role to muftis in the British legal system. A study of these two fatwas raises two important questions: What are the factors that cause a mufti to revise his opinion? And how is a fatwa revised, particularly by a mufti who is a muqallid—that is, an adherent of a school of Islamic law.

Background

In 1913, when the first fatwa was issued, apostasy did not pose a serious threat to Muslims in India. The situation worsened, however, in the years leading up to the issuance of the second fatwa. Christian missionary activities in India accelerated between 1920 and 1930. The number of conversions increased because, as I shall show, Muslim women had no recourse other than apostasy when seeking judicial divorce. Some missionaries, especially in the Punjab, encouraged Muslim women who wanted to dissolve their marriage to declare themselves Christians. A missionary by the name of Reverend Paul in Lyallpur baptized several new converts and issued certificates of baptism. The number of applications for judicial separation on the ground of apostasy increased considerably between 1920 and 1930 (Masud 1995:158ff.). Muslims in India felt threatened by these conversions and began to demand reforms in the prevailing laws.

In a public lecture delivered in Lahore in 1924, Dr. Muhammad Iqbal (d. 1938) expressed concern about these conversions. Iqbal questioned the validity of the Hanafi law that compelled Muslim women to abandon Islam to get rid of their husband. He also urged Muslim scholars to exercise ijtihad—to issue independent legal opinions that were not tied to earlier opinions of the jurists of a particular school of law—in order to reform the Hanafi law on this point (Iqbal 1982:169). This critique stimulated a debate on the subject in the press; it also compelled muftis to find a solution for hardships that were forcing Muslim women to resort to apostasy.

Mawlana Ashraf ʿAli Thanawi took an active interest in the question of relief for suffering wives. In 1931, after several years of extensive consultations with muftis in India and abroad, he published a long fatwa entitled *al-Ḥīlat al-Nājiza liʾl-Ḥalīlat al-ʿĀjiza* (A Successful Legal Device for the Helpless Wife). In the revised fatwa, Mawlana Thanawi argued that apostasy did not annul the marriage contract and could not be used as a legal device. He agreed that judicial divorce might be used to provide relief to Hanafi Muslim women, invoking Maliki doctrine in support of this point. At the same time, he observed that non-Muslim judges were not authorized—in Islamic terms—to enforce judicial separation. And he urged Indian Muslims to seek reforms in the current laws of personal status and in the judicial system in India and to demand the appointment of Muslim judges (Thanawi 1931).

In 201 pages, *al-Ḥīla* deals with all the problems related to the issue of judicial separation: the need for the appointment of Muslim judges, the possibility of adopting the doctrines of non-Hanafi jurists, the husband's delegation of the right of divorce to the wife, and the procedure and grounds for judicial separation—namely, a husband's impotence, insanity, disappearance, or cruelty, and a wife's option on reaching puberty. The Arabic texts of fatwas received from Maliki muftis in Medina, with whom he corresponded while writing the revised fatwa, are reproduced in the book. In the revised fatwa, Mawlana Thanawi distinguished three aspects of the problem: apostasy as a legal device, the suffering of Muslim women due to the unavailability of legal relief against cruel husbands, and the absence of Muslim judges. He recommended reforms on all three counts.

It was this fatwa that triggered the movement for Islamic legal reform in India. The Jamʿiyyat al-ʿUlama-i Hind, the political party formed by the ʿulamaʾ in India, acted on Mawlana Thanawi's fatwa. On behalf of the party, Qadi Muhammad Ahmad Kazimi, a lawyer and member of the Indian Parliament from Meerut, United Province (now called Uttar Pradesh), presented a bill in Parliament for this reform (Ahmed 1972:10ff.; Fyzee 1960:144). After long debates and several rounds of discussions, the bill was passed as the Dissolution of Muslim Marriage Act, 1939. The act provided that the apostasy of a Muslim wife did not annul the marriage contract, and it allowed all grounds admitted in Maliki law for a decree dissolving a marriage, including a husband's impotence, cruelty, or failure to maintain his wife (Ahmed 1972:1063).

Institutional Development

To appreciate the importance attached by Thanawi to questions of the availability of Muslim judges and adherence to the Hanafi school, it will be helpful to discuss the institution of muftis in British India. Prior to the arrival of the British, Islamic law had been administered by qadis and muftis. Under the British, qadis and muftis were replaced by judges. The position of mufti, provided for in the Regulating Act, 1772, was abolished in 1864 (Schacht 1964:95). Although one might have expected the importance of the muftis to decline, they continued to flourish, albeit in a private capacity. This may be explained by three factors. First, the continued adherence of the majority of Indian Muslims to the Hanafi school required the continued presence of muftis outside the British legal system. Second, Hanafi muftis in India did not accept the judicial authority of judges appointed by a non-Muslim ruler, especially in matters of personal status. They advised Muslims to appoint Muslim arbiters in the absence of Muslim judges, both to settle their disputes and to ratify judgments issued by the British courts (Farangi Mahalli n.d., 2:26; Rashid Ahmad Gangohi n.d.:470; Kifayatullah 1971, 5:100, 6:122, 200, 205; Lajpuri 1978, 2:121)—and who could be a more qualified arbiter than a mufti? Third, translations of Islamic legal texts and the codification of Anglo-Muhammadan law were insufficient to make British judges independent of the muftis. As is evident from the first fatwa, in difficult cases judges asked plaintiffs to seek fatwas.

As a consequence, by the first decade of the twentieth century almost every Muslim educational or political organization had established a *dār al-iftāʾ* (literally, a house in which fatwas are issued; that is, an institution in which one or more muftis answered questions about Islamic law). As is evident from the present fatwa, the dar al-iftaʾ did not completely replace the British courts, although it may have prevented some litigants from going to those courts. More significant, as the first fatwa indicates, it provided a readily available source of reference on Hanafi law, even for the British courts.

Although British judges generally did not interfere in the religious matters of the subject population, they occasionally invoked the notions of equity and justice to circumvent traditional laws that they could not endorse with good conscience. Attempts to reform Islamic law were rarely initiated by the judiciary, and British legislative attempts to reform the law were vigorously resisted by Muslims. In this case, the reform of Islamic law was initiated by the Muslims themselves through the institution of iftaʾ, which was systematically organized, using modern modes of communication to increase its popularity among the masses.

The ground for Islamic legal reform was prepared by Mawlana Ashraf ʿAli Thanawi. An outstanding scholar, teacher, Sufi, writer, and politician, Mawlana Thanawi learned all the traditional sciences, taking a special interest in logic, theology, Sufism, and law at the Hanafi school, Dar al-ʿUlum Deoband, where he studied from 1878 to 1883. He received his training in fatwa writing under the tutelage of Mawlana Muhammad Yaʿqub Nanawtawi (d. 1888). Mawlana Thanawi began writing fatwas in

1884, under the supervision of Mawlana Rashid Ahmad Gangohi (d. 1905), the founding mufti of the Deoband (on Rashid Ahmad Gangohi, see Chapter 15). The fatwas written between 1887 and 1943 were published regularly in the monthly journal *al-Nūr,* appearing from Thana Bhawan (Thanawi 1975, 1:16); subsequently, they were collected and published under the titles *Fatāwā Ashrafiyya* and *Imdād al-Fatāwā.*

The *Imdād al-Fatāwā,* published in 1927 (four volumes), 1950 (two volumes), 1949 through 1953 (six volumes), and 1965 through 1977 (six volumes), classifies fatwas under regular fiqh categories, although it adds some new categories, not customarily included in fiqh books, at the end. The accompanying table, which indicates the number of fatwas in various categories appearing in the 1949–1953 edition, gives a fair idea of the range of subjects covered and their proportions.

Ten fatwas in the *Imdād,* issued between 1883 and 1920, are related to the subject of apostasy and dissolution of marriage (Thanawi 1965, 2:229, 232, 380, 381, 382, 383, 451, 508; 1978, 5:393). Mawlana Thanawi maintained in these fatwas that apostasy annulled a marriage, that the apostate wife was to be forced to return to Islam, and that she was not allowed to marry any person other than her present husband. The revised fatwa, which was published as an independent treatise, is not included in the *Imdād al-Fatāwā* collections.

Most of the fatwas in the *Imdād* are written in Urdu, although a few are in Persian (in the first volume [1949], 25 out of 764 fatwas are written in Persian). Authorities are almost always cited in Arabic. The name of the mustafti is rarely given, but the date of the issuance of the fatwa is often

The range of subjects covered by *Imdād al-Fatāwā,* edition of 1949–1953

Subject	*No. of fatwas*	*Percentage*
Rituals	1,028	30.44
Personal status	945	27.98
Contracts	559	16.56
Marriage and divorce	376	11.13
Exegesis	138	4.08
Creeds and heresiology	116	3.43
Mysticism	96	2.84
Innovations	69	2.04
Judicial procedure	38	1.12
Penal laws	13	0.38
Total	3,378	100.00

recorded. Most of the fatwas are long, giving details of the argument and citing sources. The authorities cited belong largely to the Hanafi school, with frequent references to the Ottoman mufti Ibn ʿAbidin (d. 1836).

The removal from the question of the mustafti's name and address and the use of the third-person pronoun indicate a general and abstract approach to the activity of issuing fatwas. The citations of Arabic legal texts, without translation, suggest that the mustafti would require the services of an expert to explain the meaning of the text, thereby ensuring the need for a mufti. Mawlana Thanawi stresses this point in his revised fatwa, insisting that the book should be read by women and lay readers only with the assistance of a scholar who is also a researcher *("muḥaqqiq ʿālim")* and that no inference may be drawn from it unless this has been done. According to Mawlana Thanawi, contemporary scholars, called *mawlawī,* who had graduated from government institutions and who had read only a few books in Urdu and Persian, were not qualified to understand his fatwa (Thanawi 1931:6–7).

The questions open and close in an interrogative form and with formulaic phrases indicating the mufti's authority and status. The conventional structure of the responses—a brief answer followed by the citation of authorities—indicates that the mufti's authority is based on his ability to cite authorities of his school in support of his opinion.

Mawlana Thanawi's personality, his distinguished career as a religious guide and teacher, his political influence, and his affiliation with the Deoband all contributed to his role as a mufti. Although he was not an official mufti in the dar al-iftaʾ of the Deoband or the Jamʿiyyat al-ʿUlama-i Hind, his well-argued fatwas and their widespread publication in periodicals (and later in several editions) extended his influence as a mufti. His personal influence added to the weight of the institution of iftaʾ. As we shall see, it was difficult for Indian muftis to consider introducing changes in Hanafi divorce laws, largely because the problem of reform was related to two sensitive doctrines: taqlid[1] and apostasy. Mawlana Thanawi's personal influence and method helped to overcome this problem.

Doctrinal Context

It appears from the questions (*suwāl,* istiftaʾ) in the *Imdād al-Fatāwā* that apostasy was not the real motive for uttering words of unbelief; rather, the words were uttered by Muslim wives as a legal device to dissolve their marriages. The Anglo-Muhammadan and Hanafi laws prevailing in British India considered the question of motive immaterial. British judges discouraged investigations into whether the conversions in those cases were genuine or not (Masud 1985:209). The muftis also disregarded the real motive in order to chastise Muslim women for using apostasy as a legal device. It was only in his revised fatwa that Mawlana Thanawi took the question of motive into serious consideration. To examine why Muslim women resorted to apostasy as a legal device, I shall outline the legal doctrine relating to a Muslim woman's ability to dissolve her marriage.

In Islamic law, the right of divorce belongs largely to the husband. Hanafi law admits only one ground for a judicial divorce: the husband's impotence. Otherwise, the only way for a wife to initiate a divorce is through *khulʿ*; that is, by paying an agreed sum of money to the husband. Inasmuch as a *khulʿ* divorce is contingent on the husband's consent (ʿUthmani 1987:208), Muslim wives whose husbands were sexually potent or whose husbands refused to negotiate a *khulʿ* divorce had no legal recourse other than apostasy to dissolve their marriages.

Unlike their classical counterparts, modern Muslim jurists regard apostasy as one of the major crimes *(ḥudūd)* that entail capital punishment.[2] Apostasy changes the status of marriage, as well as the legal and personal status of the apostate, eliminating all his or her basic rights. A male apostate must be forced to return to Islam or else suffer the punishment of death. A female apostate, according to the majority view, is either punished by seventy-five lashes or imprisoned until she returns to Islam or dies.

Regarding the effect of apostasy on marriage, the *Hidāya* (n.d., 1:221) of al-Marghinani (d. 1197) and *al-Fatāwā al-ʿĀlamgīriyya* (1983, 1:339), the two most frequently used Hanafi texts in the British Indian courts, held that the marriage of a person who commits apostasy is null and void. According to Hanafi doctrine, if both spouses commit apostasy, their marriage is not dissolved. If the husband alone apostatizes, the marriage is dissolved without any judicial procedure. In the case of a wife who commits apostasy, however, Hanafi opinions are divided. The prevailing view *(ẓāhir al-riwāya)*[3] holds that the marriage is immediately dissolved and the woman should be compelled to return to Islam and then to renew her marriage. A rare view *(nādir al-riwāya)*[4] attributed to Abu Hanifa holds that an apostate wife becomes her husband's slave. A third view, held by scholars from Balkh, Samarqand, and Bukhara, argues that the marriage is not dissolved. Significantly, all three views are more concerned with punishment than with the investigation of motives for apostatizing. Even the third view, which recognizes apostasy as a legal device for dissolving a marriage, attempts to discourage use of the device. The first two views allow dissolution of marriage but do not permit the wife to marry anyone other than her previous husband.

Mawlana Thanawi dealt with three aspects of the doctrine in his first fatwa: the legal effect of apostasy on the marriage contract, the punishment for apostasy, and the different punishments for an apostate wife and for a Muslim wife of an apostate husband. The emphasis on punishment (rather than on the wife's intention to dissolve the marriage), reflects the mufti's sensitivity to the criminal aspect of apostasy. In the *Imdād al-Fatāwā,* Mawlana Thanawi generally maintains that apostasy dissolves a marriage contract.

In *al-Ḥīla,* the revised fatwa, Mawlana Thanawi studied and analyzed the Hanafi doctrine in detail. Whereas his first fatwa had been based on the prevailing view, his revised fatwa was based on the third view. Mawlana Thanawi argued that, despite their differences, the three views are unanimous on the point that an apostate wife may not marry any person other than her husband, even in the case in which her marriage is annulled (in which case the annulment would be merely a formality). As mentioned above, annulment was not possible in British India because it required the presence of the Muslim qadis. Hence, circumstances required the adoption of the third view. Whereas in his earlier fatwas Mawlana Thanawi had focused only on the effects of apostasy, in *al-Ḥīla* he was particularly concerned with the problem of how to provide relief to women who wanted to dissolve their marriages. Because Hanafi doctrine did not provide any solution, Mawlana Thanawi recommended the adoption of Maliki grounds for judicial separation. At the same time, he urged Muslims in India to seek reforms in the current laws of personal status and in the Indian judicial system.

Mawlana Thanawi appears to have forgotten that he had changed his mind on the subject between 1913 and 1931, and he expresses sarcasm with regard to those jurists who consider the marriage of an apostate wife to be annulled: "Reading only these sentences [e.g., in *al-Fatāwā al-ʿAlamgīriyya*], some persons have concluded that if a wife apostatizes, the marriage is annulled. Out of ignorance and contrary to all juristic traditions, they infer that the worthless [woman] is permitted to marry another husband after her return to Islam. [This ignorance spread] to the extent that some wretched women took apostasy for an easy solution to get rid of their husbands. As a result, they fell into the worst affliction of apostasy and destroyed their lifelong earnings of pious deeds. As a matter of fact, even legally their objective could not be achieved" (Thanawi 1931:167). This sarcasm may perhaps be explained by Mawlana Thanawi's attempt to provide a semblance of continuity to the change he had initiated. The sarcasm implies that he had never held the view that he criticizes, that his view on the subject has remained the same, and that Islamic law would not endorse a view that is harmful to religion.

The Process of Revision

It is not unusual for a mufti to revise his fatwa. In fact, the adab al-mufti literature (on this genre, see Chapter 1) deals with this phenomenon and advises the mustafti to follow the revised fatwa as soon as it comes to his knowledge. However, the adab texts stipulate that if judicial action on a fatwa has been taken before the mustafti learns of the revised fatwa, there is no need to nullify the action unless the revised fatwa states that the earlier fatwa contradicted a clear legal text—that is, Quran or hadith. On the other hand, if the revised fatwa is based on ijtihad, it does not nullify the first one, because one ijtihad cannot cancel another one (al-Nawawi 1988, 36).

The revision undertaken by Mawlana Thanawi must be viewed against the backdrop of the doctrine of taqlid. Thanawi took great care in revising the first fatwa, appointing a committee of muftis who examined his published fatwas and suggested revisions that were added to later editions under the rubric of *"tarjīḥ al-rājiḥ"* (the preferred view). The rubric indicates that the revision did not represent an ijtihad or a new opinion, but rather the adoption of an already available view that had become preferable under current circumstances. The same method is used in the revised fatwa, in which Mawlana Thanawi refers to three different views, of which he chose one. (In the first fatwa, only one view is cited). Such care was necessary because the majority of Muslims in British India practiced adherence (taqlid) to the Hanafi school, a practice that was reinforced by several factors: the British policy of noninterference in the religious matters of the colonized people; the newly institutionalized role of the muftis, who derived their authority and legitimacy from this doctrine; and the new phenomenon of the publication of fatwa collections that reached a wide public. It was therefore necessary for muftis to be careful to remain within the confines of the school. If revision was necessary, it had to be carried out with the approval of other muftis of the school.

As mentioned, Maliki law allowed more grounds for judicial separation than Hanafi law. Although the adoption of Maliki doctrines might have solved the problem for Muslim women seeking dissolution of their marriage without resorting to apostasy, taqlid did not allow this. In a case that occurred in India earlier in the nineteenth century, the wife of a missing husband was required by Hanafi law to wait at least fifty years before she could apply for judicial dissolution of her marriage. Maliki law, on the other hand, required only a three- to five-year waiting period. Sadruddin Azurda (d. 1868), a Hanafi mufti attached to a British court in Delhi, strongly opposed the adoption of Maliki doctrine in that case and wrote a long fatwa on this point (Bukhari 1990:40).

Taking these difficulties into consideration, Mawlana Thanawi appointed a committee of muftis from Deoband, Saharanpur, Thana Bhawan, and Mecca and asked them to reexamine the proposal of adopting Maliki doctrine. The committee corresponded with Maliki muftis in Medina, taking advantage of the improved means of communication available in the twentieth century. In light of the fatwas received from Medina, the committee drafted its recommendations, which served as the basis of Mawlana Thanawi's revised fatwa, *al-Ḥīla*.

The style of writing employed by Mawlana Thanawi in initiating the process of legal reform is noteworthy. In the preface to the revised fatwa, he invokes the principle of defending Islam, emphasizing that he wrote the book to refute the objection that Islam did not provide relief for women whose husbands had disappeared, were insane, or refused to provide maintenance, and who, therefore, were forced to resort to apostasy to dissolve their marriage. To justify his departure from taqlid, he sought to raise the problem to a higher level. In addition, he used the preface to counter a possible objection to his adoption of non-Hanafi doctrine, explaining that opposition to the adoption of Maliki law was based on the cautious attitude of Indian muftis who did not have access to correct information about the Maliki position. By including the Arabic texts of the fatwas received from the Maliki muftis in Medina, Mawlana Thanawi rectified this situation.

Conclusion

The two fatwas discussed here provide insight into the manner in which the institution of ifta' was used to introduce legal change in Islamic law in British India. In this particular instance, the need for legal change became acceptable to Thanawi (who was a mufti muqallid) when he became convinced of the harmful effects of a certain law on Indian Muslim women. Although far-reaching legal change occurred, it did so in a manner that posited a semblance of continuity with the past and that maintained the framework of Islamic Law. By choosing one of several Hanafi views (and a rare one at that), and by adoping aspects of Maliki legal doctrine, the Hanafi doctrine that apostasy annulls the marriage contract was amended, and the scope of judical divorce was extended. Thanawi emphasized that the reason earlier jurists had not followed such a course of action was that they were uncertain regarding the sources of the relevant legal doctrine, not because such a course of action was opposed to taqlid. The new ruling was justified on the ground that it had been undertaken after extensive research and with due caution.

The study of these two fatwas suggests that legal reform is acceptable in Islamic law—even if it is legislated by a non-Muslim government—if a semblance of continuity with the past is maintained and if it is initiated through the institution of ifta'.

CHAPTER SEVENTEEN

Are Wahhabis Kafirs? Ahmad Riza Khan Barelwi and His *Sword of the Haramayn*

USHA SANYAL

In 1902–1903, Maulana Ahmad Riza Khan Barelwi (1856–1921) wrote a treatise entitled *Al-Muʿtamad al-Mustanad* (The Dependable [Work]), in which he issued the judgment of infidelity *(kufr)* on certain contemporary South Asian Muslim scholars of Islamic law.[1] The first was Mirza Ghulam Ahmad (d. 1908), leader of the Ahmadiyya movement then emerging in Punjab (Lavan 1974; Friedmann 1989); the others were leaders of the Deoband movement, centered at the Dār al-ʿUlūm in Deoband in the North-Western Provinces (Metcalf 1982). In 1906, when Ahmad Riza went to the Haramayn on his second hajj, he submitted his work to some ʿulamaʾ there, requesting from them written testimonials *(taṣdīqāt)* in support of his verdict of kufr. After his return to the subcontinent, his verdict and the testimonials received from the Haramayn were published as a fatwa entitled *Ḥusām al-Ḥaramayn ʿalā Manḥar al-Kufr waʾl Mayn* (The Sword of the Haramayn at the Throat of Kufr and Falsehood).

ʿUlamaʾ Responses to British Rule in the Late Nineteenth Century

Ahmad Riza Khan was born in 1856, a year before the civil and military revolt of 1857 (the Mutiny) which ushered in British rule in India. He was educated in the traditional way, in his hometown of Bareilly, Rohilkhand. His father, Naqi ʿAli Khan (d. 1880), a scholar and local notable *(raʾīs)*, was an important early influence on him. Under his direction, Ahmad Riza studied the standard texts of the *dars-i niẓāmī* syllabus (Sufi 1941) at home. When he was fourteen, his father entrusted to him the task and responsibility of writing fatwas.

Fatwa writing in late nineteenth-century British India occurred in a highly charged political context. Political subjection to a non-Muslim power led the North Indian ʿulamaʾ to question whether India was *dār al-ḥarb* (a land of war) or *dār al-islām* (a land of peace). Recognizing the futility of military rebellion after the failed revolt of 1857, the ʿulamaʾ turned to internal moral reform and religious renewal *(tajdīd)* centered on education. In searching self-examination (sometimes conducted through the medium of fatwas), they sought to examine and remedy the causes for the weakness of the Indian Muslim community vis-à-vis the Hindus and, more important, the non-Muslim Western colonizers.

By the 1880s, when Ahmad Riza was in his early thirties, a number of distinct responses to the colonial situation had been articulated. The Deobandis, the Ahl-i Hadith, the Nadwat al-ʿUlamaʾ, and the Ahmadiyya were among the most important ʿulamaʾ-led movements to emerge in North India in the post-1857 period. Sir Sayyid Ahmad Khan (d. 1898), who sought to incorporate Western scientific thought into a reformed Muslim educational system, led a more westernized style of internal reform than the ʿulamaʾ (Lelyveld 1978). Each group engaged in protracted and sometimes bitter debate with those it opposed.

By the early twentieth century, the ʿulamaʾ controlled well-organized institutional structures for the dissemination of their ideas: madrasas were created by each rival "school"; annual meetings of ʿulamaʾ were organized under the auspices of regional organizations, to be followed up by the publication of the proceedings of the meeting, and sometimes by remedial action. Easy access to printing presses and postal services, which disseminated the ʿulamaʾ's writings across the country, were key to the success of these efforts. Thus by 1900 the Ahl-i Sunnat movement, led by Ahmad Riza Khan, was publishing a journal from Patna, *Tuḥfa-i Ḥanafiyya,* listing donors and reporting newsworthy events. As with other groups of ʿulamaʾ, they supplemented the written word with the oral, holding debates *(munāẓara)* on theological issues that sometimes lasted as long as three days and were attended by large numbers of local people. In these and other ways, each group of ʿulamaʾ created a complex network of influence over a wide geographical area, united by a sense of shared purpose.

The Ahl-i Sunnat Movement and Its Use of the Term "Wahhabi"

The Ahl-i Sunnat movement emerged from early nineteenth-century debates centering on Allah's omnipotence. In the 1820s, a famous debate had taken place in Delhi between Fazl-i Haqq Khairabadi (d. 1862) and Ismaʿil Dihlawi (d. 1831), on whether God could create prophets similar to Muhammad in other orders of existence. By the 1870s, the focus of debate had shifted from Allah's omnipotence to the uniqueness of the Prophet Muhammad. Ahmad Riza's father, Naqi ʿAli Khan, argued that because the Prophet Muhammad was unique, there could never be another prophet like him (an argument that Naqi ʿAli's opponents regarded as a denial of Allah's omnipotence). However, Naqi ʿAli, and likeminded ʿulamaʾ who debated the issue, identified their opponents as "Wahhabis."

Ahmad Riza, sharing his father's intellectual bent of mind, continued the battle against the Wahhabis. Indeed, the bulk of *Ḥusām al-Ḥaramayn* is devoted to condemnation of leading Deobandi ʿulamaʾ for beliefs that are said, in one way or another, to be "Wahhabi." In his view, the Deobandi interpretation of Islam could be traced back to the Arabian Wahhabis (the Muwahhidun), through the intermediacy of Maulanas Sayyid Ahmad Barelwi (d. 1831) and Muhammad Ismaʿil Dihlawi (who, as noted, had been involved in the famous debate with Fazl-i Haqq Khairabadi).

Sayyid Ahmad and Muhammad Ismaʿil had led the early nineteenth-century renewal movement they called the Tariqa-i Muhammadiyah, the order of Muhammad. The basis for their movement, as the name indicates, was the example of the Prophet Muhammad. It was "an activist movement for social and religious reform and revival of the Indian Muslim community" (Pearson 1976:48). As part of their attempt at reform, Sayyid Ahmad and Muhammad Ismaʿil had led an unsuccessful war (jihad) against the Sikh kingdom of Ranjit Singh in the Punjab in the 1820s, in the course of which they had been killed (Ahmad 1975; Pearson 1976).

In Ahmad Riza's view, Muhammad Ismaʿil, whom he scornfully described in *Ḥusām al-Ḥaramayn* as Rashid Ahmad Gangohi's *pīr-i ṭāʾifa* (Sufi master of musicians and dancing girls),[2] was the founder in India of those he called Wahhabi.[3] From his perspective, the Indian Wahhabis had been opposed ever since the emergence of their movement by ʿulamaʾ who thought of themselves as the "Ahl-i Sunnat wa Jamaʿat" (the people of the Prophet's Sunna, and the majority community). The Ahl-i Sunnat had been in existence in India ever since Islam first came to the land. In fact, they "were" true Islam. Ahmad Riza and his followers maintained that other contemporary ʿulamaʾ whose views differed from their own were deviant. In a few cases, as with the ʿulamaʾ whose views Ahmad Riza condemned in *Ḥusām*, he believed the seriousness of their offense called for the charge of apostasy.

The Context for the Writing of *Ḥusām al-Ḥaramayn*

Why did Ahmad Riza choose to renew his charge of *kufr* against Maulana Rashid Ahmad Gangohi and others in 1906? In part, it appears to have been prompted by certain recent writings by these ʿulamaʾ, passages from which he quotes in his fatwa. In part, his decision may also have followed from the situation he encountered after arriving in Mecca that year. In his

Malfūẓāt, there is a remarkably vivid account of how he came to write three fatwas (*Ḥusām al-Ḥaramayn* being one of them) while at the Haramayn.

Briefly, as he recounts it, he learned soon after his arrival that "the Wahhabis had arrived before [me], among them Khalil Ahmad Ambethwi[4] . . . They had obtained access to the ministers of the kingdom, right up to the Sharif. And they had raised the issue of the [Prophet's] knowledge of the unseen [*ʿilm-i ghayb*]" (Ahmad Riza Khan n.d.(b), 2:8). Ahmad Riza passionately believed that the Prophet had knowledge of the unseen, while the Deobandis (and others in India and Arabia) argued that this was not so. Because he found on his arrival at Mecca that a declaration of apostasy *(takfīr)* was imminent (at Khalil Ahmad Ambethwi's instigation, he implies) against an Indian scholar *(ʿālim)* who had argued that the Prophet had such knowledge, Ahmad Riza took it upon himself to convince the *ʿālim* writing the fatwa, other leading ʿulamaʾ, and, ultimately, Sharif ʿAli (r. 1905–1908) as well, that the Indian *ʿālim*'s position was the right one and he should therefore not be called a kafir, or infidel.

The intensity of the debate surrounding this question and Ahmad Riza's success in bringing some Meccan ʿulamaʾ round to his view (as he suggests) appear to have prompted him to seek their confirmation of his earlier *takfīr* in *al-Muʿtamad al-Mustanad.* There, he had charged Khalil Ahmad Ambethwi with *kufr* for his stand on the Prophet's knowledge of the unseen. If sufficient support could be garnered from the Meccan ʿulamaʾ, his position at home would be considerably strengthened on his return.[5]

If such indeed was the context in which *Ḥusām al-Ḥaramayn* was written, perhaps the Meccan ʿulamaʾ for their part found in Ahmad Riza's fatwa a means of winning a round in their own local quarrel with Wahhabi ideas. Although the Wahhabis had had no political control over the Haramayn since their ouster by the Turks in 1818, Wahhabi rulers had held Nejd during most of the nineteenth century. Under ʿAbd al-ʿAziz's (d. 1953) leadership in the early twentieth century, Arabia was united under Wahhabi-Saudi rule (Voll 1982:129–130, 172; Winder 1965:7–8).

However, in 1906 Wahhabi domination of Mecca was far from established: at this time political power in the Haramayn was still uneasily shared between the Ottoman agent and the sharif, both of whom, historically, had been hostile to Wahhabi influence in the region (De Gaury 1951:191–207, 209). The Nejd-based Wahhabis probably did not yet loom over the Meccan ʿulamaʾ as an immediate threat.[6]

Perhaps, therefore, the Meccan ʿulamaʾ's support of Ahmad Riza should not be understood as an expression of direct political interest in the Indian Wahhabis. The explanation may lie more generally in the cosmopolitan intellectual atmosphere of Mecca (Voll 1982:126), where support for differing opinions on Islamic reform could be obtained from one or another *ʿālim,* no matter what the specific situation. At any rate, Ahmad Riza apparently obtained the support of some of the leaders of the local establishment: among the twenty Meccan and thirteen Medinan ʿulamaʾ who certified *Ḥusām al-Ḥaramayn* were muftis of the Shafiʿi, Hanafi, and Maliki schools, as well as teachers (*ustādhs*) at the Haram mosque.[7] Unfortunately, we know little about them personally. One of them, Muhammad Saʿid Babasel, may be the person of the same name identified by Snouck Hurgronje in 1884–85 as the "Amin al-Fetwa (Commissioner for the publication of Fetwas) to the Shaykh al-ʿUlama in his capacity of Mufti of the Shafiʿites. In one of the courses of lectures of the Shaykh al-ʿUlama he acts also as his Muqri [repeater]" (Snouck Hurgronje 1931:185). If this is the same person, he must have been among the most eminent ʿulamaʾ when Ahmad Riza went to Mecca in 1906.[8] Although eminent, none of Ahmad Riza's signers is identified as a qadi; in other words, none appears to have been an appointee of the Ottoman government.[9]

In India, the publication of *Ḥusām al-Ḥaramayn* in 1906 apparently caused the Deobandis great embarrassment, for, as Metcalf writes, "the very name of Wahhabi, whether used legitimately or not, was deeply feared as politically disruptive" (Metcalf 1982:310). Khalil Ahmad Ambethwi, who had been declared a kafir in *Ḥusām,* was obliged to leave the Haramayn within two weeks of his arrival there, so great was the support in Mecca and Medina for Ahmad Riza's opinion. Back in India, the Deobandis wrote fatwas of their own responding to Ahmad Riza "point by point," leading, in effect, to a "*fatwa* war" (Metcalf 1982:310).

Ḥusām al-Ḥaramayn: Rhetoric and Style of Argumentation

Although Ahmad Riza's fatwa is no more than ten pages long, it appears much longer on account of the certifications printed after the fatwa proper. Technically *Ḥusām* is both a fatwa and an istiftaʾ. It is appropriate to call it a fatwa, despite the unusual circumstance that it was initially written as a commentary on a nineteenth-century work, and not generated by a question: The writer's voice is that of a mufti pronouncing judgment on an issue, supported by citations from works of jurisprudence (fiqh), as I examine below. When rewritten in 1906, it also formally became an istiftaʾ because Ahmad Riza himself (now in the role of mustafti) addressed the ʿulamaʾ of the Hijaz in its opening sentences, requesting from them confirmation of the views expressed in his treatise.

The fatwa is constructed in stages. At the outset, Ahmad Riza appeals to the ʿulamaʾ's sympathies and emotions, as in his depiction of the current state of Sunni Islam in India:

> The school [*madhab*] of the Ahl-i Sunnat is a stranger in India. The darkness of dissension [*fitna*] and trial is fearful; wickedness [*sharr*] is in the ascendency; mischief has triumphed and made it difficult to conduct one's work . . . It is incumbent [*wājib*] on [you] to help the religion and humiliate the miscreants, if not by the sword, then at least by the pen. Help us, O you who are God's and the Prophet's army, with your ink! Supply whatever we need in order to repel the enemy. Give our arms strength against this hardship. (*Ḥusām:* 9–10)

Further on, still addressing the Meccan ʿulamaʾ, the tone changes. Repeating his request for a legal opinion, he makes it plain that logic dictates that his is the only possible correct position:

> Tell me clearly whether you think these leaders of heresy are as I have portrayed them in my commentary, and if so, whether the judgment [of *kufr*] that I have passed on them is appropriate, or whether, on the contrary, it is not permissible to call them kafirs, to try to save the people from them, and to cause an aversion among the people to them—even though they deny the fundamentals of the faith [*żarūriyāt-i dīn*], speak ill of Allah, the sustainer of the universe, and His Prophet, the respected and trustworthy, and commit their slanderous talk to print. Some people, in whose hearts faith has not lodged itself, claim that the shariʿa calls upon us to respect them because they are ʿulamaʾ and learned men [*maulawīs*]—even though they are Wahhabis and even though they insult Allah and the Prophet. (*Ḥusām:* 10)

The accusations leveled against the ʿulamaʾ named further on in the text are that they had denied the "fundamentals of the faith" and had insulted Allah and His Prophet. For this, they must be declared kafirs. Not to do so, Ahmad Riza goes on to say, would constitute approval of their *kufr;* the only proper response to such tacit approval is in turn a further declaration of apostasy (*Ḥusām:* 20).

In the body of the fatwa, Ahmad Riza proceeds by first stating the general principle that anyone who professes Islam yet denies even a single one of the "fundamentals of the faith" is definitely a kafir. In the work *Iʿtiqād al-Aḥbāb* . . . he defines the "fundamentals" as beliefs based on clear verses *("nuṣūṣ")* of the Quran, on accepted and widely transmitted *("mashhūr wa-mutawātir")* hadith, and on the consensus *("ijmāʿ")* of the Muslim community (Ahmad Riza Khan n.d.[a]:77–79).[10] One may have no dealings with such a person: praying behind him or her, reading his or her funeral prayer, marrying, eating meat sacrificed by, and sitting with such a person are all forbidden. In this context, Friedmann's comment on an Ahmadi leader's view of non-Ahmadis may well be applied to Ahmad Riza: "Faith is . . . indivisible: even the rejection of one essential article places the person outside the pale" (Friedmann 1989:160). Ahmad Riza asserts that support for this general principle may be found in a variety of fiqh books, which he names.

Ahmad Riza then takes up the writings of various Indian ʿulamaʾ one by one, citing from them passages that he finds objectionable, and giving his reasons for believing that the statements made amount to *kufr.* His tone is decisive, and his opinion is often supported by citations from Quran, hadith, or fiqh. The note of personal contempt for the ʿulamaʾ he names is striking. Occasionally his mockery seems cruel, as when he repeatedly alludes to Maulana Rashid Ahmad Gangohi's blindness. For Ahmad Riza, however, an opponent's physical infirmity appears to have been a metaphor and a sign of God's just punishment for what he believed to be the person's incontrovertible lack of faith.

Ahmad Riza tells the Meccan ʿulamaʾ that the first group he wishes to call to their attention is the "Mirzaʾiyya," followers of Mirza Ghulam Ahmad. He prefers to call them the "Ghulamiyya," a play on the word *ghulām,* literally "slave," though in this context probably better understood as "knave." In his view, Ghulam Ahmad is the Antichrist or *dajjāl,* inspired by Satan.

The second group, Ahmad Riza writes, are the "Wahhabiyya Amthaliyya"—that is, those who believe that there are six or seven prophets like the Prophet Muhammad—and the "Wahhabiyya Khawatimiyya," who believe that apart from Muhammad, there is a "final prophet" *(khātam al-nabiyyīn)* in each of the other levels of the earth. Three ʿulamaʾ are named in this connection, and a passage from *Taḥzīr al-Nās* by Maulana Muhammad Qasim Nanautawi (d. 1879) is cited, to the effect that although the ignorant are under the impression that Muhammad is the last prophet in time, those with discernment know that prophetic superiority *(fażīlat)* is unrelated to being either first or last in time. Ahmad Riza's response to this is that belief in the temporal finality of Muhammad's prophethood is among the "fundamentals" of belief. Consequently, those who belong to this group are "disciples of rebellious Satan" (*Ḥusām:* 14).

The third group of kafirs, according to Ahmad Riza, are those he calls the "Wahhabiyya Kadhdhabiyya," who believe that Allah can lie. The leader of this group is Rashid Ahmad Gangohi, allegedly a follower of Ismaʿil Dihlawi. Ahmad Riza's argument against this group is that if one believes that Allah can lie, one will be inclined even to doubt the first half of the profession of faith, belief in which is essential for a Muslim.

Ahmad Riza's fourth group, which he calls the "Wahhabiyya Shaytaniyya," are explicitly described as followers of Satan. Led once again by Rashid Ahmad Gangohi, this group, he says, holds that Satan's (Iblīs's) knowledge is greater than that of the Prophet Muhammad, and that Muhammad's knowledge of the unseen (*ʿilm-i ghayb*) was only partial. In his fatwa, Ahmad Riza focuses on specific passages in *Barāhīn-i Qāṭiʿiyya,* by Khalil Ahmad Ambethwi (in fact by Rashid Ahmad Gangohi, alleges Ahmad Riza), and a pamphlet he does not name (the reference here is to *Ḥifẓ al-Īmān*) by Maulana Ashraf ʿAli Thanawi (d. 1943).

Throughout the fatwa, Ahmad Riza's argument that the ʿulamaʾ mentioned are kafirs is based on a combination of citation of authoritative texts and logical reasoning of his own. The sources cited are mainly Quran, fiqh works, and fatwa collections. In the first part of the fatwa, sources are mentioned very briefly, without complete references. Thus, at the very beginning of the fatwa, Hanafi works of fiqh and fatwa collections are enumerated (though not quoted) in defense of the general statement that any Muslim who denies even one of the "fundamentals of the faith" is a kafir, and that anyone who doubts the *kufr* of such a person is also a kafir. Among the texts he cites are: al-Marghinani's (d. 1196) *al-Hidāya,* Mulla Khusraw's (d. 1480) *Ghurar al-Aḥkām,* Ibrahim al-Halabi's (d. 1549) *Mulṭaqa al-Abḥur,* al-Haskafi's (d. 1677) *al-Durr al-Mukhtār,* Shaykhzade's (d. 1667) *Majmaʿ al-Anhur, Fatāwā-i ʿAlamgīrī,* compiled in 1664–1672, and others. In the same nonspecific manner, Ahmad Riza illustrates his description of the sorry state of Sunni Islam in India by citing a hadith on the authority of Abu Bakr: a day will come when things will be so bad that a person who was a Muslim in the morning will be a kafir in the evening, while one who was a Muslim in the evening will be a kafir the next morning. No chain of oral transmitters or source is given for this hadith—it is merely a way of bringing home to the Meccan ʿulamaʾ the extent of moral decay *(fitna)* among the Indian ʿulamaʾ.

Ahmad Riza is more specific in his discussion of the Prophet's knowledge, particularly on the *ʿilm-i ghayb* issue. He defends his argument that the Prophet had greater knowledge than Satan by quoting from *Nasīm al-Riyāḍ* by al-Khafaji (d. 1659) as follows:

> Whoever says that someone else's knowledge is greater than that of the Prophet, surely disparages him and diminishes his glory. Thus he insults him. The judgment on him will be the same as the judgment on one who insults the Prophet. There is no real difference [between them]. We make no exception in any circumstances. There has been consensus on all these judgments *(aḥkām)* from the time of the Companions to the present. (*Ḥusām:* 16)

Similarly, on the question of the Prophet's knowledge of the unseen, Ahmad Riza maintains that there is no basis for accepting the hadith in which the Prophet is reported to have said, "I do not know what lies behind this wall." Ahmad Riza argues, contrary to Rashid Ahmad Gangohi's assertion that ʿAbd al-Haqq Muhaddith Dihlawi (d. 1642) had accepted this hadith, that in fact he had dismissed it as "baseless." He also cites Shihabuddin Ahmad b. Hajar Makki's (d. 1565/66) *Afżal al-Qurā,* in which this hadith is said to have no recognizable chain of transmission (*Ḥusām:* 17).

Rebutting Ashraf ʿAli Thanawi, who had also questioned the extent of the Prophet's knowledge of the unseen, Ahmad Riza cites the Quran (72: 25, 26): "(He is) the Knower of the Unseen, and He revealeth unto none His secret, Save unto every messenger whom He hath chosen . . ." (Pickthall trans.). As Ahmad Riza argues at length in another fatwa, *Dawlat al-Makkiyya* (one of the other two written on this occasion), Allah, who alone possesses complete intrinsic knowledge of the unseen, awarded the Prophet Muhammad, inter alia, knowledge of past and present, of other worlds, and of the five hidden things mentioned in Sura 31, verse 34.[11]

To sum up Ahmad Riza's use of sources in *Ḥusām,* they consist for the most part of handbooks of Hanafi law, and commentaries thereon. Some of these were authoritative in Egypt and the Ottoman Empire. Others, such as the *Hidāya* and *Fatāwā-i ʿAlamgīrī,* were standard texts in India. Most of the works were sixteenth- or seventeenth-century texts, though the *Hidāya,* written in the twelfth century, is older. Only one work *(Nasīm al-Riyāḍ)* is directly quoted in the fatwa. For the rest, Ahmad Riza simply states as a fact that his opinion is supported by the books he cites. The Quran is quoted mainly in relation to discussion of the Prophet's knowledge of the unseen; in this connection Ahmad Riza also refers to and rejects a hadith that contradicts his position.

The argument in *Ḥusām* is also based on the use of logic, presented in such a way that the opponent's position appears untenable. In the following passage, Ahmad Riza argues that although Rashid Ahmad Gangohi considers it *shirk* (associating a partner with Allah) to believe that the Prophet had vast knowledge, he himself is guilty of the worst kind of *shirk,* because he makes Satan Allah's partner:

> When it comes to Iblis, he believes that he has comprehensive knowledge of the world [*zamīn ke ʿilm-i muḥīṭ*] but when it comes to the Prophet of Allah, he says it is *shirk,* although *shirk* is that by which a partner is assigned to Allah. So when it is established that a certain thing in the world is *shirk,* then everything else in the whole world [that conforms to the same principle] will definitely be *shirk.* There can be no partner to Allah. See then how he [Rashid Ahmad Gangohi] has faith in the partnership of the cursed Iblis with Allah. Partnership is rejected [*muntafin*] for Muhammad. See the dense black cloud of Allah's anger in his eyes [viz., Gangohi's blindness]. But see: he asks for a clear verse of the Quran in proof of Muhammad's knowledge, and isn't content with anything less than a decisive Quranic text [*naṣṣ qaṭiʿ*]. And when it comes to denying the Prophet's knowledge, then . . . he grabs hold of a false hadith [*bāṭil riwāyat*] which has absolutely no basis in the faith. (*Ḥusām:* 16–17)

Ahmad Riza's argument, therefore, is that Rashid Ahmad is willing to accept weak proofs supporting Satan's knowledge, where even strong proofs of Muhammad's knowledge are unacceptable. Furthermore, if it is *shirk* to believe that Muhammad had knowledge of everything in this world, it follows logically that belief in the vastness of Satan's knowledge is also *shirk*.

Elsewhere, Ahmad Riza uses logic to reduce his opponent's position to one of absurdity. Referring to Ashraf ʿAli Thanawi's question as to whether the Prophet Muhammad had partial or total knowledge of the unseen, he argues that the logic of this question must lead one to ask the same question about Allah. However, this is not merely absurd but an act of apostasy by consensus of the community of Muslims (*Ḥusām:* 19–20).

Conclusion

Ahmad Riza's *Sword of the Haramayn* hints by its very title at the strength of the sentiment that motivated its writing. Ahmad Riza believed passionately that worship of Allah was inseparable from love of the Prophet. Such love carried its own special responsibilities: for him as an *ʿālim,* it imposed the duty of writing fatwas against what he saw as the denigration of the Prophet by other Indian ʿulamaʾ. Feeling strongly as he did that certain ʿulamaʾ had gone beyond the pale in their writings, he saw it as his duty as an *ʿālim* to declare them to be kafirs. Thus, his love of the Prophet led directly to the intellectual activism represented by *Ḥusām.*

Ahmad Riza's love of the Prophet also led him to define what it was to be Muslim in ways quite different from those he accused of *kufr.* Some tenets of faith, such as belief in the finality of Muhammad's prophethood and in his superiority over other prophets, were in no way denied by the ʿulamaʾ concerned, Ahmad Riza's assertions to the contrary notwithstanding. On other matters, however, such as belief that Muhammad had knowledge of the unseen, the Deobandi ʿulamaʾ's position was genuinely at odds with that of Ahmad Riza. Viewing their stand on this and other issues as "denigration" of the Prophet, he considered this a clear sign that they had fallen prey to Satan's wiles and had therefore become unbelievers. In his perspective, then, two distinct, opposed groups had emerged: the Wahhabis, followers of Satan and thus kafirs; and the Ahl-i Sunnat wa Jamaʿat, followers of Allah and His Prophet and thus true believers.

CHAPTER EIGHTEEN

The Lions of Qasr al-Nil Bridge: The Islamic Prohibition of Images as an Issue in the ʿUrabi Revolt

RUDOLPH PETERS

Al-Fatāwā al-Mahdiyya fīʾl-Waqāʾiʿ al-Miṣriyya, a collection of some 13,500 fatwas issued by Grand Mufti Muhammad al-ʿAbbasi al-Mahdi of Egypt (d. 1897), contains only three fatwas whose political implications are more or less evident.[1] Here I will present one of them. Although the fatwa seems to deal with a purely religious question—namely, the obligation to remove images of human beings and animals—the underlying issue was highly political. The fatwa was given on August 31, 1882, at the request of the ʿUrabi government, during the last turbulent weeks after the attempted deposition of the Khedive and before the government's surrender to the British.

The author of this text, Muhammad al-ʿAbbasi al-Mahdi,[2] was born in the year 1827, a son of Muhammad Amin al-Mahdi (d. 1831–1832),[3] for some time the Hanafi mufti during Mehmed ʿAli's reign. In October 1848 Ibrahim Pasha appointed al-ʿAbbasi the Hanafi chief mufti *(muftīʾl-sāda al-Ḥanafiyya)*, an office he was to hold for almost half a century, until his death in 1897. Because he was only twenty-one years old at the time of his nomination, his professor of Hanafi law, Khalil al-Rashidi, was appointed head of the fatwa department *(amīn al-fatwā)* to assist him in his new office.

From the time of the Ottoman conquest of Egypt (1517), Hanafi law was applied exclusively in the law courts, and the Hanafi chief mufti was the highest ranking mufti in the country. During al-ʿAbbasi's tenure in office, this Hanafi supremacy over the other chief muftis was emphasized by the use of the new title, *muftī al-diyār al-Miṣriyya* (mufti of the Egyptian lands), or simply headmufti *(bāshmuftī)*. The primary task of the Hanafi chief mufti was to serve as a mufti at the Grand Shariʿa Court in Cairo (Mahkamat al-Qahira al-Kubra), but in the nineteenth century he also had other functions. *Al-Fatāwā al-Mahdiyya* indicates that one of the grand mufti's tasks was to attend the Khedival Council (al-Diwan al-ʿAli) in order to give advice on complicated legal questions.[4] Together with the chief muftis of the other law schools (madhhabs), the rector of the Azhar University (Shaykh al-Azhar), the dean of the descendants of the Prophet (*naqīb al-ashrāf*), and occasionally other ʿulama, the grand mufti was part of the Council of Scholars (al-Majlis al-ʿIlmi) of Cairo, which was consulted by the rulers in important religious matters (Lane 1966:121–122).

Occasionally he would be asked for an authoritative fatwa to settle controversies among jurists[5] or to deal with complaints about the misapplication of the shariʿa by qadis.[6] A decree of 1873 regulating the duties and competence of the official (and therefore Hanafi) muftis gave the grand mufti and the Alexandrian mufti unrestricted authority to issue fatwas to both the general public and government agencies, unlike other appointed muftis, who were allowed to give fatwas only in connection with the agency or court to which they were appointed.[7]

The grand mufti's power was greatly increased by the Shariʿa Courts Ordinance (La'ihat al-Mahakim al-Sharʿiyya) of 1880 (text in Jallad 1890–1895,4:145–156), which granted him the authority under certain circumstances to give binding decisions. If there was a complaint about the misapplication of the shariʿa, the matter would be investigated and decided by the Grand Shariʿa Court in Cairo. However, if there were misgivings or complaints about the decision in appeal, the case would be submitted to the grand mufti, whose fatwa would be binding. The grand mufti could also give binding fatwas in appeal from judgments of the Grand Shariʿa Court in Cairo or the Shariʿa Court in Alexandria, acting as courts of first instance (Art. 3).

Another similar procedure, which apparently had already existed for some time,[8] was formalized in Art. 22 of this ordinance: whenever a qadi was in doubt about a legal issue of a case brought before him, he first had to consult the mufti officially appointed to his court or to the district. If the qadi and the mufti could not agree on the issue, or if the mufti himself did not know the correct answer, the matter would be laid before the grand mufti, whose decision would be binding. This would also be the case if the Grand Shariʿa Court of Cairo was uncertain about a point of law in a lawsuit and consulted the grand mufti.

The result of these provisions and practices was that the function of grand mufti began to bear resemblance to the Courts of Cassation known, for example, in French or Dutch law, whose task it is to ensure the correct application of the law and who, just like the grand mufti, decide the purely legal issues and do not examine the facts as established by the lower courts. That the grand mufti did not deal with issues of fact is clear from the formula frequently to be found in his fatwas: "If the situation is as mentioned [in the question]."

Al-ʿAbbasi's biographers mention that he twice fell foul of the Khedive: once when ʿAbbas wanted to confiscate all properties of the descendants of Mehmed ʿAli (r. 1805–1848), and another time when Ismaʿil (r. 1863–1879), acting as prince-regent for Saʿid (r. 1854–1863), wanted to assimilate the family endowments *(waqf ahlī)* to public endowments *(waqf khayrī),* to gain control over them. Due to al-ʿAbbasi's opposition, nothing came of these plans. However, these must have been exceptional incidents, for his relationship with the ruling house was generally very close. This is borne out by the fact that in January 1871 Ismaʿil appointed him shaykh al-Azhar, a post usually occupied by a Shafiʿi. The reason seems to have been that Ismaʿil wanted to introduce reforms and regarded al-ʿAbbasi as the most suitable person for carrying out this task. He was not disappointed: six months later (16 Rabiʿ I 1288 [July 15, 1871]) he issued a decree, prepared by al-ʿAbbasi, introducing, among other things, the requirement that students must pass a final examination before being admitted to the ranks of the ʿulamaʾ. At the same time, al-ʿAbbasi succeeded in improving the allowances and pensions of the ʿulamaʾ at al-Azhar, no doubt in exchange for the acceptance of his reforms.

The test of al-ʿAbbasi's loyalty to the ruling house came with the ʿUrabi revolt in 1881, when he was attacked by ʿulamaʾ and Azhar students who supported the ʿUrabi movement. These people suspected him of preparing a fatwa advising that the ʿUrabi revolt was a rebellion against a legitimate government and that the rebels deserved to be put to death. The students and ʿulamaʾ of al-Azhar campaigned for his dismissal as shaykh al-Azhar, primarily on the ground that he was too outspoken in his support for the Khedive. They also wanted a candidate who was not a Hanafi, the madhhab of the ruling Turco-Circassian class against whom the ʿUrabi revolt was directed, whereas the majority of Egyptians belonged to either the Shafiʿi or the Maliki madhhab. The candidate put forward by the opposition, the Maliki chief mufti Muhammad ʿIllaysh (1802–1882),[9] was unacceptable to the government. Eighty years old, he was nevertheless an ardent and militant follower of ʿUrabi. As a compromise, the Shafiʿi scholar Muhammad al-Inbabi (1824–1896) was appointed to the office after al-ʿAbbasi's dismissal on December 5, 1881. But to attain a certain equilibrium, a council consisting of both al-ʿAbbasi and ʿIllaysh was created to assist the shaykh al-Azhar. Al-ʿAbbasi remained grand mufti (Schölch 1973:170–171; Delanoue 1982:136–137) and loyal to the Khedive. When a number of prominent Azhar ʿulamaʾ issued a fatwa advising that Tawfiq had to be deposed for disobeying the Ottoman sultan and allowing the British to take possession of the country (Engl. trans. in Broadley 1980: 175–178), al-ʿAbbasi refused to sign (Schölch 1973:350, n. 119).

The fatwa presented here is situated in the context of the ʿUrabi revolt. It is dated 16 Shawwal 1299 (August 31, 1882), two weeks before ʿUrabi's final defeat. British troops had already invaded Egypt and were advancing through the Delta, but had not yet taken Cairo. Because his supporters were motivated by Islamic religious fervor (Peters 1979:75–84), ʿUrabi apparently wanted to make a public gesture showing his Islamic zeal. This gesture took the form of an an attack on some statues that had been placed in Cairo about a decade earlier. It was a cleverly chosen move. The erection of the statue of Ibrahim Pasha in 1872 had created popular disaffection (Ebeling 1878, as quoted in Beyer 1983:262). The demolition of this and other statues was a symbolic act that carried both religious and political implications. To show that the destruction of these statues was warranted and even required by the shariʿa, and that the different madhhabs were in agreement about this issue, ʿUrabi, through the mediation of the shaykh al-Azhar, asked for fatwas based on the four madhhabs. Following is the fatwa given by the grand mufti according to Hanafi law.

Question sent to our part in a missive from the Reverend Shaykh Muhammad al-Inbabi,[10] holder of the Rectorat of the Azhar University [*mashyakhat al-Jāmiʿ al-Azhar*], with the following text:

"We have received a missive from His Excellency the Undersecretary of State for the Army [*Saʿādat Wakīl al-Jihādiyya*][11] to the effect that His Excellency the Secretary of State for the Army and the Navy [*Saʿādat al-Bāshā Nāẓir al-Jihādiyya wa'l-Baḥriyya* (Ahmad ʿUrabi)] has ordered in a telegram, which the Undersecretary of State received from him, to deal with the question of destroying and burning the idol erected in al-Azbakiyya near the minaret of the Azbakiyya Mosque,[12] as well as the question of cutting the heads of the images situated at both ends of the Qasr al-Nil Bridge,[13] and to give His Excellency the required notification that the aforementioned idol will be annihilated, so that he may be assured that the religious duties protecting the order and the hearts of the community [*umma*] are observed, for the religion of Islam forbids us to erect idols such as the ones that the Companions of the Prophet destroyed when they entered Mecca the Honorable, so as to comply with the obligations of the Religion. In the same telegram it is emphasized that no misfortunes befell our country until after the erecting of idols in Cairo and Alexandria, and it is requested that clear information be given about what the texts of the sublime shariʿa require in this matter, so that measures can be taken accordingly, etc. Because His Excellency is to be informed about the legal rules in this matter according to all law schools, it is necessary to write this missive to Your Worship [*siyādatuka*] so that you may give information on the pertinent rules according to the madhhab of the Greatest Imam [viz., Abu Hanifa].

We hope that you can give this information promptly, because at the same date we also received a request to expedite the matter."

Answer: God be praised. Our scholars have clearly stated that the acquisition of a large image of a being with a soul, which is visible to a spectator without having to look attentively, and which is in possession of all parts of the body that are indispensable for it to live, is reprehensible to the degree that it is almost forbidden [*makrūh taḥrīman*].[14] Therefore, it is legally obligatory to remove such images. The *Radd al-Muḥtār ʿalā al-Durr* [*al-Mukhtār*][15] says: "In the Supercommentary [*Ḥāshiya*] by Abu al-Suʿud[16] it is related on the authority of the *Khulāṣa*[17] that [its author] held it permissible to remove [such] an image for whomever sees it in somebody else's house. [In fact,] it ought to be his obligation. If one hires a person who produces [such] images, the latter is not entitled to wages, since his work is sinful. This has been related on the authority of Muhammad [al-Shaybani].[18] If someone destroys a house that contains [such] pictures, he is liable for the value of the house but not for the value of the pictures." From this one learns the rule regarding the removal of the aforementioned idol and the decapitation of the images [*ṣuwar*] located at both ends of the Qasr al-Nil Bridge. The Exalted God knows best.

Supplement to the Aforementioned Answer: The rulers of the Muslims must remove everything in their countries that is objectionable [*munkar*], such as practicing usury [*ribā*], the opening of places known as brothels [*karākhānāt*] and bars [*khammārāt*], and other offences [*mūbiqāt*]. [They also must] prevent God's servants from suffering wrongs contrary to the shariʿa and forbid injustice and [the application of] rules other than those revealed by God. This is more urgent.[19]

In ʿUrabi's formulation of the question, he underlines the religious aspect by referring to the equestrian statue as an idol *(ṣanam),* a term associated with the Jahiliyya period, and by mentioning the removal of idols by Muhammad's Companions after the conquest of Mecca in 630. Further, he attributes the "misfortunes" that had befallen Egypt to the erection of these statues. Although he does not specify these misfortunes, he was in all likelihood referring to the increasing foreign control over Egypt's government and finance, especially after Egypt's bankruptcy and the institution of the Anglo-French dual control in 1876. He seems to imply that this state of affairs should be regarded as God's punishment for religious neglect in tolerating these statues (and other manifestations of Western behavior).

The classical law books give two grounds for the prohibition of images: that their makers try to copy God's creation *(muḍāhāt al-khalq)* and that they thereby imitate the unbelievers *(al-tashabbuh bi'l-kuffār)* (Snouck Hurgronje 1923, 2:453). The latter ground, which provides the link between religion and politics, is highly relevant in the present context, because the erection of these statues had been part of Cairo's Western-inspired modernization.

The attack on the statues also had political implications, perhaps less obvious, but nonetheless present. The call for demolition of the statues was a political stance, first and foremost against European influence in Egypt, and, second, against the ruling house, which, among other things, was responsible for the increasing foreign presence in, and control over, Egypt. It is no coincidence that the statues in question were located in the "European" parts of Cairo: the equestrian statue in the Azbakiyya quarter, which, during the second half of the nineteenth century, was the location of consulates, foreign commercial establishments, hotels, and bars; and the lions of the Qasr al-Nil Bridge at the fringe of Ismaʿiliyya, a Western-style quarter designed and partly constructed by Ismaʿil on the model of Haussmann's Paris.[20] Because these statues were erected by Ismaʿil, ʿUrabi's action also implied criticism of the Khedival dynasty. This was obvious, because one of the statues under attack represented Ibrahim Pasha, the son of the founder of the dynasty, Mehmed ʿAli, and the father and grandfather, respectively, of ʿUrabi's adversaries, the Khedives Ismaʿil and Tawfiq (r. 1879–1892).

The grand mufti's response to the question is rather brief. It consists of the general rule with regard to images, a quotation from the *Radd al-Muḥtār* by Ibn ʿAbidin, a standard nineteenth-century Hanafi text, and a final sentence, connecting the first part of the answer to the actual issue. Although the wording of the fatwa is clear, the last sentence is not a very articulate and forceful statement, leaving the reader to draw his own conclusions. This suggests that the grand mufti may have been reluctant to issue this fatwa. He must have been in a quandary. From the legal point of view, he could not but endorse the actions envisaged in ʿUrabi's question, but politically he was loyal to the Khedive and ʿUrabi's adversary. Therefore, he did not want to lend him any ideological support.

It is significant that the fatwa is signed only by the grand mufti. In the *Fatāwā Mahdiyya,* we find several fatwas endorsed by other religious scholars: apart from the grand mufti, usually the shaykh al-Azhar (during the period that al-ʿAbbasi did not hold this position), the head of the fatwa department *(amīn al-fatwā),* and other high ranking ʿulamaʾ, not necessarily all Hanafis. These fatwas usually deal with such important matters as controversies between religious scholars or political issues, as in the aforementioned fatwa against the Sudanese Mahdi. Some were issued at the request of the highest conciliar body of state, al-Majlis al-Khususi. The topic of the fatwa under discussion here, the provenance of the question, and the circumstances under which the fatwa was requested, would certainly call for such special treatment. That the grand mufti chose to issue this fatwa separately is, I believe, indicative of his isolated political position. At the same time, it gave him the opportunity to add the supplement, which makes the fatwa unique. As a rule, a fatwa deals only with the issue expounded in the question addressed to the mufti, without digressions to other related topics. None of the fatwas contained in the *Fatāwā Mahdiyya* is followed by such a supplement. In this case, however, the grand mufti must have felt that he could not confine himself to the legal aspects of the issue and that he had to make it known where he stood politically. The grand mufti did not want ʿUrabi to increase his legitimacy by posing as a Muslim ruler faithfully carrying out the commands of Islam. He therefore pointed to a number of political and social phenomena connected with the foreign presence in Egypt that were contrary to the prescriptions of Islam, implying that ʿUrabi had in fact been slack in enforcing the religious commands and did not deserve to be regarded as a defender of Islam, his attack on the statues notwithstanding.

PART FOUR

The Modern Period

C H A P T E R   N I N E T E E N

An Argument about How to Argue

WILLIAM R. ROFF

On the face of it, the argument in the case to be discussed was simply about the permissibility, for Muslims, of keeping dogs. But the istifta' that sprang from the argument sought to clarify more than one kind of issue: not just the relatively straightforward question of what fiqh says about dogs, but, underlying this, the more complex one of how that discovery itself ought properly to be made. The case is a good example of the powerful hermeneutic and heuristic impulses that reside within the Islamic juristic tradition and are made manifest in the process of seeking and obtaining fatwas.

The request for the fatwa, directed to the Lajnat al-Fatawa of al-Azhar University, came from Kelantan, Malaysia, in the mid-1930s, as a result of a dispute between the reigning sultan's daughter, Tengku Maharani, and her brother, Raja Ibrahim, the heir apparent to the throne, who kept in his household a large Dalmatian dog. Tengku Maharani objected, holding that dogs, and in particular the secretions of dogs, notably saliva, were defiling, according to the shariʿa. Ibrahim sought an opinion in the matter from a young *ʿālim* newly returned from Mecca, Nik Abdullah b. Wan Musa, son of an ex-mufti of the state. Abdullah found in favor of Ibrahim, but his opinion was strenuously contested by other ʿulamaʾ, and eventually, after some two years of argument, a public disputation, or *majlis muzakara,* was arranged to debate the issue.

The *majlis muzakara,* which took place in the audience hall of one of the royal palaces, in the presence of the sultan, in January 1937, was attended by more than two thousand people—at that time the largest assemblage ever held in the state—and it provided the occasion for a disputation engaged in by claimants to several different kinds of authority. On the side of Ibrahim, dogs, and a view of interpretation not confined to adherence to a single *madzhab* (madhhab), were the ex-mufti Haji Wan Musa (father of Nik Abdullah, who had died in the interim) and two independent and modernist ʿulamaʾ from Singapore. On the side of Tengku Maharani, a view of dogs as polluting, and a strict mode of interpretation based on rigid adherence to a single *madzhab,* were the current state mufti and chief qadi, and two members of the ʿUlamaʾ Committee of an institution known as the Majlis Agama Islam, or Islamic Religious Council.[1]

Though the debate that ensued was certainly about dog saliva, it was quite plainly about a good deal else as well—in particular, the increasingly vexed question of how, in a changing world, one should derive one's authority for proper Islamic behavior. A little background is necessary. Kelantan, like a great many other Muslim states in the 1930s, was caught up in processes of change not of its own choosing or direction, as colonial rule and the commercialization of agriculture, and their attendant political, social, and economic transformations, impinged increasingly on public life and customary ways. The northeastern Malay states were often seen and spoken of by outsiders as isolated and remote, cut off from the rest of the world as a result of the absence of modern communications systems. So no doubt they were, when considered in terms of Britain or even the west coast of Malaysia. But these states also existed in quite another context, that of the larger Muslim world, in which they participated actively in a countless variety of ways. Kelantanese in some numbers regularly made the hajj to Mecca, and a significant proportion remained there to study for lengthy periods (all the protagonists in the fatwa debate had done so). Kelantanese ʿulamaʾ taught in the holy cities of Mecca and Medina, and also in Patani (southern Siam), Cambodia, Sumatra, and other parts of Southeast Asia, as well as in their own state, where Islamic boarding schools (*pondoks*) flourished, to which scholars from Arabia and India came to teach. Far from being isolated, the Kelantan delta and its people formed part of a complex international network of Islamic learning and exchange.

At the same time, the circumstances of British colonial rule—Kelantan had been a "protected" state, with a British adviser, since 1903—meant that Western systems of authority and administration had been implanted alongside, and were increasingly usurping, traditional Malay political and juridical institutions. This infringement did not go altogether uncontested, though Kelantanese ruling groups—the sultanate establishment, the Malay nobility associated with it, and leading ʿulamaʾ—were in no strong position to counter British influence, despite a treaty obligation that, nominally, limited that influence to the giving of "advice." Under the treaty, however, an important exclusion from this right to give "advice that had to be accepted" stipulated that there should be no interference in matters of "Malay religion and custom." In Kelantan, in consequence, as in the other peninsular states,

"Islam" became an important focus for the expression of residual Malay authority, primarily through institutions associated with the sultan as the defender of the faith.

The most important such institution was the Majlis Agama Islam, established by an enactment of the State Council (both were new, British-inspired instruments) in 1916, at the instance of a small group of the sultan's Malay ministers, officials, and leading ʿulamaʾ. The Majlis Agama was charged with the responsibility to "guard, advise, give fatwas concerning, originate, strengthen, implement, develop, and administer all matters relating to the practice and performance of the Muslim religion and Islamic law, for the benefit of the state and its people." This far-reaching brief was exercised in a great variety of increasingly centralized ways that need not detain us here, but which together made the Majlis, and those who exercised its powers of coercion and patronage, the sole arbiter of all matters Islamic in the state—as well as, in certain respects, a progressive force for social change.[2]

The establishment of the Majlis, and the putting of all Islamic authority into the hands of a central committee composed of five prominent ʿulamaʾ and seven non-ʿulamaʾ, appointed by the sultan on the advice of his senior ministers, was not greeted with universal enthusiasm. Notably absent from the Majlis was the state mufti, who had had differences with the sultan; many of his powers were now assumed by the new body. Other differences soon became apparent, reflecting the *ikhtilāf* (disagreement) often remarked on as part of God's mercy for mankind but less often accepted with equanimity by constituted authority. Under an early *notis* promulgated by the Majlis in 1917 (like enactments, notices were a new form of juridical instrument in Kelantan), all persons wishing to teach Sufi doctrines of any sort were required to obtain written authority from the Majlis—a measure framed in response to the presence in Kelantan, under the auspices of Haji Wan Musa among others, of an Ahmadiyya-Idrisiyya shaykh, Abu Hasan Azhari, who had arrived from Mecca some years earlier and was now expelled from the state.

The teachings of another arrival in Kelantan at this time also became controversial, though initially less in conflict with the Majlis Agama's authority. Abu ʿAbdullah Saʿid Hasan b. Nur Hasan b. ʿUmar al-Tukki al-Ghilazi, better known in Kelantan as Tok Khorasani, was a specialist in hadith literature who had attended the Dar al-ʿUlum, Deoband, in India, where he had studied the works of Shah Waliullah of Delhi. It appears to have been from Waliullah that the decisive characteristics of Tok Khorasani's own teachings sprang, emphasizing especially the controlling role of hadith in the interpretation and selective juridical employment of the compendious rulings of the four principle *madzhab*s. Though it was a matter of historical accident that the Shafiʿi school had come to prevail in Malaysia (as elsewhere in Southeast Asia), the principle of taqlid (unquestioned adherence) to Shafi'i doctrine was deeply entrenched in Malay society. Tok Khorasani's hadith teachings were therefore potentially in conflict with accepted practice. Among his many pupils was Nik Abdullah bin Haji Wan Musa, who later studied in Mecca with another Deobandi, 'Ubaydallah al-Sindhi, and then returned to Kelantan to give what was apparently the first opinion on the dog saliva question.[3]

As early as 1917, the Majlis Agama had issued a *notis* forbidding the issuing of any fatwa without prior approval from the Majlis, and shortly afterward it established a Meshuarat 'Ulama', or 'Ulama' Committee, to assume the Majlis' responsibility for issuing or approving all fatwas. Neither Nik Abdullah's opinion on the keeping of dogs nor his father Haji Wan Musa's related opinion on *talfīq* (the combining of doctrines from different *madzhabs*) is described contemporaneously as constituting a fatwa, perhaps for this reason. Though the Majlis's right to control all fatwas in the state was certainly objected to, it seems to have been generally observed. Along with the likely outcome of any referral to the 'Ulama' Committee (even though Raja Ibrahim was at the time committee president), this probably played a major part in Ibrahim's subsequent decision, following the *muzakara,* to seek a fatwa from al-Azhar.

At the *muzakara* itself, those "in favor of dogs" were by background and career somewhat modernist in interpretative tendency, though in varying ways. Wan Musa, in Mecca at the turn of the century, had become a member of the Ahmadiyya-Idrisiyya *ṭarīqa* (Sufi order) noted for its "Wahhabi" and irenic beliefs, and had then become closely associated with the synthesizing ideas of Waliullah, through Tok Khorasani and his own son. Abbas Taha, born in Singapore but educated as a young man in Mecca at much the same time as Wan Musa, returned to Singapore to pursue a career as a polemicist and an editor of reformist journals under the influence of the *al-Manār* circle in Cairo. Burhanuddin al-Hilmi, much younger, had been educated at a modernist madrasa in Penang before attending the Isma'iliyya Medical College in Delhi and Aligarh Muslim University.

On the other side were four men whose background and training were not markedly different. Ibrahim bin Haji Yusoff, the mufti, was a year younger than Wan Musa, and, like him, had been taken to Mecca as a boy. There they had had many of the same teachers, and Ibrahim was probably a member of the same *ṭarīqa.* Ahmad b. Haji Isma'il, the chief qadi, son of a well-known Kelantan *'ālim,* was born in Mecca in 1905, returned to Kelantan at age eleven to spend five years with local teachers, and then studied fiqh at al-Azhar for three years. Back in Kelantan from 1931, he was successively inspector of education for the Majlis and editor of their journal, before becoming chief qadi in 1935. The two members of the

Majlis's 'Ulama' Committee, Ahmad b. 'Abdul Manan and 'Abdullah Tahir, after long periods in Mecca, had returned to Kelantan to establish *pondok* schools.

Because our primary source of information about the *muzakara* is the lengthy compendium of textual materials published contemporaneously by 'Abbas b. Muhammad Taha, we know most about the "pro-dog" side of the debate. It was argued first that, Islam being not a restrictive *(ḥarāja)* faith but a facilitative *(yasāra)* one, and one moreover divinely blessed by disagreement *(ikhtilāf)* within the community (as stated by the Prophet in a hadith attested to by Ibn Hajar), it is incumbent on all conforming members of the faith *("ahl al-sunna wa'l-jama'at")* to employ reason *('aql)* in order to know and understand the shari'a. And just as al-Sha'rani, in his *Mīzān*, says that Imam Shafi'i himself held that where there exist both a strong opinion and a weaker opinion, one is free to choose between them, so may one follow one *madzhab* in certain circumstances and another *madzhab* in other circumstances. Though there are differences between *madzhab*s regarding the kinds of impurity *(najis)* and the necessity of their riddance by ablution before prayer, notably in the present instance with respect to dogs, one may, if circumstances require, follow Imam Malik in the matter in preference to Imam Shafi'i, by employing the principle of *talfīq* within taqlid.

In the absence of a similar contemporary source for the other side (beyond a restatement of Shafi'i on dogs), it is less easy to know with exactitude what the views of the "anti-dog" group were. It appears, however, that they relied principally on three contentions: that the "constitution" of the state of Kelantan required adherence to the Shafi'i school, most particularly for those in the service of the state; that the concept of *talfīq* had to be opposed, because all Kelantanese were Shafi'i; and that *talfīq* had to be opposed because, if persisted in, it was liable to encourage the growth of new *madzhab*s from the resulting mixtures.

With respect to the first of these arguments, though Kelantan did not at this time possess a formal constitution, the processes of the institutionalization of Islam that had been taking place during the preceding two decades, centered on the creation of the Majlis Agama Islam and its associated bureacracy, had resulted in the reduction to writing of instruments setting out the jurisdictions of muftis, qadis, shari'a courts, and the issuing of fatwas, some of which instruments did refer to *madzhab*. The 1917 *notis* already cited, for example, requiring that all fatwas must be issued by or with the approval of the Majlis, stipulated that fatwas issued to applicants of the Shafi'i school must follow Shafi'i doctrine, save when given by the state mufti, who must in such exceptional cases provide text and authority for his variant decision. Other examples of similar constraints embodied in statutory instruments can be cited. While there is no reason to suppose the sentiments embodied in such instruments to be foreign to Kelantan society, the force given to them by their enactment into (or contingent upon) positive law was innovatory, strengthening the ideology of conformity by casting it in additional, extra-Islamic legal forms.

The *muzakara* ended inconclusively, with the sultan directing the people of Kelantan to follow the opinion of either Haji Wan Musa or Mufti Haji Ibrahim, as they thought fit. But Raja Ibrahim was not content with this and proceeded to direct his request for a fatwa not to the ʿUlamaʾ Committee of the Majlis Agama, for the reasons suggested, but to the Fatawa Committee of al-Azhar University in Cairo.

The al-Azhar fatwa was of course written in Arabic. Though all the participants in the Kelantan debate were fluent in Arabic, as were no doubt a considerable number of others present or interested, the generality of Kelantanese had at best a "Quran school" familiarity with the the language. Both the original and a Malay translation were therefore given when the fatwa was published, first in a local monthly, *al-Ḥikma,* in May 1937, and then in the context of ʿAbbas b. Muhammad Taha's *Risāla,* which appeared around the same time.[4] The fatwa was signed by Muhammad al-Fahm, president of the Lajnat al-Fatawa at al-Azhar, and presumably embodied some kind of collective decision. As inspection of the text makes evident, authorities employed in support of the fatwa were limited to the hadith collections (mentioned simply by name, with no individual citations) of Muslim, Ibn Maja, Abu Da'ud, and al-Nasa'i. The exposition is straightforward and largely nontechnical. Reaction to receipt of the fatwa in Kelantan is not recorded.

What we have in this episode, it may be suggested, is an argument about how to argue. What was important about the argument had little enough to do with dogs—though Raja Ibrahim's Dalmation stands usefully for the problems posed by innovation—and everything to do with how in a changing world one should derive from the shariʿa correct principles of behavior. The centrality of shariʿa, of "writ," to the argument was questioned by none. Differences arose only in the realm of how writ could best be known and understood. The crucial difference related to the espousal by the "pro-dog" party of the practice of *talfīq.* For *talfīq* expressly threatened the new validator of authority and source of writ in Kelantan, the Majlis Agama. In contesting the pro-dog party's employment of a selective and combinatory use of *madzhab* to adapt to or facilitate change, the establishment ʿulamaʾ chose to appeal not simply to their own traditional view of shariʿa but also to a supposed obligation, validated extra-Islamically by another form of writ (statute or positive law), to derive the shariʿa in a particular way. It was this contention that was most seriously challenged by the al-Azhar fatwa.

[Al-Azhar University—Fatawa Committee—52] The following istifta' [request for a fatwa] has reached the 'Ulama' Committee of al-Azhar University:

First—Is it lawful to keep dogs to guard the house and the like, or not lawful?

Second—When licked or touched by a dog if someone washes with water or the like and does not wash the place licked or touched, following Imam Malik on the cleanliness of dogs and the cleanliness of their saliva, and carries out ablution for prayer and prays; and if he is not an adherent of the Maliki madhhab, but carries out ablution for prayer and prays according to the madhhab of Imam Shafi'i; and if he is [thereby] taqlid to [follows] those who combine [*talfīq*] the rulings of two instances, is this lawful or not?

Third—Does Imam Malik's pronouncement that dogs are clean contravene the religion [*dīn*] of Islam and remove him from it, or not?

[Signed] Raja Kelantan, President of the Majlis Agama, in the capital of the government of Kelantan, Kota Bharu.

The reply: Concerning the first question—Rearing dogs and keeping them for rightful use as hunters and house guards and the like is lawful according to shari'a. In truth we have [it in] the hadith books of *Ṣaḥīḥ Muslim* and *Sunan Ibn Maja* and Abu Da'ud and al-Nasa'i that the Prophet Muhammad allowed dogs for sheep [herding] and hunting and agriculture.

Concerning the second question—Combination of rulings by someone who performs *ṣalāt* [ritual prayer] in the circumstances asked about; selection from all madhhabs of one among their rulings is permissible for those who favor the madhhab of Imam Malik.

Concerning the third question—The matter of dog cleanliness is among those matters concerning which there is no definitive textual evidence; it is a matter of individual judgment on the branches of law [*far'iyya ijtihādiyya*], regarding which there are differences among the Imams. Some are of the opinion that dogs are clean [*ṭahāra*] and some of the opinion that they are unclean [*najas*], and truly each follows his own way of thinking because there is weightier evidence on his side. It is incorrect to regard Imam Malik, in saying that dogs are clean, as alienating himself from the faith or being wrong in Islam and Allah knows.

President Fatawa Committee
Muhammad al-Fahm
11 Safar 1352
22 April 1937
Fatawa Committee al-Azhar University
[Signed]

CHAPTER TWENTY

The Council of Indonesian 'Ulama' on Muslims' Attendance at Christmas Celebrations

MOHAMAD ATHO MUDZHAR

Whereas in pre-modern times fatwas generally were issued by an individual mufti, in modern times they have come to be issued by 'ulama' as a group or by institutions. This is the case in Indonesia, where fatwas are produced by the Council of Indonesian 'Ulama' (CIU). Using a fatwa of the CIU on attendance by Muslims at Christmas celebrations as a source for describing the nature of interreligious relations in Indonesia, I will analyze how the fatwa reflects broad social issues and how the emergence of the fatwa is conditioned by its social surroundings (cf. Heyd 1961; Messick 1986; Humphreys 1988). The fatwas of the CIU are an important source for the study of Indonesian national integration and interreligious harmony.

Interreligious Relations in Indonesia

According to the census in 1980, Indonesia's population was 180 million people, of whom 88 percent were Muslims, 6 percent Protestants, 3 percent Catholics, 2 percent Hindus, and 1 percent Buddhists and others. Compared with the 1971 census, the number of Muslims had increased by only 0.7 percent while that of Christians (Protestants and Catholics combined) had increased by 1.4 percent.[1]

Since the beginning of the twentieth century, the relationship between Indonesian Muslims and Christians has been cordial but competitive. One of the motives for the establishment of the reformist Muhammadiyyah movement in 1912 was to compete with Christian missionaries, who were backed by the Dutch colonial government. The Dutch provided extensive financial support to the Christians, far exceeding that given to the Muslims. In his study on Dutch policy toward Islam, Suminto (1985:32–34) showed that in 1917 the Christians received 1,235,500 guilders, compared with only 127,029 received by the Muslims. Noer (1973:170) showed that the same disparity existed in 1936 through 1939. In those four years the subsidies given to the Christians amounted to, respectively, 1,382,600, 1,373,900, 992,500, and 1,179,700 guilders, compared with 7,500, 7,500, 7,500, and 7,600 guilders for the Muslims.

Rumor has it that in the early 1960s, the Christians had a plan to convert the island of Java to Christianity within twenty years and the whole of Indonesia within fifty. While it is difficult to prove that such a plan existed, Muslims feel that the threat of Christianization is real. Boland (1982) reports that many pamphlets have been circulated by the Muslims in response to this issue. Some five years after the abortive communist coup of 1965 and the banning of communism throughout the country in 1966, it was claimed that two million Indonesians had converted to Christianity. This triggered strained relations between Muslims and Christians in many parts of the country. In 1967, difficulties arose concerning the construction of a Methodist church in Meulaboh, Acheh. In October of that year, Muslim youths in Makassar, South Sulawesi, vandalized buildings and furniture belonging to various churches (Boland 1982:230–231).[2]

Aware of the danger of escalating tension between the two religious groups, the government took the initiative in holding an interreligious group meeting on November 30, 1967, in which all of the five recognized religious groups were represented. The proposed aim of the meeting was twofold: first, to create an interreligious consultative body, and second, to produce a declaration stating that missionary activities should not be directed at those who already adhere to any of the five recognized religions. The meeting commenced with a speech by President Suharto in which he conceded the existence of conflicts between Muslims and Christians but warned the public that such conflicts may well have been instigated by the communists. The meeting turned out to be a failure, for none of the proposed aims was achieved. Although the Buddhist and Hindu representatives were agreeable to the proposals, the Muslims and the Christians were not ready to compromise. The Muslims refused to consider taking part in an interreligious body with the Christians but enthusiastically supported the second proposal to limit missionary activities. The Christians agreed to the creation of an interreligious body but would not accept any proposal limiting missionary activities (Boland 1982:234–236; Sjamsudduha 1987:141–142; Proyek Pembinaan 1978:1–2; and Basri 1978:155).

On September 17, 1975, President Suharto summoned the leaders of the CIU to a meeting where Rusjdi Hamka, the general chairman of the CIU, raised with the president the question of Christianization in Indonesia. Hamka quoted a number of quranic verses (Quran 60:7, 8, and 9) that say that God allows Muslims to be friends with non-Muslims who do not persecute or wage wars against Muslims. Hamka also mentioned the establishment of a Baptist hospital in Bukittinggi, a strong Muslim area in West Sumatra, and other missionary activities in Java intended to convert Muslims to Christianity in return for food and basic needs. President Suharto is reported to have responded positively to Hamka's courageous remarks and even agreed with him on the need for the government to purchase the Baptist hospital, then still under construction, although the purchase never took place. The raising of the question indicates that the problem of Muslim-Christian relations was a serious one for the Muslims. The dialogue between Hamka and the president was considered so important that Hasan Basri, then a vice chairman of the CIU, called it "the Ramadan Dialogue," as it took place in the month of Ramadan (Hamka 1981:171–172; Basri 1978:78–80).[3]

The CIU did not prove ready to accept the idea of creating an interreligious consultative body until February 1976, some nine years after the 1967 meeting, and the actual agreement to establish such a body was not reached until 1980. It is clear that it was not easy for the Muslims and the Christians to renounce their respective positions (Proyek Pembinaan 1978:128–129).

New developments emerged in March 1978 when Alamsjah Ratu Perwiranegara was appointed minister of religious affairs; he remained in office until March 1983. Being both a pious Muslim and an army general with a high concern for national stability and harmony among the religious groups in the country, in August 1978 Alamsjah issued two ministerial decrees on missionary activities and international support to religious bodies in Indonesia. The first decree held that missionary activities should not be directed at those who already adhered to any of the five recognized religions, and the second stated that any international financial support to religious organizations in Indonesia could be implemented only with the approval of the minister of religious affairs. Both decrees were in accord with the CIU's positions in the 1967 interreligious meeting, and were therefore supported by the CIU. Predictably, the Christians protested against both decrees and asked the government to revoke them. The reasons for this were obvious: the first decree directly contradicted their position in the 1967 meeting; the acceptance of such a decree would mean the loss of a "large field" of missionary activities. And the second decree was even worse, for much of the Christian missionary activity in Indonesia depended on international financial support.

In short, Muslim-Christian relations in Indonesia have always been characterized by rivalry. Being concerned with the obligation to preserve their faith, the Muslims are preoccupied by the threat of Christianization, while the Christians are concerned with precisely such a Christianization.

The Issuance of the Fatwa

On March 7, 1981, the CIU issued a fatwa stating that a Muslim's attendance at Christmas celebrations was forbidden *(ḥarām),* and that therefore Muslims should not be involved in any such activity. The fatwa was signed by Syukri Ghozali and H. Masudi, the chairman and the secretary, respectively, of the Fatwa Committee (Majelis Ulama Indoneisa 1984:81–89). The fatwa was issued in response to the Christian custom of inviting Muslims to formal celebrations of Christmas. Many Muslims compared Christmas celebrations to the celebration of the birth of the Prophet Muhammad *(mawlid al-nabī),* which has no ritual value. Some even took part in organizing Christmas celebrations, especially if the celebrations were held at places of work, in schools, or in the neighborhoods (rather than in churches). The Christians were happy to extend invitations to Muslims to attend such celebrations under the pretext of religious tolerance, based on the state ideology of *Pancasilaī.*[4] Many Muslims were reluctant to decline such invitations for fear of being accused of intolerance. In their confusion, many Muslims asked the CIU about the legal status of such a practice, and this led the CIU to issue the fatwa. The ʿulamaʾ thought that Muslim attendance at Christmas celebrations constituted a direct threat of Christianization.

Syukri Ghozali, the signatory of the fatwa, belonged to the conservative group of the ʿulamaʾ. He was trained in the local madrasas, and his career brought him to a number of positions. He was once a member of the parliament representing the Nahdat al-ʿUlamaʾ Party, he served at the Ministry of Religious Affairs for many years, he was appointed the dean of the Faculty of Islamic Law of the Jakarta State Institute of Islamic Studies (IAIN), and finally he was rector of the Jakarta Institute for Quranic Studies (PTIQ). But Ghozali was not the only person responsible for the fatwa, since all fatwas of the CIU were preceded by meetings at which most of the leaders of the CIU were present. In fact Hamka, the general chairman of the CIU who did not sign the fatwa, later proved to be its strongest defender.

The arguments presented in the fatwa are very elaborate. It begins by claiming that misconceptions are rife among Muslims who view Christmas celebrations as having no ritual value. For Christians, the fatwa claims, a Christmas celebration is a set of ritual activities; therefore, Muslims' attendance at such celebrations could jeopardize their faith. The fatwa argues that the promotion of religious tolerance should be carried out through social activities, not in the areas of theology and ritual. The fatwa admits that Muslims are permitted to interact and cooperate with the followers of other religions, although not in ritual and theological activities. To support the argument, the fatwa quotes three quranic verses (Quran 49:13, 31:15, 60:8) that state that Muslims may cooperate with non-Muslims on the basis of humanitarianism, provided that the interaction does not bring them to other convictions and that the nonbelievers do not drive the Muslims from their homes (Majelis Ulama Indonesia 1984:81–82).

The fatwa further argues that Muslims should not mix their ritual and theological convictions with those of other religions. In this regard, it quotes two quranic passages. The first reads, "Say: O unbelievers! I do not worship that which you worship. Nor do you worship Him Whom I worship. Nor am I going to worship that which you worship. Nor are you going to worship Him Whom I worship. You shall have your religion and I shall have my religion" (Quran 109:1–6). The second reads: "And do not mix up the truth with the falsehood, nor hide the truth while you know [it]" (Quran 2:42).

The fatwa acknowledges that Muslims should believe in ʿIsa al-Masih b. Maryam (Jesus) but only as a Messenger of God, for a number of quranic verses insist on the human character of Jesus and his being the Messenger of God. The fatwa further argues that whoever believes that God is more than one, or that God had a son, or that ʿIsa al-Masih was the son of God, is both a kafir (unbeliever) and a *mushrik* (polytheist). The fatwa also argues that, according to the Quran, on the Day of Judgment Allah will ask Jesus if he taught his people to believe in him and his mother, Maryam, as Gods, to which he will answer in the negative. The fatwa adds that the Quran clearly teaches that God is only one, on Whom all depend; He begets not, nor is He begotten, and none is like Him (Quran 112:1–4).

Having presented all these quranic quotations, the fatwa supports the argument by referring to a hadith narrated by Nuʿman b. Bashir indicating that *ḥalal* and *ḥarām* are already clear, but between the two there are things that are not clear, with regard to which Muslims should be very careful. Finally, the fatwa refers to a maxim in Islamic legal theory that states that avoiding harm should be given priority over gaining benefits. It is only after making such elaborate arguments that the fatwa concludes that a Muslim's attendance at Christmas celebrations is positively forbidden.

The fatwa's emphasis on the Quran and hadith indicates how serious the question was to the CIU. The fatwa does not refer to any other classical text, because the question addressed was thought to be a recent development in the pluralistic society of Indonesia. Actually, many pre-modern writers had touched on the question, although they were not necessarily concerned with its legal implications. Al-Maqrizi (1877:494) mentions that at the time of the Fatimid dynasty (909–1171) the Egyptian Copts celebrated Christmas and involved some Muslims in preparing the food, but he makes no mention of the legal status of the involvement. Ibn Taymiyya (d. 1328) seems to be the only pre-modern writer to deal with the legal aspect of Muslims' participation in Christmas celebrations. In his *Kitāb al-iqtidāʾ*, he states that conscious imitation of Christian festivities, with the knowledge that the object is among the particularities of the faith, is prohibited (Memon 1976:2–3, 218–219). Abu al-ʿAbbas al-ʿAzafi admits that the introduction of the *mawlid* celebration to Muslims in the Maghrib was precisely to counteract their participation in the Christmas celebrations of the local Christians (Shinar 1977:276).

Reactions to the Fatwa

The Indonesian government was not happy with the timing of the CIU fatwa, which was considered disadvantageous to the government's efforts to promote Muslim-Christian harmony after the conflicts of the late 1960s and the early 1970s. In 1967, as mentioned earlier, the government had sponsored the unsuccessful interreligious meeting. Then, in 1969 the government had launched a program called the Development of Religious Harmony Project. In the early 1970s the project succeeded in sponsoring a number of meetings and dialogues between Muslims and Christians. In 1975 the CIU was established. In 1978 decrees were issued by the minister of religious affairs to regulate missionary activities and the use of foreign funds for religious activities. In 1979 a joint decision was signed by the minister of religious affairs and the interior minister to regulate procedures for building houses of worship, including churches, as part of the effort to regain interreligious harmony. In 1980 the prospect of interreligious harmony became more promising when the Interreligious Consultative Body was created. Thus, for the government, the issuance of the fatwa was a blow to its careful nurturing of harmony (Departemen Agama 1987:72–73).

The content of the fatwa was seen by the government as even more damaging to the efforts to regain interreligious harmony. The government saw the fatwa as a reflection of the CIU's inflexibility. To the government, there was nothing wrong in Muslims' attending Christmas celebrations, so long as they did not participate in their ritual components. But how does one define ritual activities in a Christmas celebration? To this end, the minister of religious affairs issued a Letter of Circulation (Surat Edaran) on September 2, 1981, listing all religious holidays and defining their ritual parts. To show its moderate position, the letter stated that religious celebrations were to be organized, attended, and funded by the followers of the religion concerned. However, the letter further stated that if a government official had to be present at a celebration of a religious holiday that was not that of his personal faith, he might do so and remain in the audience passively but respectfully.[5]

Despite the opposing view of the government, the CIU remained firm in its fatwa. But this was precisely the situation the ʿulama' had been fearful of, namely that behind the creation of the CIU, the government had ideas to use it for its own interest. The suggestion made by the Suharto government in 1970 to create the CIU had gone unanswered until 1975 because the ʿulamaʾ had not wanted to be used by the government. The ʿulamaʾ had reasons for their reluctance. First, the suggestion was made only a year before the general election of 1971, the first of its kind in Suharto's time. Second, in 1973 the government insisted that the four existing Islamic political parties eliminate their Islamic epithet and be amalgamated into a single party called the Development United Party. Third, also in 1973, the government submitted to the parliament a draft bill on marriage; the bill allegedly was secular in nature and included many articles that were contradictory to the doctrines of Islamic law. Although the bill was revised to the satisfaction of the Muslims and finally passed, the ʿulamaʾ understood that the government would always try to limit the application of Islamic principles in the country in any way possible. When the CIU was finally established, Hamka, on the eve of his inauguration as the first general chairman of the CIU, was denounced by a group of students who demanded that he decline the chairmanship.

From its creation in 1975 until 1988, the CIU produced some thirty-nine fatwas on various issues that included ritual, marriage, culture, sectarianism, politics, and medical issues. Little or no government influence can be detected in the fatwas on ritual, culture, and medical issues, which are generally neutral and independent. The fatwas on family planning, food, and Muslim minority sects are generally very supportive of the government. It goes without saying that fatwas on political issues were highly influenced by the government. Three of the fatwas are hostile to the government, including the fatwa on Muslims' attendance at Christmas celebrations (Mudzhar 1990:254–257).[6]

Initially, the fatwa on the prohibition of Muslims' attendance at Christmas celebrations did not cause any mass controversy, as it was circulated through the monthly bulletin of the CIU, which reaches only a limited circle. Within four months, however, the fatwa was published in the mass media and began to trigger public controversy. It is not clear who was the first to distribute copies of the fatwa to the media. Some said it was Masudi, one of the secretaries of the CIU, who later was dismissed from the executive board. Tengku Muhammad Saleh, a member of the parliament, admits that one day he showed a copy of the fatwa to journalists in the parliament building; the next day it was published in the media.[7]

The government went so far as to ask the CIU to revoke the fatwa, but the CIU refused. At the request of the government, General Chairman Hamka did sign a letter limiting circulation of the fatwa, but he always insisted that the validity of the fatwa was unquestioned. On occasion he demonstrated his personal commitment to the fatwa. Once he gave a Friday sermon at the Azhar mosque in Jakarta in which he insisted on the prohibition of Muslims' attendance at Christmas celebrations. He also issued a press release about the matter, to the effect that the validity of the fatwa was maintained (Hamka 1981:192, 195).

Hamka was a well-known religious scholar long before he was elected general chairman of the CIU in 1975. Born in 1908 in the Minangkabau area of West Sumatra, he spent most of his life in Java. In 1924 he went to Yogyakarta to study Islam with Cokroaminoto, the founder of the Syarekat Islam movement; in 1927 he went on the hajj to Mecca; in 1935 he joined the reformist Muhammadiyah movement; in 1955 he was elected to the Constituent Assembly, where he represented the Masjumi until 1959; and in 1971 he was elected the advisor to the Central Committee of the Muhammadiyyah. Hamka was a successful self-educated person; he wrote 113 books, including 4 novels and 30 volumes of quranic exegeses that he completed while he was in prison for more than two years under the Sukarno regime. Although he never attended a university, his reputation earned him two honorary doctorates, one from the Azhar University of Cairo in 1959, the other from the University of Kebangsaan, Malaysia, in 1974 (Departemen Penerangan R. I. 1985:139–142; Basri 1978:283–287; Hamka 1982:317–319).

The pressure resulting from the prohibition of Muslims' attendance at Christmas celebrations apparently was sufficient to compel Hamka to resign the leadership of the CIU, under the pretext of declining health. The real reason for the resignation was a conflict with the government, as can be detected in the following letter of resignation that he himself read before a closed meeting of the CIU:

> In the name of Allah, the Gracious and the Merciful.
>
> 1. The Minister of Religious Affairs, Alamsjah Ratu Perwiranegara, at a meeting with the CIU held on April 23, 1981, expressed his disappointment with the release of the fatwa of the CIU [on Muslims' attendance at Christmas celebrations]. The minister also indicated his being furious [about the matter], and stated his intention to resign from the ministerial office.
>
> 2. In response to the statement of the minister, I said that it was not he but I who had to resign, for I am the one who is responsible for the release of the fatwa which has made the minister intend to resign.
>
> 3. Considering the fact that the existence of the CIU is still needed in Indonesia, and to secure its existence after my resignation, I have signed a letter limiting the circulation of the fatwa, with the understanding that the substance of the fatwa remains valid as has been decided upon by the CIU.
>
> 4. I saw it necessary to issue my personal press release on the validity of the fatwa, as was published by newspapers. Nevertheless, I hope that cooperation between the government and the CIU, especially the leadership of the CIU, after my resignation will be improved in the future.

5. I hereby declare my resignation from the office of the general chairmanship of the CIU before this meeting, as you are the ones who elected me for my second term of office a year ago in 1980. Thank you.[8]

The foregoing discussion shows how a single fatwa of the CIU on the prohibition of Muslims' attendance at Christmas celebrations may be used to analyze the broader issue of the complex relationships between Muslims, Christians, and the government in Indonesia in the 1980s. The fatwa depicts a picture of partial interreligious harmony.

The Decision of the Fatwa Committee of the Council of Indonesian 'Ulama' on a Muslim's Attendance at Christmas Celebrations

Having observed:

1. That Christmas celebrations are lately mistakenly understood by some Muslims as equal to the celebrations of the birth of the Prophet Muhammad peace be upon him.
2. That based on such a misconception many Muslims participated in Christmas celebrations, some even in organizing such celebrations.

Having considered:

1. That the Islamic community needs clear guidance on the issue of Christmas celebrations. It is expected that the Muslims do not mix their faith and rituals with the faith and rituals of other religions.
2. That the Muslims should always try their best to increase the quality of their faith and obedience to Allah.

Having reinvestigated the following Islamic teachings:

A. That Muslims are permitted to cooperate and interact with the followers of other religions on worldly issues, based on the following quranic verses:

1. *Sūrat al-Ḥujurāt* [Q. 49:13]: "O you men! surely we have created you of a male and a female, and made you tribes and families that you may know each other; surely the most honorable of you with Allah is the one among you most careful [of his duty]; surely Allah is knowing, Aware."
2. *Sūrat Luqmān* [Q. 31:15]: "And if they contend with you that you should associate with Me what you have no knowledge of, do not obey them, and keep company with them in this world kindly, and follow the way of him who turns to Me, then to Me is your return, then will I inform you of what you did."
3. *Sūrat al-Mumtaḥana* [Q. 60:8]: "Allah does not forbid you respecting those who have not made war against you on account of [your] religion,

and have not driven you forth from your homes, that you show them kindness and deal with them justly; surely Allah loves the doers of justice."

B. That Muslims are not allowed to mix their faith and rituals with those of other religions, based on the following quranic verses:

1. *Sūrat al-Kāfirīn* [Q. 109:1–6]: "Say: O unbelievers! I do not worship that which you worship. Nor do you worship Him Whom I worship. Nor I am going to worship that which you worship. Nor are you going to worship Him Whom I worship. You shall have your religion and I shall have my religion."
2. *Sūrat al-Baqara* [Q. 2:42]: "And do not mix up the truth with the falsehood, nor hide the truth while you know [it]."

C. That Muslims should believe in 'Isa [Jesus] the son of Maryam as a messenger of God just like Muhammad and other prophets, based on the following quranic verses:

1. *Sūrat Maryam* [Q. 19:30–32]: "He said: Surely I am a servant of Allah; He has given me the Book and made me a Prophet. And He has made blessed wherever I may be, and He has enjoined on me prayer and poor-rate as long as I live. And to be dutiful to my mother, and He has not made me insolent, unblessed."
2. *Sūrat al-Mā'ida* [Q. 5:75]: "The Messiah, son of Maryam is but an apostle; apostles before him have indeed passed away; and his mother was a truthful woman; they both used to eat food. See how We make communications clear to them, then behold, how they are turned away."
3. *Sūrat al-Baqara* [Q. 2:285]: "The apostle believes in what has been revealed to him from his Lord, and [so do] the believers; they all believe in Allah and His Angels and His books and His apostles; We make no difference between any of His apostles; and they say: we hear and obey, our Lord! Thy forgiveness [do we crave] and to Thee is the eventual course."

D. That whoever believes that God is more than one, or that God has sons, or that 'Isa [Jesus] is the son of God, he is both an unbeliever [kafir] and a polytheist [mushrik] based on the following quranic verses:

1. *Sūrat al-Mā'ida* [Q. 5:72]: "Certainly they disbelieve who say: Surely Allah, He is the Messiah, son of Maryam; and the Messiah said: O Children of Israel! worship Allah, my Lord and your Lord. Surely whoever associates [others] with Allah, then Allah has forbidden to him the garden, and his abode is the fire; and there shall be no helpers for the unjust."

2. *Sūrat al-Māʾida* [Q. 5:73]: "Certainly they disbelieve who say: Surely Allah is the third [person] of the three; and there is no god but the one God, and if they desist not from what they say, a painful chastisement shall befall those among them who disbelieve."
3. *Sūrat al-Tawba* [Q. 9:30]: "And the Jews say: ʿUzayr is the son of Allah; and the Christians say: The Messiah is the son of Allah; these are the words of their mouth; they imitate the saying of those who disbelieved before; may Allah destroy them; how they are turned away!"

E. That Allah on the Day of Judgment will ask ʿIsa if he ever taught his people in this world to believe in him and his mother as Gods, to which ʿIsa will answer in the negative, based on the following quranic verses of *Sūrat al-Māʾida* [Q. 5:116–118]: "And when Allah will say: O ʿIsa the son of Maryam! did you say to men, Take me and my mother for two gods besides Allah, he will say: Glory be to Thee, it did not befit me that I should say what I had no right to [say]; if I had said it, Thou wouldst indeed have known it; Thou knowest what is in my mind, and I do not know what is in Thy mind, surely Thou art the great Knower of unseen things. I did not say to them ought save what Thou didst enjoin me with: That they worship Allah, my Lord and your Lord. And I was a witness of them so long as I was among them, but when Thou didst cause me to die, Thou wert the watcher over them, and Thou art witness of all things. If Thou should chastise them, then surely they are Thy servants; and if Thou shouldst forgive them, then surely Thou art the Mighty, the Wise."

F. Islam teaches that Allah is only One, based on the following quranic verses [Q. 112:1–4]: "Say: He, Allah, is One. Allah is He on Whom all depend. He begets not, nor is He begotten. And none is like Him."

G. Islam teaches its adherents to stay away from things of *shubuhāt* [unclear] category, from the prohibitions of Allah, and to give priority to avoiding harm over taking benefits based on:

1. The saying of the Prophet of Muhammad narrated by Nuʿman b. Bashir, which stated: "Truly things which are permitted and forbidden are already very clear, but in between the two there exist things whose status is not clear [*mushtabihāt*], which many people do not know about. Whoever is able to stay away from the *shubuhāt,* he is maintaining the purity of his religion and dignity; whoever falls into the *shubuhāt,* he is actually falling into the forbidden areas, just like a shepherd who herds his sheep on the border to a certain forbidden area to which the sheep are likely to penetrate. Please note that each king has his own prohibitions, and the prohibitions of Allah are things which have been classified in the *ḥarām* [forbidden] category."
2. There exists a maxim in the science of Islamic legal theory which says that avoiding harm should be given priority over gaining benefits.

The Council of Indonesian ʿUlamaʾ hereby issues the fatwa:

1. Although the aim of holding Christmas celebrations in Indonesia is to pay respect to the Prophet ʿIsa, Peace Be Upon Him, the celebrations cannot be separated from Christian ritual issues.
2. Attending Christmas celebrations is forbidden [*ḥarām*] to Muslims.
3. To keep oneself from falling into things of *shubuhāt* and forbidden categories, it is urged that Muslims not be engaged in any part of Christmas celebrations.

Jakarta, Jumada al-Awwal 1, 1401 A.H. or March 7, 1981, C.E.
THE FATWA COMMITTEE OF THE COUNCIL OF INDONESIAN ULAMA

Chairman,	Secretary,
[Signature]	[Signature]
K. H. M. Syukri Ghozali	Drs. H. Masudi

CHAPTER TWENTY-ONE

A Modern Indian Mufti

GREGORY C. KOZLOWSKI

Muslims in contemporary India live in a social and political environment that sets them apart from many of their brethren in the rest of the Islamic world. They are a minority of at least 110 million living in a professedly secular nation-state.[1] Since 1947, Muslims have responded in a variety of ways to this situation. Some are eager to accommodate faith and practice to a multireligious democracy. Others seem all the more determined to preserve a distinctive pattern of religion and culture. That effort sometimes makes Indian Muslims appear "old-fashioned" in the eyes of their fellow believers living in places where the faithful form the majority and in states that are in some sense Islamic.

The governments of Yemen, Egypt, and Syria, for example, have proceeded to codify Islamic law as well as to apply it in a system of courts in which scholars educated in academies that concentrate on the Islamic sciences (madrasas) have only a marginal role. In India, Muslim personal law remains a complex mixture of judge-made legal compromises blended from a few translations, textbooks, and precedent. With all its faults from the point of view of Euro-American judicial logic,[2] the system applies to all Muslims in such crucial matters as inheritance, marriage, and divorce.

In India, legal disputes among Muslims can be settled in state-sponsored courts, but believers also have the option of seeking a legal opinion (fatwa) from a religious scholar. Courts sanctioned by the government of India can provide definitive rulings enforced by the state. Their decisions become precedents enforced throughout the nation. A mufti offers an "opinion." His word is not law, but its value may reside in its acceptance of social ambiguities and a desire for consensus that India's civil law, derived from British models, cannot countenance. For uncounted thousands of Muslims, a mufti's chamber is a court of first resort. Decisions handed down by secular tribunals—as, for example, in Shah Banu's case (Engineer 1987; Kozlowski 1989), have sparked street demonstrations, even riots. By contrast, a mufti's fatwa may agitate a particular family, a neighborhood, perhaps even a city, but it never seems to be the occasion for a national controversy that pits Muslims against the majority or against each other.[3]

Even though Muslims in India enjoy the special legal status mentioned above, a ruling in favor of Shah Banu in her attempt to secure alimony from her ex-husband (a remedy not provided for in Muslim personal law) led, almost inevitably, to contention over the nonpersonal issue of Muslims' political status in India. The original source of the case was entirely forgotten as that public identity appeared threatened and its affirmation became a matter of survival itself (Kozlowski 1993). Fatwas, by contrast, are more clearly rooted in the local communities that are the basis for the actual practice of Islam. Opinions delivered by religious scholars in one region of the Muslim world—Medina or Cairo as examples (see Kozlowski 1985; Chapter 17, this volume)—do not necessarily constitute a precedent for scholars in other countries. Within India itself, fatwas issued by scholars in one part of the country, or by one madrasa, may not be binding elsewhere or accepted by other theological schools. The majority of fatwas are delivered to specific individuals in a specific place at a specific time. As such, they may tell us more about Muslims and the strength of their faith than parliamentary machinations or the noisy politics of street demonstrations.

In themselves, fatwas are the documentary artifacts of extensive, but limited, social, political, economic, and religious interactions. Most often, their format is so spare that they reveal little about the people who asked for them and the scholars who formulated them. Rarely, they may actually describe something of the character of those exchanges over decades and centuries, and when combined with other sorts of records, they may provide insights into the social dimensions of the practice of shariʿa (Powers 1990b). Those few exceptions nevertheless demonstrate that the processes may be more significant for historians than the decisions to which they lead. Some modern scholars have had the chance either to observe the ways muftis and their clients interact (Messick 1988; Rosen 1980–1981) or to tease out the implications of a fatwa by placing it in its contemporary political and social environment (Chapter 19). In this chapter, I will follow their lead by examining a particular fatwa in the context of a series of observations of an individual mufti, the madrasa that he represents, and the ways in which both interact with ordinary believers in Hyderabad, India. The bonds linking the institution, the scholar, and the people connected to them are primarily local: focused on the exigencies established by fairly restricted sets of geographical, temporal, and social relations. The scholars and their clients do not, therefore, depend on the elaborate, and expensive, machinery of the state or an equally complex ecclesiastical bureaucracy. In rapidly changing political or economic conditions, such institutions and those loyal to them are able to preserve the ideals of Islam with a simplicity that befits a living faith.

The Mufti and the Madrasa

The Jamiʿa Nizamiyya Madrasa was founded in 1875 by a learned and holy man usually referred to as Shaykh Anwarullah Fazilat Jang (Kozlowski 1995). In 1989, the teaching faculty numbered thirty-six, and about 500 students were studying in the institution. Although Shaykh Anwarullah died in 1918, his reputation for scholarship and sanctity make his presence in the madrasa pervasive. In every subsequent generation, the shaykh al-Jamiʿa (the head of the school) and the mufti have carried on Shaykh Anwarullah's work and spirit in a unique way. If a stranger should ask, "What is the Jamiʿa?" the most junior pupil or most senior teacher would direct him to the shaykh. However, if someone is looking for a fatwa, they will send him (rarely, her) to the mufti.

An average of five or six requests for fatwas come to the Jamiʿa Nizamiyya Madrasa each day. Some of them come by post from Hyderabadis living not only in India but also in Pakistan, the Gulf, England, and the United States. Those who come in person to obtain an opinion first meet with a clerk, who checks the question (istiftaʾ) they have brought with them or drafts one for them if they have not. According to the mufti himself, most of the questions concern inheritance or marriage and divorce.

When people come in person, the mufti meets with them in his own study. He sits on a folded mat only a few inches above the floor behind a low writing desk. Everyone else sits on the floor, which is covered by a cloth sheet. He usually wears a *sherwānī* (the "Nehru coat"), baggy white trousers *(shalwār)*, and a white turban wrapped around a skull cap *(kulah)*. Unlike some scholars who have a "big turban" complex (Messick 1988), the mufti of the Jamiʿa maintains a humble demeanor, which seems to reflect the institution's identity (Kozlowski 1995). One of the school's professors criticized scholars who "make their learning a barrier between themselves and the pious but ignorant."

The current mufti, like most of the Jamiʿa's faculty, received all of his training within the madrasa. His father had served as the institution's mufti for a number of years. In addition to his formal training, the mufti served for some seven or eight years as his father's deputy. He has described himself as having become a "first-class mufti" in 1985. Besides acting as the Jamiʿa's mufti, he also serves as its shaykh al-fiqh (professor of law).

As in other Indian madrasas, since the nineteenth century the trend within the Jamiʿa has been to stress the authority of the institution over that of the individual scholar (Metcalf 1982:146–157). Even so, the mufti's personality remains a crucial aspect of the process leading to a fatwa. In more difficult cases, a board consisting of the Jamiʿa's head and several other professors signs the finished fatwa, but clients deal only with the mufti, not the board. He decides whether or not to consult the rest of the group. The mufti described here has noted that difficult cases that made such consultation necessary were rare.

Both learning and deportment can contribute to the authority a particular scholar or institution projects. The Jamiʿa carefully cultivates an atmosphere that bespeaks learning. This is reinforced when one enters the mufti's study. He is surrounded by low tables laden with folio volumes. He reveals his specialized knowledge when he picks up one of his books and begins searching through it. The book is almost always in Arabic, but the very presentation of the text (or texts, since three or four of them may be printed together) must jar the untrained eye. Most of the works he consults are printed, and they contain top-to-bottom columns surrounded with commentaries, glosses on the commentaries, and all manner of scholia. While some pages feature columns of print, the text on others is arranged in six, seven, or eight pie-shaped wedges, which become progressively narrower as they move toward the center of page. Knowledge of where to begin reading can only come from special instruction in such styles of writing and from familiarity with the text through memorization (Eickelman 1978).

Pointing to the volumes arrayed beside him, the mufti asserts that the books contain, in principle, the answers to all possible legal questions. That does not mean, however, that he would be able to find the correct answer to every problem. The mufti's view is that scholarship in the Islamic world has greatly declined since the period in which many of his books were written. "In Abu Hanifa's time, they knew thirty or forty books from memory. Who can do that today?" he asks. "No one in the present age can claim the title of mujtahid, because no one has the requisite learning." According to long-established convention, every fatwa ends with the assertion, "God alone knows the truth." Since the mufti writes this phrase on even his rough drafts, it seems to reflect genuine humility rather than a pro forma declaration.

In the interaction between the mufti and his petitioners, this humility was evident in the calm and patience that he always seems to display. He addresses those who come to him politely, on a level of ordinary etiquette. The Urdu language has several degrees of politeness or rudeness (and subtle ways of turning the former into the latter), each with its appropriate endings and tone. The mufti is not overly polite, nor is he condescending or dismissive. He also demonstrates a talent for asking the penetrating but non-threatening question.

The process of making a fatwa involves several types of ambiguity. The document may state principles and an appropriate solution to a problem that conforms to the scholar's and the institution's understanding of the "Islamic way" (shariʿa), but compliance cannot be guaranteed. A mufti has no way of making sure that his petitioners will do as they are told. He cannot punish them or prevent their seeking another fatwa. The mufti must rely on the conscience of the faithful, as well as on their loyalty to him and the institution he represents. A dismissive gesture or a harsh word might send individuals away full of resentment. A gentle demeanor can reinforce a continuing attachment to the madrasa.

Many of the Jamiʿa's faculty express the conviction that "their people" would never ignore a fatwa or seek another somewhere else. The mufti's response to a question involving those possibilities is typically neutral: "How would I know if they did that?"

A Fatwa

Whether the mufti meets with petitioners for an hour or two or even longer depends on the complexity of the case. The mufti carefully notes the actual names of the individuals involved, asks to see any relevant documents, and seeks to uncover any information that might be, intentionally or unintentionally, hidden. After considering the question, following the departure of his petitioners, he drafts his fatwa in ordinary handwriting, usually quoting an Arabic phrase or two from one of his books to clinch his opinion. A clerk then transfers the mufti's rough draft to a sheet or sheets of letterhead paper. While the stationary announces that this fatwa comes from the "Dar al-Iftaʾ-e Jamiʿa Nizamiyya" in a heavy *naskh*-style script, the body of the text is in clear *nastaʿliq*.[4] Quotations from Arabic are also placed in the *naskh* style. Below the *bismillāh* and the letterhead, including the institution's address, the same information is repeated in Roman script. To the left appears the serial number assigned to each request on its arrival. To the right, the dates are given in both Hijri and Christian years. The top half of the document is labeled *"al-Istiftāʾ,"* and the lower *"al-Iftāʾ."* The translation of this particular fatwa is as follows.

> *The Istiftāʾ:* What do the learned of the faith command[5] in the following matter? Zayd created an endowment [*waqf*] of some property. Now, this endowment's custodianship requires settlement. Zayd had no male children—[he had] only four daughters. After Zayd [died], the four daughters also passed away. Of the four daughters, one was childless. The eldest son of the first

daughter died during his mother's lifetime. He had four sons and four daughters. Can the heirs[6] of that deceased son acquire the custodianship [of this *waqf*]? The names of none of his daughters are mentioned [in the endowment deed?]. At this time the work of the custodian is changing [hands?]. What does the shariʿa command?

The Iftāʾ: According to the *shariʿat*,[7] the custodianship goes to the children of the endowment's founder. After that, it goes to an executor, and after that the *Qāẓī*. At this time the *waqf* board [the English word "board" is simply transliterated in the Urdu script as *bord*] has responsibility. It is thus on the authority of the third volume of the *Book of Waqf*,[8] page 233, "Then the children of the line of the founder, then the executor, then the *Qāẓī*."[9] If the custodianship can be placed with the children of the founder, then a stranger should not be made custodian. According to page 232 [of the book just mentioned], "So long as one of the founder's kin [*aqārib*] takes good care, then the custodianship should not be placed with a stranger."[10] With regard to this question, the above mentioned injunctions should be acted upon. Only God knows the truth.

Fatwas are often significant for what they cannot or will not say as well as for what they actually communicate. This fatwa provides only a few hints about why the custodianship of an endowment might be a matter of contention. Space does not allow for a full discussion of the institution of *waqf* or for an account of social, political, and familial conflicts that arise over *awqāf* (Powers 1990b). This fatwa passes over two potentially contentious points with seeming ease.

The first of those points concerns the rights of children whose parent has predeceased a grandparent (cf. Powers 1990b). Some Muslim scholars have asserted that individuals in that situation could acquire the benefits of a *waqf*, even though their parent, who would have held the right of succession, died before he or she could actually establish a claim. Since custodians have managerial control over an endowment's property and may take a portion of its income as a salary, is the trusteeship a benefit? Moreover, trustees are often, as in this case, members of the donor's family and beneficiaries of the *waqf* (Kozlowski 1985). Can their status as legal guardians be neatly distinguished from their role as recipients of the income? Other scholars have argued that such benefits cannot be passed on, since the parent never controlled the resources to which the children hope to succeed. The istiftaʾ and fatwa do not mention such complications. They do not list the property held in this particular *waqf*, the income derived from it, nor the ways in which the proceeds are distributed.

In India and elsewhere in the Muslim world, arguments over the control of an endowment's resources may drag on for years, decades, even centuries. During his discussions with the individuals seeking this fatwa, the mufti of the Jamiʿa would have been careful to question them concerning any kin who might have interests contrary to their own. In the event of such conflicts, the mufti always seems eager to find a compromise rather than issue an opinion that would exacerbate an argument. This concern for harmony may be one of the reasons that some Muslims seek out the mufti instead of going to the civil courts, where the adversarial approach to adjudication creates losers as well as winners.

A second controversial element concerns the brief reference to current state-supported agencies that manage endowments, "At this time the *waqf* board has responsibility." Complaints by reformers about the mismanagement of endowments go back to the previous century. Often religious and social reformers seem to have been inspired in part by an eagerness to direct the funds generated by *waqfs* to the support of their own pet causes (Kozlowski 1985). In the twentieth century, local and federal bodies whose members include Muslim government servants, local notables, self-appointed representatives, and candidates put forward by mosque committees, as well as other Muslim social service organizations, have attempted to provide for the honest management of *waqfs*. Their efforts have not been very successful (Rashid 1979). One reason for their modest record is that custodians of endowments, especially those founded and managed by a particular family, are reluctant to register their *waqf*s with the boards, fearing interference. In the present case, the fatwa shows that the mufti asserts that management of an endowment should go to the *waqf* board only as the last resort.

Both principle and personal experience seem to have influenced the mufti's preference for families over governmental institutions. As noted above, the strength of the Jamiʿa's own authority rests on direct contacts between the institution—and the people who staff it—and ordinary believers. In a sense, the *waqf* board is alien to that relationship.

From time to time, prominent Muslims in Hyderabad have criticized the officials of the board, charging them with the misappropriation of funds and the liquidation of *waqf* properties for their own profit. In 1989, many leaders accused a former president of the board of being a drinker and a womanizer. These complaints may simply be gossip, but they reveal a disposition among believers to distrust governmentally sponsored organizations. Most individuals in 1989 expressed satisfaction with the honesty and moral character of the current head of the board, although memories of the irregularities of the recent past may have inspired a certain suspicion of that body. Moreover, various members of the board in Hyderabad are affiliated with other madrasas, some of which, notably that of the Deobandis (Kozlowski 1995; Sanyal forthcoming), are rivals of the Jamiʿa. Many of the Jamiʿa's faculty are quite hostile to the Deobandis and do not consider them good Muslims. Internal conflicts within the Muslim community seem to influence the formulation of fatwas, even though the document does not refer to them directly.

In practical terms, the ʿulamaʾ of the Jamiʿa have had disagreements with the *waqf* board concerning their own endowments. Several years ago, the Jamiʿa refused to register *waqfs* dedicated to the institution. At the time, the madrasa argued that these were "gifts," rather than true *waqfs*. More recently, when legal troubles arose between the Jamiʿa and the tenants whose rents provide income for the school, some of its faculty sought a rapprochement with the board, hoping to gain its help in fighting the lawsuits. The board rebuffed the Jamiʿa, leaving a legacy of ill will on both sides.

Finally, the document does not even consider what may be the most significant problem: will the recipients act on the orders it contains? The mufti has no assurance that the individuals will put his fatwa's injunctions into practice. Though he will have done his best to avert future disputes, some among the eight surviving great-grandchildren of the endowment's founder may find that their interests are not served by the fatwa, and they might seek a second opinion from another mufti. Alternatively, they could take the matter to the civil courts. The mufti expresses his awareness of that possibility when he observes that the Jamiʿa's fatwas are accepted as evidence in the state courts. From the perspective of the courts of India, his opinion may not provide a clear decision, but the courts consider his authority and that of the Jamiʿa weighty in themselves. The respect that those governmental institutions offer seems inspired by a host of political considerations that cannot be considered here (Kozlowski 1993).

As for the mufti, his discussions with clients are laced with the Urdu pronunciations of such words as "court," "advocate," "suit," and "stamp paper." He understands the reality of contemporary society in Hyderabad and India. He strives to maintain the authority of the Jamiʿa, which is the source of his own authority, but seems to acknowledge that this has ambiguous limits. In protesting that he does not know about the consequences of his issuing an opinion, he preserves the integrity of the bond between himself, his school, and the community of believers. He assumes that they will remain loyal to him and the madrasa. By refusing, consciously or unconsciously, to place too much weight on that necessarily slender tether, he preserves the link in the face of many forces that could break it.

Conclusion

Muftis perform many tasks, depending on the place and time in which they live. Their work is, in part, the application of the norms of shariʿa to the contingencies of particular individuals living in temporally and spatially bound societies. In applying those norms, muftis adapt the "holy law" to changing circumstances (Messick 1986). Muftis also play a dynamic role in the realization of social ideals related only indirectly to the law (Rosen 1980). The mufti of the Jamiʿa does both of these things as he goes about interviewing clients, seeking compromises, and guiding his clients' perceptions of what the source of a conflict may be, as well as how it should be resolved. His final written opinion is, therefore, only part of a complicated series of exchanges in which both loyalty and authority are negotiated. The text of the fatwa may appear a thin edifice, but it rests on broad foundations.

Fatwas, therefore, are always the same and yet endlessly varied. Insofar as they advance the Islamic enterprise of doing the good and avoiding the evil, they carry out an imperative that allows no expansion or diminution. They also accommodate history, because the individual human beings who ask for opinions, as well as those who provide them, live in societies whose cultural, economic, and political foundations are shifting. Fatwas are at once the proclamation of a timeless ideal and a confession that ideals have significance only when actualized in particular times and places.

C H A P T E R   T W E N T Y - T W O

Mutʿa: Regulating Sexuality and Gender Relations in Postrevolutionary Iran

SHAHLA HAERI

In the aftermath of the 1979 Iranian revolution, the new leaders of the Islamic regime sought to "purify" Iran of Western influence. In connection with their effort to reform patterns of gender relations considered to be "corrupt" and "decadent," the revolutionary leaders approached Ayatollah Khomeini and asked him for guidance on what constitutes proper Islamic behavior. They posed the following question:

> Nowadays boys and girls study together and socialize in schools, colleges, and other institutions. They may want to conclude a temporary marriage [*mutʿa/sīgheh*][1] so that their socializing will not be sinful [*ḥarām*].[2] Your excellency has deemed a father's permission for a virgin daughter's [first] marriage necessary [*vājib*]. But there are times when many fathers are not willing to allow [this type of marriage], and so it is not possible to get their permission. Would Your Honor permit this condition to be dropped and allow temporary marriage to be contracted without a father's permission? Further, there are times when a girl who likes a boy feels embarrassed to obtain her father's permission. In this case, is it possible to avoid obtaining his permission?

The Ayatollah Khomeini answered:

> A father's permission cannot be dropped [*sāqiṭ*], and at present [*akhīran*] I see it as a necessary [*vājib*] condition. This is my fatwa. (Khomeini n.d.:510)[3]

I shall attempt to situate Ayatollah Khomeini's fatwa on temporary marriage, or *mutʿa,* in its contemporary historical context, with special reference to the history of relations between Shiʿis and Sunnis and between Iranians and the West. I argue that so long as the Shiʿis' adversaries and interlocutors were the Sunni majority, they defended the *legitimacy* of temporary marriage. Faced with greater involvement with the West in the twentieth century, and with the challenges of this complex and increasingly unequal relationship, Shiʿi jurists changed their strategy from defending the legitimacy of temporary marriage to representing it as one of the most "brilliant" and "far-sighted" aspects of Islamic thought and ideology. Specifically, I argue that the emerging internal political and religious contradictions in the Islamic regime rendered Ayatollah Khomeini's fatwa ineffective, even during his own lifetime. Almost in tandem with Ayatollah Khomeini's fatwa, the new Islamic regime made a concerted effort to rehabilitate the institution of temporary marriage (stigmatized under the previous regime) and to reintroduce it to the society from a new perspective. Evidence for this shift is found in a recent sermon *(khuṭba)* by the Iranian president, Rafsanjani, who bypasses Ayatollah Khomeini's fatwa, and, theoretically, grants greater autonomy to women.

Temporary Marriage: Sexual License or Sexual Control?

Except for one (disputed) reference to mutʿa marriage (Quran 4:24), the Quran contains no clear prescription regarding the structural elements and legal consequences of temporary marriage. Rather, during the period following the advent of Islam, such conditions gradually were conceptualized by Shiʿi jurists and given legal boundaries (Heffening 1992, 7:757–759).

The legal form of temporary marriage, as it came to be construed by Shiʿi jurists, is that of a contract between a married or unmarried man and an unmarried woman (virgin, divorced, or widowed). The duration of the marriage (anywhere from one hour to ninety-nine years) and the monetary consideration to be given to the wife must be specified at the outset. Neither witnesses nor registration is required, and the marriage contract does not envision any divorce procedure. At the end of the specified period, the partners part company without any ceremony. After the expiration of each marriage, no matter how short, the woman must maintain a period of sexual abstinence *(ʿidda)*[4] to ascertain the paternity of her child in case she is pregnant. It is the necessity of observing this condition that confers legitimacy on mutʿa and distinguishes it from prostitution, in the Shiʿi view.[5]

Of all the issues separating the Sunnis and Shiʿis, one of the most contentious and perennial has been that of mutʿa (literally, marriage of pleasure), known popularly among Iranian Shiʿis as *sīgheh*. Historical sources (Robertson Smith 1903), the early Islamic literature, and related texts indicate that mutʿa marriage was one of several types of marital relations that existed in Arabia prior to the emergence of Islam. In the seventh century, the second caliph, ʿUmar, issued an order banning mutʿa marriage soon after he assumed the caliphate. Maintaining that the Prophet outlawed all but one form of marital relation, that is, marriage by contract *(ʿaqd-i nikāḥ)*, ʿUmar identified "the mutʿa of women," as the custom was called at the time, as "fornication," which is explicitly condemned in the Quran. In theory, accordingly, the Sunnis do not practice temporary marriage. Although the Shiʿis at first did not object publicly to ʿUmar's order, they later challenged the legitimacy of the caliph's action, claiming that the Prophet permitted marriage of pleasure, pointing to Quran 4:24 as support for this view.

Classical Shiʿi jurists, with only minor variation, argued that a practice that has been mentioned in the Quran but not abrogated *(naskh)* by subsequent quranic verses or specifically banned by the Prophet Muhammad cannot be prohibited by any one else—at least not permanently.[6] In other words, even if one were to assume that ʿUmar's prohibitory order legitimately addressed the prevailing sociopolitical conditions—an argument not unanimously held by Shiʿis—that pronouncement would not have permanent applicability (al-Kashif al-Ghitaʿ 1968:268). More recently, the late Ayatollah Mutahhari (d. 1979) advanced the following rationale for ʿUmar's unilateral commandment: "The caliph's prohibitory order was political, not legal or religious. This is why the Muslims accepted such a ban. They considered the caliph's order to be a temporary political maneuver and not a permanent law. Otherwise it would have been impossible for the caliph to say that 'the Prophet has allowed something [viz., mutʿa] and I forbid you to use it,' and expect people to accept his command" (1974:49–48; see also Murata 1987; Shafaʾi 1973; Usif Makki 1963).

The Shiʿis' rejection of ʿUmar's order-cum-fatwa might also be understood within the context of their belief in the annulment of a fatwa upon the death of the religious leader proclaiming it (see below). This position, though not specifically stated by the Shiʿi ʿulamaʾ, provides them with a legitimate channel to initiate change and to offer fresh interpretations of Islamic law in the face of changing sociopolitical conditions. Temporary marriage is a case in point.

Community Control versus Individual Right: The Sunni-Shiʿi Dispute

In the contentious history of temporary marriage, one of the fundamental differences between the Sunnis and Shiʿis has centered on the issues of community control versus individual rights, paternal authority [that is, control of female sexuality and autonomy] and permissibility of temporary marriage [that is, male sexuality]. Challenged by the Sunnis, the Shiʿis consistently have maintained that temporary marriage is a legitimate form of marriage. Based on their interpretation of Quran 4:24, the Shiʿis argue that the objective of temporary marriage is to provide a moral way for men to seek sexual enjoyment—regardless of whether or not they are permanently married. Classical Shiʿi jurists justify the permissibility of temporary marriage on the ground of the irresistibility of sexual drives and human (read: male) nature. In their view, the individual (read: man) has the right to conclude as many temporary marriages as he likes.[7] This, the Shiʿi jurists argue, is the only moral and legal way to provide sexual gratification (for men) while at the same time controlling it.

Central to the Shiʿi-Sunni dispute has been the question of whether or not a father's permission is necessary for a daughter's marriage (Howard 1975), be she a virgin, a divorcée, or a widow. According to Stern (1939:37), the institution of guardianship is an Islamic creation that gives a father jural authority, control, and power over his daughter's activities. The Sunnis consistently and vociferously have maintained that a guardian *(valī)*, be he a father or someone else, must grant her permission to marry. The Shiʿis, on the other hand, have manifested uncertainty and ambivalence on the issue. Howard notes that the function and role of the guardian among the Shiʿis became intertwined with two other phenomena, namely, the necessity of witnesses for marriage and the custom of temporary marriage. In his view, the Shiʿis opposed the abolition of mutʿa marriage and the requirement of a guardian's permission for a divorced woman to remarry. But faced with a strong challenge from the Sunnis, the Shiʿis reluctantly conceded the advisability, although not the necessity, of witnesses for a permanent marriage (Howard 1975:85–87).

Noting the controversy, Shafaʾi relates the following hadith attributed to the Sixth Imam, Jaʿfar-i Sadiq: "Qamat has related from Abu ʿAbdullah, who asked the Imam, 'This virgin, unbeknownst to her parents, has invited me to go to her and expressed her interest in a mutʿa marriage. Is it permissible for me to marry [*mutʿa*] this girl?' The Imam replied, 'Yes, but refrain from having intercourse with her for mutʿa is shameful for virgins.' I asked, 'What if she is willing herself?' The Imam said, 'If she is willing, then it is not forbidden'" (1973:182, 226–229; see also Hilli 1968:518).[8]

The ideological ambivalence regarding the requirement of a guardian's permission (that is, control of women) and the custom of temporary marriage (that is, male sexuality) is reflected in the writings of different Shiʿi scholars. For example, while al-Kulaini's view (1958, vol. 5) is closer to that of the mainstream Sunnis, Tusi (d. 1067, 1964:472, 499) and Hilli (d. 1277, 1968:523) argue that a mature woman—nine years old and older—does not need her father's permission to arrange a marriage contract for herself. Both of them, however, concede that obtaining his permission is preferable.

This ambivalence has persisted to modern times. Some modern jurists make a distinction between a permanent and a temporary marriage, maintaining that a father's permission is necessary for an adult virgin's permanent marriage, but not for a temporary marriage. Others argue that an adult virgin may arrange her own permanent marriage but must obtain her father's permission for a temporary marriage (Imami 1971, 4:283–288; Langarudi 1976:23–28; Katuzian 1978:69). In his exegetical book, *Taḥrīr al-Vasīleh,* Ayatollah Khomeini presents the traditional Shiʿi view as follows: "A mature girl who is not a virgin does not need her father's or her guardian's permission. But if she is a virgin then it is best [*iḥtiyāt-i vājib;* note he does not say that it is necessary] that she should secure his permission, unless they prevent her from marrying someone who is of her status and who is willing to marry her. In this case, there is no problem if she marries without their permission" (cited in Biazar-i Shirazi 1987:55).

Iranian civil law, modified since the 1979 revolution, also adopted a variation of the classical Shiʿi interpretation, according to which an adult virgin Shiʿi woman, eighteen years of age or older, is given some degree of autonomy.[9] Although the law gives strong preference to obtaining a father's permission for a virgin daughter's first marriage, it envisions a situation in which a woman might arrange her own marriage if she can convince the court that her father (or her guardian) is unreasonable in withholding his permission (Article 1043, cited in Langarudi 1976:24). Iranian civil law remains silent on the issue of the advisability or the necessity of a guardian's permission in cases of temporary marriage.

Clashes of Worldviews: Tradition versus Modernity

As Iran became increasingly Westernized, modernized, and secular in the twentieth century, the Pahlavi shahs (1925–1979) adopted an attitude of benign neglect toward the institution of temporary marriage. Perhaps fearing a religious backlash, the state left the structure and function of the institution of temporary marriage virtually intact—while, in other respects, instituting major changes in the law of family and marriage during this period. The inability or unwillingness of the Pahlavi lawmakers to ban or to reform temporary marriage was offset by a media campaign that emphasized the backwardness of the institution and abuses relating to its practice. Subsequently, temporary marriage went underground, acquiring an aura of secrecy and fantasy and becoming further marginalized and stigmatized.

In 1963 Mohammad Reza Shah (1941–1979) proclaimed the so-called White Revolution, which included, among other things, land reform for the peasants and the political enfranchisement of women. These particular directives threatened the very foundation of the ʿulamaʾ's political and economic power, much of which had already been eroded by the secular policies of the regime. They protested strongly and vociferously, objecting to "women's liberation" and to the confiscation of religious endowments and redistribution of land among the landless peasants. They wrote extensively on why women should *not* be given the right to vote, to be elected to the Parliament, or to be appointed as judges. (It is significant that many of the same jurists, including Ayatollah Khomeini, reversed their earlier objections to women's political rights when they acquired political power, at which time they honored the existing electoral law).

Empowered by their new electoral rights, women agitated for change in the area of family law, with the result that in 1967 the Parliament (Majlis) passed the Family Protection Law (FPL), later revised in 1975. Although the law did not directly address the institution of temporary marriage, it attempted to restrict it indirectly by making the privilege of marrying a second wife contingent on a court's permission. In the mass media, particularly women's journals and magazines, the institution of temporary marriage was vilified and equated with legalized prostitution. Pundits argued that the continued functioning—often underground—of temporary marriage would lead to corruption in society and insecurity in marriage (see *Zan-i Rūz* from 1967 to 1975; Manuchihrian 1978).

Tension mounted between Shiʿi jurists, who perceived temporary marriage as a divine blessing for the community of believers, and secular authorities, who espoused legal reform in the marriage law and social change in the status of women. Threatened by the impact of Western values on the fabric of Iranian social life, Muslim jurists argued that precisely because temporary marriage is legal and religiously sanctioned, it allows men (and, as an afterthought, women) a legally and morally acceptable means to satisfy their sexual needs, making it unnecessary to resort to adultery or fornication, or, worse yet, to indulge in imitating the Western form of "free love." In their view, temporary marriage prevents prostitution and corruption (see al-Kashif al-Ghitaʿ 1968; Makarim-i Shirazi 1968; Shafa'i 1973; Mutahhari 1974; Khomeini 1982).

However, since the balance of power already had tilted in favor of the secular regime, the ʿulama''s protest and opposition resonated primarily among their own supporters and sympathizers. Secularized, educated, and urban Iranians evidently were oblivious of the religious counterdiscourse and the direction it was taking.

Some Iranian ʿulamaʾ mounted a sustained attack on both the regime and "liberated" women. They wrote articles in religious journals in defense of temporary marriage, challenging the corrupt and "West-toxicated" Iranian regime, "loose" women, and the secular elite. A leading Shiʿi scholar's book, *Our Custom,* which was translated from Arabic into Persian in 1968, contains a long section devoted to the defense of the institution of temporary marriage, while refuting various Sunni accusations. Concerned with the "corrupting" influence of the West on the fabric of social life in the major cities of Iran, the book's translator, Makarim-i Shirazi, the well-known editor of the monthly *Maktab-i Islām,* wrote an epilogue in which he discussed, perhaps for the first time in the tendentious history of mutʿa marriage, the particular relevance of temporary marriage in the modern world. Advancing a novel interpretation, Makarim-i Shirazi argued that temporary marriage represents a potential solution to the "problem of youth" (1968:381). With an eye toward the West, he argued that sexual drive peaks during adolescence and cannot be ignored, denied, or allowed to get out of hand. Because this is a period in which youth are busy with their education, they cannot be expected to accept the responsibilities associated with permanent marriage. Therefore, the best way to resolve the "problem of youth" is to allow them to make use of a contract of temporary marriage (pp. 382–383). His reformulation of the raison d'être of temporary marriage also shifted its target audience from married men who are separated from their wives to young men and women who can no longer be segregated into public and private domains, because of the necessities of modern life.

In his book *Legal Rights of Women in Islam* (1974; reprinted several times), Ayatollah Mutahhari elaborated on Makarim-i Shirazi's idea, albeit with greater clarity and conviction. He argued not only for the legitimacy of temporary marriage in an Islamic society, but also for its necessity. He characterized temporary marriage as one of the most "brilliant" laws of Islam, as a farsighted idea, and as being morally superior to its Western counterpart of "free" and "decadent" male-female relationships. In his words:

> The characteristic feature of our modern age is the lengthening of the span of time between natural puberty and social maturity, when one becomes capable of establishing a family . . . Are the young ready to undergo a period of temporary asceticism and put themselves under the strain of rigid austerity till such time as there may arise an occasion for permanent marriage? Suppose a young person is prepared to undergo temporary asceticism: will nature be ready to forgo the formation of the dreadful and dangerous psychological penalties which are found in the wake of abstaining from instinctive sexual activity and which psychiatrists are now discovering? (Mutahhari 1974:52–53)

By the time the Islamic regime wrested state power and its apparatus from the Pahlavi regime in 1979, Mutahhari's argument had become a familiar refrain among the clergy and could be heard all across the country.

Shortly after the revolution, politically secure and in control of the media, leaders of the Islamic regime, jurists, and low-ranking mullahs went public. On national television, on radio talk shows, at religious gatherings, in schools, in newspapers and magazines, and in other public forums, they made a concerted effort to discuss the moral, psychological, and physical benefits of temporary marriage. In 1980–1981, for the first time in the history of modern Iran, a religious education textbook was published with a full chapter on temporary marriage, spelling out the specifics of the institution and its benefit for youth (Bahunar 1981:35–42). Editorials appearing in various newspapers and magazines seized on the topic with zest, discussing its advantages for the (male) individual and for society at large. (The only public forum that consistently criticized temporary marriage and its adverse and potentially harmful effects on married and unmarried women was [and is] *Zan-i Rūz,* [Modern Woman] a popular weekly women's magazine).

Although statistics are lacking as to the approximate number of men and women who actually use this form of marriage, judging from the concern raised in daily newspapers, in women's magazines, and in popular discourse, it is evident that the practice of temporary marriage has found its niche in high schools, on university campuses, and in the workplace. Taking advantage of this new opportunity, and much to the chagrin of their elders and parents—indeed unbeknownst to them—an unspecified number of young men and women have engaged in this form of sexual union since the establishment of the Islamic regime in Iran.

The publicity afforded mutʿa marriage and the drive to make its use more palatable to the public and more accessible to young people has threatened parental authority and control over a young woman's choice of a marriage partner and her ability to engage in sexual activities. Such publicity has offended the sensibilities of many secularized and modernized middle-class Iranians.

This is the context in which Ayatollah Khomeini's learned opinion was sought. In the confused and chaotic conditions of postrevolutionary Iran, Ayatollah Khomeini felt the need to maintain order and provide moral guidance. Ironically, the widespread positive publicity on the merits of temporary marriage disseminated by the regime that Ayatollah Khomeini helped to bring to power rendered the effectiveness of his own fatwa negligible.

Leadership and Legitimacy: Fatwa Dead or Alive?

Ayatollah Khomeini died in June of 1989. According to the majority Shiʿi view, a fatwa dies with the mufti or mujtahid who issued it, because it is inappropriate to "follow" or "imitate" (taqlid) a dead leader. The idea is that in the presence of a living mujtahid it is morally and legally incorrect to follow a dead one, no matter how exalted his position among his followers—"A dead person cannot mediate between God and the people" (Kirmani n.d:334).[10] The majority view among the Ja'fari Shi'is is that a mujtahid's specific pronouncement remains in force only during his lifetime (Langarudi 1967:618). As sociopolitical conditions change, successive generations of mujtahids give fresh interpretations, some of which may conflict with, or negate, those issued by earlier mujtahids.

The underlying logic here is the Shi'i conviction that the Twelfth Imam, or Mahdi, is still living, although he is in occultation. Thus a mujtahid serves as his vice-regent (Kirmani n.d.:334–335; Tabataba'i 1975:104), and his fatwas and edicts are effective only so long as he is alive. This is a major difference between the Shi'i conception of futya and that of the Sunnis.[11] The Sunni-Shi'i difference over ijtihad is, in my view, also related to their dispute regarding the legitimacy of temporary marriage. If Shi'is were to accept the efficacy of a fatwa after the death of the mujtahid who issued it, they would have to recognize the legitimacy and permanency of 'Umar's prohibitory "fatwa" on temporary marriage.

That the Ayatollah Khomeini's fatwa on temporary marriage is no longer operative is supported by a controversial public sermon given by the Iranian president Hashimi Rafsanjani on November 1990—barely a year after the ayatollah's death.[12] From the politically and religiously important pulpit of the Friday mosque, Rafsanjani addressed a huge audience, drawing the people's attention, once again, to the "problem of youth" in Iranian urban areas.[13] Following in the footsteps of his "modernist" predecessors, he admonished certain unnamed self-righteous zealots who mistakenly assume that the association of young men and women is necessarily wrong:

> Nowadays, in our [modern] society, young people mature at the age of fifteen, and sexual needs awaken in them . . . Our college students are constantly exposed to the opposite sex in schools, universities, parks, buses, bazaars, and the workplace. They are continuously stimulated [by mutual proximity], but have no recourse [to satisfy their desires]. Who says this is correct? Presently, in our society, for our youth to remain pure and honorable and to respect the societal norms [of chastity and virginity] implies that they must remain unsatisfied [unable to get married] until they are twenty-five or thirty years old. They have to deprive themselves of their natural desires. Deprivation is harmful. (*Zan-i Rūz* 1294 (1990):55; Haeri 1992:202)

Rafsanjani then reiterated with rhetorical flourish the idea that temporary marriage is the answer to the moral and sexual problems of youth in the context of a modern society. He did not invoke the name of Ayatollah Khomeini to underscore the legitimacy of his assertion, despite the fact that the appeal to his authority is a cardinal principle among current Iranian leaders. In fact, unlike Ayatollah Khomeini, Rafsanjani suggested that if a young couple feels shy about going to a mullah to perform the rite or to register their temporary marriage, they may bypass this feature of the ritual by simply agreeing mutally to have a private contract "to be together for a month or two." He further proposed that if the performance of the marriage ceremony in Arabic is difficult, "the young couple can recite the marriage formula in Persian and in the absence of a mullah or other witnesses" (*Zan-i Rūz* 1294 (1990):55).

While Ayatollah Khomeini's fatwa went largely unheeded in the urban areas of Iran (temporary marriage is primarily an urban phenomenon), Rafsanjani's Friday sermon set off a storm of controversy. His comments evidently were perceived as undermining parental authority and downplaying the cultural significance and symbolic value of virginity. His repeated public attempts to rehabilitate temporary marriage and to encourage young men and women to use it, while perhaps popular with young people, met with opposition from parents and from more modernized and secular Iranians, particularly women. While parents and women's guardians perceive such publicity and argument as a threat to their time-honored authority, women understand it as a threat to the stability and security of marriage. The practice and custom of mutʿa thus continues to be a source of moral ambivalence and emotional conflict in Iran.

Conclusion

As political and religious leaders in postrevolutionary Islamic Iran, Ayatollah Khomeini and President Rafsanjani both responded to challenges emanating from the superimposition of a theocracy on an already existing secular and modern state. They also were caught in the emerging religious and political contradictions within the new Islamic state, and the unforeseen circumstances arising from the state's advocacy of temporary marriage. The two leaders approached the issue quite differently.

In his fatwa, Ayatollah Khomeini sought to achieve two objectives: to curb women's (perceived) autonomy and to reinvest the control of a woman's (sexual) activities in her guardian's care. Ironically, despite the long and contentious debate regarding the legitimacy of temporary marriage and the necessity of a guardian's permission, Ayatollah Khomeini's fatwa came very close to the view espoused by the Sunnis. Further, his fatwa echoed the strong cultural sentiment in favor of parental authority and control of female sexuality (that is, virginity). He parted company with the prevailing Shiʿi view, which does allow women, however minimally and ambivalently, a measure of autonomy to arrange a mutʿa marriage for themselves.[14]

Mindful of the economic necessity that brought an ever-greater number of women into the public domain in the aftermath of Iran-Iraq war (1980–1988), President Rafsanjani's sermon-cum-fatwa placed greater emphasis on individual autonomy, including that of women. Ignoring Ayatollah Khomeini's fatwa and the cultural stigmatization of temporary marriage, Rafsanjani drew on classical Shiʿi religious law to sanction the contracting of a temporary marriage. Rafsanjani, of course, is not a mujtahid, and he is not legally and religiously expected to issue fatwas interpreting God's law on earth. He *is,* however, the highest ranking Iranian political leader with a religious title,[15] albeit one of lesser importance. To give his comments greater influence, he chose to address the public from the pulpit rather than from the office of the president.

Due to pressing public needs and political concerns, the efficacy of Ayatollah Khomeini's fatwa was undermined during his own lifetime. Its fall into oblivion was hastened by the Islamic regime's advocacy of temporary marriage and Rafsanjani's frequent sermons in support of it. The life expectancy of Shiʿi fatwas thus depends not only on the life and death of the mujtahid, but also on the fatwa's sociopolitical significance and on other prevailing political concerns.

CHAPTER TWENTY-THREE

The Complementarity of *Iftāʾ* and *Qaḍāʾ*: Three Saudi Fatwas on Divorce

FRANK E. VOGEL

Saudi Arabia's legal system is governed by the traditional corpus of Islamic law, fiqh, to an extent equalled by no other existing national legal system. Saudi Arabia was never colonized, and, unlike virtually every other Islamic country, it has not replaced its legal system with a Western-model constitutional and legal order. Still, the Saudi system has been considerably modernized in two respects. First, the prevailing law, the fiqh of the Hanbali school, has been extensively supplemented by decree-laws issued by the king in areas where modern arrangements demand new legal provisions. Second, the legal system has undergone considerable administrative and institutional development and rationalization. Even with these changes, however, the Saudi legal system remains at heart animated by Islamic legal conceptions and practices very close to those that shaped the first Saudi state 250 years ago.

In the first part of this chapter, I present three fatwas by the Saudi mufti Shaykh ʿAbd al-ʿAziz b. ʿAbd Allah Ibn Baz on questions in the law of divorce. In the second part, I review the function of fatwas as a means of applying law, showing how *iftāʾ* and *qaḍāʾ* (adjudication) serve distinct but complementary purposes in the application of the shariʿa. Finally, I ask whether this complementarity is reflected in Saudi legal institutions, finding that, as to divorce law, the courts and iftaʾ bodies do cooperate institutionally in the application of the law. This is shown by the courts' extending of various forms of recognition, even enforcement, to Shaykh Ibn Baz's fatwas on divorce.

The Fatwas

In Saudi Arabia fatwas can be obtained from religious scholars either privately or through public agencies established for that purpose. In either case, the authority of a fatwa derives from the reputation for learning and piety of the person who issues it. Even fatwas issued by members of the public agencies for ifta᾽ are associated with their issuers.[1]

Two public agencies exist to issue fatwas (Kingdom of Saudi Arabia 1971).[2] The first is the Board of Senior ʿUlama᾽, composed of about fifteen senior religious-legal scholars appointed by the king. The board conducts studies and adopts formal fatwas on major public issues, acting either in response to an inquiry from the king or independently. The second agency for fatwas is the Standing Committee for Ifta᾽, made up of four members of the board, selected by the king, who work full-time responding to requests from private citizens for guidance on their personal affairs. The Standing Committee is administratively part of a larger independent government agency, a "General Presidency," responsible not only for private ifta᾽ but also religious research, "call" (the propagation of Islam), and "guidance" (public instruction in religion).[3] The Presidency also provides administrative support to the Board of Senior ʿUlama᾽.

Shaykh Ibn Baz is the most famous and powerful contemporary *ʿālim* in Saudi Arabia. He holds a number of important positions, including that of head of the General Presidency just mentioned, member of the Board of Senior ʿUlama᾽, and member of the Standing Committee for Ifta᾽. Owing to these positions and his general influence, he is unofficially called mufti of Saudi Arabia.

The fatwas treated here are taken from Shaykh Ibn Baz's regular column in the Presidency's weekly magazine, *al-Daʿwā*,[4] in which he answers fatwa requests sent in by readers.

The fatwas all concern divorce by *ṭalāq*—that is, divorce by the husband's repudiation. *Ṭalāq* is a purely verbal act, the pronouncing of words conveying divorce, and it requires no formality, not even witnesses. The insubstantiality of the act of *ṭalāq* occasions many difficult legal problems, three of which are dealt with in these fatwas.

Ṭalāq *by Oath*

A long-standing practice in Muslim societies is the fortifying of vows by invoking the penalty of divorce from one's wife should the vow be broken. This can be done by conditional *ṭalāq:* for example, "My wife is divorced if I ever drink wine again" or "if my wife ever talks to so-and-so." Most early fiqh authorities held that such a divorce was operative automatically on fulfillment of the condition, and this is the view generally applied in the Saudi courts.[5]

The Board of Senior ʿUlama᾽ undertook to study this issue and, based on an extensive research report, adopted a fatwa favoring the traditional ruling (Board of Senior ʿUlama᾽ 1980). A minority of the board, however, including Shaykh Ibn Baz, differed and adopted a dissenting opinion.

In the following fatwa Shaykh Ibn Baz states this position:

> Reader Kh. Kh. H. from al-Qasim sends us a question in which he states: I made an oath against my younger brother upon divorce [*ṭalāq*] if he went out of the house. Despite this he went out. When I made this oath upon divorce, I did not intend divorce, but merely intimidation, and I was in great anger. But after my anger subsided, I forgave him. I request a fatwa: has a divorce occurred or not? May God preserve and keep you.
>
> *Answer:* If the facts, questioner, are as you have described them, and you did not intend the occurrence of the divorce if your brother went out, and you intended only to restrain and frighten him, then you are obliged to perform the atonement [*kaffāra*][6] according to the more correct of the two opinions of the *ʿulamāʾ*, and no divorce of your wife occurs thereby . . . God is the giver of good fortune. (Ibn Baz 1986a)[7]

Ṭalāq *Uttered in Anger*

Many questions arise as to the validity of divorces uttered when the husband is not aware of, or does not intend, the consequences of his act. Fiqh works discuss the validity of *ṭalāq* issued by a husband who is mentally deficient, intoxicated, or jesting. A related problem, very commonly occurring, is the effect of *ṭalāq* uttered in a state of extreme anger. May the husband avoid *ṭalāq* on the ground that his anger was a sort of temporary insanity? What if he simply lost his head and now regrets what he did?

The Hanbali school as applied in Saudi Arabia's shariʿa courts is strict on this point. It nullifies the divorce only if the speaker was so angry as to have virtually lost consciousness, and, in particular, to have had no recollection of his act, drawing here an analogy to divorce uttered by one asleep or in a swoon or faint (al-Bahuti 1982, 5:235; al-Bahuti n.d., 3:120; Ibn Qudama 1983, 8:254–255).

Shaykh Ibn Baz again differs, adopting a minority view that avoids the divorce if the husband's true intent was not to divorce. This position is reflected in the following fatwa:

> Reader Muhammad al-ʿUmari sent us a question, in which he says: I became extremely angry at my wife, because of a small thing she did, and after my anger subsided, my wife told me that I pronounced a divorce during my anger, a single [and therefore revocable] divorce. I sat down to remember if this divorce had issued from me, and then remembered it, but I was not sure of it completely. I do not have the intention of divorcing my wife, but my tongue slipped, and anger overcame me without any object, while I have confidence

> that my wife was not lying. I retracted the divorce at once . . . I request from Your Eminence your fatwa whether the divorce occurred . . .
>
> *Answer:* . . . The safer course for you is to count this divorce [toward the maximum of three divorces] and consider it as having occurred, because of what you wrote about remembering it, and your confidence in the statement of your wife, in fulfillment of the Saying of the Prophet (S), "One who is wary of dubious cases is delivered in his religion and his honor," and his Saying, "Leave what causes you doubt for what does not cause you doubt." (Ibn Baz 1986b)

Note that Shaykh Ibn Baz in this fatwa reveals his own more lenient position in that he does not hold the requestor's remembering the act to be conclusive.[8] In the cautelary tradition of fatwas, he adverts to the majority view as a warning that there is an authoritative view stricter than his own.

Triple Divorce by a Single Expression

Ṭalāq divorce may be revocable (for the period of the wife's waiting period, or *ʿidda,* usually three months), or irrevocable. Irrevocable divorces are in two degrees: the lesser, which permits the parties to remarry, and the greater, which bars remarriage until after the wife has married another man and that marriage is consummated and terminated. A husband may divorce his wife twice, either revocably or irrevocably in the lesser degree, but upon a third *ṭalāq,* the divorce is of the greater degree of irrevocability. Early in Muslim history the practice arose of issuing three divorces at once, the husband ridding himself of his wife in one dramatic, fatal stroke. Historically, Sunni fiqh authorities have almost universally held that such a triple divorce has full effect as triple, even though they decry it as sinful and even forbidden.[9] However sinful, this form seems always to have been in common use, to the extent that many Muslim men today seem to know of no other form.

In Saudi Arabia this view of triple divorce has always been the majority view, being early endorsed by leaders of the Wahhabi movement (Ibn Qasim 1965, 8:379–380). It is the rule applied by most qadis in the shariʿa courts. There is, however, a minority view, even in the courts, that owes its persistence to the great Hanbali Taqi al-Din Ahmad Ibn Taymiyya (d. 1328), whose influence over the Wahhabis of Arabia has always been great. In one of his most famous opinions, Ibn Taymiyya held that the triple divorce should be counted only as a single, revocable *ṭalāq.* He was able to cite as authorities in his favor the earliest practice of the Muslim community and the opinions of a number of Companions, Successors, and early jurists (Ibn al-Qayyim al-Jawziyya 1973, 3:30–50).

Once again, the Board of Senior ʿUlamaʾ chose this issue for study and adopted a decision endorsing the majority view (Board of Senior ʿUlamaʾ 1977a). And, once again, a minority of the Board differed, among them Shaykh Ibn Baz.[10]

Thus, on all three issues, Shaykh Ibn Baz adopts positions lenient toward husbands wishing to avoid the consequences of their acts of *ṭalāq*.

Complementarity of Iftaʾ and Qadaʾ as Methods of Applying Law

Before considering the role of Shaykh Ibn Baz's fatwas in the Saudi legal system, it is useful to review key functional distinctions between iftaʾ and qadaʾ as institutions for the application of the shariʿa. (These distinctions are discussed at greater length in Chapter 1.) The following statement by Ibn al-Qayyim al-Jawziyya (d. 1350), Ibn Taymiyya's great pupil and successor, gives a good summary:

> The [mufti's] fatwa is a law [shariʿa], which is general and concerns both the requestor and others . . . The mufti opines in a ruling that is generally worded and generally applicable [*ʿāmm kullī*], that to one who does so-and-so is applicable such-and-such, or one who says so-and-so is obliged to do such-and-such. The qadi makes a particular judgment upon a particular person, [not extending to anyone but the two parties,] and his judgment is specific in terms and obligatory . . . [T]he fatwa of the scholar is general in terms and not obligatory. (Ibn al-Qayyim al-Jawziyya 1973, 1:37–38)

Ibn al-Qayyim al-Jawziyya identifies as key distinctions the following: (a) the fatwa states a *general,* abstract rule, while the judgment is *particular* and concrete; (b) the fatwa has a potentially *universal application* to the class of persons to whom the abstract ruling applies, while the judgment has *unique application,* to only the parties and event judged; (c) the fatwa is *not obligatory,* but is only advice to the person requesting it, who has the responsibility to apply it to himself or herself (in his or her "inner forum," so to speak), while the judgment is *compulsory* and enforced (in the "external forum"). I would add to this list several other distinctions, which are partly implied in Ibn al-Qayyim al-Jawziyya's statement and partly obvious: (d) the mufti deals only with *abstract fact,* as stated to him by the requestor, while the qadi engages *concrete fact;* (e) the mufti leaves the truth of *facts* to be *determined by the requestor,* while in court the *facts are tried* through evidentiary procedures; (f) the fatwa is relatively *personal and singular,* in respect to both the mufti and the requestor, while the judgment is relatively *public and multiple,* involving the qadi, the two litigants, and the functionaries of the state.[11]

Islamic law, of course, demands application not only in matters of "law" in the Western sense, but also in matters of religious conscience, ritual observance, ethics, family relations, and social manners. Given this comprehensiveness of the shariʿa, ifta᾽ is a natural complement to qada᾽ in securing the shariʿa's application. The most obvious examples are the detailed laws governing the validity of rituals like prayer, fasting, or the pilgrimage. Such laws depend ultimately on the individual's conscience for their implementation, relatively remote from issues of compulsion and proof. The individual is his or her own fact-finder and verdict-giver, guided as to the law by a fatwa (just as an Anglo-American jury decides the ultimate issues of a case, guided by the judge's instructions). But beyond such clear cases of conscience, fatwas are very often useful where more persons than one are involved and even are in contention. When the issues raised are particularly charged with religion and morality or involve psychologically subtle facts, difficulties of proof, concerns for privacy and intimacy, or strong group pressures toward conformity, resort to fatwas instead of adjudication may be natural. Here the clear example is family law. Saudi families very often forgo a binding judgment and submit internal disputes to the fatwa of a religious figure whom all members respect. Given these two examples of fatwa use, for enforcing ritual observance and resolving family disputes, it is not surprising to learn that in Saudi Arabia the great bulk of fatwas concern the laws of either ritual or the family (Puin 1977).

Complementarity between Ifta᾽ and Qaḍa᾽ Institutions

Besides providing fatwas for individual or private applications of the law, how else does the Saudi legal system employ fatwas? In particular, are there institutional arrangements in place that exploit the complementarity of ifta᾽ and qaḍa᾽? The most obvious place to look for these is in dealings between the two major institutions responsible for ifta᾽ and qada᾽, the Standing Committee and the shariʿa courts.[12] Some observations I made in the Marriage Court of the Great Shariʿa Court of Riyadh are suggestive, and call for further investigation. I found the qadi of that court not only paying respect to Shaykh Ibn Baz's fatwas on divorce, but also actively assisting parties to take advantage of those fatwas. This was made clear on two occasions.

The first occasion concerns the issue of triple divorce. A married couple came before the qadi and related that the husband had uttered a triple divorce, which they wished to avoid. It turned out that the pair had already been to Shaykh Ibn Baz, who instructed them to ask the qadi to prepare for them a statement of the facts of their case, on the basis of which the shaykh would then issue his fatwa (Marriage Court 1983). The qadi explained to me that, had the parties instead tried their case before him (as might have occurred had the wife insisted on the fact of divorce),[13] he would have been obliged to give effect to the triple divorce.

The second occasion involves the issue of the husband's intent in uttering *ṭalāq*. Appearing with his wife and their respective families, a husband stated that he had divorced his wife by *ṭalāq* three times on three different occasions. This would ordinarily entail that she is forbidden to him until after her marriage to another man. But, he added, the first divorce had been the subject of a fatwa from Shaykh Ibn Baz nullifying it on the ground of his state of anger. The qadi credited this result without further investigation, and suggested that the parties remarry (that is, conclude a new marriage contract).[14] The wife, however, would not consent to the remarriage, which left the husband helpless and terminated the case (Marriage Court 1983).

In these two cases, the parties' invocations of Shaykh Ibn Baz's advice are accepted as valid dispositions not open to reversal or upset in court—and this although the qadi himself would have reached opposite results had the cases been tried in his court.

In a number of respects, arrangements such as those exhibited here are extremely practical and useful, and deploy ifta' and qada' effectively according to the complementary functions of each. First, note that parties who desire a particular result are able to obtain it, if that result enjoys the support of a respected religious figure—even when it is in conflict with the law as applied by the courts. Second, note that such fatwa-mediated outcomes, while they add flexibility to the standard law, do not undermine it or, with it, long-standing family and social arrangements and expectations. For example, the law of the triple divorce has been intimately involved in the workings of families for centuries. Even if a Saudi qadi is attracted to Shaykh Ibn Baz's view as a matter of principle, he may, out of concern for the law's stability and predictability, feel reluctant to adopt it as his own general ruling. If the parties agree on that outcome, however, such concerns are far reduced. Third, note how Shaykh Ibn Baz's outcomes, particularly on such issues as divorce by oath or in anger, are much better suited to application in the "inner forum" than in the "outer," depending as they do on exquisitely subjective facts (chiefly, the husband's intent to divorce). If the context were instead a dispute in court about whether divorce occurred, how could the husband's claim be proved or disproved?[15] The rule might become a blank check to avoid divorce, or to make *ṭalāq* the husband's plaything, destructive of family stability and the wife's peace of mind. Fourth, a mufti, to the extent that he has interaction with the requestor or can otherwise divine the nature of the case, may be able to tailor the ruling to the moral circumstances, accounting for such factors as a wife's reluctance to resume the marriage or a husband's violence, better than a court could, with its external procedures and compulsory judgment.[16]

Conclusion

From these observations, hypotheses of various types are suggested. One has to do with applications of the shariʿa in private, familial, and communal spheres, where the fatwa is used to resolve disputes by voluntary or consensual ordering, without state compulsion. Such practices should be studied and reassessed as to their significance in the application of the shariʿa. Another type of hypothesis concerns use of the fatwa method to lend flexibility even to compulsory legal determinations—indeed to make available for such determinations multiple legal outcomes on any single issue. We should look carefully for further instances of such use, reexamining particularly those procedures, common enough historically, in which a mufti (or muftis) worked hand-in-hand with the qadi, even to the point of observing cases and offering opinions that the latter would enact as his judgment.

Investigations into both these types of hypotheses could well lead to results altering certain long-standing Western judgments about fiqh, particularly as to its rigidity, idealism, and impracticability.

CHAPTER TWENTY-FOUR

The Fatwa as an Instrument of Accommodation

AHARON LAYISH

In this chapter I wish to examine the fatwa as an instrument used to bring a semi-nomadic tribal society within the orbit of normative Islam. Though the influence of Islam on Bedouin law dates back many centuries, orthodox Islam, with its system of beliefs and institutions, plays no central role in shaping a nomadic Bedouin society. Though the Bedouin are Muslims, they generally do not fulfill ritual precepts properly or regulate matters of personal status or succession in accordance with the shariʿa. As they grow progressively more sedentary, however, the Bedouin draw closer to normative Islam, which gradually becomes their binding lifestyle as regards worship, pious duties, and law, and they express increasing acceptance of Islamic institutions and of religious functionaries as the guardians, exponents, and practitioners of the shariʿa (Layish and Shmueli 1979:32–42; Layish 1980–1982:206–221).

The fatwa is the legal opinion of a mufti. It is intended to elucidate, at the request of an inquirer, a position on a legal issue. Unlike the judgment of a qadi, it binds neither the inquirer nor anyone else. The qadi bears the primary responsibility of applying the shariʿa to a nomadic, tribal society in the process of becoming sedentary (Layish 1984:41–50; Layish, 1991a:85ff.). The mufti also plays an important role in bringing the Bedouin within the orbit of the shariʿa. He replaces the qadi where the formalities of the latter's office, and especially the school of law to which he belongs, tend to discourage the Bedouin from turning to the shariʿa for help in settling their disputes. The mufti's main function with respect to bringing the Bedouin closer to the shariʿa is to enlist the religio-legal literature in support of a mitigation of the shariʿa and a reduction of its severity so as to enable the Bedouin to absorb it into their lifestyle without undue conflict with their customary norms and rules.

The Institutional Setting

The Bedouin of the Judean Desert are subject to the jurisdiction of the shariʿa courts of Jerusalem and Bethlehem. Since the annexation of the West Bank by the Kingdom of Jordan, the Jordanian law of personal status has applied in these courts. Alongside the courts, tribal arbitrators act without any statutory status. The Bedouin of the Judean Desert resort to both the qadi and to the tribal arbitrator. In matters of personal status, the arbitrator gradually has been superseded by the institutionalized qadi, whose position has been reinforced by the execution of his judgments and by civil regulations (such as the requirement that marital status be recorded in identity cards and that government licenses be obtained for various day-to-day activities) that have prompted the Bedouin to resort to the court.

In Jordan, muftis linked to shariʿa courts in the main districts are found throughout the country. Staff lists and salary records suggest that the formal status of these muftis in the hierarchy of religious scholars is lower than that of the qadis in their respective districts. Nevertheless, the mufti's public status may be higher than that of the qadi, depending on the former's personality and legal and moral authority. In addition to the appointed muftis, religious scholars (ʿulamaʾ) and jurists *(fuqahāʾ)* serve as muftis without appointment. They are not integrated into the establishment; their status is based on their personal authority. They regard themselves as competent to decide, at the request of members of the public, all matters to which the shariʿa applies, not just matters that fall within the jurisdiction of the shariʿa court (Layish 1977:97–108).

The applicant for the legal opinion in the case under discussion here, Shaykh ʿAli Hasan, belongs to a clan *(hamoula)* of the al-Radaʾida ʿArab al-ʿUbaydiyya. This tribe is located east of Bayt Sahur in the Jerusalem-Bethlehem region. The sedentarization of the tribe began in the 1920s and is now almost complete (Layish and Shmueli 1979:30). It seems that Shaykh ʿAli Hasan chose to apply to the mufti because he surmised that he could not expect the shariʿa court to extricate him from the predicament into which he had stumbled.

The resulting fatwa was later given to me by Shaykh ʿAli Hasan. It belongs to a collection of legal documents gathered from tribal arbitrators in the Judean Desert and from the archives of shariʿa courts. Although the scholar who signed the fatwa is unknown to me, references in the legal opinion to the religio-legal literature indicate that he had a sound traditional training in Islamic law. In any case, the scholar, who identifies himself as a Shafiʿi, appears not to be a mufti by appointment, because his opinion is not written on official stationery and is not dated. This indicates that he was not affiliated with an institution but rather was acting in a private capacity. His authority derives from his generally recognized learning and probably also from his reputation as a pragmatist who resolves legal situations involving hardship. Such an independent mufti gives an opinion to every comer, in the best classical tradition, and probably receives a fee for his trouble.

Reasoning and Style of the Fatwa

The *sharʿī* mechanism of suspended repudiation distinguishes between repudiation intended to ensure the wife's obedience to the husband and repudiation involving an oath, lending additional weight to some utterances of the husband, in which case there is no intention of divorce. In both cases, the divorce becomes effective upon the fulfillment of the condition or contingency mentioned in the oath (Layish 1975:137ff., 156ff.; Anderson 1976:123ff.; Anderson 1970, 362–363). Shaykh ʿAli Hasan had divorced his wife by an oath of suspended repudiation intended to emphasize his determination in a matter that had nothing to do with his wife. He had repeated the oath several times. The condition of the repudiation materialized, and it was pointed out to him that his wife was now divorced by three successive repudiations, even though he had not intended to divorce her. It seems that the shaykh's attention was drawn to the position of the shariʿa in this matter—namely, that the only way to rehabilitate his marriage would be to have his wife marry a third party, who would then divorce her.

All the schools agree that the intermediate marriage must be contracted in good faith and must be consummated before it can be dissolved. The woman can remarry her former husband only on the expiration of the waiting period *(ʿidda)*. However, there are differences between the schools regarding the application of this principle. The Hanafi school holds that the intermediate marriage is valid even with the (unexpressed) intention to render the woman lawfully permitted again to her former husband *(bi-qaṣd al-taḥlīl),* while other schools hold that such a marriage does not meet the requirements of the intermediate marriage and hence is null and void (Layish 1991:173ff.). The Shariʿa Court of Bethlehem was bound by the Hanafi doctrine, which attaches no importance to the element of intent *(niyya)* in the oath. In other words, the wife was divorced even though there had been no intent to divorce her. Under these circumstances, the shaykh sought a remedy that would spare him the need to separate from his wife and to surrender her, albeit only temporarily, to another. It is doubtful whether the shaykh was fully aware of differences between the Hanafi doctrine prevailing in the courts (a heritage from the period of Ottoman rule in the region) and the Shafiʿi doctrine followed by the local Muslim population in matters other than personal status. It seems, however, that from the experience of other Bedouin, he had good reason to believe that a Shafiʿi mufti could solve his problem one way or another, and for this reason he decided to resort to him.

The mufti proposed a solution to the shaykh's predicament that was based on three alternative legal determinations: (1) the shaykh had not intended to divorce his wife when he uttered the suspended repudiation, which means that the marriage remains valid as if nothing had happened; (2) the divorce was a revocable divorce, which does not dissolve the marriage immediately and enables the husband to reinstate the wife within the waiting period; and (3) the shaykh conceded that the original marriage had not conformed with the requirements of Islamic law but was based on tribal custom. This conception of the matter indeed makes it necessary for the shaykh to separate from his wife and to remarry her in accordance with *sharʿī* requirements, but it does not involve heavy legal costs, because the couple's children would be considered legitimate on the strength of their being acknowledged, and, most important, the wife would not have to contract an intermediate marriage in order to be permitted again to the husband.

Being unfamiliar with Islamic law and technical terminology, the shaykh probably asked his question orally in colloquial Arabic, whereas the mufti formulated and wrote down the question very succinctly in the technical language of the law, in the third person, adding introductory and closing formulas interspersed with religious elements, as are usual in legal documents.[1]

The style of the fatwa is professional and matter-of-fact. The alternative determinations are formulated very succinctly, but in such a way as to be intelligible only to those familiar with Islamic law and Islamic legal literature. The name of a famous scholar is invoked, probably in order to lend greater authority to the legal opinion. The fatwa concludes with religious formulas expressing, inter alia, the mufti's humility and his praise of Allah as the source of all wisdom.

The translation of the fatwa follows;[2] the Arabic text can be seen on the facing page.

> [1] What is your opinion [*mā qawlukum*]—may your excellence endure[3]—[2] concerning a man between whom and between whose brother's son-in-law [or brother-in-law, *ṣihr*] ill-feeling and conflict arose because of the former's objection to the [amount of the] dower of the bride? [3] The germane brother of the groom lost his temper. His temper got the better of him; he became very angry at the bride's father [4] and said: "[I swear that] my wife, so-and-so, shall be forbidden to me [*ʿalayya al-ḥarām*]; my brother shall not marry [*yataḥallal*] that man's daughter."[4] When [people] approached the person who swore the oath, [trying to persuade him to desist from speaking as he did], [5] he repeated the oath of prohibition [*ḥarām*] and the divorce [utterance] again and again: "The groom shall not marry the bride; she shall not enter my house."[5] Afterwards [6] the contract [*ʿaqd*] with the bride was concluded[6] and, of course, his brother married her and consummated the marriage, and the bride entered the house concerning which an oath had been taken [7] that she should not enter it.

١ ما قولكم دام فضلكم
٢ في رجل وقع بينه وبين صهر اخيه عناد وشقاق بسبب اختلافه على مهر العروس.
٣ فحمق شقيق العريس واشتد عليه الحمق واعتداه غضب شديد على ابو العروس وعندها
٤ نطق قائلاً: "عليَّ الحرام من زوجتي فلانة ان اخي لا يتحلل ابنته." ولدى المراجعة مع الحالف
٥ كرر الحرام والطلاق مرارًا وتكرارًا: "ان العر[و]س لا يتحللها العريس ولا تدخل بيتي." وبعدها
٦ جرى العقد على العروس وبالطبع ان اخيه تحللها ودخل عليها ودخلت البيت المحلوف عليها انها
٧ لا تدخله. فعليه والحالة هذه افيدونا الجواب ولكم الاجر والثواب.
٨ السائل
٩ علي [محمد] حسن

١٠ **الجواب**
حيث انه كرر الحرام والطلاق فهو واقع لا محالة حيث جرى المحلوف عليه. اما الحرام فهو كناية
١١ يحتاج لنية قطع العصمة، فإن نوى به ذلك يلحق بالطلاق المكرر فإن بلغ به الثلاث يجب المحلل،
١٢ وان لم يبلغ ذلك فله مراجعتها قبل وفاء عدتها بغير اذنها وليس لها مهر في ذلك. وان خرجت فيكون
١٣ بمهر وعقد جديدين بإذنها ورضاها. والتحليل اذا كان اصل العقد صحيحًا كاملاً لجميع واجباته. واما
١٤ اذا اختل منه ركن فهو فاسد فيجوز ان يقلد الشافعي فيه بعقد ومهر جديد[ين] حيث قال القاضي ابو شجاع في شأنه
١٥ [في] **الغاية والتقريب**: "ولا يصح العقد [عقد النكاح] إلا بوَلي وشاهدَيْ عدل،" فاذا توفرت العدالة فيهم صح العقد وانواع الفسق
١٦ كثيرة معلومة، بحيث لا يتولى عليه إلا اقرب العصبات إلا اذا أذن للاجنبي. ولا تتولى بنفسها حيث الحديث:
١٧ "لا تزوج المرأة المرأه ولا المرأة بنفسها" والله اعلم.
كتبه الفقير لله
١٨ جابر ابراهيم ابو شبانة[؟]
١٩ الشافعي

Under these circumstances, we beg you to direct us by a responsum [*jawāb*],[7] and yours are the wages and the reward [*al-ajr wa'l-thawāb*].[8]

[8] The inquirer

[9] ʿAli Hasan

[10] *Answer* [*jawāb*]: As he has repeated the oath of prohibition and the divorce [utterance],[9] the repudiation has become a fact. This conclusion is inescapable, because the condition to which the oath relates [the marriage and the entry of the bride into the house] has been fulfilled. As regards the oath, it is an implicit declaration [*kināya*] [11] which, to be effective, requires [the ascertainment of] the intent [*niyya*; Schacht 1964:116] to dissolve the marriage [*qaṭʿ al-ʿiṣma*]. If he had such an intent,[10] that declaration entailed repeated [*mukarrar*][11] repudiation, and if he uttered it three times, the one who renders her [again] lawfully permitted [*muḥallil*] [to her former husband][12] is required, [12] but if he did not utter that declaration three times, he may reinstate [*murājaʿa*] the wife without her permission before the expiration of the waiting period [*ʿidda*] and without her being entitled to a dower.[13] If she has left [the conjugal home],[14] he may [reinstate her] by means of a [13] new dower and a new contract with her permission and consent. An intermediate marriage designed to render the divorced woman lawfully permitted [to her former husband] [*taḥlīl*] is required where the nature [*aṣl*] of the [original] contract was valid [*ṣaḥīḥ*], fulfilling all the legal conditions [*wājibāt*];[15] [14] where one of the essential elements [*rukn*] [of marriage] was infringed, the marriage is defective or void [*fāsid*][16] and it is permissible to follow [the Imam] al-Shafiʿi,[17] [who, under these conditions, prescribed] a new contract and dower.[18] In this connection, the Qadi Abu Shujaʿ wrote in his [15] *al-Ghāya wa'l-Taqrīb:*[19] "A contract [of marriage] is not fully valid unless it is concluded by a guardian [*walī*] and in the presence of two witnesses of good character [*ʿadl*]"; if the requirement of good character [*ʿadāla*] has been met, the contract is valid. The kinds of sinfulness [*fisq*][20] are [16] many and well-known. No one but the nearest agnate [*ʿaṣabāt*] may assume the office of marriage guardian unless a stranger has been permitted [by the court] to assume it.[21] Nor may the woman herself act as guardian, for the hadith says: [17] "A woman may not give a woman away in marriage, and a woman may not give herself away in marriage."[22]

And it is Allah who knows.[23]

Written by the poor man [who resorted] to Him [God].

[18] Jabir Ibrahim Abu Shabana [?]

[19] al-Shafiʿi[24]

Assessment of the Fatwa as an Instrument of Accommodation

The legal opinion of a mufti is not binding on either the person who commissioned it or on the shariʿa courts; its acceptance is purely voluntary. In the present case, the shaykh obtained full satisfaction. His wife was not divorced, and his sensitivity to Islamic norms was set at rest. There was no reason to ask the shariʿa court to confirm the fatwa, nor was the fatwa confirmed or registered with any state institution. It was deposited with the man who commissioned it, as evidence that his marriage was valid notwithstanding the three successive repudiations. If the shaykh had requested confirmation from the court before the enactment of the Personal Status Law of 1951 (Layish 1991b:451ff.), the qadi—bound by the Hanafi school—would have rejected the fatwa, ruling that the wife must separate from her husband, marry another man, and be divorced by him before being permitted to her first husband again.

Although the legal opinion reflects the particular circumstances of the shaykh, it is of use to the general public, since it is couched in general terms and not limited either personally or territorially. Reliance on the legal opinion of a scholar who is not officially appointed as a mufti is in itself an indication that formal status is not particularly important in the eyes of the Bedouin. What matters most is the recognized personal authority of the scholar. This resembles the institution of the independent mufti of the classical period, who was unaffiliated with any official agency.

Although the fatwa establishes no new legal norms, it plays an important role in bringing the Bedouin closer to normative Islam by bridging the gap between the shariʿa in its formal, Hanafi version and customary tribal law, under which three successive repudiations or a triple repudiation pronounced at once are not grounds for intermediate marriage. The religious transformation of the Bedouin is accomplished in several ways: through Islamic indoctrination via religious education in schools and mosques, modern communications media, the marriage solemnizers, and, of course, the shariʿa courts. Though the Bedouin may to some extent be conscious of this process,[25] it seems that it results primarily from pressures that forcibly direct the Bedouin toward the orthodox Muslim way of life. Such pressures include the strengthening of the central authority, which in turn strengthens the religious establishment; the abolition of the tribal courts (Oweidi 1982:85ff.) and the subjection of the Bedouin to *sharʿī* justice; and, finally, the geographical proximity of the Bedouin to religious, administrative, and economic centers.

The readiness of the Bedouin to accept Islam as a way of life is conditioned on its not being markedly contradictory to the way of life reflected in their customary law. In other words, the shariʿa is observed not for its own sake but to the extent that it is consistent with custom (Layish 1991a:205). The requirement that an intermediate marriage take place after three successive repudiations or a triple repudiation—a requirement which, according to the Hanafi school, must be met under any circumstances, even if the marriage is contracted with the (unexpressed) intention to render the woman lawful once again to her former husband *(bi-qaṣd al-taḥlīl)*—is a hardship for the

Bedouin community. The Shafiʿi fatwa, which takes the element of intention into account, makes it possible to render religious law more flexible, to mitigate it to such a degree that the community can digest and absorb it. Paradoxically, an institution such as the fatwa, so patently legal by Islamic standards, is enlisted by the Bedouin to uphold custom while nominally acknowledging the supremacy of the shariʿa. The Shafiʿi mufti uses the mechanism of the legal opinion as a sort of legal device *(ḥīla)* to soften harsh precepts with which the community cannot live. It is known that such devices were used by jurists in classical times as a means of bridging the gap between established legal doctrine, on the one hand, and social and economic reality, on the other (Schacht 1964:78ff.).

The utilization of the fatwa as an instrument to bring the Bedouin closer to normative Islam takes place on the private rather than the official level. Private resort to Shafiʿi jurists in order to avoid the pain of an intermediate marriage after three repudiations or a triple repudiation is a common practice, attested to by the records *(sijill)* of the Shariʿa Court of Bethlehem, to which the Bedouin of the Judean Desert are amenable (Layish and Shmueli 1979:52ff.; cf. Ziadeh 1990:13). This practice is quite natural, because the Bedouin are unaware of the differences between the schools of law and so, obviously, do not regard themselves as tied to a particular school. They seem to have discovered empirically the advantage of resorting to the Shafiʿi scholar rather than to the shariʿa court to avoid an intermediate marriage, after failing to obtain relief from the court; they had no notion of the doctrinal differences between the schools represented by the qadi and the mufti, respectively (Layish and Shmueli 1979:45).

It is easy to imagine that the qadis of the shariʿa courts, charged with applying Islamic law in matters of personal status (with the changes required by statutory legislation), do not look favorably upon the Bedouin's resort to Shafiʿi jurists, which detracts from the court's status as the sole authority for the application of the law. An inevitable consequence of simultaneously resorting to the shariʿa court and Shafiʿi jurists is perplexity and confusion due to the reference to different legal norms (reflecting differences between schools), some of which are sanctioned by the state and thus enforceable, and some of which are derived from the religio-legal authority of the jurists and thus are not enforceable. However, this situation is not new; in fact, it has always existed, because Islamic law was developed by the jurists outside the establishment.

CHAPTER TWENTY-FIVE

Postmortem Examinations in Egypt

VARDIT RISPLER-CHAIM

With the rapid development of medicine and its scientific methods in the twentieth century, postmortem examinations have become an increasingly effective instrument for learning more about the causes of death and the development of disease, and, in certain cases, ways to postpone death. In many modern states, mandatory postmortem examinations have helped to solve criminal deaths and to bring the perpetrators to justice.

Prior to the twentieth century, postmortems as an independent subject were not mentioned in the Islamic legal literature, in part because postmortems were not an issue in the legal systems of other monotheistic religions, and in part because postmortems, like organ transplants and organ donations, necessarily involve a violation of the wholeness of the human body. Islamic philosophy and Islamic medical ethics, which view the human body as a trust—and not as private property—were reluctant to discuss such violations. Once postmortems became common practice throughout the world, Islamic law could not remain indifferent. The muftis of Islam were urged to give their opinion on the legitimacy of the practice, and their fatwas have proven to be a useful tool for dealing with medical issues and other "new" questions, that is, questions which pre-twentieth-century fiqh did not recognize.

Because the fatwa is a nonbinding legal opinion, the fatwa literature is dynamic and flexible, adjusting to changing circumstances and expressing a wide range of opinions on any topic. Although this multiplicity may complicate the decision-making process of the layman, it facilitates the task of the historian by exposing the complexity of religious life in a given time and place, including internal debates, disagreements and trends.

I have selected Hasanayn Muhammad Makhluf's fatwa on postmortems

(1952, 2:219–224) as a representative example of Egyptian fatwas on mid-twentieth-century medical issues. In analyzing its structure and content, I will attempt to demonstrate that it contains many points characteristic of fatwas on medical questions.

Makhluf, who was born in Cairo in 1890, was appointed qadi in 1916, head of the *sharʿī* court in Alexandria in 1941, and chief mufti of Egypt in 1945. From 1948 he served as a member of the Supreme Council of Scholars at al-Azhar. He died in 1990. The present fatwa appears in a two-volume collection of his fatwas compiled in the 1940s. As evidenced by his education and the positions he held, Makhluf belonged to the mainstream Azhari religious establishment in Egypt, which enjoyed the support of the government. For this reason, one suspects that his fatwas were approved and, perhaps, solicited, by the government. It is also possible that his fatwas were issued in order to legitimize existing social standards. His fatwa on postmortems, which became a point of reference for later muftis, can be classified among those fatwas that helped to shape the national consensus on the subject.

The translation of the fatwa follows:

> *The Question:* According to the shariʿa, is it permitted to perform a postmortem examination for scientific purposes or in criminal cases?
>
> *The Response:* You must remember that curing the body and treating illnesses is required by the shariʿa in order to preserve mankind and enable man to live for as long as he was destined to live by God. The Messenger of God sought a cure for himself and ordered his family and Companions to cure themselves when they were sick, saying, "Cure yourselves, because God did not create an illness without a remedy" (Ibn Maja 1972, 2:1137–1138; al-Bukhari 1928, 7:222). He also said, "The Exalted God did not send down an illness without its remedy, which some people are aware of and some are not" (Ibn al-Qayyim al-Jawziyya 1970, 1:170, 3:80). His Companions followed his example in seeking cures and medical treatment.
>
> The teaching and learning of medicine was legitimized by the Messenger's approval of the science and by his personal behavior, as mentioned in the hadith; and, furthermore, through the import of quranic verses [viz., Quran 2:184–185] which give permission to a sick person to break the fast in order to enable him or her to receive medical treatment and to prevent either a worsening of the illness or death. Likewise, Quran 2:196 permits a person who is suffering from a skin illness on his head to shave his head despite the state of *iḥrām* [that is, the ritual purity required for the performance of hajj], because shaving in this case helps to cure the disease.
>
> A sick person was also allowed to replace water with sand for ablution purposes, lest his or her body be hurt. All these examples testify that the Supreme Legislator [Allah as the prime source of Islamic legislation] insisted on curing [people], on abolishing illnesses, and on protecting the human being

against anything that might harm him or her, externally or internally. This was mentioned in Ibn al-Qayyim al-Jawziyya's *Zād al-Maʿād*.[1] Medicine, both as a science and as a practice, was among the duties that a part of the *umma* [Muslim community] had to fulfill in order that the rest of the *umma* be exempt. The *umma* as a whole was sinful if medicine was not practiced in it to the same extent as all the other sciences and crafts which the Legislator required to be maintained by a part of the *umma* and which He warned not to neglect.

Among the foundations of medicine is the postmortem examination, because the doctor cannot cure or treat a disease unless he has acquired sufficient knowledge and practice in performing postmortems, and unless he has learned of the body's internal organs, the components of these organs, their interconnections, exact location, etc. These subjects are incumbent upon whoever practices medicine as required by God.

Let no one doubt it and let no one claim that medicine existed in the past without utilizing postmortem examinations because medicine was primitive and cured only external diseases. We speak here of a comprehensive medicine that provides answers to a variety of illnesses and injuries. As knowledge increases, so techniques develop and multiply.

Because postmortem examinations are required by verses which encourage the study and teaching of medicine, and because a group from among the *umma* is always required to practice medicine, it is essential that if the Legislator imposed a duty, He must have considered all issues related to it. Thus, if God, the Legislator, commanded prayer, He necessarily commanded ablution, which is a prerequisite to prayer. Likewise, if He, as we have shown, required that a group among the *umma* learn, teach, and practice medicine, He necessarily commanded them to perform, teach, and learn postmortem examinations.[2]

To this point we have demonstrated the permission to perform postmortem examinations and to study them as a science, and, moreover, their indispensability for whoever specializes in human medicine.

Postmortem examinations performed for other purposes, such as the identification of the cause of death and the investigation of its circumstances, to be used later to prove the guilt of a murderer or to acquit a suspect—are also undoubtedly legitimate if they lead to the discovery of truth in criminal cases and to establishing justice in verdicts, so that no innocent person is oppressed and no convicted criminal escapes punishment.

Frequently, a postmortem examination marks the division between truth and lies, justice and injustice. If a person is accused of poisoning another to death, witnesses may give false testimony about the crime; but the postmortem examination indicates that no trace of poison is to be found in the body and that the deceased died of natural causes. Consequently, the suspect may be acquitted. Had it not been for this examination, he would have been sentenced to death or to life in prison.

A criminal who commits a murder and then burns the body may claim that fire was the cause of death, while the postmortem proves that death was criminally caused and burning was only a cover for the crime. The criminal can thus be punished as he deserves. Had it not been for the postmortem, he would have escaped punishment and remained as a seed of evil among the public.

Another issue is respect for the human body and the possible humiliation that exposure and postmortem examinations may cause to it. An ignorant person may think that a postmortem is always forbidden, regardless of motive. However, a brief look at the laws of the shariʿa indicates that Islamic law considers both benefits and harms. Whenever the benefit outweighs the harm, permission is granted; whenever the harm outweighs the benefit, a prohibition is issued. There is no doubt that while weighing the desecration of the body that may result from a postmortem against the advantages of curing diseases, obtaining justice, and rescuing the innocent from punishment, as well as convicting a criminal, the advantages outweigh the disadvantages.

After writing this article, I came across a fatwa on the same subject by the late Shaykh Yusuf al-Dajawi, who said:

> Fiqh books do not contain conclusive texts on this subject. One might think—erroneously—that postmortems are forbidden by the shariʿa, which emphasizes the principle of maintaining human dignity, not harming it. However, one who is familiar with the spirit of the law, its good influences and intentions, knows that the shariʿa always balances the good points and the bad. The law is always the result of one aspect overriding the other, according to common sense and logic.

Therefore, our [viz., Makhluf's] opinion must be in accordance with the public good which agrees with the spirit of Islamic law in each place and generation, and which guarantees happiness in this world as well as in the world to come. Therefore, we say: Whoever views postmortems as necessary, it is because in certain circumstances, such as when a person is accused of a crime against another and he is acquitted when the examination shows that the "victim" was not criminally attacked; or when a person is criminally attacked, and then, in order to conceal the crime, he is thrown into a well, etc., postmortems are mandatory. Add to that the progress of science which accrues from postmortems, progress which humanity as a whole may enjoy and which may bring relief to many who almost died or suffered terrible pains so that they are like living dead. We say: the general picture as well as the details must lead to the conclusion that postmortems are permitted, since the benefits outweigh the disadvantages. When the postmortem is used as intended, it does not humiliate the human being, nor does it deprive him or her of dignity. The *fuqahāʾ* [jurists] concluded in their books: If before death the deceased has swallowed a sum of money, his abdomen may be opened after death to recover the money, even if it is a small amount. Some of the Maliki scholars stipulated that the sum had to be equal to the minimum establishing the crime of theft—a quarter of a dinar or three dirhams—and the Shafiʿi scholars are close to this opinion. They occupied themselves with defining the amount swallowed. If we compare that small sum of money to the benefits that accrue from postmortems, we will conclude that the latter must be considered of greater value than the recovery of a small sum of money.

We must, however, take precautions so that people do not perform postmortems too often and without giving the matter sufficient attention. Let them be carried out only when necessity requires. May the doctors and politicians in charge of such procedures fear God. Let them know that God is All-seeing, Almighty and All-guiding. And God knows best.

The Structure of Makhluf's Fatwa

The questioner asks whether postmortems are permitted for scientific purposes and for solving criminal cases. The wording indicates that the question is not general—whether or not the shariʿa approves of postmortems—but rather concerns their legitimacy for certain specified purposes, purposes that appear to be justified, humane, and indispensable.

The mufti begins by discussing medicine in general and the high esteem it was granted in the shariʿa, noting that the Prophet treated his own ailments and encouraged his Companions to seek cures for their diseases. In addition, the Quran grants several concessions to sick people, giving the preservation of their health priority over the observance of God's commandments in cases in which the latter might be harmful. Indeed, the practice of medicine is recognized as being so essential for Muslim society that it is classified in the shariʿa as one of the *furūḍ al-kifāyāt* (duties for the community as a whole),[3] which necessitates that there always be a sufficient number of people to practice it; as such it was equated with the duty of jihad and with the duty to participate in funerals. Medicine, which currently is viewed as a scientific and secular occupation, possesses a distinct religious dimension according to the shariʿa.

Only at this point does Makhluf turn to postmortems, adducing the following analogy: because medicine is essential for Muslim society, and because a doctor cannot become competent unless he has learned all the internal and external components of the human body—knowledge that can be attained only on the basis of dissection—one must conclude that postmortems are essential for medical knowledge to progress. In response to the counterclaim that medicine survived for hundreds of years without resorting to postmortems, Makhluf states that ancient medicine was primitive and responded only to external symptoms, whereas contemporary medicine is relied upon to answer all problems and to utilize modern knowledge and techniques. Postmortems are thus viewed by Makhluf as an indispensable part of a doctor's education, just as ablution is an integral part of the commandment to pray. Hence, he established the importance of postmortems for purely scientific considerations as being beyond any doubt.

The use of a postmortem to solve criminal cases is justified by Makhluf on the grounds of ensuring justice, acquitting the innocent, and convicting the guilty. This is an appeal to the reader's natural sense of justice.

Makhluf then defends postmortems against the claim that they violate the sanctity of the human body, invoking the legal principle of *maṣlaḥa*—that is, whenever benefits outnumber damages, a positive approach should be taken. Because postmortems result in more benefits than damages, the shariʿa approves of them. To this end, Makhluf cites a fatwa on the same subject issued previously by Shaykh Yusuf al-Dajawi, who also legitimized postmortems with reference to the legal principle of *maṣlaḥa.* Al-Dajawi compared the case of violating human dignity in postmortems to the permission in the shariʿa to extract a sum of money from a dead person's abdomen. By analogy, in postmortems the damage to the body is more excusable and the benefit greater.

Makhluf concludes his fatwa with al-Dajawi's assertion that doctors, politicians, and the general public should be God-fearing and perform postmortems only when necessary.

Although the initial question is specific, Makhluf begins his answer with reference to medicine in general. His conclusion is equally general, although the question receives a satisfactory answer. One senses that the question was used to introduce the general subject of postmortems. In his answer, Makhluf refers to "quranic verses" and utilizes several hadiths, *sharʿī* terminology, analogy *(qiyās), maṣlaḥa,* and a legal precedent—a fatwa issued earlier by another mufti. No quranic verses are quoted, and, except for Ibn al-Qayyim al-Jawziyya's *Zād al-Maʿād,* no specific fiqh sources are mentioned.

The fatwa develops smoothly in support of the mufti's position. It assumes a general knowledge of legal terms and principles, and it appeals more than once to the common sense and logic that are characteristic of Islamic law. This suggests that the fatwa was directed at jurists, students of law, and the educated public. For the layman, a shorter and less sophisticated fatwa would have been more appropriate.

Other Contemporary Fatwas on Postmortem Examinations

The first reference to postmortems in the twentieth century seems to have been Rashid Rida's 1910 fatwa entitled *"al-Kashf al-ṭibbī ʿan al-mawtā wa-taʾkhīr al-dafn"* (Postmortem Examinations and the Postponement of Burial),[4] which treats the political implications of obligatory postmortems in non-Muslim states for their Muslim citizens. A quarter of a century later, Shaykh Bakhit (1935) opposed postmortems in general, albeit with concessions for the purpose of preserving life and curing the sick.[5]

Following Makhluf's fatwa, which was published in the 1940s, postmortems attracted little attention until the late 1970s. ʿAbd al-Halim Mahmud (d. 1978) discussed the problem of postponement of burial, not postmortems per se (1986, 2:277). The Azhar Committee of muftis permitted postmortems for educational purposes and for criminal identification and the prevention of contagious diseases (*Majallat al-Azhar,* 1982). Shaykh ʿAbd al-Fattah (1983) limited postmortems for scientific purposes to the examination of unknown persons killed in road accidents.[6] Shaykh ʿAbd al-Hakim Naʿnaʿ (1984) supported the right to transfer the body of the deceased from one place to another (which may be required for reasons having nothing to do with postmortems). He stipulated, however, that the transfer be undertaken only for a "burning need." Shaykh Ibrahim al-Yaʿqubi (1986:98, 100), analogously to Shaykh Bakhit and to Makhluf, permitted postmortems for educational purposes, because knowledge of the human body cannot be gained from an animal's body. Toward the end of his life, Makhluf himself (1990) allowed a person to donate his body to science and authorized members of the deceased's family to grant permission for such a donation. Makhluf included such an act under the principle *"al-ḍarūrāt tubīḥ al-maḥẓūrāt"*—necessities render the prohibited permitted.

All of these muftis published their fatwas in journals and newspapers such as *Majallat al-Azhar, al-Ahrām,* and *al-Jumhūriyya,* which echo the view of the mainstream religious establishment. In general, Azhar scholars and mainstream religious circles focus on one or more of the following problems associated with postmortems: the postponement of burial, the transfer of the body after death, the violation of the sanctity of the body, postmortems for educational and juridical purposes (as opposed to postmortems for the benefit of science and the health of the general populace). Although none of these muftis issued a fatwa that was as explicit as that of Makhluf, and although their respective styles and the length of their fatwas differ, it is noteworthy that none of them rejected postmortems out of hand.

Conclusion

Makhluf and the other muftis who addressed the subject of postmortems engaged in complex legal reasoning to discover references (usually indirect) in the Quran, hadith, and shariʿa indicating that God and His Messenger gave preference to the promotion of health over religious obligations. Because postmortems are the primary means of learning about the internal anatomy of the body, they came to be recognized as promoting human health.

The muftis invoke two legal terms in their attempts to accommodate change: public benefit *(maṣlaḥa),* which signifies anything that constitutes an advantage for society at large while not overtly contradicting the shariʿa, and analogy *(qiyās),* an instrument of common sense that allows wide scope for the use of reason. The use of these terms is characteristic of Islamic writings on medical ethics in the twentieth century. Because the Quran and hadith rarely refer directly to new issues, the muftis resort to the notions of public benefit and analogy—about which there may be considerable disagreement—and seek to produce persuasive opinions. By seeking to ground the legitimation of all new phenomena (including medical issues) in *sharʿī* sources, the muftis seek to demonstrate that the shariʿa retains its validity and vitality over time and possesses the ability to adapt to modern developments. For the muftis, the shariʿa is not a cause of the alleged stagnation of Muslim societies (as some Westerners assert) but rather a source of progress, as exemplified by its attitude to medical science, which most Muslims regard as the epitome of the linking of scientific progress to the promotion of human welfare.

CHAPTER TWENTY-SIX

Tantawi on Banking Operations in Egypt

CHIBLI MALLAT

At the turn of the twentieth century, the Egyptian postal administration established the Egyptian Savings Fund (Sunduq al-Tawfir). Like similar institutions in France and other Western countries, the Savings Fund accepted cash deposits from individuals that it used for various small investments; in exchange, the fund issued savings "certificates" that yielded depositors a return on their money calculated according to a fixed and predetermined rate. When, shortly after the establishment of the fund, approximately 3,000 depositors expressed concern over the legality of the profit that they were receiving from the savings certificates, the government approached the celebrated jurist, Muhammad Abduh (d. 1905), who had been appointed mufti of Egypt in 1899, and asked him to issue a fatwa clarifying the status of such certificates in Islamic law. As subsequently reported by Abduh's disciple, Muhammad Rashid Rida (d. 1935), editor of the famed journal *al-Manār* (1917:528), Abduh issued a verbal response in 1904 in which he indicated that such operations should be carried out "according to the rules of the *muḍāraba* partnership, for the use of the monies deposited in the Fund."

Also in 1904, Rida himself published a short fatwa on this subject in which he referred to his master's recent opinion. In this fatwa, Rida characterizes Abduh as acquiescing in the operation of the Savings Fund on the ground that "the postal administration is a rich governmental administration that uses the monies deposited in the Savings Fund in a manner that is beneficial both to the depositor and to those who work in that administration and in the government" (Rida 1904:28–29). In 1906, however, Rida published an essay in *al-Manār* in which he commented on the quranic verses dealing with usury *(ribā);* in a section of that essay entitled "On the

Prohibition of *Ribā*," Rida attributed to Abduh statements in which he reportedly railed against the prevailing banking practices in Egypt, although not specifically against the Savings Fund (1906:345–352).

To the best of my knowledge, the Abduh and Rida fatwa of 1904 was the first fatwa on the subject of banking to have been issued in modern Egypt. Because of the close relationship between Abduh and Rida, there is some confusion regarding Abduh's view on the legality of savings certificates (see Eccel 1984:116; Mallat 1988:71–74), although Abduh generally is held to have allowed the scheme, which, in any event, continued to be practiced.

The fatwas issued by Abduh and Rida on the subject of banking signaled the emergence of a new field. Here, two great reformers of the early twentieth century (see Kerr 1966) became involved in a matter that marked the meeting point of certain quranic statements regarding commercial transactions and the prohibition of *ribā* (e.g., Quran 2:275) on the one hand, and a complex web of Western economic models and commercial instruments on the other. In the 1920s and 1930s, fatwas on banking appeared regularly in journals published by Islamic circles, including that of al-Azhar.[1] In subsequent years, a number of distinguished jurists contributed to the discussion. In connection with the debate over the articles on the contract of loan included in the much vaunted Civil Code by ʿAbd al-Razzaq al-Sanhuri (d. 1971; see Sanhuri 1954–1959, pt. 3; Badawi 1939 and 1964; Mallat 1988), Muhammad Abu Zahra, a traditional scholar of great repute, issued a lengthy opinion (n.d.) on subjects related to lending and Western-style banking. Also in the 1950s, the Egyptian shaykh al-Azhar, Mahmud Shaltut, issued a fatwa conferring legitimacy on the Sunduq al-Tawfir operations (this opinion is quoted at length by Tantawi in his 1989 fatwa).

The emergence of banking as a subject in the modern fatwa literature has compelled muftis to make certain changes in the mode of discourse traditionally associated with ifta'. First, the question (istifta') tends to be phrased in a very general and thematic way, asking about, for example, the validity of Western-style banking, or the influence of *ribā* on modern commercial transactions. Second, the complex nature of financial transactions makes it difficult to deal with the subject in a simple and definitive manner. Although some muftis (e.g., Abduh-Rida in 1904 and 1917) managed to respond in just a few lines, others have written full-length treatises. The longest fatwa on the subject is perhaps that of Muhammad Baqir al-Sadr, issued in 1969 in response to a query emanating from the Kuwaiti Ministry of Awqaf (Mallat 1993, Chapter 5).

In this chapter, I propose to examine a fatwa issued by the current mufti of the Egyptian Republic, Muhammad Sayyed Atiyya Tantawi.[2] As the head of Dar al-ifta', the grand mufti presides over a large and complex bureaucracy in which the practice of fatwa giving has taken on a greater collective and consensual character than it possessed in pre-modern times. The mufti of the Egyptian territories *(muftī al-diyār al-miṣriya)* is the font of ifta' in Egypt, and he commands greater respect than any other mufti in the country. Indeed, the grand mufti of Egypt is arguably the most prestigious mufti in the entire Sunni Muslim world.[3] On September 6, 1989, Tantawi issued a fatwa entitled "On Some Banking Operations." Approximately twelve pages long in its printed edition and containing no reference to a specific question, the general form and style of this text place it squarely within the modern tradition of fatwa giving on the subject of banking, replete with citations from both classical and modern jurists. In one important respect, however, Tantawi's fatwa signals a significant break with the earlier tradition of ifta'. At a critical juncture in his response, the mufti assumes the role of mustafti by addressing a question to a lay expert, in this instance, a bank manager. Tantawi includes in his fatwa both his question to the bank manager and the latter's response. Although the authority of the response resides ultimately with the mufti himself, the act of seeking clarification from a lay person with no training in Islamic law is noteworthy and may signal a new and different type of ifta'.

Born on October 28, 1925, Muhammad Sayyed Atiyya Tantawi was educated in traditional Islamic circles. He studied theology *(uṣūl al-dīn)* at al-Azhar, where he earned a doctorate in quranic commentary and hadith. In the late 1960s he taught briefly at al-Azhar. He then taught for several years in Asyut before returning to al-Azhar, where he became the dean of the theology faculty. Tantawi has written several scholarly treatises, most notably a fifteen-volume commentary on the Quran. In 1986, he was appointed mufti of the Arab Republic of Egypt, although he continued to perform various administrative roles at al-Azhar. Frequently in the public eye, Tantawi appears regularly on religious programs broadcast on television and is also seen seated next to the president on official occasions. As behooves a chief mufti of the republic, Tantawi often takes public stances on sensitive political issues. During the Gulf War, for example, he issued a fatwa in which he declared Iraq's occupation of Kuwait to be illegal and conferred legitimacy on armed opposition to the Iraqi invaders (Tantawi 1990; see Chapter 27 in this volume).

The 1990 version of Tantawi's fatwa on banking (Khudayri 1990:353–364) is divided into fourteen sections of varying lengths. In it, the mufti addresses both the general field of banking transactions and the legality of profits deriving from specific transactions. Most important, the fatwa legitimizes "capitalization certificates" *(shahādāt al-istithmār),* that is, government bonds underwritten by Egyptian banks. The fatwa was issued at a time when the validity of Western-style banking was being called into question in militant Islamic circles, and when new, Islamic financial institutions were being created in large numbers. It should be noted that Tantawi's fatwa was issued immediately prior to the scandal associated with the Islamic financial institution known as al-Rayyan, which squandered millions of pounds entrusted to it by Egyptian citizens. Because the government unofficially supported the traditional banks, the issuance of the fatwa took place in a highly charged political atmosphere. As the senior religious official in the Egyptian government, Tantawi must have been aware, as he composed his fatwa, of the political and financial challenges to the state represented by the Islamic financial institutions.

In the opening passage, the mufti discusses the crucial role of ifta' and the necessity for Dar al-ifta' to perform this role:

> There is much talk nowadays about banking transactions [*muʿāmalāt*], about the consequences of these transactions on profits, and about whether or not these transactions and profits are legal. Dar al-ifta' of Egypt has therefore found it necessary to clarify its position on some of these transactions, after the invasion of the field by those who know and those who don't know. (p. 353)

Four sections follow in which the mufti establishes, on the basis of the Quran and hadith, the obligation of wise men (literally: those who are rational, *al-ʿuqalāʾ*) to search for the truth, the principle of ijtihad, the virtue of avoiding fanaticism *(al-taʿaṣṣub),* and the importance of expertise in unraveling arcane subjects (pp. 353–354).

After citing Quran 21:7 ("ask the *ahl al-dhikr* if you do not know"), he defines the *ahl al-dhikr* as "the people of expertise and experience in all science and art." Glossing this definition, he adds, "in medicine you ask physicians, in fiqh the *fuqahāʾ,* and in economics you ask economists" (p. 354). The emphasis on expertise is supported by a prophetic hadith that is put to double use, serving, first, to reinforce the importance of expertise in the Islamic tradition and, second, to introduce the specific consequences of this expertise with relation to Dar al-ifta'.[4] Tantawi continues: "Dar al-ifta' of Egypt is responsible before God for issuing all [necessary] fatwas and rules. Thank God, Dar al-ifta' can accommodate both those who agree and those who disagree, but it cannot withhold science [*ʿilm*] which God has ordered it to pursue." Accordingly, it is the obligation of Dar al-ifta' "to answer those who ask questions." He continues, "The duty of the mufti is to reveal the legal rule . . . It is not part of his duty to impose it in all circumstances" (p. 354).

In section five, the mufti refers to the complexity of banking operations:

> Dar al-ifta' believes that it is not possible to talk about banking transactions in one single sentence, as, for example, by saying that banking transactions are all permitted or all forbidden. Each question must be addressed separately, or, at least, similar questions should be consolidated, after which, the required legal rule may be issued. (p. 355)

Reaching the heart of his subject, Tantawi places all banking transactions in three categories: (1) transactions that all ʿulamaʾ agree are legal and in which profits are *ḥalāl;* (2) transactions that the ʿulamaʾ agree are not legal and in which profits are *ḥarām;* and (3) transactions and profits about which the ʿulamaʾ are in disagreement.

In section six of his fatwa, the mufti adduces the following examples of the first category: selling and buying, commenda transactions *(muḍāraba),*[5] partnership *(mushāraka),* and lease. Included in this category, Tanatawi continues, are four types of banking operations. The first type involves transactions "in which profits are subject to increase or decrease, without being previously determined in time or quantity; [in such transactions,] all parties benefit and all bear any loss in a manner which is equitable . . . I say: these transactions and profits are *ḥalāl* and legal . . . This rule is equally applicable . . . to banks which describe themselves as Islamic and to those which do not." The second type includes the operations of "investment companies" *(sharikāt tawẓīf al-amwāl)* such as al-Rayyan: "I say: the transactions and profits of these companies are legal; Dar al-iftaʾ approves of them and wishes them luck and success." The mufti here presumes that these companies are operating in accordance with the law, without specifying what constitutes legality. He does, however, issue a warning with regard to investment companies that do not behave properly: "As for companies which are proven to have deviated from the straight path in any way whatsoever, they are not supported at all by Dar al-iftaʾ, which demands accountability and the meting out of the proper and just penalty." The third type includes "social banks [*bunūk ijtimāʿiyya*] . . . such as Bank Nasir, which offer the needy what they require in terms of money, taking in return reasonable fees, calculated by just experts [*khubarāʾ ʿudūl*], [which are used] for the salaries of employees and other expenses borne by these banks . . . I say: these sums which the banks receive to cover salary or administrative expenses are legal . . . because they are given against specific services which the bank renders to those who deal with it." Finally, the fourth type includes "specialized banks [*bunūk mutakhaṣṣiṣa*] such as industrial, agricultural, or real estate institutions which offer to the providers of various helpful services the sum they require against adequate compensation, which is assessed by just experts as salaries or administrative expenses" (pp. 355–357).

In section seven the mufti turns to transactions that are illegal (category 2) "because they are based on practices that are forbidden [*ḥarām*], such as any transaction that is based on fraud, exploitation, deceit, or injustice." This is the case with "the sale of defective merchandise," with "the sale of merchandise for twice its value," and with "taking advantage of the ignorance of one of the parties as to the market price." The mufti offers the following example of such an illegal financial transaction:

> A person lends to another 100 pounds for a specified period of time. When the time comes for repayment, the debtor is unable to pay and the creditor takes advantage of this inability. In an effort to exploit the borrower's weakness, [the creditor] tells him, "Either you pay what is due or you pay this sum with an increase of ten pounds in a month," for instance. This is clear *ribā* [*al-ribā al-jalī*] against the perpetrators of which the sharīʿa of Islam and its Prophet have called for war. (p. 357)

Transactions that fall into category 3, Tantawi continues, pose the greatest difficulty for Dar al-iftaʾ. This category, for the most part, includes "transactions that are new and innovative [*mustaḥdatha*]." At this point Tantawi refers specifically to capitalization certificates issued by the Egyptian Ahli Bank in the amount of 4 billion Egyptian pounds as of April 1989. In a significant and unusual move, the mufti here concedes that he must seek someone else's opinion before issuing his own: "Dar al-iftaʾ understands that scientific trust requires [the mufti] not to issue a fatwa in such matters before asking those who are knowledgable and possess expertise in these matters, because ruling on an issue requires [that the mufti] fully understand it." Here, Dar al-iftaʾ concedes that it could not immediately answer questions that fall beyond its area of expertise—in the present instance, in the arcane field of banking. To better understand the issues, Tantawi explains, he himself sent a detailed letter containing four questions to the chairman of the board of the Egyptian Ahli Bank. To these questions, Tantawi informs us, the chairman of the board responded as follows on August 13, 1988:

> *Question 1:* What is the nature of capitalization certificates and what is the motive for their creation?
>
> *Answer 1:* Capitalization certificates represent one type of saving, with the creation of which the government entrusted the Egyptian Ahli Bank, as a contribution to the [social] sense of saving [*al-waʿī al-iddikhārī*] and in order to finance the development plan; that is, the real relationship is between the state and the individual. The certificates were issued according to Law 8, 1965.
>
> *Question 2:* In what ways is the return on capitalization certificates used?
>
> *Answer 2:* The return is used to finance development projects that are included in the budget, and they are paid to the Ministry of Finance; that is, the return is given to the state for the financing of the development plan.
>
> *Question 3:* Who pays the profits which capitalization certificates bring to their owners?
>
> *Answer 3:* The Ministry of Finance finances the profits which capitalization certificates earn, in addition to [financing] all related expenses.

Question 4: Are capitalization certificates to be considered a loan or do they constitute a deposit which their owner is allowed to put to use?

Answer 4: A capitalization certificate is a deposit the value of which the owner is allowed to put to use. (p. 358)

After citing the bank chairman's responses, the mufti summarizes the views of Muslim jurists on the subject of capitalization certificates. In 1976, he explains, a committee of fourteen jurists belonging to the four schools of law, under the chairmanship of Shaykh Muhammad Faraj al-Sanhuri, conducted a debate on the subject of capitalization certificates. Muhammad Jirat Allah, a Shafiʿi jurist, argued that although this transaction resembles a *muḍāraba,* it is vitiated by the predetermined return on the deposit. Concurring with this view were Tantawi Mustafa, Jad al-Rabb Ramadan (also a Shafiʿi), and the Maliki jurist Sulayman Ramadan (p. 359).

The remaining nine scholars considered these certificates and their profits to be legal. According to the Maliki jurist Yas Suwaylem, a transaction in which individuals provide capital that the state puts to use is nowhere mentioned in classical law books. Thus, because all transactions are in principle allowed unless expressly forbidden, and because this particular transaction benefits both the individual and the state, the certificate is licit in its three forms—referring to three types of certificates issued by the bank, as indicated by their denomination: *a (alif), b (bāʾ),* and *c (jīm).* The Hanbali jurist Shaykh Abd al-Azim Baraka viewed the first two types of certificates as legal because they are similar "to the *muḍāraba* transaction in which the return on money is shared by the provider of capital and the worker." One cannot contend that the return, being predetermined, is illegal, because, he continued, "the matter is different here, since the projects [in which the money is invested] are based on economic projections in which results are guaranteed. The amount that the provider of capital derives from the profits is small in comparison with the overall profits that the projects generate. Both parties benefit, and exploitation and bereavement are avoided" (pp. 360–361). The assessement of the third type (denomination *c*), which includes a bonus based on a lottery, is more straightforward. According to Baraka, this bonus represents a gift from the state to the investor who holds the certificate, and therefore is legal.

The legitimacy of capitalization certificates also was confirmed by the Hanafi scholar Muhammad Salam Madkur, who, reasoning in a manner similar to Suwaylem, concluded that "the profits given by the bank are not *ribā,* because there is no exploitation and no risk of loss" (p. 361).

These views, Tantawi continues, corroborate the fatwa previously issued by Shaltut (n.d.) with regard to the Egyptian Savings Fund. Tantawi cites the following passage from Shaltut's fatwa:

> By applying legal rules and fiqh principles, we see that the profits [*arbāḥ*] of the Savings Fund [*sundūq al-tawfīr*] are legal. Such transactions are not prohibited, because money which is deposited is not a debt of the bank to its owner, nor a loan contracted by the bank. Rather, the owner presented it of his own free will to the postal administration [which managed the Savings Fund], asking the bank to accept it, with the knowledge that the administration puts the deposited moneys to use in commercial transactions in which it is rare, perhaps even impossible, for these moneys to be wasted or lost. (p. 361)

Mutatis mutandis, and on the authority of Shaltut, Tantawi compares the profits deriving from the capitalization certificates to the profits of the Savings Fund (p. 361).

In section thirteen Tantawi begins his conclusion, citing a statement of the bank chairman according to which the certificate is issued in connection with the state's financing of the development plan, to encourage the population to increase its level of savings. Legally, the certificate is not a loan but a deposit. Against the argument of those who oppose the legality of the certificate on the ground of predetermined profit, Tantawi cites jurists who argue "that the determination of the profit in advance is for the sake of the owner of the capital [that is deposited] and is done to prevent a dispute between him and the bank." The mufti cites Abd al-Wahhab al-Khallaf to the same effect: "*Muḍāraba* [used to be] carried out in accordance with an agreement between the partners. We currently live in a time in which the wills of people are weak. Thus, if the owner of capital did not receive a fixed share in the profit, he would be swallowed by his partner." To this point Tantawi adds that the share in the profit has varied from 4 to 16 percent and is not fixed. "Thus, in case of loss, there is no doubt that all [depositors] carry their share of the loss" (p. 362).

The mufti concludes the fatwa by restating the question and summarizing his own view:

> What is the opinion of Dar al-ifta' on the question of capitalization certificates and the profits deriving from them?
>
> The answer is that Dar al-ifta' has suggested to the directors of the Ahli Bank that they undertake the necessary measures to rename the profits given to the holders of capitalization certificates by calling [those profits] a capitalization return [*ʿā'id istithmārī*] or a capitalization profit [*ribḥ istithmārī*]. [Dar al-ifta' has further suggested] that [the directors] delete the word interest [*fā'ida*] because of its connection in people's minds with *ribā*, even if the rule is that transactions are judged by their truth and content, not by their name and appellation.
>
> The bank directors also should establish a fourth certificate which they should call the certificate with a variable or nonfixed return, in which a precise profit is not determined in advance, but rather profits may increase or decrease.

> In this manner, [the directors] will open the door to all transactions and put minds to rest. The people approached with these suggestions have shown their satisfaction with them and promised that they will be implemented very soon.
>
> On this basis, the Egyptian Dar al-ifta' considers the transactions involving capitalization certificates and those [commercial instruments] that resemble them in the savings houses to be legal, and [it considers] the profits deriving from them to be *ḥalāl* and legal. This is because they are either a legal *muḍāraba,* as in the opinion of Shaykh Abd al-Azim Baraka and others, or because they are a novel [and innovative] transaction that helps individuals and the Muslim community [*umma*], and that entails no exploitation of either party, as in the opinion of Dr. Muhammad Salam Madkur and others.
>
> It is beneficial that the individual buys these certificates to help the state develop worthwhile projects for all. [It also is beneficial that the individual] receives what the state gives him in return, as an encouragement for his support in a manner that benefits him and others. (p. 363)

The Mufti ends the fatwa by reiterating his reliance on both legal and economic experts and promising similar exercises on "other aspects of banking transactions, which are, as mentioned previously, varied in their ways and means" (p. 364).[6] That the fatwa was and continues to be controversial is reflected in its having recently been characterized by the Federal Shariʿat Court of Pakistan as the "solitary opinion of Shaykh Tantawi of Egypt" (1992:20).

Tantawi's fatwa legitimizing capitalization certificates adds a link to the complex chain of efforts by muftis and ʿulama' to intervene in Egyptian commerce during the course of the twentieth century. The characteristics of this chain may be summarized as follows: Egyptian muftis writing in the twentieth century acknowledge that they are treading a delicate path and are dealing with powerful economic actors and institutions that have strong supporters in new, as well as in established, commercial sectors. Because a fatwa that unilaterally condemned interest-bearing transactions would be totally ineffective, most muftis have taken care to formulate their opinions in language that is either cautious or ambiguous. The ambiguously worded fatwas issued in the early part of the century established a pattern that was followed by later muftis, with only a few exceptions (e.g., Shaltut).

The muftis of twentieth-century Egypt cannot escape the authority of their public office. Whatever religious authority he may possess, the mufti is first and foremost a public servant. Although his public function does not prevent him from occasionally voicing a discordant note, he remains a subaltern to official power. In the particular context in which Tantawi's fatwa on banking was issued, the mufti is also subordinate to the Egyptian judiciary, as demonstrated by another famous intervention that is directly related to the issue of banking and interest. In 1985, a case arose before the Supreme Constitutional Court of Egypt over the constitutionality of Article 226 of the Egyptian Civil Code. This article, which allows a fixed interest to be paid in case of default by the debtor, was attacked as unconstitutional by the rector of al-Azhar on the basis of Article 2 of the Constitution, which subjects all legislation to the principles of the shariʿa. The judges adopted the view that a retrospective invalidation of a statute could not be contemplated by the Supreme Constitutional Court (SCC, May 4, 1985, and November 16, 1985). This principle was consistently applied in the protection of civil code legislation, notably Article 227, which stipulates: "The contracting parties can agree on a different rate of interest, whether in return for a delay in payment [this is related to Article 226] or in any other situation [which includes a loan for interest], on the condition that this rate does not exceed 7 percent. If they agree on a higher interest rate, this rate will be reduced to 7 percent, and any surplus already paid must be returned [to the borrower]." This article clearly regulates fixed interest on loans, about which there was considerable controversy. The Supreme Constitutional Court also had an occasion to reaffirm its unwillingness to reconsider legislation that had been passed prior to the amendment of the Constitution in 1980 (SCC, December 21, 1985). Thus, it clearly was asserting its superior status in expounding the application of Islamic law in Egypt (see also SCC, May 16, 1991, dealing with Islamic law and property).

The position of the Supreme Constitutional Court demonstrates that the mufti and Dar al-iftaʾ continue to play a secondary role in the determination of whether Islamic law is respected in the contemporary Egyptian legal system. Although the opinion of a mufti carries significant emotional and "sociological" weight, it remains legally ineffective and subordinate to the court, even in matters relating to the interpretation of the role played by Islamic law in the state. At the same time, the ideological position of Dar al-iftaʾ remains powerful in Egypt. The issues are important and answers are eagerly awaited.

In the present instance, Tantawi was conscious of his own intellectual limitations in the field, acknowledging that, irrespective of his competence in the shariʿa, a mufti trained at al-Azhar has very little knowledge of the banking world and that the alien vocabulary associated with modern banking quickly transforms an imprudent mufti into a "fish out of water." What is significant, indeed remarkable, about Tantawi's fatwa is his candid acknowledgment of this weakness. Also significant is the manner in which he explains the method by which he researched the subject of banking and inserts into the fatwa lengthy quotations from secular "specialists." This example suggests that the mufti in late twentieth-century Egypt recognizes the limitations of religious knowledge *(ʿilm)* in the modern world and acknowledges the necessity of appealing to authorities trained in secular institutions.

Mufti Tantawi continues to issue fatwas on financial transactions that are published in daily newspapers (see, for example, a series of five fatwas on financial transactions that appeared in *al-Ahrām* in May 1991). Although the pressure to Islamize Egyptian banks may have decreased following the scandalous collapse in 1990 of the financial institution al-Rayyan, the mufti, despite his self-professed limitations, surely will continue to play an important role in Egyptian society. The modest tone of a religious expert who himself seeks the advice of experts in other fields can only strengthen the moral authority of the mufti, both in Egypt and in the Sunni Muslim world at large.[7]

CHAPTER TWENTY-SEVEN

Operation Desert Storm and the War of Fatwas

YVONNE YAZBECK HADDAD

In 1991, the mufti of the Arab Republic of Egypt, Muhammad Sayyed Tantawi, published a comprehensive fifty-page fatwa entitled *Islamic Judgment on [the] Gulf Crisis,* in which he addressed a variety of issues that had surfaced as Muslims attempted to cope with the aftermath of the Iraqi invasion of Kuwait on August 2, 1990. An English translation of the text was distributed in the United States by the Egyptian Embassy in an effort to demonstrate that policies adopted by the Egyptian government were Islamically legitimate. The main arguments of the fatwa are reproduced below. (The text has been revised to render it into idiomatic English.)

The Egyptian Dar al-ifta' ["Fatwa Office"] has found it incumbent on itself at this crucial time to shed light on Islamic statutes [*aḥkām*] in order to confront arbitrary fatwas steeped in falsehood that were issued through ignorance by unqualified persons. The most important facts to which Dar al-ifta' would like to draw attention are:

I. The worldwide community of Islam [*umma*] in general and its rulers in particular should obey the Islamic shariʿa and return to the fold of peace and security, because:

The Islamic sharʿia has established the principles that govern relationships among members of the human community at large on the basis of mutual acquaintance, cooperation, justice, mercy and the exchange of benefits made lawful by Allah [Quran 49:13]. [p. 5]

The Islamic sharʿia gives priority to the principle of making peace and maintaining security and tranquility among Muslims, in particular, and between them and others, in general [Quran 59:23, 2:208, 4:94, 8:61, 33:44, 13:23–24, 56:25–26]. [p. 6]

We urge those who have occupied the lands of others and have declared lawful that which Allah has forbidden to return to reason and restore what is right.

We also urge those who have obeyed their rulers and collaborated in wrongdoing, injustice, and aggression to abstain from such acts. For if an act of disobedience [to Allah] is imposed [by a ruler], one should neither listen to it nor obey it. [p. 10]

II. It is acknowledged by all revealed religions that peace is the rule and one cannot resort to war except to remove injustice and aggression against the faith, oneself, honor, property, or country [Quran 22:39, 40]. [p. 11]

III. The Judgment of Allah—May He be Glorified—and the Judgment of his Messenger—peace be upon him—concerning the invasion of one Muslim country by another Muslim country is perfectly clear. [p. 20]

Allah's commandment to Muslims and their rulers is unambiguous, namely, to instruct their armies to fight the party that insists on wrongdoing. [p. 23]

IV. The law of Allah—the law of truth and justice—assigns to the citizens of each country the responsibility of electing the ruler, appointing him to, and discharging him from, his office. Only they can offer the ruler a pledge of allegiance, rally round him if he acts justly and equitably, counsel him if he errs, and relieve him of his office if they find him incorrigible. No one else has the right to interfere in their choice. [p. 23]

V. The Law of Allah—Glorified be He—has made it incumbent on the ruler to adopt every lawful measure to secure the safety of his people, their property, and their honor against any aggression. [p. 27]

The principle responsibility of a ruler toward his subjects is to prepare the [military] forces and equipment that are required to defend their faith, their property, their honor, and their country against any aggression. [p. 27]

If this force is deemed adequate to defeat the aggressor and extirpate the aggression, then that is sufficient. If, however, it is deemed inadequate, then the ruler should seek the assistance of his Muslim brothers and should consolidate all efforts to confront this danger. If the situation deteriorates, and the ruler, in consultation with his supporters and experts, finds that the forces of his country and of those who were summoned to assist are unable to deal with the situation adequately, then the Muslim country, being convinced beyond any doubt of the impending danger, has every right to seek help from Muslims and non-Muslims to repel the aggression and defend that which lawfully should be defended. [p. 27]

In short, we do not deny that seeking the assistance of non-Muslims to ward off an anticipated aggression involves certain dangers. The blame for such a situation should be cast on him who has compelled his neighbors to summon foreign forces to their land as a consequence of his unprecedented invasion and occupation of Kuwait. [p. 29]

Therefore, the Egyptian Dar al-ifta' [Fatwa Office] regards the support of Saudi religious scholars ['ulama'] and judges for the measures taken to safeguard the kingdom by the Servant of al-Haramayn, Fahd Ibn 'Abd al-'Aziz, to be in accord with and conformity to the Islamic shar'ia. [p. 29]

Islam permits the seeking of help from non-Muslims whenever it is necessary to repel an evil. Such a necessity should be assessed as it is. [p. 32]

This type of assistance that Islam permits during times of weakness is different from befriending non-Muslims while excluding Muslims. [p. 32]

Evidence from the Biography of the Prophet [*Sīra*] confirms the permissibility of seeking assistance from non-Muslims whenever necessary. [p. 33]

VI. A word to rulers [Imams of Muslims]: O Majesties and Excellencies, kings and heads of Muslim states: Allah has taken an oath from the 'ulama' that they should explain to the people the rules and teachings of the faith, enjoin right conduct, and forbid indecency [Quran 3:104]. [p. 34]

Allah's Messenger commanded Muslims, especially the 'ulama' and ministers, to give sincere advice to their rulers and be brave in declaring the truth. [p. 38]

We invite you to use the power and strength that Allah has bestowed upon you to propagate peace, security, and productivity among your people and to teach them how to renounce rancor, envy, dispute, and treachery. [p. 40]

It is a sheer lie to say that they [the Iraqis] did what they did for historical reasons. Historical rights can be regained through legal channels such as the Arab League or international organizations, not through treachery, oppression, or sudden aggression. [p. 44]

VII. We appeal to you once again to seek the advice of honest 'ulama' in matters concerning Islamic statutes [Quran 21:7].

No doubt, the 'ulama' are the most knowledgeable about the rules regarding faith, deviation, transactions, finance . . . etc." [p. 44]

Wise leaders always seek the advice of others and consult with them, especially regarding decisive matters, while foolish and arrogant rulers say, "I am the state." [p. 45]

Consequently, if you ask about the judgment of Islam regarding a country that invades another without being in a state of war with it—indeed, a country to which it is bound by the bonds of faith that make Muslims "naught else than brothers," the answer is: Such action is considered null and void from the point of view of Islam as well as that of International Law. [p. 45]

If you ask about the judgment of Islamic law regarding the distribution of wealth, the answer is: Allah has favored with provisions some people more than others [Quran 16:71]. [p. 45]

> VIII. A word to the ʿulamaʾ and to those who are qualified to issue fatwas: Allah has bestowed great honor on the ʿulamaʾ: (a) He—Blessed and praised be He—"has associated them with the angels in their witness to the oneness of Allah" [Quran 2:18]; (b) He has made the ʿulamaʾ to fear him [Quran 35:28]; (c) He has given the ʿulamaʾ alone exclusive knowledge of the meaning of the similitudes in His revelation [Quran 29:43]; (d) He refuses to place the ʿulamaʾ on an equal footing with others [Quran 39:9]; (e) He raises the ʿulamaʾ to high positions. [pp. 46–47]
>
> The prophetic tradition confirms the great honor bestowed by Allah on the ʿulamaʾ. "Whoever seeks religious knowledge, Allah will make easy for him the way to Paradise. Religious scholars are the inheritors of the prophets, that is, they inherit knowledge. And whoever gains knowledge is fortunate for he gains a great thing." [p. 47]
>
> The Prophet also informed us about a time when people lacking adequate religious knowledge will provide religious instruction, following their own vain desires or interpreting Islamic statutes out of ignorance. [p. 48]

The Gulf crisis precipitated a sharp and profound division in the Arab and Muslim world, a division that transcended the struggle of various national leaders for dominance and the regional interests and preferences of the Arab "street." Despite the general condemnation of the Iraqi invasion of Kuwait, there was considerable disagreement regarding the legitimacy of the introduction of American troops into the Arabian Peninsula, an issue that produced an unprecedented fatwa free-for-all. These fatwas addressed the question of whether it is Islamically legitimate to seek help from non-Muslims and to form a coalition with non-Muslims against other Muslims, and whether the presence of non-Muslim troops in Saudi Arabia constituted defilement of the holy places. In the process, the fatwas touched on aspects of traditional Islamic political thought, as well as the role of the ʿulamaʾ. Their interpretation of what is truly Islamic varied greatly, revealing a marked difference between the worldview of "palace fatwas" and the judicious opinions issued by the majority of Islamists. These differences were also apparent in public opinion.

From the outset, professional muftis representing various governments issued fatwas providing Islamic validation for, and justification of, the policies advocated by their respective political leaders, buttressing them with reference to quranic text and prophetic precedent. These fatwas were refuted, supplemented, or reiterated by declarations and official statements issued by special congresses and conferences convened by both Iraq and Saudi Arabia. Joining the fray were independent ad hoc bodies convened for the specific purpose of providing the definitive Islamic opinion on the event; there were also numerous statements by individuals, including various noted Islamists, commentators, and opinion makers.[1]

Both Saudi Arabia and Iraq sought international Islamic sanction for their policies. The International Congress of ʿUlamaʾ convened by Iraq in December 1990 issued a declaration supporting the Iraqi position, urging Muslims to undertake jihad and revolution against the Arab Muslim leaders who had joined the coalition forces under American leadership. Those leaders were identified as traitors and agents of "Crusader" nations. Independent fatwas supporting Iraq were subsequently issued by the following countries, organizations, and individuals: Sudan, Yemen, the Jordanian Fatwa Council, the Council of ʿUlamaʾ of Hijaz (centered in Iran), Imam Abu al-Qasim al-Khoʿi (the chief marjaʿ of the Shiʿa in Iraq), Hujjat al-Islam Baqir al-Mahdi, the Council for Islamic Revolution in Iraq under the leadership of Imam Baqir al-Hakim (residing in Iran), the Islamic Council in Britain, the Jihad Movement in Jerusalem, and the mufti of Jerusalem, Shaykh Saʿd al-Din al-ʿAlami (Khalifa 1991:53).

A countercongress of ʿulamaʾ met in Saudi Arabia during the same month. ʿAbd al-ʿAziz Ibn Baz of Saudi Arabia called for war against Saddam Hussein, which he called the highest form of jihad. The mufti of Syria, Ahmad Kaftaro, issued a fatwa in which he asserted that "the Syrian position concerning the Gulf crisis and the war against Iraq is sound and in accord with the shariʿa and the judgments of Islam." The mufti of al-Azhar, Gad al-Haqq ʿAli Gad al-Haqq, as well as the mufti of Egypt, Muhammad Sayyed Tantawi, published fatwas confirming the validity of Husni Mubarak's policies.

The first issue addressed by Tantawi in his fatwa highlights the contention between the two Islamic worldviews that currently are vying for dominance in the Arab world. As a defender of the status quo, Tantawi affirms traditional Sunni teachings about the primacy of peace and security in the abode of Islam, which necessitates that Muslims grant obedience to those in authority, regardless of the error of their ways. Tantawi rules out not only the legitimacy of revolutions against tyrants and those perceived by Islamists as working against the interests of Islam, but also any opposition to those in power by those who believe that security cannot be maintained at the expense of righteousness.

Tantawi describes a pluralistic worldview that sanctions difference as part of God's goal for creation. This difference is not restricted to forms of administration of Islamic states; it also legitimates a peaceful relationship with non-Islamic states. For Tantawi there is room for nations to coexist; their role is to compete for righteousness rather than domination, and to struggle to realize peace, security, and the common good. The Islamists (generally referred to by the Western press as "fundamentalists") propose a dualistic worldview, with special emphasis on the importance of Islamic unity and the commandment to bring about an Islamic world order that will prevail over all alternative systems, which, by definition, are evil. The necessity of realizing an ideal Islamic society is perceived as God's injunction to humanity, assumed by Muslims as the select community commissioned to "command the good and forbid the evil" (Quran 3:110). Thus alien forces are not only unfit to be allies but are also intrinsic enemies of the Muslim community, since they seek to bring about its deviation from the path of obedience to the teachings of God, to render it weak, and, in the final analysis, to destroy it. From this perspective, only an Islamic order should dominate. Agreeing that nations must struggle to realize peace and security, Islamists emphasize that a higher good, the ultimate vindication of Islam over its enemies, represents the divine vision for humanity.

Tantawi justifies Egyptian and Saudi policy by affirming that in Islam, peace is the rule and that one may resort to war only in order to eradicate injustice, treachery, and aggression, especially aggression against those who have been driven out of their land because they are Muslims. While Islamists agree on the basic principle, they contend that the real aggressor is the state of Israel, which has driven Muslims out of their homeland because of their religion and which has an expansionary policy, supported and assisted by the United States, that has wreaked havoc on the lives of the people of the area.[2]

Condemnation of Iraq and support for the coalition was expressed in fatwas issued by Saudi Arabia, Egypt, and Syria, whose respective presses accused Iraq of aggression against a fellow Muslim nation, for the redress of which it was necessary to seek outside help. Iraq's behavior was illegal in terms of both Islamic law and international law. This aggression necessitated seeking help from any friendly country, Muslim or non-Muslim. The Saudi, Syrian, and Egyptian fatwas supported Saudi action as being in accordance with the shariʿa and insisted that the presence of foreign Christian forces in parts of the country did not threaten, harm, or defile the holy places (Khalifa 1991:54).

Tantawi, the ʿulamaʾ of al-Azhar, and Ibn Baz of Saudi Arabia accepted the American intervention at its face value, that is, as a temporary, surgical operation in which the foreign forces would leave once their mission was fulfilled. The Islamists, on the other hand, attributed a more sinister motive to the American forces, one that relegated the Arab forces in the coalition to a subservient role. Once the Americans get in, they said, who will guarantee their departure?

Both sides formulated their positions in a manner that addressed not only the immediate event of the invasion but also the underlying relationship of the various parties involved. Was the initial act of aggression by Iraq against a fellow Muslim state of such magnitude that it mandated seeking help from non-Muslims? Does the immediate righting of a wrong justify the introduction of an agent that might bring about the disintegration of the *umma*? Put simply, can one trust non-Muslims?

On a deeper level, many were asking if the real root of the conflict was and remains a weakness in political consciousness, an overemphasis on regionalism, or a lack of courageous leadership that could take charge and tackle the real problems of the *umma* (Ibn Nasr 1991:73). Or is the problem a lack of consensus concerning what constitutes the vital interests of the Muslims? The Islamic Council of Europe asked, "Whose interest: the preservation of the total destiny of the *umma* . . . its existence and security, its peoples and resources . . . or the preservation of the destiny of a governor or prince who fears for his throne or the loss of power?" ("Marratan" 1990:21). For Tantawi and other government muftis, the current crisis had to be addressed first, before one could speculate on the course for the future:

> When in a situation there is a clash between acting in one's self-interest and an evil, priority is given to that which is superior in weight. In the present case the protection of the stability in the Gulf region, at both the international and local levels, is superior to the [evil of a] temporary presence of foreign military forces, because it ensures the safety of the people, their honor, and properties. (Tantawi 1991:34)

The Issue of *Muwālāh*

The international congress convened in Saudi Arabia legitimated the seeking of aid from foreign forces, since such action is in conformity with all the criteria prescribed by the shariʿa. This conclusion is based on the insistence that the fundamental purpose of the shariʿa is the preservation of life, honor, and property. The congress insisted that the foreign forces were not on holy ground, since they were not close to the Haramayn ("al-Muʾtamar" 1990:9–11).

The Islamists, on the other hand, argued that seeking help from non-Muslims in a battle in which Muslims might be killed is rejected by Quran 5:51: "O ye who believe, take not the Jews and the Christians for your friends and protectors: They are but friends and protectors to each other. And he amongst you that turns to them is of them." They cited further the example of al-Andalus, where the various Muslim factions sought the help of Christian princes in fighting one another and lost the land. And they maintained that the United States was not an innocent observer but had intervened in support of Israel. "They [those who favor American intervention] claim that the United States is an ally, and we ask, an ally of whom? Of the Muslims? Of the Israelis?" (al-Zayd 1991:77).

The religious element in American society has received increased attention since the Gulf War. Muslim authors have concluded that the affirmation of the separation of religion and state is incongruent with the reality of American politics and that Christian and Jewish sentiments do play a significant role in determining United States policy, as evidenced by the American political process. Not only does the Jewish lobby have great influence on the formulation of American policy with regard to Israel, but American presidents also find it necessary to hobnob with religious organizations, bartering their powers of decision for votes. They cite the example of former president Jimmy Carter, wearing a yarmulka and assuring his audience that he worships the same God as the Jewish community and that the survival of Israel is not a political issue but a moral imperative (al-Zayd 1991:78). Religious leaders such as Jerry Falwell are cited as having announced that the establishment of the state of Israel is a fulfillment of prophecy and that any opposition to Israel is a rebellion against God's will. This coalition between the Christian Right and the Israeli lobby manifested itself in their common support of the Israeli invasion of Lebanon. Pat Robertson's support for the Gulf War therefore was interpreted as yet one more part of his "Armageddon" scenario (al-Zayd 1991:80).

The Islamists also draw attention to Billy Graham's support for the Gulf War. He not only spent the night in the White House, but also went to church with President George Bush the next day, even though it was "a Thursday and not a Sunday." The war's religious dimension was clear in Bush's speech to religious broadcasters, in which he described America as a religious nation whose "war against Iraq was a just war to confront evil with good. He repeated the expression of his Christian forebears such as St. Augustine and his successor Thomas Aquinas." At a prayer breakfast, Bush asked Americans to observe Sunday March 2, 1991, as a national day of prayer for American forces. "What was surprising was that on the same day he delivered a speech announcing the good news that those who die in this war will secure a place with the Father. After all this, is it possible to separate President Bush's decisions from their religious Crusader significance?" (al-Zayd 1991:82).

In further support of the argument that the American forces were engaged in a religious war, the Islamists observed that the United States government supports missionary organizations by providing them with tax-free status, that its embassies provide assistance to Christian missionaries who enter the Gulf countries masquerading as researchers or social workers, and that the American military in Saudi Arabia included Jewish rabbis and Christian clergy assigned by the Chaplaincy Office of the Defense Department. The troops even brought hundreds of Bibles and Christmas trees with them. Muslims also observed on American television the crosses the clergy raised on sections of the Arabian Peninsula (al-Zayd 1991:82).

According to the Islamists, American intervention changed the conflict from an inter-Arab dispute over borders and resources to one in which Arab and Muslim rulers, in coalition with Western forces under American leadership, were seeking the disempowerment of an Arab country. Although most of the Islamists initially were in favor of the rejection of conquest as a means of solving problems and condemned the Iraqi aggression, they soon saw a more grave danger in the alliance forged with the United States and other Western allies. They rejected political and economic subservience to great powers and aid from foreigners, who were depicted as having come to destroy and marginalize the strength of the Muslims and to undermine their recent achievements, as manifested in the intifada and Islamic revival (Ibn Nasr 1991:74).

Fatwas, declarations, and proclamations originated not only in Islamic countries, but also in several Islamic communities in the diaspora, including Europe and the United States. The Islamic Council of Europe called for an independent Islamic vision, absolutely rejecting the presence of foreign troops on Saudi soil. It supported the conclusion that "those who provide a fatwa that [legitimizes the] seeking of aid from non-Muslims under current circumstances have not an iota of support in either the Quran or the Sunna" (al-Majlis al-islami al-urubi 1990:19).

To the consternation of the Islamists, several prominent Muslim intellectuals with an international following, including Yusuf al-Qaradawi, rector of the University of Qatar, and Fahmi Huwaydi, the moderate Egyptian Islamist, supported the Saudi position. Al-Qaradawi indicated that the presence of the foreign forces was brought about by necessity *(ḍarūra)*. He faulted other Islamists who objected to foreign intervention, arguing that they were basing their opinion on consequences and not causes ("Majallat" 1990:23).

The Islamists found this argument vacuous. To support their interpretation, they cited Quran 60:1: "O ye who believe, take not my enemies and yours as friends offering them your love even though they have rejected the truth that has come to you and have driven out the Prophet and yourselves because ye believe in God your Lord." Hence, for some of the Islamists, the issue is not whether necessity can justify seeking help from Western forces, but that such an act is a violation of a divine injunction against forming a coalition with those deemed eternal enemies of Islam: "The question is not whether or not it is a crusading army; our concern is that these forces are those of unbelief [*kufr*]—their enmity to us and our enmity to them is established until the Hour" (al-Zayd 1991:77).

Huwaydi countered that the interpretation of the text was incorrect. The shariʿa proscription against seeking aid is contingent on the assumption that one thereby must be partial to the enemy of Islam and exchange mutual affection. That, Huwaydi argued, is not necessary. Seeking the help of the enemy while you hate him from the depth of your heart is not allegiance *(muwālāh)*, especially if this quest for aid is a necessity predicated by exigency ("Majallat" 1990:26). Huwaydi contended that the American soldiers were not defiling Saudi property, because they were 1,500 kilometers away from Mecca and Medina and were not facing toward Mecca. However, Rida Idris, an Islamist author, argued that the danger of the American presence was far greater than suggested by Huwaydi. It was, in fact, a triple danger. First, there is the colonial, Crusader-Zionist nature of American support for Israel that has resulted in the expulsion of the people of Palestine. For this reason, they cannot be chosen as allies as Quran 60:9 indicates. Second, the declared purpose of American intervention is the destruction of Iraqi power, an Israeli-American goal that threatens the Arab and Muslim *umma*. Third, American weapons of mass destruction are so powerful that they will have the final say in the resolution of the conflict (Idris 1990:28–29).

The Role of the ʿUlamaʾ

The crisis made it clear that the Muslim world does not have a central authoritative body that can negotiate unity of purpose and action. What was disconcerting to many was the fact that the Muslim world not only divided into opposite factions and warring groups, but also utilized Islamic texts and juridical understandings in a contentious manner for opposite ends. The Muslim world was divided into factions fighting one another with whatever they could muster in the way of destructive and sophisticated weaponry, while the muftis, ʿulamaʾ, and intellectuals manipulated the very quranic texts and prophetic precedents meant to create a united *umma*.

These divisions were noted by a variety of authors. Muhammad Khalifa, who wrote an article entitled, "The War of Fatwas and the Fatwas of War," observed:

> Thus, the Muslim world [not only] disintegrated into contending and warring factions, but Islam itself disintegrated into contending and contradictory texts, jurisprudence, theories, concepts, and fatwas.
>
> The Muslim world was fighting itself by referring to Islamic texts that were meant to unite it. When the various governments and political entities differed and fought for their own narrow transient interests, the ʿulamaʾ, the religious leaders, the jurists, and the Islamic organizations appeared as mere instruments and tools for the respective authorities and leaders who used them to implement their designs and interests. (Khalifa 1991:55)

Khalifa also noted that the preponderance of Islamic legal opinion, with the evident biases of its respective authors supporting various Muslim leaders, undermined public confidence in Islamic leadership. "Men of religion, the intelligentsia, and the ʿulamaʾ veered according to the wills and wishes of the rulers. They crafted fatwas to accord with the political stance of the various regimes" (Khalifa 1991:55). By contrast, despite the prevalent use of religious discourse and the fact that Iran had just brought about a new political order through "an Islamic revolution," the first Gulf war (the Iran-Iraq War of 1980 to 1988) did not turn into a conflict with sectarian or religious overtones. Muslims generally perceived it as a political struggle. The second Gulf war, on the other hand, between the coalition forces and Iraq, bore pronounced religious overtones in the West from the outset, and was seen by many Islamists as Crusaderism versus Islam. At first the religious overtones of the conflict were not so evident in the Arab context, since the debate focused on international law and the legitimacy or illegitimacy of the Iraqi invasion. But eventually all contenders inserted a massive dose of Islam to vindicate their position (Khalifa 1991:51).

Some argued that it is unseemly on the part of the ʿulamaʾ who praised Saddam on previous occasions (because he had invited them to conferences and paid them money) to suddenly express their disgust at his policies. The critics levied the same argument in regard to those who were allied to Saudi Arabia ("Malhuzat" 1990:5).

The fatwas, justifications, recommendations, and announcements concerning the Gulf crisis generally were dominated by a discourse of confrontation and combativeness rather than dialogue and a quest for resolution of conflict. The ʿulamaʾ themselves became a primary issue. Tantawi argued that the ʿulamaʾ are the final authority on what constitutes Islamic legitimacy because of their independent role. They are God's agents, having rendered an oath to Him to uphold His teachings. Their role is primarily to safeguard security and peace. While they explain the rules and give advice to the rulers, part of their task is to promote obedience to the rulers. Thus, for Tantawi, it is incumbent on the *umma* to seek the advice of the ʿulamaʾ, because their authority has been confirmed by quranic text and prophetic traditions.

Others accused the ʿulamaʾ of being fickle, self-serving, subservient, and obsequious to those in authority, that is, lacking any independent judgment. *Taḥrīr* magazine, the voice of the Palestinian Tahrir Party in the United States, referred to the Egyptian ʿulamaʾ as hypocrites whose two fatwas, one issued in the name of the Egyptian ʿulamaʾ and the other in the name of al-Azhar, were nothing but a demonstration of sycophancy. In place of proclaimers of truth, they have become the "ʿulamaʾ of the authorities" *(ʿulamāʾ al-sulṭān)* ("Marratan" 1989:9, 17).

The ʿulamaʾ were condemned for acting as "spin doctors" in justifying policies of the various regimes. "It is as though the role of the ʿulamaʾ, the intellectuals, and the popular movements was to line up in the trenches of their respective combatants. They were consulted neither before the event nor in its aftermath concerning any policies that govern the official and international situation . . . Their role was marginal; they produced a fatwa after the fact and then other fatwas after other events" ("Malhuzat" 1990:3–4).

An editorial in *al-Insān,* the organ of the Tunisian Nahda Party, published in Paris, reflects the disgust with which the ʿulamaʾ were viewed within the Islamist movement. They believed that it is wrong for the ʿulamaʾ to be subservient to those in authority and to support their decisions. "The time has come for the ʿulamaʾ to take an independent stance and confront the problems" ("Malhuzat" 1990:5). All policy decisions by those in authority should be subject to the judgment of the shariʿa, not to the whim of the ruler. The ruler should not dictate the findings and policy, nor should he decide when the fatwa is to be issued and for what purpose. While it may be true that a time of crisis is not the time to reject a ruler's request, since calamity afflicts the whole nation, the lesson to be learned "is the right of the shariʿa, the ʿulamaʾ, the intellectuals, the *daʿwa* (missionary or propaganda) movements, and the masses for consultation, to express an opinion, participate in governance, and design the internal and external policies of the state, including matters of religion, economics, culture, education, higher education, and health" ("Malhuzat" 1990:5).

It is clear that the Gulf crisis caused dramatic fissures in the Arab body politic and deepened rifts within the Muslim nations, among the various Islamic movements and between factions of the same movement. These fissures were a reflection of the division that existed among the Islamists. "The war has made it evidently clear that the *umma* is not in need of political institutions or parties to resolve the major issues facing it . . . Today's need is for leadership that can be above the fray of parties and institutions whose concern is the overall situation facing the *umma*" (Ibn Nasr 1991:74, 79).

Central to the discussion was the question of who has the right to issue fatwas and other authoritative proclamations in the modern world. Can the Muslim community trust the muftis, who have demonstrated that they are basically civil servants doing the bidding of the rulers? How is the public good defined, and by whom? Is it incumbent on Sunni Muslims to obey those in authority, regardless of their folly, in order to safeguard the security of the nation? Are the ʿulamaʾ accountable to those in authority or to a higher calling, one linked to the vision of a dominant Islamic order in the world? Of what significance, if any, are the declarations by various congresses and conferences? Can they be considered as important, relevant or authoritative as the consensus fatwas issued by al-Azhar or other fatwa councils of the various states?

The Islamists' perception of the subservience of the ʿulamaʾ to those in authority proved to be deeply disturbing. Since the majority of Islamists are "lay" persons and have no official grounding in Islamic tradition, they envisage a future revitalized Islamic society in which the ʿulamaʾ function as independent, creative adjudicators prescribing Islamic judgments *(aḥkām)* on social, economic, and political issues. The demonstration of the apparent vacillation and even untrustworthiness of the ʿulamaʾ in the wake of the Gulf crisis left the Islamists with profoundly troubling questions as to who will provide the independent judgment for the future of the Muslim nation.

CHAPTER TWENTY-EIGHT

Media Muftis: Radio Fatwas in Yemen

BRINKLEY MESSICK

> Thanks to radio broadcasting . . . it became possible for the ritual practices of the people, their contractual affairs, and the customs and traditions to which they adhere to be in accord with God's principles.
>
> MAHMUD SHALTUT (D. 1963)

> The "content" of any medium blinds us to the character of the medium.
>
> MARSHALL MCLUHAN, 1964

In one of the classic studies of "modernization," a field which saw its heyday in the 1950s and 1960s and which remains influential, in some quarters at least, to this day, Daniel Lerner (1958) identified the mass media, specifically the radio, as central to an advancing "secular trend" in Middle Eastern societies. Few would subscribe these days to Lerner's narrow, Western-based model of social change, and his "secular trend" has been complicated, to put it mildly, by widespread religious resurgences.[1] Yet, if differently argued, his focus on the transformative qualities of such mass media forms as the radio retains interest. Whereas Lerner was concerned mainly with "secular" programs, such as the news, the segment of the broadcast day to be considered here typically is classified as "religious."

Radio fatwas—that is, the opinions of contemporary muftis broadcast daily to a national listening audience—represent both a significant continuity in the venerable Islamic institution of ifta' and, I suggest, an equally significant discontinuity. To elucidate the character of the radio fatwa, I compare the interpretive work of a media mufti with that of two contemporary Yemeni muftis who deliver their opinions in the centuries-old conventional manner, in written form directly to individual questioners. To contrast the styles of broadcast and personally delivered fatwas, I translate examples of each. Although radio broadcasting began in North Yemen in the 1950s, the final decade of the Zaydi imamate, a full-fledged national service was initiated only following the Revolution of 1962 (al-Zayn 1985). Early on in the national broadcasts from the capital, San'a', the brief (ten-minute), twice-daily "Fatwa Program" ("Barnamaj Fatawa") became a mainstay.

Fatwa giving in Yemen dates to the early years of the Muslim era and is documented through the subsequent centuries in numerous biographical histories (see al-Akwa' 1980). The tradition is a diverse one, involving different schools of legal interpretation, notably the Zaydi (Shi'i) and the Shafi'i (Sunni); different degrees of institutionalization, from private to official (the ordinary scholar asked an occasional question to the Ottoman mufti of the Wilayat and the present day mufti of the republic); different levels of juristic qualification, from absolute mujtahids to modest provincial practitioners; and a full gamut of output, from preserved fatwa collections[2] to routine opinions that left no documentary record. Since there was no colonial rule in the northern Yemeni highlands, the indigenous shari'a tradition did not undergo the dislocating impositions or receptions of Western law that occurred in many other Muslim countries. As a consequence, Yemeni muftis of this century functioned in a legal world in which the shari'a retained wide relevance, with exclusive jurisdiction courts applying both civil (property, personal status) and criminal law.[3]

Conventional Muftis

The Mufti of Ibb Province

My original ethnographic research in the mid-1970s and in 1980 centered on the work of a provincial mufti, Muhammad al-Wahhabi (b. 1912), who served his native town of Ibb in the Shafi'i southern highlands of "Lower Yemen" (*al-yaman al-asfal*) (Messick 1986; 1993:135–151). At the old Ibb madrasa, al-Wahhabi (whose name implies no link to the school of Muhammad b. 'Abd al-Wahhab) studied the basic fiqh texts of the local Shafi'i school, to which he belonged, including standard manuals by Abu Shuja' (twelfth century), al-Nawawi (d. 1277), and Ibn Raslan (d. 1440),[4] and a concise treatise on jurisprudential method *(uṣūl)* by al-Juwayni (d. 1285). In addition, since his training took place during the post-Ottoman (post-1918) period of the imamate, when stipends available to students in Ibb supported the study of the ruler's madhhab, he also worked on the basic Zaydi text, *al-Azhar* (by Imam al-Mahdi al-Murtada, d. 1432), and its standard commentary by Ibn Miftah (d. 1472).[5] Finally, with Yemeni jurists of both schools, he studied a variety of works by Muhammad b. ʿAli al-Shawkani (d. 1834), the internationally known absolute mujtahid of early nineteeth-century Yemen, and his distinguished predecessor Ibn al-Amir (d. 1753), critical Zaydis who together are referred to in Yemen as "Sunnis."

After serving in the town madrasa, where he was the leading teacher of fiqh (with a special interest in inheritance law), al-Wahhabi was appointed mufti of Ibb Province following the Revolution of 1962. He occupied the post until about 1990, when old age made it difficult for him to carry out his functions. During this period, he delivered fatwas to private individuals from the town and the surrounding countryside who came to see him in his semipublic afternoon sitting room on one of the upper floors of his personal residence, a massive stone house in the center of Ibb. Some settled in on floor-level cushions for an afternoon of *qāt* chewing and waterpipe smoking with the mufti; others came, sat briefly, and then departed when their question had been answered.

His fatwa giving was based on face-to-face encounters and written communication. As the mufti was hard of hearing, there were rarely any oral exchanges accompanying the questions, although some men tried shouting in his ear. Typically, a question was written out by the questioner, or by someone else in the sitting room who was literate, and then handed to al-Wahhabi. Without pausing to refer to any books, the mufti immediately dipped his reed pen in an inkwell and commenced his answer *(jawāb)*, that is, his fatwa, which he fitted into the space left open at the top of the original slip of paper bearing the question. When he finished writing, he handed the paper back to the questioner. Since the piece of paper containing both the question and the answer was carried away by the questioner, and as al-Wahhabi had no recording secretary (except, briefly, one I myself provided), the thousands of fatwas that he issued are dispersed and untraceable.

As al-Wahhabi would readily acknowledge, his fatwas generally broke no new legal ground. Instead, they communicated the accepted position of the Shafiʿi school, occasionally supplemented by reference to Zaydi or "Sunni" views, or, in recent years, by applicable Ministry of Justice guidelines (on such matters as preemption and marriage annulment). Rather than being grand exercises in ijtihad, these short fatwas consisted of relatively simple matchings of circumstance and rule, usually with no explicit citation of sources. Despite his title and government salary, al-Wahhabi's fatwas had neither binding authority nor any formal connection with shariʿa court processes.[6] Although many of his fatwas were issued in the context of disputes, they always were delivered to single individuals rather than to adversarial pairs.

Al-Wahhabi's fatwas fall into three main topical groups: marriage and divorce matters, inheritance and endowment questions, and land ownership issues (sale contracts, leases, and preemption). Although he occasionally answered a question on a ritual *(ʿibādāt)* issue, nearly all his work pertained to the broad field of the *muʿāmalāt,* the sections of the shariʿa concerned with transactions, including both bilateral contracts (sale, marriage) and unilateral dispositions (legacy, endowment).

In the heavily terraced and well-watered countryside surrounding Ibb, there are large concentrations of private property that have been converted into inalienable, perpetual endowments *(awqāf).* The familial endowment, in particular, gives rise to innumerable disputes. In typical fashion, the question is relatively specific, but the answer is general.

> [*Question:*] What is your opinion [*mā qawlukum*], scholar of Islam, may God forgive you. We had a house endowed, until God inherits the earth and those upon it, in the name of the descendants of the endowment founder. This house has some lands whose revenues were used for the repair of the house. When the house collapsed, the heirs undertook to sell it and sell the lands. Is this sale legal? Give us a fatwa, may God reward you.
>
> *The answer* [*al-jawāb*]: The sale of an endowed property is not legal. But if [the original endowment] was invalid and the judge with jurisdiction rules on its invalidity, then its sale is legal. God knows best. Mufti of the Province. Muhammad al-Wahhabi.

Some questions involve a basic shariʿa frame that is filled in with local customary content, as in the following example dealing with the maintenance of a divorced wife:

> [*Question:*] What is your opinion, your honor, mufti of Ibb Province, may God preserve you, with regard to a man who divorced his wife and whose [financial status] is intermediate? How much is the divorced woman entitled to monthly in support [*nafaqa*], clothing, and rent? May God preserve you. The presenter [name, village]
>
> *The answer:* The requirement for the woman, per month, is ¾ *qadaḥ* of grain, by the local measure, half wheat and half sorghum; and 90 riyals each month; and she is to receive clothing valued at 120 riyals at the beginning of every year; and rent of a residence is required. Compliance must be according to what is customary. 5 February 1976. Mufti of the Province [signature]

While he is now too old to work, al-Wahhabi has not been replaced. People will continue to pose questions informally to the knowledgeable among them, but the official local muftiship may die out with al-Wahhabi.

Mufti of the Republic

In February 1992, I visited the Sanʿaʾ home of the mufti of the republic, Ahmad Muhammad Zabara (b. 1907). An adherent of the Zaydi madhhab, Zabara's early instruction began in his natal rural district of al-Kibs and continued in the Great Mosque of Sanʿaʾ. In 1926, he entered the advanced school that was opened that same year in the capital by Imam Yahya. In the 1950s, he was appointed by Imam Ahmad to head the high appeal court (then known as *al-hayʾa al-sharīʿa*), a position he held until the Revolution of 1962, after which he was appointed republican Yemen's first (and only) state mufti.[7]

Aside from his travel to international conferences and his occasional cermonial appearances, Zabara's routine work is actually similar to that of al-Wahhabi. Essentially, he is the mufti of Sanʿaʾ;[8] no legislative mandate exists for him to deliver opinions on the legal affairs of state. Afternoon discussions in Mufti Zabara's afternoon sitting room are interrupted from time to time by the arrival of questions. But whereas al-Wahhabi allowed petitioners to enter his house and approach him directly, Zabara customarily has them wait outside and convey their questions on pieces of paper carried by small children. After receiving the paper, the mufti pauses to write a short response on the piece of paper, sign his name, and apply his official seal,[9] and he gives the resulting fatwa to the child for conveyance back to the waiting petitioner. As in Ibb, there is no recording of fatwas.

On February 28, 1992, a question was posed by a man who had spent many years as a migrant worker in Kuwait. As he was illiterate, he discussed his query with a young scholar, who drafted the question.

> [*Question:*] In the Name of God. The father, mufti of the republic, may God give you success, greetings. Give us a fatwa, may God reward you, with regard to a man who emigrated [for work] from his country and provided support for his father, purchasing land for him in his home district and a house in Sanʿaʾ. The father has children by another wife, not the man's mother. Do his brothers have a right to what he has earned for himself in this situation? [Signed, name]
>
> [*Answer:*] In the name of God. All that the migrant worker earned for himself is his. Nothing of it [goes] to his young brothers or to [any] others. 28 February 1992, the grand mufti [*al-muftī al-ʿāmm*], [signed] Ahmad Muhammad Zabara [seal].

In both substance and form, the fatwas of al-Wahhabi and Zabara are conventional. After introducing a third mufti, I will compare conventional and radio fatwas with respect to both content and style.

Media Muftis

In the 1980s, four men were responsible for preparing fatwas for broadcast on the Yemeni national radio's "Fatwa Program." Questions received in the mail by the broadcasting administration were divided up and then transferred to these scholars to be answered. One of the four was the mufti of the republic, Ahmad b. Muhammad Zabara, who, as I have just described, also issued fatwas in the traditional manner.[10] The remaining three were Muhammad b. Ismaʿil al-ʿAmrani,[11] who served in the Chamber of Deputies; Hamud b. ʿAbbas al-Muʾayyad, a noted imam of a Sanʿaʾ mosque; and Muhammad b. ʿAli al-Ghurbani, a former Endowments offical and High Court adviser. The four were "chosen," according to al-Ghurbani, "to give straightforward replies; zealots [*mutaʿaṣṣibīn*] were excluded."

Al-Ghurbani was born in 1921 in the small town of Yarim, the seat of a Zaydi district on the highland plateau that later became attached administratively to Ibb Province. In Yarim, al-Ghurbani received his initial instruction in the basic Zaydi school texts, including the text and commentary of *al-Azhar* and the works of al-Shawkani. At about eighteen, some years before he actually studied the text intensively, he made his own handwritten copy of a printed Zaydi jurisprudential method treatise (*al-Kafīl,* by Muhammad b. Yahya Bahran, d. 1550) and its commentary.[12] He then bound this manuscript in leather and added decorative embossing. His career as a public functionary began with his appointment to a Public Endowments branch office in Yarim; in the 1950s he was transferred to Ibb, the provincial capital, and promoted to accounting head. When I first met him in the fall of 1974, he was still with the Ibb Province Endowments Office, but later in the decade he was transferred to the national office in Sanʿaʾ and promoted to deputy minister. Soon thereafter he moved to the High Court (Mahkamat al-Naqd) where he served nearly ten years as an advisor in the Personal Status section. His career issuing fatwas for broadcast began in the early 1980s, while he was at the High Court, and it continued after his retirement from the court until his death in late 1991. Unlike either al-Wahhabi, whom he had known in Ibb, or Zabara, his colleague as a media mufti, al-Ghurbani did not issue fatwas to people who came to his residence.

Some years ago, al-Ghurbani used a commercial metaphor to describe to me the nature of the shariʿa and the role of the interpreting jurist. In their very general and summary qualities, he explained, legal principles are similar to wholesale commodities, while the opinions and rulings necessitated by practice are like retail goods. In making interpretive interventions, the jurist breaks down bulk principle to fit the detailed trade of everyday-life situations.[13] Although this conception continued to inform his new interpretive work, al-Ghurbani observed that preparing a fatwa to be heard on a radio broadcast was a different matter from writing one for an individual to read. Whereas a conventional mufti's fatwa could be read and interpreted by the literate and knowledgeable, for themselves and for others, a fatwa heard over the radio must be immediately and generally clear. He explained that the radio audience consists of the public at large (the *jumhūr*) and therefore includes women and the uninformed. Listeners might hear the broadcast, for example, in a restaurant or while riding in a taxi. As a consequence, the radio mufti has to be relatively expansive, using examples, repetition and reference to related questions to convey his ideas. At the same time, he has to be concise and quickly summarize the issues. Al-Ghurbani said he applied techniques of the discipline of rhetoric *(balāgha)* and, occasionally, cited proverbs, poetry, and other literary references. He replied according to what he understood to be a question's legal import *(al-muqtaḍā)*, giving what he considered to be the preponderant view *(al-qawl al-rājiḥ)*, although he would not oppose existing Yemeni legislation. Reflecting on his dealings with the employees of the radio service, al-Ghurbani remarked, "Their aim is not knowledge [*ʿilm*], their aim is programming."

Upon receipt of the letters containing listeners' questions, al-Ghurbani took whatever time was necessary to consult his small personal library in the private sitting room of his Sanʿaʾ home before preparing his answers. While this library was anchored in the key works of the Zaydi school of jurisprudence, including the critical commentary on the *al-Azhar* text by al-Shawkani, it was no longer the library of a narrowly madhhab-focused jurist.[14] Also on his shelves were law works by Sunni jurists, including the Hanbalis Ibn Qudama (d. 1223) and Ibn al-Qayyim al-Jawziyya (d. 1350) and the later Hanafi Ibn ʿAbidin (d. 1842). For hadith he relied not only on familiar works by al-Shawkani and Ibn al-Amir, but also on others he had not studied in his student days, including those by the Sunnis al-Nawawi (d. 1277) and al-Suyuti (d. 1505). His new juristic range was perhaps best revealed by three fatwa collections to which he regularly referred, by al-Suyuti, by Ibn Taymiyya (d. 1328), and by the already cited twentieth-century Egyptian media mufti Mahmud Shaltut (who once wrote that "no juristic school can fully contain the message of God"). Al-Ghurbani's acquisition of a small book by al-Nawawi entitled *Adab al-fatwā wa'l-muftī wa'l-mustaftī* (excerpted from his commentary on al-Shirazi), published in Damascus (1988), evinces his interest in the theory of fatwa giving.

A partial inventory of about 400 fatwas delivered by al-Ghurbani (preserved by him as photocopies) reveals several content features that distinguish them from the fatwas I had recorded some fifteen years before in the sitting room of the provincial mufti, al-Wahhabi. First, although women used to request fatwas in Ibb, they acted through men or through al-Wahhabi's wife. Here, however, female questioners are clearly in evidence.[15] In such instances, al-Ghurbani addresses the "female questioner," or the "questioner sister." Women ask a broad range of questions, with some emphasis on marriage issues, including such topics as the implications of a husband's impotence.

A second difference in comparison with the activity of muftis such as al-Wahhabi is the incidence of questions pertaining to quranic exegesis *(tafsīr)* and hadith interpretation, issues not raised in Ibb but representing about a quarter of the total questions handled by al-Ghurbani. By contrast, as a third difference, the collection of radio fatwas contains far fewer questions touching on transactional and contractual matters *(muʿāmalāt)*, which accounted for virtually all of al-Wahhabi's fatwas. Approximately one-eighth of the radio fatwas deal with marriage and another eighth with other types of transactions, mainly in the area of family law. Examples of contractual questions pertaining to marriage and divorce addressed by al-Ghurbani include whether a woman who is divorcing her husband by *khulʿ* must be present at the transaction session, the conditions for marriage annulment *(faskh)*, and whether a woman may travel with her husband. General family law questions raise such issues as whether it is permissible for a man to divide his estate before his death or to sell property to one of his sons. Although I noted that al-Wahhabi responded to an occasional question in the field of ritual obligations, the fourth difference is that such matters predominate in the work of al-Ghurbani, accounting for fully half of his fatwas. In this category, there are questions concerning fasting in the month of Shawwal, sickness as an excuse for missing prayers, whether the prayer of a worshipper out of pace with the leading imam is invalid, the requirement of ablutions after contamination by blood, the qibla orientation of a mosque when this is different from the compass direction of north, the necessity of ablutions after a sexual dream without emission of semen, the permissibility of using snuff and tobacco in the mosque, and whether the dead "meet" one another in cemeteries. Together with the appearance of questions about *tafsīr* and hadith and the sharp reduction in the volume of *muʿāmalāt* questions, the high percentage of *ʿibādāt* questions suggests that this form of broadcast fatwa giving has become less a "legal" activity and more of a specialized "religious" one.

Al-Ghurbani's work is exemplified by his response to questions posed by a group of young women, students at a Sanʿaʾ intermediate school. After two initial questions relating to quranic exegesis, their third query is as follows:

> What do the scholars of Islam say about one who listens to and repeats Arab songs and who reads magazines? Is this licit or illicit? And is handshaking [*muṣāfaḥāt*] with foreign women teachers illicit?[16]

To this, al-Ghurbani responded:

> It is known, questioners [fem. pl.], that scholars have said many things about listening to music. Among them are those who say it is licit, and among them are those who say it is illicit, and it is clear that I hold its status to be reprehensible. Previously there have been numerous answers on this from me and from other scholars. As for the reading of magazines, it is desirable, as

> they contain diverse cultural information and the reader can get from them things that will amaze him. As for handshaking with women, generally, whether they are teachers, students, or housewives, it is illicit with respect to those not among the interdicted female relations who are forbidden for a man to marry and whom (fem.) God, in a verse from *Sūrat al-Nūr,* permits to show their ornament. God gives guidance. Muhammad ʿAli al-Ghurbani.

In the last part of this opinion, al-Ghurbani responds generically, answering from a male point of view. Another fatwa, for which no question is preserved, is a reply to a married woman:

> *The answer:* It is known, sister questioner, if the matter is as you describe, [namely,] that you cohabited with your husband for a period of three years and that he was unable to have intimacy with you due to the existence in him of a defect, namely, impotence, added to which he left you without maintenance, then this is sufficient for you to ask for annulment of the marriage in the shariʿa court of your district. It is for the court to verify the existence of the defect by a clear shariʿa method and issue a shariʿa judgment on this. God gives guidance. Muhammad ʿAli al-Ghurbani.

In conventional fatwas, questions usually are posed in the classic hypothetical manner, "with regard to a man who . . .," and then answered in the third person. Here the students are also quite formal in phrasing their question, "What do the scholars of Islam say . . .," but the married woman is answered in a comparatively direct form of second person address. In another fatwa, al-Ghurbani speaks directly to a particular woman's circumstances when he says, "You are still his wife and the mother of his seven children." Typically, the conventional mode of response is extremely concise, with none of al-Ghurbani's occasional chatty informality, "your letter arrived . . .," and so on. Whereas al-Wahhabi's or Zabara's fatwas barely constitute a sentence—it was often necessary to have such cryptic fatwas explained—al-Ghurbani endeavors to write in standard prose. His nontechnical vocabulary recalls the innovative intent in the late-nineteenth-century drafters of the Ottoman code, who strove to write in language "everyone" could understand. In the introduction to his published fatwas, many of which originally were broadcast, the former media mufti Shaltut noted that radio fatwas communicated with "the respected listeners in easy and accessible formulations, by a method that did not require difficulty or trouble."

It is ironic that comparatively personalized contacts with muftis such as al-Wahhabi in Ibb should elicit formal, impersonal replies, while the mediated fatwas of al-Ghurbani were more informal and familiar. Also, unlike al-Wahhabi's and Zabara's questioners, who carried their fatwas away on the slips of paper containing the original questions, al-Ghurbani's questioners obtained no "hard copy." The conventional muftis' questioners received immediate and private responses, while al-Ghurbani's had to wait for the mail, the mufti's research time, and their turn on the broadcast. Then they had to share their answer with thousands of other listeners.

Conclusion

Adapting to changing times and also to a novel medium, the institution of ifta' continues to provide answers. All of the fatwas translated here, conventional and broadcast alike, were routine in nature. They required no rigorous exercises of interpretation and exhibited no pronounced scholarly character. These are fatwas of the ephemeral type, which merit neither preservation nor publication, but which nevertheless serve the legal information needs of ordinary questioners. Like fatwas everywhere, they are considered responses by qualified scholars to relatively direct expressions of real-world issues and situations. Since such routine fatwas are considered of limited enduring import and usually are not reported or documented, they have received little scholarly notice. But to confine our attention to momentous fatwas alone is to overlook a major dimension of the ifta' activity, represented by the multitude of unremarkable responses, from muftis both great and small, to a host of everyday concerns.

The three Yemeni muftis, al-Wahhabi, Zabara, and al-Ghurbani, are of roughly the same generation, educated before the 1962 Revolution. All received their intellectual formation in the madhhab-based scholarship of the period, and they exemplify some important strands of the Yemeni highland's intellectual diversity. Although their training as jurists preceeded the revolution, they have worked as official muftis—provincial, republican, and media—during the postrevolutionary republican era, when they have had to contend with newly legislated forms of shari'a law. The additions to al-Ghurbani's library signal his move, as a media mufti, beyond the old madhhab confines to a broader spectrum of juristic knowledge. With the imminent passing of this older generation, however, it remains to be seen how the next generation, born after the revolution and educated in the new-style national schools and the university, will utilize or modify the institution of ifta'.

In addition to describing the marked changes in content found in the fatwas delivered some years ago by al-Wahhabi in provincial Ibb as compared to those broadcast recently by the media mufti al-Ghurbani, I have also underscored a number of discursive shifts. These latter developments, on the level of language, rhetorical style, and address, are associated with the differences between the private type of fatwa, based on the closed, mufti-mustafti dyad, and the public type, which begins as a mufti-mustafti dyad but ends as an open, mufti-jumhur (general public) relationship. Writing was the basis of all the fatwas discussed, including those designed for radio broadcast, but even the two "conventional" muftis, provincial and republican, differed in their modes of written connection, with al-Wahhabi writing in his questioner's presence and Zabara maintaining a distance. Radio fatwas begin as written questions but are delivered in the broadcast version of the spoken word, a form of "secondary orality" (Ong 1982; cf. Caton 1990:186–189). Whereas the old logocentric textual culture (Messick 1993) sought the legitimating immediacy of a human presence to secure the authoritative transmission of knowledge, the new media intervene in a distancing and alienating manner. Instead of individualized communication, the new fatwas are broadcast messages for a mass audience, the characteristic citizenry of a nation-state. The "voice" is no longer that of the mufti himself but that of a professional broadcaster. Mediated by the mail, the airwaves, and the broadcaster's even diction, the fatwa is removed from the nexus of immediate human contact. The personal matter has become public here, in much the same way that it has in the Western media.

Appendix · Notes · References
Glossary · Contributors · Index

APPENDIX

List of Fatwas

The following is a list of fatwas translated and analyzed in this book, classified according to the pattern and order of *al-Fatāwā al-Islāmiyya* (al-Azhar, 1982).

Prayer

No. 1
Subject: "Leadership of ritual prayer"
Mufti: Ibn Taymiyya (d. 1328)
Location: Egypt
Pages: 64–66
See also no. 27

Fasting

No. 2
Subject: "Expiation for breaking the fast"
Mufti: Ishaq b. Ibrahim (d. 963 or 965)
Location: Córdoba
Pages: 55–56

No. 3
Subject: "Expiation for breaking the fast"
Mufti: Yahya b. Yahya al-Laythi (d. 848)
Location: Córdoba
Page: 56

Hajj

No. 4
Subject: "Visiting Medina during the Hajj"
Mufti: Rashid Ahmad Gangohi (d. 1905)
Location: Deoband, India
Pages: 184–185

Marriage

No. 5
Subject: "Child marriage"
Mufti: Khayr al-Din al-Ramli (d. 1671)
Location: Ramlah, Palestine
Pages: 131–132

No. 6
Subject: "A husband's claim of marriage after several years"
Mufti: M. Karim Khan Kirmani (d. 1870)
Location: Kerman, Iran
Page: 168

No. 7
Subject: "Guardian's consent to mutʿa marriage"
Mufti: Ayatollah Khomeini (d. 1989)
Location: Tehran, Iran
Page: 251

Maintenance

No. 8
Subject: "Maintenance of a divorced woman"
Mufti: Muhammad al-Wahhabi (b. 1912)
Location: Ibb, Yemen
Page: 313

No. 9
Subject: "Maintenance of stepbrothers"
Mufti: Ahmad Muhammad Zabara (b. 1907)
Location: Sanʿaʾ, Yemen
Page: 314

Divorce

No. 10
Subject: "Apostasy and judicial separation"
Mufti: Ashraf ʿAli Thanawi (d. 1943)
Location: Deoband, India
Pages: 193–194

No. 11
Subject: "Divorce by oath"
Mufti: ʿAbd al-ʿAziz b. ʿAbd Allah Ibn Baz (b. ?)
Location: Riyadh, Saudi Arabia
Page: 264

No. 12
Subject: "Divorce pronounced in anger"
Mufti: ʿAbd al-ʿAziz b. ʿAbd Allah Ibn Baz (b. ?)
Location: Riyadh, Saudi Arabia
Pages: 264–265

No. 13
Subject: "Triple divorce by a single utterance of divorce formula"
Mufti: ʿAbd al-ʿAziz b. ʿAbd Allah Ibn Baz (b. ?)
Location: Riyadh, Saudi Arabia
Pages: 265–266

No. 14
Subject: "Contingent divorce"
Mufti: Sheikh ʿAli Hassan (b. ?)
Location: West Bank, Jordan
Pages: 273–275

No. 15
Subject: "Judicial divorce on ground of husband's impotence"
Mufti: Muhammad b. ʿAli al-Ghurbani (b. 1921)
Location: Sanʿaʾ, Yemen
Page: 318

Oath

No. 16
Subject: "Expiation for breaking an oath"
Mufti: Malik b. Anas (d. 795)
Location: Medina
Page: 56

No. 17
Subject: "Oath regarding debt"
Mufti: Abdurrahim (d. 1656)
Location: Istanbul
Page: 147
See also no. 11

Paternity

No. 18
Subject: "Paternity of child by a female slave not owned by father" (1)

Mufti: Abdurrahim (d. 1656)
Location: Istanbul
Page: 144

No. 19
Subject: "Paternity of child by a female slave not owned by father" (2)
Mufti: Abdurrahim (d. 1656)
Location: Istanbul
Page: 144

No. 20
Subject: "Paternity of child by a female slave not owned by father" (3)
Mufti: Abdurrahim (d. 1656)
Location: Istanbul
Page: 145

No. 21
Subject: "Paternity of child by a female slave not owned by father" (4)
Mufti: Abdurrahim (d. 1656)
Location: Istanbul
Page: 146

No. 22
Subject: "Paternity of child by a female slave not owned by father" (5)
Mufti: Abdurrahim (d. 1656)
Location: Istanbul
Page: 146

Apostasy

No. 23
Subject: "Condemnation of al-Sanusi, anathema"
Mufti: Mustafa b. Ramadan al-Bulaqi (1847)
Location: Egypt
Pages: 155–159
See also no. 10.

No. 24
Subject: "Infidelity of the Wahhabis and Deobandis"
Mufti: Ahmad Riza Khan Barelwi (d. 1921)
Location: Bareilly, India
Pages: 209–213

Mosques

No. 25
Subject: "Permissibility of discussions on religious subjects in mosques"
Muftis: Ahmad b. Muhammad Ibn Ziyad, known as al-Habib (d. 925), ʿUbaydullah

b. Yahya (d. 909), Ibn Lubaba (d. 926), Muhammad b. Walid (d. 922), Saʿd b. Muʿadh (d. 920)
Location: Córdoba
Page: 48

No. 26
Subject: "Permissibility of discussions on religious subjects in mosques"
Mufti: Abu Asbagh ʿIsa Ibn Sahl (d. 1093)
Location: Córdoba
Pages: 48–49

No. 27
Subject: "Women praying in a mosque"
Mufti: Muhammad al-Aydini (ca. 1693)
Location: Ottoman empire
Pages: 122–127

No. 28
Subject: "Use of force to protect a mosque"
Mufti: Sayyid Muhammad Nasirabadi (d. 1867)
Location: Lucknow, India
Pages: 179–180

No. 29
Subject: "Defilement of a mosque by infidels" (1)
Mufti: Sayyid Muhammad Nasirabadi (d. 1867)
Location: Lucknow, India
Page: 174

No. 30
Subject: "Defilement of a mosque by infidels" (2)
Mufti: Sayyid Muhammad Nasirabadi (d. 1867)
Location: Lucknow, India
Page: 178

Sales and Contracts

No. 31
Subject: "Manufacturing contract"
Mufti: Taqi al-Din al-Subki (d. 1355)
Location: Cairo
Pages: 73–76

No. 32
Subject: "Status as an *umm walad* of a female slave owned by a third party" (1)
Mufti: Abdurrahim (d. 1656)
Location: Istanbul
Page: 145

No. 33
Subject: "Status as an *umm walad* of a female slave owned by a third party" (2)
Mufti: Abdurrahim (d. 1656)
Location: Istanbul
Page: 145

No. 34
Subject: "Status as an *umm walad* of a female slave owned by a third party" (3)
Mufti: Abdurrahim (d. 1656)
Location: Istanbul
Page: 145

Banking

No. 35
Subject: "Permissibility of banking operations"
Mufti: Muhammad Sayyed ʿAtiyya Tantawi (b. 1925)
Location: Cairo
Pages: 289–294

Procedure

No. 36
Subject: "Payment of expenses of the defendant"
Mufti: Muhammad Karim Khan Kirmani (d. 1870)
Location: Kerman, Iran
Page: 167

Revival of Wasteland

No. 37
Subject: "Revival of wasteland"
Mufti: Muhammad Karim Khan Kirmani (d. 1870)
Location: Kerman, Iran
Pages: 169–170

Succession and Inheritance

No. 38
Subject: "Inheritance rights of the child of a female slave" (1)
Mufti: Abdurrahim (d. 1656)
Location: Istanbul
Page: 146

No. 39
Subject: "Inheritance rights of the child of a female slave" (2)
Mufti: Abdurrahim (d. 1656)

Location: Istanbul
Page: 146

No. 40
Subject: "Inheritance rights of the child of a female slave" (3)
Mufti: Abdurrahim (d. 1656)
Location: Istanbul
Page: 147

No. 41
Subject: "Transaction between parent and children"
Mufti: Ahmad al-Wansharisi (d. 1508)
Location: Banu Kanikas, al-Maghrib
Pages: 103–111

No. 42
Subject: "Inheritance of property previously gifted to the deceased"
Mufti: Muhammad Karim Khan Kirmani (d. 1870)
Location: Kerman, Iran
Page: 168

No. 43
Subject: "Inheritance versus *waqf*"
Mufti: Muhammad Karim Khan Kirmani (d. 1870)
Location: Kerman, Iran
Page: 168

Waqf

No. 44
Subject: "Custodianship of a family waqf"
Mufti: unknown
Location: Hyderabad, India
Pages: 246–247

No. 45
Subject: "Sale of *waqf* property"
Mufti: Muhammad al-Wahhabi (b. 1912)
Location: Ibb, Yemen
Page: 313
See also no. 43.

Ḍarar

No. 46
Subject: "Permissibility of postmortem examination"
Mufti: Hasanayn Muhammad Makhluf (d. 1990)
Location: Cairo, Egypt
Pages: 279–282

Permissions and Prohibitions

No. 47
Subject: "Prohibition of images"
Mufti: Muhammad al-ʿAbbasi al-Mahdi (d. 1897)
Location: Cairo, Egypt
Pages: 217–218

No. 48
Subject: "Saliva of dogs, dog-keeping"
Mufti: Muhammad al-Fahm (d.?)
Location: Cairo, Egypt
Page: 229

No. 49
Subject: "Listening to music"
Mufti: Muhammad b. ʿAli al-Ghurbani (b. 1921)
Location: Sanʿaʾ, Yemen
Pages: 317–318

No. 50
Subject: "Shaking hands with women"
Mufti: Muhammad b. ʿAli al-Ghurbani b. 1921)
Location: Sanʿaʾ, Yemen
Pages: 317–318

Non-Muslims

No. 51
Subject: "Muslim attendance at Christmas celebrations"
Mufti: Fatwa Committee of the Council of Indonesian Ulama, 1981
Location: Jakarta, Indonesia
Pages: 238–241

No. 52
Subject: "Alliances with non-Muslims *(muwālāt)*"
Mufti: Muhammad Sayyed Tantawi (b. 1925)
Location: Cairo, Egypt
Pages: 297–300

Mourning

No. 53
Subject: "Mourning practices of non-Muslim women"
Mufti: Taqi al-Din al-Subki (d. 1355)
Location: Egypt
Pages: 87–89

Notes

1. Muftis, Fatwas, and Islamic Legal Interpretation

The authors thank Norman Calder, Nissreen Haram, and Leslie Peirce for their comments and suggestions on draft versions of this essay.

1. Interesting analogues for the position of mufti are found in the Roman *jus publice respondendi* (see Cuq 1963; Weber 1978, 2:797–799; Tyan 1960:221) and the Jewish *responsa* tradition (see Ta-Shma and Tal 1972; Goitein 1971, 2:211–212, 325–326).
2. Islamic tradition teaches that the Sunna of the Prophet was transmitted orally from the first generation of Muslims to the second, that these oral reports were committed to writing during the course of the second century A.H., and that the resulting written narratives were collected, evaluated for their soundness, and arranged in six major compilations during the third century A.H. The historicity of these narratives is an issue on which Muslim and Western scholars are sharply divided (see Aʿzami 1978; Juynboll 1983; Powers 1986).
3. In a recent article, Hallaq (1994) argues that the interplay between fatwas and *furūʿ* nourished a vitality and responsiveness that was central to the continuing dynamism of Islamic law and Muslim societies.
4. See, for example, Quran 2:189, 215, 217, 219 (twice), 220, and 222; 5:5; 7:186; 8:1; 17:85; 18:84; 20:105; 79:42.
5. The efforts of Muslim scholars to determine the exact time, place, and circumstance in which individual revelations occurred are contained in the literary genre known as *asbāb al-nuzūl,* or occasions of the revelation. The following narrative is related about the revelation of Sura 4 ("Women"), verse 8, which deals with inheritance: Prior to Islam, the right to inherit reportedly was limited to adult men "who fight on horseback and seize booty." Certain Companions continued to follow this practice even after converting to Islam. When one

Companion died, his two paternal brothers seized control of his estate, refusing to share any of it with the deceased's wife and three daughters. The widow therefore approached the Prophet and complained to him about her in-laws' behavior. Muhammad summoned the two men, who explained that their actions were in accordance with the prevailing customary practices. At that point, Muhammad dismissed the litigants in order to see "what God will introduce." Shortly thereafter, God revealed: "To men a share of what parents and kindred leave, and to women a share of what parents and kindred leave" (al-Wahidi 1969:137–138; see further Powers 1986:189ff.).

6. These two verbal forms are derived from the noun *fatā,* energetic youth. The Form IV verb *aftā* signifies generally "to display abundant munificence" and "to display the qualities of freedom and nobility" (see Ibn Manzur 1979, 15:145–148; Masud 1984:130). It is perhaps because the elucidation of the truth of a matter in response to a question is considered a noble quality that this activity came to be signified by the form IV verb *aftā.*
7. Whereas traditional Muslim scholars take statements such as these at face value, many Western scholars regard the attribution of different statements and activities to Companions, Followers, and Successors as after-the-fact representations put into circulation by subsequent generations of pious Muslims. The earliest textual evidence that we have relates to the first half of the second/eighth century and to the activities of scholars such as Abu Yusuf, al-Shaybani, Abu Hanifa, Shafiʿi, Malik, and Ibn Hanbal, all of whom functioned as muftis. There is, as yet, no critical study of the historical development of *futyā.* On the problem of attribution, see Calder 1993.
8. Al-Bukhari 1862–1898, 1:441. The fatwas embedded in these narratives point to the tension between certain Muslims (known as *ahl al-raʾy)* who initially felt free to assess proper Islamic behavior on the basis of human reasoning, and others (known as *ahl al-ḥadīth*) who insisted that the indispensable benchmarks for such assessments are the Quran and the Sunna of the Prophet. Thus, Malik (d. 795), in his *Muwaṭṭaʾ*, often cites fatwas issued by Medinese scholars without making any reference to the Sunna of the Prophet (Goldziher 1967–1971, 2:198). But the growing insistence on the necessity of basing all legal assessments on an authoritative source caused muftis to support their fatwas with either a clear and unambiguous quranic verse or a prophetic Sunna (al-Qasimi 1986:37). This shift may be reflected in a narrative in which it is related that Ibn ʿAbbas was issuing fatwas on the subject of images without—at first—making any reference to the Prophet. Subsequently a man interrupted him, saying, "I make a living from selling images [so what shall I do]?" Only after the man had acceded to Ibn ʿAbbas's request to draw near did the latter say, "I heard the Messenger of God say, 'He who makes an image in this world will be required to breathe life into it on the Day of Resurrection, but he will not succeed in this task'" (Muslim 1955 3:1671; cited in Van Reenen 1990:45–46).
9. For a list of Sunni biographical dictionaries, see Schacht (1964:266); on the Twelver Shiʿis, see Calmard (1991a:555). For a general discussion of the genre and additional references, see Humphreys (1991:132–133).

10. Previously the term "shaykh ul-Islam" had been used as an unofficial title that was conferred on distinguished muftis whose jurisprudential skills were widely admired and approved (see Kramers 1934, 4:276). Thus, at a single point in time, many muftis may have held the title.
11. One Indian collection compiled in question-answer form is the *Fawāʾid/Fiqh Fīrūz Shāhī,* dedicated to Firuz Shah Tughlaq (1351–1388). Barani's *Fatāwā-i Jahāndārī* (1972), by contrast, has nothing to do with either fatwas or fiqh, but rather presents authoritative views on statecraft (Idara 1975).
12. See, for example, Ibn Khaldun 1958, 1:451–452; al-Mawardi n.d., 61–72; and al-Qalqashandi 1919, 9:255.
13. In Shafiʿi school treatises, for example, a separate section is devoted to the mufti: see al-Juwayni 1906; id. 1979, 2:1330–1551; al-Ghazzali 1980, 2:387–389; Basri 1964–1965, 2:929–992. The same holds for Maliki treatises; see, for example, al-Shatibi n.d., 4:244–293.
14. In this introduction, we rely on the following pre-modern treatises: al-Nawawi (d. 1277) (1988), which summarizes earlier treatises by al-Saymari (d. 955), Khatib al-Baghdadi (d. 1044), and Abu ʿAmr ibn al-Salah (d. 1245)—previously published as part of al-Nawawi's commentary, *al-Majmūʿ,* on al-Shirazi's *al-Muhadhdhab* (n.d.); the Shiʿi al-ʿAmili (al-Shahid al-Thani, d. 1559) (1988–1989), chap. 2; "Adab al-Mufti" in *al-Fatāwā al-ʿĀlamgīriyya* (Masud 1984:146–149); "Adab al-Mufti" in Bobakani (1962:17–30); and an anonymous manuscript discussed in Masud 1984. Other pre-modern works include those of al-Shahrazuri (d. 1243), see Brockelmann 1943–1949, 1:442; al-ʿAyntabi (cited in Heyd 1969:56); and Jahiz (Pellat 1965). Related works on fatwa drafting include al-Qalqashandi (1919, 9:255), and a treatise by Abu'l-Suʿud and the Ottoman *Qānūn-i fetvā,* both cited in Heyd (1969:47, 49). Of the many modern works, we rely primarily on those by al-Qasimi (1986) and al-Qaradawi (1988a). See also the introductions to modern collections of fatwas, such as those of Jad al-Haqq (1980:8–32), Zafir al-Din (1962), and Abu al-Ajfan (1985:65–87), in which the editors rely on the earlier treatises. On the concept of *adab,* see Metcalf (1984).
15. See, for example, al-Bukhari 1977, 1:178, 182, 192, 196, 319, 356; 3:187–188; al-Mawardi 1971–1972, 1:264, 378.
16. Ibn al-Qayyim al-Jawziyya (d. 1350) entitled his three-volume work (1969) *Advice for the Signatories* [*al-muwaqqiʿīn*] *on Behalf of the Lord of the Worlds.*
17. The Jaʿfari Shiʿis relied on their own corpus of hadith (Tabataba'i 1984:4–5). Further, their *uṣūl al-fiqh* works differ from those of the Sunnis in several respects: they contain an additional section on the *uṣūl al-ʿamaliyya,* dealing with procedural issues, which was decisively expanded in the nineteenth century by Shaykh al-Ansari (d. 1864) (Tabataba'i 1984:8–11, 57–58); their notion of consensus *(ijmāʿ)* is defined in terms of the views of Shiʿi jurists; and they rely on reason *(ʿaql)* (Tabataba'i 1984:3–4; al-ʿAmili 1988–1989:141).

The history of muftis and fatwa giving is intimately bound up with that of the madrasa, or Islamic college (Pederson and Makdisi 1986:1123–1134). On the Sunni madrasa, see Makdisi (1981), Eickelman (1985), Berkey (1992), and

Messick (1993:75–114). On the distinctive Shiʿi madrasa, see Fischer (1980) and Mottahedeh (1985). For a convenient summary and additional references, see Calmard (1991b:302).

18. Within the Usuli school, dominant among Shiʿis, ijtihad was possible at all times. Integral to the distinctive dynamism of the Jaʿfaris is the doctrine that forbids the following of positions held by a deceased jurist *(taqlīd al-mayyit)*. See Calmard (1991a:550, 554); al-ʿAmili (1988–1989:142); and Chapter 22.

19. Al-Nawawi (1988:25ff.) mentions four subtypes of mufti *muntasib:* (1) the individual who qualifies as *mustaqill,* but who prefers to adhere to a school; (2) the *ṣāḥib al-wujūh,* who commands the principles, doctrine, and reasoning of a particular school; (3) the *faqīh al-nafs,* who does not command his school's principles, but does command its doctrines and reasoning and is allowed to choose between its various views; (4) the simple *muqallid,* a mufti who knows and must follow a school's doctrines but who lacks the capacity to engage in deductive reasoning or to draw analogies (see also Jad al-Haqq 1980, 1:13). This classification may be compared to that obtained by Anderson (1970:38, 370) from twentieth-century Shafiʿi jurists in the Aden Protectorate (in descending order): *muṭlaq, fi'l-madhhab* (within the school), *bi'l-masā'il* (entitled to decide disputed points), *bi'l-fatwā* (entitled to issue fatwas). See also Calmard 1991b.

20. Al-Nawawi's authoritative Shafiʿi law manual, the *Minhāj al-ṭālibīn* (Program for Students), is subtitled *and Support for Muftis (wa-ʿumdat al-muftīn).*

21. The Jaʿfari Shiʿis allow a woman to become a *mollā,* but they disagree over whether she may become a mujtahid (Calmard 1991b:302; on Banu Amin, a noted female mujtahid, see Fischer 1980:163).

22. On the concept of *ilzām* and the discursive categories *inshā'ī* and *khabarī,* see al-Nawawi 1988:19–20, 44; al-ʿAmili 1988–1989:143; Ibn al-Qayyim al-Jawziyya 1969, 1:36; al-Wansharisi 1981–1983, 10:40; al-Qalqili 1969:*"wāw";* Heyd 1969:56; Brunschvig 1970:12; Masud 1984:146; Jackson 1992:203.

23. See, for example, al-Qarafi (1967:84), *"al-ḥukm lā yunqaḍu wa'l-futyā qābila li'l-mukhālafa";* on Ottoman *fetvas* dealing with the issue of "whether a case decided by a qadi may be heard anew," see Heyd (1969:54); on "successor review" of court judgments, see Powers 1992.

24. In such cases, "the Shaykh al-Islam first asked the *nishanji,* the official responsible for the *qānūn* and significantly called 'the mufti of the *qānūn,*' what its regulations on the point in question were and then gave his ruling in accordance with it" (Heyd 1969:55).

25. According to Gibb and Bowen (1957 [pt. 2]:137), Ottoman muftis benefited from *waqf* monies, but see Heyd (1969:52–53). In the Yemeni town of Ibb, the incumbant mufti received the annual revenue of an agricultural plot established as a *waqf* (Messick 1993:145). On the economic situation of Iranian jurists, including their access to *waqf* revenues, tax responsibilities, and relations with the *bazaaris,* see Calmard (1991a:551–552; 1991b:298–299, 302).

26. Some argue that sinfulness *(fisq)* disqualifies the incumbent but does not impair the validity of the fatwa (Masud 1984:131ff.).

27. The ʿAlamgiriyya passage, *wa-lā yajibu'l-iftā' fī-mā lam yaqaʿ*, is cited by Heyd (1969) and translated by Masud (1984).
28. The principal twentieth-century Muslim sources consulted include Rida (1970); Shaltut (1974); Makhluf (1965); al-Shaʿrawi (1981–); al-Qalqili (1969); al-Qaradawi (1982, 1988a); Ibn Baz et al. (1988); Jad al-Haqq (1980); al-Qasimi (1986); Zafir al-Din (1962); Kifayatullah (1971); and Abu al-Ajfan (1985).
29. Following the Iranian Revolution of 1979, muftis of the Jaʿfari school began to function in a radically new political context. The doctrine of the governance of the jurist *(wilāyat-i faqīh)* formulated by Khomeini (d. 1989) and institutionalized by the Islamic Republic of Iran resulted in the unprecedented consolidation of power in the hands of the leading jurist (Arjomand 1988; Calmard 1991a:553; 1991b:300; see also Chapter 22).
30. In Saudi Arabia, for example, the mufti Ibn Baz currently is head of the *idārat al-buḥūth al-ʿilmiyya wa'l-iftā' wa'l-daʿwā wa'l-irshād,* founded in 1971.
31. In 1961, Egyptian president ʿAbd al-Nasir characterized the typical Azhar shaykh as "no more than a stooge of reaction, feudalism and capitalism." He added that "some shaykhs were trying to deceive us with fatwas" (cited in Crecelius 1966:42). In 1977, under al-Qaddafi, the official Libyan newspaper published an article entitled, "No mufti, no murabits, no shaykhs," which, according to Anderson (1983:143), argues that "the powers of the mufti are incompatible with popular authority."
32. The names of these institutions are *Dār al-iftā' al-miṣriyya* and *Lajnat al-fatwā bi'l-azhar;* see also Skovgaard-Petersen 1994.
33. Committees in Southeast Asia include the *Majlis agama islam* in Malaysia. For additional examples from Southeast Asia, see Stout (1980) on Selangor, and Ishak (1989) on Trengganu. A *shūra-i fatwā* was mooted in Iran (Calmard 1991a:553).
34. From 1772 to 1864, muftis known as *mawlawī*s were attached to British courts in India (Schacht 1964:94; Chapter 16, this volume). Lane (1978:118) gives the following example of a different relationship between qadis and muftis in nineteenth-century Cairo: "The assistant judge having heard the case, desires the plaintiff to procure a 'fetwa' (or judicial decision) from the Muftee of the sect of the Hanafees, who receives a fee—seldom less than ten piastres, and often more than two hundred. This is the course pursued in all cases but those of a very trifling nature, which are settled with less trouble, and those of great importance or intricacy." Although much rests on Lane's gloss of fatwa as a "judicial decision," it is clear that the presence of such muftis was integral to court procedure and that their fatwa opinions were, in this particular historical context, both binding and conclusive.
35. In addition to unofficial fatwas provided as a "service" in what are essentially estate settlements, the courts sometimes handle inheritance disputes: "Islamic judges are perfectly willing to accept disputes and, in effect, to try them. The end result is still, on the surface, a fatwa. The difference is that there is a winner and a loser, and that the latter may decide to go to a civil court for a superceding

decision" (Lev 1972:201). Recognizing that fatwas are not by their nature judicial rulings, these Islamic judges take one additional legal step: "Because fatwas per se are unenforceable, Javanese Islamic courts have resorted to a kind of ancillary agreement by the parties to make it enforceable. That is, to strengthen a fatwa and to give it what nearly amounts to the binding power of a decision, a caveat is often entered and signed by the parties, that they shall not further contest the fatwa. As an agreement, rather than a court-issued fatwa, it can be enforced in civil court" (Lev 1972:202).

36. Some fatwa collections, such as that of al-Shaʿrawi (1981–), lack any form of categorization or indexing and present fatwas in the random order in which the questions were received.
37. On the life and work of Muhammad Rashid Rida, see Kerr (1966) and the introduction to Rida (1970).
38. For extended analyses of fatwas in general, and of fatwas on women and the Muslim family, see al-Qaradawi 1988a, 1988b.
39. See, for example, the usages of Sayyid Qutb (Kepel 1985; Haddad 1983).

2. Iftaʾ and Ijtihad in Sunni Legal Theory

1. Thus for al-Basri and others, such as Ibn al-Salah al-Shahrazuri, citing the opinion of other jurists does not constitute a fatwa, but merely a "reporting" *(ḥikāya)* of that opinion. See Ibn al-Salah al-Shahrazuri 1986, 1:38–39; Bannani 1970, 2:397.
2. It is interesting to note that of all eleventh-century positions on this issue, al-Basri's was to become better known in later centuries.
3. Text: *"wa-ʿabbarū ʿan jumlati dhālika bi-anna ʾl-muftī man yastaqillu bi-maʿrifati aḥkāmi al-sharīʿati naṣṣan waʾistinbāṭan."* Al-Juwayni 1979, 2:1332, 832, 856.
4. In addition to al-Amidi, see, for example, Ibn Amir al-Hajj 1899, 3:346ff.; al-Iji 1974, 2:308ff.; al-Shawkani n.d.(a), 269.
5. Text: *"hādha huwa al-ṣaḥiḥ alladhī ʿalayhi al-ʿamal wa-ilayhi mafzaʿu al-muftīn min mudadin madīdatin."* Ibn al-Salah al-Shahrazuri 1986, 1:33.
6. The people will "indulge themselves in their own pleasures" because there are no muftis to guide them to right conduct—a conduct dictated by the law, not by self-serving interests.
7. Text: *"yuḥtamal irādat ittiḥādihimā mafhūman wa-irādat ittiḥādihimā mā ṣadaqā wa-laʿalla al-thānī aqrab."* Al-ʿAbbadi n.d.:230.
8. See n. 1 above.
9. That commentator is very possibly al-Nawawi, whose commentary on al-Shirazi's *al-Muhadhdhab* is one of the most important Shafiʿi legal treatises.
10. Among the advocates of this view are Ibn al-Humam (d. 1456) and the commentator on his work, Ibn Amir al-Hajj (d. 1474). See Ibn Amir al-Hajj 1899, 3:347, ll. 7–10.
11. That is, Ibn ʿAbd al-Shakur (d. 1810).
12. On his call for ijtihad and opposition to taqlid, see Hallaq 1984:32–33.

13. On the theoretical and epistemological role of *wuqūʿ* in *uṣūl al-fiqh,* see al-Shatibi 1969–1970, 1:12.
14. For more on this and other related themes, see Hallaq 1992.

3. Learning at Mosques in al-Andalus

1. An abridged version of the text is also found in al-Wansharisi (1981–1983, 9:27–28).
2. A complete edition is in press, prepared by Muhammad ʿAbd al-Wahhab Khallaf, who has published several sets of documents collected from the *Aḥkām* grouped according to categories such as medicine, architecture, and heterodoxy. The fatwa that is the object of this study is found in Ibn Sahl (1983), no. 4.
3. A comprehensive study of this text would add significantly to our understanding of Andalusian society, for the documents collected by Ibn Sahl cover a wide range of activities and problems presented to the muftis and judges of his time and earlier periods. Lévi-Provençal used the manuscript of the *Aḥkām* for his *History of Muslim Spain* (1950–1957; in Spanish), and in recent years, the partial edition of the work has been exploited by scholars interested in religious and social life (Fierro 1987:50; Marín 1990; Aguirre de Cárcer 1991).
4. This word was applied to early Islamic cities, like al-Kufa and al-Basra in Iraq and al-Qayrawan in Ifriqiya. Subsequently, it became a common name for any city (Wensinck 1936). Here the text refers clearly to Eastern cities.
5. Abu al-Bakhturi Wahb b. Wahb al-Qurashi was a judge in Baghdad and Medina in the reign of Harun al-Rashid (786–809) (Ibn Khallikan 1972, no. 773).
6. On the problems raised by quranic verses that were abrogated by a later revelation and the literature produced on these questions, see Powers 1988.
7. On this famous transmitter of prophetic reports, see Veccia Vaglieri 1960: 41.
8. Ibn Sahl's introductory title to the document reads, "On people sitting in circles in mosques for [discussion of] juridical questions on Fridays." The day of the week on which these meetings were held is mentioned in the text of the fatwa only once, when the counselors of the judge mention the example of Malik b. Anas.
9. The madrasa, a specialized institution of learning, was introduced to al-Andalus only during the last period of its history and consequently never attained the importance it had in the Muslim East or in North Africa (Makdisi 1973).
10. Of the four mushawars, only Muhammad b. al-Walid never traveled outside of al-Andalus.

4. Caliphal Legitimacy and Expiation in al-Andalus

I wish to thank Brinkley Messick, Muhammad Khalid Masud, and, especially, David Powers, for their comments on draft versions of this chapter.

1. Ibn Bashkuwal's work is not specified. On his production, see Pons Boigues 1898: 248, no. 200.

2. He was the second Umayyad caliph of al-Andalus. His father, ʿAbd al-Rahman III, adopted the caliphal title in the year 929. Al-Hakam II reigned from 961 to 976. See Lévi-Provençal 1950–1953, 2:164–196.
3. He reigned from 822 to 852. See Lévi-Provençal, 1950–1953, 1:193–278.
4. It is the biography of Yahya b. Yahya al-Laythi. I follow the versions of both al-Shatibi and ʿIyad b. Musa.
5. See ʿIyad b. Musa 1981–1983?, 3:369–371; Ibn Farhun (d. 1397) 1351/1932; 2:359, no. 7. His full name is Abu Zakariyya' Yahya b. ʿAbd Allah b. Bukayr al-Makhzumi al-Misri (d. 845). He studied the *Muwaṭṭa'* of Malik with its author for seventeen years.
6. The fifth ʿAbbasid caliph, reigned 786–809. On al-Rashid, see Omar 1971, 3:232–234.
7. For a lucid description of marriage according to the different schools of law, see Ibn Rushd (Averroes) (d. 1198) n.d., 2:2–102.
8. On expiation, see Chelhod 1971a, 4:406–407, and Santillana 1938, 2:543.
9. See Chelhod 1971b, 3:53–54.
10. On ʿAbd al-Rahman II's life and personality, see Vallvé 1991, where reference is made to the favorites of the emir.
11. My inability to find any reference in al-Wansharisi (1981–1983, 1:410–429, *nawāzil al-ṣiyām*) to breaking the fast by engaging in sexual intercourse suggests that the issue was not common or was not considered important. However, Muhammad Khalid Masud refers me to a passage in al-Wansharisi (1981–1983, 6:551) in which al-Wansharisi holds "that a mufti must not exempt a person from punishment if he admits violating the sacrosanct nature of Ramadan by eating, drinking, or engaging in sexual intercourse."
12. Malik b. Anas 1981: 386–387 *("al-ʿamal fī kaffārat al-yamīn")*. See also Sahnun 1905, 3:118–123, especially p. 122 *("fī'l-ṣiyām fī kaffārat al-yamīn");* Khalil b. Ishaq 1919, 1:344–350, especially p. 346; Santillana 1938, 1:49; 2:14 (expiation of a vow, *nadhr*), 100 (expiation of an oath, *yamīn*).
13. See Schacht 1991, 6:262–265, where this information is considered to be nonhistorical. Al-Rashid would have met Malik in Medina in the very year in which Malik died (796), when the caliph was performing his pilgrimage.
14. Malik b. Anas 1981: 241–242 *("kaffārat man aftara fī ramaḍān")*. The same three possible expiations are established in the case of the husband who made an oath of sexual abstinence and broke it, and for breaking the formula of repudiation called *ẓihār:* see Santillana 1938, 1:268–269, 271; cf. Malik b. Anas 1981: 464–466.
15. The same doctrine is attributed to al-Ghazzali in a text recorded by al-Shatibi (1914, 2:285) that runs parallel to the three cases studied here. Professor Masud informs me that in *al-Sharḥ al-saghīr,* "al-Dardir favored feeding sixty needy persons over other forms of expiation. In his supercommentary on the latter text (Cairo: Dar al-Maʿarif 1392 A.H., 1: 713), Shaykh al-Sawi noted that this should hold even in the case of a caliph—*contrary to the fatwa issued by Yahya b. Yahya.* In his view, feeding is preferable to the other form of expiation because

it benefits several persons; expiation in the form of manumission would be even better."

16. See Fierro 1985: 79–102 for a case in which Yahya b. Yahya was the starting point for a peculiar practice of Andalusian Malikism, where reference is made to the issues on which Yahya b. Yahya departed from Malik's teachings. See also Fierro 1991: 119–131 for a possible explanation of Yahya b. Yahya's independent reasoning: the introduction of Berber practices into Maliki legal doctrine.
17. On the role of Ishaq b. Ibrahim during Abu al-Khayr's trial, see Fierro 1987: 149–155.
18. Ishaq b. Ibrahim's accusation that the other scholars were trying to ingratiate themselves with the caliph indicates that he, like Yahya b. Yahya, thought that they were intentionally choosing the easiest expiation. However, the degree of difficulty was not the main argument in Ishaq b. Ibrahim's choice.
19. Sunni doctrine emphasizes that the caliph is merely the administrator of the Public Treasury *(bayt al-māl)* and has no private claim on it. See Coulson (1960,1:1141–1143) for the legal aspect of this institution and Cahen (1960, 1:1143–1147) for its historical development; Cahen argues that in practice there was no distinction between the public and private property of caliphs and rulers. See also Tyan 1954–1957, 1:391–392 and 2:195, and Parfentieff 1966.
20. On this point, see Malik b. Anas 1981:241–242; Sahnun 1905, 3:123 *("fī kaffārat al-musīr bi'l-ṣiyām").* On fasting as the expiation of the insolvent person, see al-Wansharisi 1981–1983; 2:61. In the case of a slave who breaks an oath of sexual abstinence, his expiation must be fasting because, as a slave, he cannot manumit (Santillana 1938, 1:269).
21. Reigned 756–788. See Lévi-Provençal 1950–1953, 1:91–138.
22. For a description of how scholars should interact with rulers, see Ibn ʿAbd al-Barr (d. 1070) 1978, 1:163 al-Turtushi (d. 1126) 1319/1901–1902, Spanish trans. 1930–1931: 67–70. See also Lambton 1981.
23. Reigned 796–822. See Lévi-Provençal 1950–1953:39–44.

5. Ibn Taymiyya on Leadership in the Ritual Prayer

1. The Arabic text of the fatwa here presented in translation may be found in Ibn Taymiyya (1966, 2:453–455).
2. A more literal translation would be: "the maʾmum does not know that his imam did something which invalidated the prayer." My translation is based on my reading of the sense as determined by the context. Let us say, for example, that the imam has had a nosebleed. We are here dealing with a situation in which the maʾmum knows that the imam had a nosebleed but does not know that this invalidates the imam's performance of the prayer. We can say that even though he knows the imam had a nosebleed, he does not know that in having the nosebleed the imam has done something that invalidated the prayer.
3. This I gather from the fact that Ibn Taymiyya speaks of the majority *(jumhūr)*

of the ancestors as holding the view he himself favors. A majority—even an overwhelming majority—implies the existence of some sort of dissenting minority.

6. Use and Abuse of the Law

I would like to express my appreciation to Wael Hallaq and Donald Little for sharing with me their thoughtful insights on the subject, and to David Powers for his patience and support. On a special note, I am indebted to Salah al-Din al-Bashir for his significant input on the technical legal points and for his editorial remarks.

1. In fact, al-Subki is said to have presided over the Shafiʿi school in Egypt *(intahat ilayhi riyāsat al-madhhab fī miṣr)* (al-Subki, Taj al-Din, n.d., 6:156).
2. I refer in this chapter to the reprint edition of *Fatāwā al-Subkī,* which has no date. The original edition was published in Cairo in 1936–1938.
3. In the preface to *Fatāwā al-Subkī,* the original compiler explains that the fatwas in this source were either retrieved from petitioners or found in al-Subki's records. He emphatically states that the individual texts represent verbatim transcripts of the original writings and documents. Cursory acquaintance with the source lends credibilty to the former statement. Transcripts of fatwa documents in this source may be identified from the format of the question or from indications in the answer. Regarding the fatwa discussed here, see note 13 below.
4. All the paragraphing in al-Subki's fatwa is mine.
5. Text: "*Iddaʿā talafa al-baʿd biʾl-sariqa.*"
6. Text: "*Ma iddaʿā talafahu.*"
7. As shall be seen, al-Subki received three petitions about the carpetmaker's case. To reduce confusion, these have been designated as P1, P2, and P3, the numbers reflecting the order of submission. Accordingly, P3 is the last petition submitted.
8. Text: "*ajāba raḍiya allāhu ʿanhu bi-an qāla.*" Al-Subki's fatwas typically begin either with "the answer" *(al-jawāb)* or, as in this case, with "he answered" *(ajāba),* often followed by a pious formula. Apparently these introductions were sometimes provided by the person who wrote the question on the petitioner's behalf (Heyd 1969). This explains why al-Subki is occasionally referred to in the third person.
9. Thus, the fatwa was issued when al-Subki was still in Cairo, before he became a judge.
10. The Shafiʿi jurists use the terms *fāsid* and *bāṭil* interchangeably (al-Suyuti, n.d.:312).
11. Al-Subki occupied a teaching post in the Mansuriyya college in Egypt (al-Subki, Taj al-Din, n.d., 6:156).
12. "Self-employed artisan" is Joseph Schacht's term (1964:155).
13. Al-Subki's reference "to this paper," here and below, is sufficient to establish that this text represents a transcript of the response issued originally on the petitioner's sheet.
14. "*Liʾl-ḥurūbī rijālun yaʿrifūna bihā / Wa-liʾl-dawāwīni kuttābun wa-ḥussābu.*"

15. Text: *"yad al-ṣāniʿ ʿalayhi"*; the masculine pronoun suffix may refer either to the price *(al-thaman)* or to the object of sale, but not to the fee *(ujra),* which is feminine.
16. Note that the inverse of this rule is also true. Thus a contract whose valid form does not place an unconditional liability on the recipient—that is, a fiduciary contract—would not entail this liability in its invalid form (al-Suyuti n.d., 308).
17. Al-Subki must have been familiar with the author of the other fatwa, for it is highly improbable that he would have discredited the other mufti so harshly and specifically without adequate grounds. This would have constituted unjustified intellectual defamation *(jarḥ),* which was unacceptable for a man of al-Subki's intellectual caliber. Moreover, it would have been uncharacteristic of al-Subki, who tends to be very fair and prudent in ascribing fault to others.
18. If a mufti is unable to verify the credentials of an author of a fatwa on the petition sheet, he may either answer the petitioner orally, issue his fatwa on a separate sheet, or, as a last resort, issue the fatwa on the back of the petitioner's sheet.
19. Al-Nawawi (1990:61) mentions one exception to this rule: the case of an incorrect fatwa issued by someone who has managed to gain influence in the domain of iftaʾ through deception or political ties. If a mufti encounters such a fatwa on a petition sheet submitted to him, he should issue a fatwa on the same sheet in order to alert readers to the error and help prevent a misapplication of the law.
20. The following discussion is limited to the type of employee who accepts work from the general public and works on his own site, unsupervised by his client. The former qualification is significant. Muslim jurists agreed unanimously that a privately employed artisan or an artisan who works on his client's site and under the latter's supervision is not liable for accidental damages. The carpetmaker in our case is presumably a self-employed artisan working on his own site.
21. For a more detailed discussion of the *amān/ḍamān* dichotomy in Islamic law, see Chehata 1973; al-Khafif 1971; al-Zarqa 1968.
22. Al-Nawawi does not discuss the dichotomy between *athar* and *ʿayn* in his *Minhāj al-ṭālibīn,* which he composed after *al-Rawḍa* and which, arguably, became one of the most influential Shafiʿi legal works (al-Shirbini 1933, 2:351). Nor is this distinction mentioned by al-Nawawi's prominent commentators (al-Ramli 1938, 5:303; al-Haythami, n.d., 6:180). Moreover, in *Jāmiʿ al-maqāṣid,* the Shiʿi jurist al-Karaki (1410/1990, 7:267–275), drawing clearly on the discussion in *al-Rawḍa,* considers the view of workmanship as effect plausible but weak in comparison with the other view, which apparently prevailed at his time.
23. Al-Subki might at least have provided a provisional solution.
24. Two other omissions may be observed in al-Subki's answer. First, he excused himself from having to discuss the implications of the invalidity of the agency regarding the money paid, on the ground that the petitioner asked about the carpets and not about the money. This is hardly a convincing excuse; in the two former encounters with the case, al-Subki volunteered additional information

and dealt specifically with the issue of money, although the petitioner did not ask him to do so. If al-Subki had dealt with the issue of money in this case, he would have had to say that the carpetmaker (agent) had a fiduciary liability toward the money received. Therefore, the latter would not be obliged to refund the money if he is unable to do so. This is because agency contracts are fiduciary contracts in the Shafiʿi school, and an invalid contract has the same legal implications as a valid one regarding the issue of liability toward the received object (money). Second, al-Subki did not discuss what happens to the carpets that were not stolen. In the first case, the client was not obliged to take the outstanding carpets, because the contract was invalid. In the second version of the case, the client would have had to pay for the outstanding carpets if the agency proved to be valid. Here, however, al-Subki does not volunteer information that would favor the carpetmaker's case.

25. The manuals sanction certain kinds of benign legal tricks *(ḥiyal),* as, for example, a trick that may assist a petitioner to avoid a self-imposed religious obligation incurred by an oath. However, tricks that affect the rights of another person are strictly prohibited (Ibn al-Salah al-Shahrazuri 1986, 1:47, 83).

26. Muftis were cautioned against basing their written fatwas on information conveyed orally by the petitioner but not stated explicitly in the petition. In the last part of P3, al-Subki suggests repeatedly that the other mufti may have based his fatwa on information that is not provided in the question sheet: *"hākadhā fa-innaʾl-ṣūra idhā lam yakun fīhā ghayr mā dhukira . . . fa-in furiḍa ṣūra ukhrā fa-hiya lam tudhkar."* This could only further undermine the competence of the other mufti, who, by incorporating oral information, had committed a fundamental procedural error in iftaʾ.

7. Dhimmi Women and Mourning

1. Al-Subki, Taqi al-Din 1936, 2:630–632. In a preliminary study, I compared the printed version of this fatwa collection with a photocopy of one of two manuscripts used in preparing the Cairo edition of *Fatāwā al-Subkī,* a manuscript from the Zahiriyya Library in Damascus. There were no essential differences between the manuscript and the printed version of this fatwa. I am grateful to Professor Marvin Pope for his help in obtaining the manuscript copy.

2. This suggestion is based partly on grammatical considerations: "*muqayyad*" means that the term must have a qualifier; "*muṭlaq*" ("absolute") means without qualification. Thus, he claims that dhimmis may be "believers in Allah" or "believers in the Last Day," but not simply "believers."

3. Some Muslims taught that even members of the Islamic faith should express their belief in the form of "belief with a qualification," in this case *anā muʾmin in shāʾa Allāh* (I am a believer—if God wills). See, for example, al-Nawawi's commentary to Muslim's *Ṣaḥīḥ, Bāb al-īmān,* esp. the introduction (1930, 1:146ff., 1:188). For additional references see Gardet 1971, 3:1170–1174.

4. Reading: "*liʾansabahū ilā muʿayyan.*" Printed edition: "*lā nasabtuhū . . .*" I am grateful to Farhat Ziadeh for this suggested emendation.

5. Literally, if they are addressed *(mukhāṭabūn)* by the derived laws.
6. Meaning unclear; Arabic: *yajidūnahu.* Arabic dictionaries sometimes give this verb the sense of feeling—usually in connection with pain and accompanied by an appropriate noun complement in the accusative case. See Lane 1968; Ibn Manzur 1979, s.v. w-j-d. Quran translations generally follow Arberry 1955.
7. Full verse: "Fight those who believe not in God and the Last Day and do not forbid what God and His Messenger have forbidden—such men as practice not the religion of truth, being of those who have been given the Book—until they pay the tribute out of hand and have been humbled."
8. Arabic: "*ʿalā ghayr wajhihā.*"
9. Generally, the ʿulamaʾ use "*īmān*" when referring to the true belief of Muslims, and "*iʿtiqād*" when referring to a belief that may not be true. Note here that al-Subki uses "*īmānuhum*" for "their faith."
10. For example, a nonbeliever might perform all the motions of Islamic prayer, but because he does not believe, he cannot fulfill the obligation of prayer even were it to be determined that he is required to do so.
11. Note, for example, that it is not discussed by Fattal (1958) or in the comprehensive work of al-Subki's contemporary, Ibn al-Qayyim al-Jawziyya (1401/1981). It is mentioned briefly, however, by Zaydan (1963:435ff.).
12. For example, discussion of *iḥdād* does not figure in Smith and Haddad (1981). Although Goldziher discussed women's mourning practices (1967–1971, 1:235), he was primarily interested in pre-Islamic practices and their survival into Islam. Note the brevity of the discussion in Linant de Bellefonds 1971, 3:1010–1013.
13. The English text here (see al-Nawawi 1914), is not a strict translation of the Arabic original (which has been consulted). Van den Berg's translation occasionally includes glosses from major commentators of the *Minhāj* and from a work by al-Nawawi's teacher. These glosses have been retained in translation because they improve the text for my purposes, showing how it was understood.
14. "Pearl" is qualified as "*aṣaḥḥ,*" that is, "the better view," as some jurists do not include pearl on this list.
15. The word "*ʿidda*" does not occur in this verse. It is used in the Quran to indicate a divorcee's waiting period (65:1 and 4; 33:49), but in legal works, it is used to indicate the period of separation for the widow as well as the divorcee.
16. This hermeneutical rule is similar to *gezera shava* in Jewish tradition, as practiced according to Hillel: if a ruling *(gezera)* is the same in two cases, we can learn about the details of the stipulations or applications in one case by analogy from the other. *Sifra,* Introduction, 1:8 (Finkelstein 1983:10; see Finkelstein's comments *ad locum*).
17. Text: "*wa-kadhā al-dhimmiyya wa-taqyīd al-marʾa fīʾl-ḥadīth biʾl-īmān biʾllāh waʾl-yawm al-ākhar jarā ʿalā al-ghālib fa-inna al-dhimmiyya ka-dhālika wa-mithluhā fī-mā yaẓharu al-muʿāhada waʾl-mustaʾmina wa-hādhā madhhab al-shāfiʿiyya waʾl-jumhūr . . . wa-khālafa Abū Ḥanīfa qāʿidatahu hunā fī inkārihi al-mafāhīm.*"
18. This statement is based in part on an "argument from secondary-work silence."

There appears to be no reference to this as a practical legal issue (Fattal 1958, as noted above) or regarding an event in Tripoli. I found, for example, no reference to this or any possibly related event in several histories of the city that cover this period, for example, Tadmuri (1981) and Salim (1967).

19. Al-Subki 1936, e.g., 2:354–360, 360–365; see Ward 1984, esp. 11–12; Ward 1989:169–188.
20. Muhyi al-Din Isma'il b. Yahya al-Shafi'i, or Muhammad b. 'Abd al-Qadir al-Ba'labakki. Lists of the known qadis, *nā'ibs,* and other officials in Tripoli are given in Tadmuri (1981), together with extensive references. The Shafi'i qadis who served in 1337 and 1338 are found at 2:58.
21. I have been unable to identify this individual.
22. See sources in note 3.
23. On examining the wording of a claim and the importance of determining who must establish proof of his claim, see, for example, Schacht 1964:190ff.
24. See, for example, Perlmann 1982:191, where al-Munayyar insists that Jews believe that 'Uzayr (Ezra) is the son of God, even if this is denied by them.
25. The issue raised by this discussion, the validity of the belief system of another religion, has had important treatments in medieval Judaism—and in contemporary interfaith dialogue. Is it possible to reject the invalidation of another faith while remaining true to one's own tradition? Al-Subki's answer is clearly negative: even if non-Muslims' opinions about God and the Last Day are identical to those of the Muslims, they are not considered believers, even believers "with qualifications." Traditional Jewish discussions focused, for example, on whether Christianity and Islam were in the legal category of idolatry, and even whether Jewish law allows or prohibits these religions to their adherents. Modern Christian discussions have concentrated on whether there are various theological or moral imperatives to hold nonconversionary dialogues with Jews or other non-Christians. See, for example, Feldman (1990) and Novak (1989), which review some of the material discussed in Novak (1983) in the context of dialogue. Certain of the "key Lutheran statements" published by Ditmanson (1990) provide clear examples of revisionist strategies for theological validation of another religion, especially his own statement in conclusion (p. 95). It seems to me that there is need for further study of the theory and ramifications of the belief of non-Muslims in Islamic law and theology.

8. The Art of the Legal Opinion: al-Washarisi on *Tawlīj*

1. On the *Mi'yār,* see Chapter 1 of this volume. Al-Wansharisi began to compile the *Mi'yār* in 1485 and "completed" the text on July 10, 1496, although he continued to make additions, corrections, and revisions until his death in 1508. For bio-bibliographical details, see Castro 1990, 1991.
2. The translation of this term is conjectural. See Dozy 1967, 1:391–392.
3. Text: "*'alā mā aqarra bihi mawrūthuhum,*" apparently a reference to an acknowledgment by 'Uthmān in favor of his children, the nature of which is not specified in this source.

4. On *tawlīj,* see further al-Wansharisi 1981–1983, 6:79, 243–245; 8:76; 9:488; 10:351–352.
5. Text: *"rasm al-ibtiyāʿ,"* apparently a reference to the *ishhād* attached to the question.
6. Al-Wansharisi's understanding of Asbagh's disagreement with the prevailing Maliki position on this point subsequently was challenged by a jurist from Tlemcen, Abu ʿAbdallah Muhammad al-Hawdi (d. 1504–1505). A fatwa issued by al-Wansharisi in response to this challenge is found at ibid., 6:88–93. I hope to analyze this fatwa in a future work.
7. Text: *"lā yalzamu min iʿtibār al-shayʾ munḍamman li-ghayrihi iʿtibāruhu waḥdahu ʿalā anna fī riwāyat Ibn ʿĀṣim shudhūdhan fīʾl-madhab."* The translation is conjectural.
8. Although the resulting judgment may not have been accompanied by a written explanation of the grounds for the decision, to the extent that the judgment was informed by the fatwa it would have been based on rational, legal considerations. In my view, one cannot fully appreciate the cultural significance of the qadi in Muslim societies without taking into consideration the mufti's role in the judicial process (cp. Rosen 1989).
9. A distinctive feature of the Maliki law school is the importance attached by its jurists to the notion of court practice (*ʿamal*), as reflected in binding judicial decisions *(aḥkām).* Over time, Maliki jurists came to view court practice as a source of law that, in certain circumstances, might prevail over the dominant position of the school (Berque 1940, 1960; Toledano 1982:10ff.).
10. It is interesting to observe that the principle of composition employed by al-Wansharisi in producing the fatwa is analogous to that employed by him in compiling the *Miʿyār*—namely, the collection of discrete entities and their integration into a new and unique literary form. I owe this observation to Brinkley Messick.
11. Writing about the American legal system, James Boyd White (1990:224) identifies openness and a willingness to suspend judgment as important intellectual virtues that every judge and lawyer should aspire to embody in his or her writing.
12. As additional support for this hypothesis, I would draw attention to another fatwa dealing with *tawlīj* that bears a striking resemblance to the case considered in this chapter (see al-Wansharisi 1981–1983, 10:383–389). In that case, Tunisian jurists rejected the claim of plaintiffs who contended that when they were still children, their father had sold property belonging to them to strangers in a complex series of transactions designed to disinherit them. When compiling the *Miʿyār,* al-Wansharisi attached to the fatwa a long, supplementary note in which he criticized the Tunisian muftis for ignoring three indicators in the accompanying documentation which, in his view, constituted "clear signs" that the transactions did, in fact, constitute *tawlīj* (ibid., pp. 387ff.). A comparison of these two cases and a careful examination of al-Wansharisi's reasoning in them may make it possible to determine whether or not juristic bias was a factor in the present case.

9. When Women Went to Mosques

1. This assessment is based on research in the manuscript collections of the Dar al-Kutub (Egypt), the Maktabat al-Asad (Syria), and the Topkapı and Süleymaniye collections (Istanbul), and, further, on my assessment of the number and *madhhab* distribution of fatwa collections edited and published in the nineteenth and twentieth centuries.
2. Note: each treatise in the collection is cataloged individually by the Süleymaniye. The author's precise identity eludes me. Because al-Aydini appears as Muhammad b. Hamzah al-Aydini al-Güzelhsar in the old Süleymaniye catalogue, in Baghdadlı (1948, 2:216), and in Baghdadlı (1951, 2:346), he is similarly identifed in Brockelmann (1943–1949, 2:432, n. 32; 1937–1942, 2:648), and in al-Kahhalah (1958, 9:271). To the best of my knowledge, Baghdadlı Pasha is the sole source for these identifications. But he also refers, confusingly, to a Muhammad b. Hamzah Hajji Amirzadeh al-Aydini. I have checked all possible permutations of these names in the Ottoman biographical sources. Without access to Ottoman biographical works and local histories in manuscript, I cannot make a definitive determination of al-Aydini's identity. At this point, the only certain knowledge we have of the author is the fatwa's date, 1104/1693. I am grateful to the Ottoman and Turkish cataloguers at the Widener and Firestone Libraries and to Professor Cemal Kafadar, who offered helpful advice.
3. The letter *kāf* can represent either the Arabic second-person pronomial suffix, or, more likely, the Ottoman second-person singular possessive suffix, transcribed in modern Turkish as *n* or *ñ*.
4. For an interesting discussion of this issue, see al-Shawkani (n.d.[b], 3:148ff.).
5. For an example of a problematic substance—namely, coffee—that raised suspicions and was later permitted by the jurists, see Hattox (1985:46–60).
6. Süleymaniye 1038/17 ff. 23a–23b. I would like to thank Mr. Hani Azzam, who went over this text with me and saved me from many errors; Professor Muhammad Khalid Masud, whose careful reading of the text and erudition saved me from errors of typing and content, and was particularly helpful in the section on "those whose hearts are to be reconciled"; and Professor Wolfhart Heinrichs, who made many clarifying suggestions.
7. See Wensinck (1969, 6:275b).
8. Literally "those (f. pl.) of the curtains," referring to women who were secluded, possibly because they were nubile (Lane 1968, 2:708a), or, more likely, because they recently had given birth. See also al-Bukhari (n.d.:2:25), where these women are explicitly referred to as "virgins." Parturient women, that is, women who have just given birth, together with menstruating women, are excluded from ritual. I am grateful to Everett Rowson, who confirmed this reading.
9. See Wensinck (1969, 1:371b) and al-Bukhari (n.d., 1:98, *Kitāb al-Ṣalāt, bāb* 2). See also al-Nawawi (1930, 6:178–180).
10. Ibn al-Humam, *Fatḥ al-qadīr* (1970, 2:140).
11. Abu Jayb (1982:153, s.v. *ramal*).
12. See Ibn Qudama (1983, 3:385–386); Abu Jayb (1982:220). Running the first

three circumambulations is Sunna, as is hiking up the loose end of the pilgrimage garb. If one adjusts the garb on the first lap, the adjustment remains in effect throughout the rest of the circumambulation. See also Ibn al-Humam (1970, 2:410); al-Sarakhsi (1986, 4:49).

13. See Ibn al-Humam (1970, 2:259ff.).
14. I am grateful to Everett Rowson, who helped me tease the meaning from the syntax.
15. On *luqṭa,* see Abu Jayb (1982: 332); Ibn Qudama (1983, Index 2:857ff.); Ibn al-Humam (1970, 2:175); and Wensinck et al. (1969, 5:136).
16. Probably ʿAbdallah b. Wahb (d. 197/813), a companion of Malik's. See Brockelmann (1937–1942, 1:257); Kahhalah (1958, 6:162). But he might also be ʿAbdallah b. Wahb (d. 308/990); see Kahhalah (1958, 6:144).
17. May 5, 1693, in Great Britain and its cultural dependencies, where the Julian calendar remained in effect.

10. Child Marriage in Seventeenth-Century Palestine

I wish to thank David Powers for his assistance in editing this essay and for his useful comments.

1. See the articles by G. Linck-Kesting (ancient China), C. Wilcke (ancient Babylonia), R. Zoepffel (ancient Greece), E. Eyben (Greco-Roman antiquity), R. Herold (Japan), and M. Mitterauer (Europe) in Müller (1985); see also the article by W. F. Menski (Hindus) in Martin and Nitschke (1986), and Roller (1925).
2. For additional details and references, see Motzki (1985:481–483).
3. In the Roman Christian Church, eligibility for marriage was also reached—according to the *Corpus iuris canonici*—at this lower limit of puberty. See Roller (1925:4).
4. Only Abu Hanifa and some Malikis preferred the ages of seventeen and eighteen. Abu Hanifa's pupils Abu Yusuf and al-Shaybani, like the majority of jurists, preferred the age of fifteen. See Motzki (1985:494). In the *Corpus iuris canonici,* eligibility for marriage was fixed at twelve years for girls and fourteen years for boys. Since marital cohabitation might take place before these ages, these must have been maximum ages. In the law of the Roman Church, the maximum age for attaining sexual maturity was, therefore, earlier than that in Islamic law. Most secular laws of the German (and European) Middle Ages followed this example. See Roller (1925:4–11).
5. As in the laws of the Roman Church and those of the Christian Middle Ages.
6. The same is true for the laws of the Christian Middle Ages. See Roller (1925:4–11).
7. In the *Corpus iuris,* the Latin equivalent of *balagha* (to reach) is *(ad pubertatis tempora) pervenire;* in medieval German law, the equivalent is *(zu sinen/iren jaren/tagen) komen.* See Roller (1925:4–11).
8. See the fatwa discussed in this chapter. The same holds for the *Corpus iuris* and

medieval German law, with the exception that a marriage concluded for a child before the age of seven remains valid only with the later approval of the child when he or she reaches the "time of discernment" *(venit ad tempus discretionis)*. See Roller (1925:5). A similar rule is known in Muslim law.

9. The same holds for the laws of Christian Europe. See Roller (1925:4, 15).
10. The biographical information about him is based mainly on two sources: the biography by his pupil, al-Jinini, contained in the original manuscript of the *Fatāwā*, reproduced in an abbreviated form in al-Muhibbi (1284/1876, 2:134–139), and the report of the Moroccan traveler al-ʿAyyāshī (1316/1898). On Khayr al-Din's biography and its sources, see also ʿAbbas (1979:2) and Seikaly (1984:398–399).
11. According to his own report, he became sexually mature *(aḥassa biʾl-iḥtilām)* on the night of his arrival in Cairo in 1007 A.H., when he was approximately fourteen years old. See al-Muhibbi (1284/1876, 2:136). The recollection of such an incident should not be regarded as fictitious, because the beginning of sexual maturity was treated as a very important event in the life cycle and is commonly mentioned in biographies. See Motzki (1985:483–491).
12. See the introduction by Muhyi al-Din in al-Ramli (1974, 1:2).
13. See the epilogue by al-Jinini in al-Ramli (1974, 2:243–244).
14. Al-Ramli 1974, 1:66, first fatwa.
15. For additional details and references, see Motzki 1986:418–420.
16. See also al-Ramli (1974, 1:66, third fatwa; 78, first fatwa); Fahd and Hammoudi (1975:297–301); Klinkhardt (1965:17–19, 26–27); and Linant de Bellefonds (1973:162–165, 167–168, and 175–176).
17. These women would be: her grandmothers, sisters, daughters of the sisters, maternal aunts, daughters of the brothers, paternal aunts, maternal aunts of the mother, maternal aunts of the father, paternal aunts of the mother, paternal aunts of the father. The right to *ḥaḍāna* devolves in this order. For a complete table of relevant persons, see Fahd and Hammoudi (1975:295–296).
18. Similar regulations are found in the *Corpus iuris* of the Roman Church and in the German laws of the Middle Ages. See Roller (1925:4–5, 12, 15).
19. For the origin of this concept, see Motzki (1985:485); for the views of different Islamic law schools about it, see Linant de Bellefonds (1973:208–210).
20. See Brockelmann (1943–1949, 2:312; 1937–1942, 2:430/9 and Indices, 1283 (Nachträge zu Supplement 2:430/9). The name is given according to the biographical article on him in al-Muhibbi (1274/1876, 4:76); see also ibid. (2:137), where al-Hanuti is referred to as Muhammad b. Muhammad Siraj al-Din al-Hanuti.
21. Probably the *Kitāb al-Muḥīṭ al-Raḍawī* by the Syrian scholar Radi al-Din Muhammad b. Muhammad al-Sarakhsi (d. 1149), a summary of the famous *Kitāb al-Mabsūṭ* by Muhammad b. Ahmad al-Sarakhsi (d. 1090) and of texts composed by one of the fathers of Hanafi jurisprudence, Muhammad al-Shaybani (d. 805). See Brockelmann 1943–1949, 1:375; 1937–1942, 1:641.
22. The following discussion is based on Motzki (1987:82–90).
23. Al-Ramli 1974, 1:16 (4), 20 (2, 3, 6, 8), 22 (2), 27 (2, 4), 28 (2), 30 (2, 4, 5),

31 (2, 3), 32 (4), 54 (2), 55 (1), 65 (5), 70 (3), 2:43 (5), 65 (3, 4), 75 (2), 89 (2), 105 (5), 106 (1). The numbers in parenthesis refer to the ordinal number of the fatwa on that page, according to my enumeration.

24. Ibid., 1:20 (9), 21 (4), 24 (1, 2, 3, 4, 7, 8), 25 (3, 4), 26 (2), 28 (1), 32 (1), 48 (1), 59 (3), 65 (5).
25. Ibid., 1:20 (2, 6, 8), 27 (4), 28 (1), 31 (3), 69 (8).
26. Ibid., 1:23 (4), 24 (1, 6), 30 (5), 34 (4), 54 (2), 55 (1), 65 (5), 74 (2), 2:146 (1).
27. Ibid., 1:23 (4), 24 (1, 6), 30 (5), 65 (5), 74 (2), 2:146 (1).
28. Ibid., 1:24 (1, 3), 66 (1), 74 (2).
29. Ibid., 1:16 (4), 30 (4), 31 (3, 6), 32 (1, 2, 3, 4), 48 (1), 55 (1), 60 (8), 66 (1), 69 (1). See also al-Anqirawi (1281/1864, 1:38).
30. According to Hanafi legal tradition, the father or guardian of the girl is obliged to hand her over if she is physically capable of engaging in sexual intercourse. In cases of doubt, a judge settles the question with the assistance of female experts. See al-Ramli 1974, 1:32 (1, 2).
31. Khayr al-Din concludes from the question that the girl was not yet physically ready to consummate the marriage.
32. Al-Ramli 1974, 1:20 (8), 21 (4), 28 (1, 2), 30 (2, 4, 5), 31 (2, 3, 6), 32 (1), 34 (2), 69 (1, 8); 2:43 (5), 65 (3, 4), 105 (5), 106 (1), 147 (6). This practice was permitted; see the answer of Khayr al-Din in ibid., 1:32 (2).
33. Ibid., 1:25 (3), 28 (1, 2), 31 (2, 3), 32 (4), 66 (1), 69 (8), 70 (3). At 2:106 (1), Khayr al-Din himself points out that in his country most people—peasants in particular—consume the bridewealth of their wards.
34. Ibid., 1:24 (4, 7), 25 (3), 64 (6, 8).
35. Ibid., 1:22 (2), 27 (2), 34 (4), 65 (5).
36. These are the only cases of parallel cousin marriage involving children. Only 4 percent (6) of the cases that I analyzed mention parallel cousin marriages, usually regarded as preferential in Arab societies.
37. Al-Ramli 1974, 1:20 (8), 21 (4), 24 (1), 28 (2), 31 (3), 69 (8).
38. Ibid., 1:20 (3, 9), 24 (2, 3), 34 (4), 58 (6).
39. Ibid., 1:24 (3, 8), 26 (2), 28 (1), 34 (4).

11. Eleven Fetvas of the Ottoman Sheikh ul-Islam ʿAbdurrahim

1. Originally the mufti of Istanbul, the sheikh ul-Islam emerged during the reign of Süleyman I (1520–1566) as the head of the Ottoman legal establishment. See Repp (1986).
2. Most compilers presumably were *fetvā emīni*s or other permanent employees of the Fetva Office, since only they would have had access to the complete body of a sheikh ul-Islam's fetvas. The compiler of one collection, the *Netīcetū'l-fetāvā* of the sheikh ul-Islam Dürrizade Mehmed ʿArif (who held office 1785–1786 and 1792–1798), identifies himself as a *fetvā emīni.* See Dürrizade Mehmed ʿArif, *Netīcetū'l-fetāvā,* John Rylands Library, Manchester, England, Turkish ms. no. 104.
3. The headings of chapters and sections, however, are always in Arabic.

4. See note 5.
5. Because he may have a reasonable suspicion that he is the owner of the slave. The notion of *shubha* acts here solely as a legal device to prevent liability for the fixed penalty for illegal intercourse.
6. I do not present the fetvas in the order in which they appear in the text. The number in brackets that follows each fetva shows its position in the original sequence.

12. The Fatwas of Condemnation

1. Muhammad Ahmad, the "Sudanese Mahdi" (1834–1885). Allusions to fatwas against his great-grandfather can be found in al-Mahdi 1935:150. I am grateful to Heather Sharkey of Princeton University for this reference. Mirza Ghulam Ahmad (d. 1908) also claimed the distinction of Mahdi (c. 1880). A fatwa condemning his assertion that ʿIsa b. Maryam (Jesus Christ) did not die on the cross was issued in India (see Houtsma 1961:24). For fatwas against al-Ghazzali and for other fatwas of condemnation, see Trimingham 1971:47, 76, 125, 198, and 242.
2. For biographical information on al-Sanusi, see Ziadeh 1958; Evans-Pritchard 1954; and Martin 1976:99–125.
3. "*Ghulāt*" (sg. *ghālī*) is properly a Shiʿi term denoting "unusual zeal" (and quite possibly, through the Greek, the origin of the English term, "zealot"). Within the context of these fatwas, it is used to suggest someone who has "gone beyond the bounds."
4. Al-Sanusi "joined" (the term is somewhat misleading—"sought the knowledge of the organization and the blessing of its leaders") the Darqawiyya, Tijaniyya, Qadiriyya, Shadhiliyya, Jazuliyya, Nasiriyya, Habibiyya, and Idrisiyya brotherhoods (Martin 1976:101).
5. My translation is based on ʿUlaysh 1881, 1:108–111. Earlier translations can be found in Ziadeh 1958:40–44; and Depont and Coppolani 1897:546ff.: The first is incomplete (only the reply is translated) and in want of a fresh perspective; the second takes great liberties with the text.
6. *Wird:* a phrase or series of words taken verbatim from the Quran; also, a prayer or prayers peculiar to the order, the revelation of which is often bestowed in parts (the more esoteric reserved for advanced members, the more exoteric for ordinary members); the "taking of" the *wird* is a sure sign of initiation.
7. *Dhikr:* special prayers of the order recited repetitively. Some members are privy to more *dhikr*s than others.
8. Shadhiliyya: This may be a reference to the Grand Sanusi's affiliation with the Shadhiliyya *ṭarīqa* (established by Abu al-Hasan ʿAli al-Shadhili, d. 1258), whereby he most probably received an *ijāza* (license, diploma) to bestow the mysteries and magical incantation of the *ḥizb al-baḥr* (incantation of the sea), one of the most powerful and sought after of the *wird*s of Sufism.
9. Every Sunni Muslim is obliged to fashion his religious life in accordance with the legal doctrines of one of the four law schools, and, importantly, to follow

the opinions of its scholars. One may change schools (although this is discouraged), but one cannot adhere to one school while at the same time following individual practices of another.

10. *Tayammum:* ablution or "purification" by sand or earth in place of water.
11. *Wuḍū'*: the ablution made before performing appointed prayers.
12. That is, the inner self, which must be rid of its worldly inclinations.
13. The Qanut: special prayers (see Depont and Coppolani 1897:296 and 547; Wensinck 1961:271).
14. This chapter is the first of a two part series. The second part ("Fatwas That Never Were," forthcoming in the *Maghreb Review*), takes the theme to India in the post-1848 period, to British attempts to manipulate legal debate on the question of *hijra* from Dar al-Islam Algeria after 1830, and to similar efforts by the French to isolate Abd al-Qadir.
15. *Hijra:* a break off of relations (commonly rendered "flight"). For al-Shafiʿi, see Ziadeh 1958:90 and 115.
16. ʿAbd al-Qadir opposed the introduction of French influence in Algeria after the 1830s (see Martin 1976:105).
17. Cf. Trimingham 1971:119 (also 115, 116); Ziadeh 1958:95.
18. For the development of the *zāwiyas,* see Ziadeh 1958:99. There is some evidence that these *zāwiyas* might have been modeled in the past on the "*hijra*" structure of the Wahhabiyya (see Margoliouth 1961:621), though more research is required on this question.

13. Fatvas as Asymmetrical Dialogues

I would like to thank Brinkley Messick for his continuous support and David Powers for his editorial assistance.

1. On this point, see the juridical treatises of the ayatullahs Borujirdi (n.d.:11–12), Marashi (n.d.:3), and Muntaziri (1362/1983:5), who are among the most important twentieth-century Shiʿi mujtahids. All stress the duty to follow a living mujtahid. If someone follows the fatva of a mujtahid who later dies, he or she may continue to follow that fatva, although Muntaziri adds that, in this case, the follower must receive the permission of a living mujtahid.
2. To emphasize the spiritual link that tied its leaders through time, the Shaykhis usually refered to their movement as a *silsila* (chain). The term "school" adopted here follows current scholarly usage (see, for example Corbin [1972] and MacEoin [1985]), even if the Shaykhis were not a school (madhhab) in the sense used in Islamic law. Scholars use the term "school" to underline the essentially orthodox character of the Shaykhis. Scarcia (1958b:215–217), who calls them a "sect" or a "movement" (connoting issues relating to orthodoxy and heterodoxy), specifies that these terms should be understood in the context of debates between ʿulama' in nineteenth-century Iran.
3. This was the case, for example, in Yazd in 1814.
4. Shaykh Ahmad and Fath ʿAli Shah exchanged letters, and the shaykh wrote an

essay in which he responded to several questions asked by the shah (see Ibrahimi [1336/1957, 1:209, 2:31]. Note: Ibrahimi was the head of the Shaykhi school at the time of publication of his book, which contains biographies of the Shaykhis and a bibliography of their works).

5. On this transition, see Scarcia (1958b:219–220) and MacEoin (1985:675), who asserts that it is incorrect to consider Shaykh Ahmad as the founder of the Shaykhi school.

6. The school has been studied by several Western scholars, mostly from a theological perspective. The complexity of Shaykhi theological thought has led to mistakes and misunderstandings, and certain doctrinal issues are not completely clear. Most Shaykhi writings—several hundred titles—remain unstudied in the West. In the second half of the nineteenth century and the beginning of the twentieth century, the school attracted the attention of A. De Gobineau (1866:28–33), the English Orientalist E. G. Browne (1893:519–520; 1928:402–403), and A. L. M. Nicolas (1910–1911), whose work on the subject subsequently was discredited. More recently, H. Corbin, the French historian of religions, translated several Shaykhi works and studied the school extensively. Corbin views the school as the outcome of the Imami spiritual tradition that he considers to be the true foundation of Iranian spiritualism from Achaemenid times to the present. His works currently are the most extensive on the theological doctrines of the school. It is interesting to note that some of Corbin's writings on the subject were translated into Persian and accepted as theologically correct by the guide of the school, with whom Corbin had a close personal relationship (Corbin 1960; 1972:205–300). The Italian Iranist G. Scarcia also had personal contacts with exponents of the school. His two articles (1958b and 1963) are more historically oriented than the works of other scholars and contain rich information relevant to the issues discussed in this chapter. See Amanat (1989:286–294) for a detailed description of the development of the school, its position in relation to the emerging Babi movement, and Muhammad Karim Khan's condemnation of the Bab.

7. This was probably to differentiate themselves from the Babi movement, which, taking the concept of the mediator to the extreme, proclaimed a Revelation in 1844. In this regard, Corbin insists on the complete spiritual essence of the mediator, who should not be identified with any physical person. Favoring a symbolic interpretation, Corbin (1972) argues that Shaykhi thought is a "theosophy" that combines theology and philosophy and offers a rationalistic approach to metaphysics. It is "a genuine rationalistic allegory of the miraculous side of the traditional theological legends" (Bausani 1959:405). For example, the Shaykhis explain the resurrection of human beings at the end of time by means of a theory holding that man has four bodies (two *jasad*s and two *jism*s, both words meaning "body"). A complex cosmology divides the universe into climes, stations, and intermundia. Knowledge of God is rationalized as Eternal Knowledge and Created Knowledge; only the latter, which comes into being when its object comes into existence, is attainable by human beings. It is this integration of a profound spiritual dimension with a rationalistic perspective

(characterized by some scholars as "modernist" and by others as "humanist") that attracted—as they themselves indicate, although implicitly and in different ways—scholars such as Corbin, Scarcia, and Bausani. For a brief summary of Shaykhi thought, see MacEoin (1985), which contains an updated bibliography.

8. The Shaykhi attitude, particularly that of Muhammad Karim, toward ijtihad has yet to be clarified. On the basis of an extensive reading of Shaykhi works, Juan R. I. Cole has tentatively concluded that their position is essentially Usuli (personal communication).
9. For a description of the family's wealth, see Scarcia (1958b:224–225).
10. The piety and the merits of Ibrahim Khan are recalled in the first pages of *Tazkirat al-Awliyā'* (Kirmani: 1313/1934), a hagiographic work dedicated to Hajj Muhammad Karim Khan that is one of the main sources on his life (not to be confused with the book with the same title by the poet and mystic ʿAttar). I do not have access to this important work and rely on second hand information about it contained in Ibrahimi (1336/1957, 1:57–58); Corbin (1972:237 n. 38, 243 n. 43); and Scarcia (1958b:221 n. 19).
11. A Persian translation of the autobiography is included in Ibrahimi (1957, 1:61–75). For a description of the character and lifestyle of Muhammad Karim Khan, see Bayat (1982:63–65).
12. The Madrasa Ibrahimiyya, like hundreds of other madrasas in Iran, was supported by the revenues of an endowment *(vaqf)* consisting of real estate. The *vaqf* of the Madrasa Ibrahimiyah was a *vaqf-i khāṣṣ*, an endowment constituted for the benefit of a private group (as opposed to the *vaqf-i ʿāmm,* constituted for a public purpose), and remained so when the madrasa became the center of the Shaykhi school (Scarcia 1958b:223 n. 24; Scarcia 1963:221 n. 103, where he corrects his statement in 1958b:223 n. 26). The main revenues of the endowment derived from three large properties, a public bath, and several shops in the bazaar (Scarcia 1958b:225 n. 35; Scarcia 1963:221).
13. See Kirmani (1313/1934) and Scarcia (1958b:222–223). MacCoin (1985:674) suggests that it was Ibrahim Khan who put Shaykh Ahmad in contact with Fath ʿAli Shah.
14. Muhammad Baqir Hamadani, one of Muhammad Karim's disciples, fled the school and created a community of his own in the area of Isfahan; the community exists to the present day (Scarcia 1958b:224).
15. In addition to communities in the major cities (Tehran, Tabriz, and Khorramshahr), there are some Shaykhi villages in the Kerman area and in Azerbaijan.
16. I thank Juan R. I. Cole for drawing my attention to the microfilm collection of Shaykhi manuscripts at the University of Michigan Hatcher Library. The microfilm was prepared from photocopies held by the Middle Eastern Division of the Regenstein Library of the University of Chicago and is published in microform by the Middle East Documentation Center of the University of Chicago (Shaykhi Collection). The manuscript of this collection of fatvas, which consists of 205 pages, is number 23 H of the microfilmed edition. Ibrahimi (1957, 2: 602) lists the manuscript as number 894 of the works of Zayn al-ʿAbidin.
17. The Ibrahimi book (1336/1957) is an example of this attentive editorial work.

The microfilmed copy of the manuscript contains a handwritten note dated March 3, 1978, in which the head of the school at that time, ʿAbd al-Riza Ibrahimi, son of Abu al-Qasim and nephew of Zayn al-ʿAbidin, certifies the authenticity of the paper copy from which the manuscript was taken.

18. The Arabicized Persian written and spoken by Iranian ʿulamaʾ could not be understood by people who did not have a higher education. At the beginning of the twentieth century, the satirical representation of these problems of "communication," in the context of social criticism, was frequent in Persian literature. The most famous story on the subject is *Fārsi shikar ast* (Persian Is a Sweet Language), written in 1921 by Muhammad ʿAli Jamalzadah. On the use of Arabic pronunciation and words in Persian as a stylistic marker, see Beeman (1986:129–130); for a description of the contemporary social and political implications of this issue see, for example, Fischer and Abedi (1990:28, 274).
19. The page numbers refer to manuscript 23 H, cited in note 16. I place Persian terms and my textual interpolations between brackets. The punctuation is mine. I am grateful to Shiva Balaghi, Kamran Talattof, and two other readers for helping me decipher the calligraphy of the manuscript, and to Professor Gernot Windfuhr for a lively discussion.
20. See, for example, p. 203, where four generations of a family are traced in connection with an inheritance dispute.
21. A *mazraʿa* is a small farm or hamlet attached to a parent village. According to Lambton (1953:4 n. 2), "The meaning of *mazraʿah* in Qajar times when used as a technical term was a place which paid a defined sum by way of taxation for water and land as part of the assessment of a province or of a village."
22. Shiʿi law requires permission from a religious authority to acquire land as property through revivification *(iḥyāʾ)*. See Linant De Bellefonds (1980:1053).
23. Rafsanjan is the name of a town (and province) located approximately one hundred miles northwest of Kerman. Several questions deal with matters in Rafsanjan, and it is possible that a community of Shaykhi followers existed there.
24. Gardens, with their clay walls and fruit trees, are typical features of the Iranian landscape and a recurrent theme in classical Persian literature, in both realistic and in metaphorical senses. The greenness of the trees inside the garden is opposed to the dryness of the plain.
25. See Messick (1986) on the "common sense" interpretation of reality in the questions as contrasted with the "textual" interpretation of reality in the answers.

14. Sacred Space and Holy War in India

1. For background, see Elst (1990).
2. I discuss this incident briefly in Cole (1988:244–249); it has also been analyzed, from different points of view, by Bhatnagar (1968) and Fisher (1987). Here I wish to enlarge on my previous discussion and focus on the import of the fatwas issued by the Shiʿi chief mujtahid during the crisis.

3. See, for example, Sayyid Dildar ʿAli Nasirabadi, "Ajwibat al-sāʾilīn," Calcutta, Asiatic Society Library, Curzon Collection, MS 1016; id., "Najāt al-sāʾilīn," Lucknow, Nasiriyya Library, Fiqh Shiʿa, MS 256. See also Lakhnavi (1835–36); Nasirabadi (1848–49; 1860–61); Vajid ʿAli Shah (1850–51).
4. National Archives of India (NAI), New Delhi, Foreign Department Foreign Correspondence (FDFC), Dec. 28, 1855, Resident/King, Feb. 8, 1855, no. 342; Mashhadi (1896:110–111).
5. NAI, FDFC, Dec. 28, 1855, Capt. Alexander Orr/Supt. Frontier Police, July 29, 1855; Orr/Supt. Frontier Police, July 31, 1855, both in no. 341; Mashhadi (1986:111–112).
6. NAI, FDFC, Resident/Officiating Secretary to the Government (Sec. Govt.) of India, March 24, 1847, no. 94, April 17, 1847; FDFC, Dec. 28, 1855, "Notes on a Conference between the Resident and the King of Oudh," Aug. 1, 1855, no. 342; and King of Oudh/Resident, Aug. 12, 1855, no. 355.
7. NAI, FDFC, Dec. 28, 1855, Resident/King, Aug. 10, 1855, no. 355; Orr/Supt. Police, with Resident/Sec. Govt. India, Aug. 16, 1855, no. 351; Jan (1855:8–16); Mashhadi (1896:121–124).
8. NAI, FDFC, Dec. 28, 1855, "Conduct of the High Priest of Lucknow," Enclosure four with Resident/Sec. Govt. India, Sept. 8, 1855, no. 363.
9. Ibid.
10. NAI, FDFC, Dec. 28, 1855, "Conference between Minister and Resident," Aug. 30, 1855, no. 364; Captain G. K. Weston/Resident, Aug. 30, 1855, no. 365.
11. NAI, FDFC, Dec. 28, 1855, Resident/Sec. Govt. India, Sept. 8, 12, 16, 17 [1855], nos. 360, 370, 379.
12. NAI, FDFC, Dec. 28, 1855, "Report Made by Shankar Dyal of Kheree, Dated 26 Sept. 1855," appendix B to "Conference between Resident and King, 29 Sept. 1855," no. 389; Officiating Resident/Officiating Sec. Govt. India, Oct. 4, 1855, no. 394; Officiating Resident/Sec. Govt. India, Oct. 5, 1855, no. 396.
13. NAI, FDFC, Dec. 28, 1855, "Enclosure No. 1, Fatwa of High Priest," with "Conference between Resident and King, 29 Sept. 1855," no. 389.
14. NAI, FDFC, Dec. 28, 1855, "Conference between Resident and King, 29 Sept. 1855," no. 389.
15. NAI, FDFC, Dec. 28, 1855, Officiating Resident/Sec. Govt. India, Oct. 2, 1855, no. 388.
16. NAI, FDFC, Dec. 28, 1855, "Report from Daryabad, 24 Oct. 1855," no. 434; Officiating Resident/Sec. Govt. India, October 31, 1855, no. 440; Officiating Resident/Sec. Govt. India, Nov. 8, 9, and 10, 1855, nos. 448, 449, 450; Mashhadi (1896:125–128).

15. Two Fatwas on Hajj in British India

1. The marginal identification of the questioner as ʿAzizuddin is placed next to the second query, but since there is no attribution for the preceding query, both may have emanated from him.

2. Subsequent references, unless noted, are to this volume.
3. I am grateful to Gail Minault, whose copy of this edition I was able to consult in the course of surveying her excellent collection of Urdu publications.
4. Although there was discussion at the time of using the mufti to circumvent the British courts, with their hybrid Anglo-Muhammadan law, the published collections deal with issues that were not handled by the courts. Deobandis have spoken of independent courts designated to handle issues among Muslims, but I have not seen sources to document these courts, let alone their extent (Metcalf 1982: 146–147).

16. Apostasy and Judicial Separation in British India

I wish to thank David S. Powers for his comments and suggestions on earlier drafts of this essay.

1. Taqlid, often used as an antonym to ijtihad, means following and adhering to the opinion of a jurist. In the Indian context, it means adherence to a specific school of Islamic law (e.g., Hanafi) in all matters.
2. The *ḥudūd* are major crimes in Islamic law, the penalties for which are specified in the Quran and Sunna. Classical Muslim jurists recognized five *ḥudūd* crimes: unlawful intercourse *(zinā),* false accusation of unlawful intercourse *(qadhf),* consumption of alcohol *(shurb),* theft *(sariqa),* and highway robbery *(ḥarāba).* In the *Hidāya* (n.d., 2:94 ff.), al-Marghinani treats the first three crimes in the chapter devoted to *ḥudūd* and the last two in the chapter devoted to theft; and he treats apostasy and rebellion, which he does not consider to be among the *ḥudūd,* in his chapter on *siyar* (conduct). One finds the same pattern of treatment in *al-Fatāwā al-ʿĀlamgīriyya* (1983). By contrast, twentieth-century authors such as ʿAwda (1960, 2:345) regard apostasy *(ridda)* and rebellion *(baghy)* as *ḥudūd,* bringing the total number of major crimes to seven; according to ʿAwda, this is the majority opinion of Muslim jurists, with the exception of Ibn Hazm. Mawlana Thanawi seems to follow the modern enumeration of the *ḥudūd.*
3. A generally accepted view as found in the following six authoritative texts of the Hanafi school: *al-Mabsūṭ* by Muhammad al-Shaybani (d. 804), *al-Jāmiʿ al-ṣaghīr, al-Jāmiʿ al-Kabīr, al-Siyar al-ṣaghīr, al-Siyar al-Kabīr,* and *Ziyādāt.*
4. A rare or obsolete view held by the founder of the Hanafi school or his disciples, not recorded in the texts of *ẓāhir al-riwāya.*

17. Are Wahhabis Kafirs?

I am grateful to Professor Yohanan Friedmann for his comments on an earlier draft of this paper.

1. The term "Barelwi" in Ahmad Riza's name indicates that he was a resident of the town of Bareilly in Rohilkhand, western Uttar Pradesh. It should not be confused with the town of Rae Bareilly in Awadh, eastern Uttar Pradesh, where Sayyid Ahmad Barelwi (d. 1831), leader of the jihad movement of the 1830s, lived.

2. The translation of *ṭā'ifa* as "musicians and dancing girls" is controversial, as the word "*ṭā'ifa*" generally connotes a group, without any derogatory implications. I agree with Metcalf, who translates the term as "band of musicians and dancing girls" (1982:309). It is entirely in line with Ahmad Riza's strong tone of denunciation in this fatwa that he should use the term as an expression of derision. Moreover, the fact that Rashid Ahmad Gangohi's *pīr* was Hajji Imdadullah (d. 1899) indicates that the word "*pīr*" (Sufi master) is to be understood metaphorically in this context.
3. Western scholarly opinion on the validity of this view is cautious, as many scholars point out that even when intellectual influence may be assumed through residence in Mecca, which was in the eighteenth and nineteenth centuries a Sunni Muslim intellectual meeting ground, the specific reform programs supported by individual ʿulama' were informed by their own particular situations, all of which differed in terms of specific local circumstance. See, for example, Voll (1975:32–39); Ahmad Khan (1965:xlv–xlvi).
4. Maulana Khalil Ahmad Ambethwi was the principal of the Mazahir-i ʿUlum at Saharanpur, a madrasa linked to Deoband at the time. Ambethwi was a disciple *(murīd)* of Maulana Rashid Ahmad Gangohi. The book for which Ahmad Riza had attacked him in his fatwa was *Barāhīn-i Qāṭiʿiyya*. See Metcalf (1982:131–132, 309–311).
5. However, it was probably not a spontaneous decision. Ahmad Riza must have contemplated this move when the occasion presented itself. He had, in the past, obtained such confirmatory certifications of a controversial fatwa through correspondence with some Meccan ʿulama'. See Ahmad Riza Khan (n.d.[b], 2:7).
6. In a personal communication (June 23, 1989), John O. Voll expresses skepticism regarding the extent of Wahhabi influence in the Haramayn at that time: "My guess is that the Arabian Wahhabis were not a factor in influencing the views of ʿulama' in the Haramayn in 1906. This was, after all, only four years after ʿAbd al-ʿAziz had taken Riyadh and it was only in April 1906 that ʿAbd al-ʿAziz finally killed his arch-rival, the leader of the Rashid family. In 1908 Husayn became the Grand Sharif of Mecca and he was able to capture ʿAbd al-ʿAziz's brother and gain Saudi cooperation for a while. [Thus] most people in Mecca and Medina [probably] did not feel threatened by the Nejdi forces at that time."
7. A list of ʿulama' from Mecca and Medina who wrote testimonials approving Ahmad Riza's *Ḥusām al-Ḥaramayn* is given at the end of the fatwa. Ahmad Riza refers to some of them in the course of his account (n.d.[b], 2:7–20).
8. Despite the adherence of the Ottoman rulers to the Hanafi school of law, most Meccan ʿulama' followed the Shafiʿi school. Although all four schools were represented by their respective muftis, the title of shaykh al-ʿulama' was held by the mufti of the Shafiʿi school.
9. I am grateful to John Voll for bringing this point to my attention (personal communication, June 23, 1989).
10. According to these sources, the beliefs that must be embraced include: the unity of Allah, the prophethood of Muhammad, the existence of heaven and hell, the comforts and punishments of the grave, the questioning of the dead, the reck-

oning on the Day of the Resurrection, and the heavenly river and bridge. The list of "fundamentals" also includes the qualities of Allah, the Prophet, the angels, the Prophet's Companions, and his family.

11. These are: knowledge of the Hour (of Judgment), of when it will rain, of the attributes of an unborn child, of a person's earnings on the next day, and of the place of one's death.

18. The Lions of Qasr al-Nil Bridge

1. A fatwa against the Sudanese Mahdi issued at the request of the Khedival government (al-Mahdi 1304/1887, 2:28–32; 18 Dhu al-Qaʿda 1300 [September 20, 1883]). For an analysis of this fatwa, see Peters 1983. Of another one issued in 1876, we do not know the precise political context. The Khedive asked about a person claiming to have knowledge of the divine secrets *(al-mughayyabāt),* as a result of which people were busying themselves zealously with his words and committing actions that disturb public order. The grand mufti responded that such a person must be punished with *taʿzīr,* if his words do not amount to apostasy. (al-Mahdi 1304/1887, 2:7; 20 Shawwal, 1293 [November 8, 1876]).
2. Of the small number of sources on al-ʿAbbasi's life, the most important are an account by his son, Muhammad ʿAbd al-Khaliq al-Hifni, in Zaydan (n.d., 2:250–255), and that in ʿAli Mubarak (1304–1306/1886–1889, 17:12–13). For a complete list of sources, see Schölch (1973:332, n. 243). Delanoue (1982:168–174 and 136–137) summarizes the available biographical information.
3. On Muhammad Amin al-Mahdi, see Lane (1966:118–121).
4. See, for example, al-Mahdi 1304/1887, 2:449 (30 Rabiʿ II 1265 [March 25, 1849]): "We attended the Khedival Council in Cairo and the substance of the case of . . . was read to us as well as the conflicting fatwas concerning the issue . . . We considered their words and it appeared [to us] that the fatwa to the effect that . . . was the one in agreement with the stipulations of the founder of the waqf." The sources do not allow us to establish whether the grand mufti attended these council meetings on a regular basis, or only when his legal advice was required.
5. See, for example, al-Mahdi 1304/1887, 4:588 (4 Jumada I 1271 [February 3, 1855]): The Majlis al-Ahkam (one of the higher legislative and judicial councils) wants a fatwa concerning a controversy among the ʿulamaʾ of Upper Egypt regarding the law of gift.
6. See, for example, al-Mahdi 1304/1887, 3:276–281 (10 Jumada II 1289 [August 15, 1872]), where the grand mufti is consulted by the Majlis al-Ahkam about incorrect judgments of the qadi of Giza.
7. Decree of 5 Rabiʿ II 1290 (July 2, 1873); text in Jallad (1890–1895, 4:136).
8. See, for example, al-Mahdi 1304/1887, 1:222–226 (23 Jumada II 1283 [November 2, 1866]), where the grand mufti is called on to settle a dispute between the qadi and the mufti of Dumyat.
9. On ʿIllaysh, see Delanoue (1982:129–168). On the uncertain vocalization of his name, see ibid., p. 129, n. 69.

10. Muhammad al-Inbabi, 1240–1313/1824–1896; shaykh al-Azhar from 1881 to 1882 and from 1886 to 1896. See Delanoue (1982:137, n. 80).
11. This was Yaʿqub Sami (d. 1300/1882–1883), a professional soldier in the Egyptian Army, descended from a Greek family in Istanbul. During the ʿUrabi revolt he chose the side of the ʿUrabis and acted as undersecretary of state for war and president of the emergency government *(al-majlis al-ʿurfi)*. See Schölch (1973:336, n. 337).
12. This was the equestrian statue of Ibrahim Pasha, the son of Mehmed ʿAli, who ruled Egypt for about nine months in 1848. It was created by Charles Cordier in 1872 and placed at al-ʿAtaba al-Khadra' Square, opposite the ruins of the Azbakiyya Mosque, which had been partially demolished in 1869 to create a large square, part of the new layout of Cairo. The statue currently is situated at Opera Square. See Baedeker (1929:54); Behrens-Abouseif (1985:92, 111, and plate xxii, a photograph of the statue in front of the remains of the Azbakiyya Mosque).
13. These are the four bronze lion statues that can still be seen at both ends of the bridge, which was built in 1871. See Baedeker (1929:86).
14. "*Makrūh taḥrīm*" is an intermediate category between *makrūh* (reprehensible) and *ḥarām* (forbidden).
15. This is the supercommentary by Muhammad Amin Ibn ʿAbidin (d. 1836) on *al-Durr al-Mukhtār* by al-Haskafi (d. 1677), itself a commentary on the *Tanwīr al-Abṣār* by al-Timirtashi (d. 1595). See Brockelmann (suppl., 2:427–428). The *Radd al-Muḥtār* was an authoritative and widely used Hanafi text in nineteenth-century Egypt.
16. Probably *Fatḥ al-Mubīn,* the supercommentary by a certain Muhammad Abu al-Suʿud al-Misri on Muʿin al-Din Muhammad al-Harawi's commentary on the *Kanz al-Daqā'iq* of al-Nasafi (d. 1310). See Aghnides (1961:181). But Brockelmann (suppl., 2:267) identifies the author as Abu al-Masʿud and his work as a commentary, not as a supercommentary.
17. Probably the *Khulāṣat al-Fatāwā* by Tahir al-Bukhari (d. 1147). See Brockelmann (suppl., 1:641).
18. Muhammad al-Shaybani (d. 805), a "companion" of Abu Hanifa, was one of the founders of the Hanafi madhhab.
19. Al-Mahdi 1304/1887, 5:299–300 (16 Shawwal 1299 [August 31, 1882]). The episode is discussed in Schölch (1973:244) and Delanoue (1982:140). The statues were removed at the instigation of the Maliki mufti ʿIllaysh in early September. They were preserved in the Egyptian Museum and reerected after the revolt.
20. For the development of Cairo under Ismaʿil, see Abu-Lughod (1971:103–113).

19. An Argument about How to Argue

1. A detailed account of the controversy may be found in Roff (1983). The primary source of textual materials is ʿAbbas (1937). A related publication by Pejabat Kuliah al-Attas (1937) has the same starting point but does not directly discuss

the Kelantan case. Al-Azhar (1982, 7:2499–2500) records a 1968 request for a fatwa on dog keeping, based on a report in the newspaper *al-Ahrām* about twenty years earlier of a fatwa given then by the Dar al-ifta', al-Azhar, in response to "questions from Muslims in Indonesia" (I am indebted to Muhammad Khalid Masud for bringing this to my attention).

2. The history of the Majlis is set out in Roff (1974).
3. The text of Nik ʿAbdullah's opinion appears not to have survived. A related opinion on the question of *talfīq,* by ʿAbdullah's father Haji Wan Musa, is printed in ʿAbbas (1937:79ff.) and was probably given after ʿAbdullah's and immediately preceding the *muzākara.* For further Malay discussion of relevant hadiths, compare Pejabat Kuliah al-Attas (1937).
4. The text translated here is that given in ʿAbbas (1937:97–99); the Malay text in *al-Ḥikmah* (vol. 4, no. 28 May 6, 1937:10) is slightly different.

20. The Council of Indonesian ʿUlama' on Christmas Celebrations

1. Adapted from the Central Bureau of Statistics, Jakarta, 1971 and 1980; also quoted in Badan Penelitian dan Pengembangan Agama Departemen Agama (1982–1983).
2. Reports of conflicts between Muslims and Christians around this time can be found, for example, in Sydney University's *The Review of Indonesian and Malaysian Affairs* 1, no. 4 (1967):20; also in *Panji Masyarakat* (Jakarta), October 15, 1979, p. 8.
3. The quranic verses quoted by Hamka in the dialogue are concerned with the basic principles of Muslim relations with non-Muslims. The verses are as follows: "It may be that Allah will bring about friendship between you and those whom you hold to be your enemies among them; and Allah is Powerful; and Allah is Forgiving, Merciful. Allah does not forbid you respecting those who have not made war against you on account of [your] religion, and have not driven you forth from your homes, that you show them kindness and deal with them justly; surely Allah loves the doers of justice. Allah only forbids you respecting those who made war upon you on account of [your] religion, and drove you forth from your homes and backed up [others] in your expulsion, that you make friends with them, and whoever makes friends with them, these are the unjust." (Quran 60:7–9)
4. *Pancasila,* literally, "five principles," is the basis and ideology of the nation: belief in God Almighty, humanitarianism, Indonesian unity, democracy, and social justice.
5. Letter of Circulation of the Minister of Religious Affairs no. MA/432/1981 of September 2, 1981.
6. The other two fatwas hostile to the government deal with interreligious marriage and vasectomy.
7. Masudi, interviews with the author (Jakarta, October 3, 1989); and Tengku Muhammad Saleh, interviews with the author (Jakarta, November 22, 1989).
8. The letter of resignation was dated May 18, 1981, and signed by Hamka. His

son, Rusjdi Hamka, said that he had typed the letter, which had been handwritten by Hamka himself (Hamka 1981:195–196).

21. A Modern Indian Mufti

Grants from the Social Science Research Council Committee on the Comparative Study of Muslim Societies and DePaul University made possible the research for this chapter. Dr. Hasan ud-din Ahmad of Hyderabad as well as the ʿulamaʾ of the Jamiʿa Nizamiyya Madrasa deserve special thanks for their hospitality and candor.

1. Calling such a mass of people a minority is itself problematic; even so, leaders frequently complain that Muslims are undercounted in government censuses; some put the Muslim population of India as high as 150 million. Debates over the meaning of secularism are even more complicated and embittered. One of the best discussions of what "secularism" means in the modern Indian context remains V. P. Luthera (1964); as for Muslims who wish to accommodate in a radical fashion to the secular state, see Kozlowski (1974).
2. Rosen (1989) provides a critique of Euro-American legal thought as applied to the Muslim world. Though focused on Morocco, with some changes to reflect the history of Islam in South Asia, this critique could well serve as the starting point for a study of the social dimensions of shariʿa in the subcontinent.
3. In August of 1989, a local *ʿālim* caused a citywide fracas in the newspapers when he issued a fatwa arguing that it was permissible for Muslims to accept interest on bank deposits. See, for example, *Rahnāmah-ye Dakkhan,* September 9, 1989, and *Siyāsat,* September 10, 1989; see also Kozlowski (1993).
4. On the various styles of the Arabic script and the significance of the use of different scripts for decoration or emphasis, see Safadi (1978). *Nastaʿliq* is the curving and angular script often used for Persian and Urdu. Arabic can be written in *nastaʿliq,* but over the past century, due in part to the printing press, *naskh* has become increasingly identified with the Arabic language. Its use in this document no doubt stems from the Jamiʿa's as well as the mufti's concern to affirm their scholarship.
5. Urdu usage differs somewhat from Arabic style. For a translation from the Arabic of the stock opening phrase of a fatwa, see Messick (1986). Here the Urdu verb employed is *"farmānā,"* which has a sense of order or command as opposed to the Arabic say or tell.
6. The scribes of the Jamiʿa take pains to present a scholarly document. For example, the plural of *waris* (heir) is often written *warisa* in Urdu, but here the scribe has given the correct Arabic orthography: *wurathāʾ*.
7. The text itself varies the form, using *sharīʿa* in the first instance and *shariʿat* in the second.
8. I have been unable to identify the text to which the mufti is referring.
9. The quoted phrase is in Arabic.
10. The quoted phrase is in Arabic.

22. Mutʿa

The inspiration for writing this paper owes much to Muhammad Khalid Masud. I am grateful to David S. Powers, Kaveh Safa-Isfahani, Mahnaz Afkhami, and S. Veli Reza Nasr for their comments and suggestions, and to Professors Ahmad Mahdavi-Damghani and Seyyed Hossein Nasr for discussing with me the nuances and differences between the Sunni and Shiʿi positions on the issues of fatwa and ijtihad.

1. The Arabic term for the institution of temporary marriage is *"mutʿa,"* which literally means enjoyment, or pleasure. In Iran, the term *"mutʿa"* is used primarily in legal textbooks. The public has generally adopted the term *"sīgheh"* (also Arabic), which literally means the form or shape, for example, of a contract. For a description of these terms, their etymology and public usage, see Haeri 1989:50–51.
2. Shiʿi law generally restricts associations between unrelated men and women, unless appropriately segregated by a veil, and except within a specified degree of blood and marital relations. While cross-sex relations not mediated by veil or sanctioned by blood or marriage are perceived to be potentially sinful (because they may lead to illicit sex), many Iranians, in practice, find ways of circumventing the restriction by improvising on the theme of temporary marriage (see Haeri 1989:75–102).
3. The title *Tuzīḥ al-masāʾil* (Clarification of Questions) is commonly applied to a mujtahid's collected legal and religious opinions, compiled as a book by his students and devotees under his supervision.
4. The *ʿidda* for temporary marriage is two menstrual cycles or forty-five days, while that for permanent marriage is three menstrual cycles or three months. For a specific rationale regarding this discrepancy, see Haeri 1989:57–58.
5. For a comprehensive description of the institution of temporary marriage, see Tusi 1964:497–502; Hilli 1968:515–528; al-Kashif al-Ghitaʿ 1968:372–392; Khomeini 1977:491–493; Mutahhari 1974:21–52; Bihishti ca.1980:329–335; and Shafaʾi 1973. For English sources, see Levy 1931–1933; Murata 1987; Haeri 1989.
6. The Shiʿis and Sunnis both point to several hadiths attributed to the Prophet Muhammad in which he either condones or condemns temporary marriage.
7. Several contemporary Shiʿi scholars, including Ayatollah Khomeini and Ayatollah Shariʿat Madari (personal communication with the latter), have indicated their preference for a restriction on the number of temporary marriages that a man may conclude simultaneously. However, this preference has not yet been formulated as a law and retains the status of a moral recommendation.
8. This paragraph is taken from Haeri 1989:54–55.
9. According to the current civil code of the Islamic Republic, the age of maturity for women is fixed at nine lunar years (eight years and nine months, according to the solar calendar). See Office of Population and Human Resources, *Laws, Policies, and Ordinances,* Budget and Plan Organization, July 1990, p. 25.
10. Ayatollah Khomeini's fatwa calling for the assassination of author Salman Rushdie was reissued after Khomeini's death by a group of Iranian ʿulamaʾ, thereby giving it continuing legitimacy and applicability, despite the fact that,

according to Mahdavi-Damghani, this particular fatwa posseses the status of a *ḥukm* (see note 11).

11. Shiʿis, like Sunnis, distinguish between a fatwa and a binding *ḥukm*. A fatwa has general application. For example, an opinion affirming the necessity of a guardian's permission for a virgin woman's first marriage is applicable to all virgin women (Mahdavi-Damghani, personal communication, 1993). Such a fatwa may or may not be enforced by the judicial system; if it is not, following it is a matter of personal choice (Langarudi 1967:66, 495, 618). Shiʿi jurisprudence "distinguishes a *ḥukm* issued by a judge from a fatwa issued by a *mujtahid* [who is not a judge] . . . As such, the *ḥukm* may not be revoked [by ordinary citizens or lower-ranking religious or legal officials], whereas a fatwa may [be revoked]" (Langarudi 1967:243). Unlike the Sunnis, Shiʿis hold that the opinion of a mujtahid acquires the status of a *ḥukm* when issued with specific reference to a particular case, an example being Ayatollah Shirazi's famous late-nineteenth-century fatwa prohibiting the use of tobacco. A *ḥukm*, such as the death sentence that Ayatollah Khomeini imposed (in absentia) on Salman Rushdie, remains in force even after the death of the judge or mujtahid who issued it, unless it is subsequently revoked by an individual whose legal-religious credentials are equivalent to those of the first jurist. A fatwa, by contrast, generally "dies" with the individual who issued it, although adherents of the deceased man are free to follow it.
12. Although Rafsanjani had talked about this issue previously, this was the first time that he discussed it in a public forum in his capacity as president. See *Zan-i Rūz* 1045 (1985):4–5.
13. In the same sermon, Rafsanjani recommended temporary marriage for widows of the Iran-Iraq war, suggesting that women should feel confident to approach men with an offer of temporary marriage. For the complete text of his speech, see *Zan-i Rūz* 1294 (1990):55.
14. For an interesting instance of disagreement among Shiʿi ʿulamaʾ on this issue after the revolution of 1979, see Qurbani 1988:220–238.
15. His religious title is *Ḥujjat al-Islām*.

23. The Complementarity of *Iftāʾ* and *Qaḍāʾ*

This study was supported in part by a Fulbright-Hays grant for research in Saudi Arabia, 1983–1984. My knowledge of the application of family law in the courts of Saudi Arabia is based on several days' observations in 1983 in the court of Shaykh Musaʿid al-Muʿtiq, Court of Guarantee and Marriages (Mahkamat al-Daman wa'l-Ankiha), Great Shariʿa Court of Riyadh (al-Mahkama al-Kubra bi'l-Riyad). I am grateful to the Ministry of Justice of the Kingdom of Saudi Arabia for allowing me this opportunity. Because my conclusions here draw on such limited observations, they must be taken as only tentative, needing verification and extension. This chapter does not reflect changes in the latter organization occurring after the time of the study.

1. There is scant distinction between fatwas issued within the scope of one's public office and those issued privately. Shaykh Ibn Baz, for example, is approached day and night, at work and at home, in person and by telephone and letter, for

his views, all of which are valued equally. Any *ʿālim,* whether public employee or private citizen, can be so approached. Fatwas are common fare also on the radio, on television, and in the newspapers. Thus is created and constantly replenished a store of fatwas on which believers may draw to guide and legitimate behavior.

2. I am grateful to Mr. Abdulrahman al-Hussayen for clarifying the organization of Saudi fatwa institutions.
3. Al-Riʾasa al-ʿAmma li-Idarat al-Buḥuth al-ʿIlmiyya waʾl-Iftaʾ waʾl-Daʿwa waʾl-Irshad (General Presidency for the Administration of Research in the [Religious] Sciences, Iftaʾ, Call [to Islam], and Guidance).
4. More precisely, the publisher of *al-Daʿwā* is an organization predating the Presidency, founded by an earlier mufti.
5. In almost all Muslim countries, this result is changed by statute to a rule similar to Shaykh Ibn Baz's (Nasir 1990:117–118). Many present-day scholars endorse this outcome.
6. *Kaffāra* for breaking an oath consists of certain acts of charity or, failing these, fasting. See Quran 5:89.
7. In another fatwa, the requestor repeatedly swore on penalty of divorce to avoid certain sins, "trying to incite myself to abandon them," but repeatedly broke the vow. He said, "My intent was not to divorce my wife." Shaykh Ibn Baz's answer was the same in substance (Ibn Baz 1987).
8. This fatwa provides very little information on Shaykh Ibn Baz's view. His view probably resembles the opinion of Ibn al-Qayyim al-Jawziyya (1970, 4:52).
9. Again, in many Muslim countries this result is changed by statute, by declaring virtually all forms of *ṭalāq* to be single and revocable (Nasir 1990:119–121), and many contemporary fiqh scholars hold a similar view.
10. Contrary to the usual practice, the minority opinion is unsigned, but Ibn Baz's view on this issue is well known. Note that Shaykh Ibn Baz's positions on all three issues seem close to those of Ibn Taymiyya and his disciple Ibn al-Qayyim al-Jawziyya (as to triple *ṭalāq,* see Ibn al-Qayyim al-Jawziyya 1973, 3:30–38 and Board of Senior ʿUlamaʾ 1977a; as to oaths, Ibn al-Qayyim al-Jawziyya 1973, 1:279–280, 3:54–61; as to anger, Ibn al-Qayyim al-Jawziyya 1970, 4:52 and Ibn al-Qayyim al-Jawziyya 1973, 3:52–54).
11. Note that these distinctions diverge radically from, or rather cut across, the most obviously comparable distinctions from contemporary Western legal systems, such as those between legislation and adjudication, or between law-deciding and fact-finding. This may suggest how widely separate are many of the basic legal conceptions in the two types of legal systems, and how numerous the obstacles to gaining an outside understanding of systems applying the shariʿa.

    A comment is needed about characterizing the qadi judgment as unique and particular. This should not necessarily suggest that the rules applied by qadis are less general and predictable than laws stated in fatwas. Rather, characteristics of the qadi forum as external, public, and compulsory do in fact impel qadis toward adjudication by predictable, generally applicable rules, while fatwas, because they are personal, singular, and not binding, can more easily be episodic and variable, and all the more so as applied in the "inner forum."

12. Another important area of interaction is between the Board of Senior ʿUlamaʾ and the shariʿa courts. Fatwas of the former lead the courts, by force of collegial influence rather than binding statute, toward changes in legal doctrine. Such observations are suggestive as to the manner in which, in earlier Islamic legal systems, rank-and-file qadis, while deemed bound to old school doctrines, would nonetheless follow the innovative ijtihad determinations of prestigious muftis.
13. Such a suit would probably arise on the husband's complaint that the wife was *nāshiza,* or recalcitrant, for leaving the family home (Board of Senior ʿUlamaʾ 1977b).
14. The wife's waiting period had expired.
15. Proving the husband's claim would be made especially difficult by the fact that Islamic legal procedure does not allow parties to testify on their own behalf. In such situations the law often simply credits a party's word as to his or her intent.
16. A qadi can, however, achieve many of the same goals in the course of the trial by advising and exhorting the parties and urging that they settle their dispute by reconciliation *(ṣulḥ).* These and other aspects of the qadi art overlap with the fatwa functions mentioned here, and deserve similar study. Overlaps also exist with the institution of *taḥkīm,* or binding arbitration.

24. The Fatwa as an Instrument of Accommodation

This is an abbreviated version of my article, "The *Fatwā* as an Instrument of the Islamization of a Tribal Society in the Process of Sedentarization," published in *The Bulletin of the School of Oriental and African Studies,* 54, pt. 3 (1991):449–459.

1. Although the size and spacing of the letters are different in the question and the answer, the handwriting is the same; it is probably that of the Shafiʿi jurist.
2. The translation of the document is as literal as possible, with additions to elucidate the subject matter and the technical terms. Short additions appear in the body of the text, with more detailed explanations in the notes.
3. "*Mā qawlukum*" is a formula usual in requests for a formal legal opinion (istiftaʾ). When Bedouin of the Judean Desert present an oral pleading *(ḥujja)* to an arbitrator-judge, they usually employ the formula "*aysh qawlukum*" or "*aysh raʾyukum,*" which means a request for a judgment. On the similarity between a request for the legal opinion of a mufti and the *ḥujja* in a customary proceeding, see Layish (forthcoming). That formula is also usually used in requests for legal opinions from qadis in Cyrenaica. See Layish and Davis 1988:124, Document no. 158.
4. Although this formula would seem to consist of two independent sentences, it should be construed as a suspended repudiation involving an oath, intended to emphasize the man's determination to prevent his brother's marriage because of an amount of dower regarded as excessive; cf. Layish 1975:114, 138, and 235;

the literal meaning of *taḥallala* is "to render [the daughter] lawfully permitted," which should here be interpreted in the context of marriage. Confirmation of this view may be obtained from the answer of the Shafiʿi mufti; see below.

5. Under Islamic law, the wife is expected to obey her husband, which means that she must join him at the place of residence chosen by him. As the brothers lived in the same house, the bride's entry into the shaykh's house would indicate that she had indeed married his brother. This formula, too, should be understood as referring to a suspended repudiation involving an oath.
6. The suspended repudiation seems to have made an impact on the bride's father: he agreed to reduce the dower to an amount acceptable to the other party, thus removing the obstacle to the marriage.
7. "*Jawāb,*" in this document, is synonymous with fatwa. This use of the term is common among the Bedouin and occurs also in the shariʿa courts. See Layish 1991a:184; cf. Layish (forthcoming).
8. The closing passage, a typically Islamic element, refers to wages and reward in the next world. This embellishment, an expression of religious sensibility and piety that may be motivated by considerations of Islamic indoctrination, is also used among the Cyrenaican Bedouin as a closing formula in requests for a religious legal opinion. See, for example, Layish and Davis 1988:122, Document nos. 156/2–3.
9. That is, repeated the suspended repudiation involving an oath.
10. The affirmative implies the negative: if he did not intend to divorce his wife when using the oath of prohibition, then she is not divorced. This may be an allusion to the manner in which the shaykh might extricate himself from his predicament: he need only declare that he did not intend to divorce his wife.
11. A *ṭalāq mukarrar* entails the legal consequences of a revocable *(rajʿī)* divorce, which enables the wife to be reinstated without a new marriage or dower after each of the first two repudiations.
12. That is, somebody who will conclude an intermediate marriage with her and then divorce her, so that she may be permitted to her former husband again.
13. A revocable *(rajʿī)* divorce does not dissolve the marriage immediately. The husband may reinstate the wife during the waiting period (which lasts three menstrual periods) without her consent and without a new contract of marriage or dower (Schacht 1964:166; Anderson 1976:101–102; Layish 1975:177–178). The mitigating of the legal consequences of the divorce by placing it on a par with a revocable divorce may be regarded as a hint at a way to extricate the shaykh from his predicament. Another possible way of remedying the situation relates to the number of divorces: if the husband indeed intended to divorce the wife but pronounced the oath of prohibition only twice, then he may reinstate her once again during the waiting period. Only after the third repudiation is she not legally permitted to him before an intermediate marriage has taken place.
14. If she completes the waiting period without her husband's having exercised the option of reinstating her, the divorce becomes irrevocable *(bāʾin)* with all the legal consequences attending dissolution. See Layish 1975:173.

15. Conditions of the validity of a marriage are offer and acceptance *(ījāb wa-qabūl),* the use of terms expressly relating to marriage and the presence of witnesses at the session of the marriage contract. Cf. Schacht 1964:121 and 161.
16. In the case of a defective marriage, the couple must at once be separated. Under Hanafi doctrine, if the marriage has been consummated, some of the numerous legal consequences of a valid *(ṣaḥīḥ)* marriage apply, such as the payment of a dower, legitimacy of the children, and the waiting period. See Schacht 1964:163. Under Shafiʿi doctrine, there is no real distinction between *fāsid* and *bāṭil* (void). See Anderson 1970:376.
17. Muhammad b. Idris al-Shafiʿi (d. 204/820), regarded as the founder of the school of law named after him.
18. Here the mufti probably hints at a further possibility for extricating the shaykh from his quandary. If it is found, as is very likely, that the shaykh did not marry his wife in accordance with all the requirements of the shariʿa, or, in other words, if the marriage was performed according to tribal custom—that is, was a marriage by *ʿaṭāʾ* or *hiba,* very common among the Bedouin of the Judean Desert (see Layish and Shmueli 1979:35ff. and the sources indicated there)—then all that would be required to legalize it would be to separate the couple and reunite them with a flawless *sharʿī* marriage. This procedure involves some unpleasantness (inter alia, the court must affiliate the children to their father, no doubt in reliance on his acknowledgment), but considering the alternative of an intermediate marriage, it offers considerable relief.
19. Abu Shujaʿ Ahmad b. Hasan b. Ahmad (b. 434/1042–1043), a famous Shafiʿi jurist and qadi, whose family originated from Isfahan. He wrote a compendium of Islamic law, entitled *al-Ghāya fīʾl-ikhtiṣār,* or *al-Mukhtaṣar* or *al-Taqrīb,* which promoted the spread of the Shafiʿi school. It is the subject of many commentaries. The quotation cited in the fatwa may be found in Abu Shujaʿ 1955:30; see Schacht 1960:150ff.; Brockelmann 1943–1949, 1:492. For an interpretation of the quotation from his treatise occurring in the fatwa, see, for instance, al-Ghazzi 1346/1927:41–42. On questions relating to divorce by an implicit declaration *(kināya),* the validity of which is contingent on the factor of intent *(niyya),* and to revocable *(rajʿī)* divorce, see ibid., pp. 44–45.
20. *Fisq* is the opposite of *ʿadāla* for the purposes of testimony. See Schacht 1964:125.
21. Marriage guardians—like other guardians over persons or property—are natural guardians by virtue of blood relationship, in a fixed order of preference according to the degree of their relationship to the ward. The court may, under certain circumstances, appoint a nonrelative as guardian.
22. According to the Hanafi school, a fully competent woman may marry without a marriage guardian. However, the marriage guardian may oppose the marriage if the intended husband does not meet the conditions of equality in marriage *(kafāʾa).* See Schacht 1964:162.
23. An expression of modesty and piety on the part of the mufti.
24. It seems that the word "al-Shafiʿi" is not part of the scholar's name, but rather

indicates his affiliation with the Shafiʿi school, a fact of particular importance in relation to the legal opinion. The references to Shafiʿi sources reinforce this assumption.

25. Frank Stewart, who studies the tribal law of the Ahaywat in central Sinai, informs me (personal communication October 10, 1989) that some of the Bedouin there are very conscious agents of Islamization, e.g., when in town they visit the *shaykh al-dīn* and obtain from him all kinds of information about proper Muslim practice, which they then transmit to their fellow tribesmen. Sometimes they record his answers on tape so as to be sure to get them right. They are actively searching for information that will allow them to live a proper Muslim life.

25. Postmortem Examinations in Egypt

1. Ibn al-Qayyim al-Jawziyya (d. 1350 in Damascus) was a Hanbali jurist and theologian, and a disciple of Ibn Taymiyya.
2. According to the Hanafis, *sharṭ* is the prerequisite for an obligation but is independent of the obligation itself. Therefore, ablution, which is a prerequisite for prayer, is its *sharṭ*. Without ablution the prayer is not valid. *Rukn* is also a prerequisite for an obligation, but it is part of the obligation. Prostration (*rakʿa*) and Quran recitation during prayer are *rukn*s of prayer; without them the prayer is invalid (al-Zuhayli 1989, 1:54). Postmortems for educational purposes may perhaps be classified as *rukn* or even as *sharṭ* for becoming a skilled medical doctor.
3. The obligations in Islamic law can be obligations either of individuals *(farḍ ʿayn)* or of the adult community in general *(farḍ kifāya)*. Prayer, pilgrimage, and fasting, for example, belong to the first type. If an individual does not observe them, it is considered a sin. A *farḍ kifāya* is addressed to a group, although the obligation lapses when a sufficient number of people have already performed it. If no one performs the duty, the whole community is blamed. (al-Zuhayli 1986, 1:62–64).
4. This fatwa can also be found in Rida (1970).
5. After completing his studies at al-Azhar, Shaykh Muhammad Bakhit (1856–1923) subsequently served as a qadi in Alexandria, as a member of the Supreme Court of Justice in Egypt, and as the mufti of Egypt until his death.
6. Shaykh ʿAbd al-Munsif Mahmud ʿAbd al-Fattah often issues mainstream religious fatwas in *al-Liwāʾ al-Islāmī*.

26. Tantawi on Banking Operations in Egypt

1. For example, Ibrahim al-Jibali wrote several opinions in the 1930s on "the *muḍāraba*," or commenda (Jibali 1931–1933) and Yusuf al-Dajawi wrote an opinion on "commercial transactions and what they entail in terms of *ribā*" (Dajawi 1935). Similar opinions by little-known scholars have appeared in Egyptian religious journals close to al-Azhar over the course of the century.

2. The fatwa, which appeared originally in *al-Ahrām,* was reprinted in Khudayri (1990:353–364). All references in this essay are to Khudayri's text.
3. In 1980, Dar al-ifta' decided to publish the fatwas it had issued since it began to keep official records in 1895. The resulting sixteen-volume collection (the volumes dealing with the period 1895–1989 are available to me) contains a list of the muftis of modern Egypt, starting with Hassuna al-Nawawi, who was appointed on November 24, 1895 (see Dar al-ifta' 1980–1989, 1:33–35).
4. The hadith reads as follows: "God does not extract knowledge forcefully from people's hearts, but rather he extracts knowledge through the ʿulama'. Thus when there is no *ʿālim* left, the people will take for leaders ignorant people who will be asked [questions] and will answer without knowing. In this manner, they themselves will go astray and they will lead others astray."
5. The *muḍāraba* (designated *qirāḍ* by the Malikis and the Shafiʿis) is variously translated as "commenda," "partnership for profit and loss," and "trust financing." It has been defined by Muhammad Baqir al-Sadr (Sadr 1969:25) as "a nominate contract between the owner of capital [lender, *muḍārib*] and the investor-entrepreneur [borrower, *mustathmir*] to establish a trade [or enterprise] with the former's capital and the latter's labor, whereby they specify the share of each in the profit on a percentage basis. If the enterprise is profitable, they share the profit according to the agreed percentage; if the capital remains as it was, the owner of the capital receives his capital back, and the laborer gets nothing. If the enterprise incurs a loss and the capital is diminished, only the owner of the capital bears the loss" (for additional references see Mallat 1993:225, n. 26).
6. It is interesting to note that Tantawi subsequently referred to his fatwa on the subject of capitalization as his most famous fatwa (see the interview in *al-Shirā'*, Summer 1992).
7. I met Mufti Tantawi on February 9, 1993, on the occasion of his visit to the School of Oriental and African Studies, where, in a roundtable discussion, he repeated the main conclusions reached in his 1989 fatwa.

27. Operation Desert Storm and the War of Fatwas

1. The Egyptian author Khalid Muhammad Khalid, who had renounced his earlier secularist writings and espoused Islamist ideas on the relationship of religion and state, issued an opinion that was perceived as ignoring "the Crusader component" of the international coalition against Iraq and relegating to the arena of human relations the conflict over whether or not it was legitimate to seek aid from Western sources. He used images that mixed Islamic and Christian ideas about brotherhood, forgiveness, and religious pluralism. He wrote, "Greetings and thank you, O men. All of you—Arabs, Muslims, Americans, and Europeans—today carry the responsibility of liberation and securing peace. I do not know of a more noble, just, great, or lofty cause in our modern age. You are surrogates for all humanity in controlling the capacity for life, truth, freedom, goodness, and peace. Behold how great you are, as you strive to realize great hopes while suffering great pain. As for death, say to it: 'Wel-

come to death if the appointed time has come,' and say to God when he calls you to meet him, 'Greetings to a lover who has come with great yearning'" (Khalifa 1991:55).

2. The conference convened by Saudi Arabia also took note that the Iraqi invasion distracted Muslims from "their primary problems that threaten their destiny, at the forefront of which is the Masjid al-Aqsa, Jerusalem, Palestine, Afghanistan, Kashmir, and the persecution of Muslim minorities throughout the world" ("al-Mu'tamar" 1990:9).

28. Media Muftis

1. Lerner was also far off the mark in his historical understanding of the place of written texts in the Ottoman context. For example, he states (1958:113) that "oral communication was the rule under the Ottoman dispensation," and that the Ottoman elite was "*anti*-literate" (emphasis added). Part of the confusion here centers on the well-known negative attitude that existed early on in the empire toward printed texts.
2. Among the Shafiʿis, *Fatāwī al-Hubayshī* (Brockelmann 1937–1942, 2:442; al-Hubayshi ms. 1353); among the Zaydis, Shawkanī's *al-Fatḥ al-rabbānī fī fatāwī al-Shawkānī* (Brockelmann 1937–1942, 2:819). See also Maktari 1971 on the relation between Shafiʿi fatwas and water law in South Yemen.
3. For a discussion of the post-Revolution legislative continuity in the shariʿa-based legal system, see Messick 1993:68–72. Beyond the sphere of state control and within it as well, to a certain extent, tribal and other forms of customary law played an important role. See Dresch 1989; Messick 1993:182–186.
4. Well-known commentaries on al-Nawawi's *Minhāj al-ṭālibīn* are those of Ibn Hajar and al-Ramli, and on the *al-Mukhtaṣar* of Abu Shujaʿ, that of al-Ghazzi; on Ibn Raslan's *Zubād,* there was a local commentary by a nineteenth-century scholar from Ibb, al-Mufti (1988).
5. For further discussion of the relationship of the Shafiʿi and Zaydi schools in Yemen, see Messick 1993.
6. Outside of his salaried work as mufti (the fatwas were free to his questioners), he also wrote "wound evaluations," or *arsh* documents. Al-Wahhabi earned additional income writing legal instruments such as contracts and wills; preparing claims, counterclaims, and appeals for his clients to present in shariʿa court; and working to settle disputes as a mediator or arbitrator. For other examples of his fatwas and an autobiographical sketch including mention of his teachers, see Messick 1993:139, 297 n. 3.
7. His current title is *al-muftī al-ʿāmm liʾl-jumhūriyya al-yamaniyya.* During my visit, Zabara wrote a brief autobiography, which mentions his studies with specific teachers, among them, "al-Qadi ʿAbd al-Wahhab al-Shamahi, al-Qadi Husayn al-ʿAmri, shaykh al-Islam ʿAli al-Yamani, and my father the historian." The mufti also wrote that he was given licenses by these scholars and by Imams Yahya and Ahmad. After the Revolution, in addition to his appointment as mufti in Sanʿaʾ, he taught fiqh and inheritance at the University of Sanʿaʾ.

Biographies of both the father, Muhammad b. Muhammad Zabara, the famous historian, and the mufti, including details on his teachers and books studied, are found in the father's posthumously published work, *Nuzhat al-naẓar* (1979:7–15, 148–151), which was completed and edited by his son and others. On Imam Yahya's school, known as al-Madrasa al-ʿIlmiyya, and on the historian Zabara, see Messick 1993:108–109, 124, 127–131.

8. According to his biographer (Zabara 1979:151), he originally was appointed by then President ʿAbd al-Rahman al-Iryani to "*manṣib al-fatwā bi-Ṣanʿāʾ* (the position of fatwa [giver] in Sanʿaʾ."
9. The center of the seal contains the legend, "*Dār al-iftāʾ*," written across the blank pages of an open book; around the edge of the seal are written "*wizārat al-ʿadl*" (Ministry of Justice) and "*al-jumhūriyya al-yamaniyya*" (Republic of Yemen). The mufti also has bilingual official stationery, which renders Dār al-iftaʾ as "Casuistry House," and al-Mufti al-ʿAmm as "The Grand Mufti."
10. Zabara also has appeared on occasional television broadcasts, where he received, and responded orally to, unrehearsed questions.
11. See al-ʿAmrani's study *Niẓām al-qaḍāʾ fī al-islām* (1983); on the back cover is a biography of the author that mentions his fourteen years of service as a broadcast mufti.
12. Two commentaries on the *Kafīl* were printed at Imam Yahya's press in Sanʿaʾ (Rossi 1938:571–578) and were studied at al-Madrasa al-ʿIlmiyya (al-Akwaʿ 1980:288–289). On the rise of print culture in Yemen, see Messick 1993:115–131. The *Kafīl* was reprinted in Sanʿaʾ as recently as 1991.
13. This formulation may be influenced by the distinction made by Ibn Taymiyya (whom al-Ghurbani had read) between *kulliyyāt* (wholes) and *juzʾiyyāt* (parts). See also al-Qaradawi (1982) on *ijtihād juzʾī.*
14. Compare the development of the library of a local Jordanian preacher described in Antoun 1989:95–101.
15. Referring to his own broadcast activity, mufti Yusuf al-Qaradawi (1986:33–35) observes that more than half of his questioners are women.
16. Muhammad Khalid Masud informs me that the same issue is addressed in fatwas from Deoband.

References

Archives

National Archives of India. New Delhi. Foreign Department Foreign Correspondence.

Documents

Shaykhi Collection. 1990. Chicago. Middle East Documentation Center, University of Chicago.

Manuscripts

al-Aydinī, Muḥammad. *Fatāwā ʿĀlim Muḥammad al-Aydinī*. Süleymaniye Kutabhanesinde, no. 1038.

Dürrizade Mehmed ʿArif. "Netīcetū'l-fetāvā." Manchester. John Rylands Library, Turkish ms. no. 104.

al-Ḥubayshī. "Fatāwā al-Ḥubayshī." Vol. 2. Vatican Library. ms. Arab 1353.

Nāṣirābādī, Sayyid Dildār ʿAlī. "Ajwibat al-sā'ilīn." Calcutta. Asiatic Society Library, Curzon Collection ms. 1016.

———. "Najāt al-sā'ilīn." Lucknow. Nasiriyya Library. Fiqh Shiʿa ms. 256.

al-Subkī, Taqī al-Dīn ʿAlī b. ʿAbd al-Kāfī. "Mirāth Kashf al-ghimma fī mīrāth ahl al-dhimma." Cairo ms. Dār al-Kutub B 23317, 1.

Published Works

al-ʿAbbādī, Aḥmad b. Qāsim. n.d. *Sharḥ ʿalā sharḥ al-Maḥallī ʿalā al-waraqāt* (printed on the margin of al-Shawkānī, *Irshād al-fuḥūl*). Surabaya: Maktabat Aḥmad b. Saʿd b. Nabhān.

ʿAbbās, Iḥsān. 1979. "Ḫair ad-Dīn ar-Ramlī's Fatwas: A New Light on Life in Palestine in the Eleventh/Seventeenth Century," in U. Haarmann and P. Bachmann (eds.), *Die Islamische Welt zwischen Mittelalter und Neuzeit: Festschrift für Hans Roemer zum 65. Geburtstag.* Beirut and Wiesbaden: F. Steiner, pp. 1–19.

ʿAbbas, Muhammad Taha b. (ed.). 1937. *Risalah Penting pada Masʾalah Jilat Anjing diatas Empat-empat Madhhab.* Singapore: Ahmadiah Press.

ʿAbd al-Fattāḥ, ʿAbd al-Munṣif Maḥmūd. 1983. "Hal yajūz tashrīḥ al-juthāth liʾl-taʿlīm?" in *al-Ahrām* (April), 15:13.

ʿAbdurrahim. 1827. *Fetāvā-yi ʿAbdurrahim.* Istanbul: Imperial Press.

Abū al-Ajfān, Muḥammad. 1985. "Introduction," in *Fatāwā al-Imām al-Shāṭibī.* Tunis: Abū al-Ajfān.

Abū Jayb, Saʿdī. 1982. *al-Qāmūs al-fiqhī: lughatan wa-iṣṭilāḥan.* Damascus: Dār al-Fikr.

Abu-Lughod, Janet L. 1971. *Cairo: 1001 Years of the City Victorious.* Princeton: Princeton University Press.

Abū Shujāʿ, al-Ḥusayn b. Aḥmad al-Iṣfahānī. 1955. *Matn al-ghāya waʾl-taqrīb al-maʿrūf bi-ghāyat al-ikhtiṣār fī fiqh al-Shāfiʿī.* 3rd impression. Egypt: n.p.

Abū Zahra, Muḥammad. n.d. *Taḥrīm al-ribā tanẓīm iqtiṣād.* N.p.: Dār al-Saʿūdiyya.

Aghnides, Nicholas P. 1961. *Mohammedan Theories of Finance with an Introduction to Mohammedan Law and a Bibliography.* Repr. Lahore: The Premier Book House.

Aguirre de Cárcer, L. F. 1991. "Sobre el ejercicio de la medicina en al-Andalus: una fetua de Ibn Sahl." *Anaquel de estudios árabes,* 2:147–162.

Ahmad, Mohiuddin. 1975. *Saiyid Ahmad Shahid: His Life and Mission.* Lucknow: Academy of Islamic Research and Publications.

Ahmad, Muhammad Bashir. 1941. *The Administration of Justice in Medieval India.* Sulaiman Research Series, no. 1. Allahabad: The Aligarh Historical Institute.

Ahmad Khan, Muʿin-ud-Din. 1965. *A History of the Faraʾiḍī Movement in Bengal (1818–1906).* Karachi: Pakistan Historical Society.

Ahmad Riza Khan. 1985. *Ḥusām al-ḥaramayn ʿalā manḥar al-kufr waʾl mayn.* Lahore: Maktaba Nabawwiyya (originally written in 1906).

———. n.d.(a). *Iʿtiqād al-aḥbāb fiʾl jamīl waʾl muṣṭafā waʾl aṣḥāb.* Lahore: Hamid and Company Printers (originally written in 1880–1881).

———. n.d.(b). *Malfūẓāt-e aʿlā hazrat.* 4 vols. Gujarat, Pakistan: Fazl-e Nur Academy.

Ahmed, K. N. 1972. *The Muslim Law of Divorce.* Islamabad: Islamic Research Institute.

al-Akwaʿ, Ismāʿīl b. ʿAlī. 1980. *al-Madāris al-islāmiyya fiʾl-yaman.* Damascus: Dār al-Fikr.

Āl al-Shaykh, Muḥammad b. Ibrāhīm. 1979. *Fatwā fī ḥukm shurb al-dukhān.* Cairo: n.p.

Ali, Maulana Muhammad. 1977. *A Manual of Hadith.* New York: Olive Branch Press.

ʿAlī Mubārak, Bāshā. 1304–1306/1886–1889. *al-Khiṭaṭ al-tawfīqiyya al-jadīda.* 20 vols. in 4. Būlāq: al-Maṭbaʿa al-Kubrā al-Amīriyya.

Amanat, Abbas. 1989. *Resurrection and Renewal: The Making of the Babi Movement in Iran, 1844–1850*. Ithaca: Cornell University Press.

al-Āmidī, Sayf al-Dīn. 1968. *al-Iḥkām fī uṣūl al-aḥkām*. 3 vols. Cairo: Maṭbaʿat Muḥammad ʿAlī Ṣubayḥ.

al-ʿĀmilī, Zayn al-Dīn b. ʿAlī (known as al-Shahīd al-Thānī). 1988–1989. *Munyat al-murīd fī adab al-mufīd wa'l-mustafīd*. Ed. Riḍā al-Mukhtārī. Tehran: Maktab al-Iʿlām al-Islāmī.

al-ʿAmrānī, Muḥammad Ismāʿīl. 1984. *Niẓām al-qaḍā' fī al-islām*. Ṣanʿa': Maktabat Dār al-Jīl.

Anderson, Benedict. 1983. *Imagined Communities: Reflections on the Origin and Spread of Nationalism*. Rev. ed. 1991. London: Verso.

Anderson, J. N. (Norman) D. 1953. "A Draft Code of Personal Status in Iraq." *Bulletin of the School of Oriental and African Studies*, 15:43–60.

———. 1970. *Islamic Law in Africa*. 2nd ed. London: Frank Cass.

———. 1976. *Law Reform in the Muslim World*. London: Athlone Press.

Anderson, Lisa. 1983. "Qaddafi's Islam," in John L. Esposito (ed.), *Voices of Resurgent Islam*. New York: Oxford University Press, pp. 134–149.

Ando, Shiro. 1995. "The *Shaykh al-Islām* as a Timurid Office." *Islamic Studies*.

Anjuman-i Taraqqi-yi Urdu. 1961. *Qāmusu'l-kutub urdu*, vol. 1, *Mazhabiyaat*. Ed. Dr. Maulawi ʿAbdu'l-Haqq. Karachi: Anjuman.

al-Anqirāwī, Muḥammad b. Ḥusayn. 1281/1864. *Fatāwā*. 2 vols. Istanbul: n.p.

Ansari, A. S. Bazmee. 1965. "al-Fatāwā al-ʿĀlamgīriyya," in *The Encyclopaedia of Islam*. 2nd ed. Leiden: E. J. Brill.

Anṣārī, Muḥammad b. Niẓām al-Dīn. 1904. *Fawātiḥ al-raḥamūt*. 2 vols. Cairo: al-Maṭbaʿa al-Amīriyya.

Antoun, Richard T. 1989. *Muslim Preacher in the Modern World: A Jordanian Study in Comparative Perspective*. Princeton: Princeton University Press.

Anwar, H. Rosihan. 1985. "Prof. Dr. H. M. Rasjidi Pengungkap Gamblang Hubungan Antar Agama di Indonesia," in Panitya (ed.), *70 tahun Prof. Dr. H. M. Rasjidi*. Jakarta: Harian Umum Pelita.

Appignanesi, Lisa, and Sara Maitland (eds.). 1990. *The Rushdie File*. Syracuse: Syracuse University Press.

Arberry, Arthur J. 1955. *The Koran Interpreted*. New York: Macmillan.

Arjomand, Saʿid A. 1988. *The Turban for the Crown: The Islamic Revolution in Iran*. New York: Oxford University Press.

Asad, Talal. 1990. "Ethnography, Literature, and Politics: Some Readings and Uses of Salman Rushdie's *The Satanic Verses*," *Cultural Anthropology*, 5(3):239–269.

Ates, A. 1971. "Ibn al-ʿArabī," in *The Encyclopaedia of Islam*. 2nd. ed. Leiden: E. J. Brill.

ʿAwda, ʿAbd al-Qādir. 1960. *al-Tashrīʿ al-jinā'ī al-Islāmī*. 2 vols. Cairo: Dār al-ʿArūba.

ʿAyyāshī, Abū Sālim. 1316/1898. *Riḥlat al-shaykh Abī Sālim al-ʿAyyāshī*. Fez: Dār al-Ṭibāʿa.

Aʿzami, Mohammad Mustafa. 1978. *Studies in Early Ḥadīth Literature, with a Critical Edition of Some Early Texts*. 2nd ed. Indianapolis: American Trust Publications.

el-Azemmouri, Thami. 1973. "Les *Nawāzil* d'Ibn Sahl: section relative à l'*Iḥtisāb*" (part 1: introduction and Arabic text, with a presentation by M. Claude Cahen). *Hespéris Tamuda,* 14:7–107.

al-Azhar. 1980–1988. *al-Fatāwā al-Islāmiyya.* 13 vols. Cairo: al-Majlis al-Aʿlā li'l-Shu'ūn al-Islāmiyya, Wizārat al-Awqāf.

Azhar, Zahur Ahmad. 1975. "al-Fatāwā," in *Urdū Dā'ira Maʿārif Islāmiyya* (Urdu Encyclopaedia of Islam). Lahore: Panjab University, vol. 15, pp. 139–145.

al-ʿAẓīmābādī, Muḥammad. 1968–1969. *ʿAwn al-maʿbūd: sharḥ sunan Abī Dā'ūd.* 14 vols. 2nd ed. al-Madīna al-Munawwara: al-Maktaba al-Salafiyya.

Bābā, Aḥmad b. Aḥmad al-Tumbuktī. 1932. *Kitāb nayl al-ibtihāj bi-taṭrīz al-dībāj.* Cairo: n.p.

Badan Penelitian dan Pengembangan Agama, Departemen Agama R.I. 1982–1983. *Statistik Keagamaan 1981.* Jakarta: Pusat Dokumentasi dan Informasi Agama.

Badawī, Ibrāhīm Zakī. 1939. "Naẓariyyat al-ribā al-muḥarram." *Majallat al-Qānūn wa'l-Iqtiṣād,* 9:387–447; 533–566.

———. 1964. *Naẓariyyat al-ribā al-muḥarram.* Cairo: al-Majlis al-Aʿlā li-Riʿāyat al-Funūn.

Baedeker, Karl. 1929. *Egypt and the Sudan: Handbook for Travellers.* 8th rev. ed. Leipzig: Baedeker.

al-Baghdādī, Abū Muḥammad. 1308/1892. *Majmaʿ al-ḍamānāt.* Cairo: al-Maṭbaʿa al-Khayriyya.

Baghdādlı, Ismāʿīl b. Muḥammad. 1948. *Īḍāḥ al-maknūn fī dhayl ʿalā Kashf al-Ẓunūn ʿan asāmī al-kutub wa'l-funūn.* Ed. Rifʿat al-Kilīsī. 2 vols. Istanbul: al-Bahiyyah.

———. 1951. *Hidāyat al-ʿārifīn.* 2 vols. Istanbul: al-Bahiyyah.

Bāhunar, Muḥammad Jaʿfar, et al. 1981. *Taʿlimāt-i dīnī* (Religious Education). Tehran: Davarpanah Press for the Ministry of Education.

al-Bahūtī, Manṣūr b. Yūnus b. Ṣalāḥ al-Dīn b. Idrīs (d. 1641). 1982. *Kashf al-qināʿ ʿan matn al-iqnāʿ.* Ed. Hilāl Muṣaylihī Muṣṭafā Hilāl. 6 vols. Beirut: Dār al-Fikr.

———. n.d. *Sharḥ muntahā al-irādāt.* 3 vols. Beirut: Dār al-Fikr.

al-Bājī, Abū al-Walīd. 1986. *Iḥkām al-fuṣūl fī aḥkām al-uṣūl.* Ed. ʿAbd al-Majīd Turkī. 2 vols. Beirut: Dār al-Gharb al-Islāmī.

Bakhīt, Muḥammad. 1935. "Fī tashrīḥ al-mayyit," in *Majallat al-azhar* 6:627–633.

Baljon, Johannes M. S. 1991. "Indian Muftis and the Non-Muslims," *Islam and Christian Muslim Relations* 2(2):227–241.

al-Bannānī, al-ʿAllāma. 1970. *Ḥāshiya ʿalā jamʿ al-jawāmiʿ* (printed with al-Maḥallī, *Sharḥ*). 2 vols. Bombay: Molvi Mohammed Bin Gulamrasul Surtis & Sons.

Baranī, Zia ud-Din. 1972. *Fatāwā-i Jahāndārī* (Rulings on Temporal Government). Ed. Dr. Afsar Saleem Khan. Lahore: Research Society of Pakistan, University of Panjab.

Baron, Salo Wittmayer. 1980. *Social and Religious History of the Jews,* vol. 17, *Byzantines, Mamelukes and Maghribians.* 2nd ed. New York: Columbia University Press.

al-Baṣrī, Abū al-Ḥusayn Muḥammad b. ʿAlī. 1964–1965. *Kitāb al-muʿtamad fī uṣūl al-fiqh.* Ed. M. Hamidullah et al. 2 vols. (vol. 1, 1964; vol. 2, 1965). Damas: Institut français de Damas.

Basri, Hasan. 1978. "Dialog Ramadan," in Panitya (ed.), *Kenang-kenangan 70 Tahun Buya Hamka*. Jakarta: Yayasan Nurul Islam.

Bāstāni Parizi, Muhammad. 1358/1979. *Ḥamāsa-'i Kavir.* Tehran: Amir Kabir.

Bausani, Alessandro. 1959. *Persia Religiosa*. Milan: Saggiatore.

Bayat, Mangol. 1982. *Mysticism and Dissent: Socioreligious Thought in Qajar Iran.* Syracuse: Syracuse University Press.

al-Bayḍāwī, ʿAbd Allāh b. ʿUmar. 1899. *Minhāj al-wuṣūl ilā ʿilm al-uṣūl* (printed on the margin of Ibn Amīr al-Ḥājj, *Taqrīr*). 3 vols. Būlāq: al-Maṭbaʿa al-Kubrā al-Amīriyya.

al-Bayhaqī, Abū Bakr Aḥmad. 1968. *al-Sunan al-kubrā*. 10 vols. Beirut: Dār Ṣādir.

Bayly, C. A. 1983. *Rulers, Townsmen and Bazaars: North Indian Society in the Age of British Expansion, 1770–1780*. Cambridge: Cambridge University Press.

Beeman, William O. 1986. *Language, Status, and Power in Iran*. Bloomington: Indiana University Press.

Behrens-Abouseif, Doris. 1985. *Azbakiyya and Its Environs: From Azbak to Ismāʿīl, 1476–1879*. Cairo: Institut français d'archéologie orientale.

Bellamy, J. A. 1979. "Sex and Society in Islamic Popular Literature," in Afaf Lutfi al-Sayyid-Marsot (ed.), *Society and the Sexes in Medieval Islam*, Sixth Giorgio Levi della Vida Biennial Conference. Malibu: Undena Publications.

Berkes, Niyazi. 1964. *The Development of Secularism in Turkey.* Montreal: McGill University Press.

Berkey, Jonathan P. 1992. *The Transmission of Knowledge in Medieval Cairo: A Social History of Islamic Education*. Princeton: Princeton University Press.

Berque, Jacques. 1940. *Les Nawâzil el muzâraʿa du Miʿyâr Al Wazzânî: étude et traduction*. Rabat: Éditions Felix Moncho.

———. 1960. "ʿAmal," in *The Encyclopaedia of Islam*. 2nd ed. Leiden: E. J. Brill.

Beyer, Ursala (ed.). 1983. *Kairo: die Mutter aller Städte*. Frankfurt am Main: Insel Verlag.

Bhatnagar, Gaurishwar Dayal. 1968. *Lucknow under Wajid ʿAli Shah*. Varanasi: Bharatiya Vidya Prakashan.

Bhattī, Muḥammad Isḥāq. 1973. *Barr-i Ṣaghīr Pāk-o-Hind mën ʿIlm-i Fiqh*. Lahore: Idāra Thaqāfat-i-Islāmiyya.

Bīāzār-i Shīrāzī, ʿAbdul Karīm. 1987. *Masāʾil-i khānivādih: tarjumah-i bakhshhāʾi az taḥrīr al-vasīla* (Family Issues: Translation of Sections of *Taḥrīr al-Vasīla*). Tehran: Daftar-i Nashr-i Farhang-i Islamī.

Bihishtī, Muḥammad H. ca. 1980. *Shinākht-i islām* (Knowing Islam). Tehran: Daftar-i Farhangī-yi Islām.

Black, Henry Campbell. 1990. *Black's Law Dictionary.* 6th ed. St. Paul: West Publishing Co.

Blochmann, H. (ed., trans.). 1939. "Translator's Note on the *Ṣadr* of Akbar's Reign," in Abū al-Faḍl b. Mubārak, *Āʾīn-i Akbarī.* Vol. 1. Calcutta: Royal Asiatic Society of Bengal.

Board of Senior ʿUlamāʾ. 1977a. "Ḥukm al-ṭalāq al-thalāth bi-lafẓ wāḥid." *Majallat al-Buḥūth al-Islāmiyya* 1(3):27–173.

———. 1977b. "Ḥukm al-nushūz wa'l-khulʿ." *Majallat al-Buḥūth al-Islāmiyya* 1(3): 177–225.

———. 1980. "al-Ṭalāq al-muʿallaq." *Majallat al-Buḥūth al-Islāmiyya* 2(1):51–94.

Bobakāni, Makhdūm Muḥammad Jaʿfar. 1962. *al-Matāna fī maramma al-khazāna.* Karachi: Iḥyā al-Adab al-Sindī.

Boland, B. J. 1982. *The Struggle of Islam in Modern Indonesia.* The Hague: Martinus Nijhoff (slightly revised reprint).

Borujirdī, Ayatullāh Ḥusayn (d. 1961). n.d. *Risāla-i Ayatullāh Borujirdī.* Tehran: Jāvidān.

Bouhdiba, Abdelwahab. 1975. *La sexualité en Islam.* Paris: Presses universitaires de France.

Bousquet, Georges-Henri. 1966. *L'éthique sexuelle de l'Islam.* Paris: G. P. Maisonneuve.

Broadley, A. M. [Alexander Meyrick]. 1980. *How We Defended Arabi and His Friends.* Repr. Cairo: Research and Publishing Arab Centre *(sic).*

Brockelmann, Carl. 1943–1949. *Geschichte der arabischen Litteratur.* Rev. ed. 2 vols. Leiden: E. J. Brill. 1937–1942, 3 supplement vols., Leiden: E. J. Brill.

Browne, Edward G. 1893. *A Year among the Persians.* London: A. and C. Black.

———. 1928. *A Literary History of Persia.* Cambridge: Cambridge University Press.

Brunschvig, Robert. 1940–1947. *La Berbérie orientale sous les Ḥafṣides: Des origines à la fin du XVe siècle.* 2 vols. Paris: Adrien-Maisonneuve.

———. 1970. "Logic and Law in Classical Islam," in G. E. von Grunebaum (ed.), *Logic in Classical Islamic Culture.* Wiesbaden: Otto Harrassowitz.

Bukhārī, M. Fārūq. 1990. "Muftī Ṣadr al-Dīn Khān Āzurda Dehlawī awr unkā Risāla 'al-Durr al-manḍūd fī ḥukm imraʾat al-mafqūd.'" *Maʿārif,* 145:46–57.

al-Bukhārī, Muḥammad b. Ismāʿīl. 1862–1898. *Ṣaḥīḥ.* Ed. M. Ludolf Krehl and Th. W. Juynboll. 4 vols. Leiden: E. J. Brill.

———. 1928. *Ṣaḥīḥ.* 9 vols. Cairo: Idārat al-Ṭibāʿa al-Munīriyya.

———. n.d. *Ṣaḥīḥ.* 7 vols. in 3. Cairo: Dār al-Shaʿb.

al-Bukhārī, ʿUmar b. ʿAbd al-ʿAzīz b. Māza (known as al-Ṣadr al-Shahīd). 1977. *Kitāb sharḥ adab al-qāḍī li'l-Khaṣṣāf.* Baghdad: Wizārat al-Awqāf.

Butter, Donald. 1839. *Outlines of the Topography and Statistics of the Southern Districts of Oud'h and of the Cantonment of Sultanpur-Oud'h.* Calcutta: Bengal Military Orphan Press.

Cahen, Cl[aude]. 1960. "Bayt al-Māl, II: History," in *The Encyclopaedia of Isam.* 2nd ed. Leiden: E. J. Brill.

Calder, Norman. 1993. *Studies in Early Muslim Jurisprudence.* Oxford: Clarendon Press.

Calmard, J. 1991a. "Mard̲j̲aʿ-i taqlīd," in *The Encyclopaedia of Islam.* 2nd ed. Leiden: E. J. Brill.

———. 1991b. "Mud̲j̲tahid," in *The Encyclopaedia of Islam.* 2nd ed. Leiden: E. J. Brill.

Castro, Francisco Vidal. 1990. "Aproximación al Estudio Bio-Bibliografico de al Wansharīsī (834–914/1430–1508)." Granada: Memoria de Licenciatura.

———. 1991. "Aḥmad al-Wanšarīsī (m. 914/1508): Principales aspectos de su vida." *al-Qanṭara,* 12:315–362.

Caton, Steven C. 1990. *"Peaks of Yemen I Summon:" Poetry as Cultural Practice in a North Yemeni Tribe.* Berkeley: University of California Press.

Chehata, Chafik. 1973. *Études de droit musulman.* 2 vols. Paris: Presses Universitaires de France.

Chelhod, J. 1971a. "Kaffāra," in *The Encyclopaedia of Isam.* 2nd ed. Leiden: E. J. Brill, vol. 4, pp. 406–407.

———. 1971b. "Hady," in *The Encyclopaedia of Isam.* 2nd ed. Leiden: E. J. Brill, vol. 3, pp. 53–54.

Cole, Juan R. I. 1985. "Shiʿi Clerics in Iraq and Iran, 1722–1780: The Akhbari-Usuli Conflict Reconsidered." *Iranian Studies,* 18(1):3–34.

———. 1988. *Roots of North Indian Shiʿism in Iran and Iraq: Religion and State in Awadh, 1722–1859.* Berkeley: University of California Press

Corbin, Henry. 1960. *Terre celeste et corps de résurrection: De l'Iran Mazdéen a l'Iran shiʿite.* Paris: Buchel/Chastel.

———. 1972. *En Islam Iranien, aspects spirituels et philosophiques.* Vol. 4. Paris: Gallimard.

Coulson, Noel J. 1960. "Bayt al-māl, I: The Legal Doctrine," in *The Encyclopaedia of Islam.* 2nd ed. Leiden. E. J. Brill.

———. 1979. "Regulation of Sexual Behaviour under Traditional Islamic Law," in Afaf Lutfi al-Sayyid-Marsot (ed.), *Society and the Sexes in Medieval Islam,* Sixth Giorgio Levi della Vida Biennial Conference. Malibu: Undena Publications.

Crecelius, Daniel. 1966. "al-Azhar in the Revolution." *Middle East Journal,* 20(1):31–49.

Cuq, Edouard. 1963. "Prudentium Responsa," in *Dictionnaire des Antiquités.* Ed. C. Daremberg and E. Saglio. Graz, Austria: Akademische Druke, vol. 4, pp. 740–741.

Daga Portillo, R. 1987. "Aproximación a la obra *al-Aḥkām al-kubrā* del cadí ʿĪsà b. Sahl." *Miscelánea de Estudios Arabes y Hebraicos,* 36:237–249.

Dajāwī, Yūsuf. 1935. "Muʿāmalāt al-tujjār wa-mā fīhā min al-ribā." *Nūr al-islam,* 3:324–328.

Danish, Sabbar. 1978. "Hazrat Mufti Aʿzam ki Fiqhi Khidmat awr Fatwa men Ap ka maslak o mashrab" (Mufti Muhammad Shafiʿi's Contribution to Islamic Law and His Fatwa Methodology). *al-Balagh* (special issue), 13:706–787.

Dār al-iftāʾ. 1980–1989. *al-Fatāwā al-islāmiyya.* Cairo: Ministry of Awqāf.

De Gaury, Gerald. 1951. *Rulers of Mecca.* London: George Harrap and Co.

De Gobinau, A. 1866. *Les Religions et les philosophies dans l'Asie centrale.* Paris: n.p.

Delanoue, Gilbert. 1982. *Moralistes et politiques musulmans dans l'Égypte du XIXe siècle (1798–1882).* Cairo: Institut français d'archéologie orientale.

Departemen Agama. 1987. *Amal Bhakti Departemen Agama RI: Eksistensi dan Derap Langkahnya.* Jakarta: Badan Litbang Agama.

Departemen Penerangan R.I. 1985. *10 Tahun MUI.* Jakarta: Ministry of Information.

Depont, O., and X. Coppolani. 1897. *Les Confréries religieuses musulmanes.* Algiers: Adolphe Jourdan.

al-Dimashqī, Ibn ʿAbd al-Raḥmān. 1960. *Raḥmat al-umma fī ikhtilāf al-aʾimma.* Cairo: Maṭbaʿat Muṣṭafā al-Bābī al-Ḥalabī.

Ditmanson, Harald H. 1990. *Stepping Stones to Further Jewish-Lutheran Relationships: Key Lutheran Statements.* Minneapolis: Augsburg Fortress.

Dozy, R. 1967. *Supplément aux dictionnaires arabes.* 3rd ed. Leiden: E. J. Brill.

Dresch, Paul. 1989. *Tribes, Government, and History in Yemen.* Oxford: Clarendon Press.

Ebeling, Adolf. 1878. *Bilder aus Kairo.* Stuttgart: Levy and Müller.

Eccel, A. Chris. 1984. *Egypt: Islam and Social Change.* Berlin: Klaus Schwarz.

Eickelman, Dale F. 1978. "The Art of Memory: Islamic Education and Its Social Reproduction." *Comparative Studies in Society and History,* 20(4):485–516.

———. 1985. *Knowledge and Power in Morocco.* Princeton: Princeton University Press.

———. 1989. "National Identity and Religious Discourse in Contemporary Oman." *International Journal of Islamic and Arabic Studies,* 6(1):1–20.

———. 1992. "Mass Higher Education and the Religious Imagination in Contemporary Arab Societies." *American Ethnologist,* 19(4):643–655.

Elst, Koenraad. 1990. *Ram Janmabhoomi vs. Babri Masjid: A Case Study in Hindu-Muslim Conflict.* New Delhi: Voice of India.

The Encyclopaedia of Islam: A Dictionary of the Geography, Ethnography and Biography of the Muhammaden Peoples. 1913–1938. Leiden: E. J. Brill.

The Encyclopaedia of Islam. 2nd ed. 1954–. Leiden: E. J. Brill.

Engineer, Asaf Ali (ed.). 1987. *The Shah Bano Controversy.* Bombay: Orient Longman.

Evans-Pritchard, E. E. 1954. *The Sanusi of Cyrenaica.* Oxford: Clarendon.

Fabian, Johannes. 1991. *Language and Colonial Power: The Appropriation of Swahili in the Former Belgian Congo, 1880–1938.* 2nd ed. Berkeley: University of California Press.

Fagnan, E. 1923. *Additions aux dictionnaires arabes.* Alger: Bastide-Jourdan.

Fahd, Toufic, and M. Ḥammoudi. 1975. "L'enfant dans le droit islamique." *Recueils de la société Jean Bodin pour l'histoire comparative des institutions,* 35:287–346.

Farangī Maḥallī, ʿAbd al-Ḥayy. n.d. *Majmūʿat al-fatāwā.* Urdu translation, Lahore: Shahzad Publishers. 1330/1911, 3 vols., Lucknow: Yūsufī Press. 1345/1926, 3 vols. in 1, Kānpūr: Maṭbaʿ Qayyūmī.

al-Fatāwā al-ʿĀlamgīriyya al-maʿrūfa biʾl-fatāwā al-hindiyya. 1892–1893. 6 vols. Quetta: Maktaba Rāshidiyya.

al-Fatāwā al-ʿĀlamgīriyya al-maʿrūfa biʾl-fatāwā al-hindiyya. 1983. 6 vols. Quetta: Maktaba Mājidiyya Rashīdiyya. Reprint of 1311/1893, Cairo: Khadīviyya.

Fatāwā hayʾat kibār al-ʿulamāʾ biʾl-mamlaka al-ʿarabiyya al-Saʿūdiyya. 1988. Ed. Ṣafūt al-Shawādfī. Balbīs, Egypt: Dār al-Taqwā.

Fattal, Antoine. 1958. *Le Statut légal des non-musulmans en pays d'Islam.* Beirut: Imprimerie Catholique.

Federal Shariʿat Court of Pakistan. 1992. *Judgment on Interest (Riba).* Lahore: Lawyers' Book Club.

Feldman, Egal. 1990. *Dual Destinies: The Jewish Encounter with Protestant America.* Urbana: University of Illinois Press.

Fierro, Maria Isabel. 1985. "Los mālikíes de al-Andalus y los dos árbitros *(al-ḥakamān).*" *Al-Qanṭara,* 6:79–102.

———. 1987. *La heterodoxia en al-Andalus durante el periodo omeya.* Madrid: Consejo Superior de Investigaciones Cientificas.

———. 1989a. "The Introduction of *Ḥadīth* in al-Andalus." *Der Islam,* 66:68–93.

———. 1989b. "Sobre la adopción del título califal por ʿAbd al-Raḥmān III." *Sharq al-Andalus,* 6:33–42.

———. 1991. "El derecho mālikī en al-Andalus: Ss. II/VIII–V/XI." *Al-Qanṭara,* 12: 119–31.

———. 1992a. "Heresy in al-Andalus," in *The Legacy of Muslim Spain.* Ed. Salma Khadra Jayyusi. Leiden: E. J. Brill, pp. 895–908.

———. 1992b. "Tres familias andalusíes de época omeya apodadas Banû Ziyād." *Estudios Onomástico-Biográficos de al-Andalus,* 5: 85–141.

Finkelstein, Louis. 1983. *Sifra on Leviticus.* New York: Jewish Theological Seminary of America.

Fischer, Michael M. J. 1980. *Iran: From Religious Dispute to Revolution.* Cambridge: Harvard University Press.

Fischer, Michael M. J., and Mehdi Abedi. 1990. *Debating Muslims: Cultural Dialogues in Postmodernity and Tradition.* Madison: University of Wisconsin Press.

Fisher, Michael H. 1987. *Clash between Cultures.* Riverdale, Md.: Riverdale Co.

Friedmann, Yohanan. 1989. *Prophecy Continuous: Aspects of Ahmadi Religious Thought and Its Medieval Background.* Berkeley: University of California Press.

Fyzee, Asaf A. A. 1960. *Outlines of Muhammadan Law.* London: Oxford University Press.

———. 1963. "Muhammadan Law in India." *Comparative Studies in Society and History,* 5(4):401–415.

Gardet, L. 1971. "Īmān," in *The Encyclopaedia of Islam.* 2nd. ed. Leiden: E. J. Brill.

al-Ghazzālī, Abū Ḥāmid Muḥammad. 1904. *al-Mustaṣfā min ʿilm al-uṣūl.* 2 vols. Būlāq: al-Maṭbaʿa al-Amīriyya; repr. 1970, Baghdad: Muthannā.

———. 1980. *al-Mankhūl min taʿlīqat al-uṣūl.* Ed. Muḥammad Ḥasan Haytū. Damascus: Dār al-Fikr.

al-Ghazzī, Muḥammad b. Qāsim. 1346/1927. *Sharḥ al-ʿallāma al-shaykh Muḥammad b. Qāsim al-Ghazzī al-musammā fatḥ al-qarīb.* 2nd. ed. Cairo: Maṭbaʿat Muḥammad ʿAlī Ṣabīḥ.

Gibb, H. A. R., and H. Bowen. 1950 and 1957. *Islamic Society and the West.* Vol. 1 (part 1, 1950; part 2, 1957). Oxford: Oxford University Press.

Gilmartin, David. 1991. "Democracy, Nationalism and the Public: A Speculation on Colonial Muslim Politics." *South Asia,* 14(1): 141–154.

Goitein, S. D. 1971–1988. *A Mediterranean Society.* 5 vols. and index. Berkeley: University of California Press.

Goldziher, Ignaz. 1967–1971. *Muslim Studies.* Ed. S. M. Stern, trans. C. R. Barber and S. M. Stern. 2 vols. London: Allen and Unwin; Chicago: Aldine-Atherton.

Graham, William A. 1993. "Traditionalism in Islam: An Essay in Interpretation." *Journal of Interdisciplinary History,* 23:495–522.

Haddad, Yvonne Y. 1983. "Sayyid Qutb: Ideologue of Islamic Revival," in John L. Esposito (ed.), *Voices of Resurgent Islam.* New York: Oxford, pp. 67–98.

Haeri, Shahla. 1989. *Law of Desire: Temporary Marriage in Shiʿi Iran.* Syracuse: Syracuse University Press.

———. 1992. "Temporary Marriage and the State in Iran: An Islamic Discourse on Female Sexuality." *Social Research,* 59(1).

Ha'iri, Abd al-Hadi. 1977. *Shīʿism and Constitutionalism in Iran: A Study of the Role Played by Persian Residents of Iraq in Iranian Politics.* Leiden: E. J. Brill.

Ḥajjī Khalīfa. 1941–1955. *Kashf al-ẓunūn ʿan asāmī al-kutub wa'l-funūn.* 7 vols. Istanbul: Maarif Matbaasi.

Hallaq, Wael B. 1984. "Was the Gate of Ijtihad Closed?" *International Journal of Middle East Studies,* 16(1):3–41.

———. 1989. "Non-Analogical Arguments in Sunni Juridical *Qiyās.*" *Arabica,* 36(3):286–306.

———. 1990. "Logic, Formal Arguments and Formalization of Arguments in Sunnī Jurisprudence." *Arabica,* 37:315–358.

———. 1992. "*Uṣūl al-Fiqh:* Beyond Tradition." *Journal of Islamic Studies,* 3(2):172–202.

———. 1994. "From *Fatwās* to *Furūʿ*: Growth and Change in Islamic Substantive Law." *Islamic Law and Society,* 1(1):29–65.

Ḥamdān, ʿAbd al-Ḥamīd Ṣāliḥ. 1990. *Imām al-ʿulamā' Muʿādh b. Jabal.* Cairo: al-Dār al-Miṣriyya al-Lubnāniyya.

Hamka. 1982. *Ayahku.* 4th ed. Jakarta: Umminda.

Hamka, Rusjdi. 1981. *Pribadi dan Martabat Buya Hamka.* Jakarta: Pustaka Panjimas.

al-Ḥaq, Muʿīn (trans.). 1983. *Tārīkh Fīrūz Shāhī.* Lahore: Urdu Science Board.

Haram, Nissreen. Forthcoming. "Law in Practice: The Legal Method of Taqī al-Dīn al-Subkī." Ph.D. diss., McGill University.

Hardy, Peter. 1971. *Partners in Freedom—and True Muslims: The Political Thought of Some Muslim Scholars in British India, 1912–1947.* Lund, Sweden: Studentlitteratur.

———. 1972. *The Muslims of British India.* Cambridge: Cambridge University Press.

al-Ḥaṣkafī, ʿAlā' al-Dīn. 1979. *al-Durr al-mukhtār* (on the margin of Ibn ʿĀbidīn, *Radd al-Muḥtār*). Quetta: Mājidiyya. Reprint of 1321/1903, Cairo: Muṣṭafā al-Bābī.

al-Haythamī, Ibn Ḥajar. n.d. *Tuḥfat al-muḥtāj bi-sharḥ al-minhāj.* Printed with al-Shirwānī, ʿAbd al-Ḥamīd and Aḥmad b. Qāsim al-ʿAbbādī, *Ḥawāshī tuḥfat al-muḥtāj bi-sharḥ al-minhāj.* 10 vols. Cairo: Maṭbaʿat Muṣṭafā Muḥammad.

Hattox, Ralph S. 1985. *Coffee and Coffeehouses: The Origins of a Social Beverage in the Medieval Near East.* Near Eastern Studies no. 3. Seattle: University of Washington Press.

Heffening, W. 1992. "Mutʿa," in *The Encyclopaedia of Islam.* 2nd ed. Leiden: E. J. Brill.

Heyd, Uriel. 1961. "The Ottoman ʿUlema and Westernization in the Time of Selim III and Mahmud II," in *Scripta Hierosolymitana,* vol. 9. Jerusalem: The Hebrew University.

———. 1969. "Some Aspects of the Ottoman *Fetvā.*" *Bulletin of the School of Oriental and African Studies,* 32:35–56.

Ḥillī, Muḥaqqiq Najm al-Dīn Abū al-Qāsim Jaʿfar. 1968. *Sharāyʿ al-islām* (Islamic Law). Trans. from Arabic to Persian by A. Ahmad Yazdī and M. T. Dānish Pazhūh. 2 vols. Tehran: Tehran University Press.

Hopwood, Derek. 1980. "Amīn al-Ḥusaynī," in *The Encyclopaedia of Islam.* 2nd ed. Supplement. Leiden: E. J. Brill.

Houtsma, M. Th. 1961. "Aḥmadīya," in *The Shorter Encyclopaedia of Islam.* Leiden: E. J. Brill.

Howard, I. K. A. 1975. "Mutʿa Marriage Reconsidered in the Context of Formal Procedures for Islamic Marriage." *Journal of Semitic Studies* 20(1): 82–92.

Humphreys, R. Stephen. 1988. *Islamic History: A Framework for Inquiry.* Minneapolis: Bibliotheca Islamica.

———. 1991. *Islamic History: A Framework for Inquiry.* 2nd rev. ed. Princeton: Princeton University Press.

Husaini, S. A. Q. 1952. *Administration under the Mughals.* Dacca: Paradise.

Ibn ʿAbd al-Barr, Yūsuf b. ʿAbdallāh. 1968. *Jāmiʿ bayān al-ʿilm wa-faḍlihi wa-mā yanbaghī fī riwāyatihi wa-ḥamlihi.* 2 vols. in 1. Medina: al-Maktaba al-Salafiyya.

———. 1978. *al-Jāmiʿ fī bayān al-ʿilm.* 2 vols. Beirut: Dār al-Kutub al-ʿIlmiyya.

Ibn ʿAbd al-Shakūr, Muḥibb Allāh. 1904. *Musallam al-thubūt: sharḥ fawātiḥ al-raḥamūt.* 2 vols. Cairo: al-Maṭbaʿa al-Amīriyya.

Ibn ʿĀbidīn, Muḥammad Amīn. 1300/1883. *al-ʿUqūd al-durriyya fī tanqīḥ al-fatāwā al-ḥāmidiyya.* 2nd. ed. Cairo: n.p.

———. n.d. *al-ʿUqūd al-durriyya fī tanqīḥ al-fatāwā al-ḥāmidiyya.* New ed. Beirut: Dār al-Maʿrifa.

Ibn Abī Zayd al-Qayrawānī, ʿAbdallāh b. ʿAbd al-Raḥmān. 1985. *Kitāb al-Jāmiʿ fī'l-sunan wa'l-adab.* Beirut: Mu'assasat al-Risāla.

Ibn Amīr al-Ḥājj. 1899. *al-Taqrīr wa'l-taḥbīr.* 3 vols. Būlāq: al-Maṭbaʿa al-Kubrā al-Amīriyya.

Ibn Bāz, ʿAbd al-ʿAzīz b. ʿAbd Allāh. 1986a. *al-Daʿwā,* 7 Dhū al-Qaʿda 1406/July 14, 1986, p. 27.

———. 1986b. *al-Daʿwā,* 7 Rabīʿ al-Thānī 1407/December 8, 1986, pp. 26–27.

———. 1987. *al-Daʿwā,* 12 Shawwāl 1407/June 8, 1987, p. 27.

Ibn Bāz, ʿAbd al-ʿAzīz, et al. 1988. *Fatāwā islāmiyya.* 3 vols. Beirut: Dār al-Qalam.

Ibn Farḥūn, Ibrāhīm b. ʿAlī. 1351/1932. *Kitāb al-dībāj al-mudhahhab fī maʿrifat aʿyān ʿulamā' al-madhhab.* 2 vols. Cairo: Dār al-Turāth.

Ibn al-Ḥājib, Jamāl al-Dīn. 1908. *Muntahā al-wuṣūl.* Ed. Badr al-Dīn al-Naʿsānī. Cairo: Maṭbaʿat al-Saʿāda.

Ibn Hasan. 1967. *The Central Structure of the Mughal Empire and Its Practical Working up to the Year 1657.* Lahore: Oxford University Press.

Ibn al-Humām, Kamāladdīn Muḥammad b. ʿAbdalwāḥid al-Siyywāsī al-Sikandarī al-Ḥanafī. 1970. *Sharḥ fatḥ al-qadīr ʿalā al-hidāyah, sharḥ bidāyah al-mubtadā li-Burhānaddīn ʿAlī ibn Abī Bakr al-Marghīnāni* (d. 593/1197). 10 vols. Cairo: Muṣṭafā al-Bābī al-Ḥalabī wa-awlādih.

Ibn Kathīr, Ismāʿīl b. ʿUmar. 1966. *al-Bidāya wa'l-nihāya.* Beirut: Maktabat al-Maʿārif; Riyadh: Maktabat al-Nasr.

Ibn Khaldūn. 1958. *The Muqaddimah: An Introduction to History.* Trans. F. Rosenthal. 3 vols. New York: Pantheon.

Ibn Khallikān. 1972. *Wafāyāt al-aʿyān.* Ed. Iḥsān ʿAbbās. 8 vols. Beirut: Dār al-Thaqāfa.

Ibn Māja, Muḥammad b. Yazīd. 1972. *Sunan Ibn Māja.* Cairo: ʿĪsā al-Bābī al-Ḥalabī.

Ibn Manẓūr, Muḥammad b. Mukarram. 1979. *Lisān al-ʿArab.* 15 vols. Beirut: Dār Ṣādir.

Ibn Naṣr, Muḥammad. 1991. "al-Ḥaraka al-islāmiyya wa-ʿazmat al-khalīj." *al-Insān,* 1(4):73–79.

Ibn Qāsim, ʿAbd al-Raḥmān. 1965. *al-Durar al-saniyya fīʾl-ajwiba al-najdiyya.* Riyadh: Dār al-Iftāʾ.

Ibn al-Qayyim al-Jawziyya, Muḥammad b. Abī Bakr. 1969. *Iʿlām al-muwaqqiʿīn ʿan rabb al-ʿālamīn.* 4 vols. Cairo: Dār al-Kutub al-Ḥadītha.

———. 1970. *Zād al-maʿād fī hudā khayr al-ʿibād.* Ed. Ṭāhā ʿAbd al-Raʾūf Ṭāhā. 4 vols. Cairo: Muṣtafā al-Bābī al-Ḥalabī.

———. 1973. *Iʿlām al-muwaqqiʿīn ʿan rabb al-ʿālamīn.* Ed. Ṭāhā ʿAbd al-Raʾūf Saʿd. 4 vols. Beirut: Dār al-Jīl.

———. 1401/1981. 2 vols. *Aḥkām ahl al-dhimma.* Ed. Ṣubḥi al-Ṣāliḥ. 2nd ed. Beirut: Dār al-ʿIlm liʾl-Malāyīn.

Ibn Qudāma, Abū Muḥammad ʿAbd Allāh b. Aḥmad b. Muḥammad. 1983. *al-Mughnī wa-yalīhi al-sharḥ al-kabīr.* 12 vols. and 2-vol. index. Beirut: Dār al-Kitāb al-ʿArabī.

Ibn al-Qūṭīya, Muḥammad b. ʿUmar. 1926. *Taʾrīkh iftitāḥ al-Andalus.* Ed. P. de Gayangos, E. Saavedra, and F. Codera, and trans. J. Ribera. Madrid: Revista de Archivos.

Ibn Rushd (Averroes). n.d. *Bidāyat al-mujtahid wa-nihāyat al-muqtaṣid.* 2 vols. in 1. Cairo: n.p.; 1926 French trans. A. Laimèche, Algiers: n.p.

Ibn Rushd, Muḥammad b. Aḥmad. 1987. *Fatāwā Ibn Rushd.* 3 vols. Beirut: Dār al-Gharb al-Islāmī.

Ibn Saʿd, Muḥammad. 1957–1968. *al-Ṭabaqāt al-kubrā.* 9 vols. Beirut: Dār Ṣādir.

Ibn Sahl, Abū al-Aṣbagh ʿĪsā. 1983. *Wathāʾiq shuʾūn al-ʿimrān fīʾl-Andalus: al-masājid waʾl-dūr, mustakhraja min makhṭūṭ al-aḥkām al-kubrā liʾl-qāḍī Abīʾl-Aṣbagh ʿĪsà b. Sahl al-Andalusī.* Ed. Muḥammad ʿAbd al-Wahhāb Khallāf. Kuwait City: al-Markaz al-ʿArabī al-Duwalī liʾl-Iʿlām.

Ibn al-Ṣalāḥ al-Shahrazūrī, ʿUthmān b. ʿAbd al-Raḥmān. 1986. "Adab al-muftī waʾl-mustaftī," in *Fatāwā wa-masāʾil Ibn al-Ṣalāḥ fīʾl-tafsīr waʾl-ḥadīth waʾl-uṣūl waʾl-fiqh wa maʿahu adab al-muftī waʾl-mustaftī.* Ed. ʿAbd al-Muʿṭī Qalʿajī. 2 vols. Beirut: Dār al-Maʿrifa.

Ibn Taymiyya, Aḥmad b. ʿAbd al-Ḥalīm. 1381/1961. *Majmūʿ al-fatāwā.* Riyādh: Maṭābiʿ al-Riyāḍ.

———. 1966. *al-Fatāwā al-Kubrā.* Cairo: Dār al-Kutub al-Ḥadītha.

Ibrāhīmī, Abū al-Qāsim. 1336/1957. *Fihrist-i kotob-i shaykh-i Aḥmad-i Aḥsāʾī va soʾīr-i mashāyikh-i ʿizāy.* 2 vols. Kerman: n.p.

Idāra (staff). 1973. "Ṣadr al-Ṣudūr." *Urdū Dāʾira Maʿārif Islāmiyya,* 12:85–93.

———. 1975. "Fatāwā Jahāndārī" *Urdū Dā'ira Ma'ārif Islāmiyya*, 15:144-145.

Idris, Hady R. 1962. *La Berbérie orientale sous les Zirides, X^e–XIIe siècles*. 2 vols. Paris: Maisonneuve et Larose.

Idrīs, Riḍā. 1990. "Ḥiwār ma'a al-ustādh Fahmī Huwaydī." *al-Insān*, 1(3):27–35.

al-Ījī, 'Aḍud al-Dīn. 1974. *Sharḥ mukhtaṣar al-muntahā al-uṣūlī*. Ed. Sha'bān Muḥammad Ismā'īl. 2 vols. Cairo: Maktabat al-Kulliyyāt al-Azhariyya.

Imamī, Sayyid Ḥusayn. 1971. *Ḥuqūq-i madanī* (Civil Law). 4 vols. Tehran: Islāmiyah Press.

Imber, Colin. 1982. "*Zinā* in Ottoman law." *Contributions à l'histoire économique et sociale de l'empire ottoman: Collection Turcica III*. Louvain: Éditions Peeters, pp. 59–92.

———. 1993. "'Involuntary' Dissolution of Marriage and Its Solutions in Ottoman Law." *Turcica*, 25:39–73.

Iqbal, Muhammad. 1982 (reprint). *Reconstruction of Religious Thought in Islam*. Lahore: Sh. Muhammad Ashraf.

Ishak, Othman. 1989. "The Making of Fatwa in Malaysia." *Islamic Studies*, 28(4):415–419.

al-Isnawī, Jamāl al-Dīn. 1899. *Nihāyat al-sūl fī sharḥ minhāj al-wuṣūl ilā 'ilm al-uṣūl li'l-Qāḍī al-Bayḍāwī* (printed on the margin of Ibn Amīr al-Ḥājj, *Taqrīr*). 3 vols. Būlāq: al-Maṭba'a al-Kubrā al-Amīriyya.

'Iyāḍ b. Mūsā. 1981–1983?. *Tartīb al-madārik wa-taqrīb al-masālik li-ma'rifat a'lām madhhab Mālik*. 8 vols. Rabat: Wizārat al-Awqāf.

Jackson, Sherman. 1991. "In Defense of Two-Tiered Orthodoxy: A Study of Shihāb al-Dīn al-Qarāfī's *Kitāb al-iḥkām fī tamyīz al-fatāwā 'an al-aḥkām wa-taṣarrufāt al-qāḍī wa'l-imām*." Ph.D. dissertation. University of Pennsylvania.

———. 1992. "The Second Education of the *Muftī*: Notes on Shihāb al-Dīn al-Qarāfī's Tips to the Jurisconsult." *Muslim World*, 82(3–4):201–217.

Jad al-Ḥaqq, Jad al-Ḥaqq 'Alī. 1980. "Introduction," in *al-Fatāwā al-islāmiyya min dār al-iftā' al-miṣriyya*. Vol. 1. Cairo: al-Azhar.

Jallād, Fīlīb. 1890–1895. *Qāmūs al-idāra wa'l-qaḍā'*. 5 vols. Alexandria: al-Maṭba'a al-Bukhāriyya.

Jan, Mirza. 1855. *Ḥadīqa-i shuhadā'*. n.p.

Jibālī, Ibrāhīm. 1931–1933. "al-Ribā." *Nūr al-Islām*, 2:358–375, 425–431, 488–496; 3:424–429.

Johansen, Baber. 1993. "Legal Literature and the Problem of Change: The Case of Land Rent," in Chibli Mallat (ed.), *Islam and Public Law: Classical and Contemporary Studies*. London: Graham and Trotman.

al-Juwaynī, 'Abd al-Malik b. 'Abdallāh (known as Imām al-Ḥaramayn). 1906. "al-Waraqāt," in *Majmū' mutūn uṣūliyya*. Damascus: al-Maktaba al-Hāshimiyya, pp. 27–39.

———. 1400/1979. *al-Burhān fī uṣūl al-fiqh*. Ed. 'Abd al-'Aẓīm Dīb. 2 vols. 2nd ed. Cairo: Dār al-Anṣār.

———. n.d. *al-Waraqāt*. Cairo: Maktabat Muḥammad 'Alī Ṣubayḥ.

Juynboll, G. H. A. 1983. *Muslim Tradition: Studies in Chronology, Provenance and Authorship of Early Hadith*. Cambridge: Cambridge University Press.

Kably, Mohamed. 1986. *Société, pouvoir et religion au Maroc à la fin du Moyen-Age*. Paris: Maisonneuve et Larose.

al-Kaḥḥālah, ʿUmar Riḍā. 1958. *Muʿjam al-muʾallifīn*. 15 vols. in 8. Beirut: Dār al-Turāth al-ʿArabī.

al-Karakī, ʿAlī b. al-Ḥusayn. 1410/1990. *Jāmiʿ al-maqāṣid fī sharḥ al-qawāʿid*. Qum: Muʾassasat Āl al-Bayt.

al-Kāshif al-Ghiṭāʿ, Muḥammad al-Ḥusayn. 1968. *Āʾīn-i mā* (Our Custom). Trans. from Arabic to Persian N. Makārim-i Shīrāzī. Qum: Hadaf Press.

Kātūzīān, Nāṣir. 1978. *Ḥuqūq-i madanī-i khānivādih* (Family Civil Law). Tehran: University of Tehran Press.

Kepel, Gilles. 1985. *Muslim Extremism in Egypt*. Trans. Jon Rothschild. Berkeley: University of California Press.

Kerr, Malcolm. 1966. *Islamic Reform: The Political and Legal Theories of Muḥammad ʿAbduh and Rashīd Riḍā*. Berkeley: University of California Press.

al-Khafīf, ʿAlī. 1971. *al-Ḍamān fīʾl-fiqh al-islāmī*. Maʿhad al-Buḥūth waʾl-Dirāsāt al-ʿArabiyya.

Khalīfa, Muḥammad. 1991. "Ḥarb al-fatāwā wa-fatāwā al-ḥarb: al-khiṭāb al-islāmī fī ḥarb al-khalīj." *Risālat al-Jihād*, 9(97):51–55.

Khalīl b. Isḥāq. 1919. *al-Mukhtaṣar*. Trans. D. Santillana. 2 vols. Milan: U. Hoepli.

al-Khaṣṣāf Abū Bakr Aḥmad. 1978. *Kitāb adab al-qāḍī*. Ed. Farhat Ziadeh. Cairo: American University Press.

Khomeinī, Rūḥallāh. 1977. *Tawẓīḥ al-masāʾil*. Mashhad: Ḳānūn-i Nashr-i Kitāb.

———. 1982. "Non-Permanent Marriage," in *Maḥjūbi* 2(5):38–40.

Khuḍayrī, Muḥsin Aḥmad. 1990. *al-Bunūk al-islāmiyya*. Cairo: Dār al-Ḥurriyya.

Kifāyatullāh, Muḥammad. 1971. *Kifāyat al-muftī* (in Urdu). 9 vols. Karachi: Sikandar Ali.

Kingdom of Saudi Arabia. 1971. *Niẓām wa-lāʾiḥat sayr al-ʿamal fī Hayʾat Kibār al-ʿUlamāʾ*. Royal Decree A/137, 8 Rajab 1391.

Kirmānī, Mirzā Niʿmatullāh. 1313/1934. *Tazkirat al-Awliyāʾ*. Tehran: n.p.

Kirmānī, Muḥammad Karīm Khān. n.d. *Majmūʿih-i Risālāt-i farsī*. 2 vols. Kīrmān: Saʿādat Press.

Klinck, Dennis R. 1991. *Word of the Law: Approaches to Legal Discourse*. Ottawa: Carlton University Press.

Klinkhardt, Hans-Eberhard. 1965. "Die Personensorge nach islamischem Recht." *Zeitschrift für vergleichende Rechtswissenschaft*, 68:1–80.

Kozlowski, Gregory C. 1974. "Indian Secularity and the Islamic Law: A Liberal Muslim's Response." *Islamic Quarterly*, 18(3–4):33–47.

———. 1985. *Muslim Endowments and Society in British India*. Cambridge: Cambridge University Press.

———. 1989. "Shah Banu's Case, Britain's Legal Legacy and Muslim Politics in Modern India," in Yogendra Malik and Dipendra Vajpay (eds.), *Law, Politics and Society in India*. New Delhi: Chanakaya, pp. 88–111.

———. 1993. "Muslim Personal Law and Political Identity in Independent India," in Robert D. Baird (ed.), *Religion and Law in Modern India*. New Delhi: Manohar.

———. 1995. "Loyalty, Locality and Authority in Several Opinions *(Fatawa)* Delivered by the *Mufti* of the Jamiah Nizamiyyah Madrasah, Hyderabad India." *Modern Asian Studies,* 29(4):893–927.

Kramers, J. H. 1934. "Shaikh al-Islām," in *The Encyclopaedia of Islam.* 1st ed. Leiden: E. J. Brill.

Krüger, Hilmar. 1978. *Fetwa und Siyar.* Wiesbaden: Otto Harrassowitz.

Kulainī, Abū Jaʿfar Muḥammad. 1958. *al-Furūʿ min al-kāfī* (The Branches of Law in al-Kāfī). 6 vols. Tehran: Haydarī Press.

Kut, Gunay Alpay. 1991. "Maṭbaʿa, 2: In Turkey," in *The Encyclopaedia of Islam.* 2nd ed. Leiden: E. J. Brill.

Lagardère, Vincent. 1990. "La vie sociale et économique de l'Espagne musulmane aux XIe et XIIe siècles à travers les fatwas du *Miʿyār* d'al-Wanšarišī." *Mélanges de la Casa de Velázquez.* Paris: E. de Boccard.

Lājpurī, ʿAbd al-Raḥīm. 1978. *Fatāwā raḥīmiyya.* Delhi: Kutub Khana Azizia.

Lakhnavi, Musharraf ʿAli Khan (ed.). 1835–36. 3 vols. *Bayāż-i masāʾil.* Lucknow, n.p.

Lambton, Ann K. S. 1953. *Landlord and Peasant in Persia.* London: Oxford University Press.

———. 1981. *State and Government in Medieval Islam: An Introduction to the Study of Islamic Political Theory: The Jurists.* Oxford: Oxford University Press.

———. 1986. "Kermān," in *The Encyclopaedia of Islam.* 2nd ed. Leiden: E. J. Brill.

———. 1988. *Continuity and Change in Medieval Persia: Aspects of Administrative, Economic, and Social History.* London: Tauris.

Lane, Edward William. 1966. *Manners and Customs of the Modern Egyptians.* Repr. London: Dent.

———. 1968. *An Arabic-English Lexicon.* 8 vols. Beirut: Librarie du Liban.

———. 1978. *An Account of the Manners and Customs of the Modern Egyptians.* London: East-West Publications.

Langarūdī, Muḥammad Jaʿfar Jaʿfarī. 1967. *Tirmīnulūjī ḥuqūqī* (Legal Terminology). Tehran: Ibn-i Sina Press.

———. 1976. *Ḥuqūq-i khānivādih* (Family Law). Tehran: Haydarī Press.

Lavan, Spencer. 1974. *The Ahmadiyya Movement: History and Perspective.* New Delhi: Manohar.

Layish, Aharon. 1975. *Women and Islamic Law in a Non-Muslim State.* New York: John Wiley and Sons; Jerusalem: Israel Universities Press.

———. 1977. "Ha-Mimsad ha-dati ha-muslimi ba-gada ha-maʿaravit ba-tequfa ha-yardenit," *Medina, Mimshal, Viḥasim Benleumiyim,* 11: 97–108.

———. 1980–1982. "Challenges to Customary Law and Arbitration: The Impact of Islamic Law upon Settled Bedouin in the Judean Desert," *Tel Aviv University Studies in Law,* 5:206–221.

———. 1984. "The Islamization of the Bedouin Family in the Judean Desert as Reflected in the *Sijill* of the *Sharīʿa* Court," in E. Marx and A. Shmueli (eds.), *The Changing Bedouin.* New Brunswick, N.J.: Transaction, pp. 39–58.

———. 1991a. *Divorce in the Libyan Family.* New York: New York University Press; Jerusalem: Magnes Press.

———. 1991b. "The *Fatwā* as an Instrument of the Islamization of a Tribal Society in Process of Sedentarization," *Bulletin of the School of Oriental and African Studies,* 54(3):449–459.

———. Forthcoming. *Bedouin of the Judean Desert: Islamization of a Tribal Society—A Study Based on Legal Documents of Arbitrators and Sharīʿa Courts.*

Layish, Aharon, and J. Davis. 1988. *Libyan Society: A Selection of Documents from the Sijill of the Sharīʿa Courts of Ajdābiya and Kufra.* Jerusalem: Academon.

Layish, Aharon, and A. Shmueli. 1979. "Custom and *Sharīʿa* in the Bedouin Family according to Legal Documents from the Judean Desert," *Bulletin of the School of Oriental and African Studies,* 42(1):29–45.

Lelyveld, David. 1978. *Aligarh's First Generation: Muslim Solidarity in British India.* Princeton: Princeton University Press.

Lemke, Wolf-Dieter. 1980. *Mahmud Shaltut (1893–1963) und die Reform der Azhar.* Ed. Falaturi. Islam und Abendland. Frankfurt: Verlag Peter D. Lang.

Lerner, Daniel. 1958. *The Passing of Traditional Society.* Glencoe: The Free Press.

Lev, Daniel S. 1972. *Islamic Courts in Indonesia.* Berkeley: University of California Press.

Lévi-Provençal, Evariste. 1950–1953. *Histoire de l'Espagne musulmane.* 3 vols. Paris: Maisonneuve; Leiden: E. J. Brill.

———. 1950–1957. *España musulmana hasta la caída del Califato de Córdoba, Historia de España dirigida por Ramón Menéndez Pidal.* 2 vols. Madrid: Espasa Calpe.

Levy, Rubin. 1931–1933. *Introduction to the Sociology of Islam.* 2 vols. London: Williams and Norgate.

Linant de Bellefonds, Y. 1971. "ʿIdda," in *The Encyclopaedia of Islam.* 2nd. ed. Leiden: E. J. Brill.

———. 1973. *Traité de droit musulman comparé,* vol. 3. Paris and The Hague: Mouton and Co.

———. 1980. "Iḥyāʾ," in *The Encyclopaedia of Islam.* 2nd ed. Leiden: E. J. Brill.

Little, Donald P. 1984. *A Catalogue of the Islamic Documents from al-Ḥaram al-Šarīf in Jerusalem.* Beirut: Orient-Institut der Deutschen Morgenländischen Gesellschaft.

López Ortiz, José. 1931. *La recepción de la escuela malequí en España.* Madrid: Anuario de Historia del Derecho Español.

Luthera, Ved P. 1964. *The Concept of the Secular State and India.* Calcutta: Oxford University Press.

MacEoin, Denis. 1985. "Aḥsāʾī," in *The Encyclopaedia Iranica.* Boston: Routledge and Kegan Paul.

al-Maḥallī, Jalāl al-Dīn. n.d. *Sharḥ al-waraqāt.* Cairo: Maktabat Muḥammad ʿAlī Ṣubayḥ. Also see al-ʿAbbādī, *Sharḥ.*

al-Mahdī, Muḥammad al-ʿAbbās. 1304/1887. *al-Fatāwā al-mahdiyya fīʾl-waqāʾiʿ al-miṣriyya.* 7 vols. Cairo: Maṭbaʿat al-Azhar.

al-Mahdī, Ṣādiq. 1935. *Yasʾalūnaka ʿan al-mahdiyya.* Beirut: Dār al-Qaḍāyā.

Mahmassani, Ṣubḥī. 1961. *Falsafat al-tashrīʿ fīʾl-islām: The Philosophy of Jurisprudence in Islam.* Trans. F. Ziadeh. Leiden: E. J. Brill.

Maḥmūd, ʿAbd al-Ḥalīm. 1986. "*Mā raʾy al-dīn fī taʾjīl dafn juthmān al-mayyit akthar min al-ḥadd al-mafrūd,*" in *Fatāwā ʿAbd al-Ḥalīm Maḥmūd.* Cairo: Dār al-Maʿārif.

Majallat al-Azhar. 1982. (January):650.

"Majallat al-ḥaras al-waṭanī tastawjib." 1990. *al-Insān,* 1(3):22–26.

Majelis Ulama Indonesia. 1984. *Kumpulan fatwa Majelis Ulama Indonesia.* Jakarta: Pustaka Panjimas.

al-Majlis al-islāmī al-ūrūbī. 1990. "Ruʾya islāmiyya li-azmat al-khalīj." *al-Insān,* 1(3):19–21.

Makarim-i Shirazi, Nasir. 1968. "Izdivāj-i muvaqiqāt yik żarūrāt-i ijtināb napazir-i ijtimāʿī ast" (Temporary Marriage Is an Inevitable Necessity in Society), epilogue of *Ain-i Ma* by al-Kashif al-Ghitaʿ. Qom: Hadaf Press, pp. 372–390.

Makdisi, George. 1973. "The *Madrasa* in Spain: Some Remarks." *Revue de l'Occident musulman et de la Méditerranée,* 15–16:153–158.

———. 1981. *The Rise of Colleges: Institutions of Learning in Islam and the West.* Edinburgh: Edinburgh University Press.

Makhlūf, Ḥasanayn Muḥammad. 1952. "Tashrīḥ juthāth al-mawtā," in *Fatāwā sharʿiyya wa-buḥūth islāmiyya.* 2 vols. Cairo: Dār al-Kātib al-ʿArabī.

———. 1965. *Fatāwā sharʿiyya wa-buḥūth islāmiyya.* 2 vols. 2nd ed. Cairo: Muṣṭafā al-Bābī al-Ḥalabī.

———. 1990. "Fatwā." *al-Ahrām* (January 26):13.

Makhlūf, Muḥammad b. Muḥammad. 1975. *Shajarat al-nūr al-zakiyya fī ṭabaqāt al-mālikiyya.* 2nd ed. Beirut: Dār al-Kitāb al-ʿArabī.

Maktari, A. M. A. 1971. *Water Rights and Irrigation Practices in Lahj.* Cambridge: Cambridge University Press.

"Malḥūẓāt ʿalā hāmish azmat al-khalīj." 1990. *al-Insān,* 1(3):3–6.

Mālik b. Anas. 1979. *al-Muwaṭṭaʾ* (version of Muḥammad b. al-Ḥasan al-Shaybānī). Ed. ʿAbd al-Wahhāb ʿAbd al-Laṭīf. Cairo: n.p.

———. 1981. *al-Muwaṭṭaʾ* (version of Yaḥyā b. Yaḥyā). 3rd. ed. Beirut: Dār al-Gharb al-Islāmī.

Mallat, Chibli. 1988. "The Debate on *Riba* and Interest in Twentieth-Century Egypt," in Chibli Mallat (ed.), *Islamic Law and Finance.* London: Graham and Trotman, pp. 69–88.

———. 1993. *The Renewal of Islamic Law.* Cambridge: Cambridge University Press.

Manūchihrīān, Mihrangīz. 1978. *Nābarābarīhā-yi ḥuqūq-i zan va mard dar Iran va rāh-i islāh-i ān* (Legal Inequalities between Men and Women in Iran). Tehran: Penguin Press.

al-Maqrīzī, Taqī al-Dīn. 1877. *al-Khiṭaṭ al-maqrīziyya.* 2 vols. Baghdad: Maktabat al-Muthannā.

Marʿashī, Ayatullāh Shahābiddīn. n.d. *Risāla-i Ayatullāh Marʿashī.* Tehran: Farahani.

al-Marghinānī, Abū al-Ḥasan ʿAlī b. Abū Bakr. 1959. *al-Hidāya.* Delhi: Mujtabāʾī.

———. 1965. *al-Hidāya.* Cairo: Muḥammad ʿAlī Ṣubayḥ.

———. n.d. *al-Hidāya.* Beirut: al-Maktaba al-Islāmiyya.

Margoliouth, D.S. 1961. "Wahhābīya," in *The Shorter Encyclopaedia of Islam.* Leiden: E. J. Brill.

Marín, Manuela. 1985a. "*Šūrà* et *ahl al-Šūrà* dans al-Andalus." *Studia Islamica*, 62:25–51.

———. 1985b. "Una familia de ulemas cordobeses: los Banū Abī ʿĪsà." *Al-Qanṭara*, 6:292–320.

———. 1988. "Nómina de sabios de al-Andalus (93–350/711–961)." *Estudios onomástico-biográficos de al-Andalus*. Madrid: Consejo Superior de Investigaciones Cientificas, 1:23–182.

———. 1990. "Law and Piety: A Cordovan *Fatwa*." *British Society for Middle Eastern Studies Bulletin*, 17:129–136.

———. 1991. "*Zuhhād* de al-Andalus (300/912–420/1029)." *Al-Qanṭara*, 12:439–469.

———. 1992. "The Early Development of *Zuhd* in al-Andalus." *Shia Islam, Sects and Sufism: Historical Dimensions, Religious Practice and Methodological Considerations*. Ed. F. de Jong. Utrecht: M. Th. Houtsma Stichting, pp. 83–96.

"Marratan ukhrā . . . maʿa bayān ʿulamāʾ miṣr." 1989. *al-Taḥrīr*, 7(1):9, 17.

Marriage Court. 1983. (Court of Guarantee and Marriages, or Maḥkamat al-Ḍamān wa'l-Ankiḥa). Great Shariʿa Court of Riyadh (al-Maḥkama al-Kubrā biʾl-Riyāḍ), Riyadh. Personal observation, April 19, 1983.

Martin, B. G. 1976. *Muslim Brotherhoods in 19th-Century Africa*. Cambridge: Cambridge University Press.

Martin, Jochen, and August Nitschke (eds.). 1986. *Zur Sozialgeschichte der Kindheit*, Freiburg and München: Veröffentlichungen des Instituts für Historische Anthropologie e.V. 4.

Mashhadi, Kamalu'd-Din Haydar Husayni. 1896. *Qayṣar al-tavārīkh*. Lucknow: Naval Kishore.

Massignon, Louis. 1961. "al-Ḥallā<u>dj</u>," in *The Shorter Encyclopaedia of Islam*. Leiden: E. J. Brill.

Masud, M. Khalid. 1969. "Trends in the Interpretation of Islamic Law as Reflected in the *Fatawa* Literature of the Deoband School: A Study of the Attitude of the ʿUlamaʾ of Deoband toward Certain Social Problems and Inventions." M.A. thesis, Montreal: Institute of Islamic Studies, McGill University.

———. 1977. *Islamic Legal Philosophy: A Study of Abū Isḥāq al-Shāṭibī's Life and Thought*. 1995. rev. ed. *Shātibī's Philosophy of Islamic Law*. Islamabad: Islamic Research Institute.

———. 1984. "*Ādāb al-Muftī:* The Muslim Understanding of Values, Characteristics, and Role of a *Muftī*," in Barbara Daly Metcalf (ed.), *Moral Conduct and Authority: The Place of* Adab *in South Asian Islam*. Berkeley: University of California Press, pp. 124–150.

———. 1985. *Iqbal kā taṣawwur-i-ijtihād*. Rawalpindi: Ḥurmat.

———. 1990. "The Obligation to Migrate: The Doctrine of *Hijra* in Islamic Law," in Dale F. Eickelman and James Piscatori (eds.), *Muslim Travellers*. London: Routledge, pp. 29–49.

———. 1995. "Iqbal's Reconstruction of *Ijtihād*." Lahore: Iqbal Academy.

Mattar, Philip. 1987. *The Mufti of Jersualem*. New York: Garland Press.

Maudoodi, Syed Abul ʿAla. 1950–1961. *Rasaʾil o Masaʾil*. 4 vols. Lahore: Jamāʿat-i Islāmi Pākistān.

al-Māwardī, Abū al-Ḥasan ʿAlī b. Muḥammad b. Ḥabīb. 1971–1972. *Adab al-qāḍī*. Ed. Muḥyī Hilāl al-Sarhān. 2 vols. Baghdad: Maṭbaʿat al-Irshād (vol. 1); Baghdad: Maṭbaʿat al-ʿĀnī (vol. 2).

———. n.d. *Kitāb al-aḥkām al-sulṭāniyya*. Cairo: Maḥmūdiyya.

McChesney, R. D. 1991. *Waqf in Central Asia: Four Hundred Years in the History of a Muslim Shrine, 1480–1889*. Princeton: Princeton University Press.

McLuhan, Marshall. 1964. *Understanding Media*. London: Routledge.

Memon, Muhammad Umar. 1976. *Ibn Taimīya's Struggle against Popular Religion: With an Annotated Translation of His Kitāb iqtiḍāʾ aṣ-ṣirāṭ al-mustaqīm mukhālafat aṣḥāb al-jaḥīm*. The Hague: Mouton.

Messick, Brinkley. 1986. "The Mufti, the Text and the World: Legal Interpretation in Yemen." *Man* (n.s.), 21:102–119.

———. 1988. "Kissing Hands and Knees: Hegemony and Hierarchy in *Shariʿa* Discourse." *Law and Society Review*, 22(4):637–659.

———. 1990. "Literacy and the Law in Yemen," in Daisy Hilse Dwyer (ed.), *Law and Islam in the Middle East*. New York: Bergin and Garvey, pp. 61–76.

———. 1993. *The Calligraphic State: Textual Domination and History in a Muslim Society*. Berkeley: University of California Press.

Metcalf, Barbara D. 1982. *Islamic Revival in British India: Deoband, 1860–1900*. Princeton: Princeton University Press.

——— (ed.). 1984. *Moral Conduct and Authority: The Place of* Adab *in South Asian Islam*. Berkeley: University of California Press.

Minorsky, V. (trans.). 1943. *Tadhkirat al-Mulūk, a Manual of Ṣafavid Administration (circa 1137/1725)*. E. J. W. Gibb Memorial Series. New Series, vol. 16. London: Luzac and Co.

Momen, Moojan. 1985. *An Introduction to Shiʿi Islam*. New Haven: Yale University Press.

Mottahedeh, Roy P. 1985. *The Mantle of the Prophet: Religion and Politics in Iran*. New York: Simon and Schuster.

Motzki, Harald. 1985. "Geschlechtsreife und Legitimation zur Zeugung im frühen Islam," in E. W. Müller (ed.), *Geschlechtsreife und Legitimation zur Zeugung*. Freiburg and Munich: Veröffentlichungen des Instituts für Historische Anthropologie e.V. 3, pp. 479–550.

———. 1986. "Das Kind und seine Sozialisation in der islamischen Familie des Mittelalters," in J. Martin and A. Nitschke (eds.), *Zur Sozialgeschichte der Kindheit*, Freiburg and Munich: Veröffentlichungen des Instituts für Historische Anthropologie e.V. 4, pp. 391–441.

———. 1987. "Muslimische Kinderehen in Palästina während des 17. Jahrhunderts: *Fatāwā* als Quellen zur Sozialgeschichte." *Die Welt des Islams*, 27:82–90.

———. 1994. "Religiöse Ratgebung im Islam: Entstehung, Bedeutung und Praxis des *muftī* und der *fatwā*." *Zeitschrift fur Religionswissenschaft*, 94(1):3–22.

Mudzhar, Mohamad Atho. 1990. "*Fatwā*s of the Council of Indonesian Ulama: A

Study of Islamic Legal Thought in Indonesia, 1975–1988." Ph.D. dissertation, University of California, Los Angeles.

al-Muftī, Muḥammad b. ʿAlī b. Muḥsin. 1988. *Fatḥ al-mannān: sharḥ zubād Ibn Raslān*. Ed. ʿAbd Allāh Muḥammad al-Ḥibshī. Ṣanʿaʾ: Maktaba al-Jayl al-Jadīd.

Muhammad Tayyib. 1965. *Daruʾl-ʿulum deoband ki sad salah zindagi*. Deoband: Daftar Daruʾl-ʿulum.

al-Muḥibbī, Muḥammad Amīn b. Faḍl Allāh. 1284/1876. *Khulāṣat al-athar fī aʿyān al-qarn al-hādī ʿashar*. Cairo: al-Maṭbaʿa al-Wahbiyya.

———. n.d. *Khulāṣat al-athar fī aʿyān al-qarn al-hādī ʿashar*. Repr. Beirut: Dār Ṣādir.

Müller, Ernst Wilhelm (ed.). 1985. *Geschlechtsreife und Legitimation zur Zeugung*. Freiburg and Munich: Veröffentlichungen des Instituts für Historische Anthropologie e.V. 3.

Muntaẓirī, Shaykh Ḥusayn ʿAlī. 1362/1983. *Risāla-yi Ayatullāh Muntaẓiry*. Tehran: n.p.

Murata, Sachiko. 1987. "Temporary Marriage (Mutʿa) in Islamic Law." *Alserat*, 13(1).

Musallam, Basim. 1983. *Sex and Society in Islam: Birth Control before the Nineteenth Century*. Cambridge: Cambridge University Press.

Muslim b. Ḥajjāj al-Qushayrī. 1930. *Ṣaḥīḥ*. 18 vols in 6. Cairo: al-Maṭbaʿa al-Miṣriyya wa-Maktabatuhā.

———. 1955. *Ṣaḥīḥ*. Ed. Muḥammad Fuʾād ʿAbd al-Bāqī. 5 vols. Cairo: Dār Iḥyāʾ al-Kutub al-ʿArabiyya.

Muṭahharī, Murtiẓā. 1974. *Niẓām-i ḥuqūq-i zan dar islām* (Legal Rights of Women in Islam). Qum: Sadra Press.

———. 1981. "The Rights of Women in Islam: Fixed-Term Marriage." Part 3. *Maḥjūbah*, October/November.

"al-Muʾtamar al-islāmī al-ʿālamī li-munāqashat al-awḍāʿ al-ḥāḍira fīʾl-khalīj." 1990. *al-Insān*, 1(3): 8–12.

al-Nadīm, Abū al-Faraj. 1970. *The Fihrist of al-Nadīm: A Tenth-Century Survey of Muslim Culture*. Ed. and trans. Bayard Dodge. 2 vols. New York: Columbia University Press.

Naʿnāʿ, ʿAbd al-Ḥakīm. 1984. "Fatwā." *al-Jumhūriyya* (August 13):7.

Nasir, Jamal J. 1990. *The Islamic Law of Personal Status*. 2nd ed. London: Graham and Trotman.

Naṣīrābādī, Sayyid Ḥusayn. 1848–49. *Majmūʿa-i irshād al-muʾminīn*. Lucknow: Maṭbaʿ-i Muḥammadī.

———. 1860–61. *Murtażiyyāt-i Ḥusayniyya*. Ludhiana: Maṭbaʿ-i Majmaʿ al-Baḥrayn.

al-Nawawī, Abū Zakariyyāʾ Yaḥyā b. Sharaf, Muḥyī al-Dīn. 1882–1884. *Minhāj aṭ-ṭālibīn: Le guide des zélés croyant. Manuel de jurisprudence musulmane selon le rite de Chāfiʿī*. Ed. L. W. C. van den Berg with French trans. 3 vols. Batavia: Imprimerie du Gouvernement.

———. 1914. *Minhaj et Talibin: A Manual of Muhammadan Law according to the School of Shafii*. Trans. from the French by E. C. Howard. Lahore: Law Publishing Co. (reprt. 1977).

———. 1925. *al-Majmūʿ: sharḥ al-muhadhdhab.* 9 vols. Cairo: Idārat al-Ṭibāʿa al-Munīriyya.

———. 1930. *Ṣāḥīḥ Muslim bi-sharḥ al-Nawawī.* 18 vols. in 6. Cairo: al-Maṭbaʿa al-Miṣriyya bi'l-Azhar. Repr., Beirut: Dār al-Kitāb al-ʿIlmiyya 1970.

———. 1988. *Adab al-fatwā wa'l-muftī wa'l-mustaftī.* Damascus: Dār al-Fikr.

———. 1990. *Adab al-fatwā wa'l-muftī wa'l-mustaftī.* Ed. Bassām al-Jābī. 2nd. ed. Beirut: Dār al-Bashā'ir al-Islāmiyya.

———. n.d. *Rawḍat al-ṭālibīn.* 8 vols. Damascus: al-Maktab al-Islāmī li'l-Ṭibāʿa wa'l-Nashr.

"Nāzila". 1992. *The Encyclopaedia of Islam.* 2nd ed. Leiden: E. J. Brill.

Nicolas, A. L. M. 1910–1911. *Essai sur le Cheikhisme.* Paris: n.p.

Nielsen, J. S. 1990. "Maẓālim," in *The Encyclopaedia of Islam.* 2nd ed. Leiden: E. J. Brill.

Noer, Deliar. 1973. *The Modernist Muslim Movement in Indonesia 1900–1942.* Singapore: Oxford University Press.

Novak, David. 1983. *The Image of the Non-Jew in Judaism: An Historical and Constructive Study of the Noahide Laws.* New York: E. Mellen Press.

———. 1989. *Jewish-Christian Dialogue: A Jewish Justification.* New York: Oxford University Press.

Oman, G. 1991. "Maṭbaʿa, 1: In the Arab World," in *The Encyclopaedia of Islam.* 2nd ed. Leiden: E. J. Brill.

Omar, F. 1971. "Hārūn al-Rashīd," in *The Encyclopaedia of Islam.* 2nd ed. Leiden: E. J. Brill.

Ong, Walter J. 1982. *Orality and Literacy.* New York: The Free Press.

Oweidi (ʿAbbādī), A. A. S. 1982. "Bedouin Justice in Jordan: The Customary Legal System of the Tribes and Its Integration into the Framework of the State Policy from 1921 Onwards." Ph.D. thesis, University of Cambridge.

Parfentieff, B. 1966. "Étude de droit public malikite: Du droit du soverain musulman de disposer des biens appartenant au trésor *(bayt al-māl al-muslimīn).*" *Revue de l'Occident musulman et de la Méditerranée,* 1:161–204.

Pearson, Harlan Otto. 1976. "Islamic Reform and Revival in Nineteenth-Century India: The *Tariqa-i Muhammadiyah.*" Ph.D. dissertation, Duke University.

Pedersen, J. 1986. "Masd̲jid," in *Encyclopaedia of Islam.* 2nd ed. Leiden: E. J. Brill.

Pederson, J., and G. Makdisi. 1986. "Madrasa," in *The Encyclopaedia of Islam.* 2nd ed. Leiden: E. J. Brill.

Pejabat Kuliah al-Attas. 1937. *Risalah Tanbiyya al-Ṭallab fi Ahkam al-Kalb: Mas'alah Anjing.* Johor Bahru: Kuliah al-Attas.

Pellat, Charles. 1965. "À propos du *Kitāb al-Futyā* de Jāḥiẓ," in George Makdisi (ed.), *Arabic and Islamic Studies, in Honor of H. A. R. Gibb.* Cambridge: Harvard University Press, pp. 538–546.

Perlmann, Moshe. 1982. "ʿAlī al-Munayyar," in Sheldon R. Brunswick (ed.), *Studies in Judaica, Karaitica and Islamica Presented to Leon Nemoy on his Eightieth Birthday.* Ramat Gan: Bar-Ilan University Press, pp. 181–202.

Peters, Rudolph. 1979. *Islam and Colonialism: The Doctrine of Jihad in Modern History.* The Hague: Mouton.

———. 1983. "Islam and the Legitimation of Power: The Mahdi-Revolt in the Sudan," in *XXI. Deutscher Orientalistentag (Berlin, März 1980): Ausgewählte Vorträge*. Ed. F. Steppat. Wiesbaden: F. Steiner, pp. 409–20.

Pons Boigues, Francisco. 1898. *Ensayo bio-bibliográfico sobre los historiadores y geógrafos arábigo españoles*. Madrid: S. F. de Sales.

Powers, David S. 1986. *Studies in Qur'ān and Ḥadīth: The Formation of the Islamic Law of Inheritance*. Berkeley: University of California Press.

———. 1988. "The Exegetical Genre *nāsikh al-Qur'ān wa-mansūkhuhu*," in A. Rippin (ed.), *Approaches to the History of the Interpretation of the Qur'ān*. Oxford: Clarendon Press, pp. 117–138.

———. 1990a. "A Court Case from Fourteenth-Century North Africa." *Journal of the American Oriental Society*, 110:229–254.

———. 1990b. "*Fatwā*s as Sources for Legal and Social History: A Dispute over Endowment Revenues from Fourteenth-Century Fez." *al-Qanṭara*, 11:295.

———. 1992. "On Judicial Review in Islamic Law." *Law and Society Review*, 26:315–41.

———. 1993. "Legal Consultation *(Futyā)* in Medieval Spain and North Africa," in Chibli Mallat (ed.), *Islam and Public Law*. London: Graham and Trotman, pp. 85–106.

Proyek Pembinaan, Kerukunan Hidup Beragama. 1978. *Masalah hubungan antar umat beragama di Indonesia*. Jakarta: Departemen Agama R.I.

Puin, Gerd-Rüdiger. 1977. "Der moderne Alltag im Speigel Ḥanbalitischer Fetwas aus ar-Riyāḍ." *Zeitschrift der deutschen morganländischen Gesellschaft*, 3 (supp.):589–597.

Qāḍī Khān, Fakhr al-Dīn al-Ḥasan b. Manṣūr Ūzjandī. 1893. *Fatāwā Qāḍī Khān*. Kanpur: Muṣṭafā'ī.

———. 1973. *Fatāwā Ḳāḍīkhān* (printed on the margin of *al-Fatāwā al-Hindiyya* 1–3). Beirut: Dār al-Maʿrifa.

———. 1977. *Fatāwā Qāḍī Khān*. Lahore: Law Publishing Co.

Qalʿajī, Muḥammad, and Ṣādiq Qunaybī. 1985. *Muʿjam lughat al-fuqahā'*. Dār al-Nafā'is.

al-Qalqashandī, Aḥmad b. ʿAlī. 1919. *Ṣubḥ al-aʿshā fī ṣināʿat al-inshā'*. 14 vols. Cairo: al-Amīriyya.

al-Qalqilī, ʿAbdallāh. 1969. *al-Fatāwā al-urdunniyya*. Beirut: al-Maktab al-Islāmī.

al-Qaraḍāwī, Yūsuf. 1982. *Hudā al-islām: fatāwā muʿāṣira*. 3rd ed. Kuwait: Dār al-Qalam.

———. 1988a. *al-Fatwā bayna al-inḍibāt wa'l-tasayyub*. Cairo: Dār al-Ṣaḥwa.

———. 1988b. *Fatāwā muʿāṣira li'l-mar'a wa'l-usra al-muslima*. Amman: Dār al-Ḍiyā'.

al-Qarāfī, Aḥmad b. Idrīs. 1344/1925–1926. *al-Furūq*. 4 vols. Mecca: Dār Iḥyā' al-Kutub al-ʿArabiyya.

———. 1967. *al-Iḥkām fī tamyīz al-fatāwā ʿan al-aḥkām wa-taṣarrufāt al-qāḍī wa'l-imām*. Aleppo: Islāmiyya.

———. 1989. *al-Iḥkām fī tamyīz al-fatāwā ʿan al-aḥkām wa-taṣarrufāt al-qāḍī wa'l-imām*. Cairo: al-Maktab al-Thaqafī li'l-Nashr wa'l-Tawzīʿ.

al-Qāsimī, Jamāl al-Dīn. 1986. *al-Fatwā fī'l-Islām*. Beirut: Dār al-Kutub al-ʿIlmiyya.

al-Qasṭallānī, Shihāb al-Dīn Aḥmad b. Muḥammad. 1327/1909. *Irshād al-sārī li-sharḥ al-Bukhārī*. 10 vols. Būlāq: Maṭbaʿat al-Kubrā al-Amīriyya. Repr. Beirut: Dār Ṣādir, 1971.

Qurbānī, Farajullāh. 1988. *Majmūʿa-i kāmil va qavānīn va muqarrarāt-i ḥuqūqī* (Complete Collection of Laws and Directives). Tehran: Firdawsi Press.

Qureshi, Ishtiaq Husain. 1958. *The Administration of the Sultanate of Delhi*. Karachi: Pakistan Historical Society.

Raḥmān ʿAlī, Maulawi. 1961. *Taẓkira-e ʿUlamāʾ-e Hind*. Karachi: Pakistan Historical Society.

al-Ramlī, Khayr al-Dīn. 1300/1883. *al-Fatāwā al-khayriyya li-nafʿ al-bariyya*. 2nd ed. Būlāq: n.p.

———. 1974. *al-Fatāwā al-khayriyya li-nafʿ al-bariyya*. Beirut: Dār al-Maʿrifa.

al-Ramlī, Shams al-Dīn. 1938. *Nihāyat al-muḥtāj ilā sharḥ al-minhāj*. 8 vols. Cairo: Maṭbaʿat Muṣṭafā al-Bābī al-Ḥalabī.

Rashīd Aḥmad Gangōhī, Maulana. 1906. *Fatāwā-i Rashīdiyya*. 3 vols. Moradabad.

———. 1362/1943 (vol. 1), n.d. (vol. 2), 1962 (vol. 3). *Fatāwā-yi Rashīdiyya*. Delhi: Kutubkhāna Raḥimiyya.

——— n.d. (post 1960s). *Fatāwā-yi Rashīdiyya kāmil mubawwab*. Deoband: Kutubkhāna Raḥimiyya. Also (1987?) Karachi: Muhammad ʿAli Karkhanah-yi Islami Kutub.

———. n.d. *Fatāwā Rashīdiyya*. Karachi: Kārkhāna Tijārat-i Kutub.

Rashid, S. Khalid. 1979. *Wakf Administration in India*. New Delhi: Vikas.

Reinhart, A. Kevin. 1983. "Islamic Law as Islamic Ethics." *Journal of Religious Ethics*, 11:186–203.

———. 1994. "Transcendence and Social Practice: Muftīs and Qāḍīs as Religious Interpreters." *Annales Islamologiques*, 27:5–28.

Repp, R. C. 1986. *The Müfti of Istanbul*. London: Ithaca Press for the Board of the Faculty of Oriental Studies, Oxford University.

Ribera, Julian. 1928. "La enseñanza entre los musulmanes españoles." *Disertaciones y opúsculos*. 2 vols. Madrid: Impr. de E. Maestre, vol. 1, pp. 229–360.

Riḍā, Muḥammad Rashīd. 1904. "Ṣundūq al-tawfīr fī idārat al-barīd." *al-Manār*, 7:28–29.

———. 1906. "Faṣl fī ḥikmat taḥrīm al-ribā." *al-Manār*, 9:345–352.

———. 1910. Fatwā in *al-Manār*, 3:100–102.

———. 1917. "Ribḥ ṣundūq al-tawfīr." *al-Manār*, 19:527–529.

———. 1970. "al-Kashf al-ṭibbī ʿalā al-mawtā wa-taʾkhīr al-dafn," in *Fatāwā Rashīd Riḍā*. 6 vols. Beirut: Dār al-Kitāb al-Jadīd, vol. 3, pp. 851–853.

———. 1970–1971. *Fatāwā al-Imām Muḥammad Rashīd Riḍā*. 6 vols. Beirut: Dār al-Kitāb al-Jadīd.

Robertson Smith, William. 1903. *Kinship and Marriage in Early Arabia*. Boston: Beacon Press.

Robinson, Francis C. R. 1984. "The ʿUlamaʾ of Farangi Mahall and Their Adab," in Barbara Daly Metcalf (ed.), *Moral Conduct and Authority: The Place of* Adab *in South Asian Islam*. Berkeley: University of California Press.

———. 1993. "Technology and Religious Change: Islam and the Impact of Print." *Modern Asian Studies,* 27(1):229–251.

Roff, William R. 1974. "The Origin and Early Years of the Majlis Ugama," in William R. Roff (ed.), *Kelantan: Religion, Society and Politics in a Malay State.* Kuala Lumpur: Oxford University Press.

———. 1983. "Whence Cometh the Law? Dog Saliva in Kelantan, 1937." *Comparative Studies in Society and History,* 25:323–338.

———. 1988. "Whence Cometh the Law? Dog Saliva in Kelantan, 1937," in Katherine P. Ewing (ed.), *Shariʿat and Ambiguity in South Asian Islam.* Berkeley: University of California Press, pp. 25–43.

Roller, Otto. 1925. "Die Kinderehen im ausgehenden deutschen Mittelalter." *Sozialhygienische Mitteilungen,* 9:1–29.

Rosen, Lawrence. 1980–1981. "Equity and Discretion in a Modern Islamic Legal System." *Law and Society Review,* 15(2):217–245.

———. 1989. *The Anthropology of Justice: Law as Culture in Islamic Society.* Cambridge: Cambridge University Press.

Rossi, Ettore. 1938. "La Stampa nel Yemen." *Oriente Moderno,* 18:568–580.

Saeedullah. 1973. *The Life and Works of Muhammad Siddiq Hasan Khan, Nawab of Bhopal, 1248–1307 (1832–1890).* Lahore: Sh. Muhammad Ashraf.

Safadi, Yasin Hamid. 1978. *Islamic Calligraphy.* London: Thames and Hudson.

Saḥnūn b. Saʿīd al-Tanūkhī. 1905. *al-Mudawwana al-kubrā.* 17 vols. in 4. Cairo: al-Maṭbaʿa al-Khayriyya.

Sālim, ʿAbd al-ʿAzīz. 1967. *Ṭarāblus al-Shām: al-taʾrīkh al-Islāmī.* Alexandria: Ramses.

Sangilajī, Muḥammad. 1335/1916. *Āʾīn Dādrasī dar Islām.* Tehran: Dānishgah Tehran.

Sanhūrī, ʿAbd al-Razzāq. 1954–1959. *Maṣādir al-ḥaqq fiʾl-fiqh al-Islāmī.* 6 vols. in 2. Cairo: Maʿhad al-Dirāsāt al-ʿArabiyya al-ʿĀliyya.

Sanyal, Usha. Forthcoming. *In the Path of the Prophet: Maulana Ahmad Riza Khan Barelwi and the Ahl-e Sunnat wa Jamaʾat Movement in British India, c. 1870–1921.* New Delhi: Oxford University Press.

Santillana, David. 1938. *Istituzioni di diritto musulmano malichita con riguardo anche al sistema sciafiita.* 2 vols. Rome: Istituto per l'Oriente.

al-Sarakhsī, Shamsuddīn Abū Bakr Muḥammad b. Aḥmad. 1986. *al-Mabsūṭ.* 30 vols. in 15, plus index. Beirut: Dār al-Maʿrifa.

Scarcia, Gianroberto. 1958a. "Intorno alle controversie tra Akhbari e Usuli presso gli Imamiti di Persia." *Revista degli studi orientali,* 33:211–250.

———. 1958b. "Stato e dottrine attuali della setta sciita imamita degli Shaikhi in Persia." *Studi e Materiali di Storia delle Religioni,* 19(2):215–241.

———. 1963. "Kerman 1905: La 'guerra tra Şeiḫi e Bālāsari.'" *Annali dell'Istituto Universitario Orientale di Napoli,* 12:186–203.

SCC (Supreme Constitutional Court of Egypt), by date of decision. Published by the Court in three volumes, Cairo, 1986, for the decisions of May 4 and November 16, 1985 (vol. 3, pp. 209–224, pp. 245–249); December 21, 1985, (vol. 3, pp. 274–286). The decision of May 16, 1991 was published in the *Official Journal,* 1991, p. 968.

Schacht, Joseph. 1960. "Abū Shudjāʿ," in *The Encyclopaedia of Islam.* 2nd ed. Leiden: E. J. Brill.

———. 1964. *An Introduction to Islamic Law.* Oxford: Clarendon Press.

———. 1971. "On the Title of the *Fatāwā al-ʿĀlamgīriyya,*" in C. E. Bosworth (ed.), *Iran and Islam: In Memory of the Late Vladimir Minorsky.* Edinburgh: Edinburgh University Press, pp. 475–478.

———. 1987. "Nikāḥ," in *The Encyclopaedia of Islam.* 2nd ed. Leiden: E. J. Brill.

———. 1991. "Mālik b. Anas," in *The Encyclopaedia of Islam.* 2nd ed. Leiden: E. J. Brill.

Schieffelin, Olivia (ed.). 1965. *Muslim Attitudes toward Family Planning.* New York: Demographic Division, Population Council.

Schölch, Alexander. 1973. *Agypten den ägyptern! Die politische und gesellschaftliche Krise der Jahre 1878–1882 in Ägypten.* Zürich: Atlantis Verlag.

Seikaly, Samir M. 1984. "Land Tenure in 17th-Century Palestine: The Evidence from the *al-Fatāwā al-Khairiyya,*" in Tarif Khalidi (ed.), *Land Tenure and Social Transformation in the Middle East.* Beirut: American University of Beirut, pp. 397–408.

Sezgin, Fuat. 1967–. *Geschichte des arabischen Schrifttums.* 9 vols. Leiden: E. J. Brill.

Shafāʾī, Muḥsin. 1973. *Mutʿa va asār-i ḥuqūqī va ijtimāʿī ān* (Mutʿa and Its Legal and Social Effects). 6th ed. Tehran: Haydari Press.

al-Shāfiʿī, Muḥammad b. Idrīs. 1325/1907–1908. *Kitāb al-umm.* 7 vols. Būlāq: al-Maṭbaʿa al-Kubrā al-Amīriyya.

———. 1961. *Al-Umm.* 7 vols. in 4. Cairo: Maktabat al-Kulliyāt al-Azhariyya.

Shaltūt, Maḥmūd. 1974. *al-Fatāwā.* 7th Printing. Cairo: Dār al-Shurūq.

———. 1988. *al-Fatāwā.* Cairo: Dār al-Shaʿb.

al-Shaʿrāwī, Muḥammad Mutawallī. 1981–. *al-Fatāwā.* 10 vols. Cairo: Maktabat al-Qurʾān.

al-Shāṭibī, Abū Isḥāq Ibrāhīm b. Mūsā. 1914. *al-Iʿtiṣām.* 3 vols. in 1. Cairo: Maṭbaʿat al-Manār.

———. 1969–1970. *al-Muwāfaqāt fī uṣūl al-aḥkām.* Ed. Muḥyī al-Dīn ʿAbd al-Ḥamīd. 4 vols. Cairo: Maṭbaʿat ʿAlī Ṣubayḥ.

———. n.d. *al-Muwāfaqāt fī uṣūl al-aḥkām.* 4 vols. Beirut: Dār al-Maʿrifa.

al-Shawkānī, Muḥammad b. ʿAlī. 1969. *Rasāʾil.* Medina: Maktabat al-Salafiyya.

———. n.d.(a). *Irshād al-fuḥūl ilā taḥqīq al-ḥaqq min ʿilm al-uṣūl.* Surabaya: Sharikat Maktabat Aḥmad b. Saʿd b. Nabhān.

———. n.d.(b). *Nayl al-awṭār: Sharḥ muntaqā al-akhbār.* Cairo: Muṣṭafā al-Bābī al-Ḥalabī.

Shinar, P. 1977. "Traditional and Reformist Mawlid Celebrations in the Maghrib," in Myriam Rosen-Ayalon (ed.), *Studies in Memory of Gaston Wiet.* Jerusalem: Institute of Asian and African Studies.

al-Shirāzī, Abū Isḥāq Ibrāhīm. 1988. *Sharḥ al-lumaʿ.* Ed. ʿAbd al-Majīd Turkī. 2 vols. Beirut: Dār al-Gharb al-Islāmī.

———. n.d. *al-Muhadhdhab.* 2 vols. Cairo: Maṭbaʿat ʿĪsā al-Bābī al-Ḥalabī.

al-Shirbīnī, ʿAbd al-Raḥmān. 1970. *Taqrīr ʿalā ḥāshiyat al-ʿAllāma al-Bannānī.* 2 vols. Bombay: Molvi Mohammed Bin Gulamrasul Surtis and Sons.

al-Shirbīnī, Muḥammad. 1933. *Mughnī al-muḥtāj ilā maʿrifat alfāẓ al-minhāj*. 2 vols. Cairo: Maṭbaʿat Muṣṭafā al-Bābī al-Ḥalabī.

al-Shuwādafī, Ṣafwat. 1408/1987–1988. *Fatāwā hayʾat Kubbār al-ʿulamāʾ biʾl-mamlaka al-ʿarabiyya al-saʿūdiyya*. Balbīs: Dār al-Taqwā.

Sjamsudduha. 1987. *Penyebaran dan perkembangan Islam, Katolik, dan Protestan di Indonesia*. Surabaya: Usaha Nasional.

Skovgaard-Petersen, Jakob. 1994. "Defining Islam for the State: Muftis and Fatwas of the Egyptian Dār al-Iftāʾ." 2 vols. Ph.D. thesis, University of Copenhagen.

Smith, Jane I., and Y. Haddad. 1981. *The Islamic Understanding of Death and Resurrection*. Albany: State University of New York Press.

Snouck Hurgronje, C. 1915. "Islam and the Phonograph." *The Moslem World*, 5:159–165.

———. 1923. *Verspreide Geschriften*. 2 vols. Bonn and Leipzig: K. Schroeder.

———. 1931. *Mekka in the Latter Part of the 19th Century*. Leyden: E. J. Brill.

Stern, G. H. 1939. *Marriage in Early Islam*. London: Royal Asiatic Society.

Stout, Lucy Carroll. 1980. "A Question of Fact: Ascertainment of Asian Law by the English Court: A Critique of *Viswalingam v. Viswalingam*, Decided in the High Court, London, 14th March, 1979." *Malaya Law Review*, 22:34–65.

al-Subkī, Tāj al-Dīn. n.d. *Ṭabaqāt al-shāfiʿiyya al-kubrā*. 6 vols. Cairo: al-Maṭbaʿa al-Ḥusayniyya.

al-Subkī, Taqī al-Dīn ʿAlī b. ʿAbd al-Kāfī. 1936. *Fatāwā al-Subkī*. Cairo: Maktabat al-Quds (vol. 1, 1937–38; vol. 2, 1936–37).

———. n.d. *Fatāwā al-Subkī*. 2 vols. Repr. Beirut: Dār al-Maʿrifa.

Sufi, G. M. D. 1941. *Al-Minhāj: Being the Evolution of Curriculum in the Muslim Educational Institutions of India*. Delhi: Idarah-i Adabiyat-i Delli.

Suminto, H. Aqib. 1985. *Politik Islam Hindia Belanda: het Kantoor voor Inlandsche Zaken*. Jakarta: Lembaga Penelitian Pendidikan dan Penerangan Ekonomi dan Sosial.

al-Suyūṭī, Jalāl al-Dīn. n.d. *al-Ashbāh waʾl-naẓāʾir*. Cairo: Maṭbaʿat ʿĪsā al-Bābī al-Ḥalabī.

al-Ṭabarī, Muḥammad b. Jarīr. 1954–1968. *Jāmiʿ al-bayān ʿan taʾwīl āy al-qurʾān*. 30 vols. in 12. Cairo: Muṣṭafā al-Bābī al-Ḥalabī.

Ṭabāṭabāʾī, ʿAllāmah Sayyid Muḥammad Ḥusayn. 1975. *Shiʿite Islam*. Trans. from Persian to English by S. H. Nasr. Albany: State University of New York Press.

Tabatabaʾi, Hossein Modarresi. 1984. *An Introduction to Shiʿi Law: A Bibliographical Study*. London: Ithaca Press.

Tadmurī, ʿUmar ʿAbd al-Salām. 1981. *Taʾrīkh Ṭarāblus*. Beirut: Muʾassasat al-Risāla.

Taftāzānī, Saʿd al-Dīn. 1974. *Ḥāshiya* (printed with al-Ījī, *Sharḥ*). Ed. Shaʿbān Muḥammad Ismāʿīl. 2 vols. Cairo: Maktabat al-Kulliyyāt al-Azhariyya.

al-Ṭaḥāwī, Abū Jaʿfar Aḥmad b. Muḥammad. 1968. *Sharḥ maʿānī al-āthār*. Ed. Muḥammad Sayyid Jād al-Ḥaqq. 4 vols. Cairo: Maṭbaʿat al-Anwār al-Muḥammadiyya.

Tanṭāwī, Muḥammad. 1990. *al-Ḥukm al-sharʿī fī aḥdāth al-khalīj*. Cairo: Dār al-Iftāʾ.

———. 1991. *Islamic Judgment on the Gulf Crisis.* Cairo: Hajar.

Ta-Shma, Israel Moses, and Shlomo Tal. 1972. "Responsa," in *Encyclopaedia Judaica.* Jerusalem: Keter Publishing.

Tawfīq, Aḥmad. 1983. *al-Mujtamaʿ al-maghribī fiʾl-qarn al-tāsiʿ ʿashr.* Rabat: Manshūrāt Kulliyyat al-Ādāb waʾl-ʿUlūm.

Thānawī, Mawlānā Ashraf ʿAlī. 1931. *al-Ḥīlat al-nājiza liʾl-ḥalīlat al-ʿājiza.* Deoband: Dār al-Ishāʿat.

———. 1965. *Imdād al-fatāwā.* 6 vols. Karachi: Ashraf al-ʿUlūm. Also available in the following editions: 1927, Delhi: Mujtabāʾī; 1949–1953, Karachi: Ashraf al-ʿUlūm; 1974, Karachi: Dār al-ʿUlūm.

———. 1987. *Ḥīla-i nājiza yaʿnī ʿawratōn kā ḥaqq-i tansīkh-i nikāḥ.* Karachi: Dār al-Ishāʿat.

Toledano, Henry. 1982. *Judicial Practice and Family Law in Morocco: The Chapter on Marriage from Sijilmāsī's al-ʿAmal al-Muṭlaq.* Boulder: Social Science Monographs.

Torres Balbás, L. 1957. "Arte califal," in E. Lévi-Provençal, *España musulmana hasta la caída del califato de Córdoba* (*Historia de España* dirigida por Ramón Menéndez Pidal), vol. 5. Madrid: Espasa-Calpe.

Trimingham, J. Spencer. 1971. *The Sufi Orders in Islam.* Oxford: Clarendon.

Tritton, Arthur Stanley. 1970. *The Caliphs and Their Non-Muslim Subjects: A Critical Study of the Covenant of ʿUmar.* London: F. Cass.

Turkī, ʿAbd al-Majīd. 1982. "La vénération pour Mālik et la physionomie du mālikisme andalou: aspects polémiques," in *Théologiens et juristes de l'Espagne musulmane.* Paris: Maisonneuve et Larose, pp. 45–67.

al-Ṭurtūshī, Muḥammad b. al-Walīd. 1319/1901–1902. *Sirāj al-mulūk.* Cairo: al-Maṭbaʿa al-Azhariyya al-Miṣriyya; 1930–1931, Spanish trans. by Maximiliano Alarcón, 2 vols., Madrid: n.p.

Ṭūsī, Shaykh Abū Jaʿfar Muḥammad. 1964. *an-Nahāyih.* Trans. from Arabic to Persian by M. T. Dānish Pazhūh. Tehran: Tehran University Press.

Tyan, Emile. 1954–1957. *Institutions du droit public musulman.* 2 vols. Paris: Sirey.

———. 1955. "Judicial Organization," in Majid Khadduri and Herbert J. Liebesny (eds.), *Law in the Middle East.* Washington D.C.: The Middle East Institute, pp. 236–278.

———. 1960. *Histoire de l'organization judiciaire en pays d'Islam.* 2nd ed. Leiden: E. J. Brill.

———. 1965. "Fatwā (i)," in *The Encyclopaedia of Islam.* 2nd ed. Leiden: E. J. Brill.

ʿUlaysh (ʿUllaish or ʿIllaish), Muḥammad. 1881. *Fatḥ al-mālik fī fatāwā Ibn Mālik.* 2 vols. Cairo: Muṣṭafā al-Bābī; 1937, 2nd ed.

Usif Makkī, Sayyid Ḥusayn. 1963. *Mutʿa dar islām* (Mutʿa in Islam). Trans. from Arabic to Persian. Damascus: n.p.

ʿUthmānī, Muḥammad Taqī. 1987. "Islam mën khulʿ kī ḥaqīqat," in Thānawī 1987.

Vājid ʿAlī Shāh. 1850–51. *Baḥr-i hidāyat.* Lucknow: Maṭbaʿ-i Sulṭānī.

Vallvé, Joaquín. 1991. "Biografía de ʿAbd-ar-Rahmān II, emir de al-Andalus." *Boletín de la Real Academia de la Historia,* 188: 209–250.

Van Reenen, Daan. 1990. "The *Bilderverbot:* A New Survey." *Der Islam,* 67:27–77.

Veccia Vaglieri, L. 1960. "ʿAbd Allāh b. al-ʿAbbās," in *Encyclopaedia of Islam.* 2nd ed. Leiden: E. J. Brill.

Voll, John O. 1975. "Muhammad Hayat al-Sindi and Muhammad ibn ʿAbd al-Wahhab: An Analysis of an Intellectual Group in Eighteenth-Century Madina." *Bulletin of the School of Oriental and African Studies,* 38:32–39.

———. 1982. *Islam: Continuity and Change in the Modern World.* Boulder: Westview Press.

al-Wāḥidī, ʿAlī b. Aḥmad. 1969. *Asbāb nuzūl al-qurʾān.* Cairo: Dār al-Kitāb al-Jadīd.

Wakin, Jeanette A. 1985. "Fatwā," in *Dictionary of the Middle Ages.* New York: Charles Scribner's Sons.

Walsh, J. R. 1965. "Fatwā (ii)," in *The Encyclopaedia of Islam.* 2nd ed. Leiden: E. J. Brill.

al-Wansharīsī, Aḥmad b. Yaḥyā. 1981–1983. *al-Miʿyār al-mughrib waʾl-jāmiʿ al-muʿrib ʿan fatāwā ahl Ifrīqiya waʾl-Andalus waʾl-Maghrib.* Ed. M. Ḥājjī. 13 vols. Rabat: Ministry of Culture and Religious Affairs; Beirut: Dār al-Maghrib al-Islāmī.

Ward, Seth. 1984. "Construction and Repair of Churches and Synagogues under Islam: A Treatise by Taqī al-Dīn ʿAlī b. ʿAbd al-Kāfī al-Subkī." Ph.D. dissertation, Yale.

———. 1986. "Sabbath Observance and Conversion to Islam: A *Fatwa* by Taqī al-Dīn al-Subkī." *Proceedings of the Ninth World Congress of Jewish Studies.* Jerusalem: World Union of Jewish Studies, pp. 47–54 (division B, vol. 1).

———. 1989. "Taqī al-Dīn al-Subkī on Construction, Continuance and Repair of Churches and Synagogues in Islamic law," in William M. Brinner and Stephen Ricks (eds.), *Studies in Islamic and Judaic Traditions II.* Atlanta: Scholars Press, pp. 169–188.

Weber, Max. 1978. *Economy and Society.* Ed. G. Roth and C. Wittich. 2 vols. Berkeley: University of California Press.

Weiss, Bernard. 1978. "Interpretation in Islamic Law: The Theory of *Ijtihād.*" *American Journal of Comparative Law,* 26(2):199–212.

———. 1992. *The Search for God's Law: Islamic Jurisprudence in the Writings of Sayf al-Dīn al-Āmidī.* Salt Lake City: University of Utah Press.

Wensinck, A. J. 1936. "Miṣr," in *The Encyclopaedia of Islam.* Leiden: E. J. Brill.

———. 1961. "Ḳunūt," in *The Shorter Encyclopaedia of Islam.* Leiden: E. J. Brill.

Wensinck, A. J., et al. 1969. *Concordance et indices de la tradition musulmane.* 7 vols. Leiden: E. J. Brill. 1992. Paperback repr., Leiden: E. J. Brill.

White, James Boyd. 1985. *Heracles' Bow: Essays on the Rhetoric and Poetics of the Law.* Madison: University of Wisconsin Press.

———. 1990. *Justice as Translation: An Essay in Cultural and Legal Criticism.* Chicago: University of Chicago Press.

Willis, John Ralph. Forthcoming. "The Fatwas of Condemnation and the Fatwas That Never Were." *The Maghrib Review.*

Winder, R. Bayly. 1965. *Saudi Arabia in the Nineteenth Century.* London: Macmillan.

al-Yaʿqūbī, Shaykh Ibrāhīm. 1986. *Shifāʾ al-taʾrīkh waʾl-adwāʾ fī ḥukm al-tashrīʿ waʾl-aʿḍāʾ*. Damascus: n.p.

Zabāra, Muḥammad b. Muḥammad. 1979. *Nuzhat al-naẓar.* Ṣanʿāʾ: Markaz al-Dirāsāt waʾl-Abḥāth al-Yamaniyya.

Zafir al-Din, Muhammad. 1962. "Introduction," in *Fatāwā Dār al-ʿUlūm Deoband.* Vol. 1. Deoband: Dār al-ʿUlūm, pp. 51–114.

Zan-i Rūz (Modern Woman). Tehran (weekly magazine).

al-Zarqā, Muṣṭafā. 1968. *al-Madkhal al-fiqhī al-ʿāmm.* 10th ed. 3 vols. Damascus: Maṭbaʿat Tirbīn.

al-Zayd, ʿAbd al-Raḥmān. 1991. "Dawr al-Ṣalīb fī Azmat al-Khalīj." *al-Sunna,* 76(9–10):76–84.

Zaydān, ʿAbd al-Karīm. 1382/1963. *Aḥkām al-dhimmiyīn waʾl-mustaʾminīn fī dār al-Islām.* Baghdad: Jāmiʿat Baghdād.

Zaydān, J. n.d. *Tarājim mashāhīr al-sharq fiʾl-qarn al-thālith ʿashar.* 3rd ed. 2 vols. Beirut: Dār Maktabat al-Ḥayāh.

al-Zayn, ʿAbd Allāh Yaḥyā. 1985. *al-Yaman waʾl-wasāʾil al-iʿlāmīyah, 1872–1974.* Cairo: Maṭābiʿ al-Ṭubjī al-Tijāriyah. (See also El Zine, M. ʿAbdallah Yahya. 1978. *Le Yemen et ses moyens d'information: étude historique, politique, juridique, sociale et critique, 1872–1974.* Algiers: Société nationale d'édition et de diffusion.)

Zebiri, Kate. 1993. *Mahmud Shaltut and Islamic Modernism.* Oxford: Clarendon.

Ziadeh, Farhat. 1990. "*Fatāwā* and Legal Systems." Paper presented at the conference, "The Making of a *Fatwā,*" Center for Islamic Studies, Granada, Spain, January 11–14, 1990.

Ziadeh, Nicola A. 1958. *Sanūsīyah: A Study of a Revivalist Movement in Islam.* Leiden: E. J. Brill.

al-Zuhaylī, Dr. Wahbah. 1986. *Uṣūl al-fiqh al-islāmī.* Damascus: Dār al-Fikr.

———. 1989. *al-Fiqh al-islāmī wa-adillatuhu.* Damascus: Dār al-Fikr.

Zuhuruʾl-hasan Kasoli (ed.). 1950. *Arwah-i salasah.* Saharanpur.

Glossary

Adab al-muftī rules of conduct for a jurisconsult

Adab al-qāḍī rules of conduct for a judge

ʿAdāla good character, integrity

Adilla (or dalāʾil, singular: dalīl) indicators in textual sources

ʿAdl a person of good character and integrity who qualifies to serve as a witness in court. See *ʿadāla*

Aḥādīth (singular: ḥadīth) narrative reports

Aḥkām (singular: ḥukm) legal rules, assessments; judgments of a *qāḍī*

Ahl literally, "people"; when used in conjunction with a noun, "scholars": e.g., *ahl al-ʿilm,* scholars of religious science

Ahl al-dhikr people of expertise and experience in the religious sciences

Akhbārī a "Twelver" (Ithna ʿAshari) school of jurisprudence that does not allow *ijtihād* and holds that the only authoritative sources are the Quran and the Sunna

ʿĀlim see *ʿulamāʾ*

ʿAmal judicial practice

Amāna fiduciary relationship, trust

Amīn trusted person, secretary, recorder

Amīn al-fatwā superintendent of the fatwa department

ʿĀmm general; *ʿāmm kullī,* generally applicable

ʿĀmmī layman

ʿAqāʾid (singular: ʿaqīda) creeds

ʿAqd al-nikāḥ marriage contract

ʿAql reason

al-Arjaḥ al-aṣaḥḥ the weightiest and most plausible opinion in a law school

Aṣaḥḥ the better of two or more views. See *ṣaḥiḥ*

Aṣālat al-qabḍ the presumption of receipt of possession

Aṣḥāb (singular: ṣāḥib) Companions, e.g., of the Prophet

Aṣl nature, root, source, principle

ʿAṭāʾ gift

Athar effect; a tradition attributed to a Companion of the Prophet Muhammad

ʿAyn (real) object, capital asset

Bāʾin irrevocable (divorce)

Bāligh adult or major. See *bulūgh*

Barnāmaj fatāwā Fatwa Program

Bāshmuftī chief mufti

Basmala a variant of *bismillāh*

Bāṭil invalid, null and void

Bidʿa innovation

Bismillāh abbreviated form of the phrase, "In the name of God, the Merciful, the Compassionate"; *basmala*

Bulūgh puberty, adulthood, sexual maturity. See *bāligh*

Dalāʾil see *adilla*

Ḍamān liability for loss

Dār al-ḥarb Abode of War, a territory not ruled by Muslims or governed by Islamic law

Dār al-iftāʾ in modern times, an institution that issues fatwas

Dār al-islām Abode of Peace, a territory ruled by Muslims or governed by Islamic law

Dars-e Niẓāmī a syllabus for Islamic education introduced by Mulla Niẓām al-Dīn (d. 1748) in Mughal India

Ḍarūra necessity

al-Ḍarūrāt tubīḥ al-maḥẓūrāt "necessities render prohibited things permissible"

Hady ritual sacrifice, offered as expiation for transgression of the pilgrimage rites

Ḥākim-i sharʿ judge in a qadi court

Ḥalāl allowed, permitted, permissible

Ḥarām forbidden

Ḥijaj (singular: ḥujja) testimony, acknowledgment, oath, oral pleading

Ḥīla see *ḥiyal*

Ḥiyal (singular: ḥīla) legal devices, stratagems

Ḥiyāza conveyance, e.g., of property

Ḥudūd (singular: ḥadd) specific punishments for certain major crimes mentioned in the Quran

Ḥujja see ḥijāj

Ḥukm see *aḥkām*

Ḥukm-nāmeh decree

ʿIbādāt ritual practices, e.g., ablutions, prayers, tithes, fasting, and pilgrimage

ʿIdda period of sexual abstinence, waiting period for a woman after divorce or the death of her husband

ʿIddat see *ʿidda*

Iftāʾ the act of issuing fatwas

Iḥrām state of ritual purity required for performance of the *ḥajj*, or pilgrimage

Iḥtiyāt-i vājib (al-iḥtiyāt al-wājib) necessary caution

Iḥyā-i mavāt (iḥyāʾ al-mawāt) the revival of uncultivated land

Ījāb wa-qabūl offer of a contract and acceptance of the offer

Ijāza license to teach, diploma

Ijmāʿ consensus of Muslim scholars

Ijmāʿ sukūtī tacit consensus

Ijtihād independent reasoning; authentic scholarly endeavor

al-Ijtihād al-juzʾī an applied *ijtihād,* related to part of a problem

Ikhtilāf difference of opinion among two or more Muslim jurists

ʿIlla effective cause, *ratio legis*

ʿIlm knowledge, especially of the religious sciences

ʿIlm al-farāʾiḍ literally, "science of the shares," inheritance laws

Dawām al-ḥukm duration of the assessment, presumption of the continuity of rule of law

Diyāna religiosity, piety

Dukhūl consummation (of marriage)

Fāʾida interest

Faqīh see *fuqahāʾ*

Faqīh al-nafs a jurist who has not mastered his school's jurisprudential principl but does command its doctrines and reasoning, and is allowed to choose betwee its various views

al-Farʿiyya al-ijtihādiyya individual judgment on the branches of law

Farḍ kifāya a collective duty

Farz-i wājib (farḍ wājib) obligatory religious duty

Fasād corruption, deleterious consequences

Fasād al-zamān corruption of the times

Fāsid defective or void, invalid

Fāsiq a morally depraved individual, one who commits a sin *(fisq)*

Faskh annulment, e.g., of a marriage

Fatāwā (singular: fatwā) nonbinding legal opinions; authoritative or accept view of the jurists in a school of law

Fatva Persian for fatwa

Fetva Turkish for fatwa

Fetvā emīni Amīn al-fatwā

Fiqh legal doctrine(s), substantive law

Fisq see *fāsiq*

Fuḍalāʾ the learned; people of culture and refinement

Fuqahāʾ **(singular: *faqīh*)** jurists, experts in Islamic law *(fiqh)*

Furūʿ **(singular: *farʿ*)** literally "branches"; derived substantive law

Furūḍ al-kifāyāt see *farḍ kifāya*

Futyā legal consultation; fatwa

Ghayr muqallid a person or scholar who does not follow a school of law

Ḥaḍāna care, custody of a child

Ḥadīth see *aḥādīth*

Ilzām coercion, compulsion

Imām a prayer leader; when capitalized, a founder of one of the Sunni law schools; a caliph: e.g., the Great Imam; a divinely inspired descendant of the Prophet.

Iqrār legal acknowledgment in the presence of witnesses; confession

Ishhād judicial certification; summoning of witnesses to testify

Isnād chain of transmission of a hadith

Istaftā to ask a mufti for an opinion

Istiftāʾ a request for a fatwa, the question itself

Istiḥbāb preference

Istiḥsān juristic preference

Istinbāṭ derivation of rules for novel legal cases

Ittifāq agreement

Iẓhār presumption

Jāhil someone uninformed, a nonspecialist

Jawāb response to an *istiftāʾ*; fatwa

Jawāz permissibility, lawfulness

Jināyāt (singular: jināya) felonies, capital offenses; penal laws

Kafāʾa equality in marriage

Kaffāra expiation for a wrong action, sin, or crime

Kalām theology

Khāṣṣ specific; private

Khilāf mutaqaddim disagreement among the ancients

Khulʿ divorce on payment of consideration by the wife

Kināya implicit declaration

Laqīṭ lost property; foundling

Madhhab school of Islamic law; school doctrine

Maḍmūn ḍamān al-ʿaqd unconditional liability by the intrinsic terms of a (synallagmatic) contract

Madrasa institution of learning, law school

Madzhab see *madhhab*

Maḥkamat al-Ḍamān waʾl-Ankiḥa Court of Guarantee and Marriages

Maḥkamat al-naqḍ High Court

Maḥkamat al-Qāhira al-Kubrā Grand Shariʿa Court of Cairo

Mahr dower, bridewealth

Majlis Agama Islam Islamic Religious Council

al-Majlis al-ʿIlmī Council of Scholars

Majlis muzākara (mudhākara) public disputation

Makrūh taḥrīmī an intermediate category between reprehensible *(makrūh)* and forbidden *(ḥarām)*

Maʾmūm a person who is being led in prayer

Marjaʿ-i taqlīd or marjiʿ al-taqlīd literally, "source of imitation"; among the Shīʿīs, a *mujtahid* whose legal opinion is regarded as binding on his followers

Masāʾil (singular: masʾala) legal questions

Mashhūr a well-known hadith transmitted by three or more transmitters at every stage of transmission

Masjid mosque

Maṣlaḥa benefit, common good, public welfare

Mavāt (mawāt) uncultivated land

Mazāhib (or madhāhib; singular: madhhab) see *madhhab*

Maẓālim special courts of justice established by the caliph or sultan and his governors

Meshūarat ʿulamāʾ ʿUlamaʾ Committee

Mollā see *mullā*

Muʿāhada (mustaʾmina) non-Muslim woman present in Islamic lands

Muʿāmalāt transactions among human beings; contracts and obligations; banking transactions

Muḍāraba commenda transactions

Muḍārib the lender in a *muḍāraba* contract

al-Muftā bihi the subject on which a fatwa is issued

al-Muftī al-ʿāmm grand mufti

Muftī al-Diyār al-Miṣriyya mufti of the Egyptian lands

Muftī al-sāda al-Ḥanafiyya Hanafi chief mufti

Muḥallil see *taḥlīl*

Mujtahid a scholar who is qualified to exercise independent reasoning *(ijtihād)*

al-Mujtahid al-muntasib a scholar who is affiliated with a particular school of law

al-Mujtahid al-mustaqill a scholar who is qualified to exercise *ijtihād* independently without adhering to the doctrine of a particular school of law, e.g., the founders of the major *madhhabs*

al-Mujtahid al-muṭlaq founder of a school of law; independent interpreter

al-Mujtahid bi'l-fatwā a scholar who is qualified to issue a fatwa

al-Mujtahid fi'l-madhhab a scholar who is qualified to exercise *ijtihād* within a school of law

al-Mujtahid bi'l-masā'il a scholar who is qualified to decide on disputed points

Mukallaf (plural: mukallafūn) a person upon whom observance of religious practices is incumbent

Mullā religious scholar

Muntasib see *mujtahid*

Muqallid practitioner of *taqlīd;* a person who follows school doctrine because he is not qualified to engage in deductive and analogical reasoning

Muqayyad limited, qualified, e.g., as applied to a *mujtahid*

Muqtaḍā legal import of a text

Murājaʿa return of a wife to a husband from whom she has been divorced, following an intermediate marriage that has been consummated *(taḥlīl)*

Mushāʿ jointly owned property

Mushāraka business partnership

Mushāwar (plural: mushāwarūn) legal adviser, jurisconsult, mufti

Mustaftī (plural: mustaftūn) inquirer, a person who requests a legal opinion

Mustanad source text

Mustaqill see *mujtahid*

Mutʿa temporary marriage

Mutawātir A hadith transmitted by such a large number of tradents at every stage of transmission that any doubt regarding its authenticity is precluded

Muṭlaq absolute; see *mujtahid*

Muzākara (mudhākara) disputation

Nādir al-riwāya rare view

Nafaqa maintenance, support

Nāshiza a recalcitrant wife

al-Nāsikh wa'l-mansūkh abrogating and abrogated, applied to individual verses of the Quran and to hadith

Naskh abrogation. See al *nāsikh wa'l-mansūkh*

Naṣṣ (plural: nuṣūṣ) text; primary source, i.e., Quran or hadith

Naṣṣ qaṭʿī an apodictic source text, i.e., Quran or hadith

Nawāzil (singular: nāzila) cases

Nikāḥ marriage

Nishānjī official responsible for state Law *(qānūn)*; called "mufti of the *qānūn*"

Niyya intent, intention

Nuṣūṣ see *naṣṣ*

Qaḍāʾ the issuing of a judgment, the act of judging

Qāḍī judge

al-Qāʿida al-fiqhiyya legal principle, maxim

Qānūn rule, ordinance, statute

Qarāʾin (singular: qarīna) verbal or nonverbal indicators that clarify a part of speech extraneous to themselves; a given or presumed set of facts underlying a particular situation; circumstantial evidence

Qaṭʿ al-ʿiṣma termination of the marriage bond

Qawl view, opinion

al-Qawl al-rājiḥ preponderant view

Qāzī *qāḍī*

Qiyās analogical reasoning

Rajʿī revocable, e.g., as applied to divorce

Rasm al-ibtiyāʿ purchase document

Raʾy (considered) opinion

Responsum fatwa

Ribā interest

al-Ribā al-jalī clear *ribā*

al-Ribḥ al-istithmārī capitalization profit

Riyāsa juristic preeminence

Rushd maturity

Sabab occasion, e.g., of the revelation of a quranic verse; legal cause or *ratio legis*. See *ʿilla*

Ṣadr a Safavid and Mughal religious official similar to the Ottoman chief mufti *(shaykh ul-islām)*

Ṣaghīra minor girl

Ṣāḥib al-wujūh a jurist who has mastered the principles, doctrine, and reasoning of a particular school

Ṣāḥib-i fatāwā a jurist who is qualified to issue a fatwa

Ṣaḥīḥ valid, sound. See *aṣaḥḥ*

Salam contract of future sale

Shahāda testimony of faith ("There is no God but God, and Muhammad is the Prophet of God"); witness testimony

Shahādat al-istithmār capitalization certificate

Shāriʿ legislator, often applied to God

Sharʿī of or relating to *sharīʿa*

Sharīʿa Islamic law

Sharīʿat *sharīʿa*

Sharikāt tawẓīf al-amwāl investment company

Sharṭ (plural: shurūṭ) stipulation, condition, prerequisite

Shaykh elder, chief; title of scholar trained in the traditional sciences; member of a religious order; Sufi master

Shaykh al-Azhar rector of al-Azhar University

Shaykh al-fiqh professor of law

Shaykh ul-islām Ottoman chief mufti who is the ultimate source of religious authority; Mughal head of the department of religious affairs

Sheikh ul-islām see *shaykh ul-islām*

Shubha doubt, uncertainty

Shubhat al-milk quasi-ownership of property

Shūrā consultation; qadi's consilium

Shūrā-i fatwā mufti's consilium

Shurūṭ see *sharṭ*

Ṣīgheh (sīgha) literally the "form" or "shape" of a contract; *mutʿa* marriage

Sijill archival record of a qadi court

Suʾāl (masʾala) wa-jawāb question and answer

Ṣulḥ reconciliation, arbitrated settlement

Sunna exemplary behavior of the Prophet Muhammad as represented in hadith

Ṣūrat al-fatwā a legal case as described by the petitioner

Ṣūrat al-ḥāl actual case

Suwāl question. See *suʾāl*

Taḥkīm binding arbitration

Taḥlīl an intermediate marriage designed to render a divorced woman lawfully permissible to her former husband; the husband in this intermediate marriage is called *muḥallil*

Ṭalāq divorce by repudiation

Ṭalāq mukarrar repeated divorce

Talfīq combining the doctrines of different schools of law to create a new, "patchwork" rule or assessment

al-Taʾlīj see *tawlīj*

Taqlīd adherence to a school of law or to a *mujtahid*

Taqlīd al-mayyit following the doctrinal positions of a deceased jurist

Taqlīd-i shakhṣī following a single scholar as a definitive guide

Ṭarīqa (plural: ṭuruq) path, Sufi order, brotherhood, religious fraternity

Tarjīḥ al-rājiḥ opting for one legal opinion and setting aside other competing opinions that may be valid; preferred view

Taṣdīqāt testimonials

Tawḍīḥ al-masāʾil explanatory statement on issues; a treatise written by a Shiʿi *mujtahid (marjaʿ al-taqlīd)* on assuming office; a collection of fatwas issued by a Shiʿi *mujtahid*

Tawlīj (taʾlīj; plural: tawlījāt) financial transactions between parents and children designed to circumvent the Islamic inheritance laws

Taʿzīr discretionary punishment meted out by a qadi in cases not covered by the *ḥudūd* penalities

Thubūt proof

Ṭuruq See *ṭarīqa*

Tūzīḥ al-masā'il see *tawḍīḥ al-masā'il*

'Ulamā' (singular: 'ālim) scholars

Ulū al-amr "those in authority," often understood as referring to the 'ulama'

al-'Ulūm al-shar'iyya the religious sciences

Umm walad designation applied to female slave who gives birth to a child by her master

al-'Uqud al-fāsida invalid contracts

'Urf customary law

Uṣūl roots, sources, jurisprudential methods

al-Uṣūl al-'amaliyya procedural issues

Uṣūl al-dīn theology

Uṣūl al-fiqh roots of jurisprudence, methods of deriving positive law

Uṣūlīs a Shi'i school of law in which the *mujtahid* serves as a guide for the community, applying his personal interpretation to primary and secondary source texts

Vājib see *wājib*

Vaqf see *waqf*

Vaqf-i 'āmm (al-Waqf al-'āmm) see *waqf khayrī*

Vaqf-i khāṣṣ see *waqf ahlī*

Wājib obligatory, incumbent

Wājibāt legal obligations

Wakāla agency

al-Wakīl agent

Walī guardian

Waqf pious endowment, trust

Waqf ahlī family endowment

Waqf khayrī public endowment

Warisā Urdu plural of *wāris* (Arab. *wurathā'*); heirs

Wilāya authority, right of father or relative to marry his or her ward; guardianship of a minor

Wilāyat-i faqīh governance of the jurist

Yamīn decisory oath

Ẓāhir the surface or apparent meaning of a text or of the law

Ẓāhir al-riwāya the prevailing view in a school of law

Zakāt alms tax

Ẓann opinion, suspicion, probability

Ẓihār oath that is pronounced for the repudiation of a wife

Zinā adultery, fornication

Contributors

Juan R. I. Cole is Professor of History and Director of the Center for Middle Eastern and North African Studies at the University of Michigan. He is the author of *Roots of North Indian Shiʿism in Iran and Iraq* (University of California Press, 1989) and *Colonialism and Revolution in the Middle East* (Princeton University Press, 1993).

Maribel Fierro is Research Fellow at the Consejo Superior de Investigaciones Cientificas in Madrid. Her current research focuses on Maliki law, the history of al-Andalus (especially religious and intellectual developments), and Islamic ritual practices. She has edited and translated two Maliki treatises against innovations and is the author of *La heterodoxia en al-Andalus durante el periodo omeya* (Consejo Superior de Investigaciones Cientificas, 1987).

Yvonne Yazbeck Haddad is Professor of Islamic History at the University of Massachusetts at Amherst. Her publications include *Contemporary Islam and the Challenge of History, Islamic Values in the United States,* and *Mission to America: Five Islamic Sects in North America.* She is an editor of the *Oxford Encyclopaedia of the Modern Islamic World* and a past president of the Middle East Studies Association.

Shahla Haeri is Assistant Professor of Anthropology at Boston University and the author of *Law of Desire: Temporary Marriage in Shiʿi Islam* (Syracuse University Press, 1989).

Wael B. Hallaq is Professor of Islamic Law at the Institute of Islamic Studies, McGill University. He has written extensively on Sunni legal theory, logic and logical aspects of Islamic law, and Islamic legal reasoning.

Nissreen Haram is a doctoral student at the Institute of Islamic Studies, McGill University. A specialist in the history of Islamic law and jurisprudence, she is completing a dissertation on the legal practice of the Shafiʿi jurist and chief judge of Mamluk Damascus, Taqi al-Din al-Subki.

Colin Imber is Lecturer in Turkish at the University of Manchester. He is the author of *The Ottoman Empire, 1300–1481* (Isis Press, 1990) and currently is conducting research on Shaykh ul-Islam Ebussuʿud of the Ottoman empire (d. 1574).

Gregory C. Kozlowski is Professor of Islamic and South Asian History at DePaul University in Chicago. He is the author of *Muslim Endowments and Society in British India* (Cambridge University Press, 1985).

Aharon Layish is Professor of Islamic and Middle Eastern Studies at the Hebrew University of Jerusalem. He is the author of *Women and Islamic Law in a Non-Muslim State* (John Wiley and Sons, 1975), *Marriage, Divorce and Succession in the Druze Family* (E. J. Brill, Leiden, 1982), and *Divorce in the Libyan Family* (New York University Press, 1991). He is also Editor of the journal *Hamizrah Hehadash* and Executive Editor of the journal *Islamic Law and Society.*

Chibli Mallat is Director of the Centre of Islamic and Middle Eastern Law at the School of Oriental and African Studies, in London. He is the author of *The Renewal of Islamic Law* (Cambridge University Press, 1993) and editor of *Islam and Public Law* (Graham and Trotman, 1993).

Setrag Manoukian is a graduate student in the Anthropology and History Program at the University of Michigan. He is the author of *L'Argento di un Povero Cuore: Ghazal di Saʿdi Shirazi* (Instituto culturale della Republica islamica d'Iran in Italia, 1991).

Manuela Marín is Research Fellow at the Consejo Superior de Investigaciones Cientificas in Madrid and Editor of the journal *Al-Qantara.* A specialist in early Islamic history, she is the author of *Individuo y Sociedad en al-Andalus* (MAPFRE, 1992) and many articles.

Muhammad Khalid Masud is Professor of Islamic Studies at the Islamic Research Institute, International Islamic University, in Islamabad. Formerly editor of *Islamic Studies,* he is the author of *Islamic Legal Philosophy* (Islamic Research Institute, 1977).

Brinkley Messick is Associate Professor of Anthropology at the University of Michigan and author of *The Calligraphic State: Textual Domination and History in a Muslim Society* (University of California Press, 1993).

Barbara D. Metcalf is Professor and Chair of the Department of History, University of California, Davis. She is the author of *Islamic Revival in British India: Deoband, 1860–1900* (Princeton University Press, 1982), editor of *Moral Conduct and Authority: The Place of Adab in South Asian Islam* (University of California Press, 1984), and translator of and commentator on *Perfecting Women: Maulana Ashraf ʿAli Thanawi's Bihishti Zewar* (University of California Press, 1990).

Harald Motzki is Senior Lecturer in Islamic Studies at the University of Nijmegen in the Netherlands. He is the author of *Die Anfänge der islamischen Jurisprudenz: ihre Entwicklung in Mekka bis zur Mitte des 2./8. Jahrhunderts* (F. Steiner, 1991).

Mohamad Atho Mudzhar teaches at the State Institute of Islamic Studies in Jakarta and serves in Indonesia's Ministry of Religious Affairs.

Rudolph Peters is Professor of Islamic and Middle Eastern Law at the University of Amsterdam. From 1982 until 1987 he was Director of the Netherlands Institute for Archaeology and Arabic Studies in Cairo.

David S. Powers, Professor of Islamic History at Cornell University, is the author of *Studies in Qur'an and Hadith: The Formation of the Islamic Law of Inheritance* (University of California Press, 1986), translator of *The History of al-Tabari, Volume XXIV: The Empire in Transition* (State University of New York Press, 1989), and Executive Editor of the journal *Islamic Law and Society.*

A. Kevin Reinhart, Associate Professor of Religion at Dartmouth College, studies Islamic law as a religious enterprise. He is the author of *Before Revelation: Muslim Moral Thought* (State University of New York Press, 1993) and currently is conducting research on the Islamic laws of purification.

Vardit Rispler-Chaim teaches at the University of Haifa. Her research topics include Islamic law and its adjustment to changing circumstances, medical ethics, and human rights in Islam. She is the author of *Islamic Medical Ethics in the Twentieth Century* (E. J. Brill, 1993).

William R. Roff is Emeritus Professor of History, Columbia University, and an Honorary Fellow of the Department of Islamic and Middle East Studies, University of Edinburgh.

Usha Sanyal specializes in Indian Muslim history during the colonial period. She currently is revising her dissertation for publication and teaching in the Department of Religion at Rutgers University.

Frank E. Vogel is Assistant Professor of Law at the Harvard Law School. He spent nearly five years in Saudi Arabia, where he observed court sessions and discussed law and cases with judges, officials, and scholars. His doctoral dissertation, the product of this research, is entitled "Islamic Law and Legal System: Studies of Saudia Arabia."

Seth Ward teaches at the University of Denver, where he is Director of the Institute of Islamic-Judaic Studies. His area of research is the status of Jews and other non-Muslims in Islamic law and traditions.

Bernard Weiss is Professor of Arabic and Islamic Studies at the Middle East Center of the University of Utah. He has taught at the University of Toronto, McGill University, and the American University in Cairo. He is the author of *The Search* *for God's Law: Islamic Jurisprudence in the Writings of Sayf al-Din al-Amidi* (University of Utah Press, 1992).

John Ralph Willis, Professor of History and Near Eastern Studies, Princeton University, is the author of *The Passion of al-Hajj 'Umar* (F. Cass, 1989), and editor of *Studies in West African Islamic History,* volume 1, *The Cultures of Islam* (F. Cass, 1979), *Slaves and Slavery in Muslim Africa,* volume 1, *Islam and the Ideology of Enslavement* and volume 2, *The Servile Estate* (F. Cass, 1985), and founding editor of *Slavery and Abolition: A Journal of Comparative Studies.*

Index